About Island Press

Island Press is the only nonprofit organization in the United States whose principal purpose is the publication of books on environmental issues and natural resource management. We provide solutions-oriented information to professionals, public officials, business and community leaders, and concerned citizens who are shaping responses to environmental problems.

In 1999, Island Press celebrates its fifteenth anniversary as the leading provider of timely and practical books that take a multidisciplinary approach to critical environmental concerns. Our growing list of titles reflects our commitment to bringing the best of an expanding body of literature to the environmental community throughout North America and the world.

Support for Island Press is provided by The Jenifer Altman Foundation, The Bullitt Foundation, The Mary Flagler Cary Charitable Trust, The Nathan Cummings Foundation, The Geraldine R. Dodge Foundation, The Charles Engelhard Foundation, The Ford Foundation, The Vira I. Heinz Endowment, The W. Alton Jones Foundation, The John D. and Catherine T. MacArthur Foundation, The Andrew W. Mellon Foundation, The Charles Stewart Mott Foundation, The Curtis and Edith Munson Foundation, The National Fish and Wildlife Foundation, The National Science Foundation, The New-Land Foundation, The David and Lucile Packard Foundation, The Pew Charitable Trusts, The Surdna Foundation, The Winslow Foundation, and individual donors.

The Takings Issue

THE
TAKINGS
ISSUE

Constitutional Limits on Land-Use Control and Environmental Regulation

Robert Meltz
Dwight H. Merriam
Richard M. Frank

Island Press
Washington, D.C. • Covelo, California

The cover photograph by Chris Faust is from the archives of the Suburban Documentation Project. For further information and photo-use rights or purchase, contact: Frank Edgerton Martin, The Suburban Documentation Project, 308 Prince Street, #210, St. Paul, MN 55101, (612) 228–0967.

Meltz, Robert.
    The takings issue : constitutional limits on land-use control and environmental regulation / Robert Meltz, Dwight H. Merriam, Richard M. Frank.
        p.   cm.
    Includes bibliographical references and index.
    ISBN 1-55963-380-8 (cloth : acid-free paper)
    1. Land use—Law and legislation—United States.   2. Eminent domain—United States.   3. Right of property—United States.
4. Environmental law—United States.   I. Merriam, Dwight H.
II. Frank, Richard M., 1949–   .   III. Title.
KF5698.M45   1999
346.7304′5—dc21   98-34885
                                                                   CIP

Printed on recycled, acid-free paper ♾ ♲
Manufactured in the United States of America
10   9   8   7   6   5   4   3   2   1

To our wives,
Madeleine, Susan, and Connie,
and our children,
without whose unflagging patience and encouragement
this book could never have been written

Contents

Foreword   xiii
Preface   xvii
A Note to the Nonlawyer: How to Read Legal Footnotes   xxi
Acknowledgments   xxiii

Part I   Introduction   1

1   The Path to the Present   3
2   Property Protection in Federal and State Constitutions   13
3   Property and Takings Law   25

Part II   Getting to the Takings Issue   33

4   Jurisdiction   35
5   Ripeness   45
6   Other Hurdles   69
7   Section 1983 Claims   87
8   Right to Jury Trial   93

Part III   Is It or Isn't It a Taking?   101

9   Overview   103
10   Facial Versus As-Applied Challenges   107
11   Physical Takings   117
12   Regulatory Takings   129
13   Date of the Taking   161
14   Exceptions to Takings   167

Part IV   Land-Use Programs Raising Takings Issues   197

15   Planning, Zoning, and Subdivision   199
16   Physical Improvements and Exactions   241

17   Growth Management and Moratoria   263
18   Future Condemnation   281
19   Landlords and Tenants   295
20   Historic Preservation   313
21   Airplanes and Airports   337
22   Contracts and Development Agreements   357

Part V   Environmental Programs Raising Takings Issues   363

23   Wetlands   365
24   Wildlife   391
25   Mining   405
26   Billboard Controls   425
27   Rails to Trails   435
28   Hazardous Wastes and Contaminated Site Cleanup   447
29   Water Rights   457

Part VI   Remedies   471

30   Invalidation and Other Equitable Relief   473
31   Money Damages, Interest, and Fees   483

Part VII   Lessoning the Public/Private Conflict   511

32   Voluntary Initiatives, Incentives, and Direct Acquisition   513
33   Alternative Dispute Resolution   533
34   Property Rights Legislation   535

Conclusion   555

Appendix A   Key Supreme Court Takings Decisions Involving
                       Land Use: The Short Course   561

  Penn Central Transportation Co. v. New York City   561
  Agins v. City of Tiburon   562
  Loretto v. Teleprompter Manhattan CATV Corp.   563
  Williamson County Regional Planning Commission v.
    Hamilton Bank   563

First English Evangelical Lutheran Church v. County of Los Angeles 564
Nollan v. California Coastal Commission 565
Lucas v. South Carolina Coastal Council 566
Dolan v. City of Tigard 567

Appendix B **How a Court Might Analyze a Land-Use-Related Taking Claim** 569

Index 573

Foreword

As the authors of the twenty-five-year-old study of regulatory takings on which this book is modeled, we are pleased to write a foreword for such a thoughtful and readable successor. Translating the arcane "takings" jargon of judges into language that makes sense to the general reader has never been easy, but it is a much more massive challenge today than when we attempted it in 1973.

When we wrote *The Taking Issue: An Analysis of the Constitutional Limits of Land Use Control* in 1973, we were writing in a virtual federal law vacuum. The U.S. Supreme Court had decided, in quick succession, *Pennsylvania Coal* (1922), *Euclid* (1926), and *Nectow* (1928), creating regulatory takings, validating the technique of zoning, then holding that zoning can violate the Fourteenth Amendment as applied. After thus holding zoning facially constitutional on the one hand, but susceptible of being unconstitutionally applied on the other, the court then abandoned the field to the states until its cryptic and bizarre 1974 decision in *Belle Terre* (appropriately, on April Fool's Day).

As we then observed, it was left to the states to interpret—and generally to erode—Holmes's regulatory taking doctrine over the succeeding half-century, sorting out what aspects of zoning, subdivision, and other land-use controls were legal, as well as when and why. Erode they did. As Part I and chapter 9 of our 1973 report recounted with painstaking detail, regulatory takings were virtually moribund by the time the Court reexamined the concept.

The landscape has changed dramatically. As recounted in *The Takings Issue: Constitutional Limits on Land-Use Control and Environmental Regulation,* the Supreme Court has issued an even dozen opinions on regulatory takings. In 1978 and 1980, the Court suggested standards for partial regulatory takings (*Penn Central* and *Agins*). In 1985, it erected a ripeness barrier to applied challenges to land-use regulations on takings grounds (*Williamson County*) and reiterated its position in 1986 (*MacDonald, Sommer & Frates*). In 1987, it attempted to recharacterize Holmes's *Pennsylvania Coal* decision as "advisory" and raised the redoubtable "denominator issue" (*Keystone*). Also in 1987, the Court laid to rest any misconception over remedies for regulatory takings (*First English*), as foreshadowed in the famous Brennan dissent (*San Diego Gas & Electric*). Again in 1987 the Court presented us with the doctrine of unconstitutional conditions (nexus) (*Nollan*), to which it returned in 1994 to add proportionality (*Dolan*). In 1992 the Court gave us a categorical or "per se" rule on "total" regulatory takings, though with two exceptions (nuisance and background principles of a state's law of property) (*Lucas*). On top of these Supreme Court decisions, the Federal Circuit, in its relatively new role in adjudicating on appeal regulatory taking claims against the United States, has twice in the past ten years issued opinions on the nuts and bolts of such takings (*Florida Rock* and *Loveladies Harbor*).

It is fair to say that when the Supreme Court thus decided to jump back into takings and land-use controls, it largely ignored the common law of zoning created by the states. We may quibble about the whys and the wherefores, but we now have in 1998 a federal jurisprudence on regulatory takings—however incomplete or unsatisfying—that we simply did not have in 1973. It is one thing for judges to try cases and lawyers to comment in a vacuum created by a fifty-year hiatus. It is quite another to do so today. As we note below, takings litigation has exploded in the state courts, which must now consider these recent federal decisions. Whether under casual or detailed analysis, these decisions are all over the map.

State courts will have the central role, not only with respect to property and nuisance concepts and many other state law principles that are now part of federal regulatory takings law, but because the state courts are likely to be the forum for the bulk of takings litigation.

During the 1922–1973 period, state courts frequently invalidated regulations, and toward the end of that period one could barely discern a trend of judicial support for land-use regulations based on overall state or regional goals.

Twenty-five years later, however, Robert Meltz, Dwight H. Merriam and Richard M. Frank find an increasing tendency among the state appellate courts to uphold land-use and environmental regulatory programs (pp. 31, 555, *infra.*). State courts continue to discipline local regulatory practices, perhaps with more attention to procedural issues that provide equitable remedies than to outright regulatory taking demanding monetary compensation. But the state appellate decisions have almost uniformly upheld the wetland, flood plain, and other resource protection programs administered among the states. (See Part V, *infra*.) This general proposition is consistent with our 1973 conclusion that the taking issue was qualitatively different when addressing broad environmental protection objectives carefully articulated by the states.

In 1973, we speculated that "the strategy that would contribute most to a more equitable resolution of the taking cases would be simply to spend more time in the drafting of regulations and the presentation of facts supporting—or opposing—them. . . . [T]oo often these regulations take the form of sweeping prohibitions and blanket indictments of all development simply because no one has taken the time to study the problem in depth and work out a reasonable compromise between the needs of the environment and the rights of individuals." Meltz, Merriam, and Frank note that the current taking issue debate seems bound up in "absolute" positions (p. 10, *infra*.), which is not unlike the "blanket indictments" of an earlier time. The presentation of facts that can be understood in terms of rights of the individuals remains as difficult and critical today as in 1973. The misconception by the public of the taking issue, which we discussed in 1973, is still true today and often contributes to a disconnection between environmental science and policy that continues to cloud dialogue.

The most profound changes since 1973 are in the planning and regulatory processes themselves. For example, there is a closer link between planning and regulation, regulatory reform is improving administration and timing of decisions, and there is an increase in the use of market-oriented procedures such as mitigation banking and density transfer. Where these approaches are labor intensive, the shrinking public workforce may lead us to revisit the taking issue with the reinvention of many state regulatory programs.

In *The Taking Issue*, we reached a number of conclusions that were somewhat controversial at the time. First, our research suggested that the drafters of the Constitution never expected that the taking clause would be applied to *regulatory* takings. More comprehensive research by others has supported that suggestion, and in the *Lucas* decision the Court, in the majority opinion by Justice Scalia, conceded that "early constitutional theorists did not believe the Takings Clause embraced regulation of property at all." (See pp. 12–13, *infra*.). The *Lucas* court went on, of course, to uphold the application of the takings clause to regulations because the line of cases headed by *Pennsylvania Coal* was so well established. The idea that the meaning of constitutional clauses should change as they were adapted to modern conditions is hardly revolutionary, having been a fundamental tenet of the Warren court. That it should be put forth by a justice who had long advocated "originalism" is somewhat more surprising.

A second assumption that we made back in 1973 was that the remedy in takings cases could be damages. Some of our colleagues hotly contested this point, arguing that when a regulation would amount to a taking, the remedy should simply be the invalidation of the regulation. But in the *First English* case the Court supported our assumption, holding that the constitution didn't prohibit takings but only takings without compensation, and therefore the remedy should be damages rather than invalidation.

We also pointed out, however, that it was very difficult to draw a clear distinction between the line of cases applying the taking clause to regulations and another line of cases applying substantive due process to regulations. The authors of this book suggest that this distinction remains puzzling (pp. 15–18, *infra.*), and the most recent opinion of the Supreme Court in which both clauses are discussed, *Eastern Enterprises v. Apfel*, 118 S.Ct. 2131 (1998), shows how badly the Court is split on the issue. Until this distinction is satisfactorily resolved, the issue of regulatory takings will remain, as the current authors point out, a field for widely varying speculation.

Fred Bosselman, Chicago, Illinois
David Callies, Honolulu, Hawaii
John Banta, Lake Placid, New York
September 2, 1998

Preface

Over two decades ago, a book called *The Taking Issue: An Analysis of the Constitutional Limits of Land Use Control* introduced America to a then little-known constitutional provision. That provision, tucked away at the end of the Fifth Amendment in the Bill of Rights, mandates that when private property is "taken" by government action for public use, just compensation has to be paid. *The Taking Issue*, written by Fred Bosselman, David Callies, and John Banta, and published in 1973 by the Council on Environmental Quality, provided a scholarly overview, based on the limited case law of the time, of how this constitutional safeguard constrains government regulation of private land use. The book further described possible future trends and strategies with a vision that has proved to be prophetic.

As environmental and other land-use controls expanded during the 1970s and 1980s, the frequency with which landowners challenged these controls increased in tandem. Beginning in the late 1970s, the U.S. Supreme Court began an ambitious effort to develop a coherent, workable body of doctrine in the regulatory takings area, culminating in groundbreaking decisions in 1987, 1992, and 1994 that attracted media coverage on a par with the Court's more traditional high-visibility cases. At the same time, a growing "property rights movement" seized on the takings issue as the constitutional backbone for their limited-government agenda, pressing the issue in courts and legislatures alike and making the takings issue a household phrase.

Today, the rate at which property owners are filing "taking" lawsuits against government seems to be at an all-time high, and federal, state, and local regulators routinely include takings implications as one factor to be weighed in considering actions that affect private land. Though government continues to win the large majority of such suits, the landowner victories have generated political pressures that magnify their immediate effect.

With this burst in judicial activity came an almost complete transformation of the takings jurisprudence that existed when the original work was written. Principles known in embryonic form in 1973 are today greatly elaborated and, on occasion, formalized. Back then, for example, we knew only that a regulation affected a taking if it went "too far"; now, we have the three-factor balancing test and absolute rules for "total takings" and "physical takings." Other principles, completely unknown then, are now on the short list of major takings law concerns. Once, for example, there were no rules for evaluating whether the dedication and exaction conditions imposed on development permits were takings; today, such conditions must meet requirements for nexus with a permit's purpose and proportionality with a development proposal's impact. And, of course, the range of government programs against which this proliferating body of law may be invoked has itself burgeoned.

This changing situation pointed to the need for a revision of the first book. To be sure, the supernova status of the takings issue already has caught the attention of a legion of law review article and book writers. However, because of selective focus, narrow target audience, or obvious partisan slant, none of these articles and books seemed to fulfill the need for a comprehensive analysis/commentary on takings law—accessible to nonlawyer and lawyer alike. And so, *The Taking Issue* redux.

In stepping into the formidable footsteps of the original authors, we considered hewing to the general organization of their book, but quickly realized that the changes in law and policy since 1973 were too great. Our book, therefore, is an entirely new effort, not just an update. At the same time, it seeks to retain the style and "feel" of its forebear, and to emulate its objectivity and scholarship. Most important, we have attempted, wherever possible, to maintain *The Taking Issue*'s admirable quality of being a comfortable read for the nonlawyer planner, while still being informative for the practicing attorney. Put away your legal dictionary.

The federal, state, and local aspects of the takings issue, cumulatively too vast for any one person to cover, suggested a three-author collaboration—with each having a concentration of experience at one of the three levels of government and all having broad exposure to the great variety of interests and parties in land-use matters. At the same time, we sought the balance that comes from different kinds of takings-related legal practice—private versus government, develop-ment-oriented clients versus government clients. Thus, Rob Meltz's career has had a federal government focus, chiefly advising Congress with the nonpartisan Congressional Research Service on Capitol Hill. Dwight Merriam brings to the book his long experience as a pri-vate practitioner representing developers, opposition groups, envi-ronmental and conservation organizations, and governments. And Rick Frank is a senior assistant attorney general with the California Department of Justice, where he defends that state in takings litiga-tion, and a part-time law professor at the University of California at Davis and at the Lincoln Law School in Sacramento.

Of course the opinions expressed in this book are the authors' alone, and do not necessarily reflect those of their employers. The au-thors thank each other for what we each brought to this effort. We became a little like the "odd triple." Rob was the organizer, task-master, and quasi-academic, who was constantly cleaning up loose ends. This book was his idea, and its completion has been largely driven by the force of his efforts. Dwight, as a private law firm at-torney who has represented all interests in this area in his 20 years of practice, kept our feet firmly planted on the ground with what the takings issue really means in practical terms. Rick's experience as a trial and appellate lawyer and integrator of federal, state, and local law enabled his two cohorts to reach new insights and rounded out the book in a way that otherwise could not have been done. How could you write a land-use book without a Californian anyway? We are fortunate to have had the opportunity to work together.

Finally, we are grateful to the U.S. Supreme Court for declining (without even being asked) to decide any land-use takings cases over the past four years, other than the relatively narrow *Suitum v. Tahoe Regional Planning Agency* (decided in 1997). This respite from the series of thunderbolts unleashed by the Court through *Dolan v. City of Tigard* (decided in 1994) allowed the authors time to contemplate a momentarily nonmoving target.

Robert Meltz
Dwight H. Merriam
Richard M. Frank
May 28, 1998

A Note to the Nonlawyer:
How to Read Legal Footnotes

The reader without legal training may be unfamiliar with the legal citation form used by lawyers, which this book adopts. Following are a few pointers to understanding this form.

The numbers. Every legal citation (of a court decision, law review article, or treatise) has several numbers in it—for example, the U.S. Supreme Court's decision in *Penn Central Transportation Co. v. New York City*, 438 U.S. 104, 107 (1978). The number before the publication name (abbreviated "U.S.") is the volume; the number immediately after, the page number on which the case, law review article, or treatise begins. In this example, the reference is to volume 438 of the publication "United States Reports," which includes the *Penn Central* decision beginning at page 104. If there is a third number following the page number (here, "107"), that is the precise page of the cited item on which our text assertion relies. Finally, the number in parentheses is the date of the court decision, or the date of publication, as appropriate.

The publication names. Lawyers use a highly abbreviated reference style, so that footnote length doesn't overwhelm their law review articles and court opinions (it may anyway). In this book, we have spelled out more than is customary for the names of law reviews—using, e.g., "Harvard" instead of the usual "Harv." to reduce confusion. We did not do so, however, for the names of case reporters and note a few illustrations below. For case decisions from the federal courts, the citations may reference:

Publication:	*Reports decisions of the:*
U.S.	U.S. Supreme Court
S. Ct.	U.S. Supreme Court
F.2d or F.3d	U.S. Courts of Appeals
F. Supp.	U.S. District Courts
Fed. Cl.	U.S. Court of Federal Claims (renamed in 1992)
Cl. Ct.	U.S. Claims Court (created in 1982, predecessor to U.S. Court of Federal Claims)
Ct. Cl.	U.S. Court of Claims (original federal claims court, predecessor to both the U.S. Claims Court and the U.S. Court of Federal Claims)

For state court decisions the basic format is the same, except that they are often reported in two or more publications. For example, in California watch for:

Cal. 3d or Cal. 4th	California Supreme Court
P.2d	The regional (multistate) reporter that includes California Supreme Court opinions
Cal. App. 3d or Cal. App. 4th	California Courts of Appeal (official reporter)
Cal. Rptr. or Cal. Rptr. 2d	California Courts of Appeal (unofficial reporter)

Acknowledgments

Even with the authors' diverse points of view, it was plain that the universe of takings-law views today subsumes still additional vantage points. As a result, we actively sought the thoughts and criticisms of others, and wish to thank: Michael Berger, partner, Berger & Norton, P.C., Santa Monica, California; Robert Best, president, Pacific Legal Foundation, Sacramento, California; Brian W. Blaesser, partner, Robinson & Cole LLP, Boston, Massachusetts; David Brower, research professor, University of North Carolina; David Coursen, attorney-adviser, U.S. Environmental Protection Agency Office of General Counsel; John DeGrove, director, Florida Atlantic University/Florida International University Joint Center for Environmental and Urban Problems, Fort Lauderdale, Florida; John Echeverria, visiting professor, Georgetown University Law Center, Washington, D.C.; Helen Edmonds, associate, Pierce Atwood, Portland, Maine; Gideon Kanner, counsel, Berger & Norton, P.C., and professor emeritus, Loyola Law School, Los Angeles, California; Richard Lazarus, professor, Georgetown University Law Center, Washington, D.C.; R.J. Lyman, assistant secretary of environmental affairs, Commonwealth of Massachusetts; Dennis Machida, executive officer, California Tahoe Conservancy; Elizabeth Merritt, counsel, National Trust for Historic Preservation, Washington, D.C.; Douglas Porter, president, The Growth Management Institute, Chevy Chase, Maryland, and a planning and development consultant; Thomas E. Roberts, professor of law, Wake Forest University of Law; Joseph Sax, professor, Boalt School of Law, University of California at Berkeley; Glenn Sugameli, counsel, National Wildlife Federation, Washington, D.C.; and the many talented lawyers in the California Department of Justice. Many others have shared their insights with us as well; we apologize for not naming them all.

Those upon whose toil this book is founded include the following research assistants: Colin Anderson, Andrew Golden, Melanie J. Hancock, Jennifer Jewett, Diane R. Hayes, Rowena Moffett, Wayne Oakes, Karen Robbins, Peter Ruggiero, Anna Schwab, Edward Shelton, Nancy Stump, William Walker, and James H. Wehner. The ocean-sized body of takings case law accumulated in the past two decades made their sifting and selecting of court decisions and secondary materials particularly valuable.

Dwight Merriam wishes to especially thank his secretary, Sue Tenore, and two other secretaries, Sandy Paisley and Kathy Faircloth. He extends special recognition to Walter Zaborowski, who worked nearly full time on Dwight's portions of the book for a year and a half.

Rick Frank extends particular thanks to Dean Loren Smith and the staff of Lincoln Law School in Sacramento for their support—both moral and logistic.

Part I

Introduction

Chapter 1

The Path to the Present

Twelve simple words: "[N]or shall private property be taken for public use, without just compensation." Undoubtedly, this "Takings Clause," at the end of the Fifth Amendment of the Bill of Rights, has in the past two decades become the central constitutional restriction on the power of government to acquire or restrict private property rights. Almost all state constitutions have similar edicts.

The Takings Clause plays out in two procedurally distinct contexts—opposite sides of the same coin. One, the original historically, is called a condemnation proceeding (though not related to condemning buildings for health or safety purposes). Here, the government concedes it is taking the property, formally invoking its sovereign power of eminent domain as the plaintiff in a lawsuit against the property or property owner. Condemnation is used when there is no doubt that a taking is involved—when, for example, the government wants to put a highway or transmission line across private property. Usually the only seriously contested issue is how much the government must pay for the property as "just compensation."

"Takings actions," the topic of this book, are the mirror image of condemnation. They are of more recent vintage. In this instance, the government encroaches upon a property interest but emphatically *denies* any taking. Hence, it falls to the property owner to file against the government a "taking" or "inverse condemnation" action seeking compensation for an unacknowledged exercise of eminent domain. Such actions typically arise when there is doubt as to whether a taking has occurred, as with use restrictions on property or, perhaps, a short-lived physical invasion. A taking trial has not one, but two, key issues to resolve: Was there a taking? If so, how much compensation is due? Takings actions are far more likely than condemnation actions to be lightning rods; they have a David (property owner) versus Goliath (government) aspect to them.

The rise of the takings issue to celebrity status has been quite dramatic. Once a throwaway in first-year law school classes on property, the issue now garners headlines in newspaper real estate sections when a state or federal high court merely agrees to hear a case. A galaxy of reporters and TV cameras typically wait on the U.S. Supreme Court plaza after a land-use/takings case is argued, to record the postmortems of oral-argument counsel and others. Here, and later when a decision is rendered, partisans zealously seek to give the case a self-serving spin.

So, as used in the Takings Clause, what is meant by a "taking" of property? We have centuries of Anglo-American law to inform the clause's reference to "property." And we have a generally workable "fair market value" standard, invoked by the courts in the large majority of takings and condemnation cases, to give content to "just compensation." But what, pray tell, is a "taking"? Is it possible to give enduring content to this protean word, embodied in principles both general and clear? Can we move beyond a simplistic "I know one when I see one."?[1]

The answer that we hope will emerge from this book is that we can—to a point. But to have any feel for the current standards of takings law and its future possibilities, lawyers, planners, and property owners should have some notion of where the law has been.

A Brief History

Modern takings law has evolved on the heels of the rise of government-imposed land-use control in this country. It is not our purpose to question this ascending curve of government involvement (though toward the end of the book we urge a shift in approach); it seems evident that in one form or another, such involvement is called for by the corresponding upward curves of population growth, urban/suburban

---

[1]The analogy to Justice Potter Stewart's famous remark about obscenity—"I know it when I see it"—is irresistible. Jacobellis v. Ohio, 378 U.S. 184, 197 (1964) (Stewart, J., concurring).

expansion, and the impact of technology on society. When constantly rising demands and impacts intersect with a necessarily finite land base, someone must step forward with solutions. When that someone is a government entity, takings law imposes a precondition—"just compensation"—on the most intrusive of such solutions.

The seeds of the regulatory takings concept were sown when, in the early 20th century, the country's emergence from laissez-faire economics and the increasing competition between incompatible land uses in a growing nation proved an irresistible invitation to state and local governments. Government first responded in targeted fashion—prescribing for buildings such parameters as maximum height, property-line setbacks, and the materials and methods of construction, and excluding offensive enterprises from residential sections. While government had long imposed such restrictions, the pace now accelerated. Beginning in the second and third decades of this century, these selective restrictions evolved into comprehensive municipal zoning, an approach that prescribed both building characteristics and permitted uses for *all* land within the jurisdiction.

These developments of almost a century ago piqued the Supreme Court's interest, giving rise to a host of land-use decisions from 1900 to the late 1920s. Almost all these decisions upheld the government,[2] but in the Promethean case that gave us the concept of "regulatory taking," and in a later municipal zoning challenge, the Court raised a red flag of constitutional caution.[3]

Having given land-use controls this qualified blessing, the Supreme Court then departed the area for the next half-century. With only one exception, the Court appeared uninterested in regulatory impositions on landowners during this time, and certainly did not feel any need to

---

[2]In chronological order: Welch v. Swasey, 214 U.S. 91 (1909) (building height limitations); Reinman v. Little Rock, 237 U.S. 171 (1915) (ban on livery stables); Hadacheck v. Sebastian, 239 U.S. 394 (1915) (ban on brick manufacturing); Walls v. Midland Carbon Co., 254 U.S. 300 (1920) (ban on manufacture of carbon black); Village of Euclid v. Ambler Realty Co., 272 U.S. 365 (1926) (comprehensive zoning); Gorieb v. Fox, 274 U.S. 603 (1927) (building setback lines); and Miller v. Schoene, 276 U.S. 272 (1928) (requirement that infected trees be cut down).

[3]Respectively, Pennsylvania Coal Co. v. Mahon, 260 U.S. 393 (1922) (bar on development of mineral estate effected taking), and Nectow v. City of Cambridge, 277 U.S. 183 (1928) (as applied to plaintiff's land, zoning ordinance did not advance police power purposes; hence, violated due process).

articulate more concrete standards.[4] The principal reason for this hands-off approach was jurisprudential: the Supreme Court's abandonment, in the late 1930s, of the close constitutional scrutiny of economic regulation that had characterized the first decades of the century.[5] Given the new hands-off approach, it was only natural that takings challenges to regulatory control of property should be disfavored. Then, too, in the 1950s and 1960s the Warren Court focused on other parts of the Bill of Rights, concerned with individual liberties.

Meanwhile, out of the glare of national attention, the state courts in this period were actively examining the implications for land-use controls of this new idea of regulatory takings.[6] The expanding state and local government presence in the land-use area encouraged this judicial exploration.

In the decade from 1970 to 1980, the Supreme Court returned decisively to the arena of local land-use controls—first with a pair of substantive due process decisions,[7] then with two more laying out for the first time a set of regulatory takings standards and criteria of wide applicability.[8] The contrast with the inactivity of the preceding

[4]The one exception is Goldblatt v. Town of Hempstead, 369 U.S. 590 (1962). Other, *non*-regulatory land-use cases during this fallow period deserve brief mention. In Berman v. Parker, 348 U.S. 26 (1954), the Court examined whether an urban renewal project satisfied the "public use" demand of the Takings Clause. During the 1930s, the Supreme Court displayed repeated interest in appropriation/physical taking issues raised by federal treatment of Indian lands. *See, e.g.*, Chippewa Indians v. United States, 305 U.S. 479 (1939).

[5]Particularly offensive to political conservatives and libertarians is the decision in United States v. Carolene Products, 304 U.S. 144, 152 (1938), and its much-debated footnote 4. There, the Court suggested two tiers of scrutiny under substantive due process: an extremely lenient one for "ordinary commercial transactions" (presumed by commentators to include property rights) and a "more searching" one for laws directed at political activity or minorities. *See generally* DENNIS J. COYLE, PROPERTY RIGHTS AND THE CONSTITUTION 42–43 (1993); JAMES W. ELY, JR., THE GUARDIAN OF EVERY OTHER RIGHT 132–34 (1992).

[6]Fred Bosselman et al., *The Taking Issue*. Written in 1973, it provides an invaluable survey of the case law of the prior decades.

[7]Village of Belle Terre v. Boraas, 416 U.S. 1 (1974) (upholding local ban on households of unrelated persons); Moore v. City of East Cleveland, 431 U.S. 494 (1977) (invalidating local ban on households of persons not closely enough related).

[8]Penn Central Transp. Co. v. New York City, 438 U.S. 104 (1978); Agins v. City of Tiburon, 447 U.S. 255 (1980).

decades was striking, though the pendulum swing had been foreseen. Writing in 1956, Justice Frankfurter said: "Yesterday the active area in this field was concerned with 'property.' Today it is 'civil liberties.' Tomorrow it may again be 'property.'"[9]

What had happened to revive the Supreme Court's interest? First, after World War II, state and local governments began increasingly to enlist land-use controls in the service of objectives not easily characterized as abatement of common-law nuisances—that is, not readily considered prevention of threats to public health, safety, or comfort. Public concern about historic preservation, open space preservation, greenways, public beach access, growth control, vulnerable floodplains, and undesirable neighbors fueled much of the new generation of "thou shalt nots." To these were added, in the 1960s and 1970s, federal and state environmental restraints protecting wetlands, coastal zones, barrier islands, alluvial valley floors, endangered species, lands unsuitable for surface mining, and so on. These new generations of controls, embodying some novel societal goals, undoubtedly raised the judicial eyebrow. Preserving ecosystems, in the contemporary mainstream ethic that courts inevitably reflect, does not rank with zoning adult bookstores out of residential neighborhoods.

Second, the Supreme Court in the 1970s and 1980s was moving to the right, becoming more interested in using the Takings Clause to set bounds on governmental intervention in the foregoing areas.

By the late 1970s, then, two critical factors were simultaneously present: the objective need for the Court to undertake the development of a new body of constitutional doctrine, and the will on the Court for it to do so. The confluence of these factors ushered in an era that continues today, one in which the consistent characteristic of the Supreme Court's land-use takings cases has been a search for principles, standards, and, in a few instances, hard-and-fast rules.

The Results of Two Decades of Supreme Court Effort

The lead-off case in the contemporary era of doctrinal development was *Penn Central Transportation Co. v. New York City*, decided in 1978 and still probably the most important single pronouncement in takings law.[10] In this and subsequent decisions, the Court made clarifying

[9]FELIX FRANKFURTER, OF LAW AND MEN 19 (1956).
[10]438 U.S. 104 (1978).

progress on multiple fronts. When is the landowner's taking claim ripe? Once ripe, what factors should be balanced in deciding whether, in "fairness and justice," government should have to pay? Are there instances where the usual multifactor balancing analysis can be dispensed with and a simpler "bright line" test invoked? Do exactions and dedication conditions imposed on the issuance of land development permits require a specialized approach to the takings question? And finally, given that a taking has occurred, what remedy does the Constitution mandate? Before the current era we had next to no idea what the answers were to these questions; now we at least have some.

So why isn't anyone happy? There has been no safer pursuit among commentators, even well into this period of doctrinal development, than lambasting takings law as incoherent. Says one writer: "[I]t is difficult to imagine a body of case law in greater doctrinal and conceptual disarray."[11] Another proposes that, for this and other reasons, the very construct of the regulatory taking be eliminated from constitutional law wholesale.[12] Justice Stevens has said that "[e]ven the wisest of lawyers would have to acknowledge great uncertainty about the scope of this Court's takings jurisprudence."[13]

The more extreme of these negative characterizations are overdrawn, we believe. Or at least an argument can be made that they implicitly ask too much. Takings law is confusing; indeed, maddening at times. But it is not without useful guidance, even in the large majority of cases where no bright-line rule has yet been provided. The real question is whether it is reasonable to ask for black-and-white certainty in this or any other area of constitutional law that applies to an infinitude of private circumstances and countervailing public interests, and that hews to a decisional standard as metaphysical as "fairness and justice." An argument can be made that takings cases are no more ad hoc or result oriented than many of those under the First and Fourth Amendments, or than decisions applying the doctrine of standing.

---

[11]Andrea Peterson, *The Takings Clause: In Search of Underlying Principles Part I—A Critique of Current Takings Law Doctrine*, 77 CALIFORNIA L. REV. 1299, 1304 (1989).

[12]J. Peter Byrne, *Ten Arguments for the Abolition of the Regulatory Takings Doctrine*, 22 ECOLOGY L.Q. 89 (1995) (argument "III").

[13]Nollan v. California Coastal Comm'n, 483 U.S. 825, 866 (1987) (Stevens, J., dissenting).

What we now have from the Supreme Court is, for most government impacts on land, a collection of "factors [of] particular significance" to be weighed and balanced in an ad hoc, case-by-case fashion.[14] In the large majority of cases using this approach, the landowner loses. For a few special circumstances, we instead have "per se rules" that dispense with multifactor balancing and find takings based on one particular aspect of the government action's impact. Fortunate is the landowner who can convince a court that such an automatic-taking rule has been triggered in his or her case.

Some commentators discern a striving in the Court to find more such automatic rules and bemoan the loss of flexibility.[15] Others hold that the Court is not seeking to "formalize" takings jurisprudence and yearn for more bright-line tests.[16] Whichever view one holds, it is clear that the Court has not gone nearly as far as property rights partisans wish, or friends of regulation fear. This underlays the push for legislative relief by property rights activists. The decisions hailed by property rights partisans and property owners as paradigm shifting victories—*First English*, *Lucas*, *Nollan*, and *Dolan*—do indeed confer greater protection of private property. But on any objective examination, they are also doctrinally cautious and often limited in application. To this day, the Supreme Court has never found a regulatory taking based on land-use restrictions in the absence of either a physical invasion or total deprivation of economic use.

Most certainly, property rights are enjoying an ascendancy of sorts, receiving more judicial scrutiny in some contexts than purely economic regulation.[17] But they have not yet taken a place alongside non-economic civil liberties (freedom of speech, association, religion, etc.) in the degree of judicial scrutiny and distrust of government that courts deem appropriate.[18] Government continues to enjoy ample room to regulate land use responsibly without significant chance of being made to pay.

[14]*Penn Central*, 438 U.S. at 124.

[15]Frank Michelman, *Takings 1987*, 88 COLUMBIA L. REV. 1600 (1988).

[16]Susan Rose-Ackerman, *Against Ad Hocery: A Comment on Michelman*, 88 COLUMBIA L. REV. 1697 (1988).

[17]*See, e.g., Nollan*, 483 U.S. at 834 n.3.

[18]To be sure, the Supreme Court recently said: "We see no reason why the Takings Clause of the Fifth Amendment, as much a part of the Bill of Rights as the First Amendment or Fourth Amendment, should be relegated to the status of a poor relation. . . ." Dolan v. City of Tigard, 512 U.S. 374, 392 (1994).

Taken as a whole, the Court's takings cases to date reveal both broad agreement and profound division. We see broad agreement across the spectrum of justices that the jurisprudence remains a largely ad hoc one, occasional efforts by individual justices to find per se rules notwithstanding. The Court, we think, will continue to sacrifice certainty of outcome on the altar of flexibility. Further, there appears to be broad agreement that in developing a jurisprudence of the Takings Clause, government must continue to have wide latitude to pursue the public's agenda without having to compensate all those affected.

Beyond this, accord disappears. Almost all the recent Supreme Court decisions in the land-use/takings area have divided the justices—often 5 to 4—underlining the fragility of the edifice the Court has built. And the lineup has been fairly consistent: conservative justices find for the property owner, liberal justices find for the government, and the center of the Court determines the outcome. The takings issue remains a political Rorschach, rooted in one's deepest convictions about the role of government vis-à-vis the individual, of the proper boundary between public rights and private burdens.

The Court's work in this area plays out against a background of powerful history and culture. There is, of course, a strong individual rights tradition in America. In particular, a near-mythic status has been accorded to property rights, beginning with the 17th century English philosopher John Locke whose thinking, by all accounts, heavily imbued the framers of the Bill of Rights. Property rights have been seen as both the undergirding of, and conversely an emanation from, our rights of life and liberty.

Sometimes lost in the shuffle, however, are the nuances. Few legal rights, those in property included, are absolute. Recently a commentator noted an increasing tendency of our citizens, beginning with the civil rights movement of the 1960s, to speak of what is most important to them in terms of absolute rights—"to frame nearly every social controversy as a clash of rights."[19] The contrast with other Western democracies,[20] let alone with Eastern cultures, has long been

[19]MARY A. GLENDON, RIGHTS TALK: THE IMPOVERISHMENT OF POLITICAL DISCOURSE 4 (1991).

[20]Not the views of John Locke, but rather the less-admiring notions of private property propounded by Jean-Jacques Rousseau, were the most influential in continental Europe.

evident. In continental Europe, the idea of property has been described as a "paradigm of inherent limitations."[21] Here, a romanticism of property-rights absoluteness remains strong in the popular mind, even if the legal reality is far more qualified. For the Supreme Court, it simply means that its brushstrokes on takings law add to a rich and complex mural.

[21]GLENDON, *supra* note 19, at 32.

Chapter 2

Property Protection in Federal and State Constitutions

The important position of property in our culture is accorded recognition in federal and state constitutions alike, and by more than just takings clauses. What follows is a sketch of the broad constitutional landscape.

The Federal Constitution

To the men of affairs who launched the new American government, how property rights would be kept secure under an untested majoritarian system was a matter of some concern. Not only their abiding belief in property as a natural right and the underpinning of personal liberty, but their own parochial interests as major landowners, seems to have infused the framers' thinking.[1] For these reasons, direct or indirect protections for property rights are scattered throughout the Constitution. Of these, the three most prominent are the Takings Clause, the Due Process Clause, and the Fourth Amendment—all in the Bill of Rights and all initially confined to actions of the federal government. A fourth major constitutional provision directed at property was added in 1868, when the Fourteenth Amendment due process clause was adopted. That amendment was eventually interpreted to extend the Takings Clause and Fourth Amendment, along

[1] JAMES W. ELY, JR., THE GUARDIAN OF EVERY OTHER RIGHT 42–43 (1992).

13

with much of the remainder of the Bill of Rights, to actions of state and local governments.[2]

Takings Clause

Of these constitutional safeguards, the Takings Clause of the Fifth Amendment is today the dominant presence in the field. Its simple words belie the infinite array of government/private entanglements to which it applies:

> [N]or shall private property be taken for public use, without just compensation.

Observe that the clause is phrased not as a grant of new power to the federal government—the power to take private property is regarded by American courts as inherent in the nature of sovereignty, requiring no constitutional recognition.[3] Rather, the clause functions as a limitation on a power that would otherwise be absolute.[4] As is plain, those limitations are two: the property may only be taken for a "public use," and only upon payment of "just compensation."

Though by its terms the Takings Clause applies only to the federal government, its interpretation by the courts is not just of federal interest. As noted, the post–Civil War adoption of the Fourteenth Amendment due process clause had the effect, much later, of stretching the Takings Clause to reach the acts of states and localities as fully as those of the central government. Equally important, judicial interpretation of takings clauses in state constitutions usually takes its cue from how the federal counterpart is read.

As originally conceived, the federal Takings Clause probably was intended (though the evidence is not clear) to apply in only a limited circumstance—government confiscation of property for public roads and buildings and other physically invasive uses.[5] Few at the time

---

[2]Dolan v. City of Tigard, 512 U.S. 374, 383–84 & n.5 (1994) (citing Chicago, B. & Q. R.R. v. City of Chicago, 166 U.S. 226 (1897) (extension of Takings Clause to states)); Wolf v. Colorado, 338 U.S. 25 (1949) (extension of Fourth Amendment to states).

[3]Boom Co. v. Patterson, 98 U.S. 403, 406 (1878); Vanhorne's Lessee v. Dorrance, 2 U.S. (2 Dall.) 304, 310 (Cir. Ct. 1795).

[4]United States v. Carmack, 329 U.S. 230, 241–42 (1946).

[5]William M. Treanor, Note, *The Origins and Original Significance of the Just Compensation Clause*, 94 YALE L.J. 694 (1985). No less a conservative than Justice Scalia has accepted that "early constitutional theorists did not believe the Takings Clause embraced regulation of property at all." Lucas v. South Carolina Coastal Council, 505 U.S. 1003, 1028 n.15 (1992).

likely imagined that it would ever be invoked, as it routinely is today, in suits by a landowner against the government involving solely restriction of property use. Owner-initiated actions under the clause were not blessed by the Supreme Court until 1871,[6] though the Court was not yet ready then to apply the clause beyond its historical moorings in government seizure and physical occupation.[7] For the next half century, the Court confined its takings analysis largely to floodings from government water projects and other physical invasions. In 1922, however, a constitutional Rubicon was crossed with the landmark decision in *Pennsylvania Coal Co. v. Mahon*.[8] There, the Court recognized for the first time that a mere use restriction by government, in the absence of any physical occupation or appropriation of the land, could trigger a Fifth Amendment right to compensation. Thus was born the "regulatory taking" concept that is the central concern of this book.

Due Process Clauses

The rise of the regulatory taking doctrine since 1922 has mostly eclipsed its forerunners as the preeminent constitutional bound on government land-use control. Still, successful claims under the Fifth and Fourteenth Amendment due process clauses are occasionally made, even today.[9] In identical words, these clauses state:

> nor shall any person . . . be deprived of . . . property without due process of law. . . .

While these clauses are stated as procedural safeguards, the Supreme Court has long read them to have a substantive component as well—demanding that government acts be nonarbitrary and sufficiently related to a legitimate government objective. Until the Supreme Court's

---

[6]Pumpelly v. Green Bay Co., 80 U.S. (13 Wall.) 166 (1871).

[7]The most prominent case of the period rejecting use of the Takings Clause in the absence of government seizure and occupation is Mugler v. Kansas, 123 U.S. 623 (1887) (prohibition simply upon use of property for noxious purposes is not taking).

[8]260 U.S. 393 (1922).

[9]*See, e.g.,* Guimont v. Clarke, 121 Wash. 2d 586, 854 P.2d 1 (1993) (state statute requiring mobile-home park owners to contribute to tenant relocation costs is not taking, but does violate substantive due process), *cert. denied,* 510 U.S. 1176 (1994). One federal circuit, however, has limited substantive due process to situations not addressable by more specific constitutional proscriptions such as the Takings Clause. Armendariz v. Penman, 75 F.3d 1311 (9th Cir. 1996) (en banc).

recognition of regulatory takings in 1922, this "substantive due process" prong, together with the police power requirement that government acts further the public health, safety, morals, and welfare, were the prevailing theories for testing regulatory impacts on private property. Even after 1922, the Court found it hard to part with the familiar for the new. In 1926 and 1928, two challenges to the then-novel concept of comprehensive municipal zoning were decided on due process, not taking, grounds.[10] In the 1960s, decades after the demise of substantive due process, the Court took the bold step of subjecting a land-use measure to takings analysis, after comforting itself with an almost identical due process evaluation.[11]

Today, the Due Process Clause *itself* is rarely used by the Supreme Court when the issue is government curtailment of a tract's economic potential. But having exited this realm through the front door, due process is reentering through the back. In 1980, the Court announced a new takings criterion based on the degree of fit between the government's means and ends, a quintessentially due process concern. A land-use control, it said, is a taking if it fails to "substantially advance a legitimate governmental interest."[12] Though this due process–like criterion initially was ignored by lower courts, it has been spotlighted recently by the Supreme Court;[13] indeed, defined to require greater means-end scrutiny of land-use regulation than does due process analysis.[14] Some observers have suggested that the conservative wing of the Court is intent on at least this limited resurrection of the substantive due process heyday of the early 20th century, when the clause was used routinely by the Court to strike down maximum hour, minimum wage, and other social legislation as interference with "liberty of contract."[15]

[10]Village of Euclid v. Ambler Realty Co., 272 U.S. 365 (1926); Nectow v. City of Cambridge, 277 U.S. 183 (1928). *See also* Miller v. Schoene, 276 U.S. 272 (1928) (state order that infected trees be cut down did not exceed due process).

[11]Goldblatt v. Town of Hempstead, 369 U.S. 590 (1962).

[12]Agins v. City of Tiburon, 447 U.S. 255, 260 (1980).

[13]Nollan v. California Coastal Comm'n, 483 U.S. 825 (1987); Dolan v. City of Tigard, 512 U.S. 374 (1994).

[14]*Nollan*, 483 U.S. at 834 n.3.

[15]Constitutional scholars refer to this time of active judicial scrutiny of social and economic legislation as "the *Lochner* period," after the leading case of Lochner v. New York, 198 U.S. 45 (1905). There, the Court held that a state law restricting employment in bakeries to 10 hours per day and 60 hours per week was an unconstitutional interference with the right of adult laborers to contract as to their means of livelihood.

Comparison of Due Process and Takings Theories

A quick comparison of substantive due process and takings theories may be useful here, since they share the spotlight as the chief constitutional constraints on government abuse in the realm of land-use regulation. Then, too, courts themselves have long confused the two, sometimes to the point of leaving one baffled as to which theory a holding rests upon.[16] One court even flirted for some years with the hermaphroditic concept of a "due process taking," before repudiating it as irreconcilable with recent Supreme Court takings decisions.[17] Most aggrieved landowners who invoke substantive due process also argue taking.[18]

As an initial matter, due process sweeps in many more rights under the rubric of "property" than does the Takings Clause,[19] though what is important here is that land-use rights are clearly and unequivocally included under both. More fundamentally, the two clauses generally implicate very different concerns. Takings law, shorn of its recent due process graft, is largely focused on the economic impact or the intrusiveness of government control;[20] it is result

---

[16]For judicial comment on the confusion, see Tampa-Hillsborough County Expressway Auth. v. A.G.W.S. Corp., 640 So. 2d 54, 57 (Fla. 1994); Orion Corp. v. State, 109 Wash. 2d 621, 747 P.2d 1062, 1076–77 (1987) (en banc), cert. denied, 486 U.S. 1022 (1988). For other comment, see Report of the ABA Subcomm. on Land Use Litigation and Damages, *Land Use Litigation: Doctrinal Confusion Under the Fifth and Fourteenth Amendments* (1996); Michael J. Davis and Robert L. Glicksman, *To the Promised Land: A Century of Wandering and a Final Homeland for the Due Process and Taking Clauses*, 68 Oregon L. Rev. 393, 394 (1989).

A good example of the takings/due process confusion is Gerijo, Inc. v. City of Fairfield, 70 Ohio St. 3d 223, 638 N.E.2d 533 (1994), cert. denied, 513 U.S. 1150 (1995).

[17]Villas of Lake Jackson v. Leon County, 121 F.3d 610 (11th Cir. 1997).

[18]Stuart M. Benjamin, Note, *The Applicability of Just Compensation to Substantive Due Process Claims*, 100 Yale L.J. 2667, 2669 (1991).

[19]Corn v. City of Lauderdale Lakes, 95 F.3d 1066, 1075 (11th Cir. 1996), cert. denied, 118 S. Ct. 441 (1997); Pittman v. Chicago Bd. of Educ., 64 F.3d 1098, 1104 (7th Cir. 1995), cert. denied, 116 S. Ct. 2497 (1996). See due-process property cases collected in Logan v. Zimmerman Brush Co., 455 U.S. 422, 430–31 (1982).

[20]Two of the three regulatory taking factors recited in Penn Central Transp. Co. v. New York City, 438 U.S. 104 (1978)—"economic impact" and the degree of interference with "distinct investment-backed expectations"—are economic in nature.

based. Substantive due process, by contrast, examines chiefly, though not exclusively, the fit between the government's chosen means and its desired end; it is rationality based.[21] A quite irrational government act (violating due process) might have little economic impact (causing no taking), and vice versa. Again, however, the Supreme Court's insertion into regulatory takings law of the "substantially advance a legitimate governmental interest" factor blurs this distinction.

Another point of comparison is the ripeness prerequisite under each clause—a taking plaintiff must seek compensation at the state level (unless it would be futile) before bringing his or her claim in federal court, but a due process plaintiff may or may not have to do so, the courts being split on this point.[22] Finally, there are differences of remedy. Takings require government to *compensate* the landowner; invalidation of a land-use control is called for only in rare circumstances—when no avenue for obtaining compensation for the taking is available. By contrast, violation of due process means that the government act is *invalid,* rather than compensable. Thus, plaintiff's election of which theory to press determines at the outset whether the government treasury is vulnerable.

Fourth Amendment

Another constitutional locus of property rights concern is the Fourth Amendment, conferring upon the citizenry "the right . . . to be secure in their persons, houses, papers, and effects, against unreasonable searches and seizures. . . ." Protection of property rights as the moving spirit behind this Amendment was long accepted by the Supreme Court.[23] More recently, however, the "premise that property rights control the right of the Government to search and seize has been discredited."[24] Rather, what the Fourth Amendment is all about, says the modern Supreme Court, is the protection of *privacy.*[25] The Amendment's protection hinges not on a property right in the invaded place,

[21]Many courts also find in substantive due process a concern as to whether the government action is unduly oppressive, a more takings-like inquiry. *See, e.g.,* Presbytery of Seattle v. King County, 114 Wash. 2d 320, 330, 787 P.2d 907, *cert. denied,* 498 U.S. 911 (1990); Guimont v. Clarke, 121 Wash. 2d 586, 854 P.2d 1 (1993), *cert. denied,* 510 U.S. 1176 (1994).

[22]Note, *supra* note 18, at 2672–74.

[23]Boyd v. United States, 116 U.S. 616, 627 (1886); Adams v. New York, 192 U.S. 585, 598 (1904).

[24]Warden v. Hayden, 387 U.S. 294, 304 (1967).

[25]*Id.*

but upon whether the area was one in which there was reasonable expectation of freedom from government intrusion.[26] Of course, one will not be surprised to learn that there is no difference in result between many of the old cases premised on property and the new generation of cases in which the plaintiff's reasonable expectation of privacy is tied to property ownership.[27] Also not surprisingly, the prime example of a Fourth Amendment–protected interest remains the home.

State Constitutions

Over 60 years ago, U.S. Supreme Court Justice Louis Brandeis characterized the states as social and political "laboratories" that should be allowed to confront the major issues of our era with great latitude, free from unnecessary federal intervention.[28] To some degree, this "federalist" view has been reflected in a renaissance of state constitutional law over the past two decades. Long relegated to legal obscurity, state constitutions are gaining renewed interest and importance in modern American jurisprudence.[29] Couple that trend with

[26]This shift toward a Fourth Amendment jurisprudence based on reasonable expectations of privacy presaged the rise of reasonable expectations on the part of land purchasers as an explicit defining concept in Takings Clause jurisprudence. *See especially* Penn Central Transp. Co. v. New York City, 438 U.S. 104, 124 (1978) (government interference with "investment-backed expectations" a regulatory taking factor); Lucas v. South Carolina Coastal Council, 505 U.S. 1003, 1027 (1992) (takings law traditionally guided by the "understandings of our citizens" as to what rights they acquire when they buy property).

[27]*See, e.g.,* Rakas v. Illinois, 439 U.S. 128, 143–44 n.12 (1978) (privacy expectations must have source outside Fourth Amendment, as by "reference to concepts of real or personal property").

[28]New State Ice Co. v. Liebmann, 285 U.S. 262, 311 (1932) (Brandeis, J., dissenting).

[29]That trend is in large part due to the pioneering scholarship of Justice William J. Brennan nearly 50 years after Brandeis's prescient remarks. Brennan's landmark article on the significance of state constitutional law a generation ago (*State Constitutions and the Protection of Individual Rights*, 90 HARVARD LAW REV. 489 (1977)) has triggered a renewed interest in state constitutions that continues to grow. *See, e.g.,* Shirley Abrahamson, *Criminal Law and State Constitutions: The Emergence of State Constitutional Law*, 63 TEXAS L. REV. 1141 (1985); Project, *State Constitutional Law for the 21st Century* (Gormley, ed.), 67 OREGON L. REV. (No. 3, 1988); Project, *Emerging Issues in State Constitutional Law* (Nat'l Ass'n of Att'ys Gen., ed.) (No. 1, 1988).

the recent tidal wave of inverse condemnation litigation in this nation, and it was perhaps inevitable that the intersection of takings principles and state constitutional law would similarly take on heightened significance.

Takings Provisions

Forty-seven of fifty state constitutions contain a "takings clause."[30] Some of those provisions simply quote the Fifth Amendment, while the language of other state constitutional provisions varies from the federal counterpart to one degree or another.

One key textual difference is that 25 states have takings clauses that require compensation for property that is "taken *or damaged*" (emphasis added).[31] It would seem at first blush that this distinction affords private property owners an additional measure of judicial protection as compared to the Fifth Amendment. However, most states have declined to so interpret their state takings clauses, finding the level of protection afforded property owners to be coextensive with that provided under the Fifth Amendment.[32]

[30]The constitution of every state in the union except Kansas, New Hampshire, and North Carolina contains a provision mandating just compensation for private property that is "taken" by the government for public use. 8A JULIUS SACKMAN, NICHOLS ON EMINENT DOMAIN § 16.01 (rev. 3rd ed. 1997).

Even those states lacking a *constitutional* bulwark against government takings of private property afford the same type of protection by alternate means. Kansas provides such protection via a state statute that has been construed to "codify" the federal Takings Clause. Kan. Stat. Ann. § 26-513(a), *interpreted in* Garrett v. City of Topeka, 259 Kan. 896, 916 P.2d 21, 30 (1996). New Hampshire and North Carolina afford similar relief by analogizing to related constitutional provisions in their constitutions. *See, e.g.*, Burrows v. City of Keene, 121 N.H. 590, 432 A.2d 15, 18 (1981); Eller v. Board of Educ., 242 N.C. 584, 89 S.E.2d 144, 146 (1955).

[31]Those states with constitutions containing "taken or damaged" language include: Ala. Const. art. XII, § 235; Ariz. Const. art. II, § 17; Ark. Const. art. II, § 22; Cal. Const. art. I, § 19; Colo. Const. art. II, § 15; Ga. Const. art. I, § 3(a); Ill. Const. art. I, § 15; Ky. Const., § 13; La. Const. art. I., § 2; Minn. Const. art. I, § 13; Miss. Const. art. III, § 17; Mo. Const. art. I, § 26; Mont. Const. art. II, § 29; Neb. Const. art I, § 21; N.M. Const. art. II, § 20; N.D. Const. art. I, § 16; Okla. Const. art. II, §§ 23, 24; Pa. Const. art. I, § 10; S.D. Const. art. VI, § 13; Tex. Const. art. I, § 17; Utah Const. art. I, § 22; Va. Const. art. I, § 11; Wash. Const. art. I, § 16; W. Va. Const. art. III, § 9; Wyo. Const. art. I, § 33.

[32]Illustrative of the majority rule are Hensler v. City of Glendale, 8 Cal. 4th 1, 9 n.4, 876 P.2d 1043, 1048 n.4 (1994), *cert. denied,* 513 U.S. 1184 (1995); Outdoor Sys., Inc. v. City of Mesa, 997 F.2d 604, 618 (9th Cir. 1993) (citing

A few jurisdictions take a contrary view, however, concluding that the "or damaged" language provides a heightened shield of constitutional protection, over and above that offered by the federal Takings Clause.[33] The Illinois Supreme Court, for example, recently relied exclusively on that state's constitution to strike down municipal transportation impact fees as an invalid taking.[34] It did so by finding that the challenged fees were not "specifically and uniquely attributable" to the affected development—despite the fact that the U.S. Supreme Court had previously ruled in *Dolan v. City of Tigard*[35] that such a precise constitutional fit was not required by the *federal* Takings Clause. The Illinois court thereby confirmed a key principle: the Fifth Amendment provides a *floor* of property rights protection, with individual states being permitted to create a higher constitutional standard under the aegis of "independent state grounds"—i.e., a state-enacted constitutional provision.

Other jurisdictions take the view that while their state constitutions do not provide an enhanced *level* of protection for private property interests, they encompass broader *types* of property interests than those traditionally cognizable under the Fifth Amendment. The California Supreme Court found a viable, state constitution–based inverse condemnation claim arising from recurring odors attributable to a municipal sewage treatment plant. It observed that the California Constitution "protects a somewhat broader array of property values from government destruction than does the analogous federal provision."[36]

One key reason why some state courts prefer to rely on their own

---

prior state court decisions interpreting Ariz. Const. art. II, § 17); City of Northglenn v. Grynberg, 846 P.2d 175, 179–80 (Colo.), *cert. denied,* 510 U.S. 815 (1993).

[33]*See, e.g.,* Whitehead Oil Co. v. City of Lincoln, 245 Neb. 680, 515 N.W.2d 401, 408 (1994) (disjunctive language of Nebraska takings clause "obviously broader" in scope than U.S. Constitution); St. Lucas Ass'n v. Chicago, 212 Ill. App. 3d 817, 571 N.E.2d 865, 875 (1991) (declining to find a compensable taking under Illinois Constitution's "taking or damaged" language); Martin v. Port of Seattle, 64 Wash. 2d 309, 391 P.2d 540, 546 (1964), *cert. denied,* 379 U.S. 989 (1965); Knight v. City of Billings, 197 Mont. 165, 642 P.2d 141 (1982).

[34]Northern Ill. Home Builders Ass'n v. County of DuPage, 165 Ill. 2d 25, 649 N.E.2d 384, 389–90 (1995).

[35]512 U.S. 374 (1994).

[36]Varjabedian v. City of Madera, 20 Cal. 3d 285, 298, 572 P.2d 43, 52 (1977). On virtually the same facts, the Supreme Court of Rhode Island declined to find a compensable taking under either the federal or state constitutions. Harris v. Town of Lincoln, 668 A.2d 321, 327–28 (R.I. 1995).

constitutions in regulatory takings cases is that it frees them from the
sometimes difficult (or objectionable) task of reconciling their holdings with those of other state and federal courts. Illustrative is the
South Dakota Supreme Court's decision in *U.S. West Communications, Inc. v. Public Utilities Comm'n.*[37] That court found that a
state's telecommunications order preventing a regulated utility from
using its own existing telecommunications facilities to transport its
long-distance telecommunications traffic was a regulatory taking.
The South Dakota court predicated its ruling exclusively on its state
constitution, so that it would not feel constrained by "divergent law"
of regulatory takings found in other jurisdictions.[38]

There are several reasons why an aggrieved property owner might
choose to base a regulatory takings claim on state, rather than federal, constitutional provisions. Before the U.S. Supreme Court confirmed that monetary damages were a constitutionally compelled
remedy under the Fifth Amendment in 1987, several state courts applied analogous *state* constitutional provisions to compel the same
result in regulatory takings cases.[39]

While that strategy is no longer crucial, there remain several reasons why regulatory takings plaintiffs might wish to include a state
constitutional claim as part of an inverse condemnation lawsuit.
First, the often-tortuous ripeness hurdles which confront any *federal*
takings claim may be avoided. (Some state courts have not seen fit
to replicate the *Williamson County* ripeness rules discussed in
chapter 5 as part of their *state* constitutional rules.[40]) Second, as
noted above, there is always the chance that a state court will interpret its just compensation clause either to afford a higher level of
property rights protection or to encompass a broader range of property interests. In short, from the perspective of the landowner, pursuing a parallel state constitutional taking claim cannot hurt, and it
just may help.

[37]505 N.W.2d 115 (S.D. 1993).

[38]*Id.* at 127.

[39]*See, e.g.*, Ventures in Property v. City of Wichita, 225 Kan. 698, 711–12,
594 P.2d 671, 681–82 (1979). *See generally* J. Margaret Tretbar, *Calculating
Compensation for Temporary Regulatory Takings*, 42 KANSAS L. REV. 201, 203,
n.22 (1993).

[40]Williamson County Regional Planning Comm'n v. Hamilton Bank, 473
U.S. 172 (1985).

Other State Constitutional Provisions

Many state constitutions similarly contain substantive due process and "search and seizure" provisions comparable to those found in the U.S. Constitution. To date, efforts by property rights advocates to rely upon these state provisions to bolster their antiregulation position have been largely unsuccessful.

The one prominent exception has been the State of Washington. The supreme court of that state has issued a series of decisions in which it has rejected regulatory takings–based challenges to local land-use measures, only to find that the same regulatory programs raise concerns under both state and federal substantive due process provisions.[41]

A decade ago, U.S. Supreme Court Justice William Brennan observed:

> [S]tate supreme courts are increasingly evaluating their state constitutions and concluding that those constitutions should be applied to confer greater civil liberties than their federal counterparts . . . [T]his rediscovery by state supreme courts . . . is probably the most important development in constitutional jurisprudence of our times. For state constitutional law will assume an increasingly more visible role in American law in the years ahead.[42]

Justice Brennan's ruminations apply with equal force when it comes to state constitutional provisions affecting private property rights, especially state takings claims.

[41]*See, e.g.,* Guimont v. Clarke, 121 Wash. 2d 586, 854 P.2d 1 (1993), *cert. denied,* 512 U.S. 1176 (1994); Sintra, Inc. v. City of Seattle, 119 Wash. 2d 1, 829 P.2d 765, *cert. denied,* 506 U.S. 1028 (1992).

[42]Justice William J. Brennan, Address on "The Fourteenth Amendment" (Aug. 8, 1986), quoted in Robert Abrams, *Introduction,* 1 EMERGING ISSUES IN STATE CONSTITUTIONAL LAW xi (1988).

Chapter 3

Property and Takings Law

The Takings Clause is relevant only when the particular interest, expectation, or desired state of affairs which government is adversely affecting is one that can be called "property." Quite plainly, then, the essential first step for the landowner in framing a taking claim is to pinpoint a property interest—one that is protected under the state or federal constitutions' takings clauses. In the absence of such an interest, there can be no taking, no matter how great the impact of the government action (though relief under other legal theories may be available).

Property Generally

The institution of property, it hardly need be said, has rivaled love, war, and the nature of right and wrong as a favorite topic of legal philosophers. In the early 19th century, William Blackstone defined property rights as "that sole and despotic dominion which one man claims and exercises over the external things of the world."[1] John Locke saw the concept more expansively as including the products of human creativity as well as land and material possessions, and he deemed its preservation "the great and chief end of government."[2] In a similar vein, James Madison, in his essay on property, wrote that it "embraces every thing to which a man may attach a value and have a

[1]WILLIAM BLACKSTONE, COMMENTARIES ON THE LAWS OF ENGLAND 2 (1803).
[2]JOHN LOCKE, THE SECOND TREATISE OF GOVERNMENT 71 (1952) (orig. pub. 1690).

right."[3] Though our concern in this book is primarily with land—the most traditional form of property—the same questions about which rights warrant protection and what the role of government is vis-à-vis those rights remain at the forefront of the debate.

And perhaps it ever will be. To be sure, "[t]hat government can scarcely be deemed to be free, when the rights of property are left solely dependent upon the will of a legislative body, without any restraint."[4] It is difficult to imagine certain property interests being compromised to a serious degree without substantial government justification. At the same time, property rights change over time; they are not as absolute and immutable as conservatives like to describe them. By long-standing tradition, they embody a dynamic tension between public and private rights, transforming themselves in tandem with societal perceptions and needs. In particular, new scientific awareness, such as the interconnectedness of nature demonstrated by ecologists, may "shape[] our evolving understandings of property rights."[5] As we shall see at the end of this chapter, the recently hatched concepts of "background principles" and "compensable expectancies" may facilitate that evolution.

"Property" in Takings Law: The "Bundle of Sticks"

In takings analysis, "property" is used not in the "vulgar and untechnical sense of the physical thing."[6] Which is to say, the house, the parcel of land, the harvestable timber, is not itself the property. Rather, "property" refers to "the group of rights inhering in the cit-

[3]James Madison, *Property* (orig. pub. 1792) *in* 14 THE PAPERS OF JAMES MADISON 266 (Robert F. Rutland & Charles F. Hobson eds., 1983).

[4]Wilkinson v. Leland, 27 U.S. (2 Pet.) 627, 657 (1829).

[5]Lucas v. South Carolina Coastal Council, 505 U.S. 1003, 1070 (1992) (Stevens, J., dissenting). A similar sentiment is implicit in Justice Kennedy's concurring opinion. *Id.* at 1034–35. *See also* Joseph L. Sax, *Property Rights and the Economy of Nature: Understanding* Lucas v. South Carolina Coastal Council, 45 STANFORD L. REV. 1433, 1446–49 (1993) (property definitions historically have evolved to reflect new economic and social values, often to the disadvantage of existing owners); Myrl L. Duncan, *Property as a Public Conversation, Not a Lockean Soliloquy*, 26 ENVTL. L. 1095 (1996) (judges should begin to reconcile conception of property with modern science's finding that nature is interconnected).

[6]Ruckelshaus v. Monsanto Co., 467 U.S. 986, 1003 (1984) (quoting United States v. General Motors, 323 U.S. 373, 377–78 (1945)).

izen's relation to the physical thing, as the right to possess, use, and dispose of it."[7] Thus, property is the set of government-backed rights one has in the physical thing. There's a good measure of sense to this rights-based definition, since it provides a more comfortable foundation for the idea of regulatory takings than does a notion of property as the physical thing. After all, the gravamen of regulatory takings theory is that the physical thing can be eviscerated of its utility, while not taken in the physical or appropriation sense. What *has* been taken are rights.

Providing a metaphor for this rights-based vision of property is the Supreme Court's characterization of the owner's rights in a parcel as a "bundle of sticks." That image is often used to make the point that the destruction of one "strand" in the bundle generally is not a taking, because the aggregate must be viewed in its entirety (*see* chapter 12).[8] The Supreme Court has also made plain that some strands are more important than others. While there are four essential kinds of property rights—possession, use, exclusion of others, and disposal[9]—the right-to-exclude-others "strand" has been elevated to superstar status under the Fifth Amendment. As we shall see in chapter 11, even minimal government trifling with this particular right will, if sufficiently long-lived, be deemed a taking.[10] In contrast, government regulation of less-beknighted interests in land (such as rights of use) must be severe, if not total, before courts will insist on compensating the landowner (*see* chapter 12).

Sources of Property Interests

Property interests, the Supreme Court has reminded us, are not created by the U.S. Constitution itself. "Rather they are created and their dimensions defined by existing rules or understandings that stem from an independent source such as state law."[11] As suggested

---

[7]*Id.*

[8]Andrus v. Allard, 444 U.S. 51, 65–66 (1979).

[9]United States v. General Motors, 323 U.S. 373, 377–78 (1945).

[10]Another, more esoteric, property interest placed on a pedestal by the Supreme Court, at least where the abrogation is substantial, is the right to pass on land to one's heirs. Babbitt v. Youpee, 117 S. Ct. 727 (1997); Hodel v. Irving, 481 U.S. 704 (1987) (comparing right to pass on property to right to exclude others).

[11]Webb's Fabulous Pharmacies v. Beckwith, 449 U.S. 155, 161 (1980).

by its solo mention, state law is the most fertile of these extraconstitutional sources, particularly as to property interests in land. Thus, though the meaning of "property" in the U.S. Constitution has been held a federal question, it normally should be ascertained by looking to state law.[12]

Though less frequently invoked, there are nonstate sources of protected property interests in land, too. Unpatented mining claims and mineral leases on the federal lands are prime examples of *federal* law operating to create property interests.[13] Federally recognized Indian land claims are another.[14] Long-standing custom has emerged in some recent cases as an independent or buttressing source of property rights.[15]

Whatever their source, the point is that constitutionally protected property interests do not come about simply because a property owner has a unilateral expectation or abstract need—that is, because he or she fared better under the old regime.[16] There must be a government act or recognition to back up the expectation or need. As the Supreme Court put it: "[O]nly those economic advantages are 'rights' which have the law back of them."[17]

Of course, interests in land are among the most long-recognized and firmly entrenched species of property; they are not often the subject of litigation as to whether this or that right of use is a mere "unilateral expectation." Far more often, the borderline cases revolve around nonland contexts—such as the termination of a government benefit[18] or a change in an economically advantageous law.[19] On occasion, however, the property status of land-related interests is in

[12]United States *ex rel.* TVA v. Powelson, 319 U.S. 266, 279 (1943). *See generally* I. J. Schiffres, Annotation, 1 A.L.R. Fed. 479 (1969).

[13]*See, e.g.,* Clawson v. United States, 24 Cl. Ct. 366, 369 (1991) (unpatented mining claims constitute property).

[14]Tee-Hit-Ton Indians v. United States, 348 U.S. 272, 288–89 (1955); Uintah Ute Indians v. United States, 28 Fed. Cl. 768 (1993).

[15]*See, e.g.,* Skip Kirchdorfer, Inc. v. United States, 6 F.3d 1573, 1582 (Fed. Cir. 1993).

[16]Webb's Fabulous Pharmacies v. Beckwith, 449 U.S. 155, 161 (1980) ("mere unilateral expectation or an abstract need is not a property interest").

[17]Kaiser Aetna v. United States, 444 U.S. 164, 178 (1979).

[18]*See, e.g.,* Bowen v. Gilliard, 483 U.S. 587 (expectations of continued welfare benefits and child support payments not property).

[19]*See, e.g.,* Story v. Green, 978 F.2d 60 (2d Cir. 1992) (exemption from municipal peddling regulations is not property interest).

play. Examples have included whether one has a property interest or a mere expectation in the renewal of a leasehold,[20] or, following substantial capital expenditure, in the issuance of a facility operating permit,[21] or in the continuation of private benefits resulting inadvertently from a government facility.[22]

A New Approach: Compensable Expectancies

One of the most intriguing changes taking place in takings law today is the maturing of that body of law's understanding of property. For a century, the takings opinions recited the classical property interests of possession, use, right of exclusion, and disposal without further elaboration. That simple description was adequate for an earlier time, but not in today's more complex regulatory environment.

In decisions of the 1980s, reaching full flower in *Lucas v. South Carolina Coastal Council* in 1992,[23] the Supreme Court has sketched a more elaborated vision of the interests that make up Takings Clause–protected property. In particular, the Court has pointed to "background principles" of nuisance and property law as defining the range of compensable interests a plaintiff has. It is no longer enough to say in a takings claim that a government action eliminated a right of use, the Court intimates. The argument today must be that the government action eliminated a use which, notwithstanding such background principles, the plaintiff had a reasonable expectation of being able to carry out.

This new *Lucas*-emphasized perspective on what makes for a compensable property right seems to modify how takings claims should be analyzed. Where once the property owner's use expectations were examined only as part of applying the regulatory takings test, the new approach inserts an expectations analysis into the prior inquiry as to *whether plaintiff has a property interest at all*. If not, the court's task is at an end; it need not even begin the fact-intensive analysis as to how the regulation affects the particular property. Certainly, courts have always had to ask whether there was a cognizable property interest

[20]United States v. Petty Motor Co., 327 U.S. 372, 379–80 (1946).

[21]Allied-General Nuclear Services Corp. v. United States, 839 F.2d 1572 (Fed. Cir.), *cert. denied*, 488 U.S. 819 (1988).

[22]Avenal, Jr. v. United States, 100 F.3d 933, 936 (Fed. Cir. 1996).

[23]505 U.S. 1003.

before moving on to whether a taking occurred. Now, however, that first inquiry is cast by *Lucas* in more fluid, context-dependent terms.

Property rights partisans have expressed deep suspicion over the *Lucas* approach. Professor Richard Epstein sees expectations as "pav[ing] the way for the rapid elimination of all perceived entitlements by simply claiming that the enactment of a single government regulation reasonably creates an expectation that further regulations will follow."[24] On this understanding, he says, property owners may be "considered 'on notice' about the prospect of new restrictions on land use and cannot complain when they occur."[25] Justice Scalia himself hinted at this possibility in his *Lucas* majority opinion.[26] A separate implication is that the buyer of land obtains fewer rights than the seller originally acquired if the government puts new use restrictions in place during the seller's period of ownership.[27]

A prominent endorsement of the new approach is in *M & J Coal Co. v. United States*.[28] There, a mining company argued that the United States had brought about a taking by increasing the amount of coal the company had to leave in the ground to prevent any danger to public health and safety from surface subsidence. The Federal Circuit thought otherwise, concluding that an "antecedent" inquiry into the property-use interests acquired by M & J showed that it had no reasonable expectation, given the law in effect when its mineral interest was acquired, to be free of federal intervention when its operations threatened public health and safety. Thus, the federal action did not interfere with any compensable property interest, and the court did not have to launch into the second phase of the analysis, as to whether a taking occurred.

Quite arguably, the *M & J* holding could have been reached on a traditional takings analysis, citing the nuisance exemption to takings liability. The same point could be made about another leading compensable expectancies case, *California Housing Securities, Inc. v.*

---

[24]Richard A. Epstein, Lucas v. South Carolina Coastal Council: *A Tangled Web of Expectations*, 45 STANFORD L. REV. 1369, 1371 (1993).

[25]*Id.*

[26]505 U.S. at 1027 ("property owner necessarily expects the uses of his property to be restricted, from time to time. . . .").

[27]Justice Scalia apparently would not extend the expectations approach this far, at least not where dedication of a physically invasive easement is involved. *See* Nollan v. California Coastal Comm'n, 483 U.S. 825, 833–34 n.2 (1987).

[28]47 F.3d 1148 (Fed. Cir.), *cert. denied*, 516 U.S. 808 (1995).

United States.[29] Even if the court had not invoked the absence of protected expectancies there, it likely would have been unsympathetic to
claims by failed savings and loans that the physical takeover of their
premises by federal rescue agencies effected a physical taking. Still, the
doctrine of compensable expectancies is in its infancy, and the full
range of its implications unclear. The most important new decision is
Preseault v. United States, a rails-to-trails case far removed from the
traditional nuisance/public-health-and-safety exemption to takings
liability.[30] In explicitly refusing to apply expectations analysis to the
definition of title there, *Preseault* suggests that the doctrine has its
bounds. In particular, it may have limited applicability in takings actions based on outright appropriation of private property (rather than
mere restriction of use). A land purchaser does not "expect" that he
or she will be asked to suffer *that* consequence noncompensably.[31]

Under various formulations, the idea that the range of constitutionally protected property interests can be stated in terms of purchaser expectations has begun to percolate down to the state courts.
On February 18, 1997, the high court of New York State rendered no
less than three inverse condemnation decisions turning on property
owner expectations as a definitional element of title.[32] Each found no
taking. At this embryonic stage in the doctrine's development, however, the degree of difference it will make in the traditional municipal
zoning case can only be guessed.

[29]959 F.2d 955 (Fed. Cir.), *cert. denied*, 506 U.S. 916 (1992). *See* Loretto v.
Teleprompter Manhattan CATV Corp., 458 U.S. 419, 441 (1982) (property
owner generally entertains "historically rooted expectation of compensation"
for permanent physical invasions).

[30]100 F.3d 1525 (Fed. Cir. 1996) (en banc).

[31]Resistance to using the compensable expectancies concept in the nonphys-
ical, regulatory context has also surfaced. *See, e.g.*, Forest Properties, Inc. v.
United States, 39 Fed. Cl. 56, 71 (1997) (existence of "permit-based regulatory
system" when property was acquired does not of itself eliminate compensable
property interest).

[32]Gazza v. Department of Envtl. Conservation, 89 N.Y.2d 603, 679 N.E.2d
1035 (regulations existing when wetland purchased impose limits on buyer's
title), *cert. denied*, 118 S. Ct. 58 (1997); Kim v. City of New York, 90 N.Y.2d 1,
681 N.E.2d 312 (common law right of lateral support), *cert. denied*, 118 S. Ct.
50 (1997); Anello v. Zoning Bd. of Appeals, 89 N.Y.2d 535, 678 N.E.2d 870
(ordinance barring construction on steep slopes), *cert. denied*, 118 S. Ct. 2
(1997).

Part II

Getting to the Takings Issue

Chapter 4

Jurisdiction

For a half-century following the 1922 decision in *Pennsylvania Coal Co. v. Mahon*,[1] the vast majority of regulatory takings cases were filed and litigated in the state courts. Since most land-use regulation—the traditional context for regulatory takings claims—has been conducted at the local government level, this is not surprising.

That trend began to change in the 1970s, however, largely as a result of two interrelated developments. First, several states (led by New York and California) held that money damages were an inappropriate remedy to cure a regulatory taking, leaving invalidation of the offending regulation as the exclusive remedy.[2] Property owners understandably sought a more favorable forum, and federal courts provided that alternative. Second, the option of a federal tribunal became even more attractive given the advantages afforded under 42 U.S.C. section 1983—recovery of attorney fees, elimination of any exhaustion of administrative remedies requirement—and the greater comfort of federal judges with this federal provision (*see* chapter 7). While state courts have concurrent jurisdiction to hear section 1983

---

[1]260 U.S. 393 (1922).

[2]Fred F. French Inv. Co. v. City of New York, 39 N.Y.2d 587, 593–94, 350 N.E.2d 381, *cert. denied*, 429 U.S. 990 (1976); Agins v. City of Tiburon, 24 Cal. 3d 266, 272, 598 P.2d 25 (1979), *aff'd on other grounds*, 447 U.S. 255 (1980). *See also* Gold Run, Ltd. v. Board of County Comm'rs, 38 Colo. App. 44, 554 P.2d 317 (1976). That principle was subsequently overturned as deficient under federal constitutional principles in First English Evangelical Lutheran Church v. County of Los Angeles, 482 U.S. 304 (1987).

claims, section 1983 provides convenient subject matter jurisdiction in the federal court system. A veritable explosion of section 1983–based takings litigation in the federal courts thus began about 25 years ago.

State Courts

State courts nonetheless retain a major role in inverse condemnation jurisprudence. For one thing, many landowners (and an even higher percentage of their lawyers) are simply uncomfortable litigating in federal courts under federal procedures. Moreover, and of greater influence, the federal courts have developed several procedural doctrines in a none-too-subtle effort to channel as much regulatory takings litigation as reasonably possible back into the state courts. The most important doctrine for jurisdictional purposes is the second prong of the ripeness doctrine articulated by the U.S. Supreme Court in *Williamson County Regional Planning Commission v. Hamilton Bank*[3]—that plaintiffs must avail themselves of remedies made available under state law as a condition precedent to bringing takings action in federal district court (*see* chapter 5).

How then, are the state courts organized to deal with and resolve regulatory takings actions? The answer is quite mundane: state courts have done little or nothing to deal with inverse condemnation litigation in a systematic or focused way.

Unlike the federal judiciary (discussed below), state courts are generally not organized based on subject matter. Instead, all states have a court of general jurisdiction (e.g., the supreme court in New York; the superior court in California) that may hear any case brought before it, subject to limited, enumerated exceptions. In many states, there are also courts of limited jurisdiction that resolve disputes involving relatively small amounts of money or, less frequently, particular types of cases. To date, no state has apparently seen fit to create a specialized court system to handle regulatory takings or related cases. As a result, state regulatory takings cases are generally filed in the courts of general jurisdiction and, therefore, compete with the general crush of civil and criminal cases.

In recent years, a few states have taken some incremental steps to come to grips with the burgeoning volume of regulatory takings and

[3]473 U.S. 172, 194–96 (1985).

related litigation. First, a handful of jurisdictions have established specialized state *administrative* tribunals to which disaffected property owners are directed to seek redress before filing in state court.[4] Oregon's Land Use Board of Appeals (LUBA), created by the Oregon Legislature in 1983, is perhaps the most prominent example of this phenomenon. Regulatory takings claims—together with a wide array of challenges to land-use restrictions imposed by Oregon's state or local governments—are channeled into the LUBA process.[5] And, in recognition of both the complexity of such cases and the substantial expertise LUBA brings to them, Oregon law provides that appeals from administrative decisions go directly to the intermediate state *appellate* courts.[6] Mimicking the federal system, LUBA therefore serves as the functional equivalent of a state trial court in such cases under Oregon law.

This, in turn, has raised the question of whether it is constitutionally permissible for state or local governments *to require* private property owners to litigate their regulatory takings claims in administrative settings prior to bringing them in the state courts themselves. At least two states—California and Oregon—seem to suggest the answer is no. The California Supreme Court, for example, recently held that landowners could not be compelled to first adjudicate their takings claims before administrative tribunals unless those tribunals afforded roughly the same due process guarantees as are available in the courts (e.g., cross-examination of witnesses, subpoena power, application of formal rules of evidence, and so forth).[7] The Oregon courts have adopted a similar view.[8]

A variation of this trend involves specialized procedures that some state legislatures have directed state courts of general jurisdiction to utilize in adjudicating regulatory takings claims. Sometimes, these

[4]*See, e.g.,* Milardo v. Coastal Resources Management Council of Rhode Island, 434 A.2d 266 (R.I. 1981) (adverse land-use decision of administrative tribunal, together with related inverse condemnation claim, appealable to superior court under Rhode Island Administrative Procedures Act).

[5]Or. Rev. Stat. § 197.825 et seq.

[6]*Id.* at § 197.825(2)(b).

[7]Hensler v. City of Glendale, 8 Cal. 4th 1, 15, 876 P.2d 1043 (1994), *cert. denied,* 513 U.S. 1184 (1995). *See also* Healing v. California Coastal Comm'n, 22 Cal. App. 4th 1158, 27 Cal. Rptr. 2d 758 (1994).

[8]Boise Cascade Corp. v. Board of Forestry, 325 Or. 185, 935 P.2d 411 (1997) (LUBA has concurrent, though not primary, jurisdiction with state trial courts over regulatory takings claims).

procedures are unique to inverse condemnation actions;[9] in other instances, they apply to state judicial review of administrative decision-making generally.[10]

Finally, a handful of states have made halting steps toward creation of specialized courts to resolve regulatory takings and similar controversies. In California, for example, the legislature has rebuffed nascent efforts to create a specialized "Land Use Court" within the state judicial system; instead, it has decreed that the superior court in all but the most rural of California counties must "designate one or more judges to develop expertise in . . . land-use and environmental laws, so that those judges will be available to hear, and quickly resolve, actions or proceedings brought pursuant to [those laws]."[11]

Federal Courts

Until recent decades, the voice of the lower federal courts in the judicial takings chorus was an infrequent one. The reasons are plain: The United States was little involved in land-use control prior to the environmental 1970s, and use of federal section 1983 actions for state takings was not yet established.

Today, the federal case law on takings is prodigious. In contrast with state courts, however, federal courts possess strictly limited jurisdiction defined by constitution and statute. The jurisdictional hurdle is always the first one a plaintiff confronts in seeking federal court review. Precisely which jurisdictional hurdles one faces, however, depends on which federal court is chosen, who is being sued for the taking, and the specific statute under which federal jurisdiction is being invoked.

First, take the federal district courts. For a party pressing a taking claim based on state action in such courts, a threshold jurisdictional concern (noted above) is whether available state law remedies exist. If so, those state law remedies must be pursued before a district court

---

[9]*See, e.g.*, Ariz. Rev. Stat. Ann. §§ 9-500.12, 11-810 (governing administrative and judicial review of constitutionality of fees and exactions imposed by Arizona cities and counties).

[10]*See, e.g.*, N.Y. Civ. Prac. L. & R. § 7801 et seq., *applied in* Ward v. Bennett, 214 A. D. 2d 741 (1995) (N.Y. App. Div.) (governing judicial review in state court actions brought against governmental officials and entities).

[11]Cal. Pub. Res. Code § 21167.1(b).

will entertain an inverse condemnation action (*see* chapter 5).[12] Takings claims brought under 42 U.S.C. section 1983 are subject to their own jurisdictional requirements (*see* chapter 7).

When the defendant in district court is the United States, a very different set of obstacles looms, and few plaintiffs squeeze through the courthouse door. Under the "little Tucker Act," the general rule is that takings actions against the United States may be brought in district court only when the amount in controversy is $10,000 or less—an extreme rarity.[13] In special cases, other federal statutes allow district court takings actions against the federal government regardless of the amount in controversy, but few of these special cases fall into the land-use arena.[14]

The takings connoisseur will object here that Tucker Act notwithstanding, district courts once commonly addressed takings claims against the United States without any bother about jurisdictional amount. Undeniably true. The reason lies in the confusion until recently as to the proper remedy when a taking is found. Until 1987, some federal courts (and most state courts) held to the view that judicial invalidation of the government action was a constitutionally sufficient cure for a taking. Invalidation is a remedy within the jurisdiction of federal district courts. In 1987, however, the Supreme Court in *First English Evangelical Lutheran Church v. County of Los Angeles* told us that the remedy demanded by the Fifth Amendment for a taking is compensation, not invalidation.[15] Almost all compensation claims against the United States, other than those sounding in tort or admiralty, go to the Court of Federal Claims under the Tucker Act. To be sure, some plaintiffs continue to file federal takings claims in district courts seeking invalidation of the government act, often when the

[12]Williamson County Regional Planning Comm'n v. Hamilton Bank, 473 U.S. 172, 194–97 (1985); Clajon Prod. Corp. v. Petera, 70 F.3d 1566, 1575 (10th Cir. 1995).

[13]*See, e.g.,* Clouser v. Espy, 42 F.3d 1522 (9th Cir. 1994) (taking claim seeking more than $10,000 belongs in Court of Federal Claims), *cert. denied,* 515 U.S. 1141 (1995); Broughton Lumber Co. v. Yeutter, 939 F.2d 1547 (Fed. Cir. 1991) (statute vesting jurisdiction over federal questions in district court does not reach takings claims).

[14]A land-use-related example is 16 U.S.C. § 1910, giving district courts jurisdiction, regardless of the dollar amount in controversy, over certain compensation claims by holders of mining claims in national parks.

[15]482 U.S. 304 (1987).

taking argument is merely an end-of-the-complaint makeweight. And occasionally, the district courts erroneously have a go at them.

Concededly, there *are* at least two situations where takings claims may still seek injunctive remedies and be maintained in district court—both an uphill climb. First, a property owner may charge that the federal statute under which the federal action was taken withdrew the Tucker Act compensation remedy, forcing recourse to invalidation. However, the Tucker Act remedy is assumed to apply unless Congress states otherwise, which it appears never to have done in a land-use statute.[16] Second, federal district courts have jurisdiction if the plaintiff seeks to void the alleged federal taking because it does not further a "public use," as the Fifth Amendment demands.[17] This constitutional requirement has been largely eliminated by expansive judicial interpretation.

Now let's turn to the United States Court of Federal Claims. This court, once "little known" beyond disgruntled employees and contractors of the federal government,[18] today stands at the eye of the takings storm. (*See* box on pages 42–43 for background.) Its chief jurisdictional statute is the Tucker Act,[19] enacted in 1887 and little changed since, which confines the court to hearing money claims against the United States, with the major exception of torts. Plainly, the statute reaches inverse condemnation claims, though the particular Tucker Act phrase to which the Court of Federal Claims' takings jurisdiction is attributed has shifted over the years.[20] Formally, the Act has a dual function: to vest jurisdiction over taking claims in the court, and to waive federal sovereign immunity for such claims.[21]

---

[16]*See, e.g.,* Preseault v. Interstate Commerce Commission, 494 U.S. 1, 12 (1990).

[17]*See, e.g.,* Donnell v. United States, 834 F. Supp. 19, 23 n.5 (D. Me. 1993).

[18]Keith Schneider, *Environmental Laws Face a Stiff Test from Landowners,* N.Y. TIMES, Jan. 20, 1992, at A1.

[19]28 U.S.C. § 1491(a).

[20]Early decisions hung the court's takings jurisdiction on the "implied contract with the United States" phrase in the Tucker Act. Beginning in the 1940s, the judicial eye shifted to the statute's "claim . . . founded . . . under the Constitution" phrase. *See, e.g., Preseault,* 494 U.S. at 12. A transitional case, citing both, is United States v. Dickinson, 331 U.S. 745, 748 (1947).

[21]United States v. Mitchell, 463 U.S. 206, 212 (1983). To the layman, it may seem curious that a waiver of sovereign immunity is necessary to file a taking claim in federal court when the Takings Clause is said to be "self-executing." United States v. Clarke, 445 U.S. 253, 257 (1980). Further reflection, however,

Unlike the district courts, the Court of Federal Claims labors under no strictures as to the amount of compensation sought. And so the bottom line: Under the Tucker Act, jurisdiction over takings claims against the United States lies in both the district courts and the Court of Federal Claims for amounts less than $10,000, and in the latter court alone for suits seeking $10,000 or more.

A second jurisdictional hurdle at the Court of Federal Claims has lately been a flash point. Title 28 of the United States Code, section 1500, enacted soon after the Civil War, forces plaintiffs to confront an agonizing choice. Somewhat simplified, it says "File your action in the district court or in the Court of Federal Claims, but not both." More formally, it strips the Court of Federal Claims of jurisdiction over "any claim for or in respect to which the plaintiff . . . has pending in any other court any suit or process against the United States. . . ."

Section 1500 was originally aimed at the common antebellum practice of Southern plantation owners to sue in both the Court of Claims and other courts to recover compensation for cotton crops seized by the Union. In modern times, however, section 1500 has had less salutary consequences—appearing, for example, to force an election between challenging the validity of federal action in district court or filing a taking action based in claims court. Sensitive to these hardships, the claims court developed several exceptions to section 1500. One of them, announced in *Casman v. United States*, lifted the jurisdictional bar in the foregoing example on the ground that the action in district court sought a different type of remedy (invalidation) than that sought in the claims court (compensation).[22] In 1992, however, matters came to a head when the Federal Circuit ruled that section 1500 supported none of these exceptions, whereupon it overruled them and embraced a rigid, absolute reading.[23]

One year later, the Supreme Court admonished the Federal Circuit that its sweeping elimination of section 1500's case law exceptions,

---

shows that the two principles are distinguishable. "Self-executing" means that the compensation promise in the Takings Clause does not require statutory recognition. In theory, however, the United States could refuse to provide a forum for asserting this promise. In that case, the self-executing nature of the Takings Clause presumably would be given effect through a court's invalidation of the government act—relief that a district court can supply.

[22]135 Ct. Cl. 647 (1956).

[23]UNR Indus., Inc. v. United States, 962 F.2d 1013 (Fed. Cir. 1992) (en banc), *aff'd sub nom.* Keene Corp. v. United States, 508 U.S. 200 (1993).

Into the Storm: The U.S. Court of Federal Claims and U.S. Court of Appeals for the Federal Circuit

The spirited debate over the takings issue has thrown a spotlight on two courts not hitherto accustomed to public attention.

First, the U.S. Court of Federal Claims. For over a century, it languished in the judicial wings. Indeed, when created in 1855, it was a court only in name. Its key function was to relieve the pressure on Congress from the volume of private bills stemming from money claims against the United States. 10 Stat. 612. Either chamber of Congress could refer such bills to the new court, which reported back its findings and recommendations. Because the court was created under Congress's Article I power, there was no constitutional block to rendering such advisory opinions. Eight years later, at President Lincoln's recommendation, it was empowered to enter final judgments.

The enactment of the Tucker Act in 1887 greatly expanded the court's jurisdiction, to its modern scope. Now it could hear virtually all money claims against the United States, except those in tort or admiralty. In the 20th century, the court organized itself into trial and appellate divisions. The former was composed of trial judges appointed by the court; the latter, of judges nominated by the president and confirmed by the Senate under Article III of the Constitution. In 1982, Congress separated the two functions—the trial function remaining in a renamed U.S. Claims Court and the appellate function being vested in a new U.S. Court of Appeals for the Federal Circuit. In 1992, the Claims Court was given its current moniker: the U.S. Court of Federal Claims.

Since the early 1980s, takings claims in the court have been growing slowly but steadily, in both number filed annually and total number

including the different-remedy exception, had been overbroad given the facts presented.[24] However, when the Federal Circuit was later presented with a taking case that properly raised the different-remedy exception, it declined to rule as before. Rather, it reversed position and *endorsed* the exception.[25] With the resurrection of this exception, the section 1500 tiger at the claims court's gate was, for purposes of the typical taking case, rendered a mere kitten. Under this latest view, section 1500 poses no jurisdictional bar should a suit attacking the denial of a federal land-use permit in district court overlap in time with a taking action based on the same permit denial

[24]*Keene Corp.,* 508 U.S. at 216.
[25]Loveladies Harbor, Inc. v. United States, 27 F.3d 1545 (Fed. Cir. 1994) (en banc).

pending. The largest category of land-use takings cases now pending, numbering about 45, stems from the federal wetlands program. More than half of the court's takings docket, however, has little to do with land use, reflecting the large number of federal programs affecting personal property.

The Court of Federal Claims consists of 16 active judges appointed for 15-year terms (plus a varying number on senior status). All of them today are Reagan or Bush appointees (a few are reappointees from the old Court of Claims trial division), and several are now seeing their terms expire. Because a judge's political philosophy plainly may influence his or her rulings—especially so in the regulatory takings field—the judicial nomination and confirmation process can be as politicized as that for Article III judges.

The court considers itself a people's court—an equalizer between citizen and big government. Its procedures can be quite informal, allowing, for example, the argument of nondispositive motions by telephone conference call. For added accessibility, the court may hold proceedings anywhere in the country that is convenient for plaintiffs, invoking its nationwide jurisdiction. 28 U.S.C. §§ 173, 2505.

Appeals from the Court of Federal Claims are to the Federal Circuit, which also hears appeals from other courts. Unlike the Court of Federal Claims, the Federal Circuit is an Article III court, meaning, among other things, that its twelve active judges have lifetime tenure. (Not to be minimized, Court of Federal Claims judges have lifetime senior status by statute.) Because few takings cases are appealed from the Federal Circuit to the Supreme Court, the Federal Circuit has a leading role in articulating takings law in the many areas where the High Court has not yet spoken. Many of the court's key takings decisions have been authored by Judge Jay Plager.

in the Court of Federal Claims. One suspects that the last chapter in this saga has not yet been written.

Regardless of who one is suing, and in which court, a takings suit must be timely. As in state courts, failure to file within the prescribed limitations period is considered by federal courts to be a jurisdictional flaw and, as a result, necessarily fatal.[26]

[26]Crown Coat Front Co. v. United States, 363 F.2d 407 (2d Cir. 1966) (time bar for Tucker Act suits in district court is jurisdictional), *rev'd on other grounds*, 386 U.S. 503 (1967); Soriano v. United States, 352 U.S. 270, 273 (1957) (time bar for Tucker Act suits in Court of Claims is jurisdictional). *See* the more detailed discussion of statutes of limitation for takings actions in chapter 6.

Chapter 5

Ripeness[1]

Takings cases involving proposed development projects develop over time. They typically start when a developer's application for the regulatory approval of a project is denied. The initial denial may not necessarily be a taking for which just compensation must be paid. There may be some other economic use of the property that the government would approve. Until the government has reached a final, definitive position on what it will and will not approve, no one, not even the courts, can determine if there is a taking and what damages have been suffered. And even then, a property owner must seek compensation through available administrative and judicial processes, such as a state court remedy, before going forward with a taking claim.[2]

---

[1]This chapter draws from several leading articles on the doctrine of ripeness: Michael M. Berger, *The "Ripeness" Mess in Federal Land Use Cases or How the Supreme Court Converted Federal Judges into Fruit Peddlers*, INSTITUTE ON PLANNING, ZONING, AND EMINENT DOMAIN, Ch. 7 (1991); Brian W. Blaesser, *Closing the Federal Courthouse Door on Property Owners: The Ripeness and Abstention Doctrines in Section 1983 Land Use Cases*, 2 HOFSTRA PROPERTY L.J. 73 (1988); R. Jeffrey Lyman, *Finality Ripeness in Federal Land Use Cases from* Hamilton Bank *to* Lucas, 9 JOURNAL OF LAND USE & ENVIRONMENTAL LAW 101 (1993); Thomas E. Roberts, *Fifth Amendment Taking Claims in Federal Court: The State Compensation Requirement and Principles of Res Judicata*, 24 THE URBAN LAWYER: THE NATIONAL QUARTERLY ON LOCAL GOVERNMENT LAW 479 (1992); and Gregory M. Stein, *Regulatory Takings and Ripeness in the Federal Courts*, 48 VANDERBILT L. REV. 1 (1995).

[2]*See also* Bay View, Inc. v. Ahtna, Inc., 105 F.3d 1281 (9th Cir. 1997) (taking claim stemming from act of Congress not ripe until property owners seek available remedy under Tucker Act).

As applied in takings claims, the legal doctrine of ripeness has two prongs. The first, the final-decision requirement, requires that a property owner receive a final decision that is ready for adjudication; the second, the compensation requirement, requires that the property owner pursue administrative and adjudicatory relief at the local administrative level (such as by applying for a variance) and relief in state court.[3] Traditionally, ripeness goes to the jurisdiction of courts—without it a court simply has no jurisdiction to hear the case.[4] The finality of the decision-making process is key, though courts have carved out one useful exception to finality, called the futility doctrine. If it would be futile to apply for a lesser development or to ask for some variance from the law, the courts will accept the case as ripe and take jurisdiction.

Ripeness protects the courts from being overwhelmed with cases that could be resolved through further administrative proceedings with land-use authorities. And ripeness ensures that the courts will be able to measure the damages from the taking because there will always be a clear "bottom line" decision by the land-use authority. Unfortunately, ripeness can also be used by governments to keep developers from getting a fair shot.

The impact of the ripeness doctrine on the judicial process is enormous. A computer search of cases decided and reported in 1994 and 1995 in which ripeness and takings were discussed in the context of land-use permits involving zoning, subdivision, or variances, and excluding the many wetlands cases, yielded 644 decisions. And these are just the reported decisions, not the many, many unappealed and unreported trial court decisions dismissing takings claims on ripeness grounds.

Ripeness in the Context of an Application

To get a sense of what ripeness and finality mean in a typical, evolving taking case, imagine this hypothetical: Two years ago, a development company bought 150 acres of commercially zoned land in the suburban town of Ridgeville for $3 million. On the parcel it proposed to

[3]Stein, *supra* note 1, at 12–13.
[4]Lucas v. South Carolina Coastal Council, 505 U.S. 1003, 1011–14 (1992) ("unusual disposition" by lower court in deciding merits when it might have rejected claim as unripe makes it imprudent for the Court to deny review).

develop 800,000 square feet of office space in four buildings with a total of 3,200 parking spaces, a use subject to the grant of a special permit. Just after the developer purchased the property, the zoning regulations were amended to allow the proposed use, provided that the plan met numerous criteria including consideration of the impact on available infrastructure such as water, sewer, and highway access.

In applying for the special permit, the developer encountered strong resistance from a neighborhood group of residential property owners who were concerned that a development of this scale would overburden their local roads. Specifically, they said that certain intersections near the project would become significantly more congested, resulting in a substantial delay in the movement of traffic during peak hours. In addition, the neighbors raised concerns about the possible environmental impact, including the project's effect on stormwater runoff and on the water and sewer systems.

The local zoning authority ultimately voted to deny the developer's application, citing, among other reasons, the adverse impact on traffic flow and the possibility that the project would consume virtually the remaining capacity of the water system. Arguably, though, the owner could farm the land or harvest timber.

In considering a taking claim, the developer was advised that the damages could range anywhere from the $3 million that was paid for the land to approximately $40 million, the difference between the property's purchase price and its value if approved for the proposed project.

For the developer, it is unclear whether the municipality would approve a complex of less than 800,000 square feet. In terms of the ripeness doctrine, would he first be required to apply for approval of three buildings totaling 600,000 square feet and have that project denied; then apply for two buildings totaling 400,000 square feet and have that denied; and, finally, apply for 200,000 square feet and have that denied before the taking claim would be ripe for pursuit?[5] Would the developer have to try to farm the land or harvest timber to determine if it has any value and to see if those uses are the only ones acceptable to the town?

[5]In a recent decision similar to the hypothetical, a developer won $1,450,000 in just compensation after having applications for 344, 264, 224, and 190 residential units denied. Del Monte Dunes at Monterey, Ltd. v. City of Monterey, 95 F.3d 1422 (9th Cir. 1996) *cert. granted,* 66 U.S.L.W. 3639 (No. 97-1235) (U.S. 1998). An unanswered, troubling question is whether in applying for a smaller project, a developer waives the right to claim a taking for the prior denials.

For the courts, the problem also includes determining the level of compensation. Does the developer truly suffer a loss of value on the property when the 800,000 square foot project is denied? What if the municipality had approved 600,000 square feet? In such an instance there would be no taking since the value of the project would far exceed the amount paid for the property.

Policy Implications

Ripeness is mandated in part by Article III of the U.S. Constitution, which defines the "Cases [and] Controversies" that may be heard by federal courts created under that article.[6] Ripeness addresses whether a taking claim is a case or controversy and, in its prudential form, raises the question whether it is appropriate for a court to adjudicate a controversy prematurely. That is, some aspects of ripeness are constitutionally mandated—Article III requires them—and other aspects are within a court's broad discretion, within its prudential power. Prudence dictates that the courts not hear cases with incomplete records or cases that are speculative, that would lead to overly broad opinions, or that would be better resolved at the administrative level. Both federal and state courts use two criteria in determining ripeness—ascertaining whether the issues are fit for decision and whether the parties would suffer undue hardship if the court declined the case.[7]

Ripeness, in the context of takings claims, presents a difficult public policy issue. The Fifth Amendment requires that just compensation be paid where there is a taking by the government. It is intended that an owner should be made whole for the property taken, but not as to consequential damages, such as moving expenses, sentimental value, etc. It could be argued as a fundamental concept of Anglo-American justice that the property owner should be made whole as soon as possible.[8] Yet the ripeness doctrine profoundly slows the relief process and, as a practical matter, has the potential to be used by municipalities to preempt the rights of property owners.

[6]*See* U.S. Const. art. III, § 2. The U.S. Court of Federal Claims is an Article I (legislative) court but follows Article III court ripeness and standing doctrines. Massachusetts Bay Transp. Auth. v. United States, 21 Cl. Ct. 252, 257–58 (1990).

[7]Stein, *supra* note 1, at 12.

[8]Recall the adage, "Justice delayed is justice denied."

Portion of Temple Hills Country Club Estates, Williamson County, Tennessee. This was the subdivision at issue in the leading ripeness decision of *Williamson County Regional Planning Commission v. Hamilton Bank.*

Consider again our hypothetical. It could take a decade for the property owner to apply for smaller and smaller projects until the government denied all applications, or some development was approved and it became possible to demonstrate that no reasonable economic use remained in the property.[9]

Development of the Rule

Over the past 20 years the U.S. Supreme Court has created a ripeness rule for land-use cases that has made it difficult to get takings claims to trial. Initially, it appeared that ripeness was not a significant issue for the Court in land-use cases.

In 1980, the Supreme Court held that a taking claim was not ripe because the property owners never submitted development plans for their property.[10] A year later the Court reached the same result where the property owners had not availed themselves of a statutory

[9]*See* Stein, *supra* note 1, at 40.
[10]Agins v. City of Tiburon, 447 U.S. 255, 260 (1980).

administrative relief mechanism.[11] Thus, the stage was set for rulings in back-to-back decisions in 1985 and 1986 that have shaped federal and state ripeness decisions since.

In the leading case, the 1985 decision in *Williamson County Regional Planning Commission v. Hamilton Bank*,[12] the Supreme Court held that a property owner must take several steps before his or her claim is ripe. There, the developer initially received approval of a conceptual plan and laid out 469 lots in the initial phases with 212 lots receiving final subdivision approval. The developer spent $3.5 million for infrastructure improvements and constructed a golf course.

Before the developer could propose its final subdivision plans for the remaining units, the county amended the zoning ordinances to reduce the permitted development density. The Regional Planning Commission subsequently identified numerous deficiencies in the revised preliminary subdivision plat and denied approval. Although not reported in the decision, apparently there was a change in the local administration as well as increased community resistance to the large project, which made it politically difficult to approve the final phases. The developer successfully appealed the commission's ruling to the Zoning Board of Appeals, but the commission, having final say, rejected the decision of the Zoning Board of Appeals and denied approval of the revised plat yet again.

The developer sued for a taking under 42 U.S.C. section 1983 in federal district court and succeeded, in a jury trial, in proving a temporary taking and in securing an award for damages. (*See* chapter 7 for discussion of section 1983 actions; chapter 12 for temporary takings.) The court, however, held that a temporary deprivation of all use was not a compensable taking and entered a judgment notwithstanding the verdict, overturning the jury's decision. The Court of Appeals for the Sixth Circuit upheld the jury's award of compensation and set aside the district court's judgment. The U.S. Supreme Court granted review.

Justice Blackmun, writing for a six-member Court majority, noted that the developer had not sought variances from the revised ordinances that had prevented full development of the project. The Court held that the Fifth Amendment requires a final decision by the Commission before the taking issue can be reached, for only then can the economic impact of the local decision and the effect of that decision

[11]Hodel v. Virginia Surface Mining & Reclamation Ass'n, 452 U.S. 264, 297 (1981).
[12]473 U.S. 172 (1985).

on investment-backed expectations be determined. The Court said the Commission had to reach a "final, definitive position" before the case would be ripe for consideration.[13]

Williamson County actually requires the completion of *two* steps before relief is available in federal court. First, the government must reach a final decision on an application. As part of getting this final decision, the applicant must also seek relief from a restrictive decision by requesting a variance, waiver, or some other adjudicatory resolution at the local administrative level (unless it would be futile to do so).[14] Second, an applicant must pursue any remedies available in the state courts. *Williamson County* does not preclude property owners from pursuing their Fifth Amendment claim in federal courts later. However, as Gideon Kanner, an authority on takings law, has already pointed out, "[t]hat leaves open the question of whether the earlier state court litigation affects issue preclusion (i.e., does a finding of no taking by the state court give rise to collateral estoppel on the issue of taking in the later federal action?)."[15]

The requirement that a claimant must exhaust state procedures is the last element of the three-part proof of a takings claim that (1) a property interest (2) has been taken by the government (3) without just compensation.[16] A party challenging state or local action in federal court must allege that it sought and was denied just compensation under state law or that the state's "inverse condemnation procedure is unavailable or inadequate."[17]

While there have been hundreds of ripeness decisions since *Williamson County*, the case of *Southview Associates, Ltd. v Bongartz*[18] is especially interesting because it illustrates the permitting complexities developers sometimes face and the near impossibility of

---

[13]473 U.S. at 191.

[14]*See* Pearce v. Town of Bourne, Lawyers Weekly No. 11–262–96 (Massachusetts Appeals Court held no taking where conservation commission denied plan to build home near wetland and owner failed to appeal to town) *reported in* David L. Yas, *"Taking" Suit for Denial of House Plan Precluded*, MASSACHUSETTS LAWYERS WEEKLY, Nov. 11, 1996, at 1.

[15]Gideon Kanner, *Inverse Condemnation—Remedies*, JUST COMPENSATION, Nov. 1995, at 10.

[16]*See* Port Chester Yacht Club v. Iasilb, 614 F. Supp. 318, 321 (S.D.N.Y. 1985).

[17]HBP Assocs. v. Marsh, 893 F. Supp. 271, 278 (S.D.N.Y. 1995) (citing *Williamson County*, 473 U.S. at 196–97).

[18]980 F.2d 84 (2d Cir. 1992), *cert. denied*, 507 U.S. 987 (1993).

ripening some takings claims. Applying the remedies requirement of *Williamson County*, the Court of Appeals for the Second Circuit rejected Southview's contention that when no state statutory scheme exists under which compensation is provided, the plaintiff can go directly to federal court. Instead, the court held that as long as Vermont recognized a cause of action for a taking generally, the plaintiff must seek relief at the state level even if there is no precedent specifically authorizing it.[19]

The *Dodd* Case

One of the most important decisions on ripeness in recent years is *Dodd v. Hood River County*,[20] a 1995 Ninth Circuit decision in which the divided court held that the requirement of the second step in *Williamson County* (to pursue state court remedies before filing in federal court) is limited to seeking remedies on state constitutional grounds. This decision includes a California gold mine of citations on ripeness and a truly comprehensive look at the issues.

In November of 1983, Thomas and Doris Dodd purchased 40 acres of land in the Forest Use Zone in Hood River County, Oregon, with the intention of building a retirement home. At that time, they knew the property was zoned exclusively for forest use and that the county was in the process of adopting a restrictive zoning ordinance. The ordinance, adopted just over a year after the Dodds purchased

[19]Other cases of interest on this point include: James Emory, Inc. v. Twiggs County, Ga., 883 F. Supp. 1546, 1557 (M.D. Ga. 1995); Schliepper v. DNR, 188 Wis. 2d 318, 323, 525 N.W.2d 99, 101 (Ct. App. 1994); Guimont v. City of Seattle, 77 Wash. App. 74, 85, 896 P.2d 70, 79 (1995), *clarified in part and amended*, 1995 Wash. App. LEXIS 244 (Wash. Ct. App. June 9, 1995), *review denied*, 127 Wash. 2d 1023, 904 P.2d 1157 (1995); Wheeler v. City of Wayzata, 511 N.W.2d 39, 42–43 (Minn. Ct. App. 1994), *rev'd on other grounds*, 533 N.W.2d 405 (Minn. 1995).

But see Oceco Land Co. v. Department of Natural Resources, 548 N.W.2d 702, 704 (Mich. Ct. App. 1996). The court "decline[d] to hold that a trial court . . . must dismiss the claim as not ripe unless the property owner has actually taken steps to obtain all necessary permits to proceed with alternate uses, even if it has no intention of adopting any of those alternative uses." *Id.* at 703–04.

[20]59 F.3d 852 (9th Cir. 1995).

their land, required that forest dwellings be allowed in Forest Use Zones only where "necessary and accessory" to a forest use.[21]

However, when the Dodds purchased, they received no actual notice of the potential for change in the land-use restrictions, and before they purchased they received a report from the county sanitarian saying that the property was suitable for a septic system. Just a few months after the property purchase, an employee of the County Planning Department signed a land-use compatibility statement to the effect that a single-family dwelling on the property was compatible with state planning goals. Less than one month after that, the county sanitarian wrote to the Dodds stating that their plan to build in two years "would appear to leave opportunity for the water supply system to be developed."[22]

In 1990, six years after they purchased the lot and made their initial inquiries, the Dodds moved forward with their plans to develop a home on the property. They filed and were denied applications for land-use permits, and they appealed to the County Planning Commission. They lost and appealed further to the Board of County Commissioners, where they also lost.

In August 1991 they filed a notice of intent to appeal with Oregon's Land Use Board of Appeals (LUBA). Among their claims was one under the Oregon takings clause. Importantly, they did not pursue their federal taking claim, but instead "expressly reserve[d] their right to have their federal claims adjudicated in federal court."[23]

LUBA affirmed the county's decision, holding, among other things, that the timber on the property had a value of approximately $10,000 so there was no denial of a substantial beneficial use and therefore no taking. In 1992 the Dodds appealed to the Oregon Court of Appeals, which also affirmed, finding no taking under the Oregon Constitution.

While this appeal process was going on, the Dodds, consistent with their reservation of rights, filed a 42 U.S.C. section 1983 claim in federal district court claiming substantive due process, equal protection, and Takings Clause violations under the U.S. Constitution as well as a taking under the Oregon Constitution.

Before the Oregon Supreme Court decided the Dodds' case in 1993, the federal district court dismissed on ripeness grounds the

[21]*Id.* at 856.
[22]*Id.*
[23]*Id.* at 857.

Dodds' Fifth Amendment taking claim and entered summary judgment for the county and the state on all of the other counts. Later, the Oregon Supreme Court decided against the Dodds as well.

In deciding the Dodds' appeal of the federal district court's dismissal the Ninth Circuit held that the final-decision requirement, the first of the two steps of *Williamson County*, was met because the Dodds had filed land-use and conditional-use permit applications and had petitioned for zone and comprehensive plan changes.

The Ninth Circuit then discussed *Williamson County* and concluded "that under the teachings of *Williamson County* and decisions of this court in the context of ripeness, the compensation element is satisfied if remedies available under state law have been pursued."[24] The court quoted from *Williamson County*: "[I]f a state provides an adequate procedure for seeking just compensation, the property owner cannot claim a violation of the Just Compensation Clause until it has used the procedure and been denied just compensation."[25]

The court argued that the doctrine of ripeness in its prudential form is principally designed to keep cases out of court that would be "illuminated by the development of a better factual record" below. As to whether invoking ripeness to send a Fifth Amendment case to the state courts would "illuminate" it, the court said: "The Fifth Amendment action is not more 'developed' or 'ripened' through presentation of the ultimate issue—the failure of a state to provide adequate compensation for a taking—to the state court. Indeed, such a requirement would not ripen the claim, rather it would extinguish the claim."[26]

And the Ninth Circuit could not have put it more strongly than when it said: "Reduced to its essence, to hold that a taking plaintiff must first present a Fifth Amendment claim to the state court system as a condition precedent to seeking relief in a federal court would be to deny a federal forum to every takings claimant."[27]

But the state and county also argued that claim preclusion was an alternative ground to dismiss the Dodds' Fifth Amendment claim. They argued that even if ripeness did not require the presentation of the federal claim in state court, there was still a prohibition against claim-splitting that would preclude subsequent litigation of the claim in federal court.

[24]*Id.* at 860.
[25]*Id.* (citing *Williamson County,* 473 U.S. at 195).
[26]*Id.* at 860.
[27]*Id.*

The court of appeals first set out the three-part general test for claim preclusion that (1) the claim in the second action is based on the same factual transaction as the first, (2) plaintiff seeks a remedy beyond that sought earlier, and (3) the claim could have been joined in the first action. It concluded that the Dodds' Fifth Amendment claims were not subject to claim preclusion.

While claim-splitting is generally prohibited, there are two exceptions. First, was there consent or a tacit agreement for splitting the claim? The Dodds had expressly reserved their right and the county and state did not object. The county and state, along with the Dodds, made a joint request to stay the federal action until the state action was resolved. The court of appeals also found that this case fell within the second exception from the prohibition against claim-splitting in that the Oregon courts had reserved the issue for later determination.[28] The court addressed the Dodds' taking claim again in 1998, but the focus of that decision was issue preclusion, discussed later in this chapter.[29]

The *Suitum* Case

A case that may provide answers to some of the perplexing questions surrounding ripeness is *Suitum v. Tahoe Regional Planning Agency*, the U.S. Supreme Court's latest consideration of the doctrine.[30]

In the underlying fact situation, Mrs. Suitum and her husband bought a residential lot in a Nevada subdivision in 1972, planning to use it for their retirement home.[31] Mrs. Suitum first attempted to develop the lot in 1989, after the death of her husband. Her lot is surrounded by residential homes like the one she intended to build.

However, the property is within an area subject to regulation by the Tahoe Regional Planning Agency (TRPA), an entity created by an interstate compact between the states of California and Nevada. The agency operates under terms of a regional plan[32] that permits no new land coverage or permanent land disturbance within certain zones.

[28]*Id.* at 862.

[29]Dodd v. Hood River County, 136 F. 3d 1219 (9th Cir. 1998).

[30]117 S. Ct. 1659 (1997).

[31]Petitioner's Brief on the Merits, Suitum v. Tahoe Regional Planning Agency, 117 S. Ct. 1659 (1997) (No. 96–243).

[32]*Id.*; Suitum v. Tahoe Regional Planning Agency, 80 F.3d 359, 361, *vacated and remanded*, 117 S.Ct. 1659 (1997).

View of the subdivision lot sought to be developed by Bernadine Suitum, in Incline Village on the Nevada side of Lake Tahoe. The lot was the subject of *Suitum v. Tahoe Regional Planning Agency.*

After a field inspection, the agency denied Mrs. Suitum a permit to develop. She appealed, but the agency was not swayed.

Although Mrs. Suitum was offered no relief in terms of developing her property, the regulatory scheme does allow aggrieved property owners to transfer their property's development rights to property elsewhere. Mrs. Suitum had the ability to do so with a development "allocation" that she received in 1989. However, she didn't use it, and this allocation reverted back to the county. She did not apply for another.[33]

[33]The procedures for development in the Tahoe Basin state that residential allocations "not used within the year of their distribution are returned to the county and TRPA for redistribution the next year." [TRPA Attorney] Susan Scholley Aff. ¶ 8.

Instead, Mrs. Suitum filed a federal district court action under 42 U.S.C. section 1983, alleging an unconstitutional taking that violated her rights to substantive due process and equal protection. The district court granted summary judgment to the agency, finding Mrs. Suitum's claims unripe. The Ninth Circuit agreed, holding that the "final decision" requirement of *Williamson County* is not met unless a property owner who could apply to transfer development rights does so.[34]

Citing *Dodd,* the Ninth Circuit stated that without an application for transferable development rights (TDRs), the court could not determine "the extent of the use of [the] property."[35] To the court, the key inquiry was whether Mrs. Suitum's property retained "any reasonable beneficial use[.]"[36]

In upholding the district court, the Ninth Circuit also addressed another important aspect of ripeness—its futility exception, under which property owners need not pursue "idle and futile act[s]" nor unfair procedures.[37] Mrs. Suitum had unsuccessfully attempted to invoke this exception in the district court, but her contention that TDRs are a "ruse, a sham" was disregarded in favor of the agency's claim that her development rights did have value. Thus, her claims could only be made ripe if she applied to the TDR program, which she had not done.[38]

Mrs. Suitum successfully sought certiorari from the U.S. Supreme Court on ripeness, among other issues. And in a decision written by Justice David H. Souter, the Supreme Court reversed, holding that the case was "ripe for adjudication, even though [the property owner] has not attempted to sell the development rights she has or is eligible to receive."[39]

In its decision, the Court restricted its discussion of *Williamson County* ripeness principles to the "final decision" element—the only element addressed below and briefed before the Court[40]—and "emphasize[d] that the rationale adopted in the [Ninth Circuit] decision

[34]*Suitum,* 80 F.3d at 362.
[35]*Id.*
[36]*Id.* at 363, (citing MacDonald, Sommer & Frates v. County of Yolo, 477 U.S. 340, 349 (1986)).
[37]*Suitum,* 80 F.3d at 363.
[38]*Id.* at 363–64.
[39]Suitum v. Tahoe Regional Planning Agency, 117 S. Ct. 1659, 1662 (1997).
[40]*Id.* at 1664–65.

under review is unsupported by our precedents."[41] Other cases discussed by the Court included *Agins, Hodel,* and *MacDonald.*[42]

The Court found the finality element satisfied: "[T]here being no question here about how the 'regulations at issue [apply] to the particular land in question.'"[43] The agency had determined Mrs. Suitum's land to be within a Stream Environment Zone prohibiting "additional land coverage or other permanent land disturbance"[44] and had no discretion to change that restriction; thus, *Williamson County's* final-decision requirement was not implicated.[45]

The Court next considered the lower court's opinion that the agency had not made a final decision because Mrs. Suitum still needed to apply for permission to transfer her TDRs, finding that such a decision is not required by the *Williamson County* line of cases.[46] Those cases address the possible exercise of discretion by a land-use board.

In dismissing, as "a variation on the preceding position," the agency's argument that the taking claim was not ripe because no "values attributable to [Mrs. Suitum's TDRs] are known," the Court made two points.[47] First, it reiterated its earlier conclusion that "there is no discretionary decision to be made in determining whether she will get [a residential allocation that may increase the value of her TDRs]."[48] And even if she didn't get a residential allocation when she wanted one, the allocation's value "would simply be discounted to reflect the mathematical likelihood of her obtaining one."[49] Second, as to Mrs. Suitum's right to transfer her TDRs, "the only contingency apart from private market demand turns on the right of the agency to deny approval for a specific transfer . . . and the right of a local regulatory body to deny transfer approval. . . ."[50] Even if those potential actions could implicate the type of discretion discussed in *Williamson County*, the issue, to the Court, is whether the TDRs possess "saleability," and, the court noted, the agency's own position assumes many potential, lawful buyers for [Mrs.] Suitum's TDRs . . . ."[51] Thus,

[41]*Id.* at 1665.
[42]*Id.* at 1665–67.
[43]*Id.* at 1667.
[44]*Id.*
[45]*Id.*
[46]*Id.* at 1667–68.
[47]*Id.* at 1668–69.
[48]*Id.* at 1668.
[49]*Id.* at 1668–69.
[50]*Id.* at 1668.
[51]*Id.*

"valuation of [Mrs.] Suitum's TDRs is . . . simply an issue of fact about possible market prices, and one on which the [trial court] had considerable evidence before it."[52]

Focusing on the agency's denial of Mrs. Suitum's request to build a house on her lot, Justice Scalia reaches this conclusion:

[The agency] concedes that "we know the full extent of the regulation's impact in restricting [Mrs. Suitum's] development of her own land. . . ." That is all we need to know to conclude that the final decision requirement has been met.[53]

Claim Preclusion, Issue Preclusion, and Being Left with No Remedy

While the Dodds were taken off the claim-preclusion hook, they ultimately found themselves still firmly caught on the question of issue preclusion. And no one, said the Ninth Circuit, had yet decided whether the decision by the Oregon Supreme Court in the Dodds' case[54] on the taking question was an equivalent determination of the federal Takings Clause issue so as to preclude the Dodds from proceeding in federal court on that issue. To answer that question, the court of appeals remanded the case to the federal district court "to decide in the first instance whether a factual predicate is necessary to decide the question of issue preclusion."[55] The district court had determined that no additional factual findings were needed, a decision affirmed by the Ninth Circuit—with different reasoning.[56] Looking to Oregon law for the rules on issue preclusion, the Ninth Circuit found that LUBA's determination against the Dodds would be given preclusive effect if five elements were met.[57] All elements were satisfied, thus issue preclusion was proper.[58] The elements were whether:

1. The LUBA proceeding and the federal district suit involved an "identical issue";

[52]Id.

[53]Id. at 1673 (Scalia, J., concurring).

[54]The Oregon Supreme Court case is Dodd v. Hood River County, 317 Or. 172, 855 P.2d 608 (1993); the court of appeals' comment about that case is at 59 F.3d 852, 863 (9th Cir. 1995).

[55]59 F.3d at 863.

[56]Dodd v. Hood River County, 136 F. 3d 1219, 1223 (9th Cir. 1998).

[57]Id. at 1225.

[58]Id. at 1228.

2. the issue was actually litigated;
3. the Dodds had a full and fair opportunity to litigate their claim before LUBA;
4. the LUBA hearing included safeguards such as the making of independent findings on the record; and
5. issues were actually litigated before LUBA despite the reservation of a federal claim.[59]

Concluding that a further factual record was not needed, the Ninth Circuit analyzed the taking claim itself and found no taking.[60]

Requiring a developer to pursue any remedy under state law that allows for compensation before bringing an action in federal court can trigger issues of both claim and issue preclusion, formerly and more traditionally referred to as res judicata and collateral estoppel, respectively.[61] Claim preclusion prevents the bringing of a cause of action that has previously been adjudicated. Thus, a landowner who is reluctant to bring a taking claim in federal court because of the potential for claim preclusion may choose to proceed in state court. Should the state court decide the taking issue against the landowner, the landowner's claim will be precluded from further consideration in federal court by the doctrine of res judicata.[62]

Collateral estoppel, on the other hand, precludes a developer who had an opportunity to raise a taking claim in state court but failed to do so from raising that issue in a subsequent action—i.e., collaterally attacking the original decision by requesting alternative relief under the same basic set of facts. Under the Full Faith and Credit Clause of the U.S. Constitution, courts in one state are precluded from hearing cases that have been decided in other states.[63] Further, under the Full Faith and Credit statute,[64] federal courts are precluded from litigating issues that have been, or could have been, litigated at the state level. Thus, it is imperative to make the right decisions as to where to initiate suit and what claims to bring. There is no turning back, because once property owners bring takings claims in state court (as re-

---

[59]*Id.* at 1225–27.
[60]*Id.* at 1229–30.
[61]*See generally* Roberts, *supra* note 1. Res judicata means "a thing adjudged" between the same parties; collateral estoppel means "stopped by a lateral or side action" on the same issue but not necessarily between the same parties.
[62]Roberts, *supra* note 1, at 483.
[63]U.S. Const. art. IV., § 1.
[64]28 U.S.C.A. § 1738.

quired by the second step of *Williamson County*), they may find themselves unable to proceed in federal court.

For example, in *Peduto v. City of North Wildwood*,[65] the Third Circuit found no due process violation when claim preclusion denied a property owner access to the federal courts. The court held state-court exhaustion under *Williamson County* was a "necessary predicate" to the federal cause of action, and that the Due Process Clause entitles a property owner to nothing more and nothing less than full and fair adjudication in state court.

Professor Thomas E. Roberts has noted that the blocked access on the return trip to federal court can be surprising for some.[66] For example, property owners near the Sarasota-Manatee Airport brought an action in state court claiming that the impacts from engine noise constituted the taking of an airspace easement without just compensation.[67] The state court found no taking. Accordingly, the property owners brought an action in federal court under section 1983 and the Fifth and Fourteenth Amendments. The district court held, however, that they were barred by res judicata and collateral estoppel.[68]

The result in the *Sarasota–Manatee Airport* case, bad as it was for those bringing the action, is not the worst possible outcome of a ripeness claim. Someone who brings an unripe claim under section 1983 may have to pay the other side's attorney fees under a companion section, section 1988, that gives federal district courts discretion to award attorney fees to a prevailing party in a section 1983 case.[69]

A twist on the ripeness shuffle over whether to start in federal or state court occurs when a case is started at one court level and removed to the other.[70] In one case, a property owner had been operating a

[65]878 F.2d 725 (3d Cir. 1989).

[66]Roberts, *supra* note 1, at 487.

[67]Fields v. Sarasota–Manatee Airport Auth., 755 F. Supp. 377 (M.D. Fla. 1991), *aff'd*, 953 F.2d 1299 (11th Cir. 1992).

[68]*See also* Palomar Mobilehome Park v. City of San Marcos, 989 F.2d 362 (9th Cir. 1993) (same fact pattern and result; exactly the problem the Ninth Circuit was talking about in *Dodd*).

[69]42 U.S.C.A. § 1988.

[70]Under 28 U.S.C.S. § 1441(a), a defendant (such as the government) in a civil action in state court may move to remove the action to federal court if it is based on a claim over which the federal district court has original jurisdiction (such as a Fifth Amendment taking). But at least one commentator has questioned why ripeness principles require that a person bringing a taking claim must start in state court, but a defendant can remove the same case from state to federal court. Gideon Kanner, *Noted in Brief*, JUST COMPENSATION , June 1997, at 11.

nursery for eight years when he received a notice that he was violating the county's zoning laws and would be subject to prosecution and fines. He then received a letter from one of the county's lawyers saying that they were still researching the issue of whether there was a violation. Eventually the county decided there was a violation. The property owner brought an action in state court claiming due process and taking violations. The county had the case removed to federal district court, which granted summary judgment for the county.

The Court of Appeals for the Eleventh Circuit upheld the federal district court's decision that the threat of enforcement in the notice was not a final, definite decision that would lift the property owner over the ripeness hurdle because the property owner could continue to operate the nursery while the local administrative review process continued before the county's Code Enforcement Board. The court also discussed the need to have any challenges to a criminal zoning violation brought in state court to keep the federal courts from becoming "master zoning boards."[71]

Facial and As-Applied Claims

The choice between a facial or as-applied challenge presents a dilemma for any property owner with a potential taking claim. (We discuss these issues in detail in chapter 10, but for our purposes here we merely highlight the differences and their effect on ripeness.) If a property owner tries to avoid the ripeness issue by challenging a regulation as effecting a taking on its face, the chances of success are extremely limited because all the government needs to show for a complete defense is just one instance where the regulation would not effect a taking. On the other hand, if a property owner brings a takings claim based on a regulation "as applied," the property owner may either be required to make multiple sequential applications or to apply for a variance, waiver, or other relief through the ordinance itself.[72] This process can take many years to complete.

---

[71]Tari v. Collier County, 56 F.3d 1533, 1537 (11th Cir. 1995).

[72]Lyman, *supra* note 1, at 118. *See also* Gregory Overstreet, *Update on the Continuing and Dramatic Effect of the Ripeness Doctrine on Federal Land Use Litigation*, 20 ZONING & PLANNING LAW REPORT 17, 19 (Mar. 1997) [hereinafter *Overstreet I*]. Ripeness doctrine does not apply to a facial "legitimate state interest" taking claim (citing Sinclair Oil Corp. v. County of Santa Barbara,

The "State Compensation" Prong

First English,[73] a case discussed in more detail in chapter 12, is significant in terms of the "state compensation" prong of the *Williamson County* ripeness test. Prior to *First English,* it was uncertain whether the Takings Clause required states to provide just compensation for a temporary regulatory taking. After *First English,* however, it was clear that all states were required to afford compensation for temporary regulatory takings.[74] Consequently, the *Williamson County* rule applies in all states, and to fulfill the state-compensation requirement for ripeness, property owners must avail themselves of state remedies before proceeding in federal court.[75] The requirement to attempt to obtain relief under a state compensation procedure extends even to the situation where the right to such compensation "remains unsure and undeveloped"[76] and applies to physical and regulatory takings alike.[77]

---

96 F.3d 401, 406–07 (9th Cir. 1996). *Overstreet I, supra,* at 19. *But see* Sinclair at 407–09 (state–law takings claim unripe for failure to pursue administrative remedies; both federal and state takings claims for precondemnation delay also unripe for no final decision).

[73]482 U.S. 304 (1987). After remand to the California Supreme Court denied review, 1989 Cal. LEXIS 4224 (Aug. 25, 1989), and the U.S. Supreme Court denied Certiorari, 493 U.S. 1056 (1990).

[74]Roberts, *supra* note 1 at 484.

[75]*See* Christensen v. Yolo County Bd. of Supervisors, 995 F.2d 161, 164 (9th Cir. 1993); Bickerstaff Clay Prods. Co., Inc. v. Harris County, 89 F.3d 1481, 1491 (11th Cir. 1996) (federal claim not ripe because Georgia Constitution provides remedy). *See also* Gregory Overstreet, *Update on the Continuing and Dramatic Effect of the Ripeness Doctrine on Federal Land Use Litigation,* 20 ZONING & PLANNING LAW REPORT 25, 28 (Apr. 1997) (Part II of a two–part article) [hereinafter *Overstreet II*] (citing Bakken v. City of Council Bluffs, 470 N.W.2d 34, 37–38 (Iowa 1991) ("completely inappropriate" use of state–compensation element to deny a remedy in both state and federal courts)).

One Court, however, has said that seeking one's remedy under the *federal* constitution in state court is unnecessary: "the compensation element is satisfied if remedies available under the state constitution have been pursued." *Dodd,* 59 F.3d at 860.

[76]Villager Pond Inc. v. Town of Darien, 56 F.3d 375, 380 (2d Cir. 1995) (citing *Southview,* 980 F.2d at 99), *cert. denied,* 117 S. Ct. 50 (1996). For state–compensation–prong cases reaching varied results, see *Overstreet II, supra* note 75.

[77]56 F.3d at 380.

Exhaustion of Administrative Remedies

Ripeness and exhaustion both deal with the timing of judicial review, but they are not the same. Ripeness addresses the need to have a discrete dispute before courts can properly exercise their function. Exhaustion keeps a party from making an end run around the administrative agency by going directly to the courts.

Distinguishing a ripeness issue from an exhaustion defense is not always easy. Even the Oregon Supreme Court, characteristically sophisticated in land use, managed to label a ripeness issue with "exhaustion of remedies" terminology.[78]

The confusion between exhaustion and finality and ultimately ripeness is understandable. They are in some ways interrelated, and all three seek to avoid premature adjudication of claims. However, "[t]he question whether administrative remedies must be exhausted is conceptually distinct . . . from the question whether an administrative action must be final before it is judicially reviewable."[79]

Takings ripeness rules have been extended by some federal courts to substantive due process, procedural due process, and equal protection cases,[80] but other courts do not agree. In one interesting and troubling case, developers claimed that local officials deliberately and improperly interfered in the application process to block or delay issuance of permits for reasons unrelated to the merits of the application.[81] The Court of Appeals for the Third Circuit held that the standard that a property must be "conclusively barred" from development only applies to takings claims.[82]

---

[78]Nelson v. City of Oswego, 126 Or. App. 416, 419–20, 869 P.2d 350 (1994) (citing Fifth Avenue Corp. v. Washington Co., 282 Or. 591, 581 P.2d 50 (1978)).

[79]*Williamson County,* 473 U.S. at 192. The subsequent decision in *Lucas v. South Carolina Coastal Council* has not been helpful in refining the Supreme Court's ripeness doctrine.

[80]DANIEL R. MANDELKER ET AL., FEDERAL LAND USE LAW § 4A.02 [6] (Supp. 1998).

[81]Blanche Road Corp. v. Bensalem Township, 57 F.3d 253, 267–68 (3d Cir. 1995), *cert. denied,* 516 U.S. 915 (1995).

[82]*Id.* at 268. *But see* Tri County Indus., Inc. v. District of Columbia, 104 F.3d 455, 458–59 (D.C. Cir. 1997) (substantive due process claim not ripe because property owner did not seek relief from suspension of its building permit).

The Tenth Circuit recently distinguished ripeness and exhaustion after a property owner who was denied a conditional-use permit started a section 1983 action instead of seeking a variance from the local Board of Adjustment:

> Whereas exhaustion generally refers to the requirement that a litigant resort to available administrative or judicial procedures prior to filing a federal lawsuit, the finality requirement seeks to ensure that the issues and the factual components of the dispute are sufficiently fleshed out to permit meaningful judicial review.[83]

However, while the property owner in the case did not need to exhaust his available administrative remedies prior to filing the section 1983 action, he was not excused from first obtaining a final decision from the Board of Adjustment on the variance. Consequently, his taking claim was not ripe, even though he was able to file the section 1983 action.[84]

Importance of Timing

In returning once more to our hapless developer still trying to build 800,000 square feet of office space, the first question that must be answered is, When did the taking occur? At the time the proposal for 800,000 square feet of office space was denied? Probably not, for the government had not yet reached the final, definitive position on what they would approve or disapprove, as required by *Williamson County*.

Ultimately, the optimum strategy for any property owner is to make multiple, sequential applications and pursue at least one variance. Case law has not resolved how many of these rounds are necessary and whether one must always apply for a variance before a taking is ripe for adjudication.

---

[83]Bateman v. City of West Bountiful, 89 F.3d 704, 707 (10th Cir. 1996) (citing Lujan v. National Wildlife Fed'n, 497 U.S. 871, 891 (1990); Abbott Labs. v. Gardner, 387 U.S. 136 (1967)).

[84]*See also* Fowlkes v. City of Niles, 1996 U.S. Dist. LEXIS 3828 at 10–12 (W.D. Mich. Mar. 6, 1996).

The Futility Exception

The lower federal courts have adopted a futility exception similar to the one at the state level that allows a property owner to proceed directly into court to pursue a taking claim without first seeking a variance or other similar relief. The U.S. Supreme Court has yet to recognize the futility exception, and if it does so, the High Court probably will apply it only to the final-decision prong of ripeness.[85] Following the *First English* decision, it would seem to be difficult, if not impossible, to argue futility with regard to the state-compensation requirement.

The most significant case on the futility exception is *Kinzli v. City of Santa Cruz*.[86] In *Kinzli*, the Ninth Circuit held that the plaintiffs could not assert the futility exception unless they had filed a "meaningful application" with the zoning commission and had applied for a variance. In considering whether the Kinzlis' claim fell within the "futility exception" to the final-decision requirement, the Ninth Circuit discussed the two alternate tests that may be applied to determine futility—the beneficial use test and the marketability test. Under the more stringent beneficial use test, any profitable use of the land precludes futility. The marketability test considers whether any proposal could conform to the zoning regulations and still generate the interest of a potential purchaser. The court rejected the futility claim under both tests, requiring that at least one "meaningful application" as per *MacDonald* be made. Even so, the court did not specify the point at which reapplication would become futile based on the above-mentioned tests, since the plaintiffs had not even met the threshold requirement.

While the facts above support a ripeness argument, other factual patterns can prove more problematic, such as the Minnesota case involving landowners of a peninsula on Lake Minnetonka, Minnesota. The local government had zoned the property for low-density single-family residences. The landowners, who wanted to build a marina

---

[85] Arguably, the Court at least acknowledges the futility exception, though it has not decided a land-use case on the merits on the grounds of futility. *See MacDonald*, 477 U.S. at 353 n.8.

[86] 818 F.2d 1449, 1455 (9th Cir.), *amended*, 830 F.2d 968 (9th Cir. 1987), *cert. denied*, 484 U.S. 1043 (1988). *See also* Bensch v. Metropolitan Dade County, 952 F. Supp. 790, 796 (S.D. Fla 1996) (futility argument rejected because no final decision in state court on flowage–easement takings claim).

that was not permitted in that zone, instituted an inverse condemnation action claiming that the low-density residential zoning was unconstitutional and constituted a Fifth Amendment taking.[87]

The trial court granted summary judgment for the city, rejecting the taking claim and concluding that the landowners had a reasonable use because they could dock a single boat. The Court of Appeals of Minnesota reversed the trial court on the taking claim, finding that the ordinance did not permit a reasonable use. The case was remanded on ripeness grounds so local government could issue a final decision on applying the regulations to appellants' property.

The landowners unsuccessfully argued that a final decision was not required because pursuing a variance or rezoning would be futile based on a representation by city staff that the city manager had "made it clear that no permit or variance would be approved when, in 1985, they were told the city 'does not want any development of the property.'"[88] The court of appeals found that the city manager's statement did not necessarily mean a variance would not be granted nine years later in 1994. Thus, what might be a sufficient basis for claiming the futility exception to the ripeness requirement can evaporate with the passage of time because evidence of futility years ago may not remain evidence of futility in the present.

While official representations may enable the use of the futility exception, they may also disable it. One court rejected a futility claim even after a variance was rejected: "[W]e place great weight on the numerous assurances by City officials in the record that a subsequent variance application properly drawn and presented, including a development plan, would be given favorable consideration."[89]

Conclusions

Ripeness can indeed prove a trap for the unwary; it sometimes catches even the most careful and vigilant. The rules are unclear and inexact and are likely to be more of a barrier in the federal courts than in the state courts. To date, Florida is the only state to address

[87]Wheeler v. City of Wayzata, 511 N.W.2d 39 (Minn. Ct. App. 1994), *rev'd on other grounds*, 533 N.W.2d 405 (Minn. 1995).

[88]*Id.* at 43.

[89]McKee v. City of Tallahassee, 664 So. 2d 333, 334 (Fla. Dist. Ct. App. 1995).

ripeness by statute,[90] but more statutory solutions would be worth considering. If the federal and state legislatures do not address the problem, the courts would do well to attempt to craft more bright-line rules. The Ninth Circuit's *Dodd* decision from 1995 is a step in the right direction, but only one step.

[90]*See* Mark W. Cordes, *Leapfrogging the Constitution: The Rise of State Takings Legislation,* 24 Ecology L.Q. 187, 220 (1997) (section 70.001 of Fla. Stat. requires written "ripeness decision" of what economically viable uses remain after regulation).

Chapter 6

Other Hurdles

Statutes of Limitations

Of the procedural issues that occur in takings litigation, none—with the possible exception of ripeness—arises with greater frequency than the statute of limitations. In layperson's terms, the question is whether the property owner has brought the regulatory taking claim promptly enough. Three subissues are present and recurring: (1) what is the relevant limitations period; (2) when does the takings claim "accrue" (i.e., begin to run); and (3) what actions are sufficient to "toll" (i.e., suspend) the running of the statute of limitations?

Courts and scholars alike have regularly articulated the policy underpinnings of statutes of limitations. The specific utility of these time limitations in the context of regulatory takings cases has similarly been explained in several judicial decisions. The U.S. Court of Appeals for the Federal Circuit observed in a takings case that this defense:

> insures the claimants' good faith and rewards the diligent prosecution of grievances. It also encourages claimants to muster their evidence early, and to preserve it. In addition, it prevents claimants from surprising the Government with potentially stale claims based on events that transpired many years before.[1]

---

[1]Creppel v. United States, 41 F.3d 627, 633 (Fed. Cir. 1994).

A state supreme court similarly opined:

> The purpose of statutes [of limitations] is to permit and pro-
> mote sound fiscal planning by state and local government enti-
> ties. . . . The requirement that challenges to administrative ac-
> tions constituting takings be brought [within a short time
> frame] assures that the administrative agency will have the al-
> ternative of changing a decision for which compensation might
> be required. If no such early opportunity were given, and in-
> stead, persons were permitted to stand by in the face of admin-
> istrative actions alleged to be injurious or confiscatory, and
> three or five years later, claim monetary compensation on the
> theory that the administrative action resulted in a taking for
> public use, meaningful government fiscal planning would be
> impossible.[2]

Turning to the question of the applicable limitations period, one
veteran inverse condemnation attorney recently suggested (only half-
jokingly) that how lawyers view the appropriate statute of limitations
in takings cases depends on when they graduated from law school.
Most "older" land-use lawyers believe that the limitations period for
such claims is (or should be) many years in length. Newer practi-
tioners think differently—and with good reason.

These disparate perceptions actually track judicial developments
over recent years. Traditionally, courts found physical and regulatory
takings claims subject to relatively lengthy (i.e., up to 10-year)
statutes of limitations.[3] Recently, however, most state and federal
courts have begun applying far shorter statutes of limitations to reg-

[2]Hensler v. City of Glendale, 8 Cal. 4th 1, 27–28, 876 P.2d 1043 (1994), 876
P-2d 1043 (1994), *cert. denied,* 513 U.S. 1184 (1995) (quoting Patrick Media
Group, Inc. v. California Coastal Comm'n, 9 Cal. App. 4th 592, 612, 11 Cal.
Rptr. 2d 824 (1992)).

[3]*See, e.g.,* White Pine Lumber Co. v. City of Reno, 106 Nev. 778, 801 P.2d
1370 (1990) (10-year statute of limitations); Millison v. Wilzack, 77 Md. App.
676, 551 A.2d 899 (Md. Ct. Spec. App. 1989) (3 years, distinguished from 20-
year limitations period applicable to direct condemnation proceedings); Scott v.
City of Sioux City, 432 N.W.2d 144, 146 (Iowa 1988) (5 years, analogizing from
state statute pertaining to "recovery of real property"); Baker v. Burbank-Glendale-Pasadena Airport Auth., 39 Cal. 3d 862, 867, 705 P.2d 866 (1985) (5 years
for physical invasion). For a useful survey of state statutes of limitations applicable to inverse condemnation proceedings, *see* Charles C. Marvel, Annotation,
*State Statute of Limitations Applicable to Inverse Condemnation or Similar Pro-
ceedings by Landowner to Obtain Compensation,* 26 A.L.R.4th 68 (1996).

ulatory takings claims. The limitations period is in some cases derived from the enabling legislation of the regulatory entity being sued.[4] In others, abbreviated statutes of limitations generally applicable to, for example, challenges to local land-use decisions have been applied.[5]

Some plaintiffs have sought to avoid application of short limitations periods by claiming that they are not attempting to challenge the *legality* of land-use regulatory programs and, therefore, should not be subject to statutes of limitations applicable to such challenges. Instead, they say, a regulatory takings claim simply seeks compensation for the unconstitutional effect of an otherwise proper regulation. State courts to date have rejected such arguments.[6] Similar efforts to evade the application of statutes of limitations in federal takings litigation have met a similar fate.[7]

Suits brought under the federal Civil Rights Act, 42 U.S.C. section 1983, raise special questions regarding the applicable statute of limitations. In 1985, the U.S. Supreme Court decreed that in the majority of such cases, federal law should "borrow" the limitations period generally applicable to personal injury claims in the state jurisdiction in which the federal court is located.[8] Accordingly, state and federal courts around the nation have wound up applying disparate state limitations periods in determining whether particular

[4]*See, e.g.,* Tahoe Sierra Preservation Council v. Tahoe Regional Planning Agency, 34 F.3d 753 (9th Cir. 1994) (applying 60-day statute of limitations found in bi-state Tahoe Regional Planning Compact and applicable to any "legal action arising out of the adoption [of TRPA's] regional plan or of any ordinance," to bar certain regulatory takings claims brought against regional land-use agency).

[5]*See, e.g., Hensler,* 8 Cal. 4th 1, 876 P.2d 1043 (90-day statute of limitations applicable to legal challenges to subdivision map approvals); Curtis v. Ketchum, 111 Idaho 27, 720 P.2d 210 (Idaho 1986) (60-day limitations period for challenges to city council and zoning commission actions); Town of Auburn v. McEvoy, 131 N.H. 303, 553 A.2d 317 (1988) (30-day statute applicable to review of planning board action); Crystal Green v. City of Crystal, 421 N.W.2d 393 (Minn. Ct. App. 1988); Ponderosa Homes, Inc. v. City of San Ramon, 23 Cal. App. 4th 1761, 29 Cal. Rptr. 2d 26 (1994) (180-day limitations period).

[6]*See, e.g., Hensler,* 8 Cal. 4th at 26.

[7]*See, e.g.,* Gilbert v. City of Cambridge, 932 F.2d 51 (1st Cir. 1991) (rejecting argument that limitations period could be circumvented by plaintiff's styling of takings claim as one for declaratory relief); Levald, Inc. v. City of Palm Desert, 998 F.2d 680, 688 (9th Cir. 1993) (accord).

[8]Wilson v. Garcia, 471 U.S. 261 (1985).

inverse condemnation lawsuits are timely.[9] At least one court has held that this state-specific statute of limitations should be applied in section 1983 cases even when a competing and more specific federal or state limitations period is available.[10]

The situation is far less confusing with respect to inverse condemnation claims brought against the federal government in the Court of Federal Claims under the Tucker Act: The applicable limitations period is six years, by virtue of express congressional enactment.[11]

The question of when a takings claim "accrues" (i.e., when the statute of limitations begins to run) varies considerably depending on the type of takings claim involved. In cases of physical invasion of private property, most courts apply a fairly relaxed standard, finding that the claim accrues when the landowner first becomes aware of the government intrusion, or even later, when the situation "stabilizes" to a certain degree.[12]

Regulatory takings present greater problems and require further subclassification. Most courts view facial regulatory takings claims (i.e., those alleging that the mere enactment of a regulation effects a compensable taking) as accruing on the date on which the regulation is adopted or made final by the government.[13]

[9]*See, e.g.,* New Port Largo, Inc. v. Monroe County, 985 F.2d 1488 (11th Cir. 1993) (federal court would borrow four-year limitations period from Florida state law to ascertain timeliness of § 1983-based inverse condemnation claim); Azul Pacifico, Inc. v. City of Los Angeles, 973 F.2d 704 (9th Cir. 1992), *cert. denied,* 506 U.S. 1081 (1993) (§1983 claims filed in state or federal court in California subject to one-year statute of limitations); Gilbert v. City of Cambridge, 932 F.2d 51, 57 (1st Cir. 1991) (Massachusetts: three years); Perez v. Seever, 869 F.2d 425, 426 (9th Cir. 1989), *cert. denied,* 493 U.S. 860 (1989) (Nevada: two years). For a useful compendium of the statute of limitations applicable to § 1983 actions in each of the 50 states, *see* Martin A. Schwartz & John E. Kirklin, *1c Section 1983 Litigation: Claims and Defenses* § 12.9 (John Wiley & Sons, 3d ed. 1997).

[10]Tahoe Sierra Preservation Council v. Tahoe Regional Planning Agency, 34 F.3d 753 (9th Cir. 1994) (declining to apply 60-day limitations period set forth in defendant agency's enabling legislation in favor of lengthier period afforded by Wilson v. Garcia, 471 U.S. 261).

[11]28 U.S.C. § 2501. *See also* 28 U.S.C. § 2401 (prescribing six-year statute of limitations for all civil actions brought against federal government in district court).

[12]United States v. Dickinson, 331 U.S. 745, 748–49 (1947); Pierpont Inn, Inc. v. California, 70 Cal. 2d 282, 293, 449 P.2d 737 (1962).

[13]DeAnza Properties X, Ltd. v. County of Santa Cruz, 936 F.2d 1084, 1087

The question of when an as-applied regulatory taking challenge accrues is inextricably linked to ripeness principles which the U.S. Supreme Court has decreed apply to such claims.[14] Many courts have held that an as-applied claim does not accrue for statute of limitations purposes until a property owner has: (1) obtained a final administrative determination on the applicability of the regulation to the affected property, and (2) pursued and been denied compensation under available state procedures.[15]

Efforts by property owners to toll the statute of limitations in regulatory takings cases have not met with significant success. One oft-rejected theory is that an unconstitutional regulation is "continuing" in nature as long as the measure remains in effect, thus tolling indefinitely (or even starting anew) the applicable limitations period. The Court of Appeals for the First Circuit criticized that argument as obfuscating the "critical distinction between a continuing act and a singular act that brings continuing consequences in its roiled wake. . . . Whatever harms were suffered add up to nothing more than the predictable, albeit painful, consequences of the permit denial."[16]

A means by which the judiciary has mitigated the potentially

(9th Cir. 1991); Azul Pacifico, Inc. v. City of Los Angeles, 973 F.2d 704, 705 (9th Cir. 1993); *Tahoe Sierra Preservation Council,* 34 F.3d 753; Millison v. Wilzack, 77 Md. App. 676, 551 A.2d 899, 903 (Md. Ct. Spec. App. 1989). For a fuller discussion of the distinction between facial and as-applied takings challenges, *see* chapter 10; *see also* "date of the taking" discussion in chapter 13.

[14]These issues are discussed in detail in chapter 5.

[15]*See, e.g.,* Biddison v. City of Chicago, 921 F.2d 724, 728–29 (7th Cir. 1991); New Port Largo, Inc. v. Monroe County, 985 F.2d 1488, 1492–93 (11th Cir. 1993), *cert. denied,* 117 S. Ct. 2514 (1997); Levald v. City of Palm Desert, 998 F.2d 680, 687 (9th Cir. 1993), *cert. denied,* 510 U.S. 1093 (1994); Norco Construction Co. v. King County, 801 F.2d 1143, 1145 (9th Cir. 1986). *Cf.* Ponderosa Homes, Inc. v. City of San Ramon, 23 Cal. App. 4th 1761, 29 Cal. Rptr. 2d 26 (1994) section (1983–based taking claim challenging fee exaction accrues on date municipality imposed the fee); Creppel v. United States, 41 F.3d 627, 633–34 (Fed. Cir. 1994) (as-applied taking claim accrues "when the taking action occurs," i.e., when project application denied); Scott v. City of Sioux City, 432 N.W.2d 144, 147 (Iowa 1988).

[16]Gilbert v. City of Cambridge, 932 F.2d 51, 58–59 (1st Cir. 1991), *cert. denied,* 502 U.S. 866 (1992) (rejecting "continuing act" theory in as-applied takings challenge). *See also Hensler* 8 Cal. 4th 1, 21–22; *Levald,* 998 F.2d at 688 (same judicial response regarding facial inverse condemnation claim); Aiello v. Browning-Ferris, Inc., 1993 WL 463701 (N.D. Cal. Nov. 2, 1993) (accord).

difficult impact of this "no tolling" principle on property owners is to devise procedural rules that encourage plaintiffs to pursue concurrently legal challenges to invalidate the offending measure and to obtain compensation under the Takings Clause to remedy the regulation's allegedly unconstitutional effects.[17]

Abstention

One key question in inverse condemnation litigation concerns *where* the aggrieved property owner should file a lawsuit: in state or federal court. If the federal government is the defendant, the choice is usually clear, and the suit will be pursued in federal court—probably the Court of Federal Claims. Where state or local government regulations are challenged, however, the choice of courts is a significant one. Property owners often would rather litigate their regulatory takings claims in federal court, for reasons explained below. State and local government defendants, on the other hand, usually prefer the more familiar venue offered by the state courts. However, the choice is increasingly illusory under the abstention doctrine.

The abstention doctrine provides a discretionary basis upon which federal judges may decline to decide cases that are otherwise properly before the federal courts. Grounded in principles of comity and cooperative federalism, abstention is based on the notion that federal courts should not intrude on sensitive state political and judicial controversies unless absolutely necessary. Rather, say proponents of abstention, those controversies should be settled in the state court systems.

Over the years, the U.S. Supreme Court has developed several categories of federal abstention.[18] Those distinctions can be important; under some versions of abstention, the proper remedy is for the fed-

---

[17]*Creppel,* 41 F.3d at 632–33; *Hensler,* 8 Cal. 4th at 16.

[18]The categories of the abstention doctrine are generally identified by reference to the seminal U.S. Supreme Court decision which created each such subspecies. *See, e.g.,* Younger v. Harris, 401 U.S. 37 (1971) (so-called "*Younger*" abstention invoked when necessary to promote strong federal policy against federal court interference with pending state judicial proceedings); Railroad Comm'n v. Pullman, 312 U.S. 496 (1941) ("*Pullman*" abstention, allowing postponement of exercise of federal jurisdiction when federal constitutional issue could be mooted or recast by state court determination of antecedent state law issue); Burford v. Sun Oil Co., 319 U.S. 315 (1943) ("*Burford*" abstention,

eral court to dismiss the action in favor of state court adjudication, while in others the federal judge simply stays (i.e., suspends) the federal lawsuit until parallel state court litigation is concluded.[19] Yet the distinctions between the subcategories of abstention are far from clear-cut, and federal courts have on at least some occasions applied each variation of abstention to bar inverse condemnation claims brought in federal court.[20]

Historically, the federal courts' receptivity to defendants' abstention arguments has produced mixed results. Some federal judges have always been inclined to steer contentious inverse condemnation and related land-use disputes to their state counterparts.[21] Other federal courts, however, have taken the view that they are proper, indeed preferable, tribunals for the adjudication of what, after all, are principles of federal constitutional law. Older federal decisions reflecting this view often relied on the fact that state court procedures and

---

counseling against federal adjudication in cases touching on a complex state regulatory scheme); Colorado River Water Conservation Dist. v. United States, 424 U.S. 800 (1976) ("*Colorado River*" abstention, a catchall concerned with avoiding duplicative state/federal litigation and promoting wise judicial administration).

[19]The ability of federal courts to order *dismissal* of pending federal litigation in favor of state court adjudication has recently been limited in certain types of abstention cases, however. In Quackenbush v. Allstate Ins. Co, 517 U.S. 706 (1996), the Supreme Court held that in *Burford* abstention cases in which money damages are sought, federal courts may *stay* federal adjudication to allow state courts to first address important questions of state policy, but are precluded from *dismissing* the federal action in favor of state court adjudication. The judicial remedy of choice for most inverse condemnation plaintiffs is, of course, money damages.

[20]*See, e.g.,* McLaughlin v. Town of Front Royal, 21 F.3d 423 (4th Cir. 1994) (*Burford* abstention); C-Y Dev. Co. v. City of Redlands, 703 F.2d 375 (9th Cir. 1983) (*Pullman* abstention); Broadway 41st St. Realty Corp. v. New York State Urban Dev. Corp., 733 F. Supp. 735 (S.D.N.Y. 1990) (*Younger* and *Colorado River* abstention).

[21]Numerous federal courts have invoked the same policy argument in doing so. Schenck v. City of Hudson, 114 F.3d 590, 594–595 (6th Cir. 1997) ("It is not the province of a federal court to act as a super-zoning board."); Corn v. City of Lauderdale Lakes, 997 F.2d 1369, 1389 (11th Cir. 1993), *cert. denied,* 511 U.S. 1018 (1994) (same); Williams v. City of Columbia, 906 F.2d 994, 996 (4th Cir.), 1990) (accord); Raskiewicz v. Town of New Boston, 754 F.2d 38, 44 (1st Cir., *cert. denied,* 474 U.S. 845 (1985); Construction Indus. Ass'n. of Sonoma County v. City of Petaluma, 552 F.2d 897, 908 (9th Cir. 1975), *cert. denied,* 424 U.S. 934 (1976).

remedies for regulatory takings claims were not as favorable to property owners as were those in federal court.[22]

Such varying results have largely disappeared in recent years. Federal courts currently invoke abstention principles to avoid adjudication of regulatory takings cases with far greater frequency. The modern trend is largely the result of two distinct but related U.S. Supreme Court developments. The first is the Court's landmark 1987 decision in *First English Evangelical Lutheran Church v. County of Los Angeles,*[23] holding that money damages are a constitutionally compelled remedy in regulatory takings cases in state and federal courts alike. *First English* deprived both the litigants and the federal courts of the argument that constitutional remedies available in state courts are noticeably inferior to those afforded by the federal judiciary.

The second key development on this front is the Court's formulation of the ripeness doctrine, most prominently in *Williamson County Regional Planning Commission v. Hamilton Bank.*[24] Under that doctrine, regulatory takings cases are not ripe for federal adjudication until and unless a plaintiff has both: (1) obtained a final administrative determination regarding the challenged regulation's applicability to the subject property, and (2) utilized reasonably available state compensation procedures.[25]

These ripeness rules, particularly the latter, have further encouraged increasingly overburdened federal judges to apply abstention principles to shunt most inverse condemnation cases to the state court systems.[26] Indeed, federal courts have gone so far as to indicate

---

[22]For example, in the 1970s and early 1980s, states such as New York and California decreed that money damages were not available in inverse condemnation cases, and that invalidation of the offending regulation was the exclusive judicial remedy. Some federal courts cited these state law rules (since overruled by the U.S. Supreme Court) to find that federal abstention in regulatory takings cases was inappropriate. *See, e.g.,* McMillan v. Goleta Water Dist., 792 F.2d 1453, 1458–59 (9th Cir. 1986), *cert. denied,* 480 U.S. 906 (1987); Oceanic Cal., Inc. v. City of San Jose, 497 F. Supp. 962, 968 (N.D. Cal. 1980).

[23]482 U.S. 304.

[24]473 U.S. 172 (1985).

[25]*See also* MacDonald, Sommer & Frates v. County of Yolo, 477 U.S. 340, 351–53 (1986). For a more thorough discussion of ripeness principles, see chapter 5.

[26]*See, e.g.,* Tenneco Oil Co. v. Department of Consumer Affairs, 876 F.2d 1013 (1st Cir. 1989); McLaughlin v. Town of Front Royal, 21 F.3d 423 (4th Cir.

that they will invoke abstention principles to decline to hear regulatory takings cases even where plaintiffs attempt in parallel state court proceedings to reserve federal law claims for separate federal court adjudication. Such results are predicated on the express conclusion by federal judges that state courts afford property owners a fully adequate forum in which to adjudicate those federal constitutional questions.[27]

Certain competing federal court procedural rules may push regulatory takings cases into the federal courts.[28] Nevertheless, the abstention doctrine gives federal judges a powerful tool to divert takings litigation into the state judicial systems for resolution.

Authorization

What happens when a taking claim is based on government agency action that is unlawful for reasons unrelated to the alleged taking—that is, because the government had no authority to act as it did? And what happens when the agency claims immunity by arguing that it could not be liable for a taking because it does not have eminent domain power? Like many problems in the law of takings, it depends—in this case, on which court decides.

Authority to Act

In the takings court of chief interest to the federal government, the answer to our authority-to-act question has been counterintuitive—and quite different from the rule in most other courts. The Court of

---

1994); In re Eastport Assoc. v. City of Los Angeles, 935 F.2d 1071, 1075–77 (9th Cir. 1991).

[27]*See, e.g.,* Mission Oaks Mobile Home Park v. City of Hollister, 989 F.2d 359, 360 (9th Cir. 1993), *cert. denied,* 510 U.S. 1110 (1994) (citing the "strong federal policy against federal-court interference with pending state court proceedings absent extraordinary circumstances"). *But cf.* Dodd v. Hood River County, 59 F.3d 852, 860 (9th Cir. 1995) (finding that property owner not required to litigate Fifth Amendment taking claim in state court but may reserve issue for federal adjudication).

[28]*See, e.g.,* City of Chicago v. International College of Surgeons, 118 S. Ct. 523 (1997) (Fifth Amendment taking claim and related state-law administrative challenge to municipal land-use decision properly removed to federal court under 28 U.S.C. § 1441).

Federal Claims holds that the absence of agency authority to take the action generating the taking suit is fatal to litigation. "It is well settled law," it says, "that illegal acts of [federal] government officials cannot, by themselves, give rise to a taking which is adjudicable under the Tucker Act."[29] Thus, takings claimants in that court must concede the validity of the government action,[30] though they are free to pursue invalidation relief in a federal district court simultaneously.[31] If they do so, however, they can expect the claims court to stay the taking case pending resolution of the invalidation suit.

The Court of Federal Claims rule means that following a district court ruling that a federal agency acted beyond its authority, no damages will be awarded for any temporary taking while the property restriction was in effect. The reasons for the anomalous Court of Federal Claims rule appear to be several, generally rooted in the court's history. First, the claims court since the 19th century has had jurisdiction chiefly to award monetary compensation, not, for the most part, to invalidate. Second, the court has said that its rule protects Congress's constitutional power of the purse.[32] Were it to allow compensation for unauthorized government actions, it would be compelling the United States to spend money that Congress did not sanction.[33] Finally, some government actions brought to the court seem more in the nature of torts than takings. Lacking jurisdiction over torts, the court is leery of adjudicating such cases, particularly since monetary relief is available in the district court.[34]

Outside the Court of Federal Claims, the unlawfulness of the government action targeted by the landowner's taking suit seems to

---

[29]Anaheim Gardens v. United States, 33 Fed. Cl. 24, 37 (1995). The Tucker Act is the prime jurisdictional statute of the Court of Federal Claims (*see* chapter 4).

[30]Tabb Lakes, Ltd. v. United States, 10 F.3d 796, 802 (Fed. Cir. 1993). While plaintiffs must concede the validity of the government action, the government may assert invalidity as an affirmative defense. Florida Rock Ind., Inc. v. United States, 791 F.2d 893, 899 (Fed. Cir. 1986), *cert. denied*, 479 U.S. 1053 (1987).

The requirement that Tucker Act plaintiffs concede any validity issue applies regardless of whether there has been a previous adjudication of validity in the district court under the Administrative Procedure Act. Florida Rock Ind., Inc., 791 F.2d at 899.

[31]See discussion of *Casman* exception to 28 U.S.C. § 1500 in chapter 4.

[32]U.S. Const. art. I, § 9: "No Money shall be drawn from the Treasury, but in Consequence of Appropriations made by Law. . . ."

[33]NBH Land Co. v. United States, 576 F.2d 317, 319 (Ct. Cl. 1978).

[34]Anaheim Gardens *supra* note 19.

matter much less. Whether an unauthorized agency action is a taking turns on the same sort of case-by-case analysis as any other taking case. Mistakes resulting in delay does not, of itself, amount to a temporary taking.

The leading case is *Landgate, Inc. v. California Coastal Commission*.[35] There, the California Supreme Court ruled 4 to 3 that no taking resulted from a two-year delay in the issuance of a building permit resulting from the Commission's erroneous—but plausible and factually supported—determination that it had jurisdiction over lot-line adjustments. Rather, the majority said, such reasonable errors are a normal part of the regulatory process. By contrast, agency error would be a taking under *Lucas* if it indefinitely eliminated all use of the property, just as an authorized agency action would be.[36]

Landgate also follows earlier cases in rejecting the argument that unauthorized government acts are *necessarily* takings. This awkward conclusion is based on the Supreme Court precept that regulations failing to advance a legitimate governmental purpose are takings. How, the argument runs, can a mistake further a valid purpose? The *Landgate* court found that a mistake notwithstanding, the assertion of jurisdiction over lot-line adjustments advanced the proper government interest of minimizing erosion and unsightly development.

Authority to Condemn

In contrast with the authority-to-act prerequisite, some state and federal courts are more demanding of plaintiffs than the Court of Federal Claims when it comes to a defendant agency's authority to condemn. The latter court seems not to require that the agency possess authority to condemn formally the property it is being accused of inversely condemning. Other courts, however, are split. In the view of some, the frequent characterization of a taking as an unacknowledged act of

---

[35]17 Cal. 4th 1006, 953 P.2d 1188 (1998).

[36]Other cases applying ad hoc analysis to takings claim based on a regulatory mistake include Fountain v. Metropolitan Atlanta Rapid Transit Auth., 678 F.2d 1038, 1043 (11th Cir. 1982); Tampa-Hillsborough County Expressway Auth. v. A.G.W.S. Corp., 640 So. 2d 54 (Fla. 1994); Dumont v. Town of Wolfeboro, 137 N.H. 1, 622 A.2d 1238 (1993); and Steinbergh v. City of Cambridge, 413 Mass. 736, 604 N.E.2d 1269 (1992). *But see* Mac'Avoy v. Smithsonian Institution, 757 F. Supp. 60, 70 (D.D.C. 1991) (plaintiff's assertion that defendant took property unlawfully precludes taking action, citing Court of Federal Claims rule).

eminent domain logically requires that the agency accused of taking have eminent domain (condemnation) authority in the circumstances giving rise to the alleged taking. A leading commentator endorses this view,[37] and some recent cases agree.[38]

The better, and more modern, view is that it should make no difference whether the agency accused of taking has condemnation authority. After all, the presence or absence of condemnation authority is plainly irrelevant to the justice of the landowner's cause,[39] and the rule might encourage governments "to avoid . . . the Constitution through the expedient of delegating regulatory powers, but not the power of eminent domain. . . ."[40] Moreover, unlike the case of unlawful government action, where the property-use constraint is terminated, there appears to be no alternative relief for the landowner. One court, in rejecting the condemnation authority prerequisite, called it "nonsensical" to condition the success of a regulatory taking action on whether the agency has the power to condemn.[41]

Standard of Review and Burden of Proof

In some ways these "procedural" issues are the most important of all, because they quite often dictate the outcome of a particular case on its merits. How high the courts place the legal hurdles that takings lit-

---

[37]"The remedy of inverse condemnation, by the very premise which gives rise to it, is available only as against defendants who possess the power of eminent domain." 3 JULIUS L. SACKMAN, NICHOLS ON EMINENT DOMAIN § 8.01[4][a] (rev. 3rd ed. 1997).

[38]See, e.g., Environmental Indus., Inc. v. Casey, 675 A.2d 392 (Pa. Commw. Ct. 1996); State v. The Mill, 809 P.2d 434, 439 (Colo. 1991) (en banc); Green Acres Land & Cattle Co. v. State, 766 S.W.2d 649, 651 (Mo. App. 1988). See also Clajon Prod. Corp. v. Petera, 70 F.3d 1566, 1575 (10th Cir. 1995) (state agency lacking eminent domain power could not be sued under state inverse condemnation procedure).

[39]The landowner "suffers no less a taking merely because the defendant was not authorized to take." Baker v. Burbank-Glendale-Pasadena Airport Auth., 39 Cal. 3d 862, 864 705 P.2d 866, 868 (1985), cert. denied, 475 U.S. 1017 (1986).

[40]Tahoe-Sierra Preservation Council, Inc. v. Tahoe Regional Planning Agency, 911 F.2d 1331, 1341 (9th Cir. 1990), cert. denied, 499 U.S. 943 (1991).

[41]Boise Cascade Corp. v. Board of Forestry, 131 Or. App. 538, 886 P.2d 1033, 1041 (1994), aff'd in part, rev'd in part, 325 Or. 185, 935 P.2d 411 (1997) (affirming as to authority-to-condemn). Accord, Fountain v. Metropolitan Atlanta Rapid Transit Auth., 678 F.2d 1038, 1044 (11th Cir. 1982); Tahoe-Sierra

igants must surmount, and on whom the obligation to overcome those hurdles is placed, can strongly influence the ultimate outcome even before the first piece of evidence is introduced.

Until quite recently, the standard of review was well established in inverse condemnation law, allocation of the burden of proof between the parties even more so. Some key recent cases, however, have unsettled the law on both points and reflect at least a gradual shift in favor of property owners.

Standard of Review—An Incremental Shift in the Law

Let us first focus on the standard of review. We speak here not directly of the substantive takings law principles identified later (particularly in chapters 11 and 12) but, rather, on how skeptically or deferentially a court is to view a litigant's case.

Until the 1930s, American courts took a fairly dubious view of the legality of governmental efforts to regulate private economic behavior. Many such regulations were struck down by skeptical courts, often under the guise of substantive due process (a constitutional cousin of the Takings Clause).[42] The political and legal turmoil associated with the Depression of the 1920s and 1930s marked a sea of change in such judicial thinking, with the courts adopting a much more deferential view toward exercises of the police power to regulate economic conduct, including land use.[43]

It was in this latter era that the doctrine of regulatory takings first took root. Accordingly, in the decades following *Pennsylvania Coal Co. v. Mahon*,[44] courts applied to Takings Clause cases many of the same deferential standard of review principles that governed constitutional challenges to government regulation generally. Key among these is the long-standing rule that ordinarily a government regulation need only be rationally related to a legitimate governmental objective

---

Preservation Council, Inc. v. Tahoe Regional Planning Agency, 911 F.2d at 1341 (asserting conflict between condemnation authority prerequisite and *First English*); *Baker*, 705 P.2d at 868–69.

[42]The most famous—or infamous—such case was Lochner v. New York, 198 U.S. 45 (1905), in which the Supreme Court invalidated a state labor protection law on substantive due process grounds.

[43]The key decision reflecting this shift is Carolene Prods. v. United States, 304 U.S. 144, 152. n.4 (1938).

[44]260 U.S. 393 (1922).

to pass constitutional muster.[45] Courts actually have gone even further at times, concluding that a state's exercise of the police power demands only that the government "could rationally have decided" that the regulation might achieve the state's objective.[46]

The only long-standing exception to such a "hands-off" standard of review is found in those cases in which government regulates private conduct implicating fundamental rights, or if there is a "suspect classification," such as race, at issue. In such cases, a far more exacting standard of review has traditionally been applied by the courts—i.e., whether the regulation is necessary to achieve a compelling government objective.[47] Takings Clause challenges, however, were not deemed to warrant that exacting standard of review. Instead, the "reasonable relationship" test has generally been applied to inverse condemnation cases, just as it has been to so-called "economic regulation" litigation generally.

Illustrative is the Supreme Court's 1962 regulatory takings case, *Goldblatt v. Town of Hempstead*.[48] There a unanimous Court, "[i]ndulging in the usual presumption of constitutionality," upheld a city ordinance limiting open-pit mining. After reiterating the "reasonable relationship" standard it deemed applicable, the Court went on to observe: "Even this rule is not applied with strict precision, for this Court has often said that 'debatable questions as to reasonableness are not for the courts but for the legislature. . . .'"[49] With such a minimal standard of review (from the government's standpoint), is it any wonder that government regulations generally withstood takings challenges in the past?

In recent years, that situation has begun to change—albeit incrementally. The shift has been most pronounced in the case of exactions

---

[45]*See, e.g.,* Minnesota v. Clover Leaf Creamery Co., 449 U.S. 456, 466 (1981), *cited with approval in* Nollan v. California Coastal Comm'n, 483 U.S. 825, 865 (1987) (Blackmun, J., dissenting).

[46]*Clover Leaf Creamery Co.,* 449 U.S. at 466, *cited with approval in Nollan,* 483 U.S. at 843 (Brennan, J., dissenting).

[47]*See, e.g.,* Moore v. City of East Cleveland, 431 U.S. 494 (1977), in which the Supreme Court applied the latter test to invalidate on freedom-of-association grounds a municipal ordinance limiting occupancy of dwelling units to members of a single family.

[48]369 U.S. 590.

[49]*Id.* at 594–95. *See also* City of College Station v. Turtle Rock Corp., 680 S.W.2d 802, 808 (Tex. 1984) ("An extraordinary burden rests on one attacking a city ordinance.")

challenged under the Takings Clause (discussed in detail in chapter 16). In its 1987 *Nollan v. California Coastal Commission* decision, the Supreme Court articulated a new takings standard requiring that exaction conditions on development permits advance the same governmental objective as the permit to which they are attached.[50] In announcing this standard, the Court took pains to distinguish it from the traditional, more lenient test applied to constitutional challenges to government regulation generally.[51]

The Supreme Court expanded upon this theme in its next "unconstitutional condition" case, decided in 1994: *Dolan v. City of Tigard.*[52] In *Dolan,* the Court announced a second component of the *Nollan* test, one addressing the required degree of connection between the impact of the exaction and the projected impact of the development project under review. The Court eventually settled on a "rough proportionality" touchstone, but only after examining and rejecting—Goldilocks style—competing standards of review as being either too stringent or excessively lax in protecting private property rights.[53] Nevertheless, the standard of review has become more formidable for government defendants—at least when it comes to takings challenges based on certain land-use development conditions.

Underlying this evolution of standard of review principles in inverse condemnation law is the Supreme Court's obvious rethinking of takings jurisprudence generally. Recently the Court has taken pains to place the Takings Clause higher in the constitutional firmament than other provisions of that charter protecting "mere economic" interests.[54] It is problematic whether property rights will receive the same degree of judicial protection under the Takings Clause as, say, freedom of religion is currently afforded under the First Amendment. Nonetheless, the Takings Clause is receiving unprecedented attention from the courts, and that is unquestionably influencing the shifting standard of review principles.

Burden of Proof—Major Evidentiary Changes Afoot

Equally as "outcome determinative" as the standard of review is the courts' allocation of the burden of proof between Takings Clause

[50]483 U.S. 825, 837 (1987).
[51]*Id.* at 834–35 n.3 (questioning holding in *Goldblatt*).
[52]512 U.S. 374.
[53]*Id.* at 389–93.
[54]*Id.* at 392.

litigants. For example, is it the plaintiff property owner's responsibility to demonstrate the unconstitutionality of the challenged regulation? Or does the government defendant have the obligation to affirmatively demonstrate that the measure is constitutionally valid?

Courts routinely characterize regulatory programs as having a "strong presumption of constitutionality."[55] Traditionally, the burden has been on an inverse condemnation plaintiff to demonstrate a regulation's unconstitutionality. Accordingly, judges have typically allocated the burden of proof in takings cases to those who challenge regulatory measures under the Fifth Amendment: "[I]n evaluating most generally applicable zoning regulations, the burden properly rests on the party challenging the regulation to prove that it constitutes an arbitrary regulation of private property."[56] The Supreme Court's other recent takings decisions have generally echoed this burden of proof rule.[57]

At the same time, judges have traditionally placed the burden on the government to prove the existence of affirmative defenses that would shield it from an otherwise viable taking claim.[58]

But in recent years, the Supreme Court has moved slowly but steadily toward a reallocation of the burden of proof—from the property owner to the government—in at least some types of regulatory takings litigation. The issue was joined most directly in the

[55]Goldblatt v. Town of Hempstead, 369 U.S. 590, 594–95 (1962); Dolan v. City of Tigard, 512 U.S. 392, 409–411 (Stevens, J., dissenting); City of College Station v. Turtle Rock Corp., 680 S.W.2d 802, 808 (Tex. 1984).

[56]Dolan, 512 U.S. at 391–92, n.8 (citing Village of Euclid v. Ambler Realty Co., 272 U.S. 365 (1926)).

[57]Keystone Bituminous Coal Ass'n. v. DeBenedictis, 480 U.S. 470, 485 (1987); Lucas v. South Carolina Coastal Council, 505 U.S. 1003, 1016 n.6 (1992).

[58]See, e.g., Aptos Seascape Corp. v. County of Santa Cruz, 138 Cal. App. 3d 484, 499–500, 188 Cal. Rptr. 191 (1982), appeal dismissed, 464 U.S. 805 (1983) (burden on county to demonstrate that TDR program provides sufficient landowner options to avoid taking); Loveladies Harbor v. United States, 21 Cl. Ct. 153, 157–58 (1990), aff'd, 28 F.3d 1171 (Fed. Cir. 1994); Leppo v. City of Petaluma, 20 Cal. App. 3d 711, 718–19, 97 Cal. Rptr. 840, 844 (1971) (government defendant in flood damage case has burden to demonstrate its actions were necessary to abate threat to public health and safety). But cf. Kinzli v. County of Santa Cruz, 818 F.2d 1449, 1454 (9th Cir. 1987), cert. denied, 484 U.S. 1043 (1988) (plaintiff property owner has burden to show futility of pursuing administrative relief in response to government's assertion of ripeness defense to regulatory takings claim).

Court's 1994 *Dolan* decision, again involving the "unconstitutional conditions" situation. In parsing through the potential standards of review to be applied in such cases, the *Dolan* majority repeatedly stressed that it was the city's obligation to demonstrate the requisite connection between project impact and government exaction.[59] Having eventually settled on the "roughly proportionate" test, the Court went on to conclude that the "city has not met its burden" in demonstrating that its real property exactions were roughly proportionate to the perceived environmental impacts of Mrs. Dolan's commercial expansion.[60] The majority based its burden-shifting on the seemingly tenuous distinction that in *Dolan* the city had imposed the challenged conditions as part of a quasi-adjudicative land-use decision rather than a quasi-legislative (i.e, generally applicable) one.[61]

Four members of the Court in *Dolan* took umbrage at what they perceived as the majority's unprecedented and unsupported reallocation of the burden of proof to the government. Justice Stevens observed on behalf of three dissenting justices: "The Court decides for the first time that the city has the burden of establishing the constitutionality of its conditions. . . ."[62] He later protested:

> The burden of demonstrating that . . . conditions have unreasonably impaired the economic value of the proposed improvement belongs squarely on the shoulders of the party challenging the state action's constitutionality. That allocation of burdens has served us well in the past.[63]

In a separate dissent, Justice Souter similarly took the *Dolan* majority to task for what he considered an unprecedented and unwise shifting of the burden of proof to the government.[64]

But two years earlier, in *Lucas v. South Carolina Coastal Council*,[65] the Supreme Court had at least implied that it was rethinking the burden of proof question. The majority in *Lucas* strongly suggested

[59]*Dolan*, 512 U.S. at 388

[60]*Id.* at 394–95.

[61]*Id.* at 393. *Cf.* Parking Ass'n. of Georgia v. City of Atlanta, 515 U.S. 1178, 115 S. Ct. 2268 (1995) (Thomas, J., dissenting from denial of certiorari) (arguing that *Dolan's* "rough proportionality" should also be applied to quasi-legislative government decisions).

[62]*Dolan*, 512 U.S. at 398 (Stevens, J., dissenting).

[63]*Id.* at 411 (Stevens, J., dissenting).

[64]*Id.* at 414 (Souter, J., dissenting).

[65]505 U.S. 1003 (1992).

that the burden would be on the government to demonstrate the existence of "background principles of nuisance and property law" that might insulate it from takings liability.[66] In dissent, Justice Brennan complained that the Court had thereby effectively shifted the burden of proof to the government to demonstrate the nonexistence of a taking.[67]

Similarly problematic is the venerable principle, noted above, that government's regulatory enactments are presumed valid and constitutional. That standard can no longer be considered firmly established, given the skeptical treatment the Supreme Court and individual justices have given to various legislative pronouncements.[68]

In the wake of these recent Supreme Court cases, the key unresolved question is whether the above-described shift in standard of review and burden of proof principles will be limited to "unconstitutional condition" cases like *Nollan* and *Dolan,* or extended more broadly through inverse condemnation law generally. The smattering of recent lower court decisions that have addressed this question is divided on the point.[69] How the evidentiary questions are resolved will go far in determining the success or failure of future takings plaintiffs and defendants.

---

[66]*Lucas,* 505 U.S. at 1031–32.

[67]*Id.* at 1045–46 (Brennan, J., dissenting).

[68]*See, e.g., Lucas,* 505 U.S. at 1031 (strong disinclination to defer to legislative findings on public interest supporting regulation under attack). *See also* Stevens v. City of Cannon Beach, 510 U.S. 1207 (1994) (Scalia, J., dissenting from denial of certiorari).

[69]*Cf.* City of St. Petersburg v. Bowen, 680 So. 2d 421 (Fla. 1996), *cert. denied,* 117 S. Ct. 1120 (1997) (government defendant failed to carry burden of demonstrating that closure of apartment complex to deter drug trafficking constituted proper nuisance under *Lucas,* or that private owner lacked reasonable expectancy of use of property upon acquisition); Marshall v. Board of County Comm'rs, 912 F. Supp. 1456, 1473 (D. Wyo. 1996) (plaintiff has burden in regulatory taking case to prove ordinance unconstitutional).

Chapter 7

Section 1983 Claims

In recent years, a federal statute—42 U.S.C. section 1983—has taken on increasing significance in takings litigation, as so-called "section 1983 actions" have come to represent an ever-larger percentage of regulatory takings cases. It is therefore essential that litigators and government decision-makers alike be aware of this statute and its implications regarding Takings Clause controversies.[1]

During the Reconstruction Era following the Civil War, Congress enacted legislation designed to provide redress for people whose civil rights had been violated. That law, the Civil Rights Act of 1871, is codified in pertinent part as 42 U.S.C. section 1983 *et seq.* Commonly referred to as "section 1983," the statute provides:

> Every person who, under color of any statute, ordinance, regulation, custom, or usage, of a state or territory or the District of Columbia, subjects, or causes to be subjected, any citizen of the United States or other person within the jurisdiction thereof to the deprivation of any rights, privileges, or immunities secured by the Constitution and laws, shall be liable to the party injured in an action at law, suit in equity, or other proper proceeding for redress.

Elements of a Section 1983 Claim

In order to analyze the legal basis and sufficiency of a section 1983 claim, three key elements of the statute must be met. A plaintiff must

---

[1]For an excellent discussion of how section 1983 principles apply to regulatory takings litigation, see Kenneth Bley, *Use of the Civil Rights Acts to Recover Damages for Undue Interference With the Use of Land,* SB14 ALI–ABA 261 (1996).

be able to show that: (1) there has been a deprivation of some right, privilege, or immunity secured either by the U.S. Constitution or federal statute; (2) deprivation has occurred "under color of state law," which can take the form of a statute, ordinance, regulation, custom, or usage; and (3) a "person" has violated plaintiff's protected right(s).[2] For a section 1983 action to succeed, there must be a causal link between these essential elements. In other words, the defendant's act under color of state law must be the legal cause of the plaintiff's claimed deprivation of a protected right.[3]

Section 1983 thus provides a federal remedy for deprivations of federal constitutional and statutory rights that occur under color of state law. Section 1983 is based on the constitutional authority of Congress to enforce the Fourteenth Amendment. It creates no additional substantive civil rights but, rather, is solely a *remedy* for deprivation of those rights created in the U.S. Constitution or other federal law.[4]

Section 1983 and Regulatory Takings Litigation

For the first 90 years following its enactment, section 1983's impact outside the field of race relations was very limited. The statute's impact on state and local agencies and officials was severely constrained by judicial interpretations that limited the types of wrongs section 1983 addressed and remedied. That situation has changed dramatically over the past three decades, as a direct result of several key U.S. Supreme Court decisions that have expanded dramatically the scope of government liability under section 1983.[5] Now, section 1983 has

---

[2]The "state law" element of § 1983 liability can, under settled legal principles, actually be promulgated at either the state *or local government* level. *Id.*

[3]Gomez v. Toledo, 446 U.S. 635, 640 (1980); Monell v. New York City Dep't. of Social Serv., 436 U.S. 658, 692 (1978).

[4]*See, e.g.,* City of Oklahoma City v. Tuttle, 471 U.S. 808, 816 (1985); Chapman v. Houston Welfare Rights Organiz., 441 U.S. 600, 617–18 (1979).

[5]*See, e.g.,* Maine v. Thiboutot, 448 U.S. 1 (1980) (term "laws" in § 1983 encompasses virtually all federal laws, not just those related to constitutional rights); Monroe v. Pape, 365 U.S. 144 (1961) ("under color of state law" encompasses misuse of power by state and local officials, even if acts were beyond scope of their authority); *Monell,* 436 U.S. 658 (local governmental entities are "persons" under § 1983, and liability may be based on governmental "custom", even unwritten or otherwise not formally approved); Owen v. City of Indepen-

become the single most commonly invoked congressional statute in the federal courts.

Beginning in the 1970s, property owners came to rely on section 1983 as a principal means of pursuing regulatory takings claims against state and local governments. (*Federal* regulatory decisions are not subject to attack under section 1983, given the statute's express language limiting its coverage to deprivation of federally protected rights committed under color of *state* law.) This is largely the result of two distinct features of the Civil Rights Act. First, the statute makes clear that money damages are appropriate to redress violations of section 1983. (By comparison, the *constitutionally* compelled nature of a damages remedy in successful inverse condemnation cases was not made clear until the U.S. Supreme Court so held in 1987.[6]) Second is the fact that the Civil Rights Act contains a provision allowing a court to award attorney fees to the successful party in a section 1983 lawsuit.[7] This attorney fee provision stands in sharp contrast to the so-called American Rule, which generally requires that each party to a civil lawsuit bear its own attorney fees regardless of outcome.

In years past, a number of federal courts expressed considerable skepticism about the propriety of invoking section 1983 in inverse condemnation litigation. Illustrative is *Raskiewicz v. Town of New Boston*, in which the federal appeals court held that litigants may not ordinarily obtain judicial review of local land-use disputes under the guise of section 1983: "Federal courts do not sit as a super zoning board or a zoning court of appeals."[8]

Federal court antipathy toward section 1983/regulatory takings litigation has largely abated in recent years. Numerous federal and state court decisions have now held that section 1983 is a proper

---

dence, 445 U.S. 622 (1980) (municipality cannot assert good faith defense when one of its citizens has violated federally protected rights of another citizen).

[6]First English Evangelical Lutheran Church v. County of Los Angeles, 482 U.S. 304 (1987).

[7]*See* 42 U.S.C. § 1988 (authorizing discretion to award attorney fees).

[8]754 F.2d 38, 44 (1st Cir. 1985), *cert. denied*, 474 U.S. 845 (1985). *See also* Hubenthal v. County of Winona, 751 F.2d 243 (8th Cir. 1984) (declining to permit federal court § 1983 action when state remedies available to address claim against local officials); Rymer v. Douglas County, 764 F.2d 796, 803 (11th Cir. 1985).

procedural mechanism for bringing regulatory takings claims against state or local governmental officials.[9]

Some recent federal cases go even further, finding that section 1983 is the *exclusive* jurisdictional remedy under the Takings Clause to address an alleged unconstitutional deprivation of property by state or local governments.[10] Those decisions suggest that neither the Takings Clause nor the Fourteenth Amendment generally support a direct cause of action under the Constitution for a regulatory taking.

Opportunities and Limitations in Using Section 1983 in Takings Cases

Sometimes overlooked is the fact that section 1983 litigation is not limited to the federal courts. State courts have concurrent jurisdiction to hear 1983 actions.[11] This is increasingly important, given the federal courts' growing disinclination to hear regulatory takings cases for reasons unrelated to section 1983.[12] Similarly, section 1983 has been invoked to pursue challenges to the regulation of private prop-

[9]Cordeco Dev. Corp. v. Santiago Vasquez, 539 F.2d 256 (1st Cir. 1976), *cert. denied*, 429 U.S. 978 (1976); Rogin v. Bensalem Township, 616 F.2d 680 (3d Cir. 1980), *cert. denied*, 450 U.S. 1029 (1981); Scott v. Greenville County, 716 F.2d 1409 (4th Cir. 1983); National W. Life Ins. Co. v. Commodore Cove Improvement Dist., 678 F.2d 24 (5th Cir. 1982); Gordon v. City of Warren, 579 F.2d 386 (6th Cir. 1978); Barbian v. Panagis, 694 F.2d 476 (7th Cir. 1982); Westborough Mall, Inc. v. City of Cape Girardeau, 794 F.2d 330 (8th Cir. 1986), *cert. denied*, 480 U.S. 918 (1987); McDougal v. County of Imperial, 942 F.2d 668 (9th Cir. 1991); Executive 100, Inc. v. Martin County, 922 F.2d 1536 (11th Cir. 1991), *cert. denied*, 502 U.S. 810 (1991); Anastasio v. Planning Bd., 197 N.J. Super. 457, 484 A.2d 1358 N.J. Super. Ct. Law Div. (1984).

[10]Azul Pacifico, Inc. v. City of Los Angeles, 973 F.2d 704, 705; Bieneman v. City of Chicago, 662 F. Supp. 1297, 1299 (N.D. Ill. 1987). *Cf.* Amen v. City of Dearborn, 718 F.2d 789, 792 n.4 (6th Cir. 1983), *cert. denied*, 465 U.S. 1101 (1984). ("Because an alleged 'taking' in violation of the Fifth and Fourteenth Amendments presents a serious constitutional question, a direct cause of action lies within the district court's federal question jurisdiction.")

[11]Felder v. Casey, 487 U.S. 131, 139 (1988); Williams v. Horvath, 16 Cal. 3d 834, 548 P.2d 1125 (1976); Lange v. Nature Conservancy, Inc., 24 Wash. App. 416, 601 P.2d 963 (1979), *cert. denied*, 449 U.S. 851 (1980); T & M Homes, Inc. v. Township of Mansfield, 162 N.J. Super. 497, 393 A.2d 613 (N.J. Super. Ct. Law Div. 1978).

[12]See discussion in Chapters 5 and 6.

erty based on a variety of constitutional and statutory theories other than just the Takings Clause.[13]

Inverse condemnation suits brought via section 1983 nevertheless present often-formidable obstacles for property owners. Government defendants may invoke numerous defenses to liability under section 1983. Some of these defenses—ripeness, statute of limitations, abstention, and standing—are available in regulatory takings litigation generally and are discussed elsewhere in this text.[14] Others are unique to section 1983–based inverse condemnation actions. One example is provided by the Supreme Court's 1989 decision in *Will v. Michigan Dept. of State Police,* holding that neither a state nor a state official sued in his or her official capacity is a "person" subject to suit under section 1983.[15]

Some of the most important sets of defenses currently available to defendants in regulatory takings cases under section 1983 are the immunities that have been developed under case law. Individuals sued under section 1983 may be entitled to either an absolute or a qualified immunity from liability under that statute.[16] (This becomes especially crucial when money damages are sought.) Absolute immunity defeats a suit at the outset, and state and local officials acting in a legislative, prosecutorial, or judicial capacity may assert absolute immunity under section 1983. For example, state or local officials who adopt zoning ordinances have absolute immunity.[17] State judges are

---

[13]*See, e.g.,* Tellis v. Godinez, 5 F.3d 1314 (9th Cir. 1993), *cert. denied,* 513 U.S. 945, (1995) (successful § 1983–based challenge to vindicate due process rights to property); Falls v. Town of Dyer, 875 F.2d 146 (7th Cir. 1989) (equal protection).

[14]*See* chapters 5 and 6.

[15]491 U.S. 58. This defense is not available to *local* governmental entities and officials, however. Moreover, the *Will* defense has been somewhat circumscribed by the Court's subsequent holding that state officials *are* subject to suit under section 1983 in their *individual* (as opposed to official) capacity. Hafer v. Melo, 502 U.S. 21 (1991).

[16]Imbler v. Pachtman, 424 U.S. 409, 413 n.13 (1976). Governmental entities themselves, however, are strictly liable for violations of section 1983 and cannot assert immunities available to public officials. Owen v. City of Independence, 445 U.S. 662 (1980).

[17]Lake Country Estates, Inc. v. Tahoe Regional Planning Agency, 440 U.S. 391 (1979) (members of bi-state regional land-use agency acting in quasi-legislative capacity absolutely immune); Gorman Towers, Inc. v. Bogoslavsky, 626 F.2d 607, 608 (8th Cir. 1980); Crymes v. Dekalb County, 923 F.2d 1482, 1485–1486 (11th Cir. 1991).

similarly entitled to absolute immunity from damage actions brought under section 1983.[18]

Absolute immunity is not available to state and local officials, however, when they are acting in an administrative or "executive" capacity. Individual defendants are instead entitled to invoke "qualified immunity" in such cases. In *Harlow v. Fitzgerald*, the Supreme Court established an objective standard for determining when qualified immunity is available: governmental officials performing discretionary functions "are shielded from liability from civil damages [but not equitable relief] insofar as their conduct does not violate clearly established statutory or constitutional rights of which a reasonable person would have known."[19] A contrasting set of examples makes the point: An unprovoked prison guard who savagely beats an inmate is not likely to win qualified immunity, inasmuch as the beating rather obviously violates the inmate's "clearly established" rights under *Harlow*. On the other hand, given the often-elusive Constitutional standards for what does and doesn't constitute land-use regulation violative of the Fifth Amendment, a government planner seems more likely to fall within the protections of *Harlow*.

It is fair to say that the majority of regulatory takings lawsuits now brought against state or local governments in both state and federal courts involve causes of action explicitly brought under section 1983. The Civil Rights Act of 1871, a venerable piece of federal legislation, is likely to play an even more prominent role in inverse condemnation litigation in the years to come.

[18]Pulliam v. Allen, 466 U.S. 522 (1984); Stump v. Sparkman, 435 U.S. 349, 360–363 (1978).

[19]Harlow v. Fitzgerald, 457 U.S. 800, 818 (1982). *See also* Davis v. Scherer, 468 U.S. 183, 191 (1984).

Chapter 8

Right to Jury Trial

There is relatively little case law on the question of whether property owners are entitled to have their regulatory takings claims tried to a jury, rather than to a judge. The likely reason for this dearth of authority is that, until recently, most inverse condemnation cases were resolved via pretrial motion, short of a full trial. That phenomenon is slowly changing, however, for reasons described elsewhere in this book.

As a matter of both policy and litigation strategy, the issue is very important. Juries tend to bring a pragmatic, nonideological view to legal disputes. They are less concerned with precedent and legal consistency than are judges. And, perhaps most important, juries tend to sympathize with "the little guy and gal," as opposed to an often-faceless government bureaucracy. It is therefore little wonder that, given a choice, many landowners and their attorneys would rather have their regulatory takings disputes decided by juries than judges.

Any analysis of litigants' right to a jury trial in inverse condemnation litigation begins with the Seventh Amendment to the U.S. Constitution:

> *In Suits at common law,* where the value in controversy shall exceed twenty dollars, *the right of trial by jury shall be preserved,* and no fact tried by a jury, shall be otherwise re-examined in any Court of the United States according to the rules of the common law. (Emphasis added.)

As the Supreme Court and numerous experts have routinely noted, the Seventh Amendment thus did not *create* a right to jury trial in civil cases beyond that extant at the time the Bill of Rights was ratified. Rather, "the seventh amendment *preserves* the right to jury trial only for 'suits at common law.'"[1] (Emphasis added.)

Rules 38 and 39 of the Federal Rules of Civil Procedure further govern the right to jury trials in federal courts. Rule 38(a) provides that: "The right of the trial by jury as declared by the Seventh Amendment to the Constitution or as given by a statute of the United States shall be preserved to the parties inviolate." Rule 39 describes the procedure once a jury trial has been demanded pursuant to Rule 38.

Right to Jury Trial in Direct Condemnation Actions

The Federal Rules of Civil Procedure further and specifically limit the right to a jury trial in *direct* condemnation cases. Rule 71A governs the specific procedure for federal condemnation of real and personal property. Rule 71A(h) describes which issues a jury may properly consider:

> If the action involves the exercise of the power of eminent domain under the law of the United States, any tribunal specially constituted by an Act of Congress governing the case for trial of the issue of just compensation shall be the tribunal for the determination of that issue; but if there is no such specially constituted tribunal any party may have a trial by jury of the issues of just compensation. . . . *Trial of all issues shall otherwise be by the court*. (Emphasis added.)

The question of whether an eminent domain proceeding is one properly for a jury to hear on issues other than the amount of compensation was addressed by the U.S. Supreme Court in *United States v. Reynolds*.[2] In *Reynolds*, the United States brought suit in federal district court to condemn more than 250 acres of land for a federal development project. The landowner claimed that 78 acres of the land taken for the project had not been within the original scope of

---

[1]Etalook v. Exxon Pipeline Co., 831 F.2d 1440, 1447 (9th Cir. 1987) (citing Beacon Theaters, Inc. v. Westover, 359 U.S. 500 (1959)).
[2]397 U.S. 14 (1970).

the project. "The parties agreed that if the acreage at issue was 'probably within the scope of the project from the time the Government was committed to it,' substantially less compensation is due than if it was not."[3]

The Supreme Court determined that it was the district judge's responsibility to determine the scope-of-the-project factual issue, and that the jury was to be "confined to the performance of a single narrow but important function—the determination of a compensation award within ground rules established by the trial judge." The Court found that "[i]t has long been settled that there is no constitutional right to a jury in eminent domain proceedings." *Reynolds* instead cited and relied upon the Federal Rules of Civil Procedure; as noted above, Rule 71A(h) provides that "except for the single issue of just compensation, the trial judge is to decide all issues, legal and factual that may be presented."[4]

Inasmuch as the Seventh Amendment confers no right to a jury trial in direct condemnation actions, any such right must be specifically conferred by federal statute or rule.[5] Notably, state courts have adopted the same principle under their constitutional and statutory law: There is no right to a trial by jury in eminent domain actions brought by state or local governments, except to the extent that right is conferred by state statute or rule.[6]

Right to Jury Trial in Regulatory Takings Cases

It is perhaps unsurprising that courts would apply right-to-jury-trial principles first developed in direct condemnation cases in inverse condemnation litigation as well. The U.S. Supreme Court, after all, has

---

[3]*Id.* at 18.

[4]*Id.* at 18–20. *See also* 7 WEST'S FEDERAL PRACTICE MANUAL § 7696 (1979); 5 MOORE'S FEDERAL PRACTICE ¶ 38.32[1] (2d ed. 1994).

[5]5 MOORE'S FEDERAL PRACTICE ¶ 38.32[3] (2d ed. 1994) (citing Fed. R. Civ. P. 71A).

[6]*See, e.g.,* People v. Ricciardi, 23 Cal. 2d 390, 402, 144 P.2d 799, 805 (1943); 5 MOORE'S FEDERAL PRACTICE ¶ 38.32[1] (2d ed. 1994)("In dealing with a comparable problem arising under state constitutions with provisions similar to the Seventh Amendment, the state courts have quite uniformly held that there is no state constitutional right to jury trial."); 12 A.L.R.3d 7, 11 (1967).

described an inverse condemnation action as an eminent domain pro-ceeding initiated by the property owner rather than the condemnor.[7] The basis of both a direct condemnation action and an inverse con-demnation action is the same: the Fifth Amendment's prohibition of taking of private property without just compensation.

A handful of reported decisions have addressed the issue of whether there exists a right to a jury trial in regulatory takings cases. Those cases have consistently concluded, with one exception, that there is no constitutional or statutory right to have a jury determine a government defendant's *liability* in inverse condemnation cases. If the trial judge finds liability, however, the appropriate *amount of damages* is generally considered a matter for a jury. Most courts agree that the only exception to the latter rule is when the federal govern-ment is the defendant in a regulatory takings case; in that instance, the question of damages is similarly one for resolution by the trial judge.

Federal Courts—Suits Against the Federal Government

Regulatory takings claims brought against the federal government in federal courts raise unique jurisdictional and procedural questions. Illustrative is the Ninth Circuit's decision in *KLK, Inc. v. U.S. De-partment of the Interior*.[8] In *KLK*, a corporate owner of unpatented mining claims alleged that the U.S. Department of the Interior had taken those mineral interests by failing to approve KLK's mining plans. The company sued in federal court under the Mining in the Parks Act, 16 U.S.C. § 1910, seeking money damages.

The court of appeals expressly held that the plaintiff had no con-stitutional or statutory right to have any portion of its regulatory taking claim tried before a jury. In a unanimous opinion, the Ninth Circuit analogized to federal eminent domain principles and settled case law to determine that the case was properly litigated before the district judge, sitting as the trier of fact.[9]

---

[7]Kirby Forest Indus. v. United States, 467 U.S. 1, 5 (1994); Agins v. City of Tiburon, 447 U.S. 255, 258 n.2 (1980); Armstrong v. United States, 364 U.S. 40, 49 (1960); United States v. Causby, 328 U.S. 256, 262 (1946). *See also* Breidert v. Southern Pacific Co., 61 Cal. 2d 659, 663 n.1, 394 P.2d 719, 721 n.1 (1964) (accord).

[8]35 F.3d 454 (9th Cir. 1994).

[9]*Id.* at 457–58.

The Court of Appeals for the Fourth Circuit previously reached the same conclusion in *Fulcher v. United States*. After summarizing the close conceptual and jurisprudential link between direct and inverse condemnation actions, the Fourth Circuit observed that "[t]he trials for both [types of actions] are conducted by a judge without the intervention of a jury."[10]

This rule is a subset of the general principle that there exists no constitutional right to trial by jury in any action against the United States. The Seventh Amendment is not applicable because it applies only to "suits at common law," and at common law there was no right of action against a sovereign enforceable by jury or otherwise. Accordingly, a right to jury trial in an action against the United States can only be found in federal statute or rule.[11]

Federal Courts—Suits Against State and Local Governments

Most federal courts have applied a similar rule in regulatory takings cases brought against *state and local* governmental entities. Reported federal decisions have almost uniformly adopted the model from eminent domain proceedings brought under Rule 71A of the Federal Rules of Civil Procedure. Specifically, they hold that inverse condemnation challenges are properly heard in two phases. The first phase deals with the question of whether the governmental defendant has indeed "taken" the plaintiff's property; that issue is properly tried without a jury. Assuming liability is found, the question of the *amount* of just compensation is then determined by a jury.

Illustrative of this principle is the Eleventh Circuit's decision in *New Port Largo, Inc. v. Monroe County*.[12] In that case a developer brought a regulatory taking challenge to a local government's zoning decision. It further claimed a right to have a federal jury decide the issue of the county's liability for the taking and the proper amount of compensation. The court of appeals disagreed with the first premise: "[N]o jury fact-finding is required in regulatory takings cases. . . .

---

[10]Fulcher v. United States, 632 F. 2d 278, 284 (4th Cir. 1980).

[11]Charles A. Wright & Arthur R. Miller, Federal Practice and Procedure § 2314 (1971). *See also* 28 U.S.C. § 2402 (generally any action brought against United States shall be tried by the district court, without a jury); Fed. R. Civ. P. 71A.

[12]95 F.3d 1084 (11th Cir. 1996), *cert. denied*, 117 S. Ct. 2514 (1997).

'The [c]ourt determines all issues, legal and factual, in an inverse condemnation suit, save the question of just compensation. . . .'"[13]

Most other federal courts that have faced the jury-trial question have taken the identical view. In *Mid Gulf, Inc. v. Bishop*, for example, a property owner sued city officials in inverse condemnation, alleging that defendants' denial of a building permit and related approvals was a taking. The district court observed:

> The issue of whether the City's regulations are unreasonable and effect a taking is a question of law for the court. . . . If so, then damages are a question of fact for a jury.[14]

Another federal district court reached the identical conclusion: "[T]here is no right to a jury trial on a determination of liability on an inverse condemnation claim. . . ."[15]

Standing in marked contrast to this line of federal cases is the Ninth Circuit's 1996 decision in *Del Monte Dunes v. City of Monterey*.[16] *Del Monte Dunes* is significant because it appears to be the first reported federal court decision—at least in a regulatory taking case brought under section 1983—holding that the issue of liability is properly decided by a jury rather than the trial judge. Rejecting the above-described cases analogizing inverse condemnation cases to eminent domain actions, the court of appeals in *Del Monte Dunes* found the question of liability in regulatory takings cases to constitute a "mixed question of fact and law" for which a right to jury trial exists.[17] *Del Monte Dunes* thus directly conflicts with numerous other federal court decisions on this key procedural issue, such as *New Port Largo*.

It thus came as no surprise when, in early 1998, the U.S. Supreme Court agreed to review the *Del Monte Dunes* case and resolve the intercircuit conflict created between *New Port Largo* and *Del Monte Dunes*.

Expert commentators on the subject of regulatory takings law

---

[13]*Id.* at 1092 (citing Resolution Trust Corp. v. Town of Highland Beach, 18 F.3d 1536, 1550 (11th Cir. 1994)).

[14]Mid Gulf, Inc. v. Bishop, 792 F. Supp. 1205, 1215 (D. Kan. 1992) (citing Naegele Outdoor Advertising v. City of Durham, 844 F.2d 172 (4th Cir. 1988), *cert. denied,* 513 U.S. 928 (1994); Brock v. State Highway Comm'n, 195 Kan. 361, 404 P.2d 934 (1965)).

[15]Warner/Elektra/Atlantic Corp. v. County of DuPage, 771 F. Supp. 911, 913 (N.D. Ill. 1991).

[16]95 F.3d 1422 (9th Cir. 1996), *aff'd on rehearing,* 127 F.3d 1149, *cert. granted,* 118 S. Ct. 1359 (1998).

[17]95 F.3d at 1427–30.

The 38-acre oceanfront property at issue in *City of Monterey v. Del Monte Dunes at Monterey Ltd.*

advocate the majority rule regarding a landowner's right to trial by jury in such actions—even when the litigation is brought under section 1983.[18]

State Courts

State courts have routinely adopted the majority rule espoused by federal courts concerning regulatory takings cases: The issue of liability is to be tried to the court, sitting as the trier of fact. If and when the governmental defendant is found to have committed an unconstitutional taking of property, a jury is then impanelled, but for the sole purpose of determining the appropriate amount of compensation.[19]

The reasoning behind this long-standing rule of state law has been often stated and would seem to apply equally to federal court

[18]*See, e.g.,* Kenneth Bley, *Use of the Civil Rights Act to Recover Money Damages for the Overregulation of Land,* REGULATORY TAKING: THE LIMITS OF LAND USE CONTROLS 63 (G. Hill. ed., 1990), SB 14 ALI–ABA 261 (1996).

[19]*See, e.g.,* Brock v. State Highway Comm'n, 195 Kan. 361, 366, 404 P.2d 934, 940; Artway v. Scheidemantel, 671 F. Supp. 330, 336 (D.N.J. 1987); Hensler v. City of Glendale, 8 Cal.4th 1, 15, 876 P.2d 1043, 1052 (1994), *cert. denied,* 513 U.S. 1184 (1995). *See also* Healing v. California Coastal Comm'n, 22 Cal. App. 4th 1158, 1169, 27 Cal. Rptr. 2d 758, 765 (1994).

proceedings—the question of whether a government regulation has triggered an unconstitutional taking of private property entails a complex set of mixed questions of law and fact.[20]

Concluding Thoughts

The rules that have thus evolved to limit the right to trial by jury in regulatory takings cases are, to a large extent, unique to this area of the law. They stand in marked contrast to cases brought in other constitutional and statutory contexts, in which a right to trial by jury has been found with far greater consistency. In *Tull v. United States*,[21] for example, the U.S. Supreme Court held that in an enforcement action brought under the Clean Water Act to bar unauthorized filling of wetlands, the Seventh Amendment afforded the landowner defendant a right to jury trial on the question of civil penalties. On the other hand, said the Court, subsequent assessment of the appropriate *amount* of such penalties is properly a matter for the trial judge rather than a jury. *Tull* therefore establishes a rule directly contrary to that adopted by federal and state courts in regulatory takings cases. Thus, when it comes to the right to trial by jury, the rules applicable to regulatory takings litigation are quite unique.

Until recently, then, the law limiting the right to jury trial in regulatory takings cases was settled. *Del Monte Dunes* threatens to upset that stability. The U.S. Supreme Court could relegate the Ninth Circuit's opinion on the right-to-jury-trial issue to the status of Constitutional curiosity. Or the Supreme Court could effect a major expansion of the right to trial by jury in Takings Clause cases. And, depending on the scope of the court's decision, that expansion could affect takings cases decided in federal and state courts alike.[22]

[20]*See, e.g., Healing,* 22 Cal. App. 4th at 1169. Cf. Bateson v. Geisse, 857 F.2d 1300, 1302–03 (9th Cir. 1988) (characterizing as "questions of law" or "mixed questions of law and fact" district court's determination that city council's decision to withhold building permit was arbitrary, capricious); Village of Euclid v. Ambler Realty Co., 272 U.S. 365, 395 (1926); Greenbriar, Ltd. v. City of Alabaster, 881 F.2d 1570, 1578 (11th Cir. 1989); Naegele Outdoor Advertising v. City of Durham, 844 F.2d 172, 174, 176; Midnight Sessions, Ltd. v. City of Philadelphia, 945 F.2d 667, 682 (3d Cir. 1991), *cert. denied,* 503 U.S. 984 (1992).

[21]481 U.S. 412 (1987).

[22]For a vigorous argument in favor of expanding the right to jury trial in inverse condemnation cases under the Seventh Amendment, see Eric Grant, *A Revolutionary View of the Seventh Amendment and the Just Compensation Clause,* 91 NORTHWESTERN U. L. REV. 144 (1996).

Part III

Is It or Isn't It a Taking?

Chapter 9

Overview

So now the preliminary hurdles described in Part II have been cleared. The court has jurisdiction, the taking claim is ripe, there are no statute of limitations or abstention problems, the plaintiff was the owner of the property as of the date of the alleged taking, the government action was authorized (i.e., in suits against the United States), and no other barriers to reaching the taking issue exist.

Is it or isn't it a taking?

The body of judge-made law that has grown up around this question is complex, to put it mildly. At bottom, however, it all derives from the judicial sensibility about what is the fairest way to allocate the burdens of public regulation between the landowner and the broader society acting through its government. When, in other words, should the costs be left with the property owner, and when should they be more broadly distributed? This is takings law's central quandary. As stated in one of the field's most famous quotes, opening the analysis section in countless court opinions on takings—the Takings Clause:

> was designed to bar Government from forcing some people alone to bear public burdens which, in all fairness and justice, should be borne by the public as a whole.[1]

Right away, it is obvious that this quote doesn't take one very far. To say that "fairness and justice" are subjective states the obvious—even what should go into the determination is debatable. Courts, in assessing takings claims, are explicitly or (more often) implicitly feeling their way among a host of social and government concerns

---

[1]Armstrong v. United States, 364 U.S. 40, 49 (1960).

that the property owner, understandably focused on his or her own injury, may not be. The law of takings requires one to step back and view the big picture—the broad fabric of concerns and policies that it seeks to advance. To the property owner, such matters may seem abstract and remote, and "fairness and justice" in his or her particular case not achieved at all.

In addition to the need for a proper vantage point, what is fair and just depends on many things. The range of circumstances in which government may affect property values is incredibly diverse—e.g., the problem underlying the government action, the degree of harmfulness of different land uses, the types of property interests that may be limited. In the usual case, takings law opts for a full accommodation of these factual nuances, concededly at the expense of outcome predictability. The takings law reprise, endlessly intoned, is that except in special circumstances, whether a taking has occurred can be determined only after an "ad hoc, case-by-case" analysis.

The following chapters of Part III, setting out the tests that courts use to decide which government actions are takings, form the heart of this book. Parts IV and V describe how these criteria play out in selected areas of frequent government/landowner conflict. As you go through these criteria, note a few cross-cutting themes.

First, only the most severe regulatory restrictions on land use are generally held to be takings. Courts may differ as to just how severe, but this is a minor quibble. They are almost all in the same ballpark. It is significant that the ascent to the bench of many conservative judges in recent decades has made for little adjustment to the takings orthodoxy on this point, at least so far.

Why is this so? To some extent, the point made earlier—that "fairness and justice" is a two-way street—offers an explanation. Courts seem to understand that a low threshold for compensability would make government and social change quite difficult, though whether the threshold needs to be as high as it is now is an important and evolving question. As the estimable Justice Oliver Wendell Holmes put it: "Government could hardly go on if to some extent values incident to property could not be diminished without paying for every such change in the general law."[2]

The required severe impact on the landowner may also be the result of historical factors. A half-century ago, the newborn concept of regulatory takings took its baby steps in a judicial world familiar with only physical occupations and formal appropriations as Fifth

[2]Pennsylvania Coal Co. v. Mahon, 260 U.S. 393, 413 (1922).

Amendment takings. It was only natural, therefore, that the courts should have confined regulatory takings to land-use restrictions of a similarly high degree of intrusiveness—the functional equivalents of physical occupation and appropriation.

Courts also may sense implicitly that using an easy-to-satisfy test for regulatory takings runs counter to the restraint appropriate to the judicial branch. If the legislature deems a regulatory program to be in the public interest, judges may suppose (rightly or wrongly) that it is not their function, without compelling reason, to undercut it through the frequent imposition of compensation liability. To be sure, however, this point largely restates the different way in which courts view property rights and individual liberties. Courts show little reticence in throttling the lawmakers when First Amendment liberties are at stake.

Second, note the constant tension in takings law between the usual case by case, ad hoc approach to resolving takings cases and the allure of "bright line" rules (situations that are automatic takings). Certain justices of the Supreme Court have pushed successfully for more bright-line rules—in the areas of "total takings," permanent physical occupations, and development-permit conditions of improper nature or degree. Landowners understandably try to shoehorn their cases into an existing bright-line category, to avoid the unpredictability of an ad hoc case. This creates expansionary pressure on the existing per se categories. It is doubtful, however, that the courts will go much further than they have already in embracing per se taking rules. Yes, they provide greater certainty, but at a price— that of reduced sensitivity to individual circumstances. Such sensitivity is the very hallmark of takings law.

Above all, don't expect it all to make perfect sense. It doesn't. Many have pointed out the anomalies in takings law—for example, the fact that a landowner suffering a just-below-threshold impact on land value gets nothing, while someone incurring a slightly larger, above-threshold impact gets the full reduction in market value. Or the fact that a miniscule physical occupation of land is compensated, while a severe use restriction may not be. Or that two landowners in the same all-economic-uses-prohibited position may be treated in sharply different fashion by takings law, depending on the order in which government regulated away such uses. Takings law may be out of its infancy, but it still has much growing to do.

Chapter 10

Facial Versus As-Applied Challenges

Consider the owner of land who has just learned of a newly enacted statute or regulation, or perhaps an historic district or wetlands designation, that threatens some day to thwart activity on the property. The landowner has a fateful choice. He or she can challenge the law right away, attacking it as a taking "on its face." Or the owner can wait until some future time when the government seeks to apply the law to the specific parcel, as through a permit denial, and raise an "as applied" taking claim then. Every taking claim falls into one of these two categories. Which label a court attaches is crucial because it likely will determine the plaintiff's burden of proof and whether the plaintiff must demonstrate ripeness.[1]

A swift resort to the courts, arguing that a law works a facial taking, is unlikely to prevail. To succeed, a facial challenge must meet a tough burden of proof: that the challenged law is so restrictive that it necessarily effects a taking of plaintiff's property under any conceivable implementation scenario. (In an alternative phrasing, a facial challenge is said to assert a taking of all affected properties.[2]) As a result, the argument runs, a taking can be found without the bother of an evidentiary battle between the litigants about the specifics of how the law will affect plaintiff's property.

[1]This chapter assumes familiarity with the ripeness concepts discussed in chapter 5.

[2]*See, e.g.,* Taylor v. Village of North Palm Beach, 659 So. 2d 1167, 1170, 1171 n.1 (Fla. Dist. Ct. App. 1995).

Further, the facial taking concept logically dictates that the landowner does not have to meet the usual ripeness requirements before a court can reach the merits of the claim. If the claim is that a law takes the plaintiff's parcel under any assumption—under any conceivable scenario of government action under the law—why should the landowner have to run the gauntlet of permit and variance applications for the proposed activity and successive versions? Such an exercise is destined, by the definition of a facial taking, not to yield approval for any economic use sufficient to deflect the taking claim. The facial claim is by its very nature ripe.[3]

Being able to dispense with ripeness headaches makes facial claims highly attractive to landowners, but showing that a law will take one's land under any conceivable implementation scenario is quite difficult. In the majority of cases, where the taking claim turns on economic impact, one can imagine the difficulty of showing that no matter how administered, the law or regulation will deprive the landowner of all or nearly all economic use.[4] Indeed, the challenged law seemingly would have to take the blatant form: "No economic use may be made of land in such-and-such area—no exceptions."[5] Today, with awareness of takings law widespread among bill drafters and planners, few such absolute and inflexible laws and plans are being adopted.

For that reason, if a facial challenge is to have decent prospects of prevailing, it may have to be based on takings criteria other than economic impact—for example, the alleged failure of the law "to sub-

---

[3]Some exceptions to this principle, embraced by some courts, are discussed later in this chapter.

[4]In a bit of understatement, Justice Scalia has noted that a claim of total deprivation of economic use is "easier" to establish in an as-applied claim. Pennell v. City of San Jose, 485 U.S. 1, 18 (1988) (Scalia, J., dissenting). A rare, but unsatisfying, example of a successful facial taking claim founded on economic impact is Seawall Assocs. v. City of New York, 74 N.Y.2d 92, 542 N.E.2d 1059 (1989) (finding facial taking based on three independent grounds: economic impact, failure to substantially advance a legitimate state interest, and physical invasion).

[5]See, e.g., Taylor, 659 So. 2d 1167 (facial takings claim fails because conservation/open space designation "does not unequivocally turn the island into a passive park"); Del Oro Hills v. City of Oceanside, 31 Cal. App. 4th 1060, 1076, 37 Cal. Rptr. 2d 677 (1995) (ordinance is safe from facial takings challenge if it preserves, through permit procedure or otherwise, some economic use of parcel), cert. denied, 516 U.S. 823 (1995).

stantially advance legitimate state interests,"[6] or an effective appropriation of land through statutory text alone. *Those* claims may be ripe and provable solely on the face of the law.[7]

Alternatively, and more commonly, the landowner may allege an as-applied taking. That is, the owner may claim that the government action worked a taking once it was applied to his or her property, as through a permit denial or subdivision plat disapproval. For example, the broad land-use prescriptions in a town's comprehensive plan and implementing ordinances may leave open the possibility of a wide range of development intensity on a lot. On its face, therefore, it does not preclude economic use of the parcel and is not a taking. But the zoning board's application of its ordinances to limit development on a lot to no more than X dwelling units, after denial of variances, may be a taking if X units are not a sufficient number to yield a profit. This gives rise to an as-applied taking claim, and two ripeness requirements are often held to apply. To recap from chapter 5: Plaintiff must show a "final and authoritative determination" by the government agency of the type and intensity of development permitted and, if suing in federal court, must demonstrate that any state-level avenues for compensation were pursued. The overwhelming bulk of land-use takings litigation falls into the as-applied category.

Yet another distinction between facial and as-applied takings claims, worth passing mention, is how they relate to statutes of limitations. Quite naturally, a facial claim based on the mere adoption of a statute, regulation, or area designation fixes the date when the limitations period starts to run at the time of adoption. Equally plain, the limitation period in an as-applied claim generally starts at the time of permit denial, development proposal disapproval, or the like.

If there's any comfort to takings claimants, they do not deal with the facial/as-applied distinction alone. The distinction arises as well in other constitutional challenges to land-use controls, such as those

---

[6]Agins v. City of Tiburon, 447 U.S. 255, 260 (1980).

[7]*See, e.g.,* Yee v. City of Escondido, 503 U.S. 519, 534 (1992); *Pennell,* 485 U.S. at 18 (Scalia, J., dissenting); Guimont v. Clarke, 121 Wash. 2d 586, 854 P.2d 1, 12 and n.8 (1993), *cert. denied,* 510 U.S. 1176 (1994). However, claims based on the failure of a government action to substantially advance a proper interest may run into the deep-seated judicial deference toward legislative enactments. *See, e.g.,* Westwinds Mobile Home Park v. City of Escondido, 30 Cal. App. 4th 84, 35 Cal. Rptr. 2d 315 (1994).

Parcel of land, known as "Tiburon Headlands," owned by Bonnie and Donald Agins in the City of Tiburon, California. Development of this lot overlooking the San Francisco Bay was at issue in *Agins v. City of Tiburon.*

based on due process and equal protection. The broad parameters of the dichotomy—as, for example, the need to demonstrate ripeness only in an as-applied case—remain the same in each constitutional area,[8] though important details may vary.

The Supreme Court Canon

The Supreme Court's liturgy on facial and as-applied takings challenges is contained in three key decisions. The seminal case is still *Agins v. City of Tiburon*,[9] where following the Aginses' purchase of a prime five-acre lot overlooking San Francisco Bay, the city amended its zoning ordinance to allow the building of between one and five single-family homes on the lot. The ordinance envisioned that landowners first would submit a development plan. The Aginses declined to do so; instead filing a court challenge to the amended ordinance on its face.

The absence of a submitted plan, said the *Agins* Court, meant that the only issue properly before it was whether the "mere enactment" of the zoning ordinances constitutes a taking. "Mere enactment," unfortunately for the Aginses, created a situation where as many as five homes might be permitted on their lot if the approval process were pursued, and they had not demonstrated that five homes was an uneconomic use. Thus, the Court could not conclude, on the facial challenge, that a taking had occurred.[10]

---

[8]*See, e.g., Pennell*, 485 U.S. at 11–15 (facial due process and equal protection challenges to rent control scheme addressed on merits; no landlord had ever been affected); Kawaoke v. City of Arroyo Grande, 17 F.3d 1227 (9th Cir.) (ripeness requirements not relevant to facial challenge based on substantive due process), *cert. denied*, 513 U.S. 870 (1994); Eide v. Sarasota County, 908 F.2d 716 (11th Cir. 1990) (as-applied due process and equal protection challenges unripe because landowner never submitted development proposal).

[9]447 U.S. 255 (1980).

[10]The *Agins* decision is better known for having articulated two per se rules of regulatory taking law. Because the Court confined itself to plaintiff's facial challenge, some commentators have suggested that the *Agins* rules have some special connection with facial takings. However, later Supreme Court elaborations upon the *Agins* rules in *Nollan*, *Dolan*, and *Lucas* belie this view. *See* chapter 12.

Since *Agins*, the Court has continued to disapprove of facial, or "mere enactment," takings attacks.[11] Ruling on a facial claim, says the Court, means ruling in the absence of specifics as to how a plaintiff's land has been affected, and such specifics lie at the very heart of the Court's takings criteria. Thus, it prefers to wait for concrete harm to occur in the context of an as-applied challenge. To be sure, the Court will usually acquiesce in reaching the merits of the facial claim, but is rarely willing to sustain it.

The two important facial takings decisions after *Agins* involve mining regulation. In *Hodel v. Virginia Surface Mining & Reclamation Ass'n*, the Court rebuffed a pre-enforcement takings attack on the federal surface mining law.[12] The Court explained that the constitutionality of statutes ought not be adjudicated when unnecessary, and that this rule is especially important in takings cases, given the ad hoc, factual analysis used. As in *Agins*, the "mere enactment" of the statute effected no taking—here because a mining prohibition leaves open the possibility that other economic uses of plaintiffs' properties remain.

In *Keystone Bituminous Coal Ass'n v. DeBenedictis*, a state anti-subsidence law met the same fate.[13] In spurning the facial takings challenge, the Court felt content to simply quote its 1981 discussion in *Agins* and note that plaintiffs face an "uphill battle" in facial suits.[14] Interestingly, plaintiffs had filed both a facial and an as-applied challenge. When the trial court dismissed the facial claim, both parties asked to have it certified for appeal, in the hope of sparing themselves the unnecessary preparation of "complex and voluminous proofs" involved in the as-applied case.[15]

The Court's most recent land-use/takings case reaffirms the absence

---

[11]A half-century before *Agins*, the Supreme Court presaged its current preference for as-applied takings in its companion decisions in Village of Euclid v. Ambler Realty Co., 272 U.S. 365 (1926) and Nectow v. City of Cambridge, 277 U.S. 183 (1928). In *Euclid*, a facial challenge to a municipal zoning scheme was rejected on a standard highly deferential to the legislative judgment; in *Nectow*, an as-applied attack on a similar scheme was successful.

[12]452 U.S. 264 (1981).

[13]480 U.S. 470 (1987).

[14]*Id.* at 495.

[15]*Id.* at 493. Of course, a holding that no facial taking has occurred in no way precludes the landowner from later asserting an as-applied challenge based on the same regulatory scheme. *Hodel*, 452 U.S. at 297 n.40.

of a ripeness hurdle for facial takings claims, but cites once more the "uphill battle" in succeeding on the claim itself.[16]

Comments and Confusion

An ample number of lower court decisions reiterate the Supreme Court litany in this area. Most such courts assert: that a facial taking claim is vitiated if the statute/regulation does not by its terms eliminate nearly all economic use,[17] or if it otherwise permits those administering it to avoid takings;[18] that facial takings claims dispense with the need to show a final and authoritative agency ruling (or indeed any implementing ruling) on the type and intensity of development allowed on the particular parcel;[19] that, generally, takings cases involving land-use controls must await as-applied challenges to succeed; that as-applied challenges are usually not ripe until a "final and authoritative determination" as to permitted development is obtained, and, if brought in federal court, until state avenues for compensation are exhausted.[20]

Closer inspection of the decisions, however, reveals that the significance of the facial/as-applied dichotomy is not fully settled. For one thing, there are a few cases that depart, partially or fully, from the

[16]Suitum v. Tahoe Regional Planning Agency, 117 S. Ct. 1659, 1666 n.10 (1997) (dictum).

[17]See, e.g., Maryland Aggregates Ass'n v. State, 337 Md. 658, 655 A. 2d 886, cert. denied, 514 U.S. 1111 (1995).

[18]See, e.g., Tahoe-Sierra Preservation Council v. State Water Resources Control Bd., 210 Cal. App. 3d 1421, 259 Cal. Rptr. 132 (1989).

[19]See, e.g., Taylor v. Village of North Palm Beach, 659 So. 2d 1167, 1172 n.3 (Fla. Dist. Ct. App. 1995). Several decisions have noted the facial-taking plaintiff's dispensation from having to exhaust administrative remedies: Guimont v. Clarke, 121 Wash. 2d 586, 854 P.2d 1 (1993), cert. denied, 510 U.S. 1176 (1994); Robinson v. City of Seattle, 119 Wash. 2d 34, 830 P.2d 318 (1992), cert. denied, 506 U.S. 1028 (1993); Del Oro Hills v. City of Oceanside, 31 Cal. App. 4th 1060, 1077–78, 37 Cal. Rptr. 2d 677, cert. denied, 516 U.S. 823 (1995).

[20]Even limiting ourselves to decisions that explicitly address the text proposition, the number of cases is daunting. A few make the point: Dodd v. Hood River County, 59 F.3d 852, 858 (9th Cir. 1995); Eide v. Sarasota County, 908 F.2d 716 (11th Cir. 1990), cert. denied, 488 U.S. 1120 (1991); Trail Enter., Inc. v. City of Houston, 907 F. Supp. 250, 251 (S.D. Tex. 1995); Sierra Club v. California Coastal Comm'n, 12 Cal. App. 4th 602, 15 Cal. Rptr. 2d 779, review denied (1993).

orthodoxy that facial takings claimants need not demonstrate ripeness. The Ninth Circuit has held that while a facial taking claim dispenses with final-determination ripeness, it does not eliminate the pursuit-of-state-compensation prerequisite—assuming the latter is properly before the court.[21] Elsewhere, a state court seems to have jettisoned entirely the no-ripeness-requirement rule for facial takings.[22]

Doubtless, courts face a temptation to manipulate the facial and as-applied name tags based on whether they wish to address the merits of the taking claim. In *Pennell v. City of San Jose*, for example, a landlord saw a taking in a rent control ordinance that required the city to consider tenant hardship in deciding whether to approve above-ordinary rent increases.[23] Notwithstanding the plaintiff's plausible characterization of his claim as facial, the majority opinion avoided any labeling. Rather, it cited lack of ripeness, thus treating the claim as as-applied, and declined to reach what surely would have been a difficult taking issue. In dissent, Justice Scalia fumed that the claim was plainly facial, and that the Court should have addressed the merits.

There is also definitional confusion as to the very concept of a facial claim. On the one hand, many courts describe facial challenges as being aimed at the "mere enactment" of a statute or regulation. This concept of facial takings keys on the fact that the property owner's

---

[21]Southern Pacific Transp. Co. v. City of Los Angeles, 922 F.2d 498, 505–07 (9th Cir. 1990), *cert. denied*, 502 U.S. 943 (1991). More recently, the Ninth Circuit sliced the facial-takings pie still finer, depending on which of the *Agins* takings criteria is involved. In Sinclair Oil Corp. v. County of Santa Barbara, 96 F.3d 401 (9th Cir. 1996), it held that while pursuit of state compensation is a ripeness prerequisite for state takings claims based on denial of a property's economic use, it is not when the taking claim is based on the government action's failure to substantially advance a legitimate state interest. *Cf.* Levald, Inc. v. City of Palm Desert, 998 F.2d 680, 686 (9th Cir. 1993) (pursuit of state compensation prior to filing facial claim *not* required where compensation remedy repudiated by state courts as of date of taking), *cert. denied*, 510 U.S. 1093 (1994).

Refusing to divide up the facial-takings pie at all is Crow-New Jersey 32 Ltd. Partnership v. Township of Clinton, 718 F. Supp. 378 (D.N.J. 1989) (facial takings challenges dispense with *both* final-determination and state-compensation ripeness).

[22]Estate of Tippett v. City of Miami, 645 So. 2d 533 (Fla. Dist. Ct. App. 1994) (facial challenge to designation of historic district rejected because claimants did not seek permits), *review dismissed*, 652 So. 2d 819 (Fla. 1995).

[23]485 U.S. 1 (1988).

claim does not hinge on any post-adoption implementation of the statute or regulation—that is, on some agency's formal application of the law to the owner's specific tract. Call it the "no implementation" definition. The other notion of a facial claim is that the government action can be seen by its terms ("on its face") to work a taking; looking at the specifics of the impact on claimant's property is unnecessary. Under this view, the more parcel-specific data the property owner must present to make his or her case, the less appropriate to label the claim a facial one. Call this the "no specifics" view.

The foregoing distinction makes clear why it is perfectly possible to have, say, a taking suit that is *both* "mere enactment" (hence facial to some courts) and as-applied. Imagine a statute that by its terms prohibits mining in certain areas, with no provision for exceptions. The prohibition is self-executing; no administrative procedure is needed to give it effect. A taking action based on this prohibition would, by definition, be a mere-enactment challenge. It may also, to have a chance at success, be as-applied, since many specifics as to the tract in question may have to be offered by the claimant to rule out any nonmining economic uses of the property that remain.[24]

Of course, as a practical matter most challenges will be tagged the same—facial or as-applied—under either the no-implementation or no-specifics view. If a law has not been implemented, the owner of land likely has fewer specifics as to its precise impact on such land. Doubtless this correlation between the two approaches is one reason for the definitional confusion.

The no-specifics view also suggests that the concepts of facial and as-applied challenges are but opposite poles with intervening shades of gray. No takings claim is purely facial; at the very least, the plaintiff must put forward enough specifics about his parcel to show that it is subject to the contested land-use restriction. In the federal courts, Article III standing requirements demand no less.[25] But where the

[24]The text illustration is modeled after an actual as-applied, mere-enactment case: Whitney Benefits, Inc. v. United States, 926 F.2d 1169 (Fed. Cir.) (enactment of surface mining law found to deprive company of all economic use of its mineral estate, but only after "complex and voluminous proofs"), *cert. denied*, 502 U.S. 952 (1991).

[25]Article III of the U.S. Constitution limits the power of federal courts created under that article (including the federal district courts) to the adjudication of "Cases" and "Controversies." This restriction is construed to mean that a plaintiff in such courts must be able to allege past or threatened "injury in fact." An owner whose land is not within the scope of a challenged land-use control necessarily fails this requirement, and hence cannot maintain suit.

plaintiff marshals a few parcel-specific facts beyond that rock-bottom minimum, courts should not reflexively brand the claim as as-applied and, as a result, demand that a *Williamson County* "final and authoritative determination" have occurred. If the plaintiff can show that the relevant takings criteria are satisfied at a particular legal stage, no matter how early, then it is pointless for a court to insist formalistically on further proceedings because the claim, under a no-specifics view, is not a facial one.

A final note: The facial taking claim, we have seen, is often resolved with little reference to the particulars of the landowner's piece of land. Consider, however, that if the facial argument prevails, the court must switch gears. It must fully immerse itself in the specifics of the plaintiff's property and how the government action affected it—in order to assess market value and figure the compensation due. The point is merely that the need for this subsequent, specifics-intensive stage does not undercut the facial nature of the original taking claim.

Chapter 11

Physical Takings

The permanent physical invasion of private property by the government should be the easiest of takings to recognize. Physical takings are just that—physical entry upon and occupation of private property by the government, or by something set in motion or authorized by the government (floodwaters, the general public, cable television companies, etc.).[1]

When permanent, these intrusions are generally so open and obvious that none of the usual takings tests are used. There is seldom balancing of public and private interests, no consideration of investment-backed expectations, no threshold questions of diminution in value, no "relevant parcel" issue. The only question is, is it a *permanent* physical taking, and if so, how much does the government owe. In most circumstances, the permanent physical invasion is a per se taking.

Why the virtual per se rule? Because in takings law, there can be no greater assault on private property rights than permanent physical invasion by the government. Physical invasion takings are an affront to one of the most revered incidents of ownership—the right to exclude others—a right that should be "tenaciously guarded by the courts."[2]

---

[1]The takings issue is not implicated in the routine public health and safety requirements that mandate private installation of equipment such as fire extinguishers, smoke detectors, and fire escapes. The difference is that the government or someone/something put in motion by the government does not physically invade private property under such regulation.

[2]Cable Holdings of Georgia v. McNeil Real Estate Fund VI, 953 F.2d 600 (11th Cir.) (taking found where government attempted to expand its use of easement through private property), *cert. denied*, 506 U.S. 862 (1992).

"Physical invasion cases are special and . . . any permanent physical invasion is a taking."[3]

So, when residential homes are destroyed by government-created floods, there is a physical taking.[4] When apartment building owners are forced to provide a place on their property for television and telephone cables—another physical taking.[5] When airplanes fly low over private property, that too may be a physical taking,[6] as discussed in chapter 21.

At the far end of this long continuum of physical takings cases, we have the case of a family who upon returning home discovered that the local government had excavated and carted away half of their property in the process of widening the street.[7] An exasperated court found the street-widening program to be a per se physical taking.

[3]Loretto v. Teleprompter Manhattan CATV Corp., 458 U.S. 419, 432 (1982).

[4]Singleton v. United States, 6 Cl. Ct. 156, 162–64 (1984) (for taking by flooding, floods must be intermittent, frequent, inevitably recurring); United States v. Dickinson, 331 U.S. 745 (1947) (taking where government caused intermittent flooding); Hawkins v. City of La Grande, 315 Or. 57, 843 P.2d 400 (1992) (sewage-laden water, released from city holding ponds onto private property, a taking); Hamblin v. City of Clearfield, 795 P.2d 1133 (Utah 1990) (city-authorized subdivision changing drainage and flooding property may be taking). *But see* Bunch v. Coachella Valley Water Dist., 15 Cal. 4th 432, 63 Cal. Rptr. 2d 89 (1997) (no taking because public entity acted reasonably); Bodin v. City of Stanwood, 79 Wash. App. 313, 901 P.2d 1065 (1995) (no taking in sewage spill caused by heavy rains), *aff'd*, 927 P.2d 240 (Wash. 1996); Diamond K. Corp. v. Leon County, 677 So. 2d 90, 91 (Fla. Dist. Ct. App. 1996); Bennett v. Tarrant County Water Control & Improvement Dist. No. 1, 894 S.W.2d 441, 449 (Tex. App. 1995).

[5]*Loretto*, 458 U.S. 419; Century Southwest Cable Television, Inc. v. CIIF Assoc., 33 F.3d 1068, 1071 (9th Cir. 1994) ("[I]ntrusion of cable service onto rental property is a taking. . . ."); *Cable Holdings of Georgia*, 953 F.2d 600 (taking where government forced property owner to allow television cable through dedicated utility easement), *cert. denied*, 506 U.S. 862 (1992); Media General Cable of Fairfax, Inc. v. Sequoyah Condominium Council of Co-owners, 737 F. Supp. 903 (E.D. Va. 1990) (applying *Loretto* and finding a per se taking where town authorized placement of unwanted cables through private property), *aff'd*, 991 F.2d 1169 (4th Cir. 1993).

[6]United States v. Causby, 328 U.S. 256 (1946) (taking where low-flying planes passed over a chicken ranch, scared chickens so that they flew into walls, often killing themselves); Brown v. United States, 73 F.3d 1100 (Fed. Cir. 1996) (remand for taking determination where low-flying aircraft disrupted seclusion and quietude of recreational property).

[7]Kruse v. Village of Chagrin Falls, 74 F.3d 694 (6th Cir. 1996), *cert. denied*, 117 S. Ct. 71 (1996).

Permanent physical invasions and outright appropriations were the *only* recognized takings in the early days of takings law. This changed when the Supreme Court decided *Pennsylvania Coal Co. v. Mahon*,[8] announcing the doctrine of regulatory takings. Under that doctrine, a regulatory restriction on the use of land, as distinguished from a physical invasion, can also be a taking.

The rights associated with landownership include the right to dispose of property, the right to use, the right to leave property to heirs, and the right to exclude others.[9] It is this last right that is most obviously wiped out with physical takings.

The Right to Exclude

If the benefit of an intrusion is enormous compared to the intrusion itself, some might mistakenly apply the multifactor analysis for regulatory takings. However, a landmark case shows why physical invasion precludes such an analysis. In 1971, Jean Loretto purchased a New York City apartment building, upon which the former owner had allowed cable companies to attach cable wire and a junction box.[10] She did not discover the cable paraphernalia until some time after she purchased the property. Nearly two years after the purchase, the cable company attempted to attach more cable wire to Mrs. Loretto's building.

Cable wire presumably provides great public benefit; without the connections Mrs. Loretto and other apartment owners could not provide cable television service to their tenants. State law prohibited landlords from interfering with the citywide cable service. In most cases, the government-required intrusion was minor. The junction box mounted on Mrs. Loretto's roof took up less than one eighth of a cubic foot of space, about the size of a shoe box.

Mrs. Loretto objected to the government giving the cable companies permission to install anything on her building, no matter how small. The Court concluded:

> [A] permanent physical occupation authorized by government is a taking without regard to the public interests that it may serve. Our constitutional history confirms the rule, recent cases

---

[8]260 U.S. 393 (1922).
[9]United States v. General Motors Corp., 323 U.S. 373, 378 (1945).
[10]Loretto v. Teleprompter Manhattan CATV Corp., 458 U.S. 419 (1982).

Apartment building owned by Jean Loretto, in Manhattan, New York City. Installation of cable-TV cable and boxes on the outside of this building was the issue in the leading physical taking case of *Loretto v. Teleprompter Manhattan CATV Corp.*

do not question it, and the purposes of the Takings Clause compel its retention.[11]

In other words, the government can require submission to regulation, but where the regulation results in a permanent physical occupation, the government must pay. You may ask, why does this minute intrusion warrant compensation when even some of the most severe of regulatory restrictions fail to meet the takings test? The answer lies in the sacrosanct status of the right to exclude.

Shades of Gray

Three cases suggest the problems that can occur in deciding whether there is a regulatory taking, physical-invasion taking, or no taking at all.[12] The first is *FCC v. Florida Power Corp.*,[13] which effectively narrows the *Loretto* holding. The subject of the dispute was a federal statute governing what owners of utility poles could charge others for use of the poles. Under it, the FCC dramatically reduced the permitted rents in a number of per-pole contracts. Citing *Loretto*, the pole owners alleged a per se taking. The Court ruled against them, concluding that "nothing in the [applicable federal law] . . . gives cable companies any right to occupy space on utility poles."[14] Regarding the contracts as a voluntary submission to the occupation, the Court observed:

> [I]t is the invitation [by the pole owner to the lessee], not the rent, that makes the difference. The line which separates [this case] from *Loretto* is the unambiguous distinction between a . . . lessee and an interloper with a government license.[15]

There are only two ways in which the Court could have reached the conclusion that *Loretto* did not apply. The Court either interpreted

---

[11]*Id.* at 426.

[12]One recent case from the U.S. Court of Federal Claims "appears close to the conceptual border" of physical and regulatory takings. The Stearns Co., Ltd. v. United States, 34 Fed. Cl. 264, 272 (1995) (government required mineral rights owner to obtain determination of rights or compatibility per federal statute; owner claimed either physical or regulatory taking).

[13]480 U.S. 245 (1987).

[14]*Id.* at 251.

[15]*Id.* at 252–53.

Loretto as applying only to that equipment attached to Mrs. Loretto's building subsequent to her purchase,[16] or it distinguished Mrs. Loretto's case as one in which the landlord wanted to remove the cables, changing or terminating the use, while in *FCC* the petitioners planned to continue the same use. But the Court never reached this second issue, stating that until the pole owners attempted to change the use, the claim was not ripe.

Still missing is an answer to the question of how *Loretto* would apply to cases where private owners of heavily regulated businesses such as utilities are required, over objection, to enter into, renew, or refrain from the continued use of their property.

In the second case, *Yee v. City of Escondido*[17] (chapter 19), the Supreme Court considered a California law limiting the ability of a mobile-home park owner to terminate a tenancy. John Yee contended that the law resulted in a per se occupation of his land by unwanted tenants.

The Court disagreed, finding just enough voluntariness, not in letting the tenants stay, but in the contract which put the mobile-home owners on the land initially. The Court applied *FCC*, holding that although the government could not require the landowner to submit to the physical occupation, it could regulate the property once the landlord-tenant relationship was voluntarily established, for as long as that relationship continued.

The final case in our trilogy of gray-area cases is *Nollan v. California Coastal Commission*[18] (chapter 16). The Nollans leased beachfront property with an option to buy. The option was conditioned on their promise to replace the small bungalow on the property, which had fallen into disrepair. To do the work, they were required to obtain a permit from the California Coastal Commission. They submitted a permit application to demolish the existing structure and replace it with a three-bedroom house in keeping with the rest of the neighborhood. The commission granted the permit, conditioned on the Nollans' granting the public the right to pass across the beach portion of their property between public beaches to the north and south. The Nollans claimed a physical taking.

---

[16]The *Loretto* Court included equipment installed *before* Mrs. Loretto purchased in the physical invasion. This was clearly inconsistent with the law and was a mistake. In physical invasion cases, the date of taking is generally the time of the invasion, and takings law allows only the owner on the date of taking to maintain the taking action.

[17]503 U.S. 519 (1992).

[18]483 U.S. 825 (1987).

Beachfront bungalow (top, view from road) in Ventura County, California, demolished to make room for the property owners' current home (bottom, view from beach). Conditions imposed on this demolition were at issue in *Nollan v. California Coastal Commission*.

The Court ruled that where the granting of a land-use permit is conditioned upon some physical invasion, the condition must substantially advance the same government purpose as that advanced by the permit itself. Under the *Nollan* facts, no such nexus existed. The commission argued that its purpose was to protect the public's ability to see the beach, assist the public in overcoming the psychological barrier to using the beach created by a developed shorefront, and prevent congestion on the public beaches. The Court concluded, however, that the easement requested—along the beach rather than at right angles to it from the road—did not advance any of these objectives.[19] Said the Court: "[I]f it wants an easement across the Nollans' property, it must pay for it."[20]

Duration and Extent of Physical Takings

Both physical and regulatory takings can be permanent or temporary, partial or complete. Where the courts have found an invasion to be temporary, they have not found a taking. That is not to say that short-term or finite invasions are not compensated as physical takings.

[19]*Id.* at 836. *Nollan* brings out the point that you do not have to have a single occupier in order to establish a permanent physical taking. It is enough to have different people invading the property with some regularity.

[20]*Id.* at 842. Two other "right to exclude" cases are noteworthy. One finds a taking; the other, decided a mere one year later, does not. In Kaiser Aetna v. United States, 444 U.S. 164 (1979), the owners of the land surrounding a pond proposed to develop a marina, opening their pond to the ocean and potentially subjecting themselves to the federal navigational servitude. This servitude creates a public right of access to navigable waters (*see* chapter 14). Here, however, the Court focused on the history of the Hawaiian fishponds and the owners' investment-backed expectation of a right to exclude, holding that the imposition of the navigational servitude, in this context, would result in a physical invasion taking.

In the second case, Pruneyard Shopping Center v. Robins, 447 U.S. 74 (1980), a shopping center banned the distribution of handbills on its property, even though the California Supreme Court had held that the state constitution permits such activity. Influenced by the sanctity of the right to free speech and the commercial character of the property, the Court held that the shopping center failed to demonstrate that the right to exclude others was so essential to the use or economic value of its property that the state-authorized limitation of it was a physical taking. Taken together, these cases mark the opposite, outer reaches of the Court's analysis of the physical takings issue.

Rather, the courts take some liberty and classify these as permanent takings.

This element of permanency appears to go back to the language in *Loretto*, under which a *permanent* physical occupation of private property by the government is a per se taking. Courts have latched onto *Loretto* as the lead physical takings case, lending great weight to its "of a permanent nature" language. Hence, most courts feel a need to find permanency in the physical occupation before they will grant compensation. They find it in the common law of property.

As expressed in *Hendler v. United States*, "permanent does not mean forever, or anything like it."[21] What has been permanently taken is not the land, but the rental value of the land for the term of occupation or an estate for years—a term of finite duration. This definition of permanent is nonsensical to most people, but real estate lawyers may appreciate the point—the physical invasion is complete and permanent for a fixed term, just as an apartment lease gives the tenant a complete and permanent right to occupy for the period of the lease.

There is a reason for all the fuss and litigation. Generally, where a private party physically although temporarily occupies private property, the owner of the property has a recourse in trespass. However, where the invader is a government entity, sovereign immunity may apply, leaving only the Takings Clause as a weapon.

Focusing on the temporary nature of the government's taking in *YMCA v. United States*,[22] the Court subtly illustrated the importance of permanency. The U.S. Army was ordered to clear rioters from the YMCA building in the Panama Canal Zone. After being ejected, the looters turned on the soldiers, who moved back into the building and set up positions. The building remained under siege throughout the night.

When the fight was over, the building was in ruins. The Court found that "the temporary occupancy of [the] buildings and the damage inflicted on them by the rioters during such occupancy did not constitute a taking."[23] The rationale primarily relied on the fact that the building owners were the intended beneficiaries of the governmental activity, and fairness and justice did not require compensation. The Court also pointed out that the government did not cause

---

[21]952 F.2d 1364, 1376 (Fed. Cir. 1991).
[22]395 U.S. 85 (1969).
[23]*Id.* at 89.

the deprivation of use; the rioters did. However, in the end the Court again mentions the *temporary* nature of the occupation.

Police Power, Physical Invasion, or Both

Some state courts are still wrestling with the intractable problem of whether the legitimate exercise of the police power can coexist with a holding of a physical taking. One of the more dramatic cases on this question came to us recently from California's highest court.[24] A felony suspect took refuge in a store and refused to surrender. The police fired tear gas into the store, causing much damage.

The court boldly stated that in California, "just compensation has . . . never been applied to require a public entity to compensate a property owner for property damaged resulting from the efforts of law enforcement officers to enforce criminal laws."[25]

Similarly, the Florida Supreme Court found no taking where trees exhibiting physical symptoms of a bacterial disease, and trees within 125 feet of them, were ordered destroyed.[26] The government destroyed all of the property owner's trees, and the court found a taking only for trees destroyed in excess of the 125-foot radius.

A Pennsylvania court also cited the police power in its finding that no taking had occurred even when the property owners' building was demolished by the city without notice.[27] The owners had lived in the building and operated a retail meat market there. But they vacated the property in 1963, and in 1973, the city demolished it.[28] The owners made a taking claim, but it was dismissed by the trial court.

---

[24]Customer Co. v. City of Sacramento, 10 Cal. 4th 368, 895 P.2d 900 (1995), *cert. denied*, 116 S. Ct. 920 (1996).

[25]*Id.* at 377–78.

[26]Department of Agric. & Consumer Serv. v. Polk, 568 So.2d 35 (Fla. 1990). *Cf.* Miller v. Schoene, 276 U.S. 272 (1928) (property owner ordered to cut down trees per statute to prevent spread of plant disease; statute upheld due to public interest in protecting orchards, which were important to state's economy).

[27]German v. City of Philadelphia, 683 A.2d 323 (Pa. Commw. Ct. 1996), *appeal denied*, 700 A.2d 444 (Pa. 1997). *See also* Hoeck v. City of Portland, 57 F.3d 781, 787 (9th Cir. 1995). *But see* City of Houston v. Crabb, 905 S.W.2d 669, 674–75 (Tex. Ct. App. 1995) (taking where "[c]ity failed to prove it validly exercised its police power"); Blanchard v. City of Ralston, 559 N.W.2d 735, 739–40 (Neb. 1997) (taking based on city's emergency demolition of building).

[28]*German*, 683 A.2d at 325.

The court found that an application to demolish the property showed that the demolition was an exercise of the police power, and such an exercise is not compensable under the eminent domain code.[29] The appeals court affirmed, noting that the property owners had not met their burden of proving a taking by eminent domain.[30] The appeals court referred to the trial court's determination that the owners had abandoned the building for ten years before it was demolished. The owners disputed the abandonment finding, but the appeals court disagreed: "[C]onsidering the length of time between the abandonment of the building and its demolition, we believe the trial court's position is justified."[31]

In a Minneapolis case, the police used a bulldozer to make their entry.[32] After making the arrests, they patched up the holes with plywood. Nowhere was it alleged that the landlords did anything illegal. Contrary to the decisions by the California, Florida, and Pennsylvania courts, however, the Minnesota court found a taking:

> [I]t would be unfair to force an innocent person to bear the entire cost of a benefit conferred upon the community as a whole, namely the apprehension of a dangerous felon.[33]

Similarly, a New Jersey court held that where a search for drugs was conducted under a no-knock search warrant, the property owner is entitled to compensation. However, the court did qualify its holding:

> [E]very time property is destroyed by a governmental official such action will not automatically require payment of just compensation. The holding herein is limited to a physical taking of property belonging to an innocent third party for a public purpose.[34]

---

[29]*Id.* at 327.

[30]*Id.* at 328.

[31]*Id.* at 329.

[32]McGovern v. City of Minneapolis, 480 N.W.2d 121 (Minn. Ct. App. 1992).

[33]*McGovern*, 480 N.W.2d at 127 (citing Wegner v. Milwaukee Mut. Ins. Co., 479 N.W.2d 38 (Minn. 1991)).

For a taking involving loss, rather than destruction, of use, *see* City of St. Petersburg v. Bowen, 675 So. 2d 626 (Fla. Dist. Ct. App.) (in fight against illegal drug use, board ordered apartments closed for one year; if board wants to do so, it must pay), *review denied*, 680 So. 2d 421 (Fla. 1996), *cert. denied*, 117 S. Ct. 1120 (1997).

[34]Wallace v. City of Atlantic City, 257 N.J. Super. Ct. Law Div. 404, 484 (1992).

These police power cases are difficult factually and troubling because the property owners are indeed damaged but are not compensated in all states for physical invasions. This may be why some courts have decided that acts of police power and physical invasion takings can coexist on the same facts, in the same case. For more on emergency exceptions, see chapter 14.

Conclusion

While physical takings appear to be obvious, scratching the surface of these cases brings us through the veneer into an amalgam of complexities, ranging from what is physical as compared to what is regulatory, permanent takings that are not truly permanent, and temporary takings that are not temporary at all but merely the permissible exercise of good public regulation.

The most difficult of these cases are ones in which physical invasion by the government greatly damages private property, but the loss is seen as secondary or incidental to a lawful government activity, such as crime fighting. Whether or not these invasions are compensable is left to courts on a state-by-state basis. Frequently, the property owner is left with no remedy or a remedy less desirable than just compensation. This is one of those areas of takings law in which the federal and state legislatures might effectively address the problem of compensation for physical invasion by the government.[35]

---

[35]*See* chapter 34. An adequate remedy may be had through a tort claims statute.

Chapter 12

Regulatory Takings

In this chapter we survey the evolution of regulatory takings, a doctrine conceptually distinct from the physical takings principles described in chapter 11, though not always so in practice.[1] We then identify key components of regulatory takings jurisprudence: "total" v. "partial" takings; "temporary" takings; the doctrine of "unconstitutional conditions" under the Takings Clause; the "relevant parcel" issue. The chapter concludes with a brief analysis of two "cutting edge" questions surrounding regulatory takings law—"judicial" takings and regulatory "givings."

Origins and Early Case Law of Regulatory Takings

The Founding Fathers likely would be amazed at the very notion of regulatory takings. It is now widely believed that the drafters of the Bill of Rights intended the Takings Clause to limit only government's actual physical seizures of private property without payment of

---

[1]*See, e.g.,* Nollan v. California Coastal Comm'n, 483 U.S. 825, 832 (describing case as a physical taking dispute), 834 (giving regulatory takings analysis) (1987). *Cf.* Seawall Assoc's. v. City of New York, 74 N.Y.2d 92, 542 N.E.2d 1059, 1065, *cert. denied,* 493 U.S. 976 (1989) (construing apartment conversion/rent control measure as physical occupation); Clajon Prod. Corp. v. Petera, 70 F.3d 1566, 1578 (10th Cir. 1995) (*Nollan* "extend[s] the analysis of complete physical occupation cases to those situations in which the government achieves the same end . . . through a conditional permit procedure").

compensation.[2] Supreme Court justices have similarly conceded the point in their regulatory takings opinions.[3] Some have argued that the entire notion of regulatory takings represents a fundamental misstep in constitutional thinking and that the entire doctrine should be abolished.[4]

No matter. Our task is not to bury the doctrine of regulatory takings, but to explain it. Regardless of its constitutional pedigree, the notion that government regulation may effect a taking of property is by now firmly ingrained in constitutional and natural resource law. It is not likely to be abandoned by the Supreme Court any time soon.

Penn Central and the Advent of Specific Criteria for Regulatory Takings

To this day, the 1978 decision in *Penn Central Transportation Co. v. New York City*[5] is the most important regulatory takings opinion ever handed down by the Supreme Court. Significantly, Justice William Brennan's majority opinion begins with a candid admission that "this Court, quite simply, has been unable to develop any 'set formula' for determining when 'justice and fairness' require that economic injuries caused by public action demand compensation."[6]

The majority in *Penn Central* then proceeded to offer three relevant factors to consider when measuring regulatory takings:

> The *economic impact* of the regulation on the claimant and, particularly, the extent to which the regulation has interfered with distinct *investment-backed expectations* are, of course, relevant considerations. [Citing *Goldblatt*.] So, too, is the *character of the governmental action*. A 'taking' may more readily

[2]Joseph Sax, *Takings and the Police Power*, 74 YALE L.J. 36, 58–60 (1964); William M. Treanor, *The Origins and Original Significance of the Just Compensation Clause of the Fifth Amendment*, 94 YALE L.J. 694 (1985); J. Peter Byrne, *Ten Arguments for the Abolition of the Regulatory Takings Doctrine*, 22 ECOLOGY L.Q. 89, 91–96 (1995); William M. Treanor, *The Original Understanding of the Takings Clause and the Political Process*, 95 COLUMBIA L. REV. 782 (1995).

[3]Lucas v. South Carolina Coastal Council, 505 U.S. 1003, 1014–15 (1992). *See also id.* at 1055–60 (Blackmun, J. dissenting).

[4]*See, e.g.*, Byrne, *supra note 2*.

[5]438 U.S. 104 (1978). See Appendix A for case summary.

[6]*Id.* at 124.

South facade of the Grand Central Terminal, Manhattan, New York City. Expansion of this designated historic landmark was the issue in *Penn Central Transportation Co. v. New York City.*

be found when the interference with property can be characterized as a physical invasion by government . . . than when interference arises from some public program adjusting the benefits
and burdens of economic life to promote the common good.
(Emphasis added.)[7]

The Supreme Court did not indicate in *Penn Central* that the
above-quoted factors were necessarily exclusive. Nevertheless, the
Court has not seen fit to expand upon them; and lower state and federal courts have routinely cited and applied the *Penn Central* trilogy
of factors in subsequent decades. It therefore seems worthwhile to
spend a moment discussing each of the key *Penn Central* criteria in a
bit more detail.

Economic Impact of the Regulation

Experience demonstrates this to be the most significant of the three
Penn Central factors, but not in and of itself dispositive absent a
"total taking."[8] The Court has also failed to provide any general explication of the criterion. How *much* economic impact from a government action is required in order to find a regulatory taking? And
do all economic impacts count equally? To date, economic impact
tends to enter judicial takings analyses in the form of inquiry into the
impact of the government's action on: (1) the rate of return, (2) economic uses of the property, or (3) fair market value.

Illustrative of the reasonable-return rule is *Penn Central* itself, in
which the Court found that even without the development proposed
by the landowner, a "reasonable return" could be earned from the existing facility.[9] To similar effect is *Keystone Bituminous Coal Ass'n v.
DeBenedictis*, which, in upholding a state requirement that coal companies leave 50 percent of the coal in the ground to prevent surface
subsidence, relied in part on the coal companies' failure to claim that
their mines had been made unprofitable as a result.[10]

Turning to the question of economic use, modern courts have generally held that it is only the elimination of *all* (or nearly all) beneficial use of property that is a taking. A well-settled corollary to the
rule that takings require virtually complete elimination of a prop-

---

[7]*Id.*

[8]Keystone Bituminous Coal Ass'n v. DeBenedictis, 480 U.S. 470, 490 (1987).

[9]*Penn Central*, 438 U.S. at 136–137.

[10]480 U.S. at 496 (1987). *Accord,* Atlas Corp. v. United States, 895 F.2d 745,
758 (Fed. Cir. 1990).

erty's economic use is that barring *the most profitable use* of property is not, alone, a taking.[11] Similarly, the loss of future profits unaccompanied by a *physical* taking provides a "slender reed" upon which to base a taking claim.[12]

Diminution of a property's fair market value is a more fluid concept. Traditionally, both the U.S. Supreme Court and lower courts have taken the view that even when government regulation causes a substantial reduction in a property's fair market value, no taking has transpired.[13] As the Court observed in *Penn Central*, its land-use decisions "uniformly reject the proposition that diminution in property value, standing alone, can establish a taking."[14] But that notion is beginning to change. In its 1992 *Lucas* decision, the Court suggested for the first time (albeit in dicta) that regulatory action which triggers diminution in property values falling short of total elimination of value *might* nonetheless be compensable under the Takings Clause.[15] Some lower courts have held that such nontotal reductions in market value due to government regulation may indeed be violative of the Takings Clause.[16]

Distinct Investment-Backed Expectations

The second of the regulatory takings criteria identified in *Penn Central*—the degree to which government interferes with the "distinct investment-backed expectations" of the private property owner—is

[11]Andrus v. Allard, 444 U.S. 51, 66 (1979).

[12]*Id.*; *Penn Central*, 438 U.S. at 127, 130.

[13]Hadacheck v. Sebastian, 239 U.S. 394 (1915) (zoning ban's 90% reduction of property value not a taking); Haas v. City & County of San Francisco, 605 F.2d 1117, 1120 (9th Cir. 1979), *cert. denied*, 445 U.S. 928 (1980) (95% reduction in parcel value not a taking); Pace Resources, Inc. v. Shrewsbury Township, 808 F.2d 1023, 1031 (3d Cir. 1987), *cert. denied*, 482 U.S. 906 (1987) (89% reduction); Gardner v. New Jersey Pinelands Comm'n, 125 N.J. 193, 210–11, 593 A.2d 251, 259 (1991).

[14]438 U.S. at 131.

[15]Lucas v. South Carolina Coastal Comm'n, 505 U.S. 1003, 1019–20, n.8.

[16]*See, e.g.,* Florida Rock Indus., Inc. v. United States, 18 F.3d 1560 (Fed. Cir. 1994) (62% reduction in land value may be a taking); Loveladies Harbor, Inc. v. United States, 21 Cl. Ct. 153 (1990), *aff'd*, 28 F.3d 1171 (Fed. Cir. 1994) (99% reduction in land value plus additional factors a taking); Kavanau v. Santa Monica Rent Control Bd., 16 Cal. 4th 761, 774–775, 941 P.2d 851 (1997), *cert. denied*, 118 S. Ct. 856 (1998). *Cf.* Yancey v. United States, 915 F.2d 1534 (Fed. Cir. 1990) (personal property's value reduced by 54% a taking).

more amorphous. The phrase derives from an early and influential law review article on inverse condemnation law.[17] Its parameters remain uncertain even today.

How the "distinct investment-backed expectations" criterion is applied can be illustrated with some simple hypotheticals, however. Assume that an individual buys a parcel of land knowing that it is too small to qualify as a legal lot under applicable zoning regulations. The landowner would thereafter lack a viable regulatory takings claim, notwithstanding her inability to develop, because she knew what she was getting into in buying the illegal lot. Similarly, a person buying land that has been dedicated and duly recorded as open space by the prior owner lacks a reasonable investment-backed expectation to build on the property. This would seemingly apply whether or not the buyer had actual knowledge of the open space restriction; a reasonable purchaser is on notice of property restrictions that are of public record.[18]

The only U.S. Supreme Court regulatory takings decision in which "investment-backed expectations" has played a prominent role is *Ruckelshaus v. Monsanto Co.*[19] *Ruckelshaus* involved trade-secret data submitted to government in support of applications for pesticide registration. After concluding that such trade secrets constitute "property," the Court embarked on a takings analysis closely tied to the expectations of the applicant, based on the confidentiality protections afforded by statute when the trade secrets were submitted. The Court concluded that the government's use of the corporate data was a taking, given the express guarantee of confidentiality contained in the statute, coupled with the fact that the guarantee gave rise to a reasonable investment-backed expectation that was substantially breached.[20]

---

[17]Frank Michelman, *Property, Utility, and Fairness: Comments on the Ethical Foundations of "Just Compensation" Law,* 80 Harvard L. Rev. 1165, 1233 (1967).

[18]*See* Leonard v. Town of Brimfield, 423 Mass. 152, 155, 666 A.2d 1300 (1996), *cert. denied,* 117 S. Ct. 582 (1976) (no reasonable expectation to develop within floodplain when plaintiff bought property with constructive notice of its zoning). *See also* McNulty v. Town of Indialantic, 727 F. Supp. 604, 612 (M.D. Fla. 1989) (same result re preexisting beach setback ordinance); Kim v. New York, 90 N.Y.2d 1, 681 N.E.2d 312, *cert. denied,* 118 S. Ct. 50 (1997) (same).

[19]467 U.S. 986 (1984).

[20]*Id.* at 1012–13. *Cf.* Penn Central Transp. Co. v. New York City, 438 U.S.

One of the more intriguing questions involving this *Penn Central* criterion is whether it is ever an interference with reasonable investment-backed expectations when government acts within a regulatory scheme existing and known to a private property owner at the time the plaintiff purchased the property.[21] Even where acquisition of private property predates a new regulatory restriction, expectations, to be reasonable, must "take into account the power of the state to regulate in the public interest," including recognition of "the legitimate interest of municipalities in being able to modify land-use planning rules when they perceive the need for change."[22]

Lower courts have struggled to apply the "reasonable investment-backed expectations" factor announced in *Penn Central*. The Federal Circuit has suggested it is relatively unhelpful in adjudicating regulatory takings claims.[23] Some courts, on the other hand, have specifically relied on this criterion to reject a regulatory takings claim.[24]

Character of the Governmental Action

The character of the governmental action seems the most straightforward of the three *Penn Central* factors. At the simplest level, and as the *Penn Central* Court expressly noted, a taking is far more likely to

---

104, 136 (1978) (building's designation as landmark doesn't interfere with developer's expectation); Connolly v. Pension Benefit Guar. Corp., 475 U.S. 211, 226–27 (1986) (retroactive imposition of liability on employers who withdrew from multiemployer pension plans).

[21]*See, e.g.*, Claridge v. New Hampshire Wetlands Bd., 125 N.H. 745, 485 A.2d 287 (1984) (buyer with notice of possible regulatory barriers to wetlands development has no legitimate investment-backed expectation). Mayhew v. Town of Sunnyvale, 964 S.W. 2d 922 (Tex. 1998) (accord), Virginia Beach v. Bell, 255 Va. 395, 498 S.E. 2d 414 (Va. 1998) (same).

[22]Pace Resources, Inc. v. Shrewsburg Township, 808 F.2d 1023, 1033 (3d Cir. 1987).

[23]Florida Rock Indus., Inc. v. United States 18 F.3d 1560, 1564, 1567 (Fed. Cir. 1994).

[24]*See, e.g.*, Alegria v. Keeney, 687 A.2d 1249 (R.I. 1997); Gazza v. New York Dept. of Envtl. Protection, 89 N.Y.2d 603, 679 N.E.2d 1035, *cert. denied*, 118 S. Ct. 58 (1997); Basile v. Town of Southampton, 89 N.Y.2d 974, 678 N.E.2d 489, *cert. denied*, 118 S. Ct. 264 (1997).

be found when government physically occupies private property than when it merely regulates private use.[25]

But subsequent cases indicate that as to purely regulatory actions, some government programs are entitled to less deference under the Takings Clause than others. For example, the Court has shown particular skepticism toward government programs that abrogate the right to devise property[26] or the right of private landowners to exclude the public from their property.[27]

The same is true with respect to land-use programs perceived by the courts as preserving privately owned lands as open space or wildlife habitat for the benefit of the public.[28] Conversely, those instances in which government acts to abate a nuisance or proscribe nuisance-type activity are the kinds of regulatory actions most likely to survive constitutional attack.[29]

The difficulty, of course, is with those regulatory programs that fall somewhere between. The Supreme Court recently observed that "the distinction between 'harm-preventing' and 'benefit-conferring' regulation is often in the eye of the beholder."[30] As to these intermediate government programs, therefore, the first two *Penn Central* factors are likely to take on heightened significance for a reviewing court.

Advent of the *Agins* Two-Part Test

Had the Supreme Court stopped with its *Penn Central* test, regulatory takings law would not be the muddle it is today. But a mere two years after *Penn Central*, in *Agins v. City of Tiburon*, the Court articulated a new, seemingly distinct constitutional standard against which to measure regulatory takings challenges:

[25]Penn Central Transp. Co. v. New York City, 438 U.S. 104, 124 (1978).

[26]Hodel v. Irving, 481 U.S. 704 (1987); Babbitt v. Youpee, 519 U.S. 1232 (1997).

[27]Kaiser Aetna v. United States, 444 U.S. 164 (1979); Nollan v. California Coastal Comm'n 483 U.S. 825, 832 (1987).

[28]Lucas v. South Carolina Coastal Council, 505 U.S. 1003, 1024–25 (1992).

[29]*See, e.g.,* Miller v. Schoene, 276 U.S. 272 (1928) (compelled destruction of trees infected with communicable disease not a taking); United States v. Central Eureka Mining Co., 358 U.S. 858 (1958) (wartime closing of nation's gold mines to free up needed workers not a taking); Keystone Bituminous Coal Ass'n v. DeBenedictis, 480 U.S. 470 (1987) (state prohibition on underground mining causing subsidence damage to surface structures not a taking).

[30]*Lucas,* 505 U.S. at 1024.

> The application of a generally zoning law to particular property effects a taking if the ordinance does not substantially advance legitimate state interests . . . or denies an owner economically viable use of his land. . . .[31]

Agins thus articulates a two-part regulatory takings test, under which government action meeting either part of the test is usually considered a taking.[32]

The first prong of the *Agins* test is of controversial origin and has been applied inconsistently. Whether a government regulation "substantially advances a legitimate governmental interest" sounds suspiciously like the "rational basis" standard traditionally applied—and almost invariably deemed satisfied—in cases challenging government regulation under the substantive due process provisions of the U.S. Constitution.[33] Indeed, in *Agins* the Supreme Court seemed to apply its newly minted "substantially advances" test in precisely that manner to uphold a zoning ordinance against the landowner's taking claim.[34]

In the handful of regulatory takings cases that immediately followed and cited *Agins*, the Supreme Court declined to mention the "substantially advances" criterion, choosing instead to focus on the second factor: whether the regulation denied the property owner all economically viable use."[35] But the "substantially advances" prong regained prominence with the Court's 1987 decision in *Nollan v. California Coastal Commission*.[36] *Nollan* was the first case in which

---

[31]447 U.S. 255, 260 (1980). Significantly, the Court cited Nectow v. Cambridge, 277 U.S. 183 (1928), a substantive due process case, as authority for the first criterion and *Penn Central* for the second.

[32]At least one lower court has construed the *Agins* test as requiring that *both* elements be satisfied in order to find a regulatory taking. Del Oro Hills v. City of Oceanside, 31 Cal. App. 4th 1060, 1079, 37 Cal. Rptr. 2d 677, *cert. denied,* 516 U.S. 823 (1995). Most courts, however, have read the *Agins* standard in the disjunctive. *See, e.g.,* 152 Valparaiso Ass'n. v. City of Cotati, 56 Cal. App. 4th 378, 65 Cal. Rptr. 2d 551 (1997); Seawall Assoc's. v. City of New York, 74 N.Y. 2d 92, 542 N.E.2d 1059, 1065, *cert. denied,* 493 U.S. 975 (1989).

[33]*See, e.g.,* Minnesota v. Clover Leaf Creamery Co., 449 U.S. 456, 466 (1981). *See generally* discussion in chapter 2.

[34]*Agins,* 447 U.S. at 261.

[35]*See, e.g.,* Hodel v. Virginia Surface Mining & Reclamation Ass'n, 452 U.S. 264, 296 (1981); Hodel v. Indiana, 452 U.S. 314, 335 (1981).

[36]483 U.S. 825 (1987).

the "substantially advancing" prong of the *Agins* test was actually relied upon to find a regulatory taking.

The second prong of the *Agins* test, the requirement that land-use regulations not deny landowners all economically viable use of their property, finds its roots in an obscure footnote from *Penn Central*.[37] Whether and how that criterion relates to the three-factor *Penn Central* test described above has been the subject of considerable uncertainty. It has been argued that the former is a substitute for the latter.[38] Alternatively, some courts have construed this part of the *Agins* standard as subsuming the entire three-pronged *Penn Central* standard.[39] Other decisions interpret the *Agins* deprivation of all economically viable use criterion as encompassing only the "economic impact" and "reasonable investment-backed expectations" elements of the *Penn Central* rule.[40]

Both prongs of the *Agins* test have generated criticism, some from members of the Supreme Court itself. The "substantially advances" criterion has been disparaged as importing into Takings Clause analysis expansive substantive due process notions that the Court had rejected early in this century.[41] The second prong ("denial of all economically viable use") arguably "predicates the conclusion of unconstitutionality purely on the ground of economic loss, without regard to the need for the regulation or the expectations of the owner. . . ."[42]

Doctrinal Confusion—and Still Other "Partial Takings" Tests

Not surprisingly, the existence of these two parallel takings standards has sowed substantial confusion in the state and federal courts. Certain of the U.S. Supreme Court's regulatory takings cases that came

[37]Penn Central Transp. Co. v. New York City, 438 U.S. 104, 138 n.36 (1989).

[38]Byrne, *supra* note 2, at 104; Andrea Peterson, *The Takings Clause: In Search of Underlying Principles,* 77 CALIFORNIA L. REV. 1301, 1330–33 (1989).

[39]*See, e.g.,* City of Waynesville, 900 F.2d 783, 787 (4th Cir. 1990).

[40]Reahard v. Lee County, 968 F.2d 1131, 1136 (11th Cir. 1992), *cert. denied,* 514 U.S. 1064 (1995). *cf.* Florida Rock Indus., Inc. v. United States, 791 F.2d 893, 900 (Fed. Cir. 1986).

[41]Dolan v. City of Tigard, 512 U.S. 374, 409–411 (1994) (Stevens, J., dissenting).

[42]Byrne, *supra* note 2, at 104.

after *Penn Central* and *Agins* cite and purport to apply the three-factored *Penn Central* test; others rely upon and attempt to apply the *Agins* two-part test. Lower state and federal courts fall into the same pattern. Moreover, none of the Court's numerous regulatory takings decisions since 1980 attempt to integrate or otherwise reconcile the two competing tests. The result is both predictable and unfortunate: widespread uncertainty and confusion among legal and planning communities alike.

In the face of this uncertainty, some state and federal courts have decided to go it alone, attempting to formulate their own rules governing regulatory takings.[43] Some jurisdictions have pretty much abandoned regulatory takings claims altogether, preferring to review (and sometimes strike down) government regulations on other constitutional grounds.[44] Yet in the vast majority of cases, the *Penn Central* standard seems both appropriate and workable. The Supreme Court could do all affected groups a service by jettisoning the *Agins* and other regulatory takings criteria in favor of *Penn Central's* regulatory takings trilogy.

Total Takings

So far, we have been discussing so-called "partial takings," i.e., those situations in which government regulation is claimed to have *reduced* but not *eliminated* the economic value or use of private property.[45] Most regulatory takings challenges fall into that category. It is the extreme situation in which it can be argued that land-use or other

[43]*See, e.g.,* Florida Rock Indus., Inc. v. United States, 18 F.3d 1560, 1571 (Fed Cir. 1994); *Reahard,* 968 F.2d at 1136 (proposing eight-part test); 152 Valparaiso Ass'n. v. City of Cotati, 56 Cal. App. 4th 378, 65 Cal. Rptr. 2d 551 (1997).

[44]The State of Washington is perhaps the most prominent example of this trend. *See, e.g.,* Guimont v. Clarke, 121 Wash. 2d 586, 854 P.2d 1 (1993), *cert. denied,* 510 U.S. 1172 (1994) (mobile-home relocation statute valid under regulatory takings law principles, but violates park owners' right to substantive due process).

[45]The term "partial taking" is inherently misleading. One might understandably believe that a partial taking is a violation of the U.S. Constitution. Not so. Courts instead have come to use the term as legal shorthand for a situation in which a regulation *reduces,* but does not *eliminate,* the value of private property. Whether such a partial taking is or isn't compensable depends on application of the *Penn Central/Agins* ad hoc criteria to the facts of a particular case.

The two empty beachfront lots owned by David Lucas in the Isle of Palms subdivision, Charleston County, South Carolina. Mr. Lucas' effort to build homes on these lots prompted *Lucas v. South Carolina Coastal Commission.*

government regulation will have the effect of rendering real property wholly valueless.

But what about government rules that *do* trigger an economic "wipeout" of a private property owner, reducing the value of land to nothing? The Supreme Court answered this question in its 1992 decision *Lucas v. South Carolina Coastal Council.*[46] There the state trial court had determined that South Carolina's Beachfront Management Act, which barred developer Lucas from building any permanent structures on his two barrier island lots, had rendered those lots completely valueless. On review, the U.S. Supreme Court viewed itself bound by that factual determination. The Court then proceeded to announce a new takings standard to address this situation.

For "the relatively rare situations where the government has deprived a landowner of all economically beneficial use,"[47] the Court created a (nearly) bright-line rule standing in marked contrast to its "partial takings" jurisprudence. The Court specifically decreed in

[46]505 U.S. 1003 (1992).
[47]*Id.* at 1018.

Lucas that there should be a presumption that a taking has occurred "in the extraordinary circumstance when *no* productive or economically beneficial use of land is permitted. . . ."[48] (Emphasis in original.)

Why just a *presumption* of compensability for such "total takings"? The Supreme Court conceded in *Lucas* that there are some circumstances where government regulation is necessary and appropriate under the Takings Clause, even when its effect is to eliminate totally the value of private property. The Court articulated two relatively narrow grounds upon which government could avoid liability for such a "total" regulatory taking: (1) where the proposed uses of private property contravene traditional notions and limitations found in state property law, and (2) where regulation is necessary to forestall "grave threats to the lives and property of others."[49] (The parameters of these exceptions are discussed in detail in chapter 14.)

Predictably, *Lucas's* "total takings" rule has had far less impact on regulatory takings law generally than the *Penn Central/Agins* "partial takings" jurisprudence. This is because total takings arise in relatively few cases. In the occasional instance where this does happen, however, lower courts have not hesitated to find government liability.[50] Perhaps of greater long-term significance is Justice Scalia's intimation in dicta that the *Lucas* presumption-of-a-taking rule might apply in at least some extreme "partial takings" situations as well.

Temporary Takings

The phrase "temporary taking" actually encompasses several disparate strands of regulatory takings law. In one sense, the phrase refers to principles established in *First English Evangelical Lutheran Church v. County of Los Angeles*.[51] There the Supreme Court held that once a court concludes that a regulation goes too far and effects a taking, money damages are a constitutionally required remedy. But *First English* went on to provide a government defendant with two discrete options in this situation: (1) it can leave the offending regulation in place, thus making the taking permanent; or (2) it can repeal the measure, in which case the taking is "temporary"—extending

[48]*Id.* at 1017.
[49]*Id.* at 1027–29.
[50]*See, e.g.,* Bowles v. United States, 31 Fed. Cl. 37, 49–50 (1994).
[51]482 U.S. 304 (1987).

from the time of the regulation's enactment or application to the subject property until the time it was found by the reviewing court to violate the Takings Clause.[52]

A second, conceptually distinct type of alleged temporary taking was identified in *First English* and distinguished there from the type of temporary taking for which *First English* mandates monetary compensation. The former consists of "normal delays in obtaining building permits, changes in zoning ordinances, variances, and the like. . . ."[53] In most such circumstances, delays are considered part of the burden of living in a regulated society, and compensation is generally not required.[54]

A third variant of an alleged temporary taking is closely related to the second: it involves a government's *erroneous* assertion of regulatory jurisdiction over a particular piece of property. When a court determines that government regulators lack authority to issue or deny permits concerning a particular parcel of land, is the landowner entitled to compensation for the time during which the property remained subject to the flawed claim of regulatory jurisdiction? Most courts have answered this question in the negative, at least where the government's assertion of regulatory jurisdiction is the product of a good faith mistake.[55]

Finally, temporary takings can arguably arise in the context of development moratoria enacted by government to halt development of lands on an interim basis. Claims that such moratoria effect a temporary taking of property are adjudicated on an ad hoc basis; relevant factors include the length of the challenged moratorium, its justifica-

[52]*Id.* at 317–18.

[53]*Id.* at 321.

[54]*See, e.g.,* Guinnane v. City & County of San Francisco, 197 Cal. App. 3d 862, 868–70, 241 Cal. Rptr. 787, 790–91 (1988), *cert. denied,* 488 U.S. 823 (1988). *Cf.* Dufau v. United States, 22 Cl. Ct. 156 (1990); Philric Ass'n. v. South Portland, 595 A.2d 1061 (Me. 1991); Alexander v. Town of Jupiter, 640 So. 2d 79, 80–81 (Fla. 1994).

[55]Tabb Lakes, Ltd. v. United States, 10 F.3d 796 (Fed. Cir. 1993); Landgate, Inc. v. California Coastal Commission, 17 Cal. 4th 1006, 953 P.2d 1188, (1998); Littoral Dev. Co. v. San Francisco Bay Conservation & Dev. Commission, 33 Cal. App. 4th 211, 221–22, 39 Cal. Rptr. 2d 266, 272 (1995) Cannone v. Noey, 867 P. 2d 797, 801; Steinbergh v. City of Cambridge, 604 N.E. 2d 1269, 1274–1277 (Mass. 1992).

tion(s), whether it is fixed in duration or open-ended, etc. (Land-use moratoria are examined in detail in chapter 17.)

Nollan/Dolan and the Doctrine of "Unconstitutional Conditions"

Starting in 1987, the U.S. Supreme Court created a new and conceptually distinct category of regulatory takings. This doctrine has come to be known alternatively as the *Nollan/Dolan* standard or the doctrine of unconstitutional conditions. Under this principle,

> "the government may not require a person to give up a constitutional right—here the right to receive just compensation when property is taken for a public use—in exchange for a discretionary benefit conferred by the government where the property sought has little or no relationship to the benefit."[56]

The unconstitutional conditions standard was imported into regulatory takings law in two key inverse condemnation decisions, *Nollan v. California Coastal Commission*[57] and *Dolan v. City of Tigard*.[58] The *Nollan/Dolan* requirement takes the form of a two-part test. To survive scrutiny under the Takings Clause, a dedication/exaction condition imposed by government: (1) must have an "essential nexus" to a legitimate state interest; and (2) be "roughly proportionate" to the projected impacts of the proposed development.[59] In *Nollan*, the Supreme Court found that a permit condition imposed by the California Coastal Commission failed the "essential nexus" component. In *Dolan*, by contrast, the Court found that the City of Tigard had satisfied the "essential nexus" requirement in imposing certain permit conditions, but that those conditions lacked the requisite "fit" when compared to the projected land-use impacts of the private landowner's proposed development project.

Accordingly, the *Nollan/Dolan* unconstitutional conditions subset of regulatory takings law possesses its own legal standards and is

---

[56]Dolan v. City of Tigard, 512 U.S. 374, 385 (1994).
[57]483 U.S. 825 (1987).
[58]512 U.S. 374 (1994).
[59]*Id.* at 386–91.

conceptually distinct from "partial," "total," or "temporary" regulatory takings principles. (*Nollan/Dolan* and its progeny are discussed in considerably more detail in chapter 16, dealing with exactions.)

The Relevant Parcel Issue

Before the question of whether a particular regulation has "taken" private property can be answered, one must establish the relevant property interest against which the regulation's effect is to be measured. This issue of the "relevant parcel," or "denominator,"[60] in inverse condemnation law was once considered relatively settled. That is no longer the case.

The threshold question of determining the relevant parcel or increment of property for purposes of analysis under the Takings Clause is actually deceptively complex. A simple example frames the issue. Assume a property owner owns three rural, ten-acre parcels. The first parcel consists of nine acres of developable uplands and one acre of fragile wetlands. The second is contiguous to the first and fully developable. The third, also fully developable, is located down the road, a mile away. Assume further that the landowner seeks to develop solely the one-acre wetlands portion of the first ten-acre parcel, but that the development would destroy a pristine marsh the government seeks to maintain as open space and wildlife habitat. The owner subsequently sues the government, alleging a compensable taking.

What is the relevant parcel, or "denominator," for the reviewing court to assess in determining the economic impact and other relevant takings factors concerning the challenged government decision? The one acre of wetlands? The entire ten-acre parcel? Or the aggregate thirty acres of the three plots owned by the landowner?

To a considerable degree, the answer to this question dictates whether a taking will be found. If, for example, the relevant parcel for purposes of determining a regulation's economic impact is the single acre of wetlands, existing precedents strongly suggest that the court will find a total or near-total elimination of all economic use.[61] And

---

[60]As the Supreme Court explained in Keystone Bituminous Coal, Ass'n v. DeBenedictis, 480 U.S. 470, 497 (1987), a threshold question in any regulatory takings inquiry is defining the unit of property whose value furnishes the denominator of the fraction for the economically beneficial use analysis.

[61]*See, e.g.*, Tabb Lakes, Ltd. v. United States, 10 F.3d 796, 802 (Fed. Cir. 1993).

under the presumption-of-a-taking standard announced in *Lucas*, government liability will almost inevitably follow. On the other hand, if the court examines the full ten-acre property, the regulation reduces the value much less and thus triggers the courts' traditional, multi-faceted balancing analysis. The likelihood of the property owner prevailing is dramatically reduced. And if the court views all three parcels as the relevant denominator, the landowner is even less likely to prevail. In any of these situations, how the court perceives the relevant property interest plays a critical role in modern takings analysis.

Supreme Court Analysis of the Denominator Issue

Until recently, the U.S. Supreme Court had dealt with the denominator question in a consistently broad fashion. The landmark decision on the "relevant parcel" issue remains *Penn Central Transportation Co. v. City of New York*.[62] In *Penn Central*, the landowner argued that the city's refusal to permit construction of an office tower above Grand Central Terminal worked a compensable taking of its "air rights," i.e., its property interest in the unbuilt area atop the terminal. Justice Brennan, speaking for the Court, disagreed:

> "Takings" jurisprudence does not divide a single parcel into discrete segments and attempt to determine whether rights in a particular segment have been entirely abrogated. In deciding whether a particular governmental action has effected a taking, this Court focuses rather both on the character of the action and on the nature and extent of interference with rights in the parcel as a whole. . . .[63]

The Supreme Court built on its *Penn Central* holding a mere year later, in *Andrus v. Allard*.[64] Here, however, the Court's attention shifted from the physical attributes of the subject property to the jurisprudential "bundle of sticks" that collectively constitute ownership of property. In *Allard*, the issue was whether a federal ban on the sale of certain bird artifacts triggered a taking. The Court answered in the negative, relying in principal part upon the fact that the statute

[62]438 U.S. 104 (1978).
[63]*Id.* at 130–31. Justice Rehnquist argued for a contrary result in dissent. *See id.* at 112 n.13 (Rehnquist, J., dissenting).
[64]444 U.S. 51 (1979).

permitted the owner of the artifacts uses of the property other than sale: "where an owner possesses a full 'bundle' of property rights, the destruction of one 'strand' of the bundle [in *Allard*, the right to sell property] is not a taking because the aggregate must be viewed in its entirety."[65]

There matters stood until the Supreme Court's 1992 decision in *Lucas v. South Carolina Coastal Council*.[66] *Lucas* did not raise the relevant parcel issue at all. Nonetheless, Justice Scalia opined in dictum:

> Regrettably, the rhetorical force of our "deprivation of all economically feasible use" rule is greater than its precision, since the rule does not make clear the "property interest" against which the loss of value is to be measured. . . . Unsurprisingly, this uncertainty regarding the composition of the denominator in our "deprivation" fraction has produced inconsistent pronouncements. . . .[67]

Justice Scalia's ruminations in *Lucas* might well be seen as judicial encouragement to litigants to revisit the denominator issue in future regulatory takings cases. But that interpretation is undercut by the Supreme Court's decision the following term in *Concrete Pipe & Products of California, Inc. v. Construction Laborers Pension Trust*,[68] a pension fund case in which a unanimous Court held:

> To the extent that any portion of the property is taken, that portion is always taken in its entirety; the relevant question, however, is whether the property taken is all, or only a portion of the parcel in question.[69]

What, then, is one to make of the available Supreme Court precedent on the "relevant parcel" issue? With the exception of the Scalia dictum in *Lucas*, the Court has uniformly taken the view that the denominator in regulatory takings cases should be viewed expansively, both to afford government regulators deference and to avoid a mode

---

[65]*Id.* at 65–66. *See also* Keystone Bituminous Coal Ass'n v. DeBenedictis; 480 U.S. 470 (1987).

[66]505 U.S. 1003 (1992).

[67]*Id.* at 1016–17 n.7.

[68]508 U.S. 602 (1993).

[69]*Id.* at 644.

of analysis in which virtually every government regulation could be viewed as a taking.[70]

How Lower Federal and State Courts Have Viewed the Denominator Issue

The relative uniformity of Supreme Court precedents on the relevant parcel question has not been replicated in the lower federal and state courts. The Court of Federal Claims and the Court of Appeals for the Federal Circuit, in particular, have been inconsistent on the topic.

How, for example, is one to reconcile the takings decisions from those tribunals which involve mining and wetlands regulation[71] and adopt a narrow interpretation of the denominator issue (i.e., one more favorable to the private property owner)[72] with other cases from the same courts which construe the relevant parcel expansively in the context of federal wetlands regulation?[73]

This inconsistent treatment is unfortunate, for two related reasons. First, the Federal Circuit and Court of Federal Claims are currently deciding a greater number of important regulatory takings cases than any other state or federal courts in the nation. Second, the disparate precedents emerging from these courts inject considerable uncertainty into takings litigation.

Such has been the case in the U.S. Court of Appeals for the Ninth Circuit. In at least two cases, the Ninth Circuit has ruled that distinct

[70]*Penn Central* was not the first Supreme Court decision to identify and grapple with the relevant parcel issue. That distinction probably belongs to Goldblatt v. Town of Hempstead, 369 U.S. 590, 596 (1962), in which the Court held that a landowner's loss of his quarry rights did not constitute a taking, given the remaining rights he retained to the property as a whole. Even before *Goldblatt*, many courts endorsed a no-segmentation rule in the context of direct condemnation *valuation* proceedings. Reference to the parcel-as-a-whole for purposes of calculating severance damages provides one such example.

[71]A more extended discussion of the relevant parcel question in the context of wetlands regulation can be found in chapter 23.

[72]Whitney Benefits, Inc. v. United States, 18 Cl. Ct. 394, *aff'd*, 926 F.2d 1169 (Fed Cir.), *cert. denied*, 502 U.S. 952 (1991); and Loveladies Harbor, Inc. v. United States, 21 Cl. Ct. 153 (1990), *aff'd*, 28 F.3d 1171 (Fed. Cir. 1994).

[73]*See, e.g.*, Tabb Lakes, Ltd. v. United States, 10 F.3d 796 (Fed. Cir. 1993); Deltona Corp. v. United States, 657 F.2d 1184 (Fed. Cir. 1981), *cert. denied*, 455 U.S. 1017 (1982); Ciampitti v. United States, 22 Cl. Ct. 310 (1991).

parcels owned by a single owner should be treated separately for purposes of analyzing a regulatory takings claim. In both cases, the court predicated that result in principal part upon the fact that the local government had zoned each property differently.[74] Other federal court decisions—including some others from the Ninth Circuit—have taken a different, more expansive approach.[75]

State court decisions on the denominator question generally track the evolving jurisprudence of the lower federal courts: Most older precedents adhere to a broad construction of the relevant parcel in regulatory takings cases, while more recent decisions take more disparate positions. New York's experience is illustrative. Earlier cases consistently adopted the *Penn Central*-type analysis advocated by government defendants.[76] In contrast, the New York courts have taken a more restrictive approach in more recent decisions. In *Seawall Associates v. City of New York*,[77] for example, the New York Court of Appeals cited the principle of "conceptual severance"—focusing upon the value of the rights affected by the regulation without regard to the law's relationship to the value of the entire property—in striking down a municipal tenant occupancy law.[78]

Some states have developed seemingly inconsistent jurisprudence on the relevant parcel question. California is one example. In one California decision, the court embraced the approach previously adopted by the Ninth Circuit and described above—ruling that parcels disparately zoned by the government defendant should be considered

---

[74]*See* American Sav. & Loan Ass'n v. County of Marin, 653 F.2d 364 (9th Cir. 1981) (contiguous parcels); Kaiser Dev. Co. v. City & County of Honolulu, 649 F. Supp. 926 (D. Haw. 1986), *aff'd*, 898 F.2d 112 (9th Cir. 1990) *supp. opinion*, 899 F.2d (9th Cir.), *amended*, 913 F.2d 573 (9th Cir. 1990), *cert. denied*, 499 U.S. 947 (1991), (noncontiguous parcels).

[75]*See, e.g.*, McLeod v. County of Santa Clara, 749 F.2d 541 (9th Cir. 1984), *cert. denied*, 472 U.S. 1009 (1985); McAndrews v. Fleet Bank of Mass., 796 F. Supp. 613 (D. Mass. 1992), *aff'd*, 989 F.2d 13 (1st Cir. 1993); Zilber v. Town of Moraga, 692 F. Supp. 1195, 1204–05 (N.D. Cal. 1988).

[76]*See, e.g.*, Spears v. Berle, 422 N.Y.S.2d 636, 640, 397 N.E.2d 1304, (1979); Pecora v. Gossin, 356 N.Y.S.2d 505 (1974), *aff'd*, 370 N.Y.S.2d 281, 49 A.D.2d 668 (1975).

[77]74 N.Y.2d 92, 544 N.Y.S.2d 542 N.E.2d 1059, 550–51 (1989).

[78]*See also* Manocherian v. Lenox Hill Hosp., 84 N.Y.2d 385, 400, 643 N.E.2d 479 (1994), *cert. denied,* 514 U.S. 1109 (1995) (destruction of reversionary property interest can trigger regulatory taking).

separately.[79] Several other California cases, on the other hand, have viewed the relevant parcel issue expansively and, on that basis, have declined to find a taking.[80]

Key Issues in the "Relevant Parcel" Inquiry

A number of issues arise in the course of the relevant parcel inquiry. One relates to the nature of the property interest being asserted. A review of the pertinent cases reveals that the courts are far more likely to view the denominator issue broadly if real property is involved than if the nature of the property interest is a more discrete interest such as a water, mining, or grazing right, or similar property right. Most jurisdictions seem fully prepared, for example, to view a claimed water right separate from the land to which that right is appurtenant,[81] and an asserted right to maintain a billboard independently from the parcel of land on which it is located.[82]

A second issue derives from the fact that how broadly the judiciary views the relevant property interest quite often depends on the nature of the property right being circumscribed by governmental action. Stated another way, some "sticks" in the property rights "bundle"

[79]Twain Harte Assoc., Ltd. v. County of Tuolumne, 217 Cal. App. 3d 71, 85–88, 265 Cal. Rptr. 737, 744–45 (1990).

[80]See, e.g., Aptos Seascape Corp. v. County of Santa Cruz, 138 Cal. App. 3d 484, 497, 188 Cal. Rptr. 191, 197 (1982), appeal dismissed, 464 U.S. 805 (1983); City & County of San Francisco v. Golden Gate Heights Inv., 14 Cal. App. 4th 1203, 1209, 18 Cal. Rptr. 2d 467 (1993), cert. denied, 510 U.S. 928; Ramona Convent of Holy Names v. City of Alhambra, 21 Cal. App. 4th 10, 26 Cal. Rptr. 2d 140 (1993), cert. denied, 513 U.S. 927 (1993). See also K&K Construction, Inc. v. Department of Natural Resources, 456 Mich. 570, 581 n.6, 575 N.W. 2d 531, 537 N.6 (1998) (separate zoning of separate parcels irrelevant because owner had intended to use all three parcels in one development plan); American Dredging Co. v. Department of Envtl. Quality 169 N.J. Super 18, 404 A.2d 42, 43–44 (N.J. Super Ct. App. Div. 1979); State Dept. of Envtl. Regulation v. Schindler, 604 So. 2d 565, 567–68 (Fla. 1992) (accord); Zealy v. City of Waukesha, 201 Wis. 2d 365, 548 N.W.2d 528 (1996).

[81]See Fallini v. United States, 31 Fed. Cl. 53, 57 (1994), vacated, 56 F.3d 1378 (Fed. Cir. 1995), cert. denied, 517 U.S. 1243 (1996).

[82]See, e.g., Patrick Media Group v. California Coastal Comm'n, 9 Cal. App. 4th 592, 11 Cal. Rptr. 2d 824 (1992); Tahoe Regional Planning Agency v. King, 233 Cal. App. 3d 1365, 285 Cal. Rptr. 335 (1991); Naegele Outdoor Advertising, Inc. v. City of Durham, 844 F.2d 172 (4th Cir. 1988).

are apparently worth more than others under the Takings Clause. Courts are particularly sensitive to those "sticks" which constitute an "essential attribute of ownership." The U.S. Supreme Court has repeatedly so characterized, for example, the owner's right to exclude others and has been willing to define the relevant property interest rather narrowly when the regulation at issue impinges upon that right.[83] The Court has similarly portrayed the right to devise private property.[84] It is therefore unsurprising that in each of these cases, the Court has found an unconstitutional taking when that "essential attribute of property" has been infringed upon by government regulation.

A third issue that arises in denominator-related litigation pertains to the often-multidimensional aspect of the inquiry. The relevant parcel can, for example, be considered "horizontally," e.g., are the affected parcels geographically contiguous or dispersed, commonly or disparately zoned? But the relevant parcel can also be viewed "vertically"; that, after all, was how the issue arose in *Penn Central*, where the landowner sought to view the air rights independently from the existing, low-rise structure. Subsurface mining rights can raise the same concerns.[85]

The relevant property interest can also be viewed in *temporal* terms. At what point in time, for example, should the relevant parcel be defined: when the property restrictions took effect, when the current owner acquired the property interest, etc.?[86] In the case of temporary moratoria, should the moratorium period be viewed in isolation in cases where governmental restrictions precede or follow it?[87] Finally, when government exercises its police power to re-create conditions extant at a prior time (such as when reintroducing animal

---

[83]*See, e.g.*, Kaiser Aetna v. United States, 444 U.S. 164 (1979); Nollan v. California Coastal Comm'n, 483 U.S. 825 (1987); Dolan v. City of Tigard, 512 U.S. 374 (1994).

[84]Babbitt v. Youpee, 519 U.S. 1232, 117 S. Ct. 727 (1997); Hodel v. Irving, 481 U.S. 704 (1987).

[85]Keystone Bituminous Coal Ass'n v. DeBenedictis, 480 U.S. 470 (1987).

[86]*See, e.g.*, Loveladies Harbor, Inc. v. United States, 21 Cl. Ct. 193 (1988), *aff'd*, 28 F.3d 1171 (Fed. Cir. 1994).

[87]*See, e.g.*, Tahoe Sierra Preservation Council v. Tahoe Regional Planning Agency, 808 F. Supp. 1474 (D. Nev. 1992), *aff'd in part and rev'd in part*, 34 F.3d 753 (9th Cir. 1994), *amended*, 42 F.3d 1360 (9th Cir. 1994), *cert. denied*, 514 U.S. 1036 (1995); Woodbury Place Partners v. City of Woodbury, 492 N.W.2d 258 (Minn. 1992), *cert denied*, 508 U.S. 960 (1993).

species to their historic range(s)), are the public and private interests appropriately considered in light of those historic conditions or as of the present time?[88]

"Ad hoc-ery" Versus Objective Criteria to Determine the Relevant Parcel

Despite the critical nature of the relevant parcel inquiry, few courts have attempted to establish guidelines or an analytical framework that would assist in resolving the issue in particular cases. Instead, most reported decisions that have addressed the issue at all simply state that an ad hoc, fact-based inquiry is required. In *Loveladies Harbor, Inc. v. United States*,[89] the Federal Circuit indicated that it would adhere to a flexible approach to account for factual variances in particular cases. Similarly, the court in *Tabb Lakes, Ltd. v. United States*,[90] eschewed determining as a matter of law a definition of the "whole parcel," in favor of a fact-based inquiry.

One of the few decisions that attempts to create *some* legal guidance as to the relevant parcel conundrum is *Ciampitti v. United States*.[91] In that wetlands/regulatory takings case, the Court of Federal Claims identified several factors in determining the relevant parcel: the degree of contiguity of the various property interests; the date(s) on which the property interests were acquired; the extent to which the parcel(s) have been treated as a single unit, both by the landowner and government regulators; and the extent to which the lands rendered undevelopable by government regulation enhance the value of the remaining, less-restricted lands.[92] To these might be added: the reasonable expectations of the property owner (i.e., at the time the investment was made or the property purchased); economic efficiency; and whether or not the landowner has combined otherwise unrelated parcels into a single unit for purposes unrelated to the inverse condemnation action.[93]

---

[88]*See, e.g.*, Moerman v. California, 17 Cal. App. 4th 452, 21 Cal. Rptr. 2d 329 (1993), *cert. denied*, 511 U.S. 1031 (1994) (rejecting taking claim for property damage arising out of Tule elk relocation program).

[89]28 F.3d 1171, 1181 (Fed. Cir. 1994).

[90]10 F.3d 796 (Fed. Cir. 1993).

[91]22 Cl. Ct. 310 (1991).

[92]*Id.* at 318.

[93]*See also* Zealy v. City of Waukesha, 201 Wis. 2d 365, 548 N.W.2d 528, 533 (1996).

Disparate Views on the Denominator Issue

The discordant conclusions that various courts have reached on the relevant parcel question are perhaps most starkly illustrated by the contrasting, decisions of two U.S. Circuit Courts of Appeals.

In *Florida Rock Industries, Inc. v. United States*, 18 F.3d 1560 (Fed. Cir. 1994), *cert. denied,* 115 S. Ct. 898 (1995), the dispute concerned the U.S. Army Corps of Engineers' refusal to issue a dredge-and-fill permit under section 404 of the Clean Water Act that would have allowed the private property owner to extract limestone from a 98-acre wetlands parcel. The Federal Circuit reversed the Court of Federal Claims' earlier finding of a compensable taking and remanded the case to the latter court for further factual deliberations. In so doing, however, the majority opinion analogized the case to physical invasion case law to suggest that the relevant property interest in regulatory takings cases can and should be construed quite narrowly:

> By taking some portion of Florida Rock's economic use of the property—its power to disturb the overlying wetlands, and with it the common law property right to mine its subsurface minerals—the Government appears to have destroyed *part of* the value of Florida Rock's holdings. If that proves to be the case, and if the application of the *ad hoc* tests previously described so warrant, the property interest taken belongs to the Government, and the right to just compensation for the interest taken belongs to Florida Rock. (18 F.3d at 1572 (emphasis added).)

The Federal Circuit elaborated on the point by noting that:

> Identification of a specific property interest to be transferred to the Government should pose little problem for property lawyers. Property interests are about as diverse as the human mind can conceive. (18 F.3d at 1572, n.32.)

This somewhat novel philosophy on the denominator issue drew a vigorous dissent, which argued that the majority's views were inconsistent with prior Supreme Court precedent. (*Id.* at 1573, 1578–79 (Nies, C.J., dissenting)).

The view articulated by the Federal Circuit majority in *Florida Rock* stands in stark contrast to the Tenth Circuit's decision in *Clajon Production Corp. v. Petera,* 70 F.3d 1566 (10th Cir. 1995). In *Clajon,* the dispute concerned the State of Wyoming's strict limits on the number of hunting permits that could be issued to out-of-state hunters. Wyoming ranch owners who depend heavily on out-of-state hunters for their clientele challenged the permit limits under the Takings Clause:

> Plaintiffs argue that the complete evisceration of a single stick in the bundle of property rights—i.e., the right to hunt on one's property—can constitute such a taking. The linchpin of this argument is Plaintiffs' contention that courts can and should analyze each stick in the bundle of property rights separately in order to determine whether the regulation at issue effects a taking of a given stick. [citing *Florida Rock*] Plaintiffs argue that we must focus only on [the Wyoming law's] impact on their property "right to hunt." Therefore, Plaintiffs continue, their "right to hunt" is the appropriate denominator for our determination of whether [the restriction] deprives them of complete beneficial use of their property. (70 F.3d at 1577.)

A unanimous Tenth Circuit disagreed, concluding that *Florida Rock* departs from longstanding U.S. Supreme Court jurisprudence on the denominator question:

> "[W]e believe that the relevant denominator must be derived from the entire bundle of rights associated with the parcel of land. [citing *Penn Central* and *Keystone Bituminous Coal*] Thus, we reject the *Florida Rock* approach and adhere to the more traditional analysis outlined in *Penn Central.* (*Ibid.*)

The result is an inter-circuit conflict on a constitutional issue of considerable moment. Juxtaposition of the *Florida Rock* and *Clajon* decisions reflects a desultory fact of life for the planners, lawyers, and decision-makers who labor in the land-use vineyard: absent further clarification from the U.S. Supreme Court, it is difficult if not impossible to discern many of the applicable ground rules in regulatory takings law.

Until the courts provide greater certainty to the denominator debate, they will likely continue to address the relevant parcel issue in disparate fashion.[94] The question is certain to arise with considerable frequency, given its critical importance to resolution of the ultimate issue of taking liability. Pending some definitive resolution,

> [O]ne thing is clear—as a strategic matter, property owners will always claim that a destruction of one strand of the owners bundle of rights or loss of the ability to develop one portion of the property is a taking. Conversely, government will always attempt to show that what has been destroyed is minor when compared to the value of the property as a whole.[95]

The above-quoted commentators distill the current precedents to conclude: "At this point, when the right to exclude others is not implicated and zoning or other land-use controls are involved, the courts still tend to apply the classic 'whole parcel' focus articulated in *Penn Central.*"[96]

Judicial Takings

Can *courts* "take" property?

It is by now well settled that the legislative branch of government can affect a compensable taking of property purely through enactment of a statute[97]; that the executive branch can trigger a Fifth Amendment taking when it carries out government police powers[98]; and that the executive and legislative branches can suffer joint liability in some circumstances where the former implements an unconstitutional statutory program enacted by the latter.[99] Far less clear is

---

[94]Legislatures have a potential role to play here as well. At least two state legislatures have attempted to codify the relevant parcel concept. *See* chapter 34.

[95]Daniel Reisel & Steven Barshov, "When Does Government Regulation Go 'Too Far,'" *reprinted as part of the program materials for Environmental Litigation* (SA 85ALI-ABA June 1996) at 14.

[96]*Id.*

[97]Hodel v. Irving, 481 U.S. 704 (1987) (Indian Land Consolidation Act).

[98]Nollan v. California Coastal Comm'n, 483 U.S. 825 (1987) (imposed coastal access condition insufficiently related to police power).

[99]Lucas v. South Carolina Coastal Council, 505 U.S. 1003 (1992) (addressing constitutionality of building setback requirements mandated by state's Beachfront Management Act and enforced by state land-use agency).

whether the *judiciary* can similarly contravene the Takings Clause. The relatively few reported decisions which have addressed the point fail to chart a clear course.

The starting point, and the Supreme Court opinion which most explicitly suggests that courts can "take" property, is the Court's 1967 decision in *Hughes v. Washington*.[100] The issue in *Hughes* was the question of whether federal or state law controlled in a riparian landowner's boundary dispute with the State of Washington. The Washington State Supreme Court had previously held that state law controlled, under which the land at issue was owned by the state. The U.S. Supreme Court disagreed, finding that federal law applied and that under the federal boundary rules the riparian owner prevailed.

It is the concurring opinion of Justice Potter Stewart, however, which is significant for present purposes. Justice Stewart expressed concern about the Fifth Amendment consequences of the Washington Supreme Court's state law rule. Stewart opined that by interpreting Washington state law in a manner which dispossessed the riparian owner of his title claim, the Washington Supreme Court may effect a compensable taking. Observed Stewart, "a State cannot be permitted to defeat the constitutional prohibition against taking property without due process of law by the simple device of asserting retroactively that the property it has taken never existed at all."[101] He concluded with the admonition that "the Due Process Clause of the Fourteenth Amendment forbids such confiscation by a State, no less through its courts than through its legislature. . . ."[102]

Justice Stewart's ruminations are dicta, not binding on any state or federal court. Nevertheless, the concept he identified over three decades ago has intrigued academicians and caught the attention of at least a few lower courts.

The principle of judicial takings received its most enthusiastic reception in long-fought litigation over Hawaiian water rights. In a major 1973 water rights decision, *McBryde Sugar Co. v. Robinson*, the Supreme Court of Hawaii overruled prior, contrary case law and adopted as the state law of Hawaii the English common law doctrine of riparian rights.[103] A subsequent, related case brought in federal district court in Hawaii, *Robinson v. Ariyoshi*, involved a dispute over rights to water diverted from a river on the island of Kauai. One

[100]389 U.S. 290 (1967).
[101]*Id.* at 296–97 (Stewart, J., concurring).
[102]*Id.* at 298.
[103]54 Haw. 174, 504 P.2d 1330 (1973), *cert. denied*, 417 U.S. 976 (1974).

of the theories advanced by Robinson, the agricultural landowner plaintiff, was that the state court decision in *McBryde* had made a radical change in that state's water rights law, which in turn deprived Robinson of his constitutionally protected rights under the now-discredited Hawaiian water rights system. The federal district court agreed, finding that the state supreme court had effectively taken Robinson's property when it rendered its decision in *McBryde*.[104]

On appeal, the Ninth Circuit affirmed, characterizing the question as being whether the "state, by a judicial decision which creates a major change in property law, [can] divest property interests?"[105] The federal court of appeals first noted that the Supreme Court of Hawaii was "acting well within its judicial power under the state constitution when it overruled earlier cases and declared for the first time, after more than a century of different law, that the common law doctrine of riparian ownership was the law of Hawaii. . . . New law, however, cannot divest rights that were vested before the court announced the new law."[106] The Ninth Circuit concluded that Robinson had in fact acquired a vested right to divert water and, as such, "cannot be divested of this right without just compensation."[107] Instead, said the appellate court, the State of Hawaii must bring "condemnation proceedings before it can interfere with vested water rights and the enjoyment of the improvements made in reliance thereon."[108]

The precedential effect of *Robinson v. Ariyoshi* is seriously clouded by the fact that the Ninth Circuit's decision was subsequently vacated and remanded by the U.S. Supreme Court for consideration of whether the takings claim was ripe for judicial review.[109] On remand, the court of appeals concluded that Robinson's takings challenge was indeed premature inasmuch as the Hawaiian state courts had not yet issued a final decision that "interfered in any way with the parties' use of diversions" of water claimed to be theirs.[110]

Other courts have taken a more skeptical view of the notion of judicial takings. Illustrative is the decision of the Court of Appeals for

---

[104]Robinson v. Ariyoshi, 441 F. Supp. 559, 585–86 (D. Haw. 1977). *See also* Sotomura v. County of Hawaii, 460 F. Supp. 473, 482–83 (D. Haw. 1978).

[105]Robinson v. Ariyoshi, 753 F.2d 1468, 1471 (9th Cir. 1985).

[106]*Id.* at 1474.

[107]*Id.*

[108]*Id.* at 1475.

[109]Ariyoshi v. Robinson, 477 U.S. 902 (1986).

[110]Robinson v. Ariyoshi, 887 F.2d 215, 219 (9th Cir. 1989).

the Fifth Circuit in *Reynolds v. Georgia*, in which that federal tribunal rejected the Ninth Circuit's holding in *Robinson* and instead applied long-standing jurisdictional principles to bar a collateral attack on an alleged judicial taking by a state court.[111]

Several state and federal courts have simply raised the legal issue without finding the need to resolve it. Illustrative is the District of Columbia Circuit's 1987 decision in *Corporation of the Presiding Bishop of the Church of Latter-Day Saints v. Hodel*.[112] In that case a church had purchased land in American Samoa in 1953. When the church filed a trespass action against a native Samoan family in 1979, the High Court of American Samoa determined that the church lacked legal title to the land. The church then challenged the High Court's ruling in federal district court; one ground of that challenge was that by "failing to recognize the rights that had thus vested in the Church . . . the High Court 'violated the Church's rights under both the due process and taking clause of the Fifth Amendment.'"[113]

The federal district court rejected the church's taking claim "on the ground that a court cannot 'take' property when it resolves a title dispute between private parties."[114] On appeal, the church moderated its position somewhat, claiming that a judicial action which meets the test of "gross or arbitrary error" raises a valid claim of judicial taking. The District of Columbia Circuit responded as follows:

> The question of whether courts, as opposed to legislative bodies, can ever "take" property in violation of the Fifth Amendment is an interesting and by no means a settled issue of law. We have no occasion, however, to decide this issue today. Under appellant's own criteria, a judicial action cannot qualify as a "taking" absent "gross" or "arbitrary" error. If there was no such error . . . then there was no taking under appellant's own analysis.[115]

[111]640 F.2d 702, 707 n.2 (5th Cir. 1981), *cert. denied*, 454 U.S. 865 (1981). *See also* Scogin v. United States, 33 Fed. Cl. 285, 291 (1995). The Ninth Circuit has itself recently suggested some equivocation regarding the judicial takings principles it espoused in *Robinson*. *See* Kesselring v. F/T Arctic Hero, 30 F.3d 1123, 1126 (9th Cir. 1994) (rejecting claim that judicial enforcement of seaman's wage liens constitutes taking).

[112]830 F.2d 374 (D.C. Cir. 1987), *cert. denied*, 486 U.S. 1015 (1988).

[113]*Id.* at 379.

[114]*Id.* at 381 (quoting district court decision). Reported at 637 F. Supp. 1398 (D.D.C. 1986).

[115]*Id.* at 381.

The court of appeals found the complained of decision failed to meet this standard of error.[116]

State courts on several occasions have similarly raised the issue—without deciding it—of whether courts can take property.[117] Some of these decisions imply a fair degree of antipathy toward the concept of judicial takings, however.

Numerous arguments have been advanced by academics both in support of and in opposition to the notion of judicial takings. Proponents argue that the Takings Clause does not distinguish among the various branches of government, and that the Constitution has been extended to state judicial decisions in certain other contexts, such as racial discrimination and freedom of speech.[118] Skeptics counter with several points: that courts serve simply as neutral arbiters over disputes between litigants; that courts don't "create" new law but simply discern what the correct law should be (and theoretically always was); etc.[119]

Two aspects of judicial takings theory seem especially problematic. The first is that courts whose decisions are declared (by other courts) to have "taken" private property, unlike the legislative and executive branches, possess no source of revenue with which to compensate aggrieved property owners. This would seem to present a major conceptual and practical problem, inasmuch as the Supreme Court has now decreed that money damages are a constitutionally required remedy in a regulatory takings case.

Second, and even more compelling, are the federalism implications of judicial takings theory. Most judicial takings claims, if deemed viable, would likely play out in precisely the manner that they did in Hawaii: disaffected litigants who lose in state court will seek a second bite of the judicial apple by filing a new claim in federal court, claiming that the state judiciary (rather than the party who originally contested their claim) "took" their property and now must pay com-

---

[116]*Id.*

[117]*See, e.g.,* California v. Superior Ct. (Lovelace), 11 Cal. 4th 50, 76, 900 P.2d 648 (1995); National Audubon Soc'y v. Superior Ct., 33 Cal. 3d 419, 440 n.22, 658 P.2d 709 (1983), *cert. denied,* 464 U.S. 977 (1983); *See also,* Village of Wilsonville v. SDA Sers, 86 Ill. 2d 1, 426 N.E. 2d 824, 841 (1981).

[118]*See* Barton H. Thompson, *Judicial Takings,* 76 VIRGINIA L. REV. 1449 (1990).

[119]*Id.*

pensation. This would seem to constitute a most serious intrusion into state affairs, especially since it is by now well settled that federal courts are not especially well suited to interpret and apply state property law principles.[120] Such "horizontal" federal court review of state court decisions has been generally disapproved by the U.S. Supreme Court.[121] In the past few years, the U.S. Supreme Court has expressed heightened concerns about federal court intrusions upon the state judicial process, invoking general principles of federalism.[122]

The notion that courts can affect a regulatory taking of private property is provocative. Nevertheless, it seems unlikely for reasons both practical and philosophical that the concept of judicial takings will generate broad support from the courts.

Regulatory "Givings"

We conclude this chapter by identifying a nascent notion of inverse condemnation law: the notion of "regulatory givings."

It is axiomatic that government regulation produces winners and losers. By proscribing development on parcel A, a community general plan necessarily enhances the economic value of parcel B. And if government builds a publicly financed subway system or freeway interchange, those fortunate enough to own property in the immediate vicinity will similarly experience a consequential appreciation in land value. These actions of government can be characterized as "givings." The concept of regulatory "givings" is related to the "reciprocity of advantage" principle identified by Justice Holmes in *Pennsylvania Coal* and discussed previously. In a sense, then, we have come full circle in our travels through the law of regulatory takings.

However, inverse condemnation principles are decidedly one-sided. Regulatory takings law focuses primarily on the *negative*

---

[120]Lucas v. South Carolina Coastal Council, 505 U.S. 1003, 1029 (1992); *see also,* Arizonans for Official English v. Arizona, 117 S. Ct. 1055, 1073–74 (1997).

[121]Rooker v. Fidelity Trust Co., 263 U.S. 413 (1923); District of Columbia Ct. of Appeals v. Feldman, 460 U.S. 462 (1983); Reynolds v. Georgia, 640 F.2d 702, 706 (5th Cir. 1981).

[122]Arizonans for Official English, 117 S. Ct. 1055 (1997); *cf.* Printz v. United States, 117 S. Ct. 2365 (1997).

economic impacts government decisions can have on private property
and tends to ignore the salutary effects of government givings.[123]

Some jurists and scholars advocate reforms in regulatory takings
principles that would address this conceptual imbalance. In his dissent in *Dolan v. City of Tigard,* for example, Supreme Court Justice
John Paul Stevens suggested that regulatory givings should be factored into the takings equation.[124]

The seminal academic treatment of this subject is *Windfalls for
Wipeouts,* a thoughtful work co-authored by Dean Misczynski and
the late Donald Hagman.[125] More recently, other proponents of a
more balanced economic approach to regulatory takings principles
have also stepped forward.[126]

Translating this kind of economic theory into jurisprudential reality remains a formidable challenge. Seemingly most daunting are
the questions of precisely how government "givings" would be quan-
tified, and how monetary transfers from regulatory "winners" to regulatory "losers" could feasibly be effectuated. Difficult issues, to be
sure. But an intriguing note on which to conclude this discussion of
regulatory takings.

[123]By contrast, the law relating to *direct* condemnation is beginning to recognize and incorporate the favorable economic impact of public works on adjacent
private property. *See, e.g.,* Los Angeles County Metro. Transp. Auth. v. Continental Dev. Corp., 16 Cal. 4th 694, 94 P.2d 809 (1997) (government may reduce
eminent domain damages by deducting increased value its public works project
brings to adjacent parcel).

[124]512 U.S. 374 at 399–400 (1994) (Stevens, J., dissenting), *See also* Jordan
v. Village of Menomonee Falls, 28 Wis. 2d 608, 619–20, 137 N.W. 2d 442
(1965); Collis v. Bloomington, 310 Minn. 5, 11–13, 246 N.W.2d 19, 448
(1976).

[125]DONALD HAGMAN & DEAN MISCZYNSKI, WINDFALLS FOR WIPEOUTS: LAND
VALUE CAPTURE AND COMPENSATION (American Planning Ass'n 1978).

[126]Donald Elliot, *Givings and Takings,* LAND USE LAW & PLANNING DIGEST
Jan. 1996 at 3.

Chapter 13

Date of the Taking

Not uncommonly, a taking case stands or falls on a single, mundane, historical issue: the date of the alleged taking. Who is a proper plaintiff, whether the time for filing an action has expired, and other make-or-break questions can turn on this unglamorous item. But though obvious in many takings cases, the precise date on which the taking should be deemed to have occurred can be elusive in others. This chapter deals with the twin questions of how courts fix the date of taking (as sometimes said: "when the taking cause of action accrues"), and the many important consequences of that date.

Determining the Date of Taking

When government interference with private property comes about in a single bold stroke of unequivocal application to a particular property owner, the date of the taking is blessedly clear. Suppose, for example, that the U.S. Army Corps of Engineers rejects a wetlands permit application. The legal impact of the government action hits with full force on that date, particularly since the wetland owner has no administrative recourse.[1] Similarly, the effective date of an agency rule that applies to the property owner without further agency action would be the date of any taking, even if it takes some time before its

[1]Even in this straightforward circumstance, there may be exceptions. *See, e.g.,* Marks v. United States, 34 Fed. Cl. 387 (1995) (statute of limitations on temporary taking claim begins to run not upon denial of wetland permit, but rather upon later court decision resolving plaintiff's property interest), *aff'd without opinion*, 116 F.3d 1496 (Fed. Cir. 1997), *cert. denied*, 118 S. Ct. 852 (1998).

impact becomes pronounced. And not surprisingly, when the alleged taking is in the form of a physical invasion or entry into possession by the government, the cause of action arises at the time of the physical invasion or entry.[2]

But in many cases, the taking date is not so neat and clean.[3] Overlapping to a great extent with ripeness analysis (chapter 5), the date-of-taking determination may require the court to examine whether the property owner, following denial of a land development approval, has exhausted available avenues for variances and special exceptions. Murkier is when it appears that the government, though rejecting the landowner's initial development proposal, might yet approve a scaled-down version of it. How many rejections before the taking occurs? Or, the question may arise whether a particular statute's effect can be adequately gauged in the absence of any implementing administrative action at all.[4]

Other situations obscuring the date of taking happen where the full legal consequences of a government edict do not take effect for a while,[5] where enforcement occurs through a series of escalating actions against a landowner, or where the existence or nature of the property interest in question is not immediately clear.[6]

In other instances, the date of taking is uncertain because the phys-

---

[2]*See, e.g.,* Martin v. United States, 30 Fed. Cl. 542, *aff'd by unpub. op.* 41 F.3d 1519 (Fed. Cir. 1994); Carr v. Town of Fleming, 122 A.D.2d 540, 504 N.Y.S.2d 904 (1986).

[3]*See, e.g.,* Catellus Dev. Corp. v. United States, 31 Fed. Cl. 399 (1994) (fixing date of taking "must often be done in a somewhat imprecise manner").

[4]*Cf.* Whitney Benefits, Inc. v. United States, 18 Cl. Ct. 394, 406–07 (1989) (enactment of surface mining statute constitutes date of taking, where later denial of permit required under statute was "mere formality"), *aff'd,* 926 F.2d 1169 (Fed. Cir.), *cert. denied,* 502 U.S. 952 (1991) *with* Chevy Chase Land Co. v. United States, 37 Fed. Cl. 545 (1997) (enactment of "rails-to-trails" statute is not date of taking, since implementing events must occur before impact on plaintiff is known).

[5]*See, e.g.,* Naegele Outdoor Advertising, Inc. v. City of Winston-Salem, 340 N.C. 349, 457 S.E.2d 874 (1995) (cause of action arose on date zoning ordinance enacted, rather than at end of amortization period for bringing billboards into compliance).

[6]*See, e.g.,* Marks v. United States, 34 Fed. Cl. 387 (1995), *aff'd without opinion,* 116 F.3d 1496 (Fed. Cir. 1997), *cert. denied,* 118 S. Ct. 852 (1998); W.H. Pugh Coal Co. v. State, 157 Wis. 2d 620, 460 N.W.2d 787 (1990) (taking claim accrued when plaintiff prevailed in earlier litigation), *review denied,* 464 N.W.2d 423 (1990).

ical situation that is the basis for the claim is an evolving one. A common example is the gradual growth, over several decades, in an airport's physical size and the daily number of flights, plus increases in the size and noisiness of aircraft operating there.[7] In such a case, courts may affix the taking label to any discrete event giving rise to a significant increase in the level of property owner injury. Plainly, there is the possibility in many long-term scenarios of multiple taking dates.

With physical takings, there may be an issue whether the intrusion is a one-time aberration; hence at best a tort. A taking does not occur, say most courts, until the invasion first appears to be permanent or regularly recurring. Paradigmatically, this is the government flooding case: The government dam causes one flood of the landowner's property, then another, then another. Only when flooding is "inevitably recurring," say most courts, is there a taking.[8] Judging from the federal flooding cases at least, this requirement is better phrased as "sufficiently frequent" flooding that is almost annual, or more frequent, is often held a taking,[9] while flooding that occurs less often is rarely so held.[10]

The other common issue with physical takings concerns not the frequency of government action, but its extent. Sticking with the flooding prototype, when is the full scope of the physical invasion known? The rule, as stated in *United States v. Dickinson*, is that the date of taking is when "the situation becomes stabilized."[11] In this way, a landowner may postpone suit until the consequences of the government action "have so manifested themselves that a final account may be struck."[12]

How far *Dickinson* extends beyond the recurring flooding case,

[7]*See* further discussion in chapter 21.

[8]United States v. Cress, 243 U.S. 316, 318, 328–29 (1917); Turner v. United States, 17 Cl. Ct. 832 (1989), *rev'd on other grounds*, 901 F.2d 1093 (Fed. Cir. 1990).

[9]*See, e.g.,* Barnes v. United States, 538 F.2d 865 (Ct. Cl. 1976).

[10]*See, e.g.,* Baird v. United States, 5 Cl. Ct. 324, 329 (1984). "It is settled that a single flood does not, nor indeed one, two, or three floods by themselves do not, constitute a taking," said Singleton v. United States. 6 Cl. Ct. 156, 162–63 (1984).

[11]331 U.S. 745, 749 (1947).

[12]*Id. See, e.g.,* Cooper v. United States, 827 F.2d 762 (Fed. Cir. 1987) (claim for taking of timber accrued when government-caused flooding ended *and* extent of timber damage could be ascertained); McDonald v. United States, 37 Fed. Cl. 110 (1997) (same), *aff'd without pub. op.*, 135 F.3d 778 (Fed. Cir. 1998).

however, is a long-fought and still unsettled issue. A decade later, the Supreme Court gave it a narrow reading,[13] and the important Court of Appeals for the Federal Circuit seems to have fallen in line.[14] Judicial acceptance of the *Dickinson* holding in cases arising outside the context of physical takings is particularly qualified. The concern is that read too broadly, the doctrine may overly delay the ripening of claims, and hence relief for property owners, whenever the extent or effects of the government action (or resulting damages) is not immediate and full blown.[15] Thus, it is fairly settled right now that the damages from the taking need not be complete and fully calculable before the cause of action accrues.[16] Still, some minimal insistence by the courts as to the certainty and stability of the government action's impact seems inevitable.

Consequences of the Date of Taking

Why do we care when the date of the taking falls? No less than three independent reasons.

First, the date on which the taking cause of action ripens determines who may maintain the action and collect compensation. Only those with an ownership interest as of the date of taking, not those holding interests only before or afterwards, may do so.[17] The rationale is straightforward: Only the owner on the taking date suffers a loss. A subsequent buyer is presumed to have purchased at a dis-

---

[13]United States v. Dow, 357 U.S. 17, 27 (1958).

[14]Fallini v. United States, 56 F.3d 1378, 1381 (Fed. Cir. 1995) (in *Dow*, Supreme Court "more or less limited [*Dickinson*] to the class of flooding cases to which it belonged"), *cert. denied*, 517 U.S. 1243 (1996). *See* Applegate v. United States, 25 F.3d 1579 (Fed. Cir. 1994) (*Dickinson* stabilization rule applies to government-caused erosion from private beach).

[15]*See, e.g.,* Persyn v. United States, 34 Fed. Cl. 187 (1995) (continually expanding airport operations), *aff'd without pub. op.*, 106 F.3d 424 (Fed. Cir. 1996), *cert. denied*, 117 S. Ct. 1697 (1997).

[16]*Fallini*, 56 F.3d at 1382 (enactment of statute protecting wild horses, not their continuous drinking of plaintiff's well water in subsequent years, constituted taking).

[17]*Dow*, 357 U.S. at 20–21 (1958); Cooper v. United States, 827 F.2d 762, 764 (Fed. Cir. 1987). Finding the roots of this requirement in the personal injury component of constitutional standing analysis is Maniere v. United States, 31 Fed. Cl. 410, 420 (1994).

counted price reflecting the government action; to compensate the buyer would be to confer a windfall. Where the facts show otherwise, however, as when the buyer was not reasonably on notice of the pre-purchase taking and the seller was never compensated, courts have been known to abandon the owner-at-date-of-taking rule and award damages to the post-taking buyer.[18]

Second, the date of taking starts the running of the statute of limitations.[19] Takings plaintiffs, like others, often wait too long before acting. However, where the limitations period as reckoned from the start of the conflict has expired, hope is not necessarily lost for the property owner. Plaintiffs may nonetheless be able to pin the taking label on some more recent event, thus resurrecting the action, at least for damages occurring since that event.[20]

Third, the taking date defines how much money the property owner gets—in two ways. Under the Fifth Amendment, the amount of compensation owed is the market value of the property at the time the taking occurs. Thus, for example, improvements placed on property after the date of taking may not be eligible for compensation.[21] In addition, the taking date begins the period during which interest on the compensation award accumulates. Such interest, sometimes called "delay compensation," is required by the Takings Clause in order to put the plaintiff in as good a position now as if compensation had been paid contemporaneously with the taking. Other factors aside, one supposes that to maximize the awarded interest, plaintiffs should argue for a date of taking as early as possible within the limitations period.

[18]See, e.g., Vern Reynolds Constr., Inc. v. City of Champlin, 539 N.W.2d 614 (Minn. App.), review denied (1995); Upper Eagle Valley Sanitation Dist. v. Carnie, 634 P.2d 1008 (Colo. App. 1981). Cf. Hoover v. Pierce County, 79 Wash. App. 427, 903 P.2d 464 (1995) (purchaser denied recovery for flooding conditions, since he knew or should have known of condition when property was bought), review denied, 129 Wash. 2d 1007, 917 P.2d 129 (1996).

[19]See fuller discussion of the date of taking for purposes of the statute of limitations in chapter 6.

[20]See, e.g., Townsend v. State, 117 N.M. 302, 871 P.2d 958 (N.M. 1994) (rejecting state's argument that limitations period should run from first time state entered plaintiff's land to remove gravel; each subsequent act of removal gave rise to new taking).

[21]See, e.g., Jones v. United States, 1 Cl. Ct. 329 (1983) (recovery denied for irrigation system installed after it was apparent that government-caused flooding permanent).

Chapter 14

Exceptions to Takings

Over the past century, courts have developed principles under which some types of government action, regardless of their economic impact on private property, will not be considered compensable takings. While these "exceptions" to takings most commonly arise in the context of regulatory takings claims, they can come into play in physical takings cases as well.

Historically, these exceptions were diffuse, of amorphous parameters, and difficult to place in the takings paradigm. The U.S. Supreme Court clarified matters significantly in its 1992 decision, *Lucas v. South Carolina Coastal Council*.[1] After first establishing a presumption that regulatory action which totally eliminates private property's economic value triggers a compensable taking, the *Lucas* majority then proceeded to limit that presumption:

> Where the State seeks to sustain regulation that deprives land of all economically beneficial use, we think it may resist compensation only if the logically antecedent inquiry into the nature of the owner's estate shows that the proscribed use interests were not part of his title to begin with. This accords, we think, with our "takings" jurisprudence, which has traditionally been guided by the understandings of our citizens regarding the content of, and the State's power over, the "bundle of rights" that they acquire when they obtain the property.[2]

[1]505 U.S. 1003.
[2]*Id.* at 1027 (footnote omitted).

The Court thus made a critical analytical point: Before a court can determine whether private property has been "taken" by virtue of governmental action, it must know what the nature and parameters of that property interest are. This "logically antecedent inquiry" will sometimes indicate that the affected private property right is limited as a result of circumstances that are wholly independent of, and predate or transcend, the government action being challenged. Stated differently, government cannot "take" a property interest that the private claimant never legitimately possessed.

Lucas went further, identifying two broad categories of exceptions to the Takings Clause, categories that independently limit the "bundle of rights" the private party brings to the taking conflict. The first involves proposed uses of private property that contravene traditional notions—and limitations—found in state and federal property law:

> In light of our traditional resort to "existing rules or understandings that stem from an independent source such as state law" to define the range of interests that qualify for protection as "property" under the Fifth and Fourteenth Amendments [citations omitted], this recognition that the Takings Clause does not require compensation when an owner is barred from putting land to a use that is proscribed by those "existing rules or understandings" is surely unexceptional.[3]

The second and more controversial deviation from the Court's newly articulated "total taking" rule involves what is known as the "nuisance exception." In a century-long line of cases beginning in 1887, the Supreme Court has rejected a number of property rights claims in deference to arguments that the government was invoking its police power to address key public health, safety, and welfare concerns.[4] In such cases, the challenged regulation was deemed valid regardless of its economic impact on the affected private property.[5] The

---

[3]*Id.* at 1030.

[4]*See, e.g.*, Mugler v. Kansas, 123 U.S. 623 (1887) (closure of brewery); Plymouth Coal Co. v. Pennsylvania, 232 U.S. 531 (1914) (miner safety regulation); Hadacheck v. Sebastian, 239 U.S. 394 (1915) (closure of brickyard in urban area); Miller v. Schoene, 276 U.S. 272 (1928) (government directive to cut down infected trees in order to prevent disease's spread); Keystone Bituminous Coal Ass'n v. DeBenedictis, 480 U.S. 470 (1987) (coal mining subsidence regulation upheld).

[5]*Keystone*, 480 U.S. at 488, 491–92.

rationale for the nuisance exception was and is that "all property in this country is held under the implied obligation that the owner's use of it shall not be injurious to the community."[6] Significantly, and somewhat paradoxically, the Court in *Lucas* simultaneously circumscribed the boundaries of the nuisance exception and elevated it to newfound constitutional significance.[7]

Lucas, therefore, provides a clear analytical model through which these "exceptions to takings" can be viewed and applied. The threshold questions, however, are what are those exceptions, and what are their origins.

State Law–Based Limits on Use of Private Property

Lucas and other recent Supreme Court decisions do not short-circuit an inverse condemnation plaintiff's threshold obligation to demonstrate the nature and scope of the property interest claimed to have been "taken" by the government. Indeed, they reinforce it. Thus, for example, a landowner must be able to demonstrate that a proposed development is located on land he or she owns, rather than on the property of the public or third parties.[8] Similarly, a property owner whose development proposal is rejected by government regulators on the ground that the owner previously conveyed a valid open-space easement for the parcel to third persons would presumably lack a viable taking claim under *Lucas*.[9]

---

[6]*Mugler*, 123 U.S. at 665.

[7]Some have viewed *Lucas* as only addressing the nuisance exception. But state and federal laws, beyond just nuisance law, impose many limitations on the use of private property. *Lucas* explicitly acknowledges this. Lucas v. South Carolina Coastal Council, 505 U.S. 1003, 1028–30 (1992).

[8]*See, e.g.,* Lechuza Villas West v. California Coastal Comm'n, 60 Cal. App. 4th 218, 70 Cal. Rptr. 2d 399 (1997) (regulatory takings challenge to commission's denial of development permit defective due to landowner's failure to establish clear title to coastal property).

[9]*See* Ojavan Investors, Inc. v. California Coastal Comm'n, 54 Cal. App. 4th 373, 62 Cal. Rptr. 2d 803 (1997), *cert. denied,* 118 S. Ct. 601 (1997) (deed restrictions agreed to by predecessor-in-interest precluded claim of current development right).

Even without specific acts by the private landowner, there may exist inherent limits on private property rights cognizable under the Fifth Amendment. As *Lucas* aptly observes, the majority of these limitations are grounded in *state* property law.[10] A brief overview of some of those principles follows.

The Public Trust Doctrine

Simply stated, the public trust doctrine provides that certain natural resources are held by the sovereign in special status. Government may neither alienate those resources nor permit their injury or destruction by private parties. Rather, public officials have an affirmative, on-going duty to safeguard those resources for the benefit of the general public.[11]

The public trust doctrine first achieved prominence in American jurisprudence in an 1892 U.S. Supreme Court decision, *Illinois Central Railroad v. Illinois*.[12] It is generally considered a principle of state law, however, and in recent years has received far more attention from the state courts than from their federal counterparts. California is at the forefront of this trend. It is therefore unsurprising that California courts have more frequently addressed the interrelationship of public trust principles and the Takings Clause than have other state jurisdictions.

California courts first applied the public trust doctrine to limit government transfer, and private development, of California's coastal

---

[10]*Lucas*, 505 U.S. at 1027–28. The Supreme Court has repeatedly stressed that rights of private property are generally based on state, rather than federal, law. *See, e.g.*, Stevens v. City of Cannon Beach, 510 U.S. 1207 (1994) (Scalia, J., dissenting from denial of certiorari).

[11]For a discussion of the historic underpinnings of the public trust doctrine and an analysis of its modern scope, see Joseph Sax, *The Public Trust Doctrine in Natural Resource Law: Effective Judicial Intervention*, 68 MICHIGAN L. REV. 471 (1970); and Jan S. Stevens, *The Public Trust: A Sovereign's Ancient Prerogative Becomes the People's Environmental Right*, 14 U.C. DAVIS L. REV. 195 (1980).

[12]146 U.S. 387 (1892). *See also* Summa Corp. v. California *ex rel*. State Lands Comm'n, 466 U.S. 198 (1984); Phillips Petroleum Co. v. Mississippi, 484 U.S. 469 (1988) (both revisiting the doctrine).

tidal and submerged lands.[13] These restrictions under the public trust doctrine have similarly been found applicable to California's inland navigable waterways.[14] For the most part, California decisions have not found lands imbued with the trust to be wholly incapable of alienation to private parties. Rather, the view has been that the private grantee obtains but a "naked fee" interest in such real property, with the state necessarily reserving a public trust interest that has been characterized as an easement.[15]

After tidelands and the beds of navigable waterways, fish and wildlife are the natural resources most traditionally associated with the public trust doctrine. While it may be that states probably do not "own" fish and wildlife in a proprietary sense, courts have held such resources subject to important, publicly held rights under trust principles, and that they are not—at least while in the wild—in private ownership.[16]

The most controversial, recent application of the public trust doctrine under California law has been to that state's complex system of allocating water rights. In the landmark *National Audubon Society v. Superior Court* decision,[17] the California Supreme Court expressly declared the public trust doctrine to exist as an additional constraint

[13]*See, e.g.*, Oakland v. Oakland Water Front Co., 118 Cal. 160, 50 P. 277 (1897); People v. California Fish Co., 166 Cal. 576, 138 P. 79 (1913). *See also*, Donnell v. United States, 834 F. Supp. 19, 25 (D. Maine 1993) (recognizing existence of public trust doctrine under state's law).

[14]Colberg, Inc. v. California, 67 Cal. 2d 408, 432 P. 2d 3 (1967), *cert. denied*, 390 U.S. 949 (1968); California v. Superior Ct. (Lyon), 29 Cal. 3d 210, 220–22, 625 P.2d 239, *cert. denied*, 454 U.S. 865 (1981).

[15]*See, e.g.*, *California Fish Co.*, 166 Cal. at 584–85, 598–99, 138 P. 79, 82–83, 88–89; City of Berkeley v. Superior Ct., 26 Cal. 3d 515, 521–25, 606 P.2d 362, 364–67 (1980), *cert. denied*, 449 U.S. 840 (1980).

[16]Geer v. Connecticut, 161 U.S. 519, 529 (1896), *rev'd on other grounds*, Hughes v. Oklahoma, 441 U.S. 322 (1979); Mountain States Legal Found. v. Hodel, 799 F.2d 1423, 1426 (10th Cir. 1986); In re Steuart Petroleum Co., 495 F. Supp. 38, 40 (E.D. Va. 1980); People v. Truckee Lumber Co., 116 Cal. 397, 399–401, 48 P. 374, 374–75 (1897); People v. Brady, 234 Cal. App. 3d 954, 961, 286 Cal. Rptr. 19, 21 (1991). *See also* MICHAEL J. BEAN, THE EVOLUTION OF NATIONAL WESTERN WILDLIFE LAW, 10 (1983); Gary D. Myers, *Variations on a Theme: Expanding the Public Trust Doctrine to Protect Wildlife*, 19 ENVTL. L. 723 (1989).

[17]33 Cal. 3d 419, 658 P.2d 709 (1983), *cert. denied*, 464 U.S. 977 (1983).

on the allocation and use of water rights in California. Other states have similarly embraced the public trust doctrine as a component of their property law system, to one degree or another.[18]

In several California cases, private landowners have raised the Takings Clause in an effort to defeat public trust claims advanced by government and environmentalists. Those claims have been consistently rejected by the California Supreme Court to date, principally on the ground that the public trust doctrine inherently reserves in the public certain rights to trust resources—rights that never passed into private ownership.[19] The few decisions in other jurisdictions that have addressed the intersection of public trust and takings principles have generally come to the same result.[20]

---

[18]*See, e.g.*, United Plainsman v. North Dakota State Water Comm'n, 247 N.W.2d 457 (N.D. 1976) (applying doctrine to state's water allocation system); Kootenai Envtl. Alliance, Inc. v. Panhandle Yacht, 105 Idaho 622, 671 P.2d 1085, 1094 (1983) (same); Gould v. Greylock Reservation Comm'n, 350 Mass. 410, 215 N.E.2d 114 (1966) (proposed lease of rural parklands for ski resort beyond power of legislature); State Dep't of Envtl. Protection v. Jersey Cent. Power & Light Co., 133 N.J. Super. 375, 336 A.2d 750 (N.J. Super. A.D. 1975) (limiting discharge of power plant wastewater into creek); Just v. Marinette County, 56 Wis. 2d 7, 16–17, 201 N.W.2d 761, 768 (1972) (filling of wetlands barred); Payne v. Kassab, 11 Pa. Commw. 14, 28, 312 A.2d 86, 93 (1973) (right of citizens to "clean air, pure water, and to the preservation of the natural, scenic, historic and aesthetic values of the environment"); Conn. Gen. Stat. § 22a-15 ("public trust in the air, water and other natural resources").

Some states have found only certain public resources impressed with public trust values and responsibilities. *Cf.* Arizona Center for Law in the Public Interest v. Hassell, 172 Ariz. 356, 837 P.2d 158, 168–69 (Az. Ct. App. 1991) (applying public trust doctrine to beds of navigable waterways) *with* Seven Springs Ranch, Inc. v. Arizona, 156 Ariz. 471, 753 P.2d 161, 165 (Az. Ct. App. 1987) (public trust doctrine inapplicable to groundwater adjudications).

[19]*See e.g., California Fish Co.*, 166 Cal. at 599–601; *City of Berkeley,* 26 Cal. 3d at 532; California v. Superior Ct. (Lyon), 29 Cal. 3d 210, 231–32; *National Audubon Society,* 33 Cal. 3d at 440.

[20]In re Guadalupe River Basin, 642 S.W.2d 438, 445–46 (Tex. 1982) (water rights); In re Opinion of the Justices, 139 N.H. 82, 649 A.2d 604, 608–09 (1994) (state sovereign tidelands). *But cf.* Orion Corp. v. Washington, 103 Wash. 2d 441, 693 P.2d 1369, 1380 (1985), *cert. denied,* 486 U.S. 1022 (1988) (creation of state sanctuary encompassing tidelands might result in regulatory taking if it prevents economic uses consistent with public trust).

Public Access to Waterways

The constitutions, statutes, and common law of many states afford the public a right of access to tidelands, rivers, bays, streams, and other navigable waterways.[21] For example, numerous cases have confirmed the existence of a public navigational easement over such areas—even if the bed of a river is privately owned, members of the public have a right to navigate and to exercise the incidents of navigation on such waterways.[22] Such rights are often codified in state statutes as well.[23]

Denial of private development of areas subject to such rights would not appear to trigger a compensable taking. The handful of cases that have considered the issue to date have so held.[24] These cases draw in major part from the far more numerous decisions that consider clashes between the Takings Clause and the *federal* navigational servitude, discussed later in this chapter.

Public Access to Shorelines and Uplands

Several state courts have expanded upon public-access-to-waterways principles to hold that the public has a right of access to and use of

[21]*See, e.g.*, Cal. Const. art. X, § 4; Graham v. Estuary Properties, Inc., 399 So. 2d 1374 (Fla. 1981), *cert. denied*, 454 U.S. 1083 (1981); Nevada v. Bunkowski, 88 Nev. 623, 628, 503 P.2d 1231, 1234 (1972).

[22]*See, e.g.*, Bohn v. Albertson, 107 Cal. App. 2d 738, 757, 238 P.2d 128, 140–41 (1951); People *ex rel.* Baker v. Mack, 19 Cal. App. 3d 1040, 1050, 97 Cal. Rptr. 448, 454 (1971); Nevada v. Bunkowski, 88 Nev. 623, 503 P.2d 1231 (1972); Southern Idaho Fish & Game Ass'n v. Picabo Livestock Co., 96 Idaho 360, 528 P.2d 1295 (1974).

[23]*See, e.g.*, Cal. Harbors & Nav. Code § 131; Cal. Pub. Resources Code § 6339(a); Massachusetts Bay Colony Ordinance of 1631-47 (17th century ordinance, still applicable in Massachusetts, Maine, and New Hampshire, decreeing that any pond containing more than 10 acres is a "great pond" held in common by public).

[24]*See* Peterman v. State Dep't of Natural Resources, 446 Mich. 177, 521 N.W.2d 499, 508–09 (1994) (riparian landowner's rights subject to state navigational servitude; neither public's exercise of navigational rights nor damage to properties arising from public navigational improvements necessarily result in compensable taking); Miramar Co. v. Santa Barbara, 23 Cal. 2d 170, 172–73, 143 P.2d 1, 2–4 (1943) (accord).

upland areas under state law, and that these public rights trump private property rights under the Fifth Amendment. The most prominent examples are recent decisions from Oregon and Hawaii.

In *Stevens v. Cannon Beach*,[25] an Oregon city denied a beachfront seawall permit that would have facilitated commercial development of the privately owned site. The city rejected the application because the seawall was to be built on land to which members of the public had a continuing right of access under Oregon's long-standing, common law doctrine of "custom." The Oregon Supreme Court rejected the private landowners' regulatory takings claim, concluding that because they lacked the fundamental private property right on which an inverse condemnation claim is necessarily based—i.e., the right to exclude the public—no takings claim could be stated. The *Stevens* decision, moreover, expressly found Oregon's law of custom to constitute a background principle of state property law of the type contemplated by the U.S. Supreme Court in *Lucas* as immunizing the government from a successful takings claim.[26]

Native gathering rights were at issue in *Public Access Shoreline Hawaii v. Hawaii County Planning Commission* (*"PASH"*).[27] In *PASH*, the Hawaii Supreme Court was confronted with a conflict between Native Hawaiians and a developer of a proposed 450-acre shoreline community complex on the Big Island of Hawaii. The natives, concerned that the project would infringe upon their claimed, centuries-old gathering rights (including food gathering and fishing), challenged the project. The developer argued that no such rights existed under modern Hawaiian law or, if they did, those gathering rights must yield to more traditional property interests under the English common law tradition.

The Hawaii Supreme Court disagreed, in a unanimous decision. The court explained the historic basis of Native Hawaiian gathering rights, which it analogized to the English doctrine of custom.[28] The

[25]317 Or. 131, 854 P.2d 449 (1993), *cert. denied*, 510 U.S. 1207 (1994).

[26]317 Or. at 142, 854 P.2d at 456. *Stevens,* apparently, was the first post-*Lucas* state court decision to do so. *See also* Neptune City v. Borough of Avon-by-the-Sea, 61 N.J. 296, 294 A.2d 47 (1972).

[27]79 Haw. 425, 903 P.2d 1246 (1995), *cert. denied*, 517 U.S. 1163 (1996).

[28]903 P.2d at 1259–63. Ironically, that principle of English common law forms the basis of Oregon's state law of custom, applied by the Oregon Supreme Court in Stevens v. City of Cannon Beach (discussed in note 26).

PASH court next proceeded to conclude that Hawaiian land use officials had an affirmative duty to protect those aboriginal rights under
the Hawaii Constitution and statutes,[29] and that those same rights
could properly be reconciled with Western concepts of property
rights that are also an important element of Hawaiian common law.
Part of that reconciliation, observed the court, was the recognition
that the fee interest conveyed under Hawaiian land grants is inherently limited:

> Our examination of the relevant legal developments in
> Hawaiian history leads us to the conclusion that the western
> concept of exclusivity [of possession] is not universally applic-
> able in Hawaii. [Citing *Stevens v. City of Cannon Beach*.] In
> other words, the issuance of a Hawaiian land patent confirmed
> a limited property interest as compared with typical land
> patents governed by western concepts of property.[30]

Finally, the Hawaii Supreme Court turned to the question of
whether legal recognition and protection of Native Hawaiian gathering rights worked a taking of the developer's shoreline property,
but found it unnecessary to resolve that issue, given the procedural
posture of the litigation. However, the court left little doubt as to its
views on the subject, citing *Lucas* for the proposition that native
gathering rights constituted just the type of background principle of
state property law that circumscribe private property rights:

> Hawaiian custom and usage have always been a part of the
> laws of this State. . . . [T]he government "assuredly [can] . . . as-
> sert a permanent easement that [reflects] a pre-existing limita-
> tion upon the landowner's title."[31]

PASH thus represents one of the most vivid and novel examples to

---

[29]*Id.* at 1256–59. In some jurisdictions, the right to hunt or fish is guaranteed
by the state constitution. *See, e.g.*, Cal. Const. art. I, § 25 (public right to fish on
and from public lands). That constitutional provision, in turn, has been interpreted as affording a reasonable right of access to such fishing areas. *See* California v. San Luis Obispo Sportsman's Ass'n, 22 Cal. 3d 440, 584 P.2d 1088
(1978). Such state constitutional guarantees would appear to pass muster as exemptions under the *Lucas* standard.

[30]*PASH*, 903 P.2d at 1268.

[31]*Id.* at 1272–73 (citing *Lucas*).

date of the extent to which traditional state law principles can limit private interests in property, and how such principles can defeat an inverse condemnation claim at the outset.[32]

Archaeological and Historic Sites

Some states afford special status to lands having particular archaeological or historic significance, even when title to such sites is held by private parties. Conflicts over these properties can trigger novel questions under the Takings Clause.

Illustrative is the Iowa Supreme Court's recent decision in *Hunziker v. Iowa*.[33] The plaintiffs in *Hunziker* were developers who had purchased farmland to develop it. Three years later, the state archaeologist made "a significant find"—a burial mound made by Native Americans between 1000 and 2500 years ago. Pursuant to state statutes enacted a decade before plaintiffs purchased the property, state officials required the site to be left undisturbed and the developers were denied a building permit. The developers responded with a regulatory takings lawsuit. The state supreme court relied on the *Lucas* long-standing state-property-law exception to reject the taking claim: "[I]mplicit in the Supreme Court's 'bundle of rights' analysis [in *Lucas*] is that the *right* to use the land in the way contemplated is what controls."

Hunziker makes two important refinements (some would argue, extensions) to the *Lucas* threshold rule. *Lucas* suggested that when property law–based principles are advanced to defeat a takings claim at the outset, those principles must be both long-standing and grounded in common law.[34] Yet the Iowa Supreme Court in *Hunziker*

---

[32]There are limits to the reach of such state law principles, however. 'Ohana v. United States, 76 F.3d 280 (9th Cir. 1996), illustrates this point. In *'Ohana*, Native Hawaiians relied on the *PASH* decision for the proposition that their gathering rights included the right to *exclusively* occupy and use for fishing certain areas within a national historic park in Hawaii. The Ninth Circuit disagreed, finding that "Ancient custom did not include the right to remain upon and exclude others from the land." *Id.* at 282.

[33]519 N.W.2d 367 (Iowa 1994).

[34]*See, e.g.*, Lucas v. South Carolina Coastal Council, 505 U.S. 1003, 1029 (1992): "Any limitation so severe cannot be newly legislated or decreed (without compensation), but must inhere in the title itself, in the restrictions that back-

considers state *statutes* to qualify as immunizing background principles of state property law sanctioned under *Lucas*, even those code provisions that predate a landowner's acquisition of a subject property or taking claim by just a few years.[35]

Other State Property Law Principles

There are a host of other background principles of state property law that will undoubtedly be advanced by government defendants in an effort to defeat inverse condemnation claims.[36] Those principles run the gamut from English common law rules embraced with particular fervor by the former colonies; to civil law principles imported from French law to the parishes of Louisiana; to Native Alaskan hunting, fishing, and property rights unique to our 49th state. Accordingly, the examples discussed above should be viewed as illustrative rather than exhaustive.

Limiting State Law–Based Limits on Private Property Rights: A Warning from the U.S. Supreme Court

A cynical view of *Lucas*'s state property law–based exception might suggest that state and local government efforts to foreclose inverse condemnation claims are limited only by officials' imaginations and creative thinking. Two justices of the Supreme Court recently signalled, however, that there may be limits to the elasticity with which that Court will review state property law principles designed to forestall a taking claim under *Lucas*.

---

ground principles of the State's law of property . . . already place upon land ownership." This passage seems inconsistent with earlier language from the same majority: "[T]he property owner necessarily expects the uses of his property to be restricted, from time to time, by various measures newly enacted by the State in legitimate exercise of its police powers. . . ." *Id.* at 1027.

[35]In this sense *Hunziker* seems more faithful to Justice Kennedy's concurring opinion in *Lucas*, in which Kennedy advocated a more flexible and contemptorary view of state property law principles than the majority appeared willing to embrace. *Lucas*, 505 U.S. at 1035 (Kennedy, J., concurring).

[36]*See, e.g.*, Hoeck v. City of Portland, 57 F.3d 781, 789 (9th Cir. 1995), *cert. denied*, 516 U.S. 1112 (1996), (regulatory takings claim arising out of municipality's demolition of dilapidated building rejected; owner "had no right to use his property to maintain an abandoned structure [citing *Lucas*]" and citing municipal ordinances rather than state common law).

Recall *Stevens v. City of Cannon Beach*, the decision in which the
Oregon Supreme Court held that Oregon's common law of custom
deprived the landowners of a property right upon which a viable
taking claim was necessarily based. The landowners asked the U.S.
Supreme Court to review the case. The Supreme Court refused. However, Justice Scalia—who authored the majority opinion in *Lucas* two
years earlier—wrote a bitter dissent.[37] Justice Scalia began by acknowledging that property rights are generally defined under state
rather than federal law, but said:

> [A] State may not deny rights protected under the Federal Con-
> stitution . . . by invoking nonexistent rules of State substantive
> law. Our opinion in *Lucas* . . . would be a nullity if anything
> that a State court chooses to denominate "background law"
> . . . could eliminate property rights.[38]

The Oregon Supreme Court's decision in *Stevens* presented that
exact danger, maintained Justice Scalia in typically forceful terms:

> To say that this case raises a serious Fifth Amendment takings
> issue is an understatement. The issue is serious in the sense that
> it involves a holding of questionable constitutionality; and it is
> serious in the sense that the land-grab (if there is one) may run
> the entire length of the Oregon coast.[39]

Justice Scalia's dissent in *Stevens*, in which he was joined by Justice
O'Connor, seems to view the Supreme Court's role as appropriately
looking behind—and second-guessing—property law pronouncements made by state courts for purposes of testing the *Lucas* property
law–based exception to takings law. Traditionally, this is a role the
Court has declined to play. If and when a majority of the Court is prepared to review state property law rules *de novo* in connection with
inverse condemnation challenges, the effectiveness of state law–based
defenses to such takings claims will be circumscribed. This, in turn,
raises some of the same federalism themes that have been discussed in
chapter 12, in the context of "judicial takings."

---

[37]Stevens v. City of Cannon Beach, 510 U.S. 1207 (1994) (Scalia, J., dissenting from denial of certiorari).
    [38]*Id.* at 1208–09.
    [39]*Id.*

Federal Law–Based Limits on Use of Private Property

While *Lucas* devoted primary attention to *state* law–based limits on rights of private property, the Supreme Court has noted both in *Lucas* and a host of earlier decisions that *federal* law can have much the same effect. Those federal law–based limits can take several forms.

Federal Navigational Servitude

One such preexisting, inherent limitation on the use and enjoyment of private property is the federal navigational servitude. Unlike state law principles, the navigational servitude is grounded in the U.S. Constitution, specifically its "commerce clause."[40] It is a paramount right,[41] permitting the United States to regulate, modify, or build in navigable waters, without liability to private landowners under the Takings Clause, when in the interests of navigation or commerce.[42] Government programs that commonly benefit from the servitude include the building of dams and locks, the dredging of channels and ports, and the removal of navigational obstructions.

The rule of no compensation derives from the fact that property damage from such programs "results not from a taking of the riparian owner's property in the stream bed, but from the lawful exercise of a power to which the property has always been subject."[43] The servitude is held to be a dominant one that can be asserted to the exclusion of any conflicting property rights.

Illustrative is the Federal Circuit's decision in *Confederated Tribes*

---

[40]U.S. Const. art. I, § 8, cl. 3.

[41]*See generally* Julius Sackman, I.A. Nichols on Eminent Domain, § 2.2[11] (3d ed. Rev. 1997); 4 Waters and Water Rights § 305 *et seq.* (R. Clark ed., 1970). The servitude is sometimes referred to as a "dominant servitude" or a "superior navigational easement." *See also* Marks v. United States, 34 Fed. Cl. 387 (1995).

[42]Navigation need not be the sole purpose of the federal project, or even the most important one. Confederated Tribes v. United States, 20 Cl. Ct. 31, 43 (1990), *aff'd*, 964 F.2d 1102 (Fed. Cir. 1992).

[43]United States v. Cherokee Nation, 480 U.S. 700, 703–05 (1987). *See also* United States v. Rands, 389 U.S. 121, 123 (1967) (same).

of the Colville Reservation v. United States.[44] In *Confederated Tribes,* tribes living along the Columbia River challenged the federal government's decision to build the Grand Coulee Dam. The court of appeals concluded that "construction of the Grand Coulee Dam does not entitle the tribe to compensation under the Fifth Amendment for the water power value of the land where the United States has invoked its sovereign right to exercise its navigational servitude." Rather, said the court, "the tribes' claims in law and equity were subordinate to the Government's exercise of its navigational servitude."[45]

It is therefore unsurprising that the Supreme Court in *Lucas,* while focusing mainly on state law–based rules, specifically identified the navigational servitude as an effective federal law defense to a takings challenge—even one alleging a physical invasion of private property.[46]

While the federal navigational servitude is therefore more powerful than its state law cousin, it is not without limits. For example, the servitude does not extend to lands above the ordinary high-water mark of a waterway. The taking of such "fast lands" must be compensated, even when the adverse impact results from government activity entirely within the waterway.[47]

The status of the federal navigational servitude was muddled somewhat by the Supreme Court's decision in *Kaiser Aetna v. United States.*[48] At issue there was a private lagoon which, through private funds, had been dredged and connected to a navigable bay as part of a private marina community. The U.S. Army Corps of Engineers invoked the navigational servitude, claiming a public right of access to the newly navigable lagoon. Allowing that Congress doubtless had

---

[44]964 F.2d 1102 (Fed. Cir. 1992).

[45]*Id.* at 1109.

[46]Lucas v. South Carolina Coastal Council, 505 U.S. 1003, 1028–29 (1992) (citing Scranton v. Wheeler, 179 U.S. 141, 163 (1900)).

[47]Kaiser Aetna v. United States, 444 U.S. 164, 177 (1979); Owen v. United States, 851 F.2d 1404, 1412 (Fed. Cir. 1988). This distinction between fast and water-covered lands has been imported to cases interpreting the *state* navigational servitude as well. *See, e.g.,* Peterman v. State Dep't of Natural Resources, 446 Mich. 177, 521 N.W.2d 499 (1994), in which the Michigan Supreme Court found state officials to have acted within their power to promote access to and construct improvements on waterways, but imposed liability under the Takings Clause for property damage to riparian uplands.

[48]444 U.S. 164 (1979).

Panoramic view of Hawaii Kai development, including Kuapa Pond. Access of the boating public to the pond was at issue in *Kaiser Aetna v. United States*.

the *power* under the Commerce Clause to insist on public access, the Supreme Court said that nonetheless it would be a taking to do so in the circumstances presented. Specifically, the private developer in *Kaiser Aetna* had invested substantial amounts in improvements to connect a private, previously isolated pond to the ocean.[49]

The unique facts of *Kaiser Aetna*, noted at several points by the Court, argue for delimiting its impact on settled navigational servitude jurisprudence.[50] Still, *Kaiser Aetna* represents a crack in the dike of noncompensability for use of the navigational servitude below the high-water mark. The Supreme Court has done little to resolve the uncertainty,[51] and some lower courts are reflecting the

[49]*Id.* at 176–78. In a companion decision, Vaughn v. Vermillion Corp., 444 U.S. 206 (1979), the Court applied *Kaiser Aetna* to reject the argument that manmade channels, built on private land and privately funded, are subject to a public right of access under the federal navigational servitude where they connect with navigable waterways.

[50]In the Court's most recent word on the servitude, United States v. Cherokee Nation, 480 U.S. 700 (1987), the Court laid out a rather traditional, pre-*Kaiser Aetna* litany of navigational servitude principles.

[51]For example, *Lucas* cites both *Kaiser Aetna* and the Court's more traditional navigational servitude precedents without attempting to reconcile them. Lucas v. South Carolina Coastal Council, 505 U.S. 1003, 1029 (1992).

same ambivalence over the federal navigational servitude's constitutional relationship to the Takings Clause.[52]

Indian Tribes

Indian tribes often bring takings claims, typically against the federal government. Like many legal issues relating to Native Americans, the special status of Indian tribes adds unique questions to the takings analysis and can limit the legal rights of Indians.

A key, threshold issue is whether the Indian claim to the land in question has been recognized by Congress. This is because, as the Supreme Court has noted, "Indian occupancy, not specifically recognized as ownership by action authorized by Congress, may be extinguished by the Government without compensation."[53] Thus, the fact of occupancy since time immemorial is not, in and of itself, sufficient to sustain a taking claim against the federal government.[54]

A second question is whether the federal government, in depriving Indians of property rights, is simply managing tribal property in its trustee role. If that is the case, the Supreme Court has ruled, the Takings Clause is inapplicable and just compensation is not required.[55]

---

[52]The recent jurisprudence of the Federal Circuit is illustrative. *Cf.* Florida Rock Indus., Inc. v. United States, 791 F.2d 893, 900 (Fed. Cir. 1986) (effect of *Kaiser Aetna* is that "the old navigation servitude, often used to excuse what looked suspiciously like takings, is no longer available for that duty in regulatory takings cases") *with* Owen v. United States, 851 F.2d 1404, 1408 (Fed. Cir. 1988) (navigational servitude defines boundaries within which United States can supersede private interests without taking liability). For a recent case taking a more expansive and conventional view of the federal navigational servitude, *see* Donnell v. United States, 834 F. Supp. 19, 27 (D. Maine 1993) (Corps of Engineers–ordered removal of private pier in navigable waters does not trigger a taking). *See also* Marks v. United States, 34 Fed. Cl. 387 (1995) *aff'd,* 116 F.3d 1496 (Fed. Cir. 1997), *cert. denied,* 118 S. Ct. 852 (1998).

[53]Tee-Hit-Ton Indians v. United States, 348 U.S. 272, 288–89 (1955).

[54]However, against private parties and the states, the distinction between congressionally "recognized" and "unrecognized" title has been deemed irrelevant; here, the Indian right of occupancy is as enforceable as a fee simple title. *See generally* FELIX COHEN, HANDBOOK OF FEDERAL INDIAN LAW 491 (1982); NATIONAL ASSOCIATION OF ATTORNEYS GENERAL, INDIAN LAW DESKBOOK (2d ed., 1998).

[55]United States v. Sioux Nation, 448 U.S. 371, 416 (1980).

Accordingly, the rights of tribes and individual Native Americans under the Takings Clause are often circumscribed by virtue of the unique nature of their relationship with the federal government.[56]

Restricting Private Property to Protect Public Lands

Occasionally, the federal government will impose restrictions on the use of private property in order to prevent damage to or otherwise protect adjacent, *publicly* owned lands. Such restrictions can lead to claims of a compensable taking by the United States. To date those claims have been rejected by the federal courts on a fairly consistent basis.[57] The decisions seem to place great weight on the government's broad powers under the Property Clause of the Constitution to manage the public lands.[58]

"Federalizing" the *Lucas* Property Law Exception

Discussed earlier were several state court decisions that have applied and perhaps expanded the principle, reaffirmed in *Lucas*, that limitations on the bundle of private property rights imposed by long-settled state law can defeat a taking claim at the outset. In a recent, important case, *M & J Coal Co. v. United States*,[59] the Federal Circuit indicated that *federal* laws imposing similar limits to the use of private property can have the same legal effect.

The facts of *M & J Coal* offer an uncanny echo of several earlier, seminal Supreme Court takings decisions. Federal regulators had cited a private coal company for violations of the Surface Mining Control and Reclamation Act (SMCRA);[60] those violations had, in turn, led to subsidence of surface lands owned by third parties and to

---

[56]Adding to the irony is the fact that Indian tribes themselves, in exercising powers of self-government, are statutorily barred from "tak[ing] any private property for public use without just compensation." 25 U.S.C. § 13025.

[57]Reichelderfer v. Quinn, 287 U.S. 315 (1932); Stupak-Thrall v. United States, 70 F.3d 881 (6th Cir. 1995); United States v. 62.50 Acres of Land, 953 F.2d 886 (5th Cir. 1992); Clouser v. Espy, 42 F.3d 1522 (9th Cir. 1994), *op. vacated,* 81 F.3d 651 (6th Cir. 1996), *cert. denied,* 117 S. Ct. 764 (1997).

[58]U.S. Const. art. IV, § 3, cl. 2. *See also* Duncan Energy Co v. U.S. Forest Serv., 50 F.3d 584, 591 (8th Cir. 1995).

[59]47 F.3d 1148 (Fed. Cir. 1995), *cert. denied,* 516 U.S. 808 (1995).

[60]30 U.S.C. §§ 1201–1328.

related safety hazards. The coal company, while acceding to the government's power to regulate the company's operations to prevent such consequences, nonetheless argued that compensation was due under the Fifth Amendment. Citing the important public health and safety underpinnings of the challenged federal regulations, the Federal Circuit Court of Appeals rejected the regulatory taking claim.

Critical for present purposes was the analytical path followed by the court of appeals. It cited *Lucas* for the proposition that an otherwise compensable regulation is not a taking if the owner's proposed use is proscribed by existing rules that qualify the nature of the property interest. Significantly, the court held that these inherent limitations can flow from *federal* as well as state law. *M & J Coal* cited the statutory restrictions found in SMCRA, enacted by Congress in 1977 (and prior to plaintiff's acquisition of the property), to qualify as such an inherent limitation on the company's property rights:

> [A] court should inquire into the nature of the land owner's estate to determine whether the use interest proscribed by the governmental action was part of the owner's title to begin with. . . . In this case, M & J never acquired the right to mine in such a way as to endanger the public health and safety. . . . [61]

Accordingly, and like the state court in *Hunziker*, the Federal Circuit has opined that it views the *Lucas* exemption expansively. *M & J Coal* sweeps even recently enacted federal legislation within the ambit of legal restrictions that, properly viewed, can limit an owner's property interest. Again, this decision and others like it[62] seem more consonant with Justice Kennedy's expansive concurrence in *Lucas* than

---

[61]147 F.3d at 1154. While *Lucas* concerned a "total taking" of economic value by government regulation, the Federal Circuit in *M & J Coal* came to the unremarkable conclusion that reference to inherent limitations on private property rights was equally relevant in the far more common situation when government regulation eliminates only a fraction of the value of private property. *Id.* at 1153.

[62]*See, e.g.*, Lake Pleasant Group v. United States, 32 Fed. Cl. 429 (Fed. Cl. 1994), *aff'd*, 79 F.3d 1166 (Fed. Cir. 1996) (no private easement to cross state-owned trust lands); California Housing Sec. v. United States, 959 F.2d 955, 956 (Fed. Cir.), *cert. denied*, 506 U.S. 916 (1992). *But cf.* Preseault v. United States, 100 F.3d 1525, 1538–39 (Fed. Cir. 1996) ("Nothing in *Lucas* suggests that the background principles of a state property law include the sweep of a century of federal regulatory legislation. . . ."). For a general discussion of the role of federal statutes in the *Lucas* "background principles" analysis, see Lynn E. Blais, *Takings, Statutes and the Common Law: Considering Inherent Limitations on Title*, 70 So. CALIFORNIA L. REV. 1, 49. (1996).

with Justice Scalia's more circumscribed majority opinion. In any event, *M & J Coal* represents an important development in regulatory takings law.

The "Nuisance Exception" to Takings Liability

The most venerable—and certainly the most controversial—exception to takings liability is the so-called "nuisance exception." The doctrine finds it origins in an old Latin maxim: "sic utere tue ut alienum non laedas"—use your own property in such a manner as not to injure that of another.[63] When the nuisance exception is successfully invoked, it cuts off a taking claim.

Historical Roots of the Nuisance Exception

The Supreme Court first explored the intersection of the Takings Clause and nuisance doctrine over a century ago, in *Mugler v. Kansas*.[64] *Mugler* involved a federal constitutional challenge to a Kansas law that made illegal the operation of Mugler's profitable, and previously legal, brewery. The state had banned the business in a purported effort to protect public health, morals, and safety. Mugler challenged the law under the Takings Clause. Justice Harlan, writing for the Supreme Court, rejected the argument:

> A prohibition simply upon the use of property for purposes that are declared, by valid legislation, to be injurious to the health, morals, or safety of the community, cannot, in any just sense, be deemed a taking or an appropriation of property for the public benefit. . . . The power which the States have of prohibiting such use by individuals of their property as will be prejudicial to the health, the morals, or the safety of the public, is not—and, consistently with the existence and safety of organized society, cannot be—burdened with the condition that the State must compensate such individual owners for pecuniary losses they may sustain, by reason of their not being permitted, by a noxious use of their property, to inflict injury upon the community.[65]

Thus was the nuisance exception to the Takings Clause born.

[63]1 BLACKSTONE'S COMMENTARIES 306.
[64]123 U.S. 623 (1887).
[65]*Id.* at 668–69.

In the early 20th century, the Supreme Court repeatedly upheld a variety of property rights claims in deference to government's argument that it was invoking its police power to address key public health, safety, and welfare concerns.[66] And in a dissent to Justice Holmes' landmark majority opinion in *Pennsylvania Coal Co. v. Mahon* establishing the principle of regulatory takings, Justice Brandeis invoked the nuisance exception to argue that no taking existed in *Pennsylvania Coal* as a matter of law.[67] The full Court re-embraced the nuisance exception in 1962, when it rejected a regulatory takings claim brought in response to local zoning that restricted dredging and gravel pit excavation.[68]

The scope and limits of the nuisance exception were next addressed in a trilogy of Supreme Court cases spanning the late 1970s to the early 1990s—*Penn Central, Keystone*, and *Lucas*. It was in *Penn Central* that Justice Rehnquist first coined the phrase "nuisance exception to the taking guarantee," though only to argue that the city's historic preservation ordinance failed to constitute such a regulatory response.[69] Justice Rehnquist traced the origins of the exception back to the 1887 *Mugler* decision.

A decade after *Penn Central*, the Supreme Court in *Keystone Bituminous Coal Ass'n v. DeBenedictis*[70] seized upon powerful facts to address the exception directly. The facts in *Keystone* are nearly a carbon copy of those confronting Justice Holmes six decades earlier: a Pennsylvania-based coal company was once again challenging a state regulation requiring that certain underground coal deposits remain unmined in order to provide support to surface lands and prevent damaging subsidence. The same basic facts as *Pennsylvania Coal*, but a very different result. In a 5-to-4 decision, the Supreme Court in *Keystone* upheld the very type of regulation it had struck down in 1922. Critically, the Court relied in major part upon the

---

[66]Plymouth Coal Co. v. Pennsylvania, 232 U.S. 531 (1914) (miner safety regulation); Reinman v. City of Little Rock, 237 U.S. 171 (1915) (abatement of livery stable operation in residential neighborhood); Hadacheck v. Sebastian, 239 U.S. 394 (1915) (closure of brickyard in urban area); Miller v. Schoene, 276 U.S. 272 (1928) (government directive to cut down infected trees in order to prevent disease's spread).

[67]260 U.S. 393, 417 (Brandeis, J., dissenting).

[68]Goldblatt v. Town of Hempstead, 369 U.S. 590, 593–95 (1962).

[69]Penn Central Transp. Co. v. New York City, 438 U.S. 104, 144–46 (1978) (Rehnquist, J., dissenting).

[70]480 U.S. 470 (1987).

nuisance exception to uphold the Pennsylvania regulations. Justice Stevens, speaking for the majority, noted that the modern Pennsylvania regulation contained the very type of "harm-prevention" legislative findings and justifications absent from the measure invalidated in *Pennsylvania Coal*.[71]

Now–Chief Justice Rehnquist dissented in *Keystone*, in the process retreating from his categorical embrace of the nuisance exception in *Penn Central*. While acknowledging the continuing viability of the principle, Rehnquist took great pains in his *Keystone* dissent to try to circumscribe its application. He repeatedly characterized it as a "narrow exception" to Takings Clause liability. He also opined that "our cases have never applied the nuisance exception to allow complete extinction of the value of a parcel of property."[72]

Lucas and the Evolving Role of the Nuisance Exception

There matters stood until the Supreme Court's 1992 decision in *Lucas*. As was the case with the "background principles of property law" exception discussed above, *Lucas* makes clear that government's assertion of the nuisance exception can defeat an inverse condemnation claim at its inception.[73]

This, however, is the only good news *Lucas* provides devotees of the nuisance exception. Justice Scalia's majority opinion limited the Court's prior rule that under the Takings Clause government regulation can totally eliminate economic value of property whenever the challenged measure is claimed to avert public harm or terminate a noxious use of that property. Instead, the *Lucas* Court embraced a more narrow rule: that liability for a "total" taking can be avoided only where, based on a fact-specific inquiry, the proposed use of

---

[71]*Id.* at 488. The Court also went on to uphold the regulation for two other reasons: The law had not made it impossible for the company to profitably engage in mining, and the company had not demonstrated an undue interference with its investment-backed expectations. *Id.* at 493–502.

[72]*Id.* at 512–13 (Rehnquist, C.J., dissenting).

[73]Lucas v. South Carolina Coastal Council, 505 U.S. 1003, 1027 (1992). As one commentator has aptly noted, "the *Lucas* majority transformed the nuisance exception into a true, categorical exception to the Takings Clause." Scott R. Ferguson, *The Evolution of the "Nuisance Exception" to the Just Compensation Clause: From Myth to Reality*, 45 HASTINGS L. J. 1539 (1994).

property would not have been permitted under *traditional* nuisance law principles.

Scalia's majority opinion found the nuisance exception applicable where regulation is necessary to forestall "grave threats to the lives and property of others,"[74] such as the required dismantling of a nuclear power plant situated astride an earthquake fault. In principal part, Scalia's dissatisfaction with the traditional "noxious use" standard was based on the suspicion that many regulatory measures represent but covert attempts to confer public benefits at the expense of private property rights: "the distinction between 'harm-preventing' and 'benefit-conferring' regulation is often in the eye of the beholder."[75]

One of the most notable passages from *Lucas* is the Court's fashioning of a new, multifaceted constitutional test by which lower state and federal courts are directed to assess the applicability of the revised nuisance exception.[76] Speaking for the Court, Justice Scalia went further to add a key restriction to the nuisance exception: any such change must be justified based on land-use limitations of the type recognized under *preexisting* state law,[77] seeming to imply that such restrictions must be creatures of common (i.e., judge-made) law rather than legislation, and must be predicated on well-settled state nuisance rules. Yet later in the opinion, Justice Scalia appeared to draw back from this absolutist view, noting that "changed circumstances or new knowledge may make what was previously permissible no longer so."[78] Finally, the Court in *Lucas* cautioned that application of state

---

[74]*Lucas*, 505 U.S. at 1029 n.16.

[75]*Id.* at 1024.

[76]According to the Court, the relevant factors include:

> the degree of harm to public lands and resources, or adjacent private property, posed by the claimant's proposed activities, the social value of the claimant's activities and their suitability to the locality in question, and the relative ease with which the alleged harm can be avoided through measures taken by the claimant and the government (or adjacent private landowners) alike. . . .

Id. at 1030–31 (citations omitted).

[77]*Id.* at 1029.

[78]*Id.* at 1031 (citing RESTATEMENT (SECOND) OF TORTS § 827, comment. (g)). Elsewhere Justice Scalia noted that "the property owner necessarily expects the uses of his property to be restricted, from time to time, by various measures *newly enacted* by the State in legitimate exercise of its police powers. . . ." *Id.* at 1027 (emphasis added).

nuisance or property law principles to defeat a taking claim must be "objectively reasonable."[79]

The majority's extended discussion of the nuisance exception in *Lucas* drew statements of concern by a number of justices. Justice Kennedy concurred in the judgment, but stressed that he would have articulated the Court's newly circumscribed nuisance exception in a more flexible and expansive manner.[80] Justices Blackmun and Stevens both wrote lengthy dissents, in which each took vigorous exception to the scope of the nuisance exception articulated in the majority opinion.[81] Justice Souter wrote a separate statement, in which he, too, seemed uncomfortable with the absolutist statement of nuisance principles reflected in the majority opinion.[82] Thus, to one extent or another, the revised nuisance law exception announced in *Lucas* apparently represents the view of a narrow 5-to-4 majority of the Court.

The Nuisance Exception in the Post-*Lucas* Era

The *Lucas* majority narrowed the scope of the "nuisance exception" that had been reaffirmed by the Court as recently as 1987 in *Keystone Bituminous Coal*. In so doing, however, the Court neither overruled or even criticized its earlier opinion in *Keystone* and prior, similar precedents. This will undoubtedly produce confusion for lower courts and litigants in future cases.

The Court declared in *Lucas* that any reliance on property or nuisance law principles to overcome a "total takings" claim must be founded on "background principles" of state nuisance law; yet, from state to state wide dissimilarities permeate nuisance and other property law principles, and the disparities in resulting inverse condemnation decisions are likely to be pronounced. Inasmuch as the nuisance exception applies not just to "total takings" but to "partial takings" as well, the number of cases in which the exception will be invoked should also prove substantial.

Other uncertainties are exhibited in this same portion of the Court's *Lucas* opinion. For example: what, precisely, constitutes a "background" principle of state nuisance and property law for

---

[79]*Id.* at 1032 n.18.

[80]*Id.* at 1034–36 (Kennedy, J., concurring).

[81]*Id.* at 1047–55 (Blackmun, J., dissenting) and at 1067–71 (Stevens, J., dissenting).

[82]*Id.* at 1077–78 (separate statement of Souter, J.).

purposes of takings analysis? One that was firmly established when a given state was admitted to the Union? Or one that was articulated at the turn of the century? Or a decade ago? And what *types* of law fall under this exception? Just judge-made (i.e., "common") law? Statutes? Federal and state constitutional provisions? Administrative decrees?[83]

A central shortcoming of the *Lucas* analysis of the nuisance exception is that common law nuisance principles are continually evolving to reflect societal changes, technological advances, newly discovered hazards, etc. The Court regularly acknowledged this reality in its decisions prior to *Lucas*.[84] Freezing state-law property and nuisance principles at some past, indeterminate date—as the majority seems to be dictating in *Lucas*—ignores this fact. Moreover, using traditional nuisance law as a way of regulating land use has been criticized for its draconian, "all-or-nothing" effect: Either the challenged use is allowed to continue, or is proscribed.[85] A final, complicating factor is the amorphous nature of nuisance law generally.[86]

The Nuisance Exception in Lower State and Federal Courts

Both before and since *Lucas*, a host of state and federal courts have had occasion to address the nuisance exception in takings litigation. Perhaps the most traditional and recurring example is the case of floodplain zoning, in which development of flood-prone areas is barred in order to protect human lives and property. That, for example, was precisely the situation in *First English Evangelical Lutheran Church v. County of Los Angeles*,[87] the landmark case in which the Supreme Court ruled money damages to be a constitutionally compelled remedy for a regulatory taking. What is perhaps less

---

[83]For an expansionist answer to these inquiries, see Blais, *supra* note 62.

[84]*See, e.g.*, Milwaukee v. Illinois, 451 U.S. 304, 317 (1981). *See also* Justice Kennedy's concurring opinion in *Lucas*, 505 U.S. at 1035 (Kennedy, J., concurring). For an analysis proposing that Justice Kennedy's view of the nuisance exception ultimately is likely to prevail in takings jurisprudence, *see* Richard Lazarus, *Putting the Correct "Spin" on* Lucas, 45 STANFORD L. REV. 1411, 1425 (1993).

[85]*See* Boomer v. Atlantic Cement Co., 26 N.Y.2d 219, 257 N.E.2d 870 (1970).

[86]*See* PROSSER AND KEETON ON TORTS 616 (5th ed. 1984).

[87]482 U.S. 304 (1987).

known is that, on remand, the state court upheld the local development ban in a flood-prone canyon in express reliance on the nuisance exception.[88]

Another application of the nuisance exception, this one post-*Lucas*, is illustrated by *Bernardsville Quarry v. Borough of Bernardsville*.[89] There, a landowner was prevented by a local ordinance from quarrying below a certain depth. The New Jersey Supreme Court, while acknowledging that the regulation might otherwise constitute a regulatory taking, noted that it was expressly designed to protect persons and property. Citing *Keystone* and related U.S. Supreme Court decisions, the state court observed that "the public interest in preventing activities similar to public nuisances is a substantial one, which in many instances has not required compensation."[90] It further concluded, "In this case, the evidence amply demonstrated a reasonable basis for the borough to believe the operations of the quarry below the permissible level would create genuine and substantial risks of harm to the public in general and the environment in particular."[91] As such, ruled the court, the local ordinance did not amount to a taking.

Perhaps the most extreme application of the nuisance exception is the Wisconsin Supreme Court's famous opinion in *Just v. Marinette County*,[92] which predates *Lucas* by two decades. In *Just*, the state court held that government could prevent a landowner from changing the natural character of private property—i.e., through the filling of

---

[88]First English Evangelical Lutheran Church v. County of Los Angeles, 210 Cal. App. 3d 1353, 1370–72, 258 Cal. Rptr. 893, 904–05 (1989), *cert. denied*, 493 U.S. 1056 (1990). *See also* Helix Land Co. v. City of San Diego, 82 Cal. App. 3d 932, 147 Cal. Rptr. 683 (1978); Turner v. Del Norte County, 24 Cal. App. 3d 311, 101 Cal. Rptr. 93 (1972).

[89]129 N.J. 221, 608 A.2d 1377 (1992).

[90]*Id.* at 1384.

[91]*Id.* at 1385.

[92]56 Wis. 2d 7, 201 N.W.2d 761 (Wis. 1972). *See also* M & I Marshall & Ilsey Bank v. Town of Sommers, 141 Wis. 2d 271, 414 N.W.2d 824, 830 (Wis. 1987) (reaffirming *Just*). The *Just* holding was subsequently adopted in several other states as well. *See, e.g.*, Gardner v. New Jersey Pinelands Comm'n, 125 N.J. 193, 593 A.2d 251, 254 (N.J. 1991). Its reasoning has been expressly rejected in others. *See* Gil v. Inland Wetlands & Watercourses Agency, 219 Conn. 404, 593 A.2d 1368 (1991); Vatalaro v. Department of Envtl. Regulation, 601 So. 2d 1223 (Fla. 1992). *See generally* Joseph Sax, *Property Rights and the Economy of Nature: Understanding* Lucas v. South Carolina Coastal Council, 45 STANFORD L. REV. 1433 (1993).

The Nuisance Exception in Gold Rush California

California's case law relating to nuisance dates back to 1850 when the state was admitted into the Union. The first reported public nuisance case in California is *Gunter v. Geary*, 1 Cal. 462 (1851), a decision with ironic parallels to the facts in *Lucas*: The plaintiff in *Gunter* had built a house, on pilings, on San Francisco Bay. City officials pitched the house into San Francisco Bay, claiming it to be a public nuisance. The state Supreme Court held that the house was constructed on that part of the bay constituting a public highway, and that if a person appropriates such land to private use, the presumption is that there is a detriment to the public, the use is a public nuisance, and that the use can be lawfully removed. (*Id.* at 468–69.)

Public nuisance law was also at the heart of California's first major environmental battle: the fight by farmers and city dwellers to halt the massive flooding and downstream destruction triggered by hydraulic mining in the Sierra Nevada. Perhaps California's most significant state court nuisance decision is *People v. Gold Run Ditch & Mining Co.*, 66 Cal. 138, 4 P. 1152 (1884), in which the California Supreme Court upheld a permanent injunction against a company that had created a public nuisance due to its hydraulic mining activities. In the same year, a federal district judge came to the same conclusion in a quite similar factual setting, and in the process set forth a thorough analysis of applicable public nuisance principles. (*Woodruff v. North Bloomfield Gravel Mining Co.*, 18 F. 753 (D. Calif. 1884).) The *Gold Run* and *Woodruff* decisions spelled the end of the hydraulic mining industry in California, fundamentally and irrevocably changing the state's economy. (For a fascinating account of the 19th-century legal and political wars over hydraulic mining, *see* Robert Kelley, *Gold vs. Grain* (1959).)

wetlands—if the proposed change would harm the public interest in its waterways and natural resources.

Some recent federal court decisions have been more reticent to apply the nuisance exception, at least in the threshold, categorical manner contemplated in *Lucas*, so as to defeat an inverse condemnation claim at the outset.[93]

[93]*See, e.g.*, McDougal v. County of Imperial, 942 F.2d 668, 676 (9th Cir. 1991) (rejecting nuisance rationale as blanket defense to attack on floodway ordinance); Whitney Benefits, Inc. v. United States, 926 F.2d 1169, 1176 (Fed. Cir. 1991), *cert. denied*, 502 U.S. 952 (1991).

Destruction by Necessity—the Emergency Exception

A first cousin of the nuisance exception is the principle that liability for a taking will not attach when one destroys private property as a necessary consequence of addressing some disaster-like situation. "In the case of fire, flood, pestilence, or other great public calamity, when immediate action is necessary to save human life or to avert an over-whelming destruction of property, any individual may lawfully enter another's land and destroy his property, real or personal, providing he acts with reasonable judgment."[94] The most common instance of destruction by necessity occurs in the case of fire, where both neighbors and government firefighters freely trespass on adjoining land, and structures may even be destroyed to prevent the fire from spreading. Similarly, in a variety of circumstances during wartime, the sovereign has the power to take and destroy property without payment of just compensation.[95] The safety of the state and general citizenry in such cases overrides all considerations of private loss.[96] It is in this context that we see most prominently how the nuisance exception can apply to physical as well as regulatory takings.

Two decisions illustrate the broad array of situations that can bring the destruction-by-necessity rule into play under the Takings Clause. *Miller v. Schoene*,[97] decided a mere five years after *Pennsylvania Coal*, is perhaps the most famous application of this exception. The Supreme Court in *Schoene* unanimously held that the Takings Clause did not require the State of Virginia to compensate owners of cedar trees for the value of the trees that the state had ordered destroyed to prevent a disease from spreading to nearby apple orchards, which represented a far more valuable resource to the region. In rejecting the claim, the Court did not consider it necessary to "weigh with nicety the question whether the infected cedars constitute a nuisance according to common law; or whether they may be so declared by statute."[98] Rather, the Court observed, the state's exercise of its police power to prevent the impending danger was justified and did not require compensation.

[94]JULIUS SACKMAN, NICHOLS ON EMINENT DOMAIN § 1.43 (3d ed. Rev. 1997). *See also* Omnia Commercial Co. v. United States, 261 U.S. 502, 508 (1923).
[95]Caltex, Inc. v. United States, 344 U.S. 149 (1952).
[96]United States v. Pacific R.R., 120 U.S. 227, 234 (1887).
[97]276 U.S. 272 (1928).
[98]*Id.* at 280.

The convenience store in Sacramento, California, that was the site of the police action challenged in *Customer Company v. City of Sacramento.*

The relevance of the emergency exception in a wide array of situations is seen by fast-forwarding seven decades from *Schoene* to a far grittier and urbanized setting. In *Customer Company v. City of Sacramento,*[99] local law enforcement officials in California had tracked a felony suspect into a convenience store. When negotiations to dislodge the miscreant failed, the police lobbed a fuselage of tear gas and mace into the store. The suspect was apprehended, but the store suffered over $200,000 in damage. The store owner responded by suing city officials, claiming a taking under the California Constitution. A closely divided California Supreme Court disagreed, invoking the emergency exception to conclude that the police had acted properly.

As the close vote in *Customer Company* suggests, application of the emergency exception does not always coexist comfortably with the modern, more expansive view of takings principles generally. Some recent federal cases demonstrate renewed efforts to rein in the scope of this potentially broad exception to Takings Clause liability.[100]

---

[99]10 Cal. 4th 368, 895 P.2d 900 (1995), *cert. denied,* 516 U.S. 1116 (1996).

[100]*See, e.g.,* Yancey v. United States, 915 F.2d 1534 (Fed. Cir. 1990) (taking found when government quarantine forced sale of breeder turkeys for slaughter at a 75% loss); Hendler v. United States, 952 F.2d 1364 (Fed. Cir. 1991) (government's locating of equipment on private property as part of monitoring and

Fines and Forfeitures

Numerous federal, state, and local laws provide for criminal fines and the forfeiting of property used in the commission of crimes. Almost invariably, courts uphold such penalties as a reasonable means of effectuating law enforcement authority and assert that no exercise of the power of eminent domain is involved.[101]

A vexing problem raised by the forfeiture exception to takings liability arises when an innocent party has an interest in property that is forfeited through the criminal act of another. Most courts have held that forfeiture of property even in this instance effects no taking.[102]

Conclusion

In all of the above-described situations, then, a takings claim can be defeated by government officials who are able to justify their actions under one or more of the above-described "exceptions to takings." Yet the uncompensated forfeiture of property by innocent third parties seemingly cannot be squared with the Supreme Court's modern Takings Clause jurisprudence generally. It appears impossible to reconcile these cases, for example, with the Court's oft-recited view in *Armstrong v. United States* that it is inequitable to force "some people alone to bear public burdens which, in all fairness and justice, should be borne by the public as a whole."[103]

---

cleanup activities on adjacent hazardous waste site triggered temporary, compensable taking).

[101]*See, e.g.,* United States v. One 1962 Ford Thunderbird, 232 F. Supp. 1019, 1022 (N.D. Ill. 1964).

[102]Calero-Toledo v. Pearson Yacht Leasing Co., 416 U.S. 663, 687–88 (1974). For a particularly extreme application of this rule, *see* Bennis v. Michigan, 516 U.S. 442 (1996).

[103]364 U.S. 40, 49 (1960).

Part IV

Land-Use Programs Raising Takings Issues

Chapter 15

Planning, Zoning, and Subdivision

At the very core of local land-use regulation is the process of developing and adopting comprehensive plans and official maps, zoning for land uses, and subdividing land for development. One would expect that the takings landscape would be littered with cases claiming takings as a result of these ubiquitous, profoundly local processes. But while a large number of takings cases do tangentially touch these regulatory spheres, there are relatively few cases in which planning, zoning, or subdivision in their purest forms are at issue.

That result perhaps occurs because traditional local land-use regulation has been kind to property rights, focusing largely on avoiding nuisances and providing for orderly development. In contrast, more recent regulation, particularly outside traditional land-use controls, has sought to protect natural resources, preserve landmarks, limit or redirect growth, and force property owners to bear a greater share of the costs of the impacts of their developments. It is these "cutting edge" regulatory programs that have most wounded property rights and that generate more takings litigation. It is still important, however, to recognize the limits of planning, zoning, and subdivision in the takings context.

Planning

The rational planning model identifies ideals, goals, and objectives; assesses existing resources; forecasts future trends; offers alternatives for reaching community ends; recommends implementation strategies; and continuously reassesses and revises the plan.[1] This sweeping approach is in contrast with municipal zoning, which, by its very nature, deals with specific parcels of real estate in the here and now (although implications for the future are also evident in some aspects of most local zoning ordinances). Courts have typically treated land-use planning and zoning as separate functions:[2] "Land use planning and zoning are different exercises of the sovereign power. . . ."[3] Plans are created to control and direct the use and development of property within a county or municipality, and to serve as a "constitution" for all future development within that jurisdiction.[4] Zoning, on the other hand, is considered a means rather than an end.[5] Its function—to implement a plan for the future development of the community[6]—involves the exercise of discretionary powers within limits imposed by the plan.[7]

While Americans generally accept zoning, many remain ambivalent about planning. This attitude is unfortunate, since the two practices are, or should be, intricately connected. The Standard State Zoning Enabling Act (SSZEA),[8] promulgated by the U.S. Department of Commerce in the early 1920s and still used today as a model enabling act for the majority of states, recognized the importance of joint planning and zoning and attempted to mandate that zoning be "in accordance with a comprehensive plan."[9] However, the Act failed to define what a "plan" was or how one was to be developed, let alone how the two functions were to be "in

[1]*See* Schyktz v. Pritts, 291 Md. 1, 19–20, 432 A.2d 1319 (1981).

[2]Charles M. Haar, *In Accordance With A Comprehensive Plan*, 68 HARVARD L. REV. 1154, 1154–58 (1968).

[3]Machado v. Musgrove, 519 So. 2d 629, 631 (Fla. Dist. Ct. App. 1987) (citing Baker v. City of Milwaukee, 271 Or. 500, 533 P.2d 772 (1975), *review denied*, 529 So. 2d 693 (Fla. 1988).

[4]O'Loane v. O'Rourke, 231 Cal. App. 2d 774, 782, 42 Cal. Rptr. 283 (1965); deBottari v. Norco City Council, 171 Cal. App. 3d 1204, 1212, 217 Cal. Rptr. 790, 795 (1985).

[5]Udell v. Haas, 21 N.Y.2d 463, 469–70, 235 N.E.2d 897 (1968); Asian Americans for Equality v. Koch, 72 N.Y.2d 121, 131, 527 N.E.2d 265 (1988).

[6]City of Jacksonville Beach v. Grubbs, 461 So. 2d 160, 163 (Fla. Dist. Ct. App. 1984), *review denied*, 469 So. 2d 749 (Fla. 1985); Roberson v. City of Montgomery, 285 Ala. 421, 233 So. 2d 69 (1970); Seligman v. Belknap, 288 Ky. 133, 155 S.W.2d 735 (1941); Mills v. City of Baton Rouge, 210 La. 830, 28 So. 2d 447 (1946); Roselle v. Wright, 21 N.J. 400, 408, 122 A.2d 506 (1956).

[7]*Baker*, 533 P.2d at 778.

[8]Standard State Zoning Enabling Act (SSZEA) (1924). *See* 8 PATRICK J. ROHAN, ZONING AND LAND USE CONTROLS § 53.01[1] (1994).

[9]SSZEA at § 3. *See* 8 ROHAN, *supra* note 8, at § 53.01[1].

accord." Years passed before any guidance was forthcoming. The Standard City Planning Enabling Act was not promulgated until four years after the Standard State Zoning Enabling Act,[10] leaving the horse to push a cart that had left long before.[11]

The "in accord" dilemma was compounded by judicial acquiescence in the common municipal practice of zoning without a comprehensive plan.[12] Courts have repeatedly held that absent specific statutory authority, the plan need not be a written document[13] nor be embodied in a separate document.[14] In fact, the courts became quite adept at "finding" comprehensive plans where none in fact existed.[15] Many state courts have used their finest judicial sleight of hand to hold that the comprehensive plan referred to in the SSZEA could be found in a variety of places, ranging from the zoning ordinance itself to the preamble of a zoning amendment. Thus, state courts have found that regardless of a plan's language, the comprehensive planning requirement was met by the zoning regulations in whatever form they might be after they were enacted or amended,[16] an approach that is still followed in some states today.[17]

[10]Standard City Planning Enabling Act (1928).

[11]The enabling legislation of most states includes the "in accordance with" requirement, or some variation. A few states have omitted the comprehensive plan provision (see, e.g., Noona v. Mouton, 348 Mass. 633, 639, 204 N.E.2d 897 (1965)), and some have substituted the term "well considered plan" (see, e.g., N.Y. GENERAL CITY LAW § 20 subd. 25) or have required that a master plan be adopted prior to zoning regulations (see, e.g., Martz v. Butte Silver Bow Gov't, 196 Mont. 348, 641 P.2d 426 (1982)).

[12]See KENNETH H. YOUNG, ANDERSON'S AMERICAN LAW OF ZONING § 5.03 (1996).

[13]Tulsa Rock Co. v. Board of County Comm'rs, 531 P.2d 351, 357 (Okla. Ct. App. 1974); Chestnut Hill Co. v. Snohomish, 76 Wash. 2d 741, 745, 458 P.2d 891 (1969), cert. denied, 397 U.S. 988 (1970).

[14]Baker v. Milwaukie, 17 Or. App. 89, 94, 520 P.2d 479 (1974), modified on other grounds, 271 Or. 500, 533 P.2d 772 (1975).

[15]DAVID L. CALLIES, ROBERT H. FREILICH & THOMAS E. ROBERTS, CASES AND MATERIALS ON LAND USE 372 (1994).

[16]Lazy Mountain Land Club v. Matanuska-Susitna Borough Bd. of Adjustment & Appeals, 904 P.2d 373, 379–80 (Alaska 1995); Hyland v. Mayor of Township of Morris, 130 N.J. Super. 470, 327 A.2d 675, 678–79 (App. Div. 1974).

[17]In some jurisdictions, a local governing body may enact zoning ordinances, approve subdivisions and public works, and otherwise regulate land use without preparing and adopting a separate plan. The plan is at most advisory. These

Other states[18] have chosen a middle ground, encouraging or requiring separately developed plans, not necessarily insisting on total plan control over zoning and other local land-use enactments. In these states the plan's degree of influence can range from guidance to a kind of super zoning.[19]

In states where planning is not required by statute and local governments are not bound by any comprehensive planning process when they enact land-use regulations, plans are not generally regarded as regulatory actions. Courts view plans as guides, not straitjackets; as no more than general ideas about the possible future uses of land in the community.[20] Claims that a particular designation of a landowner's property in the local comprehensive plan constitutes a taking are therefore not usually upheld.[21] Nor generally may a landowner claim a taking solely on the basis that a rezoning of land

---

states include Alabama, Alaska, Colorado, Connecticut, Illinois, Indiana, Kansas, Louisiana, Michigan, Massachusetts, Mississippi, Missouri, New Mexico, New York, North Dakota, Ohio, Oklahoma, Pennsylvania, Tennessee, Utah, Washington, West Virginia, Wisconsin, and Wyoming. 2 EDWARD H. ZIEGLER, JR., RATHKOPF'S THE LAW OF ZONING AND PLANNING § 12.04 (1996).

[18]*Id.* (These states include Arkansas, Georgia, Iowa, Maryland, Minnesota, Nebraska, New Hampshire, North Carolina, South Carolina, South Dakota, Texas, and Virginia).

[19]States that do not mandate planning or require zoning to conform with a comprehensive plan may have a different stance as to certain designated areas, most notably environmentally sensitive areas (*e.g.*, wetlands), or high-hazard areas (*e.g.*, ocean beaches). *See, e.g.*, §§ 113A-100, -102, -106 through -108 of the North Carolina General Statutes.

[20]Cochran v. Planning Bd., 87 N.J. Super. 526, 535, 210 A.2d 99 (Law Div. 1965) (adoption of master plan not a taking); Dale v. City of Mountain View, 55 Cal. App. 3d 101, 107, 127 Cal. Rptr. 520 (1976) (no taking because planning is accepted practice authorized by legislature); Love v. Board of County Comm'rs, 108 Idaho 728, 730, 701 P.2d 1293 (1985) (plan need not be followed precisely); Stuart v. Board of County Comm'rs, 699 P.2d 978, 980 (Colo. Ct. App. 1985) (comprehensive plan advisory); Theobald v. Board of County Comm'rs, 644 P.2d 942 (Colo. 1982) (comprehensive plan advisory); Burgess v. Gallatir County Comm'n, 215 Mont. 503, 698 P.2d 862 (Mont. 1985) (comprehensive plan advisory); Blue Ridge Realty & Dev. Corp. v. Lower Paxton Township, 51 Pa. Commw. 349, 353, 414 A.2d 737 (1980) (master plan only recommendatory).

[21]Allen Family Corp. v. City of Kansas City, 525 F. Supp. 38 (W.D. Mo. 1981) (mere designation of plaintiff's farmland for eventual use as park not grounds for inverse condemnation suit).

is inconsistent with the municipality's plan.[22] General land-use planning, feasibility studies, and even adoption of a general plan indicating potential use of private property will not alone support a claim for inverse condemnation.[23] Moreover, where a landowner shows that a plan has resulted in a decline in a property's market value, the prevailing view is there is no taking unless the government has otherwise acted with impropriety.[24] This is not to say that in jurisdictions where comprehensive planning is not a legal prerequisite to zoning there are no plan-initiated limits on a municipality's regulatory activities; the municipality must still pay heed to the community's comprehensive plan. While such a plan's guidelines do not totally bind the local legislative body, they do establish parameters within which the legislature can exercise discretion with safety.[25] In amending a zoning ordinance, for instance, the local government must be cognizant of the comprehensive plan.[26] For the most part, however, an ordinance will typically be upheld so long as it is consistent with the planning strategy of the community, even if not entirely consistent.[27] In fact, a local government that has drawn up a comprehensive plan and is attempting to regulate land use according to it, although not mandated by the state to do so, may be able to use the plan as an affirmative defense to claims that its regulatory programs are confiscatory.[28]

[22]*Blue Ridge Realty,* 51 Pa. Commw. at 353.

[23]Cambria Spring Co. v. City of Pico Rivera, 171 Cal. App. 3d 1080, 1091–92, 217 Cal. Rptr. 772 (1985); Selby Realty Co. v. City of San Buenaventura, 10 Cal. 3d 110, 119–20, 514 P.2d 111 (1973); Rancho LaCosta v. County of San Diego, 111 Cal. App. 3d 54, 168 Cal. Rptr. 491 (1980), *cert. denied,* 451 U.S. 939 (1981).

[24]Klopping v. City of Whittier, 8 Cal. 3d. 39, 51–52, 500 P.2d 1345 (1972) (planning can require compensation if part of government scheme to decrease land value prior to condemning it); Suess Builders Co. v. City of Beaverton, 294 Or. 254, 656 P.2d 306 (1982); Burrows v. City of Keene, 121 N.H. 590, 432 A.2d 15 (1981) (city's pre-zoning activities depressed land values).

[25]YOUNG, *supra* note 12, at § 5.06; Zetrouer v. Alachua Co., 408 So. 2d 1065 (Fla. Dist. Ct. App. 1982), *petition denied,* 417 So. 2d 331 (Fla. 1982); Taylor v. Head of Harbor, 104 A.D.2d 642, 480 N.Y.S.2d 21 (1984), *appeal denied,* 64 N.Y.2d 609 (1985); State *ex rel.* MacQueen v. Dunbar, 167 W. Va. 91, 95, 278 S.E.2d 636 (1981).

[26]YOUNG, *supra* note 12, at § 5.06. Cheney v. Village 2 at New Hope, Inc., 429 Pa. 626, 632, 241 A.2d 81 (1968).

[27]Ferguson v. Board of County Comm'rs, 110 Idaho 785, 788, 718 P.2d 1223 (1986); Bedford v. Mt. Kisco, 33 N.Y.2d 178, 188, 306 N.E.2d 155 (1973).

[28]Neuzil v. City of Iowa City, 451 N.W.2d 159 (Iowa 1990) (court recognized justification for downzoning in part by its consistency with comprehensive plan).

We have thus far discussed the comprehensive plan and its litigation potential for Fifth Amendment takings claims in the context of states that do not mandate planning or that do not insist that local land-use regulations strictly adhere to a comprehensive plan. However, the relationship between confiscation and land-use planning can be different in states where planning and zoning are legislatively coupled.

Some states have taken the "in accordance with" language of the Standard State Zoning Enabling Act seriously. Where state law mandates a separate plan, and it becomes a prerequisite to valid land-use regulation, the jurisdiction is said to follow the "consistency doctrine."[29] Florida and California are among the leaders in consistency. In these states and a few others,[30] a very close relationship between planning and zoning and other land-use controls is mandated; land-use regulation must reflect, be harmonious with, follow, and carry out designations in the plan.[31]

In the consistency states the takings issue can be found in planning controversies because the plan can actually control the zoning, special permits, and conditional uses granted under that zoning; site plan approval; and even the issuance of building permits. Consistency requirements potentially move the taking claim up to an earlier point in the planning-regulation-development process because the regulatory impact of comprehensive plans is clearer in such jurisdictions. Thus, if a plan is amended to change a medium-density residential area to preservation, the zoning must conform. The takings issue battle line consequently is drawn not in the sand of the beachhead of zoning, but further back, in the planning process that dictates the zoning.[32]

Consistency in the takings context typically rears its head when a landowner's development ideas are threatened by a local comprehensive plan for a different sort of land use. As required by statute in a consistency state, a zoning or other restrictive ordinance implements

[29]*See* JOSEPH F. DiMENTO, THE CONSISTENCY DOCTRINE AND THE LIMITS OF PLANNING 2 (1980).

[30]The consistency states include Arizona, California, Delaware, Florida, Hawaii, Idaho, Kentucky, Maine, Montana, New Jersey, Oregon, Rhode Island, and Vermont.

[31]Florida statutorily defines "consistency" in chapter 163.3194(3)(a) of the Florida Statutes.

[32]Despite the increased importance of planning and its elevated role in the regulatory hierarchy, the general observation that takings claims are mostly unsuccessful against well-thought-out, nonarbitrary plans and implementing ordinances is still valid, even in consistency states. *See* 2 ZIEGLER JR, *supra* note 17, § 12.09.

the plan, thwarting contradictory development plans. At this point, an alleged taking occurs.

In Ohio, a convenience store was opened at a mobile home park without a required zoning permit.[33] The permit had been required since 1983, when the zoning commission amended its zoning resolution and changed the property's classification. Before then, the property's classification permitted commercial establishments. Also, the property owner's father had occasionally run a store at the site. The owner eventually received a nonconforming-use permit. Nevertheless, he sued the township and various officials in 1991, alleging a taking. One of his claims was that the township failed to enact a comprehensive plan prior to enacting its zoning resolution. However, the state court of appeals agreed with the trial court that the plan requirement is satisfied where a zoning resolution and map "provided for land uses for the entire township, and that these land uses were identified on the zoning map."[34] As to the owner's takings claims, both the trial and appellate courts found no taking since the owner continued to operate a profitable mobile home park, thus no deprivation of economically viable use had occurred.[35]

Inconsistency between a plan and a regulatory decision is not in itself enough to prove a taking. Merely showing that a landowner's proposed use conforms to the comprehensive plan and yet has been denied is not enough.[36] Conversely, a showing that a rezoning has been denied because of inconsistency with the plan does not constitute a taking. Also, showing that an ordinance is inconsistent with the comprehensive plan will not alone support a takings claim.[37]

We have established that when local governments in a consistency state enact zoning and other land-use ordinances, they must conform to the comprehensive plan. Problems may arise, however, when the local legislative body is slow in issuing consistent enactments. How long is too long for a local government to get its act together, thereby

[33]Curtis v. Geneva Township Trustees, 1996 Ohio App. LEXIS 2447 (Ohio Ct. App., June 14, 1996), *dismissed*, 77 Ohio St. 3d 1474 (1996).

[34]*Id.* at 6–7, quoting from an unreported decision.

[35]*Id.* at 10–11.

[36]Chandis Sec. Co. v. City of Dana Point, 52 Cal. App. 4th 475, 60 Cal. Rptr. 2d 481 (1996), *review denied*, 1997 Cal. LEXIS 1907 (Cal. Apr. 2, 1997). *But see* Del Monte Dunes at Monterey, Ltd. v. City of Monterey, 95 F.3d 1422, 1430–32 (9th Cir. 1996) (evidence supports jury's finding of taking; application consistent with comprehensive plan), *cert. granted*, 118 S. Ct. 1359 (1998).

[37]Machado v. Musgrove, 519 So. 2d 629 (Fla. Dist. Ct. App. 1987).

exposing itself to constitutional attack for unreasonable delay? This question was found ripe for review in a Florida case, *Alexander v. Town of Jupiter*.[38] For eight years the Town of Jupiter had failed to resolve the inconsistency between its comprehensive plan, which designated certain property for conservation, and its zoning ordinance, which did not include provisions for development within a conservation district. For two years the plaintiff attempted to obtain a tree-clearing permit for his property within the conservation district. The town refused to issue a permit pending resolution of the inconsistency. The court found that the permit denial created a temporary taking issue ripe for adjudication. Seeking evidence as to what could be considered a reasonable amount of time for resolving zoning and planning inconsistencies, the court looked to the Florida statutes, which require adoption of land-use regulations in conformity with the plan within one year after the state has approved the local plan.[39] The case was remanded to the trial court to decide whether a compensable taking had occurred.

While the consistency doctrine may open the door earlier and perhaps admit more takings claims, this potential burden is outweighed by the advantages of comprehensive planning and zoning. The consistency doctrine has rescued local governments caught in difficult situations, such as trying to regulate and plan for land use in the face of fierce landowner opposition.

Sometimes property owners couldn't care less if their local ordinance conforms to the comprehensive plan; they just do not want to be regulated at all. In some areas of the country, citizens have enacted, or have attempted to enact, anti-takings resolutions, declaring their communities confiscation-free zones. In California, the consistency doctrine was invoked in an attempt to defeat certain provisions of a "Landowners' Bill of Rights."[40] In Tehama County, voters enacted an ordinance by initiative to limit governmental regulation of private property. Proponents of the initiative published a statement of reasons, which included the following assertion:

---

[38]640 So. 2d 79 (Fla. Dist. Ct. App.), *dismissed on other grounds*, 648 So. 2d 725 (Fla. 1994).

[39]*Id.* at 83 (citing Fla. Stat. § 163.3202).

[40]Patterson v. County of Tehama, 190 Cal. App. 3d 1298, 235 Cal. Rptr. 867 (1987). This decision has been withdrawn by the court and therefore cannot be cited in litigation and has no value as precedent. However, we can find no other case on point and use the case here only for an example of the type of claim that might be made.

[T]hrough the passage of the Landowners' Bill of Rights, it is our intention to limit the power of public entities—to effectively destroy the value of property through zoning.[41]

After deciding that the initiative had referred to only the county through the term "public entity" and thereby had not attempted to abrogate the authority of the State of California, the court found that certain provisions of the ordinance conflicted directly with various provisions of the California Government Code requiring counties in California to adopt and enforce general plans. The initiative effectively repealed the existing Tehama County General Plan, as well as prohibited future adoption and enforcement of a general plan meeting the requirements of state law. The court held that the voters of Tehama County could not impede acts of the Legislature. Therefore, the offending portions of the resolution were declared invalid.

A comprehensive plan and attendant regulations in a consistency state may be used to foreclose a taking claim by showing that the pre-taking value of the property is not significantly higher than the value of the property after the alleged taking. To illustrate, let us consider the facts of *City National Bank of Miami v. United States*.[42] Property was purchased with the intention of mining limerock. The activity was to take place in a wetlands area, requiring both a section 404 permit from the U.S. Army Corps of Engineers pursuant to the Clean Water Act and a permit from the Florida Department of Environmental Regulation. The county also restricted limerock mining by regulation and required an amendment to the master plan and issuance of an unusual-use permit for such an activity, if it were allowed at all. The federal permit was denied, and the landowner filed a takings claim against the federal government.

The court cited the rule of *Keystone Bituminous Coal Association v. DeBenedictis*[43] that the "test for regulatory taking requires . . . [the court] to compare the value that has been taken from the property with the value that remains in the property. . . ."[44] The plaintiff asserted that the value of the land before the permit denial should not

---

[41]*Id*. at 1299, 235 Cal. Rptr. at 873.

[42]33 Fed. Cl. 224, *mot. denied, summ. j. granted*, 33 Fed. Cl. 759 (1995).

[43]480 U.S. 470 (1987).

[44]*Id*. at 497. *See* Florida Rock Indus., Inc. v. United States, 18 F.3d 1560 (Fed. Cir. 1994) (remand to determine whether taking occurred by comparing fair market value before to fair market value after the alleged taking), *cert. denied*, 513 U.S. 1109 (1995).

be based on the state and county restrictions then in place. The court, however, declared that it could not ignore a most basic local planning tool, the comprehensive plan, in valuing the property.[45]

The *City National Bank of Miami* court held that if the federal government established that either the comprehensive plan flatly prohibits limerock mining, or that the plaintiff would have failed to obtain the required master plan amendment or redesignation and unusual-use permit, the taking claim must fail because there would be no diminution in value attributable to the government's action. The court thus treated locally enacted land-use restrictions carried out under the mandate of consistency as a controlling factor in determining whether a landowner's property had been taken by an act of the federal government.

Mandated planning along with the consistency requirement may help buffer local governments from takings claims. Comprehensive plans addressing all of a community's land-use needs, and backed by extensive studies and recorded findings, tend to indicate that the local government is acting to further the public health, safety, and general welfare. Zoning and other regulatory measures that conform to a well-designed plan are much more likely to win judicial approval than ad hoc, narrowly focused and uncoordinated controls.[46]

An official map specifically identifies the location of future streets, parks, drainage systems, and other basic public facilities on vacant land within a municipality. State-level agencies may also use official maps, or "maps of reservation," to indicate the location of future public infrastructure, such as highways and thoroughfares. In contrast with the maps in a comprehensive plan, which may vary in precision according to their intended use, or local zoning maps, which often follow street and lot lines, the official map must be accurate in scale, location, and dimension. "Such a map must be the product of surveys rather than estimates."[47]

The local legislative body adopts the official map as an ordinance or resolution, effective for a specified period of time. Local enabling

---

[45]33 Fed. Cl. 224, 232 (citing United States v. 320.0 Acres of Land, More or Less, 605 F.2d 762, 818 (5th Cir. 1979)), *complaint dismissed*, 33 Fed. Cl. 759 (1995); United States v. Eden Memorial Park Ass'n, 350 F.2d 933, 936 (9th Cir. 1965); United States v. Meadow Brook Club, 259 F. 2d 41, 45 (2d Cir.) (if existing zoning precludes more profitable use, ordinarily such use should not be considered in valuation), *cert. denied*, 358 U.S. 921 (1958).

[46]Lee County v. Sunbelt Equities, 619 So. 2d 996, 1002 (Fla. Dist. Ct. App. 1993).

[47]ROBERT M. ANDERSON, AMERICAN LAW OF ZONING § 26.01 (1986).

statutes govern the official-map adoption process, which notifies
landowners and developers that the municipality intends to acquire
specified property for public use sometime in the future. In addition,
installation of improvements or erection of buildings within areas reserved for future public acquisition is prohibited.[48] One court has
characterized the official map as "essentially a tool of planning,
rather than zoning."[49]

Some early proponents of the official map advocated its usefulness
in growth management, while others emphasized the map's potential
to reduce government's future property acquisition costs by freezing
land values at current prices. Two versions of the official map
emerged from this professional and academic debate: one based on
the government's power of eminent domain, the other based on the
police power of government to regulate nuisances.[50]

In 1928, the U.S. Department of Commerce published A Standard
City Planning Enabling Act (the "Act") to facilitate investment and
stimulate economic growth.[51] Section 21 of the Act offered model
language for an official-map enabling statute for local governments.
The Act's version was predicated upon the government's power of
eminent domain.[52] The Act's drafters were concerned, however, that
municipal adoption of an official map might be construed as a taking
under the Fifth Amendment.[53]

The Act conceded that the official map created a temporary encum-
brance by the government on private property and encouraged municipalities to provide just compensation to affected landowners.[54]
However, due to the expense of this approach, its use by local governments was not widespread.

The Municipal Mapped Streets Act (the "Streets Act") was an alternative to the Standard City Planning Enabling Act and was based

---

[48]*Id.* at § 26.02.

[49]Nigro v. Planning Bd. of Saddle River, 122 N.J. 270, 276, 584 A.2d 1350
(1991).

[50]Joseph C. Kucirek & J.H. Beuscher, *Wisconsin's Official Map Law*, 1957
WISCONSIN L. REV. 176, 183 (1957). *See also* EDWARD M. BASSETT, ZONING: THE
LAWS, ADMINISTRATION, AND COURT DECISIONS DURING THE FIRST TWENTY YEARS
26–27 (1940).

[51]6 ROHAN, *supra* note 8, § 37.01[2][b] (1994).

[52]Kucirek & Beuscher, *supra* note 50, at 183 n.24.

[53]Standard City Planning Enabling Act at § 21.

[54]DONALD G. HAGMAN & JULIAN C. JUERGENSMEYER, URBAN PLANNING AND
LAND DEVELOPMENT CONTROL LAW § 7.9 (1986).

on the police power of local government to regulate nuisances.[55] The Streets Act maintained that municipalities could adopt an official map without compensating affected landowners. Advocates of the Streets Act posited that reserving private property for possible future acquisition was not a government action constituting a physical taking but rather a police power regulation to provide for the health, safety, and welfare of the community.[56]

The Streets Act model language also provided that variances to the official map could be issued if the reservation posed a hardship to the landowner. A hardship was defined as either lack of reasonable return or a balancing-test determination of whether the owner's use of the property outweighed the interest of the municipality to preserve the integrity of the official map.[57] Additionally, affected landowners could apply to delete their property from the official map by amendment.[58]

Most states that use the official-map planning technique have adopted the police power, Streets Act version as the enabling statute.[59] By controlling the location of streets through an official map, a municipality arguably acts in the public interest, planning for the orderly and efficient future development of the community. However, this objective is achieved by restricting development of private property, sometimes for many years. Landowners whose property is encumbered by an official-map designation often complain that their property is taken by this designation when they are unable to get development approval in the reserved areas. Furthermore, land identified on an official map for future public acquisition necessarily suffers some diminution in value, or can become virtually unmarketable, further precipitating takings challenges.

The central issue considered by most courts has been whether adoption of an official map constitutes a confiscatory regulation requiring just compensation under the Takings Clause. At the time the official-map technique was first introduced, a taking was generally defined as the physical invasion of private property by the govern-

[55]EDWARD M. BASSETT ET AL., MODEL LAWS FOR PLANNING CITIES, COUNTIES AND STATES INCLUDING ZONING, SUBDIVISION REGULATION AND PROTECTION OF OFFICIAL MAP 15–25, 89–92 (1935). *See also* Kucirek & Beuscher, *supra* note 50, at 183–84.

[56]BASSETT ET AL., *supra* note 55, at 20–25, 89–92.

[57]HAGMAN & JUERGENSMEYER, *supra* note 54, at § 7.9.

[58]*Id.*

[59]Kucirek & Beuscher, *supra* note 50, at 183.

ment.[60] However, as the official-map technique came into more general use, the U.S. Supreme Court further developed takings law doctrine to include in some cases government regulations that affect property value.

Early Fifth Amendment challenges to the mapping of future streets and public improvements generally failed. The courts consistently held that official maps, in and of themselves, did not take private property.[61] A 1930s case, *Headley v. Rochester*, provides the classic rationale in support of the constitutionality of the official map, at least in the abstract.[62]

Many of these early court decisions upholding "paper streets" emphasized that landowners are served with constructive notice of future possible condemnation through publication of the official map. One court made the following observations:

> The object of the recording of the map is to give notice to all persons of the systems of highways proposed to be established by subsequent proceedings of condemnation. It does not restrict in any way the use or improvement of lands by their owners before the commencement of proceedings for condemnation of lands for such highways; nor does it limit the damages to be awarded in such proceedings.[63]

Some decrease in property value due to an official map will be tolerated.[64] However, while an official map may prevent development of land that a municipality expects to acquire in the future, regulatory action may not purposely devalue property.[65] Such restrictions on development cannot be used to minimize the value of land actually taken for public use;[66] nor may the government make systematic threats of eminent domain to lower property values.[67]

When a map of reservation is not implemented solely for freezing current land prices for future acquisitions by the government, courts have recognized that some cost reductions do adhere to such foresight.

[60]Note, *The Origins and Original Significance of the Just Compensation Clause*, 94 YALE L.J. 694, 708 (1985).

[61]Erie R. Co. v. Passaic, 79 N.J.L. 19, 21, 74 A. 338 (1909).

[62]272 N.Y. 197, 5 N.E.2d 198 (1936).

[63]Baumann v. Ross, 167 U.S. 548, 597 (1897).

[64]Palm Beach County v. Wright, 641 So. 2d 50, 53 (Fla. 1994).

[65]*See, e.g.*, State *ex rel.* Tingley v. Gurda, 209 Wis. 63, 243 N.W. 317 (1932).

[66]Rochester v. Hennen, 56 A.D.2d 719, 720, 392 N.Y.S.2d 943 (1977).

[67]*See, e.g.*, Reservation Eleven Assocs. v. District of Columbia, 420 F.2d 153, 157 (D.C. Cir. 1969).

In *Palm Beach County v. Wright*,[68] the Florida Supreme Court acknowledged that the comprehensive planning of future transportation needs greatly benefited the community and reduced costs. The *Palm Beach* thoroughfare map was distinguished from the invalid maps in *Joint Ventures*[69] because it limited development only to the extent necessary to ensure compatibility with future land use and included some flexibility to deal with hardship cases.

It is well-settled law that the mere adoption of an official map does not constitute a taking per se.[70] But the courts will find a taking when the restriction is unreasonable.[71] State and federal courts have looked to several factors to determine the reasonableness of an official map's impact on a particular piece of land. Some courts have recognized that denial of a building permit under an official map may have so great an impact that a taking occurs.[72] Other state courts have detected no taking where a property owner was denied a permit to build in a mapped street.[73] If, however, an official-map statute that precludes issuance of building permits in designated corridors is found invalid, the landowner may have a temporary takings claim for the time in which the owner was not permitted to build on the property, provided the owner can show that "[t]he authority's action in recording the reservation map invaded some property right of [the landowner]."[74]

Another factor is how much of the property is actually restricted. Generally, application of an official map is invalid when the develop-

[68]641 So. 2d 50.

[69]*Id.* at 53.

[70]Franco-Italian Packing Co. v. United States, 130 Ct. Cl. 736, 128 F. Supp. 408 (1955); Krieger v. Planning Comm'n of Howard County, 224 Md. 320, 167 A.2d 885 (1961); *Palm Beach,* 641 So. 2d 50.

[71]In re Sansom Street in Philadelphia, 293 Pa. 483, 143 A. 134 (1928) (ordinance left owner with only two and one-half feet of land outside limits of projected street); Caperton v. Lawrence, 161 Misc. 23, 290 N.Y.S. 1016 (Sup. Ct. 1936) (map depicting streets cutting through dwelling).

[72]Kirschke v. Houston, 330 S.W.2d 629 (Tex. App. 1959), *appeal dismissed,* 364 U.S. 474 (1960); Miller v. Beaver Falls, 368 Pa. 189, 194, 82 A.2d 34 (1951) (general plan that froze private land for three years invalid); Ward v. Bennett, 214 A.D.2d 741, 625 N.Y.S.2d 609 (1995).

[73]State *ex rel.* Miller v. Manders, 2 Wis. 2d 365, 376, 86 N.W.2d 469 (1957) (valid exercise of police power). *See also* Hilltop Properties, Inc. v. State, 233 Cal. App. 2d 349, 361, 43 Cal. Rptr. 605 (1965).

[74]Orlando/Orange County Expressway Authority v. W & F Agrigrowth-Fernfield, Ltd., 582So. 2d 790, 792 (Fla. Dist. Ct. App.), *review denied,* 591 So. 2d 183 (Fla. 1991).

ment restrictions affect a substantial portion of private property,[75] while lesser impacts might be acceptable.[76]

An official-map restriction does not constitute a taking when the desired use of the property can be accomplished elsewhere on the site.[77] In addition, takings claims can be avoided if a property use can be allowed by variance or through an amendment to the official map. Such "safety-valve clauses" make it much more likely that a court will uphold mapping as a constitutional means of planning future streets and other public improvements.[78]

If there is any trend in the relationship of planning to zoning, it is in the direction of more consistency, rather than less. Consequently, we are likely to see the takings issue more often in planning.

Zoning

Controlling land use to protect the public health is not a new phenomenon. State and federal courts were upholding a wide variety of restrictions on private property long before the introduction of zoning as a local government tool. Many of these cases were predicated on nuisance law, which was and still is the common law's method of ensuring that a landowner's use of private property will not injure his neighbors or the public in general.

Inherent in nuisance law is the principle of "sic utere tuo ut alienum non laedas"—one must so use his property as not to injure that of another.[79] Cases based at least in part on a nuisance theory and holding government exempt from paying compensation have included fact scenarios such as closing an illegal brewery,[80] destroying infected cedar trees,[81] banning an urban brickyard operation,[82]

---

[75]Roer Const. Co. v. City of New Rochelle, 207 Misc. 46, 136 N.Y.S.2d 414 (Sup. Ct. 1954); Rand v. City of New York, 3 Misc.2d 769, 155 N.Y.S.2d 753 (Sup. Ct. 1956); Jensen v. New York, 42 N.Y.2d 1079, 369 N.E.2d 1179 (1977).

[76]Corbett v. New York, 114 A.D.2d 435, 494 N.Y.S.2d 348 (1985).

[77]R.B.I. Enter. Inc., v. City of Rochester, 25 A.D.2d 97, 267 N.Y.S.2d 274, 279 (1966).

[78]But see Forster v. Scott, 136 N.Y. 577, 32 N.E. 976 (1893) (mapping statute void for impairing property's value, interfering with owner's power of disposition).

[79]Bove v. Donner-Hanna Coke Corp., 236 A.D. 37, 39, 258 N.Y.S. 229 (1932).

[80]Mugler v. Kansas, 123 U.S. 623, 668 (1887).

[81]Miller v. Schoene, 276 U.S. 272 (1928).

[82]Hadacheck v. Sebastian, 239 U.S. 394, 411 (1915).

restricting gravel and sand mining,[83] limiting underground coal mining,[84] and drastically limiting use of a flood-prone campground.[85] It is clear from these cases that some courts have used the nuisance doctrine to engage in a little "judicial zoning" in order to control land uses when the legislature has failed to do so.[86]

This is not to say that the common law of nuisance is the sole basis for land-use controls in America today. While nuisance doctrine has provided some definitions and standards for judicial review,[87] the true mother of zoning and other land-use regulations is the police power. It is the inherent right of the sovereign state to regulate for the public health, safety, morals, and general welfare.[88] Once duly delegated with police power from the state, its political subdivisions are authorized to regulate locally.

Like nuisance cases, early police power cases focused on protecting the public health and safety, and, to a lesser degree, public morals and general welfare. Courts generally would support government regulations made for these reasons, absent arbitrary and capricious behavior. Under the police power umbrella, many communities enacted building height limitations,[89] established minimum construction standards,[90] imposed setback requirements,[91] required emergency ingress and egress,[92] excluded certain uses from designated residential or commercial areas,[93] and otherwise regulated activities on pri-

---

[83]Goldblatt v. Town of Hempstead, 369 U.S. 590 (1962).

[84]Keystone Bituminous Coal Ass'n v. DeBenedictis, 480 U.S. 470 (1987).

[85]First English Evangelical Lutheran Church v. County of Los Angeles, 210 Cal. App. 3d 1353, 258 Cal. Rptr. 893 (1989), *review denied*, 1989 Cal. LEXIS 4224 (Aug. 25, 1989), *cert. denied,* 493 U.S. 1056 (1990).

[86]CALLIES, FREILICH & ROBERTS, *supra* note 15, at 5 (1994).

[87]*Id.*; Village of Euclid v. Ambler Realty Co., 272 U.S. 365, 387–88 (1926) (nuisance law used by analogy to measure police power). *See* Lucas v. South Carolina Coastal Council, 505 U.S. 1003, 1029–30 (1992) (law of nuisance important in defining meaning of property).

[88]*See, e.g.,* City of Chicago v. Clark, 359 Ill. 374, 376, 194 N.E. 537 (1935); Schmidt v. Board of Adjustment, 88 A.2d 607 (N.J. 1952).

[89]*See, e.g.,* People *ex rel.* Kemp v. D'Oench, 111 N.Y. 359, 361, 18 N.E. 862 (1888).

[90]People *ex rel.* Namm v. Carlin, 182 A.D. 626, 169 N.Y.S. 295 (1918). *See also* Detroit Edison Co. v. Wixom, 382 Mich. 673, 172 N.W.2d 382 (1969); Motor Lodges, Inc. v. Willingham, 509 P.2d 901 (Okla. 1972).

[91]*See, e.g.,* City of St. Louis v. Hill, 116 Mo. 527, 22 S.W. 861 (1893).

[92]Robinson v. Jagger, 293 N.Y.S.2d 258 (1968).

[93]Reinman v. Little Rock, 237 U.S. 171 (1915) (livery stables); Hadacheck v.

vate property.[94] Courts ruled that the police power was sufficiently broad to include these new laws, and that they could be considered reasonable preventative measures against harm to the public health and safety.[95] One court summed up the general consensus by observing that the police power is as broad as the public needs.[96]

Most of the nuisance and police power cases discussed above illustrate how the courts and legislatures dealt with incompatible land uses in the era before zoning. And most were decided before the era of "regulatory takings," ushered in by *Pennsylvania Coal Co. v. Mahon* in 1922.[97] Such cases did not, therefore, often raise the takings issue under the Fifth Amendment. Instead, most early land-use control cases were decided on common law principles, or involved procedural and substantive due process challenges.[98] However, these first permutations of government control over private property provide a useful perspective from which to study the modern versions of land-use regulation.

In 1926, the U.S. Supreme Court decided *Village of Euclid v. Ambler Realty Co.* upholding the use of zoning under the police power.[99] That same year the Zoning Advisory Committee of the U.S. Department of Commerce issued its revised version of the Standard State Zoning Enabling Act,[100] and zoning was off and running. Zoning

---

Sebastian, 239 U.S. 394 (1915) (brick kilns). For a more modern regulatory effort, *see* 1995 Venture I, Inc. v. Orange County, 947 F. Supp 271 (E.D. Texas 1996) (sexually oriented businesses).

[94]In re Opinion of Justices, 103 Me. 506, 69 A. 627 (1908) (cutting or destruction of trees); St. Louis v. Fisher, 167 Mo. 654, 67 S.W. 872 (1902) (dairies), *aff'd*, 194 U.S. 361 (1904), *overruled in part*, Hays v. Poplar Bluff, 263 Mo. 516, 173 S.W. 676 (1915) (ordinance invalid if it fails to provide "rule applicable to all alike under the same circumstances"); Quintini v. Mayor, etc. of Bay St. Louis, 64 Miss. 483, 1 So. 625 (1887); People v. Levine, 119 Misc. 766, 198 N.Y.S. 328 (Rensselaer County Ct. 1922).

[95]*See, e.g.,* Welch v. Swasey, 214 U.S. 91 (1909) (height limitations).

[96]Ex parte Quong Wo, 161 Cal. 220, 118 P. 714 (1911). *See also* Parking Ass'n of Georgia, Inc. v. City of Atlanta, 450 S.E.2d 200, 202–03 (Ga.) (aesthetics part of public welfare element of police power), *cert. denied*, 515 U.S. 1116 (1995).

[97]260 U.S. 393, 415 (1922).

[98]Most modern land-use cases are also decided on other constitutional grounds, most notably procedural and substantive due process, and to a lesser degree, equal protection.

[99]272 U.S. 365 (1926).

[100]Standard State Zoning Enabling Act (1926). *See* 8 ROHAN, *supra* note 8, § 53.01[1] (1994).

soon became a ubiquitous tool of local governments, until today almost every state and major city uses zoning as its primary instrument of land-use regulation. Houston, however, steadfastly proclaims its freedom from zoning, but so far remains the exception.

Ever since *Euclid*, state and federal courts have consistently upheld comprehensive zoning, finding that as long as procedural due process is not violated and the regulations are not arbitrary or irrational, zoning is a valid exercise of the police power that does not require compensation.[101] Courts have recognized that while zoning imposes a burden on landowners,[102] all property is held subject to state authority to regulate so the property does not unnecessarily endanger people.[103]

This is not to say that zoning ordinances are not subject to takings claims. Remember, ever since 1922 the Supreme Court has held that regulations can effect a taking if they "go too far."[104] Exactly how far is too far has never been conclusively defined, and the courts have employed a variety of tests to determine whether a particular regulation has effected a taking.

As far back as the early nuisance and police power cases, landowners were expected to absorb any loss attributable to the restrictions placed against use of their property. In return, the landowners allegedly received reciprocal benefits from other landowners in the community who were also burdened by government regulation, a theory known as average reciprocity of advantage.[105] According to this principle, land-use ordinances do not give rise to a constitutional challenge either because the benefits received

---

[101]Nectow v. City of Cambridge, 277 U.S. 183 (1928) (zoning regulations improper for not bearing substantial relation to public health, safety, morals, or general welfare). *But see* City of Pharr v. Tippitt, 616 S.W.2d 173 (Tex. 1981) (city did not act arbitrarily, capriciously, or unreasonably).

[102]Robin Corp. v. Board of Supervisors, 17 Pa. Commw. 386, 397, 332 A.2d 841 (1975).

[103]Ellis v. W. University Place, 141 Tex. 608, 610–11, 175 S.W.2d 396 (1943).

[104]Pennsylvania Coal v. Mahon, 260 U.S. 393, 415 (1922). *Cf.* Texas Manufactured Hous. Ass'n, Inc. v. City of Nederland, 101 F.3d 1095 (5th Cir. 1996) (ordinance restricting placement of manufactured housing is not taking), *cert. denied*, 117 S. Ct. 2497 (1997).

[105]*See, e.g.*, Keystone Bituminous Coal Ass'n v. De Benedictis, 480 U.S. 470, 491–93 (1987) ("reciprocity of advantage" is among reasons why property owners do not succeed in takings claim).

by the landowner outweigh the burdens imposed by the restriction or the benefits from mutual regulations provide the compensation to satisfy the Fifth Amendment.[106] Even where a landowner has suffered economic loss due to regulation, the owner need not necessarily be "compensated" by a direct reciprocal advantage, so long as the owner still retains some economically viable use of the property considered as a whole.[107]

This early justification for police power restrictions carried over to zoning once that came into the forefront of land-use law and has continued to be used as a rationale by commentators and courts alike.[108] For instance, in *Agins v. City of Tiburon*,[109] the Court found that an open-space zoning ordinance restricting development did not effect a taking, noting that the zoning restrictions benefited the plaintiffs as well as the public by "serving the city's interest in assuring careful and orderly development of residential property with provision for open-space areas."[110]

In general, courts will uphold an otherwise valid zoning ordinance that causes some reduction in the value of property. These cases are often based on a finding that the general welfare of the public is more important than the pecuniary profits of the individual.[111] While protecting property values is the objective of most zoning, applying a zoning ordinance will not be deemed unconstitutional simply because it reduces the value of a particular piece of real estate, so long as the regulation relates to the public health, safety, and general welfare. As one court put it: "Properly administered zoning power by local authorities may legally leave in its wake scars of lost profits to land owners as well as restricted uses causing inconvenience and disappointments but that is the exact meaning of zoning."[112]

[106]Raymond R. Coletta, *Reciprocity of Advantage and Regulatory Takings: Toward A New Theory of Takings Jurisprudence*, 40 AMERICAN U.L. REV. 297, 302 (1990). *See also* Penn Central Transp. Co. v. New York City, 438 U.S. 104 (1978).

[107]*See, e.g.*, Lucas v. South Carolina Coastal Comm'n, 505 U.S. 1003 (1992).

[108]*See* Coletta, *supra* note 105, at 301–02.

[109]447 U.S. 255 (1980).

[110]*Id.* at 262.

[111]Geneva Inv. Co. v. St. Louis, 87 F.2d 83, 90 (8th Cir.), *cert. denied*, 301 U.S. 692 (1937); Case v. Los Angeles, 142 Cal. App. 2d 66, 298 P.2d 50 (1956); Board of County Comm'rs v. Kay, 240 Md. 690, 215 A.2d 206 (1965); Style/Rite Homes, Inc. v. Zoning Bd. of Appeals, 54 Misc. 2d 866, 283 N.Y.S.2d 623 (Sup. Ct. 1967).

[112]Little v. Young, 82 N.Y.S.2d 909, 916 (Sup. Ct.), *aff'd*, 274 A.D. 1005 (1948), *aff'd*, 299 N.Y. 699 (1949).

To what degree property values may be diminished by a zoning ordinance without crossing into confiscatory territory is not subject to precise calculation. The court must consider the difference between the value of the property as zoned and its value if zoned as proposed.[113] Such determinations naturally turn on the facts of a case, and courts will decide such an issue only on an ad hoc basis.[114] In general, however, proof of a very large difference in value is insufficient by itself to overcome the presumption of validity of a zoning ordinance.[115]

While a zoning ordinance does not effect a taking solely on the basis of a reduction in land value, this rule assumes that the ordinance does not destroy value altogether. "Although phrased in slightly differing terms in the cases, the rule emerging . . . is that a regulation must deny the landowner all or substantially all practical uses of a property in order to be considered a taking for which compensation is required."[116] A zoning ordinance that deprives the landowner of the entire use of the property constitutes a "categorical taking."[117] Such a restriction will generally be considered confiscatory even if it is enacted for the legitimate police power purpose of protecting the public health, safety, morals, and general welfare.[118]

Where circumstances make a parcel of real estate unsuitable for any purpose allowed in the zoning ordinance, the court may find that no economically viable use is available, and that a taking has oc-

[113]St. Lucas Ass'n v. City of Chicago, 212 Ill. App. 3d 817, 825, 571 N.E.2d 865 (1991), citing Oak Park Trust & Sav. Bank v. Village of Palo Park, 106 Ill. App. 3d 394, 435 N.E.2d 1265 (1982).

[114]DePaul v. Board of County Comm'rs, 237 Md. 221, 205 A.2d 805 (1965); Gardner v. Leboeuf, 24 Misc. 2d 511, 204 N.Y.S.2d 468 (Sup. Ct. 1960), aff'd, 15 A.D.2d 815, 226 N.Y.S.2d 678 (1962); Bauer v. Waste Management, 234 Conn. 221, 662 A.2d 1179 (1995); Threatt v. Fulton County, 467 S.E.2d 546, 550 (Ga. 1996).

[115]DuPage Trust Co. v. County of DuPage, 31 Ill. App. 3d 993, 999–1000, 335 N.E.2d 61, 66 (1975).

[116]Zealy v. City of Waukesha, 201 Wis. 2d 365, 374, 548 N.W.2d 528 (1996) (citing Lucas v. South Carolina Coastal Council, 505 U.S. 1003, 1015; Dolan v. City of Tigard, 512 U.S. 374, 383–85 (1994); Zinn v. State, 112 Wis. 2d 417, 424, 334 N.W.2d 67 (Wis. 1983); Reel Enters. v. City of La Crosse, 146 Wis. 2d 662, 674, 431 N.W.2d 743 (Ct. App. 1988)); FIC Homes of Blackstone, Inc. v. Conservation Comm'n, 673 N.E.2d 61 (Mass. Ct. App. 1996), review denied, 424 Mass. 1104 (1997).

[117]Lucas, at 1026.

[118]Id. at 1029 n.16.

curred. For instance, physical features that may render a property undevelopable under an existing ordinance include parcel size[119] and shape,[120] but not topography that renders development hazardous,[121] or difficult.[122]

Much more common than the relatively rare categorical takings are cases in which some use is left, albeit not the owner's preferred use. The Fifth Amendment does not guarantee that an owner may put his property to its "highest and best use," nor does it require that local governments permit or require the most profitable use of each parcel of real estate in the jurisdiction.[123] If, for example, a landowner can prove the highest and best use for his property is an apartment house, but zoning permits only single-family dwellings, this is insufficient to prove the ordinance is unconstitutional.[124]

Often, whether or not an ordinance that leaves the landowner some use of the property will be sustained depends upon how the court weighs the benefit to the public against the burden placed on the landowner. If a zoning ordinance sufficiently contributes to the public health, safety, or welfare, while the detriment to the landowner is slight, the ordinance will not constitute a taking.[125] However, where the "gain to the public is small—compared to the

[119]Robyns v. Dearborn, 341 Mich. 495, 67 N.W.2d 718 (1954); *Lucas*, 505 U.S. 1003; Householder v. Grand Island, 36 Misc. 2d 862, 114 N.Y.S.2d 852 (Sup. Ct. 1951) (setback restrictions leave no space to build), *aff'd*, 280 A.D. 874 (1952), *aff'd*, 305 N.Y. 805 (1953); Samuels v. Harrison, 195 N.Y.S.2d 882 (Sup. Ct. 1959) (mere lessening of profits does not render ordinance confiscatory).

[120]LaSalle Nat'l Bank v. Evanston, 24 Ill. 2d 59, 179 N.E.2d 673 (1962); Smith v. Wood Creek Farms, 371 Mich. 127, 123 N.W.2d 210 (1963).

[121]Forde v. Miami Beach, 146 Fla. 676, 1 So. 2d 642 (1941) (where shoreline erosion made lots unstable for residential purposes, ordinance limiting use to residential invalid); Little Rock v. Hocott, 220 Ark. 421, 247 S.W.2d 1012 (1952) (restricting use of steep-grade property to single-family residential unconstitutional).

[122]Alsenas v. Brecksville, 29 Ohio App.2d 255, 281 N.E.2d 21 (1972) (classification as single-family residential not invalid where land extremely irregular and terrain made providing roadway difficult).

[123]*See, e.g.,* Tanner v. Green Forest, 302 Ark. 170, 788 S.W.2d 727 (1990); Sellon v. Manitou Springs, 745 P.2d 229 (Colo. 1987).

[124]YOUNG, *supra* note 12, § 3.25.

[125]Meyer Material Co. v. County of Will, 51 Ill. App. 3d 821, 366 N.E.2d 1149 (1977); Prairie Vista, Inc. v. County of Sangamon, 43 Ill. App. 3d 343, 356 N.E.2d 1323 (1976).

hardship imposed upon the property owner, courts are fully justified in declaring the ordinance unreasonable, confiscatory and void."[126]

Rezoning

When a landowner opposes current restrictions and petitions for a change in the zoning ordinance, or when a community decides that the zoning classification of certain areas should be changed, the local government may change the zoning ordinance, or carry out a "rezoning," as authorized under the enabling legislation for regulating land use. Rezonings are subject to the usual takings tests. Rezonings have the potential, however, to raise a few additional takings concerns.

Many courts treat rezoning as different from original zoning in terms of procedures, which in turn affects how the two activities are classified for purposes of judicial review. In *Fasano v. Board of County Commissioners of Washington County*,[127] the Oregon court recognized, then created an exception to, the general rule that ordinances laying down general policies without regard to a specific piece of property are usually an exercise of legislative authority, are subject to limited review, and may only be attacked on constitutional grounds as an arbitrary use of authority.[128] A determination whether the permissible use of a *specific* piece of property should be changed is usually an exercise of judicial authority and therefore is not accorded the traditional presumption of validity.[129]

While *Fasano*-type reasoning is not followed in most jurisdictions,[130] the Oregon case does illustrate a general trend at both state

[126]First Nat'l Bank v. County of Cook, 46 Ill. App. 3d 677, 683, 360 N.E.2d 1377 (1977).

[127]264 Or. 574, 507 P.2d 23 (1973). *See* Neuberger v. City of Portland, 288 Or. 155, 603 P.2d 771 (1979) (judicially created *Fasano* test superseded by Or. Rev. Stat. § 227.175(3), present version of which now at 1997 Or. Laws 844 § 5(4)).

[128]Although the *Fasano* court recited the general rule, it rejected the idea that judicial review was limited to a determination whether the change at issue was arbitrary and capricious. *Fasano*, 264 Or. at 581.

[129]*See* Lee County v. Sunbelt Equities II, Ltd. Partnership, 619 So. 2d 996 (Fla. Dist. Ct. App. 1993) (finding site-specific, owner-initiated rezoning sufficiently judicial in character that final administrative orders thereafter appropriate for appellate review).

[130]*See* Hall Paving Co. v. Hall County, 237 Ga. 14, 226 S.E.2d 728 (1976) (downzoning legislative); Meyer Material Co. v. County of Will, 51 Ill. App. 3d 821, 366 N.E.2d 1149 (1977) (rezoning primarily legislative); Tealin Co. v. City of Ladue, 541 S.W.2d 544 (Mo. 1976) (rezoning legislative); Todd Mart, Inc. v.

and federal levels to blur the lines between activities classified as quasi-judicial,[131] and those traditionally considered legislative. The trend may open the door to courts rethinking more local land-use decisions as courts use a stricter standard of review.[132] An accompanying trend is the courts' predilection to look for site-specific, individualized analysis by the local government when it is applying its regulatory scheme to a particular parcel, rather than allowing the government to rely on a whole-plan analysis to justify restrictions placed on an individual landowner.[133] Whether treating more cases as adjudicatory and requiring site-specific analysis will lead to an increase in takings legislation in the rezoning context remains to be seen.

Historically, zoning has been based on a notion that the community would follow a blueprint of development dictated by the comprehensive plan and accompanying zoning ordinance. The ordinance was to be uniformly applied to all real estate in each particular district, and landowners could develop their property within the parameters of the ordinance.

This method would work well for a jurisdiction that can plot its future development on a clean canvas. More often, however, a zoning ordinance is imposed on an already-established community. Buildings have been constructed, neighborhoods have been formed, streets and railroads have been laid out, and factories have been operating, often for generations before the zoning ordinance.

In the real world, then, most development does not occur "as of right" according to preset zoning regulations. Instead, most communities zone developed property according to its existing use and grandfather-in exceptions. The remaining vacant land is then underzoned, or "short-zoned," under a highly restrictive classification, such as agriculture, or large-lot single-family residential. In order to put vacant land to more intensive use, landowners must procure a change in the zoning or otherwise receive permission from the government. Whereas prior to zoning the burden is on government to

---

Town Bd. of Webster, 49 A.D.2d 12, 370 N.Y.S.2d 683 (1975) (denial of upzoning legislative).

[131]Coffey v. Maryland Nat'l Capital Park & Planning Comm'n, 293 Md. 24, 441 A.2d 1041 (Md. 1982); Board of County Commr's v. Gaster, 285 Md. 233, 401 A.2d 666 (Md. 1979).

[132]Weeks Restaurant Corp. v. City of Dover, 119 N.H. 541, 404 A.2d 294 (1979); In re Great Waters of America, Inc., 140 Vt. 105, 435 A.2d 956 (1981).

[133]Dolan v. City of Tigard, 512 U.S. 374, 383–86 (1994).

prove that protecting the public requires restricting the use of private property, after zoning the roles are reversed, and not only is the use of land frozen but the burden to obtain governmental permission to re-zone private property is shifted to the landowner. If the landowner proves that a proposed rezoning conforms to both the municipality's comprehensive plan and the procedural requirements of zoning, the burden shifts to the government to show that the zoning achieves a legitimate public purpose.[134] When the landowner fails to obtain a change in zoning, the landowner may allege that a taking has oc-curred.

The takings issue may also arise when the government initiates a change in zoning for an entire area, a change that does not suit a par-ticular landowner. Such changes may be either "upzonings" or "downzonings." Upzoning is a term used by some people to mean the rezoning of property to more intensive uses, while other people be-lieve it means just the opposite—the rezoning to less intensive uses.[135] We choose to use the word upzoning to mean rezoning to increase de-velopment density. Consequently, by downzoning we mean a re-zoning that decreases development density.[136] There are few takings cases arguing that increasing development density effects a taking.[137] Most of the rezoning-related takings cases result from downzonings.

A comprehensive rezoning, or the refusal to rezone at the request of an individual landowner, will not give rise to a taking claim without more than the landowner's inability to use property as planned. No property owner has a cognizable vested interest in the

---

[134]Board of County Comm'rs of Brevard County v. Snyder, 627 So. 2d 469 (Fla. 1993) (landowners permitted to file new application for rezoning). *But see* Jacobi v. City of Miami Beach, 678 So. 2d 1365, 1366 (Fla. Dist. Ct. App. 1996) (takings claim regarding disapproval of lot reconfiguration rejected because owners expanded existing house, thus "were not denied substantially all use").

[135]A search in the MEGA file of the MEGA library of LEXIS (July 15, 1997) produced 11 cases using the term "upzone." Six of these interpreted upzoning as increasing the density of development while the other four cases—all from New York—treated it as a decrease in intensity of use. The last of the 11 cases did not clearly explain what was meant by the term. Citation list on file with the au-thors.

[136]A search in the MEGA file of the MEGA library of LEXIS (July 15, 1997) produced 50 cases using the term "downzone." From those cases, the 11 most recent decisions were reviewed. All generally interpreted downzoning as de-creasing the intensity of development. Citation list on file with the authors.

[137]Note, *The Unconstitutionality of Transferable Development Rights*, 84 Yale L. J. 1101 (1975).

existing zoning of property,[138] nor in some hoped-for change in that zoning, even when the government intimates that such a change will be forthcoming.[139] Furthermore, landowners should anticipate that some regulation cannot be avoided, and regulations may change, as expressed by the U.S. Supreme Court: "[I]t seems to us that the property owner necessarily expects the uses of his property to be restricted, from time to time, by various measures newly enacted by the State."[140]

There are limits, however, to government rezoning. A government-initiated zoning change or refusal to rezone upon request of a landowner may be found unconstitutional where restrictions are so burdensome that they in effect confiscate private property.[141] As we have pointed out, all land-use regulations, including rezonings, must "substantially advance legitimate state interests" or not "den[y] an owner economically viable use of his land."[142] So long as the ordinance has a legitimate comprehensive planning objective, there is no taking unless all reasonable uses of property have been proscribed.[143]

As to the first part of the test, courts have accepted a variety of public purposes to justify downzoning, including bringing the subject area into conformance with the local comprehensive plan,[144]

---

[138]Orange Lake Assocs., Inc. v. Kirkpatrick, 21 F.3d 1214 (2d Cir. 1994); Dean Tarry Corp. v. Friedlander, 826 F.2d 210 (2d Cir. 1987). *See also* RRI Realty Corp. v. Incorporated Village of Southampton, 870 F.2d 911, 919 (2d Cir.), *cert. denied*, 493 U.S. 893 (1989); Ellentuck v. Klein, 570 F.2d 414, 429 (2d Cir. 1978).

[139]Furey v. City of Sacramento, 780 F.2d 1448 (9th Cir. 1986).

[140]Lucas v. South Carolina Coastal Council, 505 U.S. 1003, 1027 (1992).

[141]Cardon Oil Co. v. City of Phoenix, 122 Ariz. 102, 593 P.2d 656 (1979); D'Addario v. Planning & Zoning Comm'n of the Town of Darien, 25 Conn. App. 137, 593 A.2d 511 (1991); Petersen v. City of Decorah, 259 N.W.2d 553 (Iowa Ct. App. 1977) (city to enact zoning amendment permitting property owner productive use); Bickerstaff Clay Products Co., Inc. v. Harris County, Ga., 89 F.3d 1481, 1488 (11th Cir. 1996).

[142]Agins v. City of Tiburon, 447 U.S. 255 (1980).

[143]McShane v. City of Faribault, 292 N.W.2d 253, 257 n.2 (Minn. 1980) (rule of no taking unless owner deprived of all reasonable uses discussed and distinguished from rule for regulations that solely benefit government enterprise); Larson v. County of Washington, 387 N.W.2d 902, 907 (Minn. Ct. App. 1986).

[144]C. Thomas Williamson III, *Constitutional and Judicial Limitations on the Community's Power to Downzone*, REGULATORY TAKING: THE LIMITS OF LAND USE CONTROLS, 1, 3 (G. Richard Hill ed., 1993) (citing Haar, *supra* note 2, at 1157).

upgrading the community's economy,[145] protecting against the dangers of inadequate health facilities,[146] promoting orderly growth,[147] maintaining aesthetic character,[148] and preserving the environment.[149] This "legitimate state interest" prong of the takings test is often not even challenged by landowners who claim that a rezoning or refusal to rezone has taken their property.[150]

As to the second part of the test, the burden is on the property owner to show that all primary uses, as well as all secondary uses (those allowed through a special use permit, variance, or similar device) are unavailable. This is generally a difficult hurdle to overcome since almost always some use remains. For instance, in *Long Cove Club Assocs., L.P. v. Town of Hilton Head Island, South Carolina*,[151] the owner of a ten-acre commercial parcel that had been downzoned alleged a loss of all economically beneficial use of a development permit issued by the town prior to the zoning change. The South Carolina Supreme Court, citing a Fourth Circuit decision, held that the development permit was personal property but subject to the *Lucas* analysis, contrary to the argument made by the property owner.[152]

There is a limit, however, to what the courts will consider reasonable uses left to the owner. For instance, one New York court[153] upheld a declaratory judgment that the town board's rezoning of a portion of plaintiff's property from business to residential was unconstitutional where the site was not suitable for residential use. The court rejected an argument that the property owner should prove the property was not suitable for various public or quasi-public uses permitted by the residential zoning classification, such as churches,

[145]*Id.* at 3 (citing Chucta v. Planning Comm'n of Seymour, 154 Conn. 393, 225 A.2d 822 (1967) (increase minimum lot size)).

[146]*Id.* at 3, (citing Pacific Blvd. Assocs. v. Long Beach, 48 A.D.2d 857, 368 N.Y.S. 2d 867 (1975) (residential downzone)).

[147]*Id.* at 3 (citing Carty v. City of Ojai, 77 Cal. App. 3d 329, 143 Cal. Rptr. 506 (1978) (commercial downzone)).

[148]*Id.* at 3 (citing Maher v. City of New Orleans, 516 F.2d 1051 (5th Cir. 1975), *cert. denied*, 426 U.S. 905 (1976)).

[149]*Id.* at 3 (citing Moviematic Indus. Corp. v. Board of County Commr's, 349 So. 2d 667 (Fla. Dist. Ct. App. 1977)).

[150]*See, e.g.,* Long Cove Club Assocs., L.P. v. Town of Hilton Head Island, S.C., 319 S.C. 30, 458 S.E.2d 757 (1995), *cert. denied*, 516 U.S. 1029 (1995); Lucas v. South Carolina Coastal Council, 505 U.S. 1003, 1015 (1992).

[151]*Long Cove,* 458 S.E.2d 757.

[152]*Id.* at 758.

[153]Grimpel Assocs. v. Cohalen, 41 N.Y.2d 431, 361 N.E.2d 1022 (1977).

schools, colleges, libraries, and municipal parks. The court said, "To confine private property to public uses alone amounts to an appropriation of property rights for the benefit of the public without compensation therefor."[154]

In order to prevail on a takings claim, a property owner must also show more than that the current zoning classification (in a landowner-initiated rezoning request) or the new zoning restriction (in a government-initiated downzoning) has caused a significant diminution in value, or that a substantially higher value could be obtained in an alternative use.[155] In one Oregon case, the landowners conceded that their property, rezoned for agricultural uses, could be beneficially used for agriculture, and thus retained some value. Although the property would not be as profitable as before the zoning change, the court found the change did not constitute a taking.[156]

As always, however, courts do not cotton to regulatory actions that deliberately attempt to reduce land values to procure a cheap piece of real estate for the government. As we have seen in planning contexts, such a practice encounters automatic judicial disfavor. The phrase "predatory zoning" has been used to epitomize the courts' reaction to such conniving. For instance, in an Iowa case,[157] a city council denied a request to rezone from agricultural to commercial that would have allowed a shopping center on land that was unsuitable for agriculture. The court found the agriculture classification was designed to freeze development until the city could use the property as an industrial area. Rather than buy the land to hold it in reserve, the city "has used the zoning power to accomplish the result without 'paying for' the taking," the court noted.[158]

If only a portion of a landowner's property is downzoned to the extent there is no reasonable use left in that portion, but the remainder of the parcel is still available, has a taking occurred? The first step for a court in such an instance is to determine what, precisely, is the property. The U.S. Supreme Court has never endorsed a test that "segments" a contiguous property to determine the relevant parcel.

[154]*Id.*, 41 N.Y.2d at 433.

[155]McGowan v. Cohalen, 41 N.Y.2d 434, 436–37, 361 N.E.2d 1025 (1977) (land has economic value).

[156]Joyce v. City of Portland, 24 Or. App. 689, 546 P.2d 1100 (1976).

[157]Petersen v. City of Decorah, 259 N.W.2d 553 (Iowa Ct. App. 1977).

[158]*Id.* at 555. *See also* Kissinger v. City of Los Angeles, 161 Cal. App. 2d 454, 327 P.2d 10 (1958); Department of Pub. Works & Bldgs. v. Exchange Nat'l Bank, 31 Ill. App. 3d 88, 334 N.E.2d 810 (1975).

Rather, the Court has consistently held that a landowner's property in such a case should be considered as a whole.[159]

While *Lucas*[160] has been cited for the proposition in its footnote 7, that courts should use a flexible approach in deciding when to segment property in takings cases, that issue was not before the *Lucas* court, rendering the footnote statement purely dicta. It is important to note, too, that Justice Scalia, author of the *Lucas* opinion, joined in the following opinion after *Lucas*:

> We rejected this analysis [that the property should be segmented] years ago in *Penn Central* . . . [T]he relevant question . . . is whether the property taken is all or only a portion of the parcel in question.[161]

One of the most volatile issues under the takings clause in the rezoning context involves municipal designation of private property as "open space," a designation limiting or precluding all development. Courts in zoning cases in the earlier part of this century may have struggled with the concept of regulations enacted under a local government's police power that were designed to protect amenities such as scenic views that did not fall squarely within the definition of public health and safety. However, in the 1950s urban renewal case, *Berman v. Parker*, the U.S. Supreme Court gave its unqualified support to aesthetics as a legitimate regulatory concern, stating that the public has an interest in assuring that the community is "beautiful as well as clean, well-balanced as well as carefully patrolled."[162] It has since been noted that the public has an interest in municipal open-space zoning to preserve and conserve valuable, and disappearing, open space.[163] Such an interest is legitimate and substantial.[164]

[159]Zealy v. City of Waukesha, 201 Wis. 2d 365, 378–80, 548 N.W.2d 528 (1996) (parcel viewed as whole retains combination of uses); Quirk v. Town of New Boston, 140 N.H. 124 (1995) (perimeter of campground not discrete segment).

[160]505 U.S. at 1016 n.7.

[161]Concrete Pipe & Prods. v. Construction Laborers Pension Trust, 508 U.S. 602, 644 (1993), *quoted in* Zealy, 201 Wis. 2d at 377. For a more general discussion of this issue, *see* chapter 12.

[162]348 U.S. 26, 33 (1954) (agency can take title to buildings but must compensate owners). *See also* Village of Euclid v. Ambler Realty Co., 272 U.S. 365 (1926) (zoning ordinance valid; trend seems to be toward broadening police power).

[163]*See generally* Karl E. Geier, *Agricultural Districts and Zoning: A State-Local Approach to a National Problem*, 8 ECOLOGY L.Q. 655 (1980).

[164]Agins v. City of Tiburon, 447 U.S. 255, 261 (1980).

In *Agins v. City of Tiburon*, a landowner challenged the munici-pality's open-space protective zoning ordinance. In response to state mandate, the City of Tiburon had classified the plaintiff's ridgetop land in an open-space zone. The landowner challenged the ordinance on its face, claiming the change rendered the property valueless by limiting the number of residences he could build on the ridgetop to between one and five on five acres. The U.S. Supreme Court upheld the California Supreme Court's holding that there was no taking, based in part on the fact that there was some value left in the property.

The *Agins* Court laid out a two-part test identifying a regulation as a taking if the restriction either fails to substantially advance a legiti-mate state interest or denies the owner economically viable use of the land.[165] This test involves weighing public and private interests.[166] In weighing the interests, the Court found that, in light of legislative purposes and the shared benefits and burdens on Agins and adjacent landowners, the ordinance substantially advanced a legitimate state interest and did not prevent Agins from developing the land com-pletely. The court noted that the conversion of open space to urban use has numerous resultant adverse impacts, such as noise, water pol-lution, destruction of scenic beauty, and increased flood hazards that lower-density development would help to avoid.

Like open-space ordinances, local floodplain regulations can se-verely restrict the use of private property. Floodplain regulations are almost universally used by local governments either to curtail poten-tially unsafe development in areas prone to flooding or to mitigate flood damage. Relatively few cases have invalidated floodplain regu-lations on takings grounds, based in large part on the health and safety aspect of such regulations.

Protecting the health and safety of the public is the foremost justi-fication for all police power regulations, and floodplain regulations have long been recognized in this category. Court decisions up-holding such restrictions implicitly recognize the public hazard cre-ated by developing flood-prone and mitigative areas,[167] and ac-knowledge the legitimate state interest in reducing such hazards through regulation.[168] In threats to life, the legislature may take "the

---

[165]*See* Steel v. Cape Corp., 677 A.2d 634, 651 (Md. Ct. Spec. App. 1996) (open-space zoning ordinance and regulations satisfied "reasonable relationship test," but as applied, left owner with "no viable economical uses").

[166]*Agins*, 447 U.S. at 261–63.

[167]1 ZIEGLER, JR., *supra* note 17, § 7.07.

[168]*See, e.g.*, Dolan v. City of Tigard, 512 U.S. 374, 385–86 (1994).

most conservative course which science and engineering offer."[169]

This "harm-prevention" purpose has been used to justify many floodplain regulations, including the one that prevented the First English Evangelical Lutheran Church[170] from rebuilding its flood-destroyed campground. On remand from the U.S. Supreme Court, the California appeals court judge compared floodplain zoning to the "harm-prevention" purposes of early nuisance cases, and found no taking.[171] The Wisconsin court, in *Just v. Marinette County*, has gone even further, holding that property owners have no inherent right to change the nature of their land in detriment to the public.[172]

Numerous low-density land uses have been accepted as reasonable uses left to land subject to floodplain regulations. Takings claims have been defeated, for example, when landowners were left with such indigenous, nondevelopmental uses as forestry, woodlands, grasslands, wetlands, agriculture, horticulture, recreational, open space, density-credit transfer, nature trails, scenic vistas, hunting, fishing, wildlife observation, and parking—even where these were not typical uses.[173]

---

[169]Queenside Hills Realty Co. v. Saxl, 328 U.S. 80, 83 (1946), *cited in* 1 ZIEGLER, JR., *supra* note 17 at § 7.07[1][a].

[170]First English Evangelical Lutheran Church v. County of Los Angeles, 482 U.S. 304 (1987).

[171]*First English*, 210 Cal. App. 3d 1353, 1365–66, 258 Cal. Rptr. 893 (1989), *review denied*, 1989 Cal. LEXIS 4224 (Aug. 25, 1989), *cert. denied*, 493 U.S. 1056 (1990).

[172]56 Wis. 2d 7, 201 N.W.2d 761, 768 (Wis. 1972) (prohibition against filling wetlands constitutional).

[173]*See* Brecciaroli v. Connecticut Comm'r of Envtl. Protection, 168 Conn. 349, 362 A.2d 948, 952–53 (1975); Turnpike Realty Co., Inc. v. Dedham. 284 N.E.2d 891 (Mass. 1992) ("[a]ny woodland, grassland, wetland, agricultural, cultural or recreational use of land or water not requiring filling" allowed), *cert. denied*, 409 U.S. 1108 (1973); Krahl v. Nine Mile Creek Watershed Dist., 283 N.W.2d 538, 543 (Minn. 1979); Sibson v. State, 115 N.H. 124, 336 A.2d 239 (1975) (uses include "wildlife observation, hunting, haying of marsh grass, clam and shellfish harvesting, and aesthetic purposes"), *overruled in part*, Burrows v. Keene, 121 N.H. 590, 432 A.2d 15 (1981) (generally, leaving some uses may preclude a taking, but "[g]overnment may not violate the requirements of the [state] constitution . . . under the guise of the so-called 'police power'"); Claridge v. New Hampshire Wetlands Bd., 125 N.H. 745, 485 A.2d 287 (1984); Usdin v. State Dep't of Envtl. Protection, 173 N.J. Super. 311, 414 A.2d 280, 290 (Law Div. 1980), *aff'd*, 179 N.J. Super 113, 430 A.2d 949 (App. Div. 1981). *But see* Vatalaro v. Department of Envtl. Regulation, 601 So. 2d 1223 (Fla. Dist. Ct. App.) (taking where denial of permit left owner with no viable economic use of land except "just looking at it"), *review denied*, 613 So. 2d 3 (Fla. 1992).

The courts will also consider whether the use proposed in a flood zone area is reasonable. A permit denial to build in a floodplain will not give rise to a takings claim if the proposed use is unreasonable. Unreasonable uses have included constructing dwellings in flood-prone areas,[174] filling wetlands,[175] obstructing floodways,[176] and other harmful activities.

A floodplain ordinance that seeks to accommodate landowners who have been denied proposed uses can help buffer the regulatory scheme from constitutional attack. Permits are often available for uses that are not banned or permitted as of right. For instance, a permit may be issued for construction in the floodplain if the building is elevated or otherwise adequately flood-proofed.

In addition to uses permitted as of right, a zoning ordinance may also provide for conditional uses. If the property meets certain conditions, a conditional use permit is granted. Conditional uses are designed to cope with situations where a particular use, although not inherently inconsistent with the use classification of a particular zone, may, if uncontrolled, create problems.[177] Most courts have held that there is no meaningful difference between a special exception and a conditional-use permit.[178] Conditional-use permits in many cases are "confined to uses of public concern, such as airports, cemeteries, development of natural resources, public utilities, educational institutions, libraries, and governmental enterprises."[179]

In *Community Concerned Citizens, Inc. v. Union Township Board of Zoning Appeals*,[180] the Zoning Board of Appeals had denied a

[174]Turner v. Del Norte County, 24 Cal. App. 3d 311,101 Cal. Rptr. 93 (1972); Spiegle v. Borough of Beach Haven, 46 N.J. 479, 218 A.2d 129, *cert. denied*, 385 U.S. 831 (1966).

[175]Subaru of New England, Inc. v. Board of Appeals, 8 Mass. App. Ct. 483, 395 N.E.2d 880 (1979); N.Y.C. Office Park v. Planning Bd. 144 A.D. 2d 348, 533 N.Y.S.2d 786 (1988).

[176]Young Plumbing & Heating Co. v. Iowa Natural Resources Council, 276 N.W.2d 377 (Iowa 1979).

[177]*See* Louis W. Doherty, Comment, Chrismon v. Guilford County *and* Hall v. City of Durham: *Redefining Contract Zoning and Approving Conditional Use Zoning in North Carolina*, 68 N.C. L. Rev. 177, 180 (1989).

[178]101A C. J. S. *Zoning & Land Planning* § 229 (1979).

[179]*Id.* at § 191. *See* Public Access Shoreline Hawaii v. Hawai'i County Planning Comm'n, 903 P.2d 1246, 1273 (Haw. 1995) (recognizing gathering rights no judicial taking because western property principles not universally applicable in Hawaii), *cert. denied sub nom.* Nansay Hawaii v. Public Access Shoreline Hawaii, 116 S. Ct. 1559 (1996).

[180]66 Ohio St. 3d 452, 613 N.E.2d 580 (1993).

conditional-use permit for a day-care center. The Supreme Court of Ohio held that this denial was not a taking.[181] Prohibiting construction of a day-care center did not deny the property owners all economically beneficial use of their land, thus no taking occurred, the court concluded.[182]The Commonwealth Court of Pennsylvania has also recently addressed the issue of when a conditional use becomes a taking in *Pennridge Development Enterprises v. Volovnik*.[183]

Rights in a conditional permit may be cut off by police power regulations. The Supreme Court of North Dakota faced this issue in *Buegel v. City of Grand Forks*.[184]

In *Bach v. County of St. Clair*,[185] the property owner attempted to establish that the denial of a special-use permit resulted in a taking. The owner contended that a fourteen-foot-width zoning requirement for mobile homes prevented him from placing one on his property, thus depriving him of its "essential use."[186] The court concluded that the plaintiff had not shown that the mobile home would meet the other requirement of the ordinance, compliance with HUD standards.[187]

Subdivision Control

The subdivision of land for sale and development does not directly raise the taking issue very often because subdivision regulations themselves do not typically effect a taking. It is the interplay with other regulations, such as lot size controlled by zoning and exactions required to mitigate adverse impacts of subdivision development (as discussed in chapter 16) that usually trigger the loss and the claim.

---

[181]*Id.*, 613 N.E.2d at 583–84. *See also* Nello L. Teer Co. v. Orange County, 1993 U.S. App. LEXIS 12525 (4th Cir. May 26, 1993) (no property interest in issuance of special permit because land-use board had "significant discretion").

[182]*Id. See also* Estate & Heirs of Isabel Sanchez v. County of Bernalillo, 120 N.M. 395, 902 P.2d 550 (1995) (no taking because use restriction applies to public generally).

[183]154 Pa. Commw. 609, 624 A.2d 674 (1993).

[184]475 N.W.2d 133 (N.D. 1991).

[185]217 Ill. App. 3d 291, 576 N.E.2d 1236 (1991).

[186]*Id.*, 576 N.E.2d at 1241.

[187]*Id.* For more information on special-use permits, see BRIAN W. BLAESSER, DISCRETIONARY LAND USE CONTROLS: AVOIDING INVITATIONS TO ABUSE OF DISCRETION §§ 3.01 to -.11 (1997).

The term "subdivision" generally refers to dividing one tract of land into two or more parcels.[188] Whether a subdivision is subject to regulatory control varies among the states.[189] For example, the creation of segmented estates and transfers of less than fee-simple property interests may not constitute a subdivision subject to regulatory control.[190] Thus, whether creating new lots is subject to subdivision control can only be determined from relevant state and local statutes.[191]

Subdivision controls regulate the division of land and improvements needed to serve such developments.[192] Contemporary subdivision controls regulate the design standards of streets and utilities, reservation of land for public use, and other matters related to the physical layout and economic impacts of a subdivision plat.[193] Subdivision regulation is intended to assist in the orderly sale and transfer of land and in title registration by providing for the surveying and platting of lots and other tracts of land. The subdivision process also protects the consumer and the larger community by ensuring that land to be developed will be adequately supported with all necessary infrastructure, including roads, sidewalks, water, sewer, storm-water control, and electric and gas utilities. Subdivision regulation also can control land design, avoid development of steep slopes and shallow depth-to-bedrock areas, preserve scenic vistas, and protect natural resources.

The first public subdivision-control laws were intended to provide accurate identification of land divisions.[194] Early subdivision regulations required that any land divided for sale or conveyance had to be platted by survey and shown on a plat map. A typical map would

[188]Metzdorf v. Borough of Rumson, 67 N.J. Super. 121, 125,170 A.2d 249 (App. Div. 1961). *See* HAGMAN & JUERGENSMEYER, *supra* note 54, § 7.5.

[189]*See, e.g.,* Conn. Gen. Stat. Ann. § 8-18; Mass. Gen. L. ch. 41, § 81L; Wash. Rev. Code Ann. § 58.17.020. *See also* HAGMAN & JUERGENSMEYER, *supra* note 54, § 7.5 (1986) (regulatory application varies by state for failure to define the term subdivision in the Standard City Planning Enabling Act).

[190]Kiska v. Shrensky, 145 Conn. 28, 138 A.2d 523 (1958); Town of Arundel v. Swain, 374 A.2d 317 (Me. 1977) (creation of campsites within campground); Dube v. Senter, 107 N.H. 191, 219 A.2d 456, 458 (1966) (land divisions without new streets). *See also Metzdorf,* 170 A.2d at 252 (testamentary or intestate land divisions exempted).

[191]*See* HAGMAN & JUERGENSMEYER, *supra* note 54, § 7.5.

[192]*See* Richard Ducker, *Land Subdivision Regulation,* THE PRACTICE OF LOCAL GOVERNMENT PLANNING 198 (Frank S. So & Judith Getzels eds., 1988).

[193]*Id.*

[194]*See* HAGMAN & JUERGENSMEYER, *supra* note 54, § 7.2.

show the subdivided lots, all roadways within the plat, and any other improvements. The map also had to be recorded in the land records office. These early subdivision regulations seldom provided for review or approval of plats by public authorities.

As a precondition to approval and acceptance of any plat for recording, modern subdivision controls require substantive and procedural review by public authorities.[195] Land subject to subdivision regulation and recorded in a plat cannot be sold or transferred unless the plat is approved and accepted for recording by designated public authorities. Subdivision controls emphasize a holistic regulatory approach relating the plat to the local community and are an integral part of any community's comprehensive planning to manage development.[196]

The primary *procedural* purpose of subdivision review is to provide for the due process rights of the applicant and any parties-in-interest. This is accomplished through information dissemination, notice to abutters, and public hearings.[197] Subdivision review involves a three-step review and approval process (i.e., preapplication, preliminary application, and final application) by designated planning entities.[198] Authorities vary regarding whether a subdivision application vests under the common law upon preliminary approval or only upon final approval.[199] State enabling statutes often define how rights are vested. An applicant may have a limited period of time after the preliminary approval to seek final approval.[200] Local subdivision control authorities may be required to act within a specified time or the subdivision application passes by default. Typically, the final plat must be recorded in the land records by the applicant within a certain time after final approval.[201]

The primary *substantive* purpose of subdivision review is to determine and regulate the plat's physical and economic impacts on the host community. Specifications of all site improvements must be pro-

---

[195]*Id.* § 7.6.

[196]*See* Golden v. Planning Bd. of Ramapo, 30 N.Y.2d 359, 369–70, 285 N.E.2d 291 (1972) (phased growth enabled by state statutes), *appeal dismissed*, 409 U.S. 1003 (1972).

[197]*See* HAGMAN & JUERGENSMEYER, *supra* note 54, § 7.6.

[198]Ducker, *supra* note 191, at 226–36.

[199]*See* HAGMAN & JUERGENSMEYER, *supra* note 54, § 7.6 (preliminary approval). *See also* B. & W. Assocs. v. Planning Bd. of Hackettstown, 242 N.J. Super. 1, 4, 575 A.2d 1371 (App. Div. 1990) (subsequent zoning amendment does not apply to final plat).

[200]*See, e.g.*, R.I. Gen. Laws § 45-23-41(H).

[201]*See* HAGMAN & JUERGENSMEYER, *supra* note 54, § 7.6.

vided to the designated subdivision control authority. It can then either deny the plat or condition plat approval on the provision of certain improvements—called conditions or exactions. This may involve privately financed on-site and off-site improvements to offset the subdivision's impacts on the host community, or either the uncompensated dedication of land or the private construction of public-service facilities for the host community. In the alternative or in addition, a fee-in-lieu-of land dedication may be collected by the host community and placed in an escrow account to be used for future public-service expenses. Land developers sometimes challenge the imposition of such conditions as violations of due process or as takings. These challenges have driven both the case law and scholarly discussion.[202]

The power of government to regulate subdivisions was originally based on two separate legal theories: the privilege doctrine and the police power doctrine.[203] It is well settled in modern case law that land subdivision control is a valid exercise of the local government's police power.[204]

Local subdivision regulation is limited by the state legislature's statutory delegation of authority.[205] Neither conditions of approval nor denials of subdivisions not authorized by state enabling statutes will be enforced by the courts.[206] The power of a planning board to review and approve subdivisions is further limited by the constitutional standards of due process and reasonableness.[207]

---

[202]*Id.* § 7.8.

[203]5 NORMAN WILLIAMS, JR. & JOHN M. TAYLOR, AMERICAN LAND PLANNING LAW: LAND USE AND THE POLICE POWER § 156.02 (1985).

[204]Ridgefield Land Co. v. City of Detroit, 241 Mich. 468, 472–73, 217 N.W. 58 (1928); Krieger v. Planning Comm'n of Howard County, 224 Md. 320, 324, 167 A.2d 885 (1961). *See also* Martha Lester, Comment, *Subdivision Exactions in Washington: The Controversy Over Imposing Fees on Developers*, 59 WASHINGTON L. REV. 289, 290 (1984).

[205]Kelber v. Upland, 155 Cal. App. 2d 631, 638, 318 P.2d 561 (1957) (authority limited to enabling legislation terms); Pennobscot, Inc. v. Board of County Comm'rs, 642 P.2d 915, 919 (Colo. 1982) (en banc) (regulatory power limited to statutory delegation); Smith v. Zoning Bd. of Appeals, 227 Conn. 71, 84–85, 629 A.2d 1089 (1993), *cert. denied*, 510 U.S. 1164 (1994); Eyde Constr. Co. v. Charter Township of Meridian, 149 Mich. App. 802, 807, 386 N.W.2d 687 (1986).

[206]*Eyde*, 149 Mich. App. 802. *See also* Robbins Auto Parts, Inc. v. Laconia, 117 N.H. 235, 236, 371 A.2d 1167 (N.H. 1977); Board of Supervisors v. Rowe, 216 Va. 128, 138, 216 S.E.2d 199 (1975).

[207]*See* Davis Enters. v. Karpf, 105 N.J. 476, 485, 523 A.2d 137 (1987); Brous v. Smith, 304 N.Y. 164, 106 N.E.2d 503 (1952); Admiral Dev. Corp. v. City of

Courts have established a two-step constitutional standard of review to determine whether government control of a subdivision is valid. A court will inquire (1) was the power to act delegated; and (2) was the action a reasonable exercise of the police power?[208]

Conventional conditions that adequate circulation, drainage control, water supply, and sewage treatment be included on a plat and provided without capital cost to the host community are generally considered a reasonable exercise of the police power.[209] Some regulations also govern the rate, location, and sequence of development. These controls are often justified as furthering a community's comprehensive planning.[210] Communities condition plat approvals on exactions or improvements on-site and off-site to offset alleged adverse community impacts. These conditions may involve land dedications—even physical improvements—for roads, water, sewer, storm water, parks, schools, and general community facilities. When land dedication is not practical, a fee condition, in lieu of land dedication, is often imposed.[211] These latter conditions are sometimes subject to judicial attack as a taking or a denial of due process.[212]

The courts have established three different standards of review to determine whether a subdivision condition is invalid or constitutes a taking requiring just compensation.[213] These traditional state standards may have been altered by the *Nollan/Dolan* "essential nexus"/"rough proportionality" requirements.

The narrowest exaction test requires that the benefit accruing from the exaction be "specifically and uniquely attributable" to the development. The second, and least demanding test, is the "reasonably related" test which finds no exaction when the "proposed development is a contributing factor to the problem sought to be alleviated." Last,

---

Maitland, 267 So. 2d 860, 863 (Fla. Dist. Ct. App. 1972); Evans v. Town of Tully Planning Bd., 140 Misc. 2d 400, 531 N.Y.S.2d 660, 664 (Sup. Ct. 1988).

[208]*See* Ira M. Heyman & Thomas K. Gilhool, *The Constitutionality of Imposing Increased Community Costs on New Suburban Residents Through Subdivision Exactions*, 73 YALE L.J. 1119, 1122 (1964).

[209]*Id.*

[210]WILLIAMS, JR. & TAYLOR, *supra* note 202, § 156.04. *See* HAGMAN & JUERGENSMEYER, *supra* note 54, § 7.3.

[211]*See* Ducker, *supra* note 191, at 217.

[212]*See* Heyman & Gilhool, *supra* note 207, at 1134–41.

[213]Batch v. Town of Chapel Hill, 92 N.C. App. 601, 376 S.E.2d 22, 30–31 (1989), *rev'd without considering taking claim*, 326 N.C. 1, 387 S.E.2d 655 (1990), *cert. denied*, 496 U.S. 931 (1990). This case has been in three North Carolina courts and in three federal courts for most of a decade and no court has yet to decide whether there was a taking.

the "rational-nexus" test provides that a subdivider can be required "to bear that portion of the cost which bears a rational nexus to the needs created by, and benefits conferred upon, the subdivision."

The legislative deference doctrine also applies to court reviews of whether a local government has conformed to the judicial standards of due process and reasonableness.[214]

These standards of judicial review yield different results depending upon the facts.[215] Regardless of the standard, any dedication or exaction imposed as a condition of subdivision approval must be closely related to the harm caused by the development. Failure to clearly justify the need for the condition imposed may result in a judicial decision that a taking has occurred.[216] Few subdivision cases allege a taking directly on the issue of subdivision itself rather than on exactions or growth management, because so long as the underlying zoning allows some use, all the typical subdivision approval does is multiply the intensity of that use.

In the first instance, as with all land-use cases, the plaintiff must show a property interest worthy of constitutional protection before a taking can be proved.[217] There is no authority that a property owner has a vested right in a contemplated development or subdivision. In fact, all authority suggests no such broad and loosely defined property right exists.[218]

It is clear, then, that the plaintiff in a taking action must show more than a thwarted desire to subdivide the property. Instead, the plaintiff must show that the regulation does not advance a legitimate public purpose or that it denies all economically viable use of the land.[219]

[214]See Golden v. Planning Bd. of Ramapo, 30 N.Y.2d 359, 377 (1972).

[215]For decisions upholding land dedications or exactions, see Associated Home Builders, Inc. v. City of Walnut Creek, 4 Cal. 3d 633, 484 P.2d 606, *appeal dismissed*, 404 U.S. 878 (1971); Weingarten v. Town of Lewisboro, 144 Misc. 2d 849, 542 N.Y.S.2d 1012 (Sup. Ct. 1989), *aff'd without opinion*, 160 A.D.2d 668, 559 N.Y.S.2d 807 (1990), *appeal dismissed*, 76 N.Y.2d 934 (1990).

[216]See New Jersey Builders Ass'n v. Bernards Township, 211 N.J. Super. 290, 511 A.2d 740 (Law Div. 1985), *aff'd*, 219 N.J. Super. 539, 530 A.2d 1254 (App. Div. 1986), *aff'd*, 108 N.J. 223, 528 A.2d 555 (1987).

[217]Marshall v. Board of County Comm'rs for Johnson County, Wyo., 912 F. Supp. 1456, 1464 (D. Wyo. 1996) (citing Martinez-Velez v. Simonet, 919 F.2d 808, 810 (1st Cir. 1990).

[218]*Marshall*, 912 F. Supp. at 1464 (citing MacDonald Sommer & Frates v. Yolo County, 477 U.S. 340, 25 (1986); Lucas v. South Carolina Coastal Council, 505 U.S. 1003, 1014–19, (1992); Snake River Venture v. Board of County Commr's, Teton County, Wyo., 616 P.2d 744, 751 (Wyo. 1980).

[219]Agins v. City of Tiburon, 447 U.S. 255, 260 (1980).

A landowner may be hard pressed to prove that a subdivision regulation enacted with precision, and applied in strict compliance with all due process requirements, fails to serve a legitimate public purpose. Subdivision regulations must be enacted pursuant to enabling legislation that grants the power to regulate from the state to local governments;[220] but once that delegation of power is established, most courts will hold that subdivision regulations are an exercise of the local government's police power, and can use different means to further the public's health, safety, general welfare, and morals.[221] These purposes should ideally be spelled out as precisely as possible in the local subdivision ordinance to guide the local decision-maker who grants or denies subdivision approval.[222] Even where every purpose is not detailed in the local ordinance, however, courts are often willing to extend the police power to uphold a local government's denial of a subdivision application so long as there is no arbitrary or capricious action involved.

Even when an ordinance substantially advances a legitimate state interest, to withstand constitutional attack a land-use regulation must also not deny all economically beneficial use of the property. A showing that a would-be subdivider will suffer some diminution in return due to denial of the development as proposed is not sufficient to prove no viable use remains in the property.[223] In *Marshall v. Board of County Commissioners for Johnson County, Wyoming*, for instance, the court found that "[a]lthough the lot restrictions may have diminished the number of lots available for sale in the proposed subdivision from 23 to perhaps as few as seven, this fails to demonstrate a complete destruction of plaintiff's investment backed expectations."[224]

---

[220]*See* Bella Vista Ranches, Inc. v. City of Sierra Vista, 126 Ariz. 142, 613 P.2d 302, 303 (Ariz. Ct. App. 1980); El Dorado at Santa Fe, Inc. v. Board of County Commr's, 89 N.M. 313, 551 P.2d 1360, 1367 (1976).

[221]ROBERT H. FREILICH & MICHAEL M. SHULTZ, MODEL SUBDIVISION REGULATIONS, PLANNING, AND LAW 25 (1995) (citing Ayres v. City Council, 34 Cal. 2d 31, 207 P.2d 1 (1949). *See also* Beaver Meadows v. Board of County Commr's, 709 P.2d 928 (Colo. 1985).

[222]*Marshall*, 912 F. Supp. at 1468.

[223]A.J. Czyr, Inc. v. Ridgefield Planning & Zoning Comm'n, 1995 Conn. Super. LEXIS 3115 (Conn. Super. Ct. Nov. 7, 1995); Coleman v. Town of Forest Lake, 1994 Minn. App. LEXIS 628 (Minn. Ct. App. July 5, 1994) (unpublished opinion without precedential value).

[224]*Marshall*, 912 F. Supp. at 1474.

In *Cannone v. Noey*, the court found that many reasonable uses remained for an owner whose subdivision application had been temporarily denied because of inadequate wastewater treatment and disposal proposals, thereby negating any temporary taking claim.[225]

An unpublished Minnesota case provides an excellent example of why the typical subdivision case does not support a successful taking claim. In the Town of Forest Lake, Minnesota, Donald Coleman in 1977 platted a residential subdivision of forty-two lots.[226] Four lots were larger than the others and Coleman had planned to either sell them or further subdivide them into lots of a size similar to the rest in his subdivision. In May 1992, Coleman applied to resubdivide the four larger lots into eight lots. The lots met all the existing zoning requirements and the town board considered the application on June 23, 1992.

The town's attorney advised the board that the only way it could deny the application would be by ordinance. So, the board told the town's administrator and the town's attorney to draft an ordinance prohibiting this type of subdivision. On August 26, 1992, three months after the application for the subdivision and two months after the town board first considered the application, the board adopted an ordinance. It prohibited resubdivisions that would increase the density of an existing plat unless there had been a specific reservation at the time of the original subdivision.[227] After it adopted the new ordinance, the town board denied Coleman's application for failure to conform.

The appellate court found that there was a rational basis for the ordinance and that Mr. Coleman had no protection under the "reasonable reliance" doctrine of the Minnesota statutes, which give a vested right to an approval for one year following a preliminary approval and for two years following a final approval. The vested right allows a subdivider to proceed under those approvals without regard to any subsequent amendment to the comprehensive plan or "official control." The court indicated that Mr. Coleman was not trying to complete his project as it was approved in 1977, but was trying to complete a new and different project.

Although comprehensive subdivision regulation is widespread in this country, vast areas still exist, particularly in the West, with very little subdivision regulation. What power does a local government

---

[225]867 P.2d 797, 801 (Alaska 1994) (*citing Lucas*, 112 S.Ct. 2894).
[226]*Coleman*, 1994 Minn. App. LEXIS 628.
[227]*Id.* at 3–4.

have to restrict subdivisions when there is little or no regulation? Can local governments impose conditions or additional requirements on subdividers when there is little or no guidance in state or local regulations? The answer is suggested in a recent decision of the U.S. District Court for the District of Wyoming.[228]

Although we do not separately discuss takings created or alleged to be created by the government enforcing its own regulations, claims do arise from such actions. In one instance, subdividers claimed damages, but the court found no taking when a city temporarily stopped a subdivision. Public health and safety were threatened when a lagoon emerged because of springs uncovered during excavation.[229]

Temporary takings (discussed in greater detail in chapters 11 and 12) can arise in the subdivision context. A partnership proposed subdividing its land in a remote area of Alaska into a recreational subdivision of sixteen one-acre lots.[230] The State Department of Environmental Conservation rejected the plans due to inadequate wastewater treatment and disposal. The Alaska Supreme Court held that the department had rejected the proposal arbitrarily and in violation of the law.[231] The partnership then filed a taking suit that was rejected on ripeness grounds. Then a series of applications involving both administrative agencies and the courts occurred. Ultimately, the partnership alleged that a temporary taking occurred from May 23, 1989, when the plans were rejected for the second time by the Department of Environmental Conservation, to March 31, 1991, when a state hearing officer ultimately approved the project.

The Alaska Supreme Court expressly held that the partnership had not been denied all economically feasible use of the property and could not claim a categorical taking under *Lucas*. There was no evidence that the partnership could not sell the parcel for a substantial price or that a purchaser could not have used the entire parcel for recreation. Furthermore, the partnership produced no evidence that it could not have subdivided the property into larger lots or used the property for recreation or as a commercial lodge.

---

[228]Government may be able to regulate in the absence of such guidance as long as owner's investment-backed expectations have not been completely destroyed. Marshall, 912 F. Supp. 1456, 1474.

[229]Gosnell v. City of Troy, Ill., 59 F.3d 654 (7th Cir. 1995). *See also* Kenneth B. Bley, *The Search for Constitutionally Protected "Property" in Land Use Law*, 29 URBAN LAWYER 251 (1997) (concern that implementation of zoning might be capable of evading constitutional review).

[230]Cannone v. Noey, 867 P.2d 797 (Alaska 1994).

[231]*Id.* at 798–99.

One of the most significant problems in land-use regulation generally is regulating cumulative effects. How can the government effectively regulate when a series of small transactions or approvals individually have negligible impact but collectively and cumulatively have significant impacts? The U.S. Army Corps of Engineers, for example, considers cumulative impacts and prohibits applications that "piecemeal" a project to avoid review of its total impacts. This issue, which can arise in subdivision approval, was central to an important recent case in Montana, *Dreher v. Fuller*, upholding a county's review of cumulative impacts.[232]

It is sometimes said that land use is more regulated than the securities industry, but much more difficult to learn because there is no single body of statutory and regulatory rules. One of the most interesting aspects of land-use law, and the takings issue in particular, is the overlap, even among areas of apparently disparate regulation. A good example of this overlap can be found in the subdivision context. In *Smith v. Zoning Board of Appeals of Town of Greenwich*, a planning commission denied a subdivision proposed within a separately regulated historic district, citing historic factors.[233] The Smiths proposed to subdivide their land into three lots and the planning commission granted them preliminary approval subject to the resolution of fourteen issues. The Smiths were required to meet with the Historic District Commission because the parcel was within the district, although the commission could not act on the appropriateness of developing one of the lots until approval of a final subdivision plan by the planning commission. Still, the Historic District Commission expressed opposition. The planning commission then rejected the subdivision, stating that approval would "permit construction of a house in the . . . significant open space, thereby disrupting the essential characteristic of the historic district."[234] In its review, the Connecticut Supreme Court looked to a provision in the subdivision regulations that permitted the commission to require a twelve-point environmental assessment, including "historical and archeological factors." The court held that the regulation allowed the planning commission to consider impacts on the historic district. The court found no taking because there was no evidence of an absence of other viable options to develop the property.[235]

---

[232]257 Mont. 445, 849 P.2d 1045 (1993).

[233]227 Conn. 71, 76, 629 A.2d 1089 (1993), *cert. denied*, 510 U.S. 1164 (1994).

[234]227 Conn. at 76.

[235]*Id.* at 99.

Planning, zoning, and subdivision in and of themselves precipitate few direct takings claims, but they are active launching pads for takings claims when their traditional nuisance-avoiding, development-facilitating framework is embellished with conditions, exactions, and protections of resources in the natural and built environments.

Generally, subdivision conditions for on-site improvements to offset negative impacts of the subdivision are a valid exercise of the police power. But, as conditions expand beyond the geographic boundaries of a plat or constitute a public benefit not related to a plat-created harm, they become exactions subject to invalidation or a requirement to pay just compensation.

Chapter 16

Physical Improvements and Exactions

New developments create new burdens, on-site and off-site, including the need for more utility infrastructure[1] (water, sewer, storm water, electric, telephone, cable television); greater road capacity; more schools; increased fire, police, and emergency services; and more passive and active recreational facilities and open space. Historically, developers have routinely provided for some of these needs. The typical in-kind, on-site exaction so readily accepted is the developer's contribution of roads and utility infrastructure internal to the site. To the best of our knowledge, no subdivider has ever claimed that building and then dedicating the roads within a subdivision to the government is a taking. Why? One answer is that it simply has been that way from the beginning. Another is that the exaction of the roads is on-site, it is in-kind (the developer builds the roads, rather than paying others to do it), and virtually all of the benefit is conferred onto the developer and the developer's purchasers.

But what happens when the development causes adverse effects away from the site? Suppose the subdivision will create traffic that will congest an intersection a quarter of a mile away. Can the subdivider be required to construct a turning lane at that intersection or contribute a fee-in-lieu-of this off-site, in-kind exaction? What if the intersection is already functioning poorly—should the subdivider be required to improve the already-bad situation?

There are thousands of exactions cases. Most are substantive due process cases—did the local government have the proper authority to

---

[1]*See also* DONALD G. HAGMAN & JULIAN C. JUERGENSMEYER, URBAN PLANNING AND LAND DEVELOPMENT CONTROL LAW § 9.6 (1986).

require the exaction and if so, was it related to the impact of the land use? Exactions cases have increased as the types of exactions have multiplied. Exactions themselves became increasingly important as the on-site and off-site impacts of development increased, existing infrastructure proved inadequate, and fiscal shortfalls became more common.

The cases suggest the range of these "new" types of controversial exactions. Examples include cases involving: a floodplain,[2] bicycle path,[3] beachfront pedestrian path,[4] strip of land for road widening in return for granting access to water service,[5] nonresidential development impact fee to subsidize housing for low-income employees related to new development,[6] coastal setback line,[7] elimination or modification of nonconforming sign,[8] oceanfront rip-rapping,[9] preservation of single-room occupancy units,[10] recreational open-space dedication,[11] and a one and one-half million dollar payment in return for permission to demolish single-room occupancy building.[12]

[2]Dolan v. City of Tigard, 512 U.S. 374 (1994) (dedication for flood control invalid).

[3]*Id.* (no reasonable relationship between proposed development and dedication).

[4]Nollan v. California Coastal Comm'n, 483 U.S. 825 (1987) ("if [government] wants an easement . . . it must pay for it").

[5]Walz v. Town of Smithtown, 46 F.3d 162 (2d Cir. 1995) (upheld compensatory and punitive damages against town for voiding permit in attempt to coerce land conveyance), *cert. denied*, 515 U.S. 1131 (1995).

[6]Commercial Builders of N. Cal. v. City of Sacramento, 941 F.2d 872 (9th Cir. 1991) (linkage fee of $6,000 per low-income household not a taking), *cert. denied*, 504 U.S. 931 (1992).

[7]McNulty v. Town of Indialantic, 727 F. Supp. 604 (M.D. Fla. 1989) (no taking; uses remain and purchaser knew about restrictions).

[8]Circle K Corp. v. City of Mesa, 166 Ariz. 464, 803 P.2d 457 (Ariz. Ct. App. 1990) (no taking).

[9]Delaware v. Putnam, 552 A.2d 1247 (Super. Ct. Del. 1988) (statute unenforceable, but would effect taking).

[10]Seawall Assocs. v. City of New York, 74 N.Y.2d 92, 542 N.E.2d 1059 (1989) (facially invalid physical taking).

[11]Auburn v. McEvoy, 131 N.H. 383, 553 A.2d 317 (1988) (recovery barred by statute of limitations).

[12]City of New York v. 17 Vista Assocs., 192 A.D.2d 192, 599 N.Y.S.2d 549 (1993) (agreement void as against public policy), *later proceeding*, 197 A.D.2d 369 (1993), *modified, aff'd*, 84 N.Y.2d 299 (1994) (upholding invalidation).

Legal History of Exactions[13]

The Supreme Court has used both the "substantially advances" standard and the "reasonable relationship" test in its land-use cases. We first trace the use of these phrases by the Court to unearth the precedential foundation for each. Then we will look at one way of interpreting *Nollan* (in conjunction with *Lucas*[14]) to perceive the potential ramifications of the Court's new approach to reviewing land-use exactions.

Underlying this history is an unresolved tension between substantive due process and the takings issue. Both sometimes arise in the same cases. The fundamental result is usually different—winning a substantive due process claim typically yields invalidation and another run at the regulators; a successful taking claim provides "just compensation." The doctrinal history in land-use cases is a messy merger of the two constitutional theories, with often profoundly different results from succeeding on one theory over the other. What we have in *Dolan* is the invocation of one theory (substantive due process) coupled with a claim for a remedy under the other theory (just compensation for a taking) in a correspondingly conflated factual situation (run-of-the-mill floodplain exaction accompanied by a physical-invasion bicycle and pedestrian pathway).

The Court's substantive due process reviews of land-use regulations have typically employed the "substantially advances" or an equivalent standard.[15] The Court has coupled this formulation with the "fairly debatable" approach to upholding legislative judgments, making clear that its respect for the separation of powers doctrine and its recognition of its institutional limitations generally keeps the

---

[13]Text is based on three articles: Dwight H. Merriam, AICP & R. Jeffrey Lyman, *Testing the Constitutionality of Land-Use Exactions in Dolan and Nollan*, 17 ZONING & PLANNING LAW REPORT 17 (Mar. 1994); Dwight H. Merriam, AICP & R. Jeffrey Lyman, *Dealing with Dolan, Practically and Jurisprudentially*, 17 ZONING & PLANNING LAW REPORT 57 (Sept. 1994); Dwight H. Merriam, AICP & R. Jeffrey Lyman, *Constitutional Principles for Land-Use Exactions*, 22 ENVIRONMENTAL & URBAN ISSUES 13 (Winter 1995).

[14]Lucas v. South Carolina Coastal Council, 505 U.S. 1003 (1992).

[15]*See* Village of Euclid v. Ambler Realty Co., 272 U.S. 365 (1926) (zoning ordinance upheld); Nectow v. Cambridge, 277 U.S. 183 (1928) (ordinance invalid as applied because no "substantial relation to the public health, safety, morals, or general welfare"); Gorieb v. Fox, 274 U.S. 603 (1927).

Court from intruding on the business of other branches of government.[16]

For example, in one early case, the Court upheld an ordinance creating an exclusive residential zone in a rapidly urbanizing area, refusing to "substitute its judgment for that of the legislative body charged with the primary duty and responsibility of determining the question."[17] The Court upheld building set-back requirements shortly thereafter, noting that increased urban population density had provoked new regulatory responses:

> State legislatures and city councils . . . are better qualified than the courts to determine the necessity, character and degree of regulation which these new and perplexing conditions require; and their conclusion should not be disturbed by the courts unless clearly arbitrary and unreasonable.[18]

Only where the record created below expressly found that a zone classification failed to serve *any* police power goals was a city's action invalidated, and then in part because it also precluded any "practical use" of the land.[19]

Although the Supreme Court stayed out of the land-use field for nearly fifty years after the *Euclid*-era flurry of cases, its continuing review of economic regulations generally stressed a deferential approach, often invoking the "reasonableness" standard.[20] In its sole pronouncement on a land-use regulatory matter during this hiatus,

---

[16]*Euclid*, 272 U.S. at 388. *See also* Zahn v. Board of Pub. Works, 274 U.S. 325 (1927) (court will not substitute its judgment for "fairly debatable" determination by legislative body).

[17]*Zahn*, 274 U.S. at 328.

[18]*Gorieb*, 274 U.S. at 608.

[19]*Nectow*, 277 U.S. at 187–88.

[20]City of New Orleans v. Dukes, 427 U.S. 297 (1976) (ordinance prohibiting pushcart vendors from French Quarter upheld), *overruled on other grounds* as stated in, Intercommunity Relations Council v. U.S. Dep't of Health & Human Sers., as stated in, 859 F. Supp. 81 (S.D.N.Y. 1994); Williamson v. Lee Optical Co., 348 U.S. 483 (1955) (law forbidding optician from fitting lenses without prescription from opthalmologist or optometrist upheld); Day-Brite Lighting, Inc. v. Missouri, 342 U.S. 421 (1952) (state law allowing employees to leave work, with pay, to vote upheld); United States v. Carolene Prods Co., 304 U.S. 144 (1938) (federal statute prohibiting interstate shipment of certain types of skimmed milk upheld).

Goldblatt v. Hempstead,[21] the Court strongly emphasized this aspect of its jurisprudence:

> "To justify the State in . . . interposing its authority in behalf of the public, it must appear, first, that the interests of the public . . . require such interference; and, second, that the means are reasonably necessary for the accomplishment of the purpose, and not unduly oppressive upon individuals."
>
> Even this rule is not applied with strict precision, for this Court has often said that, "debatable questions as to reasonableness are not for the courts but for the legislature."[22]

The *Goldblatt* opinion exemplified the Supreme Court's respect for other branches of government. The *Goldblatt* Court reviewed a public safety ordinance that prevented further extraction from an existing water-filled excavation. There was no evidence that the ordinance might mitigate any actual or potentially increased danger. Despite this "indecisive" foundation, the Supreme Court sustained the ordinance after affirming that the property owner, not the town, bore the burden of proving unreasonableness.[23]

A decade and a half later, the Supreme Court's self-proclaimed "useful . . . review" heralded its re-entry into the takings field on the solid foundation of its historic standard. Harkening back to the *Euclid*-era substantive due process cases, the Court noted in *Penn Central Transportation Co. v. New York City* that a taking might result if a regulation were "not reasonably necessary to the effectuation of a substantial public purpose."[24] Perhaps even more importantly, *Penn Central* was mostly about an "ad hoc" balancing of interests that was consistent with a deferential threshold inquiry into "reasonableness," and not about a result-defining "substantially advances" requirement.[25]

In a series of other land-use decisions founded on other constitutional provisions, the Court similarly suggested that "reasonableness"

[21]369 U.S. 590 (1962).

[22]*Id.* at 594–95 (citations omitted).

[23]*Id.* at 596.

[24]438 U.S. 104, 127 (1978) (no taking because restrictions "substantially related to the promotion of the general welfare") (citing Nectow v. Cambridge, 277 U.S. 183 (1928)).

[25]*Id.* at 123.

was the proper test, absent implication of fundamental rights or reliance upon suspect classifications.[26]

Two terms after *Penn Central*, in *Agins v. City of Tiburon*, the Court worked the due process "substantially advances" standard into the takings analysis:

> The application of a general zoning law to particular property effects a taking if the ordinance does not substantially advance legitimate state interests, [citing *Nectow* at 188], or denies an owner economically viable use of his land, [citing *Penn Central* at 138 n.36].[27]

In *Agins*, however, the Court did not apply this two-part formulation because the developer's as-applied claim was deemed unripe. The Court recited the two-part formulation in later takings cases, although not always reaching the takings issue or finding a taking.[28] Even in these cases, however, the Court apparently believed that the "substantially advances" standard was consistent with the conventional presumption of validity and accompanying judicial deference to legislative judgments.[29]

This great body of exactions law as it applies to the takings issue has now been largely distilled in two U.S. Supreme Court cases and one recent decision from California's highest court. Read and understood together they provide useful guidance as to when an exaction may effect a taking and how government and private property owners might work together to avoid litigation.[30]

[26]Moore v. East Cleveland, 431 U.S. 494, 520 (1977) (Stevens, J., concurring in judgment) (ordinance restricting housing occupancy invalidated as not having "substantial relation to the public health, safety, morals or general welfare"); Schad v. Borough of Ephraim, 452 U.S. 61, 68 (1981); Arlington Heights v. Metropolitan Hous. Dev. Corp., 429 U.S. 252, 263 (1977).

[27]447 U.S. 255, 260 (1980) (no taking because use remains).

[28]*See, e.g.*, Keystone Bituminous Coal Ass'n v. DeBenedictis, 480 U.S. 470, 485 (1987); United States v. Riverside Bayview Homes, Inc., 474 U.S. 121, 126 (1985); San Diego Gas & Elec. Co. v. San Diego, 450 U.S. 621, 647 (1981) (Brennan, J., dissenting).

[29]*See, e.g.*, *Keystone*, 480 U.S. at 486.

[30]*See* Nollan v. California Coastal Comm'n, 483 U.S. 825 (1987); Dolan v. City of Tigard, 512 U.S. 374 (1994); and Ehrlich v. City of Culver City, 12 Cal. 4th 854, 911 P.2d 429, *cert. denied*, 117 S. Ct. 299 (1996).

The Meaning of *Nollan*

Does it really matter which test the Court uses? After all, *Euclid* employed the theoretically more demanding "substantially advances" standard, yet upheld residential zoning. Meanwhile, *Nollan* relied upon the putatively more deferential "reasonable relationship" test, and invalidated the Coastal Commission's permit condition.

Comparing other constitutional tests doesn't clarify matters. The "substantially advances" standard sounds like middle-tier equal protection analysis.[31] Yet Justice Brennan accused the *Nollan* majority of using the "reasonable relationship" test to invoke strict scrutiny.[32]

What Is the Quantity of the Nexus?

On June 24, 1994, the Supreme Court handed down its eagerly awaited *Dolan v. City of Tigard* decision,[33] a case that represents a significant victory for the property rights movement. Departing from the traditional rule that deference is given to governments in their administrative decision-making, the Court shifted the burden onto governments to prove they are "substantially advancing legitimate governmental interests" when they impose permit conditions requiring dedications. But the practical import of *Dolan* for planners and developers is less clear. The *Dolan* dissenters feared grave consequences from the majority's new rule of law. While it is not certain that *Dolan*'s long-term impact will be so severe, most would agree that there will be some practical difficulties for those involved in zoning.

The Facts and Decision in *Dolan*

Despite its potential constitutional importance, the *Dolan* case began with an unremarkable set of facts. Florence Dolan (a self-styled "elderly widow") owns a 1.67-acre commercial lot on Main Street in Tigard, Oregon, where she operates a 9,700-square-foot plumbing and electric supply store. The lot is within the city's Commercial Business District and its "Action Area" overlay zone. A small stream, known as Fanno Creek, flows along the lot's western boundary.

[31]*See* Craig v. Boren, 429 U.S. 190, 197–99 (1976) (classifications by gender).
[32]Nollan v. California Coastal Comm'n, 483 U.S. 825, 842–43 (1987).
[33]512 U.S. 374 (1994).

Plumbing and electric supply store (top) owned by Florence Dolan in the city of Tigard, Oregon, and Fanno Creek (bottom), which flows through the southwestern corner of the lot and along its western boundary. Redevelopment of this property was at issue in *Dolan v. City of Tigard*.

In April 1991, Mrs. Dolan and her now-deceased husband John applied to the Tigard Planning Commission for approval to tear down their store and replace it with a 17,600-square-foot building to expand their business. The Dolans proposed to create thirty-nine new, paved parking spaces. This constituted the first stage in a multi-phase project, which would later include an additional building and more paved parking.

The planning commission approved the Dolans' application, subject to several conditions. One was that the Dolans dedicate an area within the 100-year floodplain along Fanno Creek for a greenway. Another required dedication of an additional fifteen-foot strip for a pedestrian and bicycle pathway. In total, the conditions required the Dolans to dedicate about 10 percent of their lot. The Dolans sought a variance, not by offering alternative mitigation measures as the city's code directed, but by asserting that their proposal was consistent with the city's comprehensive plan.

The planning commission denied the variance and issued findings, the basis and accuracy of which the Dolans did not challenge. It issued a finding to justify the floodplain dedication. The finding also supported the pathway dedication. There was no further support in the record for either dedication requirement.

However, the dedication requirements did reflect several of Oregon's comprehensive statewide land-use goals.[34] The goals developed by the state Land Conservation and Development Commission (LCDC), must be incorporated in comprehensive land-use plans for every county and city.[35] Several commission goals were directly relevant to the Dolans' plans, including directives to conserve open space and protect natural and scenic resources; guard against storm-water pollution; allow only appropriate uses in areas prone to natural disasters and hazards; and provide for a transportation system including alternative transit. Tigard adhered to these requirements in its comprehensive land-use plan, which called for vegetation buffers along streams and drainage ways for purposes including flood control.

The Dolans appealed the planning commission's decision to the Tigard City Council, which affirmed with minor modifications. The Dolans next took their claims to the statewide Land Use Board of Appeals ("LUBA"). The Dolans still did not challenge either the planning commission's findings or evidence. They argued only that

[34]*Id.* at 377 (citing Or. Rev. Stat. §§ 197.005–197.860).
[35]*Id.* at 377 (citing Or. Rev. Stat. §§ 197.175(1), 197.250).

the dedication requirements constituted a taking. LUBA disagreed, finding a "reasonable relationship" between the dedication requirements and the city's plans.

The Oregon Court of Appeals affirmed, rejecting the Dolans' argument that the U.S. Supreme Court's *Nollan* decision had established a more stringent "essential nexus" requirement. The Oregon Supreme Court also affirmed, holding that the "reasonable relationship" test applied and had been satisfied and that *Nollan* had not created any new tests. The U.S. Supreme Court granted Mrs. Dolan's petition for certiorari.

The *Dolan* Court was split into three parts. Chief Justice Rehnquist authored the majority opinion, joined by Justices O'Connor, Scalia, Kennedy, and Thomas. Justice Stevens dissented vehemently (taking the unusual step of reading his opinion from the bench) and was joined by Justices Blackmun and Ginsburg. Justice Souter dissented separately.

Under *Dolan*, permit conditions that require a developer to "deed portions of [her] property" to the government can be justified only if the government "make[s] some sort of individualized determination that the required dedication is related both in nature and extent to the impact of the proposed development."[36] Applying this test, the Court found that the City of Tigard had not shown that its dedication requirements were "roughly proportional" (a new term in *Dolan*) to the impacts of the development. Without an individualized determination, the city would have to pay to take Mrs. Dolan's land.

This holding continues and expands the Court's importation of the due process test—invalidating land-use regulations not "substantially advancing legitimate governmental interests"—into takings law.[37] Taken together, *Nollan* and *Dolan* establish two elements for the "substantially advancing" test—from *Nollan*, the nature of the advancement; from *Dolan*, the degree. *Nollan* requires an "essential nexus" between the dedication and a legitimate state interest. *Dolan* demands "rough proportionality" between the dedication and the impacts of the proposed development. *Dolan* also creates a site-specific, heightened scrutiny requirement for exactions imposed on a single property.

To understand the context for applying the "substantially advancing" test, we look at the points on which the *Dolan* majority and dissents agreed: First, protecting floodplains and encouraging trans-

[36]*Id.* at 391.
[37]*See* Agins v. City of Tiburon, 447 U.S. 255, 260 (1980).

portation alternatives are legitimate public interests supporting regulation of private property. Second, development that increases impervious surfaces and generates additional traffic can be prohibited because of potential adverse effects—e.g., increased runoff and traffic congestion—on the environment and infrastructure. Third, permits for such development can be conditioned by dedication requirements, so long as there is a sufficient relationship between the development's impacts and the dedications.

Understanding when to apply the "substantially advancing" requirement is apparently easier than deciding how to apply it, because the Court split nearly down the middle on this. All the justices agreed that Tigard's exactions satisfied the "essential nexus" test. But Chief Rehnquist went beyond *Nollan* by asking "whether the *degree* of the exactions demanded . . . bear the required relationship to the projected impact" from the proposed development.[38] (Emphasis added.) He acknowledged that his inquiry found no precedent in Supreme Court doctrine, so he turned to "representative" state court decisions on subdivision exactions for guidance in fashioning a test. He rejected the two extreme schools of thought—the "lax" reliance of some courts upon "very generalized statements" to support an exaction and the "exacting scrutiny" imposed by the Illinois courts under the "specifically and uniquely attributable test."[39] The Chief Justice favored instead the intermediate approach, often called the "reasonable relationship" test, which is used in many jurisdictions.[40]

Despite this extensive support from the state courts, the Court did not adopt the reasonable relationship test per se, fearing it would be confusingly similar to deferential "rational basis" review under the Equal Protection Clause. The Court found that "a term such as 'rough

---

[38]*Dolan,* 512 U.S. at 388.

[39]*Id.* at 389–90 (citing Billings Properties, Inc. v. Yellowstone County, 144 Mont. 25, 394 P.2d 182 (1964); Jenad, Inc. v. Scarsdale, 18 N.Y.2d 78, 218 N.E.2d 673 (1966) (for lax standards) and (citing Pioneer Trust & Sav. Bank v. Mount Prospect, 22 Ill. 2d 375, 380, 176 N.E.2d 799, 802 (1961)) (for the exacting scrutiny standard).

[40]*Dolan,* 512 U.S. at 390–91 (citing Simpson v. North Platte, 206 Neb. 240, 245, 292 N.W.2d 297, 301 (1980); Jordan v. Menomonee Falls, 28 Wis. 2d 608, 137 N.W.2d 442 (Wis. 1965); Collis v. Bloomington, 310 Minn. 5, 246 N.W.2d 19 (1976); College Station v. Turtle Rock Corp., 680 S.W.2d 802, 807 (Tex. 1984); Call v. West Jordan, 606 P.2d 217, 220 (Utah 1979); Parks v. Watson, 716 F.2d 646, 651–53 (9th Cir. 1983)).

proportionality' best encapsulates" the requirements of the Takings Clause.[41]

Justice Stevens took the majority to task for its transformation of "reasonable relationship" into "rough proportionality," arguing that none of the cited cases "announce[d] anything akin" to the Court's new test. His dissent also excoriated the majority for failing to follow the lead of state courts in "consider[ing] what the property owner gains" from the permit-for-a-dedication exchange and "requir[ing] that the entire parcel be given controlling importance" when assessing a taking claim.[42] Justice Stevens accused the majority of establishing a *Lochner*-type test under which judges assume "superlegislative power."[43]

Applying its new standard, the majority found Tigard had not satisfied its obligation to justify either of the permit conditions. The Court struggled to understand "why a public greenway, as opposed to a private one, was required" to protect the floodplain.[44] The majority's analysis of the pathway dedication acknowledged that Tigard had calculated the number of trips to be generated by the expanded store, but faulted the city for failing to determine how many workers or shoppers might use the pathway. Tigard could not sustain its dedication requirement without at least "some effort to quantify" this offset.

Justice Souter's dissent focused not just on the creation of the "rough proportionality" test but also on its application, noting that the Court found a taking relating to the pathway based on a single word (actually, a single letter—the majority opinion said "could offset" instead of "would offset"). Justice Souter found the Court's approach inappropriate in light of its traditional deference to municipal decision-making.

But the majority rejected its tradition of deference in an important passage tucked in a footnote:

> [I]n evaluating most generally applicable zoning regulations, the burden properly rests on the party challenging the regulation to prove that it constitutes an arbitrary regulation of property rights. [Citing *Euclid*.] Here, by contrast, the city made an adjudicative decision to condition petitioner's application for a

[41]*Dolan*, 512 U.S. at 391.
[42]*Id.* at 399 (Stevens, J., dissenting).
[43]*Id.* at 409.
[44]*Id.* at 393.

building permit on an individual parcel. In this situation, the burden properly rests on the city. *See Nollan*, 483 U.S. at 836.[45]

This shift in allocating the burden of proof is truly revolutionary, upsetting constitutional doctrine firmly established since at least 1938, in another famous footnote.[46] The *Dolan* majority was frank in explaining its dramatic departure:

> [The Court acted,] see[ing] no reason why the Takings Clause of the Fifth Amendment, as much a part of the Bill of Rights as the First Amendment or Fourth Amendment, should be relegated to the status of a poor relation [when applied to the regulation of economic enterprise].[47]
>
> The Court affirmed the Takings Clause as a member of the family of preferred constitutional rights: Under the well-settled doctrine of "unconstitutional conditions," the government may not require a person to give up a constitutional right . . . in exchange for a discretionary benefit conferred by the government where the [right sacrificed] has little or no relationship to the benefit.[48]

This doctrine of unconstitutional conditions, discussed later in this chapter, may not even be well settled, as Justice Stevens was quick to point out. It certainly has no history of application to takings claims, as the majority's reliance on free speech cases implied.[49] Even so, the Court applied the doctrine to find that Tigard had not justified requiring Mrs. Dolan to sacrifice her "right to exclude others" in order to obtain a permit.[50]

Dolan continued the Supreme Court's explanation of how dedica-

---

[45]*Id.* at 391 n.8.

[46]*See* United States v. Carolene Prods. Co., 304 U.S. 144, 152–53 n.4 (1938) ("There may be narrower scope for operation of the presumption of constitutionality when legislation appears on its face to be within a specific prohibition of the Constitution . . .").

[47]*Dolan*, 512 U.S. at 392.

[48]*Id.* at 385.

[49]*Id.* (citing Perry v. Sinderman, 408 U.S. 593 (1972) (dispute as to whether exercise of free speech caused teacher's termination); Pickering v. Board of Educ., 391 U.S. 563, 568 (1968) (public school teachers' free speech rights)).

[50]*Dolan*, 512 U.S. at 384 (citing Nollan, v. California Coastal Comm'n, 483 U.S. 825, 831 (1987); Kaiser Aetna v. United States, 444 U.S. 164, 176 (1979) (even if government invades only easement, it must pay just compensation)).

tions and exactions that "substantially advance legitimate governmental interests" possess a constitutionally sufficient relationship to the impacts of proposed development, a test first explored in *Nollan*.

Nexus and Proportionality Requirements

The "substantially advancing" requirement now has two elements—from *Nollan*, the nature of the advancement; from *Dolan*, the degree.

The takings claims successfully prosecuted in *Dolan* and *Nollan* suggest that planners and developers must focus on a few key points when dealing with dedications and other exactions. Before turning to the jurisprudential issues and the refinements offered by *Ehrlich v. City of Culver City*,[51] let us look at some of the practical lessons from *Nollan* and *Dolan*.

Dolan, like *Nollan* before it, was concerned with dedication of an interest in land, as in deeding an easement, not regulation of the use of land. The use of regulation alone in *Dolan* could have included the prohibition of development in the floodplain. While lawyers for property owners will undoubtedly try to extend the *Nollan/Dolan* reasoning to all land-use controls, it presently appears that regulation remains the constitutionally safer way to proceed. However, some regulation may still be suspect after *Dolan*, such as incentive zoning systems where a developer "volunteers" to dedicate some land in exchange for a density bonus. Importantly, more conventional regulatory techniques ordinarily suffice to serve important public needs, and dedications are superfluous in most circumstances. For example, Tigard already precluded development in the floodplain on Mrs. Dolan's property, even before she sought to expand her store. *Dolan* emphasizes that regulation should remain the primary tool of land-use planners and government officials.

Trying to implement innovative land-use controls is one of the most challenging parts of a planner's job. The *Dolan* decision underscores that these new techniques bring an added responsibility to ensure protection of private property. The new burden of justification will require government regulators to rely upon sound planning and to demonstrate its relationship to the tools they use.

Of course, requiring that regulation be consistent with planning—even if only to determine an "essential nexus" and "rough propor-

---

[51]12 Cal. 4th 854, 911 P.2d 429, *cert. denied*, 117 S. Ct. 299 (1996).

tionality"—takes time and money. All too often, governments do not have enough money, and developers do not have time. The studies that *Dolan* appears to make necessary call to mind the environmental impact statements required under the National Environmental Policy Act (NEPA). These "property rights impact statements," if we may coin a phrase to apply to this *Dolan* requirement, may likewise prove useful in protecting important interests, but they will also be costly and time-consuming to prepare. It may come to pass, post-*Dolan*, that developers will prepare a "property rights impact statement" in anticipation of governmental takings. Still, there may be circumstances in which only a dedication will serve the public interest, as when Tigard wanted a recreational greenway and a pedestrian/bicycle pathway. Yet it may be impractical or impossible to demonstrate the required "essential nexus" or requisite "rough proportionality." The government can still take the land, but it must pay for it. Planners and regulators should not forget that eminent domain is an important tool for land-use control.

Dedications and other "in-kind" requirements are indivisible. You cannot require just half a travel lane for a new road or only the red light on a traffic signal. But impact fees can be calibrated to the penny, albeit sometimes with greater apparent, than real, precision. The increasing use of impact fees across the country may have received a significant (if inadvertent) boost from *Dolan* in demonstrating their efficiency as planning tools and their constitutional defensibility.[52]

However, the Supreme Court made it clear in both *Dolan* and *Nollan* that regulators may deny development applications outright when legitimate governmental interests would otherwise be harmed, even if regulators cannot meet their new burden for justifying conditions to an approval. This blunt instrument may not be advisable in many instances, however, since new development often brings important benefits to the community. Planners should hesitate before recommending that socially beneficial development be forbidden simply because of some adverse impacts. But sometimes outright denial may still be appropriate, when impacts upon the environment or infrastructure are too great and conditions to mitigate them cannot be justified.

[52]See Noreen A. Murphy, *The Viability of Impact Fees After* Nollan *and* Dolan, 31 NEW ENGLAND L. REV. 203, 254 (1996).

Unconstitutional Conditions Doctrine

Analyzing *Dolan's* practical ramifications is important in the short term, but the jurisprudential question is ultimately of greater concern. The logic of applying the unconstitutional conditions doctrine to a taking claim may be startling, but it also may become more common.

The doctrine permits a court to invoke a heightened level of scrutiny triggered by the constitutional right where a more deferential standard related to the provision of a discretionary benefit might otherwise apply. As Professor Richard Epstein has said, it is the property rights movement's "second best" alternative to a direct assault on the modern regulatory state.[53] In the Takings Clause context, this means that it can justify the demanding "substantially advancing" test where such judicial rigor might not otherwise be appropriate. In order to explore the full ramifications of the doctrine, we look at the two deeper issues inhering in the doctrine: What is the constitutional right given up? And, what is the discretionary benefit conferred?

It is evident from *Nollan*[54] and *Dolan,*[55] that the Court is willing to eschew the "parcel as a whole" rule established in *Penn Central,* focusing instead on a single stick in the bundle of property rights. (*See* our discussion of the relevant-parcel question in chapter 12.)

So, the jurisprudential question becomes whether there are sticks in the bundle other than the right to exclude that are sufficiently "essential" to trigger unconstitutional conditions analysis. This problem is compounded by the uncertain identity of the sticks. The traditional triumvirate is possession, use, and disposition, but leading scholars typically see the sticks as numbering nearly a dozen.[56] And, "property lawyers have for centuries been able to devise permutations and combinations [of the sticks] . . . com[ing] to 2047 in number. . . ."[57]

---

[53]Richard A. Epstein, *Unconstitutional Conditions, State Power, and the Limits of Consent,* 102 HARVARD. L. REV. 4, 28 (1988).

[54]483 U.S. at 831–32.

[55]512 U.S. at 384.

[56]*See* A.M. Honoré, *Ownership,* OXFORD ESSAYS IN JURISPRUDENCE 107, 113–28 (A.G. Guest ed., 1961) (rights to possession, use, management, income, capital, security, incident of transmissibility, absence of term, prohibition of harmful use, liability to execution, and residuary character).

[57]James L. Oakes, *"Property Rights" in Constitutional Analysis Today,* 56 WASHINGTON L. REV. 583, 590 (1981).

These daunting numbers underscore the problem with focusing on a single stick.

But focus on individual sticks we must because the Court is doing it. If the Court is willing to invoke the unconstitutional conditions doctrine for other sticks, then the *Nollan/Dolan* reasoning might be extended from the dedications context to the regulatory context. Currently, the Court's reasoning applies only when a property owner must grant an easement to the public in order to receive a permit, though as we shall see, the California Supreme Court's decision in *Ehrlich* extends the *Nollan/Dolan* site-specific, heightened scrutiny analysis to impact fees without using the unconstitutional conditions framework. Regulatory restrictions such as zoning appear safe, as the *Dolan* Court suggested by noting that "the conditions imposed were not simply a limitation on the use petitioner might make of her own parcel, but a requirement that she deed portions of the property to the city."[58] We have no doubt that "police power hawks," to use Professor Daniel R. Mandelker's own term, will take comfort in this language, but they must understand that the *Ehrlich* case is likely to have a profound effect on how other states interpret *Nollan/Dolan*.

The flip side of unconstitutional conditions deals with the discretionary benefit being conditioned. Unlike the constitutional rights aspect, which reveals how far the doctrine might be extended, the benefit component relates to how often the doctrine is necessary to justify rigorous constitutional protection of property. In *Dolan*, the Court never explained what discretionary benefit Mrs. Dolan sought. But the assumption that any local land-use permit is a discretionary benefit is undercut by an aside in *Nollan*.[59]

Differentiating the Nollans' permit request from Mrs. Dolan's in constitutionally recognizable terms is easy. The Nollans were proposing to build a house, while Mrs. Dolan was proposing to build a store. As the Court recently observed in a different context, "[a] special respect for individual liberty in the home has long been part of our culture and our law. . . ."[60] The Nollans' existing building "had

[58]*Dolan*, 512 U.S. at 385.

[59]483 U.S. at 833 n. 2. *See also* Art Piculell Group v. Clackamas County, 922 P.2d 1227, 1234 (Or. Ct. App. 1996) (hearings officer can properly consider benefits to developer in evaluating legality of approval condition); Patrick A. Randolph, Jr. *Oregon Court Wrestles with* Dolan (May 8, 1997) at http://www.prandolph@cctr.umkc.edu.

[60]City of Ladue v. Gilleo, 512 U.S. 43, 58 (1994) (ban on almost all residential signs violates First Amendment).

fallen into disrepair, and could no longer be rented out."[61] Mrs. Dolan's expansion plans appeared to result from the economic success of her existing store. And, as we all know, economically viable use of land is a constitutionally significant concern.[62]

So, the unconstitutional conditions doctrine was unnecessary in *Nollan* in order to invoke the "substantially advancing" test. Where a property owner's only option is building a house or losing any economic return on its property, the heightened scrutiny of the "substantially advancing" test is justified. But where a property owner seeks to intensify the commercial use of land, as did Mrs. Dolan, then she seeks a discretionary benefit for which ordinary judicial deference may be appropriate, unless she is called upon to sacrifice an "essential" stick in the bundle of her constitutionally protected property rights.

Post-*Dolan* Decisions

While a complete analysis of the post-*Dolan* decisions is beyond the scope of this work, it is interesting to see how the Oregon courts have treated *Dolan*. It helps us in understanding how "rough proportionality" may be interpreted and applied.[63]

In short, impact fees, though not mandated by *Dolan*, are probably a surer way of meeting the test of rough proportionality.[64] As stated by Professor Patrick A. Randolph, Jr: "[A] broad based legislative determination . . . reduces the possibility of gross unfairness in particular cases."[65]

[61]*Nollan*, 483 U.S. at 827.

[62]*See* Lucas v. South Carolina Coastal Council, 505 U.S. 1003, 1019 (1992) ("when the owner of real property has been called upon to sacrifice all economically beneficial uses in the name of the common good . . . he has suffered a taking").

[63]*See* Schultz v. City of Grants Pass, 131 Or. App. 220, 884 P.2d 569 (1994); J.C. Reeves Corp. v. Clackamas County, 131 Or. App. 615, 887 P.2d 360 (1994).

[64]*See also* Home Builders Ass'n of Cent. Ariz. v. City of Scottsdale, 930 P.2d 993, 999–1000 (Ariz. 1997) (water resource development impact fee, applicable to all new realty development, not subject to analysis under *Dolan*), *cert. denied*, 117 S. Ct. 2512 (1997).

[65]Patrick A. Randolph, Jr., *Development Fees After* Dolan, DAILY DEVELOPMENT 3, ¶ 3 (Feb. 26, 1996) at <http://www.urich.edu/~jolt/vlil/burk.html>.

A New Turn in the Road—The *Ehrlich* Decision

Interestingly, right after the U.S. Supreme Court handed down *Dolan*, it vacated a decision by an appellate court in California in a case involving an impact fee for public art, *Ehrlich v. City of Culver City*.[66] The case was remanded for a determination of the impact of *Dolan*. This remand came as a surprise to some who figured that *Dolan* only had to do with in-kind exactions and dedication of land, not with the payment of money, which would not involve any public access to private property.

Richard Ehrlich bought a vacant parcel of about 2.4 acres in Culver City, California, in 1975 and built a private tennis club on the property (commercially zoned for a sports facility); but the business failed and he closed it. He then sought a permit to build thirty townhouses on the property, but the city denied the application because public recreational facilities would be lost.

Mr. Ehrlich ultimately offered to build four tennis courts, but the city imposed conditions on his approval, including payment of a $280,000 "mitigation fee," purportedly to offset loss of the recreational facilities.

In an important, but unpublished decision about six months after the remand by the U.S. Supreme Court, the California Court of Appeal held that the mitigation fee must be judged by what the court saw as a *Nollan/Dolan* two-part test.[67] The first part was whether the city had the power to deny the zone change request outright without causing a taking. The court reasoned that refusal to rezone the property would not constitute a taking, even if Mr. Ehrlich couldn't successfully operate a private tennis facility there, because he purchased the property with the zoning and had no other investment-backed expectations.

As to the second part, the "essential nexus" and "roughly proportional" criteria, the court found that the mitigation fee met the test. The city, said the court, would use the funds to replace recreational facilities, and the amount to be paid was about equal to the cost of building the courts.[68]

---

[66]The California appeals court decision is 15 Cal. App. 4th 1737 (1993), but it is not citable per rules 976 and 977 of the California Rules of Court. The U.S. Supreme Court decision vacating the California decision is *Ehrlich*, 512 U.S. 1231 (1994). The California appeals court decision has been superseded by 12 Cal. 4th 854, 911 P.2d 429, *cert. denied*, 117 S. Ct. 299 (1996).

[67]No. B055523 (Cal. Ct. App. Dec. 23, 1994).

[68]*Id.*

Ehrlich then successfully petitioned the California Supreme Court for review.[69] In its decision, the California high court concluded that the *Nollan* and *Dolan* tests for a regulatory taking were relevant to analyzing the monetary exaction imposed by the city as a condition for rezoning[70] and offered this observation about exactions:

> [I]t is well accepted in both the case and statutory law that the discontinuance of a private land use can have a significant impact justifying a monetary exaction to alleviate it. We perceive no reason why the same cannot be said of the loss of land devoted to private recreational use through its withdrawal from such a use as a result of being "up zoned" to accommodate incompatible uses.[71]

Applying the *Nollan/Dolan* test, the California Supreme Court found that the city had met its burden of showing the required nexus between the rezoning and the monetary exaction. Using zoning "to facilitate the availability of private recreational facilities . . . is within the scope of the city's police power."[72] However, the court found the specific $280,000 mitigation fee to be unsupported by the evidence and rejected an argument that the fee related to the cost of replacing lost tennis courts. That cost "would have been paid for by the fees of the private club members and the [tennis] courts would have been private, not open to all members of the public free of charge."[73] The high court expressed concern about making one property owner pay for benefits gained by the general public, although it acknowledged the possibility that some fee might be justified. In the case before it, however, more information was needed to establish "what if any recreational fee the evidence might establish."[74] Therefore, the court remanded the case for additional proceedings.[75]

---

[69]*Ehrlich*, 911 P.2d 429, 433 (Cal. 1996).

[70]*Id.* at 440.

[71]*Id.* at 446.

[72]*Id.* at 447.

[73]*Id.* at 448–49.

[74]*Id.* at 449.

[75]*Id.* at 449–50. *See also* Gideon Kanner, *Tennis Anyone? How California Judges Made Land Ransom and Art Censorship Legal,* 25 REAL ESTATE L.J. 214, 226, 227 (Winter 1997) (pointing out that city did not seek recreation fee when tennis club shut down and facilities were lost, but only when developer sought permission to build townhouses).

Floodplain Controls

In general, lands adjacent to or near waterways are often subject to special regulations to prevent flooding. Such regulations often surface after a severe flood. The leading case on floodplain controls today is *Dolan*.[76] Prior to *Dolan*, other courts examined floodplain control issues, with varying results.[77]

To prevent homes from being located in the area mostly likely to flood, a floodplain overlay zone is created along the watercourse, typically bounded at its outer limits by the topographic contour (elevation above mean sea level) where a flood might reach on average once in one hundred years. Development of homes in the floodplain protection zone is prohibited, and other uses are restricted to protect the public's health and safety.

What Lies Ahead

Exaction cases will continue to be a source of takings claims. The substantive due process test is probably unchanged, regardless of the way courts at all levels have toyed with new labels. Fiscal constraints on governments, the increased desire to preserve natural resources, and continuing efforts to get developers to contribute more will cause more conflicts and takings challenges.

---

[76]512 U.S. 374 (1994).

[77]*See* Elsmere Park Club Ltd. Partnership v. Town of Elsmere, 771 F. Supp. 646 (D. Del. 1991); Beverly Bank v. Illinois Dep't of Transp., 579 N.E.2d 815 (Ill. 1991); Vatalaro v. Department of Envtl. Regulation, 613 So. 2d. 3 (Fla. 1992).

Chapter 17

Growth Management and Moratoria

Growth management programs, which often include development moratoria, have been adopted to overcome problems with traditional zoning. Under traditional zoning, development can occur at any rate in any place and at any time, so long as the use is permitted and the standards of the regulations are met. Because traditional zoning has little effect on individual land-use decisions, most communities are "over-zoned" for most uses—far more land is zoned for far greater development intensity than the community actually wants or needs. This is necessary to ensure that opportunities are available for development when individual landholders decide to keep their land out of production.

Another problem with traditional land-use regulatory mechanisms is that they do not link development of infrastructure with the pace and location of development, so development may outstrip a local government's ability to provide supporting services. With the increasing financial pressures on federal, state, and local governments and the shifting of economic burdens from federal to state, and from state to local, governments, many communities have been driven to the brink of bankruptcy by development that costs far more than it returns in tax and other revenues.

The solution to these manifold problems has become growth management and its principal tool, the development moratorium. The Standard State Zoning Enabling Act promulgated by the U.S. Department of Commerce in the mid-1920s does not address growth management regulations and moratoria. The authority has been found elsewhere, such as in a constitutional home-rule provision.[1] While growth management programs are increasingly accepted as an appropriate regulatory approach to the problems of uncontrolled development, the takings issue has been implicated in many cases because growth management and moratoriums generally tend to slow or stop development.[2]

A common misunderstanding is that growth management is designed to only slow growth. Growth management is also used to increase the pace of development, encourage development in specific areas, and prevent the loss of buildings that might be razed or converted to other uses.[3] In this last category we have the historic district and historic landmark preservation ordinances, which are unique enough to be discussed separately in chapter 20. We also have the special problems arising from the potential loss of affordable housing, including single-room-occupancy units. This problem is addressed in part in chapter 19, but it is also discussed here because moratoria on demolition or conversion of apartment and single-room-occupancy units are fundamentally growth management ordinances.

Growth Management Defined

Growth management, which controls the "rate, amount, type, location and/or quality of future development,"[4] uses regulatory strategies including development moratoria, caps on the number of building permits issued, requirements that infrastructure be con-

---

[1]Boulder Builders Group v. City of Boulder, 759 P.2d 752 (Colo. Ct. App. 1988) (city can adopt growth management regulations under its home-rule charter).

[2]See DOUGLAS R. PORTER, PROFILES IN GROWTH MANAGEMENT (1996). See also ERIC D. KELLY, MANAGING COMMUNITY GROWTH: POLICIES, TECHNIQUES, AND IMPACTS (1993).

[3]See, e.g., Maine's state enabling legislation for growth management, title 30-A, § 4312 of the Maine Revised Statutes.

[4]TIMOTHY C. BEATLEY, DAVID J. BROWER & LOU ANN BROWER, MANAGING GROWTH: SMALL COMMUNITIES AND RURAL AREAS 7 (1988) (includes appendix of ordinances and other growth-management documents from municipalities in 11 states). See also James H. Wickersham, Note, The Quiet Revolution Continues: The Emerging New Model for State Growth Management Statutes, 18 HARVARD ENVTL. L. REV. 489, 512–45(1994) (discussing The American Land Institute's Model Land Development Code, and the Planning Consistency Model).

structed concurrently with new development, and growth boundaries.[5] The goals of growth management may include protecting and enhancing aesthetic resources, protecting historic and cultural resources, preserving farmland and open space, protecting the natural environment (by reducing air pollution; preventing groundwater contamination; and protecting sensitive habitats such as wetlands, coastal beaches, and dunes), and providing affordable housing.[6]

Proponents of growth management argue that such programs harmonize the purposes of environmental protection and private property rights by redirecting development into a more efficient pattern. Proponents also assert that by intensifying urban centers, open spaces are preserved, the natural environment is protected and enhanced, and farming and other rural industries remain viable. In addition, it is claimed that restricting new development to areas where public services are already available helps keep taxes and other costs low.

As with zoning, growth management regulations are often defended against takings claims as being the reasonable exercise of the police power.[7] Courts have held that growth management regulations advance legitimate state interests when they protect the environment; enhance the quality of life; promote public health, safety, or welfare and general well-being of the community by limiting the rate, distribution, quality, and type of residential development; improve air quality; reduce traffic congestion; and ensure the availability of essential services including water and sewer.[8] And courts generally uphold growth management regulations as valid exercises of the police power when they protect the public welfare in these diverse ways.[9]

[5]See KELLY, *supra* note 2, at 43–71.

[6]See BEATLEY, ET AL., *supra* note 4, at 15–24.

[7]DONALD G. HAGMAN & JULIAN C. JUERGENSMEYER, URBAN PLANNING AND LAND DEVELOPMENT CONTROL LAW § 9.3 (1986).

[8]Construction Indus. Ass'n v. City of Petaluma, 522 F.2d 897 (9th Cir. 1975) (annual limitation on housing units upheld), *cert. denied*, 424 U.S. 934 (1976); Long Beach Equities, Inc. v. Superior Ct. of Ventura County, 231 Cal. App. 3d 1016, 1030, 282 Cal. Rptr. 877 (1991), *review denied*, 1991 Cal. LEXIS 4556 (Sept. 26, 1991), *cert. denied*, 505 U.S. 1219 (1992); Associated Home Builders of the Greater Eastbay, Inc. v. City of Livermore, 18 Cal. 3d 582, 557 P.2d 473 (1976) (upheld building-permits ban linked to water, sewer, etc.); Golden v. Planning Bd. of Ramapo, 30 N.Y.2d 359, 285 N.E.2d 291 (upheld adequate-public-facilities ordinance), *appeal dismissed*, 409 U.S. 1003 (1972).

[9]Agins v. City of Tiburon, 447 U.S. 255, 261 (1980); *Long Beach Equities, Inc.*, 231 Cal. App. 3d at 1030.

Tougher questions emerge when growth management programs and moratoria restrict development to the point where property values are diminished.

In *Long Beach Equities, Inc. v. Superior Court of Ventura County*, the court upheld the growth management ordinance against a takings challenge, finding that the ordinance promoted a pattern of development that would benefit the public welfare.[10] The growth management plan limited the number of building permits issued annually in an attempt to protect natural resources and to discourage the premature conversion of open space to urban uses.[11] The court held that local legislation, including the growth management ordinance at issue, is constitutional on its face as long as (1) it bears "a substantial relationship to the public welfare," and (2) it inflicts no irreparable injury on the landowner. The court added that this is true even if the plaintiff alleges a substantial diminution in property value.[12]

Moratoria

A moratorium is an authorized delay in the provision of governmental services or development approval. While we concentrate on local-government moratoria affecting land use, moratoria are found at all levels of government in all manner of activities—from federal offshore oil leases,[13] to a county's moratorium on landfills,[14] to a state-imposed development ban,[15] to a local sewer program temporarily preventing sewer connections or extensions.[16]

So does a moratorium effect a temporary taking? The U.S. Supreme Court made plain in *First English*, discussed in chapter 12, that simply because a government land-use restriction is temporary, compensation is not precluded. If a temporary restriction is sufficiently onerous, it is a taking—"not different in kind from permanent takings, for which the Constitution clearly requires compensa-

---

[10]231 Cal. App. 3d at 1030–31.

[11]*Id.* at 1031.

[12]*Id.* at 1030.

[13]Union Oil Co. v. Morton, 512 F.2d 743, 750–52 (9th Cir. 1975).

[14]Pro-Eco v. Board of Comm'rs of Jay County, Ind., 956 F.2d 635 (7th Cir. 1992).

[15]Joint Ventures Inc. v. Department of Transp., 563 So. 2d 622 (Fla. 1990).

[16]Peduto v. City of North Wildwood, 878 F.2d 725 (3d Cir. 1989).

[17]First English Evangelical Lutheran Church v. County of Los Angeles, 482

tion."[17] But *First English* did not elaborate on the all-important prior question: When does a temporary restriction effect a taking?

Under police powers local governments may enact reasonable interim zoning measures to limit development for short periods without causing a taking, provided these measures are enacted in good faith and without singling out properties.[18]

However, vested rights, may allow a property owner to proceed with development even during a moratorium. For example, in *Western Land Equities, Inc. v. City of Logan*,[19] a moratorium case, Utah's highest court held that "an applicant is entitled to a building permit or subdivision approval if his proposed development meets the zoning requirements in existence at the time of his application and if he proceeds with reasonable diligence, absent a compelling, countervailing public interest."[20]

Although a moratorium on apartment construction within a particular district for a reasonable period of time has been upheld, cities must ordinarily refrain from enacting ordinances banning apartment construction altogether.[21] A moratorium on the destruction of apartments can also constitute a taking.[22]

A development moratorium prior to condemnation can effect a taking, particularly where it is seen as a way for government to reduce the cost of the later condemnation. (Precondemnation takings are discussed in more detail in chapter 18). In *Joint Ventures, Inc. v. Department of Transportation*,[23] the Supreme Court of Florida held that a state statute[24] imposing a five-year development moratorium in a transportation corridor during preacquisition planning was a taking. Florida had argued that without the development moratorium, land-acquisition costs could rise to the point of jeopardizing

---

U.S. 304, 318 (1987) (invalidation without paying for use of property constitutionally insufficient remedy), *review denied*, 1989 Cal. LEXIS 4224 (Aug. 25, 1989), *cert. denied*, 493 U.S. 1056 (1990).

[18]Almquist v. Town of Marshan, 308 Minn. 52, 245 N.W.2d 819 (1976).

[19]617 P.2d 388 (Utah 1980).

[20]*Id.* at 396.

[21]Willistown v. Chesterdale Farms, Inc., 7 Pa. Commw. 453, 300 A.2d 107 (1973) ("exclusionary" zoning ordinance unconstitutional).

[22]Seawall Assocs. v. City of New York, 74 N.Y.2d 92, 542 N.E.2d 1059, 1061 (1989) (interference with rights to possess, exclude effects taking).

[23]563 So. 2d 622 (Fla. 1990).

[24]Fla. Stat. Ann §§ 337.241(2) and (3) found unconstitutional.

[25]563 So. 2d at 625.

the project. As we will see in chapter 22 in the discussion of the contracts cases, courts are wary of governments regulating to reduce their costs, essentially as interested parties rather than as neutral arbiters. The *Joint Ventures* court found that the moratorium was an attempt by the state "to circumvent the constitutional and statutory protections afforded private property ownership under the principles of eminent domain."[25]

In *Tampa-Hillsborough County Expressway Authority v. A.G.W.S. Corp.*,[26] the Florida Supreme Court explained that *Joint Ventures* did not hold that merely filing a map of reservation delineating land for future condemnation was a per se taking.[27]

Because land sellers and developers can plan around a year or two's delay without much economic impact, short-term moratoria are much easier to defend. Landowners must prove that a map of reservation is effectively a taking, in that it denies substantially all economically beneficial or productive use.

The Importance of Defined Duration

In the frequently cited post-*Lucas* case of *Woodbury Place Partners v. Woodbury*,[28] the Court of Appeals of Minnesota held there was no facial taking in the adoption, pursuant to a state statute, of a two-year moratorium on acceptance or consideration of subdivision approval, site plan review, or rezoning of undeveloped areas adjacent to a highway to preserve the corridor. In *Lucas*, the U.S. Supreme Court had held that a regulatory action could constitute a compensable taking even without a multifactor analysis or a balancing of public and private interests if the regulation "denies all economically beneficial or productive use of land."[29] Despite the City of Woodbury's stipulation that the moratorium would deny all economically viable

[26]640 So. 2d 54 (all landowners within boundaries of invalidated maps not entitled to per se declarations of taking), *corrected*, 19 Fla. L. Weekly 5343 (Fla. 1994).

[27]*See also* Palm Beach County v. Wright, 641 So. 2d 50, 52–53 (Fla. 1994) (thoroughfare map of future transportation corridors). These map-of-reservation cases are akin to the official-map-act cases discussed in chapter 15.

[28]492 N.W.2d 258 (Minn. Ct. App. 1992), *review denied*, 1993 Minn. LEXIS 20 (Jan. 15, 1993), *cert. denied*, 508 U.S. 960 (1993).

[29]*Woodbury*, 492 N.W. 2d at 260.

use of the property from March 23, 1988 to March 23, 1990,[30] the court still found no *Lucas*-type categorical taking:

> We interpret the phrase "all economically viable use for two years" as significantly different from "all economically viable use" as applied in *Lucas*. The two-year deprivation of economic use is qualified by its defined duration. . . . "All economically viable use from March 23, 1988 to March 23, 1990" [the language from the stipulation] recognizes that economic viability exists at the moratorium's expiration.[31]

This is an important point—*Lucas* does not dictate that a moratorium on all use is necessarily a taking because a moratorium is usually for a defined, short period.

How Long Is Not Too Long?

How long can a moratorium last and still not effect a taking? The short answer is that it probably depends on the nature of the government activity to occur during the moratorium.

In *Golden Valley Lutheran College v. City of Golden Valley*,[32] a one-year moratorium on all development was held not to cause a taking under either the *Lucas* categorical test—because the property had value at the end of, and could be put to beneficial use during, the moratorium—or the multifactor balancing test of *Penn Central*.

Offen v. County Council for Prince George's County, Maryland held that an eight-year sewer moratorium on development in most of the county did not cause a taking.[33] In one New York county, a moratorium on sewer extensions, including main-line extension permits,

---

[30]*Id.* at 260, Stipulation 47.

[31]*Id.* at 261. *Accord* Williams v. City of Central, 907 P.2d 701 (Colo. Ct. App. 1995) (no taking by 10-month interim gaming moratorium), *cert. denied*, 1995 Colo. LEXIS 830 (Dec. 4. 1995). *See also* Union Oil Co., 512 F.2d at 750–52 (moratorium may be taking where imposed without specifying when it would end).

[32]1994 Minn. App. LEXIS 92 (Minn. Ct. App. Jan. 25, 1994), *review denied*, 1994 Minn. LEXIS 221 (Mar. 15, 1994), *cert. denied*, 513 U.S. 819 (1994).

[33]96 Md. App. 526, 562, 625 A.2d 424 (1993) ("all economically viable uses are not prohibited"), *rev'd on grounds unrelated to the withdrawn constitutional takings claim*, County Council Prince George's County, Md. v. Offen, 334 Md. 499, 639 A.2d 1070 (Md. 1994).

has remained in effect since 1986 by state order. A property owner who sued for compensation has been rebuffed on ripeness grounds.[34]

In *Kawaoka v. City of Arroyo Grande*, a one-year water moratorium on some development applications has been upheld as not violative of substantive due process and equal protection.[35] The Ninth Circuit, however, did not limit its ruling to the due process and equal protection claims, extending its view on the moratorium that even if it could be argued that the moratorium delayed development of their property for one year, such a short-term delay does not rise to constitutional dimensions.[36] An eighteen-month moratorium on developing parcels of two or more acres, giving the city time to develop a plan to preserve scarce land for affordable housing, did not cause a taking.[37] A four-month moratorium on special-use applications has also been successfully used during development of a new plan and regulations for quarries.[38]

The amazing expansion of the gaming industry over the last few years has created not only political, social, and economic turmoil, and some windfalls for both the public and private sectors, but also an interest in moratoria. The City of Central, Colorado, imposed a moratorium on development in the gaming district to study growth induced by the gaming industry. This moratorium was held not to be a temporary taking absent "extraordinary delay."[39]

A good example of an appropriate time period for a development moratorium is found in *Santa Fe Village Venture v. City of Albuquerque*.[40] In 1989 the Albuquerque City Council adopted a property-acquisition policy and building moratorium for one year for private properties within the Petroglyph National Monument. The council then extended the moratorium for six months and then, at the end of that extension, extended it for another year. The time limits

---

[34]HBP Assocs. v. Langdon Marsh, 893 F. Supp. 271 (S.D.N.Y. 1995).

[35]17 F.3d 1227 (9th Cir. 1994) (evidence of irrationality, racial discrimination insufficient), *cert. denied*, 513 U.S. 870 (1994).

[36]*Id.* at 1237.

[37]Tocco v. New Jersey Council on Affordable Hous., 242 N.J. Super. 218, 576 A.2d 328 (App. Div. 1990), *certification denied*, 122 N.J. 403 (1990), *cert. denied*, 499 U.S. 937 (1991).

[38]Nello L. Teer Co. v. Orange County, 1993 U.S. App. LEXIS 12525 (4th Cir. 1993).

[39]Williams v. City of Central, 907 P.2d 701 (Colo. Ct. App. 1995), *cert. denied*, 1995 Colo. LEXIS 830 (Dec. 4, 1995).

[40]914 F. Supp. 478 (D.N.M. 1995).

were carefully crafted to follow the anticipated time periods for Congress to act on legislation creating the Petroglyph National Monument, and during the last year of the moratorium, all property owners who applied for building permits were assured of approval within twelve months from the date of application. The court found no taking. A development moratorium for a limited period seems most justified in this type of situation—an irreplaceable natural resource and a moratorium that extends for a well-defined, limited period with opportunities for property owners to lock in a final action on their applications.

An equally compelling type of "temporary moratorium," to use the terminology of the Tahoe Regional Planning Agency (TRPA), is the restriction adopted by TRPA from June 25, 1981 until June 26, 1984, while TRPA developed its regional plan for the Lake Tahoe Basin.[41]

The moratorium decision on remand of the U.S. Supreme Court in *First English*, holding that a delay of more than two years was not unreasonable,[42] has not been widely cited because it is seen as the epilogue to a much bigger story. As the Colorado Court of Appeals analyzed the remand in *First English* as well as *Agins* and *Woodbury Place Partners*:

> [A]n interim regulation prohibiting construction or development is not a temporary taking even if such restrictions would be held too onerous to survive scrutiny had they been permanently imposed. [Citing the remand in *First English*.] Absent extraordinary delay, fluctuations in value that occur during a temporary moratorium enacted to effect the process of governmental decisionmaking are, simply, incidents of ownership. [Citing to *Agins* and *Woodbury Place Partners*.][43]

---

[41]Tahoe-Sierra Preservation Council, Inc. v. Tahoe Regional Planning Agency, 938 F.2d 153 (9th Cir. 1991) (takings claim dismissal reversed, remanded), *compl. dismissed*, 808 F. Supp. 1474, 1484 (D. Nev. 1992) (time barred, etc.), *aff'd in part and rev'd in part on other grounds, remanded*, 34 F.3d 753 (9th Cir. 1994) (takings claim time barred).

[42]First English Evangelical Lutheran Church v. County of Los Angeles, 210 Cal. App. 3d 1353, 258 Cal. Rptr. 893 (1989) (interim ordinance no taking), *review denied*, 1989 Cal. LEXIS 4224 (Aug. 25, 1989), *cert. denied*, 493 U.S. 1056 (1990).

[43]*Williams*, 907 P.2d at 704.

Defensible Moratoria

A so-called "planning pause" moratorium can give the government breathing room while it considers comprehensive zoning changes in the face of uncontrolled development or potential loss of natural and cultural resources.[44] "Planning pause" moratoria cases are truly fact-driven. As a New York court recently said in *Schulz v. Lake George Park Commission*: "[W]hile the use of emergency rules imposing construction moratoriums is likely to recur, whether such moratoriums are justified is a fact-sensitive inquiry to be evaluated on a case-by-case basis."[45]

Here as elsewhere, courts will support moratoria when there is a clear public need and the period of the moratorium is no longer than necessary. In Crawford County, Georgia, for example, the board of County Commissioners grew deeply concerned about the unregulated development of mobile-home lots in the county and the effect of such development on the property values of conventional subdivision homes.[46] The board directed the county attorney to draft a resolution placing a "temporary moratorium" on issuing mobile-home permits for the southeastern portion of the county. The moratorium was to be effective until completion and review of a comprehensive development plan.

The Crawford County moratorium is a model defensible "planning pause" moratorium. It was carefully drawn to stop development only where necessary. It included only properties smaller than twenty-five acres unless a property was part of a subdivision that had already received final plat approval and one or more lots had been deeded to individual purchasers by the developer. The moratorium also excepted developments where an application for a mobile-home permit had been made prior to the passage of the moratorium and the applicant had expended funds or otherwise substantially changed position based on assurances from local officials. Most importantly, the

---

[44]*See also* 119 Dev. Assocs. v. Village of Irvington, 171 A.D.2d 656, 566 N.Y.S.2d 954 (1991) (valid exercise of police power).

[45]180 A.D.2d 852, 579 N.Y.S.2d 761, 763 (1992) (moratorium repealed; issue moot), *modified sub nom.* Schulz v. N.Y. State Dep't of Envtl. Conservation, 200 A.D.2d 793, 606 N.Y.S.2d 459 (1994) (storm-water regulations valid), *appeal dismissed without op.*, 83 N.Y.2d 848, 634 N.E.2d 607, *appeal denied*, 83 N.Y.2d 758 (1994).

[46]Brown v. Crawford County, Ga., 960 F.2d 1002 (11th Cir. 1992) (absolute immunity to establish moratorium).

moratorium was limited to a mere ninety days, with a potential
ninety-day extension, if the Board of Commissioners had not acted
on the recommendations of its consultant by adopting a revised
zoning plan. When the Board of Commissioners adopted the moratorium, they were already updating their local plan and regulations.

Although the case was decided on issues other than the taking
claim, the court expressed its approval of the moratorium:

> Voting to establish the temporary moratorium was prudent to
> allow time to review the commissioned development plan. . . .
> The facts show nothing more than the conscientious effort of
> the county commissioners to investigate a potential county
> zoning problem requested by petition of a significant number
> of Crawford County residents.[47]

Defensible moratoria are the rule, rather than the exception. A
Cook's tour of a few recent cases may help in understanding the
boundaries of acceptable moratoria.

In *Villas of Lake Jackson, Ltd. v. Leon County*, a moratorium has
been used to stop the issuance of permits while local government
studied ways to reduce adverse impacts on lake water quality.[48] In
Mid Gulf, Inc. v. Bishop, a federal trial court upheld a ninety-day
moratorium on accepting applications for permits to drill for gas and
oil. Local officials expressed concern about the effect on residents,
cleanup problems the government had encountered with one well,
and "the general lack of knowledge among the City's leaders regarding gas and oil drilling. . . ."[49]

A moratorium for site-specific enforcement of development requirements is also not a taking. For example, a moratorium held not
to be a taking prohibited the sale of lots in a subdivision with an inadequate storm-water system that did not conform to the developer's
plans and specifications.[50]

Sometimes it is not at all clear whether a moratorium is uncon-
scionably designed to stop a particular project, or whether it is truly
in the public interest. The *Corn v. City of Lauderdale Lakes* case is a

[47]*Id.* at 1012–13.

[48]Villas of Lake Jackson Ltd. v. Leon County, 796 F. Supp. 1477 (N.D. Fla.
1992), *recons. granted in part, modified, takings counts dismissed in part,
summ. j. granted in part*, 906 F. Supp. 1509 (N.D. Fla. 1995).

[49]1992 U.S. Dist. LEXIS 14127 at 6 (D. Kan. August 11, 1992).

[50]Foster v. Board of Comm'rs of Warrick County, Ind., 647 N.E.2d 1147
(Ind. Ct. App. 1995).

good example.[51] Perhaps what is most startling is the trial court's straight-up critique of the moratorium itself:

> The moratorium seems nothing more than an attempt at post hoc rationalization [citation omitted]. In short, the City Council was motivated solely by an irrational desire to thwart Corn's plans.[52]

The *Corn* case, with all of its history dating back to 1977, made its way to the U.S. Court of Appeals for the Eleventh Circuit in 1993—yet another example of the long gestation period for takings cases. The property owner had proposed building a 900-unit mini-warehouse on a parcel zoned for such a use.[53] The proposal was rejected by the city council both because of a change in zoning as well as enactment of a moratorium. The court of appeals reversed both the federal trial court's holding that there was a violation of substantive due process and its dismissal of the claims against individual city council members on legislative immunity grounds.[54] While the decision does not address the remanded just compensation claim, there is a useful analysis of the case law, the standards to be applied by local land-use decision-makers, the degree to which local decision-makers must investigate development proposals, the standard for deferential review of local decision-making and the application of legal precedent. But most of all, the case illustrates how difficult it is at times to draw the line between what is good government and what violates property rights.

On remand, the federal trial court held that the ordinances did not effect a taking of either the parcel or the project.[55] That decision was appealed to the court of appeals, which vacated the judgment that the moratorium caused a temporary taking of the parcel. The appeals court remanded for the trial court to make further findings on that claim, stating that it could not effectively review the claim without

---

[51]771 F. Supp. 1557 (S.D. Fla. 1991) (temporary-taking damages awarded), 997 F.2d 1369 (11th Cir. 1993) (reversed substantive due process holding; just compensation claim remanded), *cert. denied*, 511 U.S. 1018 (1994).

[52]771 F. Supp. at 1569.

[53]*Corn*, 95 F.3d at 1066, 1068 (11th Cir. 1996), *cert. denied*, 118 S. Ct. 441 (1997).

[54]*Corn*, 997 F.2d 1369 (11th Cir. 1993), *cert. denied*, 511 U.S. 1018 (1994).

[55]*Corn*, 95 F.3d 1066, 1070–71 (11th Cir. 1996), *cert. denied*, 118 S. Ct. 441 (1997).

such findings.[56] The appeals court did affirm the trial court decision that no taking of the project, as distinguished from the parcel, had occurred:

> We hold that, regardless of what vested rights Corn may have had in the Project under Florida law, a denial of permission to build a particular development project does not, by itself, state a just compensation claim.[57]

Importance of Uses Available During and After a Moratorium

It is useful to reach back to the U.S. Supreme Court's 1980 decision in *Agins v. City of Tiburon*[58] because the famous footnote 9 of that decision seems to suggest that temporary restrictions on the use of property do not constitute a taking:

> The State Supreme Court correctly rejected the contention that the municipality's good-faith planning activities, which did not result in successful prosecution of an eminent domain claim, so burdened the appellants' enjoyment of their property as to constitute a taking. . . . Mere fluctuations in value during the process of governmental decisionmaking, absent extraordinary delay, are "incidents of ownership. They cannot be considered 'taking' in the constitutional sense." [Citations omitted.][59]

The importance of what happens to value during the time when a property cannot be developed or further developed shows up in numerous cases. In *Kelly v. Tahoe Regional Planning Agency*, a property owner at Lake Tahoe in Nevada was unable to further develop his property for thirteen years and even then because of new regulations the development potential was greatly reduced.[60] The Nevada Supreme Court found no taking and held that the Tahoe Regional Planning Agency (TRPA) can postpone building in critical areas for a "reasonable period of time" so long as the "benefit received by the property from the ordinances is direct and substantial and the burden imposed is proportional." The court noted that the owner had paid $500,000 for his property, lived in the main house for almost 20

[56]*Id.* at 1073.
[57]*Id.* at 1074.
[58]447 U.S. 255 (1980).
[59]*Id.* at 263 n.9.
[60]109 Nev. 638, 855 P.2d 1027 (1993), *cert. denied*, 510 U.S. 1041 (1994).

years and sold the main house alone for $1.1 million.[61] He had also received another $5.6 million from prior sales of parcels in the planned unit development.

The courts have tried to find meaning in the 1969 interstate compact that created the TRPA and in the subsequent compact and the regional plans promulgated by TRPA. Many TRPA cases have involved takings; one of the more interesting, especially in the moratorium context, is *Carpenter v. Tahoe Regional Planning Agency*.[62]

Alice Carpenter purchased a parcel at Lake Tahoe in 1973 for $27,950, recorded the deed in 1980, and decided to build a house in 1981. By then, an ordinance creating a case-by-case review for development in the basin was in place and the 1980 Compact between California and Nevada had replaced the 1969 Compact. The 1980 Compact was intended to establish "environmental carrying capacities" within the Lake Tahoe Basin while providing for orderly and environmentally safe growth.

On August 26, 1983, the TRPA governing board temporarily suspended all project permits. In 1984, the TRPA passed the 1984 Regional Plan, which never took effect because the day it was adopted, the Attorney General of California filed suit alleging that the plan violated the 1980 Compact. To resolve these complexities, the TRPA adopted the 1987 Regional Plan with several new elements including an Individual Parcel Evaluation System, transfers of development rights, a system by which property owners could challenge the land capability classification of their parcels, and a provision for amending plans.

Carpenter applied for a building permit in 1982, but she never received it because of the initial ordinance, effective June 25, 1981; a moratorium on all new building that ran from August 29, 1983 through April 26, 1984; the 1984 Regional Plan; and the injunction from April 27, 1984 through July 14, 1987 brought on by the Attorney General's suit. Ultimately, she sold her lot to the State of Nevada in 1990 for $185,000 as part of the state's buyout program of environmentally sensitive Lake Tahoe area properties.

Ruling on motions for summary judgment from TRPA, the federal trial court ultimately held that Carpenter could maintain her taking claims, though they were not yet ripe, for the period from June 25, 1981, when the ordinance went into effect, through the end of the

[61] *Id.* at 650–51.

[62] 804 F. Supp. 1316, 1319 n.2 (D. Nev. 1992) (listing other TRPA takings cases).

subsequent moratorium on April 26, 1984, during which time no development was allowed.

In the court's reasoning, *First English* required that the government compensate a landowner for a temporary taking if during the period of land-use restriction the property owner was deprived of all economically viable use of the land. Carpenter, who had no existing permitted use, suffered such a deprivation.

In other words, even if use of the property is eventually restored, the owner can still sue for a temporary taking. The temporary prohibition, and the temporary loss, still occurred, it was a taking, and it must be compensated. Thus, the fact that the plaintiff sold her property should have no impact on any temporary taking claim, although the court allowed in a footnote that "[t]he result would probably differ in the case of a claimed permanent taking."[63]

The *Carpenter* court is not saying that every moratorium causes a temporary taking and, indeed, on the facts of the case no facial taking was found. What the court did say is that if a long period of prohibited use includes a short time during which use is totally precluded by a moratorium, and there is no economically beneficial permitted use, then if there is a temporary taking, the property owner can be compensated—even if the property has value later when it is sold. This is still consistent with the view that a moratorium is not necessarily a temporary taking, particularly where there is some economic use during the time of the moratorium.

For a moratorium case illustrating the importance of the uses remaining during a moratorium and the potential for further development, see *Merriam Gateway Associates v. Town of Newton, New Jersey*.[64] In that case, a truly hapless developer purchased a former shoe factory with the intent of converting it into 100 residential condominium and commercial units. The developer proceeded with the project in 1987, four years after purchasing the property and after learning that a sewer moratorium had been lifted. Construction began in March 1988 and final site-plan approval was granted in December 1988. Just three months later, when the project was about 80 pecent complete, the developer learned that the New Jersey Department of Environmental Protection ("DEP") had reimposed the sewer moratorium almost two years earlier and no certificates of occupancy could be issued. The developer, in claims against its architects,

[63]*Id.* at 1327 n.15.
[64]1992 U.S. Dist. LEXIS 21562 (D.N.J. June 1, 1992), *aff'd*, 91 F.3d 124 (3rd Cir. 1996). The developer is not related to any of the coauthors.

engineers, and law firms for malpractice and breach of contract and against the Town of Newton, alleged more than $13 million in damages.[65] The federal trial court held that the developer had failed to state a Fifth Amendment taking claim because it did not contend that the property had been rendered useless. The town had received a special concession from the New Jersey DEP during the moratorium and had secured hookups for sixteen units (with other units served by hauling sewage to another treatment facility), and when the ban was lifted in November 1990, the plaintiff had been free to pursue the project, though it did not.[66]

The importance of reasonable and beneficial economic uses remaining during a moratorium arises again and again. For example, the City of Pearl, Mississippi, adopted a two-year moratorium on locating new mobile-home sales establishments.[67] The owner of two parcels sued, claiming a taking and seeking injunctive relief to permit him to place mobile-home sales establishments on his parcels. During his deposition, the owner conceded that there were other uses for his two properties during the moratorium even though he did not believe they were as profitable as ground leasing the properties for mobile-home sales establishments.[68] Furthermore, the plaintiff acknowledged that he had paid $250,000 for one of the properties that was appraised for $825,000 in 1990. He further testified that although he could not remember what he paid for the other parcel, it was appraised at $750,000 at the time of his deposition, just after the end of the moratorium.[69] Thus, the court found no taking because other uses remained for the property.

Exhaustion

The exhaustion doctrine, requiring a claimant to establish a complete administrative record as a prerequisite to a claim, is particularly important in a taking claim based on a moratorium. The New York State Legislature imposed a moratorium on development along Beaverdam Creek in the town of Brookhaven so the creek could be studied for possible inclusion in New York State's Wild, Scenic and

[65]*Id.* at 3.
[66]*Id.* at 9–10.
[67]Herrington v. City of Pearl, 908 F. Supp 418 (S.D. Miss. 1995).
[68]*Id.* at 425.
[69]*Id.* at n.10.

Recreational Rivers System.[70] A property owner's claim for just compensation was dismissed on the ground that he had not exhausted administrative remedies and had, therefore, not established a regulatory taking. The owner had not proven that he had applied for an exemption from the moratorium before filing suit. The New York appeals court affirmed, stating that it could not consider the owner's takings claim without an adequate administrative record. The state had not denied the property owner an exemption from the moratorium, thus the owner had not yet been denied "an economically viable use of its land."[71]

Damages

Can a landowner win significant money damages in a moratorium case? Emphatically, yes. River Oaks Marine, Inc. was successful in a claim against the Town of Grand Island, New York, for the town's prohibition against removing soil substances from Grand Island under the Grand Island Natural Resources Moratorium, with an award of $1,149,149.43, including $298,919.43 in prejudgment interest.[72]

Conclusions

Growth management programs that cause a loss in value by slowing down the rate of growth and by limiting growth in specific locations will be defensible in most cases against taking claims because they will be judged based on the *Penn Central* multifactor balancing test. Growth management programs typically do not destroy all value but cause some reductions in value, often for limited periods.

A moratorium may be merely a short, stopgap measure, totally defensible under the police power, to avoid adverse impact to the public's health, safety, and general welfare while the government plans and implements regulations. As such, a moratorium may or may not be a temporary taking.

[70]Timber Ridge Homes at Brookhaven, Inc. v. New York, 223 A.D.2d 635 (1996), *appeal denied*, 88 N.Y.2d 802 (1996).

[71]*Id.* at 636.

[72]River Oaks Marine, Inc. v. Town of Grand Island, 1992 U.S. Dist. LEXIS 18974 (W.D.N.Y. Nov. 24, 1992). *See also* chapter 31.

When that line is crossed, the line between valid police power regulation and a temporary taking largely depends on whether there are underlying reasonably beneficial and economic uses available during the moratorium and whether the moratorium is for as short a period as reasonably necessary for the government to plan and act. There may be cases where no underlying use remains and there is still no taking, particularly if the moratorium is of short duration and the danger to public health and safety is great. And there may be a taking even if there is an underlying use if the moratorium is long, not reasonably related to permissible governmental objectives, and causes great economic impact on the property owner.

Just as good planning may require a moratorium now and again, a moratorium requires good planning. A moratorium's objectives should expressly identify critical public health and safety issues, the moratorium should be for as short a time as necessary, and every moratorium should do all that is possible to encourage the reasonable economic use of affected property, including allowing interim uses and waivers or exemptions from the moratorium on a case-by-case basis.

Chapter 18

Future Condemnation

Precondemnation Activity

Unlike government action that results in property being taken *indirectly* through the impact of land-use and development regulations, condemnation (eminent domain) is government acquisition of property *directly* through the formal steps of either a negotiated purchase or through a judicial proceeding to determine the fair market value of the property, announce a redevelopment plan or the intent to acquire, and then designate areas for condemnation. The results are predictable. Tenants depart the area, owners "disinvest" or cut back on routine maintenance and repair, property sales and rentals evaporate, and mortgage money is nowhere to be had.[1]

The threat of condemnation can cause as much if not more economic harm to a property as condemnation itself because of the loss of income during the period of the threat or on-site and off-site changes that reduce the value of the property. First, people thinking about renting in the potentially condemned building lose interest because they foresee having to move in the near future. Tenants terminate their leases early and those who complete their terms do not

---

[1]*See* Sayre v. City of Cleveland, 493 F.2d 64, 68 (6th Cir. 1974) (urban renewal program alone does not effect taking), *cert. denied*, 419 U.S. 837 (1974).

renew. Rents are depressed because of the waning interest in the building and the deteriorating neighborhood. Vacancies and vandalism increase.

Faced with the announced condemnation of the building and its demolition, owners naturally reduce maintenance. Why replace worn tile in the hallways when the whole building is going to be torn down anyway? Some of the tenants who occupy the few remaining rented units seem to care little for the property, and the building suffers beyond the reduced maintenance. But then after ten years, the city abandons its redevelopment project. Not long thereafter, because the building has fallen into such poor repair, the city orders it razed at the owner's sole expense.

Now that the site has been cleared and your investment except for a small residual value in the land has disappeared, the city decides to renew its redevelopment plans. Your vacant lot is designated as part of the redevelopment project and eventually taken through eminent domain at a low price.

Fact Patterns of Precondemnation Cases

This not-so-hypothetical fact pattern is derived in part from a real case.[2] But this is just one fact pattern that can be identified from the precondemnation activity cases, sometimes labeled as de facto taking,[3] acquisitory intent, or precondemnation-blight cases.[4] The following are other, typical fact patterns:

  1. Regulatory review of development, condemnation announced.[5]

---

[2]See Foster v. Detroit, 405 F.2d 138 (6th Cir. 1968) (city's actions effected a taking).

[3]"De facto" adds nothing—a de facto taking is still just a taking. (*But see infra* note 4).

[4]The New York courts distinguish between de facto takings and takings based on precondemnation blight. In Beaux Arts Properties, Inc. v. United Nations Dev. Corp., 68 Misc. 2d 785, 790–91, 328 N.Y.S.2d 16 (Sup. Ct. 1972), aff'd, 39 A.D. 2d 844, 332 N.Y.S.2d 1008, *appeal denied,* 31 N.Y.2d 643 (1972), the court found no taking when the plaintiff's property, first included in a plan for redevelopment, was removed from the plan three years later.

[5]San Francisco v. Golden Gate Heights Invs., 14 Cal. App. 4th 1203, 18 Cal. Rptr. 2d 467 (1993) (at time of subdivision preapplication meeting, city staff discovered property was omitted from open-space map; three years later city adopted resolution to acquire property; owner not entitled to precondemnation damages because no evidence that value decreased due to city's conduct), *review*

2. Downzoning alleged as precondemnation activity, condemnation never announced.[6]
3. Reduction in development potential, condemnation announced.[7]
4. More restrictive zoning adopted, condemnation announced, condemnation abandoned.[8]
5. Condemnation proposed, but property never taken.[9]
6. Condemnation proposed, property ultimately taken but only after a long delay.[10]
7. Condemnation proposed, taking delayed, increased enforcement of building or housing codes, property taken.[11]
8. Condemnation proposed, tenants notified, filing of condemnation delayed, tenants vacate building, property taken.[12]
9. Condemnation proposed, public services reduced, area buildings razed, condemnation proposed again, and property taken.[13]

---

denied, 1993 Cal. LEXIS 2663 (May 20, 1993), *cert. denied*, 510 U.S. 928 (1993).

[6]Kaiser Dev. Co. v. Honolulu, 649 F. Supp. 926 (D. Haw. 1986), *aff'd*, 898 F.2d 112 (9th Cir.), *supp. op.*, 899 F.2d 18 (9th Cir.), *amended*, 913 F.2d 573 (9th Cir. 1990), *cert. denied*, 499 U.S. 947 (1991).

[7]San Diego Gas & Elec. Co. v. City of San Diego, 450 U.S. 621, 628 (1981).

[8]Agins v. City of Tiburon, 447 U.S. 255 (1980) (no taking).

[9]Peacock v. County of Sacramento, 271 Cal. App. 2d 845, 77 Cal. Rptr. 391 (1969) (county actions restricting usable height of property owners' land constitute taking); County of Bernalillo v. Morris, 117 N.M. 398, 872 P.2d 371 (Ct. App. 1994) (property owner should receive temporary takings damages), *cert. denied*, 873 P.2d 270 (N.M. 1994).

[10]Ream v. Handley, 359 F.2d 728 (7th Cir. 1966) (takings complaint dismissed, court lacks subject-matter jurisdiction), *holding overruled by* Lynch v. Household Fin. Corp., 405 U.S. 538 (1972).

[11]City of Cleveland v. Hurwitz, 19 Ohio Misc. 184, 249 N.E.2d 562 (Prob. Ct. 1969); City of Buffalo v. Manguso, 42 A.D.2d 673, 344 N.Y.S.2d 248 (1973) (compensation due for value lost from blight where nearby properties condemned first, code enforcement was unrealistic, and government kept shifting between rehabilitation and condemnation policies).

[12]Sayre v. United States, 282 F. Supp. 175 (N.D. Ohio 1967).

[13]In re Elmwood Park Project, 376 Mich. 311, 136 N.W.2d 896 (1965) (property owner entitled to just compensation). However, in E & J Inc. v. Redevelopment Agency of Woonsocket, 122 R.I. 288, 290, 405 A.2d 1187 (1979), the Rhode Island Supreme Court found "nothing more than noncompensable consequential damages" to a drive-in hamburger stand located outside, but on the edge of, a redevelopment area when the business failed after the neighborhood was left "barren" and in a "desert like condition," streets were closed, and traffic diverted.

10. Condemnation proposed, taxes on property increased.[14]
11. Condemnation proposed, property owner conveys portion of property in contemplation of condemnation to mitigate damages, property condemned.[15]

Judicial recognition of condemnation blight in these troubling scenarios is increasing, but primarily in those instances where the threat of condemnation can be demonstrated to have worked a substantial and unreasonable interference with property rights. Previously, the courts largely ignored the problem. As the U.S. Supreme Court said in *Danforth v. United States:*

> [A] reduction or increase in the value of property may occur by reason of . . . [precondemnation activities, but s]uch changes in value are incidents of ownership. They cannot be considered as a "taking" in the constitutional sense.[16]

Several state courts followed *Danforth* for many years and it is still cited today.[17]

As a general rule, the "mere" threat of condemnation or the announcement of an impending condemnation does not amount to a "de facto" taking requiring the payment of just compensation, even if the threat or expression of intent to condemn results in damage to property or diminution in its value.[18] No taking results from the mere declaration that property will be taken because compensation for such a declaration is speculative in nature.[19] This theory is uti-

---

[14]Kohl Indus. Park Co. v. County of Rockland, 710 F.2d 895 (2d Cir. 1983); Peacock v. County of Sacramento, 271 Cal. App. 2d 845, 77 Cal. Rptr. 391 (1969).

[15]Wilmot v. New York, 32 N.Y.2d 164, 297 N.E.2d 90 (1973) (owner should be compensated as if property were whole, should not be prejudiced for choosing to mitigate damages through conveyance).

[16]308 U.S. 271, 285 (1939). The early state cases were equally unsympathetic.

[17]*See, e.g.,* In re the County of Nassau, 68 Misc. 2d 405, 326 N.Y.S.2d 946 (Sup. Ct. 1971) (display of map of proposed area to be condemned not a taking); Florio v. City of Miami Beach, 425 So. 2d 1161, 1162 (Fla. Dist. Ct. App. 1983) (no condemnation blight and no taking through inclusion in redevelopment area where property owner not restricted as result of designation), *pet. denied,* 434 So. 2d 887 (Fla. 1983); National By-Products Inc. v. City of Little Rock, 323 Ark. 619, 626, 916 S.W.2d 745 (1996).

[18]Pitman v. United States, 211 Ct. Cl. 357, 358 (1976); Heimann v. City of Los Angeles, 30 Cal. 2d 746, 185 P.2d 597, 602 (Cal. 1947); Gully v. Southwestern Bell Tel. Co., 774 F.2d 1287, 1292 n.12 (5th Cir. 1985).

[19]Marion & R.V. Ry v. United States, 270 U.S. 280 (1926) (war-emergency

lized by government particularly in those cases where the property owner is not deprived of use and enjoyment or economic benefits of his property.[20]

Courts' willingness to find takings as a result of precondemnation activities began to increase about thirty years ago, as the complexities of redevelopment and renewal became more obvious.[21] As one federal court put it:

> An abuse of the exercise of the power of eminent domain would constitute a taking of property without just compensation if that abuse directly and proximately contributes to, hastens, and aggravates, acting alone or in combination with other causes, the deterioration and decline in value of the area and the subject property.[22]

Courts have wrestled with substantive issues in trying to find the middle ground.

Unreasonable Government Conduct

To effect a taking as a result of precondemnation activity, the government's conduct must be "unreasonable."[23] What is unreasonable, both in terms of conduct and delay, is a question of fact.[24]

Certain activity by government may be so oppressive or conducted in such bad faith as a part of precondemnation activity that a taking may be deemed to have occurred. For example, in anticipation of condemnation activities, a city used its power to issue or deny building permits to encourage people to move out, verbally discouraged repairs, caused unreasonable delay in the issuance of permits, represented that a fixed maximum price for homes in the area to be condemned would be paid, represented that occupancy permits

---

law authorizing President "to take possession and assume control of any railroad").

[20]Schultz v. United States, 5 Cl. Ct. 412, 419 (1984); In re Condemnation of Premises, 449 A.2d 820 (Pa. Commw. Ct. 1982).

[21]Gideon Kanner, *Condemnation Blight: Just How Just Is Just Compensation?*, 48 NOTRE DAME LAWYER 765 (1973), *reprinted in* C730 A.L.I.-A.B.A. 219, 248–49 (1992).

[22]Sayre v. United States, 282 F. Supp. 175, 185 (N.D. Ohio 1967).

[23]Klopping v. City of Whittier, 8 Cal. 3d 39, 52, 500 P.2d 1345 (1972).

[24]Cambria Spring Co. v. City of Pico Rivera, 171 Cal. App. 3d 1080, 217 Cal. Rptr. 772 (1985).

would be difficult to obtain due to the city's desire to clear a certain area, posted signs encouraging people to sell to the city, and conducted other activities in the same vein. Because of these activities, the court held that a taking had occurred even though no formal eminent domain proceedings had been instituted.[25]

Because reasonableness is a question of fact and of degree, it is possible to find that during the pendency of the condemnation the government acted reasonably. In one case it was found that property owners could not recover compensation even with allegations and some proof at trial that they lost rental income and suffered a reduction in market value while the condemnation was pending. The local government interrupted utility service, held a public auction on the property owners' premises without their consent, piled construction materials around the building, and interfered with access to the building as a result of the construction.[26]

Also, where the government has deliberately acted to reduce the value of property by filing a notice of a pending claim, publishing a threat of condemnation, mailing letters and other communications to neighborhood residents, refusing to issue building permits while intensifying building code–violation inspections, reducing municipal services to the area, and condemning and razing buildings in piecemeal fashion, the court will likely find a taking.[27]

Continuous Versus Mere Threat of Condemnation

As the *Danforth* Court held, merely announcing a proposed condemnation action does not rise to the level of a taking. This doctrine has been followed in most states.[28] Telling tenants about a proposed condemnation, followed by their moving out and the building falling into decline, is not a taking unless proof is presented that the prop-

---

[25]Amen v. City of Dearborn, 718 F.2d 789 (6th Cir. 1983), *cert. denied,* 465 U.S. 1101 (1984).

[26]O'Brien v. City of Syracuse, 54 A.D.2d 186, 388 N.Y.S.2d 866 (1976), *cert. denied, appeal dismissed,* 434 U.S. 807, *appeal dismissed,* 41 N.Y.2d 1008 (1977).

[27]Board of Educ. v. Clarke, 89 Mich. App. 504, 508–09, 280 N.W.2d 574 (1979) (citing In re Elmwood Park Project, 376 Mich. 311, 317, 136 N.W.2d 896 (1965)).

[28]Barsky v. City of Wilmington, 578 F. Supp. 170 (D. Del. 1983); Tierney v. Planned Indus. Expansion Auth., 742 S.W.2d 146, 154 (Mo. 1987) (passage of

erty owner's inability to rent was caused by "prospective tenants' fear of future condemnation."[29] It is also not a taking even if the government lies to a property owner about its intent when the owner could not justifiably have relied on the alleged misrepresentations.[30]

However, the continued commencement and cessation of proceedings in eminent domain has been held to be a *continuous,* and not a "mere," threat of condemnation, thus causing an unreasonable and substantial interference with property rights—a taking.[31] Similarly, a decline in business directly related to precondemnation activity combined with publicity in a local newspaper of the impending demolition of the business improvements on the property and repeated postponements of the date of a formal taking have been held to be a "de facto" taking because of the unreasonable delay and interference with property rights.[32]

The voluntary nature of the property owner's action can be decisive when an owner cuts off his own rights to recover against a government entity that proposes to take his or her property. In one case, a property owner had spent about $250,000 in beginning to demolish his building when he received word from the mayor that the city proposed to acquire his property. The mayor asked how much he would take for the property; the owner never responded. The mayor

---

blighting ordinance and ordinance approving initial redevelopment plan causes no taking), *appeal dismissed,* 486 U.S. 1040 (1988); Orfield v. Hous. & Redevelopment Auth. of St. Paul, 305 Minn. 336, 232 N.W.2d 923 (1975); City of Buffalo v. Clement Co., 28 N.Y.2d 241, 255–58, 269 N.E.2d 895, 903–05 (1971), *appeal after remand,* 40 A.D.2d 753, 337 N.Y.S.2d 642, *appeal dismissed,* 31 N.Y.2d 958, 293 N.E.2d 252 (1972).

[29]Heinrich v. City of Detroit, 90 Mich. App. 692, 701, 282 N.W.2d 448, 452 (1979).

[30]Oregon v. Hewett Professional Group, 321 Or. 118, 130, 132, 895 P.2d 755 (1995) (state agency misrepresented that it would not take property). A similar situation arose in Fitger Brewing Co. v. Minnesota, 416 N.W.2d 200 (Minn. Ct. App. 1987) (property owner claimed that state misrepresented federal regulations relating to condemnation; no taking because owner's freedom of choice about making improvements not substantially destroyed by state's actions), *cert. denied,* 488 U.S. 819 (1988).

[31]Osborn v. City of Cedar Rapids, 324 N.W.2d 471, 474 (Iowa 1982) (taking found in four successive eminent domain proceedings; "nearly continuous threat").

[32]Com. Dep't of Transp. v. DiFurio, 555 A.2d 1379, 1381 (Pa. Cmmw. Ct. 1989), *appeal denied,* 574 A.2d 72–73.

then notified the owner that the city and county would be purchasing the property. A few months later, the property owner was told that the county alone would purchase the property and on that basis he negotiated a voluntary sale. He then sued the city for the demolition expense. The property owner cited the *Foster* case,[33] but the court was unconvinced, holding that the damage was not compensable and that the owner should have negotiated the demolition expense with the county.[34]

What ultimately seems to be most important in weighing the reasonableness of the government's condemnation actions is how affirmative and numerous those actions might be. A quintessential case arose in New York almost thirty years ago. The city had notified tenants by letter and telephone that it would soon condemn the property, notified the owner that it would start demolishing the building, sent notices to the tenants to look for other quarters, approved removal of the railroad siding from the building, and cut off garbage pickup—all of which cumulatively drove the tenants out and virtually destroyed the value of the property before the condemnation was complete.[35]

Delay

Where the record is devoid of any evidence that the government intentionally delayed acquisition, the delay is not unreasonable.[36] A property owner cannot recover for damages caused by delay, for example, where the delay results from a cease-and-desist order of the federal government, not from actions of the acquiring governmental

---

[33]Foster v. Detroit, 405 F.2d 138 (6th Cir. 1968).

[34]Greenwood v. City of Seattle, 73 Wash. 2d 741, 745–47, 440 P.2d 437 (1968).

[35]City of Buffalo v. George Irish Paper Co., 31 A.D.2d. 470, 473, 299 N.Y.S.2d 8 (1969) (de facto taking), *aff'd*, 26 N.Y.2d 869, 258 N.E.2d 100 (1970). Like many other things in the law, reasonableness in the context of condemnation blight claims is a question of degree.

[36]San Francisco v. Golden Gate Heights Invs., 14 Cal. App. 4th 1203, 18 Cal. Rptr. 2d 467 (1993).

entity.[37] If the government, however, purposely delays the acquisition simply to drive down land value, there is a taking.[38]

The *length* of the delay from the announcement of the condemnation to the completion of the acquisition, including the time of payment, is central to many precondemnation blight cases.[39] A one-year delay causes no taking.[40] An almost two-year delay from when the condemnation action was filed in court until payment is made in an escalating market is not compensable.[41] Allowing almost two years to transpire from taking the preliminary steps in an airport expansion plan to the first offer of purchase is not a taking.[42]

Three years' delay from announcement of a project to commencement of condemnation may not be a taking.[43] Approximately the same time period—three and a half years—has also been found not to cause a taking even when the property included in an urban renewal area suffered lost rents in a declining area made worse by the exodus of tenants and landlord disinvestment encouraged by the city.[44] Clearly, delay alone is not always determinative.

At five years there may be a taking.[45] Try six years from the announcement of an urban renewal program to notification to the property owner that the property would not be taken. During the period

[37]*But see* West Jefferson Levee v. Coast Quality Constr. Corp., 640 So. 2d 1258, 1299 (La. 1994) (Army Corps of Engineers prohibits further development of levee pending satisfaction of requirements; property owner complies with requirements; in meantime, creation of national park authorized; owner's application to Corps denied; owner entitled to compensation for taking), *cert. denied*, 513 U.S. 1083 (1995).

[38]Department of Transp. v. Diversified Properties Co. III, 14 Cal. App. 4th 429, 17 Cal. Rptr. 2d 676 (1993), *review denied* (1993).

[39]*See*, e.g., Thompson v. Tualatin Hills Park & Recreation Dist., 496 F. Supp. 530, 543–44 (D. Or. 1980) (one-year delay is not enough to find a taking), *aff'd*, 701 F.2d 99 (9th Cir. 1983).

[40]*Id.*; P & L Properties, Inc. v. City of New Haven, 1996 Conn. Super LEXIS 1255 (Conn. Super. Ct. May 13, 1996).

[41]Lazy Mountain Aviation, Inc. v. City of Palmer, 618 P.2d 570 (Alaska 1980).

[42]City of Brookings v. Mills, 412 N.W.2d 497 (S.D. 1987).

[43]City of Muskegon v. DeVries, 59 Mich. App. 415, 229 N.W.2d 479 (1975).

[44]Gould v. Redevelopment Auth., 610 S.W.2d 360, 365 (Mo. App. 1980).

[45]Thomas W. Garland, Inc. v. City of St. Louis, 596 F.2d 784 (8th Cir. 1979) (physical invasion not needed for de facto taking; remand), *cert. denied*, 444 U.S. 899 (1979), *on remand*, 492 F. Supp. 402 (E.D. Mo. 1980) (city not liable for acts of developer in redevelopment plan).

the tenants vacated, the property became unmarketable, and its intended uses became severely limited because of the impending condemnation and consequential deterioration of the neighborhood. Not surprisingly, a federal court found a taking.[46] The U.S. Court of Appeals in that case found that government action had caused a substantial burden on the owner's property right—a threshold test in moving from acceptable delay to a taking. Sometimes merely the passage of time, if that period of time is long enough, is sufficient for the parties to litigate the alleged taking.[47]

Once you move into the high end of the range, the courts tend to find a taking or at least a cause of action for a taking, especially if the long delay is coupled with actions that make it difficult or impossible for the owner to make reasonable use of the property. Ten years of delay—coupled with publication of notices that the property would be taken, and that no compensation would be awarded for any improvements to it; dismantling of properties in the area; creation of noise, dust, and confusion that encourage decay and desertion; bringing in heavy equipment for use in demolishing nearby buildings; sending notices to tenants that they would be required to vacate; and publishing notice that the property owner would be paying the tenants moving expenses and other compensation when they vacated—can support a cause of action for inverse condemnation based on condemnation blight.[48]

However, where the delay is unintentional and no taking occurs before institution of an eminent domain proceeding, to assure the award of just compensation the court may move the date of valuation back in time. Valuation is then made where the precondemnation activities have substantially impaired marketability and the condemning authority has expressed an unequivocal intention to take the property.[49]

---

[46]Richmond Elks Hall Ass'n v. Richmond Redevelopment Agency, 561 F.2d 1327 (9th Cir. 1977). *See also* Broadway 41st Street Realty Corp. v. The N.Y. State Urban Dev. Corp., 733 F. Supp. 735 (S.D.N.Y. 1990) (delay of nearly ten years may be a taking).

[47]Levine v. City of New Haven, 30 Conn. Supp. 13, 15, 294 A.2d 644 (1972). ("This court is of the opinion that if long periods of time elapse after initial condemnation proceedings and there is no 'taking' for as long as, in this case, nine years, the property owner has a constitutional right to have his claim litigated").

[48]Lincoln Loan Co. v. State Highway Comm'n., 274 Or. 49, 545 P.2d 105 (1976).

[49]Lange v. Washington, 86 Wash. 2d 585, 588, 595, 547 P.2d 282 (1976).

Finally, where a property owner causes the delay through repeated court challenges of government attempts to acquire his property, the delay is not unreasonable and not a taking.[50]

Abandonment

Abandonment of eminent domain proceedings is not a taking if the government acted reasonably and in good faith.[51] But such a result is fact-driven. The opposite conclusion was reached after the City of Trenton initiated a redevelopment project in 1958. A declaration of blight was made in 1967. By 1973, the city had acquired and demolished about half the properties in the area, but not plaintiff's, which like many others had suffered rapid deterioration, increased vacancies, and lost rents. In 1973, the city abandoned the project. The New Jersey Supreme Court remanded to the trial court, holding that plaintiff's takings claim merited consideration.[52]

Value Change

Sometimes the issue is the change in value from the time of the announcement to the time of either filing the action to condemn or paying damages.[53] Evidence that there has been no decrease in value because of the government's conduct has precluded a supplemental award of damages for expenses incurred during a two-year delay.[54]

Mapping and Planning

As with the threat of condemnation, the mapping, planning, or platting of certain property for public use typically does not alone constitute a taking. But activity that works a substantial and unreasonable

[50]Simmons v. Wetherall, 472 F.2d 509 (2d Cir.), *cert. denied,* 412 U.S. 940 (1973).

[51]Agins v. City of Tiburon, 447 U.S. 255, 263.

[52]Washington Market Enters., Inc. v. City of Trenton, 68 N.J. 107, 343 A.2d 408 (1975) (if plaintiff succeeds in proving a taking, damages should be awarded).

[53]*Lange,* 86 Wash. 2d 585 (when pending action has significantly affected the valuation of property prior to trial, court may properly discount this effect by fixing value at some prior time when only the prevailing market value would obtain).

[54]San Francisco v. Golden Gate Heights Invs., 14 Cal. App. 4th 1203, 1213, 18 Cal. Rptr. 2d 467 (1993).

interference with property rights may, given the appropriate set of facts, constitute a de facto taking requiring compensation. Generally, however, planning by itself is never deemed a taking. Thus, a hazardous waste siting commission's designation of property as a potential site for a hazardous waste facility under a state sitings act was not a taking in the absence of extraordinary delay or other unreasonable conduct on the part of the commission, evidence of imminent condemnation, or of severe injury or hardship to the owners.[55]

However, there have been cases where planning activities were held to have caused a taking. The City of Beaver Falls, Pennsylvania, upon learning that a property owner intended to construct 72 dwelling units on certain property, passed an ordinance adopting a general plan for parks and playgrounds. The ordinance provided that the city council had three years from the passage of the ordinance to determine if it desired to actually appropriate the land. The court held that the plotting of the subject property for a park or playground coupled with the freezing of potential development for three years constituted a taking of property "by possibility, contingency, blockade and subterfuge."[56]

In another case the federal government approved and publicized a plan to build a public square on private property, making it impossible for the owner to sell the property. Furthermore, the government prohibited the owner from demolishing the building or putting the property to a new use, all the while assuring the owner that the property would be acquired. The government even discussed trading property with the owner. The court found a taking.[57] In a similar case, a taking was found when the owner was informed that coastal legislation would require taking his land, and he was prevented from subdividing and developing it (the government also told prospective purchasers of the impending condemnation and told the owner it would be fraudulent to sell his property).[58]

---

[55]Littman v. Gimello, 557 A.2d 314 (N.J. 1989), *cert. denied,* 493 U.S. 934 (1989).

[56]Miller v. City of Beaver Falls, 82 A.2d 34, 37 (Pa. 1951).

[57]Benenson v. United States, 212 Ct. Cl. 375, 548 F.2d 939 (1977).

[58]Drakes Bay Land Co. v. United States, 191 Ct. Cl. 389, 444, 424 F.2d 574 (1970).

Cutting the Gordian Knot

Professor Gideon Kanner noted almost a quarter century ago that the "soundest—legal analysis of the problem has been enunciated by the California Supreme Court in *Klopping v. City of Whittier.*"[59] That remains true today. When the City of Whittier decided to develop public parking facilities, it initiated condemnation proceedings to acquire the land. A third party challenged the bond financing and consequently the city was unable to market its bonds and pay for the property. The condemnation was dismissed, but at that time, the city announced plans to renew condemnation if the bond litigation succeeded.

Two years after the city first began to condemn the property, owners of properties to be acquired brought inverse-condemnation actions to recover for the losses attributed to condemnation blight from the announcement and delay of the condemnation. The actions were dismissed and the intermediate appellate court affirmed, applying a rule reflecting the *Danforth* rule:

> [T]he mere fact that a condemning authority announces its intention to condemn in the future, thereby depreciating the value of property between the date of the announcement and the actual filing of the action, is *damnum absque injuria* [a loss for which the law gives no remedy].[60]

But the California Supreme Court reversed, holding that injury from condemnation blight was compensable. In so doing, it truly refined the analysis of these difficult cases. Unlike the more recent cases that have logically linked condemnation blight and de facto takings into a single construct, the *Klopping* court followed the *Clement* position of segregating the two.

---

[59]Kanner, *supra* note 21, C730 A.L.I.-A.B.A. at 256 (citing *Klopping*, 8 Cal. 3d 39 (1972)).

[60]Klopping v. City of Whittier, 100 Cal. Rptr. 363, 365 (Cal. App.), *superseded*, 8 Cal. 3d 39, 500 P.2d 1345 (1972). The same line of reasoning and invocation of the weighty Latin phrase was followed on the opposite side of the country two years later in Fischer v. City of Syracuse, 78 Misc. 2d 124, 129–30, 355 N.Y.S.2d 239 (Sup. Ct. 1974) (compensation sought for condemnation blight because although property was in urban renewal area, condemnation was not initiated; dismissed for failure to state cause of action), *aff'd*, 46 A.D.2d 216, 361 N.Y.S.2d 773 (1974), *appeal denied*, 36 N.Y.2d 642, *cert. denied*, 423 U.S. 833 (1975).

The court still identified a middle ground: Damage could occur to property in condemnation that would not be capable of being accounted for by adjusting the market value of the blighted property within the context of the condemnation proceeding. The *Klopping* approach thus recognizes the importance of balance in protecting private property rights and in not unnecessarily fettering government, especially in its need for public input before taking private property.

The court in *Klopping* also recognized the problem of determining where the property owner should bring the action to recover damages. The court pointed out that a property owner generally should attempt recovery within the condemnation proceeding. If there is no condemnation proceeding or if it is not moving forward to a final conclusion, the owner can recover through an inverse-condemnation action.

Conclusions

This is one notable area of takings jurisprudence where the courts have done an especially good job in fashioning rules and solutions to a difficult problem. Delay in and of itself—which is often occasioned by the complexities of public acquisition and the need for public participation—does not effect a taking, but unreasonable delay can. Regardless of the length of delay, if it is accompanied by unreasonable activities that reduce the property's value, the courts will likely find a taking. The burden is on the property owner to challenge the reasonableness of the government's conduct. The property owner in more progressive jurisdictions can proceed to recover during a condemnation action and, if there is no pending condemnation action, to bring an inverse-condemnation claim for just compensation.

Chapter 19

Landlords and Tenants

One common theme appears in all landlord-tenant battles: disagreement about who should benefit or be burdened by newly created laws and regulations. The confusion and frustration between landlords and tenants, worsened by the takings issue, has thrust the courts into the role of peacemaker between war-weary opponents.

This chapter addresses how courts have disposed of takings claims not only in cases of rent control ordinances, but also in cases of vacancy or eviction-control restrictions, as well as building conversion restrictions. Finally, we review a few takings cases that transcend our general understanding of who is a landlord and who is a tenant.

The Landlord–Tenant Relationship

Landlord-tenant relationships are created in several ways. In most cases, the relationship is established and governed by an oral or written contract. However, there is a second group of cases where, absent an agreement between two parties, a court determines that a landlord-tenant relationship exists by considering the "intent" of the property owner prior to his allegations of a taking.[1] Lastly, statutes sometimes control the relationship, providing rights or obligations, such as when a holdover tenant occupies the premises after the lease has ended or the rental status of the unit has changed.[2]

Obviously, the landlord is the property owner directly affected by physical and regulatory takings. Hence, the landlord is often the party trying to invoke the Takings Clause based upon "the right to *exclude* strangers, or for that matter friends, but especially the Government."[3]

The famous case of Mrs. Loretto, the apartment building owner in New York City who triumphed in her physical taking claim because a television cable system junction box was placed on her roof, is a good example of a landlord exercising her right to exclude or to be compensated for a government-approved intrusion.[4] A full discussion of the case is in chapter 11.

However, landlord takings claims are not always as cut-and-dried as in *Loretto*. There are many cases where landlords were not compensated for an intrusion, or were unable to exercise their right of exclusion, because a court found that government action was intended to benefit tenants. Some examples of tenant-protection legislation include the Americans with Disabilities Act (ADA) and the Fair Housing Amendments Act.[5]

---

[1]Seawall Assocs. v. City of New York, 74 N.Y.2d 92, 542 N.E.2d 1059, *cert. denied*, 493 U.S. 976 (1989); Golden Gate Hotel Ass'n v. City & County of San Francisco, 864 F. Supp. 917 (N.D. Cal. 1993), *rev'd on other grounds*, 18 F.3d 1482 (9th Cir. 1994).

[2]Troy, Ltd. v. Renna, 727 F.2d 287 (3d Cir. 1984).

[3]Hendler v. United States, 952 F.2d 1364, 1374 (Fed. Cir. 1991) (substantial physical occupancy of private property is taking). However, the property owner in that case did not receive compensation. Hendler v. United States, 38 Fed. Cl. 611 (1997). *See also* Federal Home Loan Mortgage Corp. v. New York State Div. of Hous. & Community Renewal, 83 F.3d 45 (2d Cir. 1996) (FHMLC argued that applying rent-control law to previously exempt property constituted taking; no taking).

[4]Loretto v. Teleprompter Manhattan CATV Corp., 458 U.S. 419 (1982), *appeal denied*, 71 N.Y.2d 809, *cert. denied*, Loretto v. Group W Cable, 488 U.S. 827 (1988).

[5]The ADA is codified at 42 U.S.C.S. § 12101–12213;. the Fair Housing Amendments Act at 42 U.S.C.S. § 3601–31.

Rent Regulation Defined

Regulation of rents has been used to alleviate typical economic pressures during wartime.[6] However, rent regulations have continued and expanded during other times.[7]

Defining rent regulation can initially pose problems because of different, but related terms. "Rent regulation," "rent stabilization," and "rent control" often are used interchangeably—in error. Rent regulation is the generic term for rent control and rent stabilization. Properties subject to rent control are generally limited to the maximum rent stated by a rent control board, regardless of any previously signed lease.[8] In contrast, rent stabilization contemplates a current written lease and allows a percentage increase in rent based in part on market conditions. Rent stabilization has generally been described as a more market-efficient response to changing economic conditions than rent control regulations, which have been perceived as failing to achieve their stated purpose.[9]

---

[6]Block v. Hirsch, 256 U.S. 135 (1921) (World War I housing emergency allowed Washington, D.C. ordinance to withstand takings challenge); Bowles v. Willingham, 321 U.S. 503 (1944) (World War II emergency allowed rent regulations to be deemed not a taking).

[7]See, e.g., Yee v. City of Escondido, 503 U.S. 519 (1992) (rent-control ordinance is not per se taking; regulatory taking issue not decided); Rent Stabilization Ass'n v. Dinkins, 5 F.3d 591 (2d Cir. 1993); Cienega Gardens v. United States, 33 Fed. Cl. 196 (1995) (prepayment restrictions on mortgages), partial summ. j. granted, 37 Fed. Cl. 79 (1996) (trial needed for takings claim).

[8]Resolution Trust Corp. v. Diamond, 18 F.3d 111, 114 (2d Cir.) (RTC can repudiate tenancies rooted in lease or contract), vacated, remanded sub nom. Solomon v. Resolution Trust Corp., 513 U.S. 801 (U.S. 1994), on recons., reinstated, in part, modified, remanded, 45 F.3d 665 (2d Cir. 1995) (RTC repudiation rights upheld; change made regarding term of tenancies), cert. denied, 515 U.S. 1158 (U.S. 1995).

[9]"The purpose of rent control is to permit an efficient landlord to pay all actual and reasonable expenses and receive a fair profit while, at the same time, protecting the public interest in having affordable and properly maintained rental housing available to the citizens of the community." Cotati Alliance for Better Hous. v. City of Cotati, 148 Cal. App. 3d 280, 296, 195 Cal Rptr. 825 (1983). The Cotati rent-control laws are being challenged again, however. 152 Valparaiso Assocs. v. City of Cotati, 56 Cal. App. 4th 378, 65 Cal. Rptr. 2d 551 (1997) (dismissal of takings claim remanded to trial court), review denied, 1997 Cal. LEXIS 7533 (Oct. 29, 1997).

Since rent regulations are usually created to protect the public during times of hardship, courts have generally found that they are reasonably related to permissible governmental objectives.[10]

The Inherent Economic Aspects of Rent Regulation

Most rent regulation takings claims are of the regulatory type, and the multifactor analysis from *Penn Central* is routinely applied.[11] Application of the *Penn Central* test to rent regulation cases has involved complicated economic considerations. Rent regulation boards often consider interrelated economic factors, making it difficult to discuss the economic arguments within takings. Some factors include the cost of debt service, the mortgage interest rate, inflation trends, reasonable profits for landlords in the local area, the impact of tax laws, and the current value of property in the regulated area.[12]

Court Decisions on Regulatory Takings Claims

While standards applicable to formal condemnation have typically remained constant, we have noted that regulatory takings cases, including economically complex rent regulation cases, are fact-sensitive and subject to ad hoc analysis. While there are scores of rent regulation/takings cases, the following cases illustrate much about where the law has been, where it is, and where it may go.

[10]Specific findings of the need for rent regulation bolster such determinations. For example, the New York State Legislature does a study every three years of the rental-housing vacancy rate in New York City to justify rent regulation there. Alan S. Oser, *Reconfirming the Unending "Housing Emergency,"* N.Y. TIMES, Sept. 8, 1996, at 7. *See also* R.S. Radford, *Why Rent Control Is a Regulatory Taking,* 6 FORDHAM ENVTL. L.J. 755, 769 (1995); William K. Jones, *Confiscation: A Rationale of the Law of Takings,* 24 HOFSTRA L. REV. 1, 83 (1995) (rent control "obvious taking"); Pennell v. City of San Jose, 485 U.S. 1, 22 (J. Scalia, dissenting) (rent control "establish[es] a welfare program").

[11]Penn Central Transp. Co. v. New York City, 438 U.S. 104 (1978) (no taking; restrictions substantially relate to promoting general welfare and reasonable uses remain).

[12]*See, e.g.,* City of Berkeley v. City of Berkeley Rent Stabilization Bd., 27 Cal. App. 4th 951, 959–61, 33 Cal. Rptr. 2d 317 (1994) (board did not abuse discretion in adopting rent regulations), *review denied,* 1994 Cal. LEXIS 6417 (Dec. 1, 1994).

The first rent regulation takings case that the U.S. Supreme Court reviewed was *Block v. Hirsch*.[13] There, the Court upheld a District of Columbia rent law that restricted a landlord's ability to regain possession of his leased premises during the First World War. The Court found that because of a housing-shortage emergency in Washington, D.C., and the need for affordable housing for wartime workers there, the public interest required that the law be sustained. Although the *Block* decision is an old one, the precedent it established—that government can regulate housing conditions to maintain or improve living conditions—still carries great weight today. The precedent established by *Block,* which allows the government substantial leeway in regulating the housing market in times of demonstrated need, has frustrated many landlords' takings claims.

In some cities, regulated landlords have organized nonprofit associations to fight for relief from rent regulations. Probably the leading organization of this type is the Rent Stabilization Association of New York City (RSA), with a membership of more than 25,000 New York City landlords.[14] In one case, the RSA sued the city contending that its rent regulations worked a taking by not allowing for a "just and reasonable" return on the landlords' property. The RSA argued that many of its members could never qualify for the regulations' hardship exemption, which the city asserted was available to landlords in dire economic straits.

The U.S. Court of Appeals for the Second Circuit rejected the association's claim and found that the organization did not have standing, nor had it established a facial or as-applied taking. The court reasoned that the purported practical unavailability of the hardship provisions, standing alone, could not effect a taking because rent was still received and the provisions did not limit a landlord's rent in the first place.[15]

In what landlords see as adding insult to their injury, it is possible that a local rent regulation agency can make the situation worse for landlords by ordering a *reduction* of the regulated rent in a particular landlord's building when conditions are found to be substandard. In *Sterling v. Santa Monica Rent Control Board*, tenants successfully

---

[13]256 U.S. 135 (1921).

[14]Rent Stabilization Ass'n v. Dinkins, 5 F.3d 591, 592 (2d Cir. 1993).

[15]Although the complaint was dismissed, the court left open the option of individual members of RSA bringing claims in their individual capacity or as a class based upon economic hardship.

sought a rent reduction for allegedly inadequate housing.[16] Although an appeal resulted in a remand for further administrative proceedings, these did not occur because the landlord obtained a court order against any rent reduction. The rent control board appealed, and a court held that "substantial deterioration (*i.e.*, breach of the implied warranty of habitability) or violations of housing, health and safety codes may . . . be considered as a basis for rent decreases."[17]

A common theme running through many takings claims against purely regulatory action by the government is the great deference courts give to programs of agencies charged with administering the rent laws and regulations. As a result, landlords have had little success in such takings claims.[18]

The U.S. Congress has created a type of rent regulation in statutory protections for low- and moderate-income families. The federal Department of Housing and Urban Development (HUD) has implemented programs in conjunction with congressional policy to maintain and/or further initiate the development of low- and moderate-income rental housing. In *Cienega Gardens v. United States*, landlords brought a taking claim against the United States based on breach of contract.[19] The property owners and HUD had worked out a plan that stipulated the allowable rents and mortgages for a designated period of years in return for financial incentives in developing the property.[20] However, in the 1980s, Congress became concerned that developers would use prepayment clauses within these contracts to release them from their contract with HUD and to allow them to lease or sell their housing at a market rate. The unilateral change made by Congress did not sit well with the developers who asserted, among other claims, that Congress took their property.

The U.S. Court of Federal Claims considered the possibility of a regulatory taking by applying the *Penn Central* test. As to the "character of the governmental action," the court found that the action—

[16]168 Cal. App. 3d 176, 214 Cal. Rptr. 71 (1985).

[17]*Id.* at 186.

[18]*See* Kavanau v. Santa Monica Rent Control Bd., 16 Cal. 4th 761, 782–83, 941 P.2d 851 (1997) (landlord won due process argument, but lost on taking), *cert. denied*, 118 S. Ct. 856 (U.S. 1998). *But see* Michael M. Berger, *Lack of Increasing Sensitivity: Court Hands Down 'Remedy' that Pushes Landlord Back to Rent Board*, SAN FRANCISCO DAILY JOURNAL, Sept. 3, 1997, at 4 ("The [California] Supreme Court's decision adds a new wrinkle: You can't win anyway.").

[19]33 Fed. Cl. 196 (1995), *partial summ. j. granted*, 37 Fed. Cl. 79 (1996).

[20]33 Fed. Cl. at 203.

prepayment restrictions—was regulatory like the historic preservation ordinance in *Penn Central*. As to the "economic impact" of that action, although the developers could not put the property to its most profitable use, they could still receive rents plus financial incentives, the court found. Finally, in discussing the extent of government interference with the developers' "investment-backed expectations," the United States argued that the developers' expectations were unreasonable because they should have "expected that the government might change its mind about allowing plaintiffs to exercise the rights set forth in their deed of trust notes."[21] However, the court agreed with the developers that the "reasonableness" of expectations was not the issue; the issue was whether the developers' expectations were "investment-backed."[22] The court ordered a new trial to determine the "investment-backed expectation" as well as how developers were affected by the Congress's change in the prepayment policy.

California has had a tremendous amount of rent regulation litigation, probably because it first established or extensively used many of the country's programs related to the housing market. California's experimentation with different economic structures of housing programs has agitated both landlords and tenants.[23]

Rent Regulation and Mobile-Home Parks

An interesting twist in the mobile-home rent-control cases is the physical invasion taking argument. Rent control in the mobile-homes context occurs when the government regulates the rental price for the "pad"—the land that the mobile home occupies. Mobile-home park

---

[21]*Id.* at 222.

[22]The "investment-backed" component of the developers' expectations was more important than "reasonableness" because their prepayment expectations were based on language within the deed of trust notes, authorized by HUD, and in force for most of the 20 years of their mortgages.

[23]The Berkeley, California, rent control program was upheld in City of Berkeley v. City of Berkeley Rent Stabilization Bd., 27 Cal. App. 4th 951, 33 Cal. Rptr. 2d 317 (1994). In *Berkeley*, the city rent stabilization board attempted to regulate the city's rents and avoid an unconstitutional confiscatory effect on landlords, giving them a fair investment return. *But see* Richardson v. City & County of Honolulu, 759 F. Supp 1477, 1492–96 (D. Haw. 1991) (enactment of ordinance controlling rents only on residential condominiums a regulatory taking because rent ceiling "arbitrary," and ordinance "does not provide any mechanism to ensure that its formula will yield a fair rate of return").

owners, like their apartment owner counterparts, are often frustrated and economically damaged by such rent regulations. The mobile-home park owners' challenges are based not only on their objection to the regulated pad rental price, but also on the belief that any long-term benefits from the rent regulations go overwhelmingly to the tenants.

The Physical Invasion Argument

There are two cases that for a time legitimized the argument that mobile-home rent-control regulations effect a physical invasion of property. In *Pinewood Estates of Michigan v. Barnegat Township*,[24] a federal appeals court held that the park owners lost the possessory interest in their land partly because of a state law that allowed rent control boards to regulate the rents of pads in mobile-home parks. Similarly, in *Hall v. City of Santa Barbara*,[25] the Ninth Circuit found that certain local ordinances in California caused physical invasions of mobile-home park owners' property.

Mobile-home park owners successfully argued the physical invasion theory before several courts by demonstrating that most of the relevant rent control ordinances essentially constituted a grant to tenants of a right to occupy the pads in perpetuity. Park owners can use the special landlord-tenant relationship in the takings argument:

> [In the relationship between mobile-home park owners and mobile-home owners,] [p]ark owners may no longer set rents or decide who their tenants will be. As a result, . . . any reduction in the rent for a mobile home pad causes a corresponding increase in the value of a mobile home, because the mobile home owner now owns, in addition to a mobile home, the right to occupy a pad at a rent below the value that would be set by the free market. [Citations omitted.][26]

The physical occupancy in perpetuity, and the supposed loss of pre-

---

[24]898 F.2d 347 (3d Cir. 1990). *See also* Aspen-Tarpon Springs Ltd. Partnership v. Stuart, 635 So. 2d 61, 68 (Fla. Dist. Ct. App. 1994) (statute constitutes physical taking because it "authorizes a permanent physical occupation of the park owner's property and effectively extinguishes a fundamental attribute of ownership").

[25]833 F.2d 1270 (9th Cir. 1986) (remand as to whether ordinance constitutes taking), *cert. denied*, 485 U.S. 940 (1988).

[26]Yee v. City of Escondido, 503 U.S. 519, 526 (1992).

miums, led frustrated mobile-home park owners to argue, and early court decisions to find, that the effect of the regulations worked a physical invasion of the park owners' property.

The basis for the mobile-home park owners' temporary success was their ability to persuade the courts that the effect of the rent ordinances was analogous to the permanent physical occupancy in *Loretto*. (*See* chapter 11 for further discussion of *Loretto*.)

The Landmark Case of *Yee v. City of Escondido:* A Shift in Regulatory Takings Law

The U.S. Supreme Court's 1992 decision in *Yee v. City of Escondido*,[27] wiped out the physical takings argument in mobile-home rent regulation cases. In *Yee*, the city adopted an ordinance that rolled back mobile-home park rents to their 1986 levels and prohibited increases without prior approval. Park owners complained that the rent control ordinance, coupled with its vacancy decontrol provisions, granted tenants a right to permanently occupy and use the land. The Supreme Court rejected the park owners' attempts to invoke *Hall* and *Pinewood*, holding that the rent control ordinance in *Yee* did not compel the mobile-home park owners to continue renting the property: "[P]ut bluntly, no government has required any physical invasion of [the plaintiffs'] property."[28] Moreover, the court added that the inability to exclude others from one's property is not a physical taking when the property owner "voluntarily open[s] its property to occupation by others[.]"[29] However, the Court recognized that "a different case would be presented where the statute compelled a landowner to rent his property or to refrain in perpetuity from terminating a tenancy."[30]

[27]503 U.S. 519 (1992).

[28]*Id.* at 528.

[29]*Id.* at 531.

[30]*Id.* at 528. Also, in the typical mobile-home case it is unlikely that physical invasion claims will be made so long as the mobile-home park owner can cease doing business, or the burdens placed on the owner are not too onerous. However, for a more in-depth explanation of the possibility of compelling government regulations effecting a physical taking, *see* the section on *Housing Preservation Regulations* later in this chapter (specifically the *Seawall* case).

Sunset Terrace Mobile Home Park in the city of Escondido, California, owned by John and Irene Yee. This was one of several such parks in the city at issue in *Yee v. City of Escondido.*

Although *Yee* resolved the "physical occupation" question for subsequent mobile-home park cases,[31] it did not address all issues of the takings analysis. The Court explicitly left open the possibility of rent regulations being challenged through a *regulatory* takings claim.

The *Penn Central* test is the key to analyzing such claims. In any case, though, it is not likely that the claims of mobile-home park owners will succeed more often than the claims of apartment building owners. But as discussed later in this chapter, there may be other options for making a successful taking claim.

Vacancy decontrol provisions coupled with eviction restrictions have also frustrated mobile-home park owners.[32] However, like the

---

[31]Levald, Inc. v. City of Palm Desert, 998 F.2d 680 (9th Cir. 1993) (*Yee* extinguished any chance that mobile-home park law could be attacked on physical invasion theory), *cert. denied*, 510 U.S. 1093 (1994); Carson Harbor Village v. City of Carson, 37 F.3d 468 (9th Cir. 1994).

[32]Vacancy decontrol provisions prevent park owners from charging market rents to tenants who may be the new occupants of their pads when the previous tenant has left his or her mobile home.

landlords of apartment buildings, mobile-home park owners have had little success in proving a taking.[33]

Regulations Restricting Evictions

A commonality—eviction restrictions—links apartment rent regulation and mobile-home park rent regulation. In both instances, legislators and regulators have enacted restrictions to protect residential tenants during perceived housing shortages. Such restrictions should be interpreted in a way that achieves that goal, otherwise the public may actually be harmed.[34] Too narrow a restriction may exacerbate the problems that rent regulations are designed to alleviate.

The recent New York case, *Manocherian v. Lenox Hill Hospital*,[35] dealt with a law that New York's highest court found did not further its stated goal of resolving a housing shortage. Apartment building owners leased apartments that a nonprofit hospital subleased to its employees. The building owners challenged a statute that gave an exceptional benefit to the hospital. The landlord asserted that the state law allowed an entity with a perpetual corporate existence to lease his apartments forever. The owner argued that this created a regulatory taking by permanently depriving him of a reversionary interest in his property. The high court agreed with the landlord and found an unconstitutional taking because the law failed to achieve its stated purpose of alleviating a severe housing shortage. Further, the law's effect, benefiting corporate tenants, did not substantially advance a legitimate state interest. Therefore, the court's real problem with the New York law was that a corporate entity was named as a primary tenant who could sublease the premises at will. Furthermore, the potential never-ending existence of the corporate hospital, as a tenant, was quite different from the human character contemplated during creation of most anti-eviction/rent regulations. The court also used a dissent in the lower court to explain its position:

---

[33]*See* Troy Hill, Ltd. v. Renna, 727 F.2d 287 (3d Cir. 1984) (taking claim by owners of apartment complex fails); *Levald*, 998 F.2d 680 (no physical taking; regulatory taking claim not ripe).

[34]*See* Manocherian v. Lenox Hill Hosp., 84 NY 2d 385, 394, 643 N.E.2d 479 (1994) (state statute intended to help residential tenants actually benefited nonprofit hospital), *cert. denied*, 514 U.S. 1109 (1995).

[35]*Id.*

A statutory interpretation which encourages the deployment of rent stabilized apartments in perpetuity as temporary dormitory space for an ever changing roster of hospital employees and promotes the displacement of these employees, some of whom may be long term tenants, when they leave their employment does a disservice to rent stabilization's underlying purpose of protecting residential tenants from evictions during an acute housing shortage.[36]

Accordingly, the regulation creating the perpetual tenancy was held to be invalid. In addition, the court found the regulation to be an unconstitutional taking, "though we need not decide this issue on a stand-alone basis because we do not consider it dispositive by itself in this case."[37]

The human element of a tenant in most other rent regulation cases has influenced courts to defer to the eviction control regulations created by state and local authorities. In *Troy Hill, Ltd. v. Renna*,[38] long-term statutory tenancies were held not to work a taking. The Tenancy Act of New Jersey was created to protect certain citizens, including disabled persons, against evictions from a residential building.[39] The court found no taking because, notwithstanding the statute, the landlord was receiving compensation through rent. And because people die, there was no permanent physical occupation of the property. The statutory tenancy law merely regulated the use of private property.

Despite the adverse precedent, a landlord challenging eviction restrictions can find success on rare occasions. However, successful landlords in such cases have also been government corporations. In *Resolution Trust Corporation v. Diamond*,[40] a court dealt with state and local rent regulations creating statutory tenancies—or noneviction conversion plans—that protect rental tenants when their units are converted to condominium or cooperative ownership. The ten-

[36]*Id.* at 394–95.

[37]*Id.* at 398.

[38]727 F.2d 287 (3d Cir. 1984). *See also* Dawson v. Higgins, 197 A.D.2d 127, 135–37, 610 N.Y.S.2d 200 (1994), *appeal dismissed*, 640 N.E.2d 143 (N.Y. 1994), *cert. denied*, 513 U.S. 1077 (1995).

[39]The Tenancy Act dovetailed with a preexisting Anti-Eviction Act, by creating a "protected tenancy status" for qualified individuals to obtain the right to remain as tenants in their units for 40 years beyond what was required by the Anti-Eviction Act. *Troy Hill*, 727 F.2d at 289–92.

[40]45 F.3d 665 (2d Cir. 1995), *cert. denied*, 515 U.S. 1158 (1995).

ants in this case alleged that as long as they continued to pay rent, they could continue to occupy their apartments pursuant to the statute.

However, the Resolution Trust Corporation (RTC), which acts as receiver, or conservator, for distressed federally insured thrift institutions, tried to repudiate the tenancies of nine condominiums that it controlled, pursuant to its statutory authority to repudiate burdensome contracts. The tenants and the State of New York raised a taking claim that unsuccessfully opposed RTC's actions. The argument that had been persuasive in so many other cases, i.e., the state's legitimate interest in protecting tenants, was virtually preempted by the federal authority given to RTC, and the court held that RTC could repudiate the tenancies.

Relocation Assistance Regulations

Relocation assistance programs, funded by property owners, create other problems for the owners and have been the source of disputes in several locales, particularly the State of Washington. The City of Seattle adopted a regulation requiring all landlords to provide reasonable relocation assistance to low-income tenants upon the demolition, substantial rehabilitation, or other change in a housing development.[41] The stated purpose was to encourage economic opportunity, maintain affordable housing, and preserve housing.[42] Landlords argued that a regulatory taking had occurred and sought review under a higher standard than the typical reasonable relationship standard for regulatory

[41]Garneau v. City of Seattle, 897 F. Supp. 1318 (W.D. Wash. 1995); Guimont v. Clarke, 121 Wash. 2d 586, 854 P.2d 1 (1993) (no taking in Mobile Home Relocation Assistance Act), cert. denied, 510 U.S. 1176 (1994). But see Aspen-Tarpon Springs Ltd. Partnership v. Stuart, 635 So. 2d 61, 68 (Fla. Dist. Ct. App. 1994) (statute regulatory taking for "singl[ing] out mobile home park owners to bear an unfair burden").

[42]Garneau, 897 F. Supp. at 1321. See also Conn. Gen. Stat. § 21-70a (relocation expenses for displaced mobile-home tenants); Arcadia Dev. v. City of Bloomington, 552 N.W.2d 281 (Minn. Ct. App. 1996) (mobile-home park owners must pay relocation expenses when park closes per ordinance; no taking), review denied, 1996 Minn. LEXIS 795 (Oct. 29, 1996); Greenfield Country Estates Tenants Ass'n v. Deep, 666 N.E.2d 988, 992 (Mass. 1996). But see Gideon Kanner, Noted in Brief, JUST COMPENSATION, Dec. 1996, at 11 (court fails to realize mobile homes are cheaper than fixed homes because of risk park may close).

takings. The court used the lesser standard and indicated that even under a higher standard, the government would have met its burden.

Regulations Preventing Apartment Building Conversions

Landlords who have lost profits and have been frustrated by rent regulations sometimes have sought relief by converting their apartment buildings to condominiums or cooperative ownerships. From the 1960s well into the 1980s, a condominium and cooperative craze swept the country, through new construction and conversion of existing rental buildings to condominiums, cooperatives, or some other form of common-interest ownership.

The landlords' perceived window of opportunity for improved profits through conversion was gradually stifled by local and state governments. In fear that the rental stock would be severely depleted by continued conversions, governments tightened the regulation of conversions. Rather than enacting an absolute prohibition on rental apartment conversion, laws often require that the building owner apply for a special permit.

The application process for receiving special conversion permits often has been enough of an impediment to cause landlords to raise takings claims. In *Griffin Development Company v. City of Oxnard*, a special-use permit was needed to convert Griffin's apartment building.[43] However, the city had very strict standards for obtaining the permit; the landlord did not meet them. The Supreme Court of California denied Griffin's taking claim because Griffin could still make reasonable use of his property because he was still able to rent his apartments.[44] In general, "takings clause challenges in the [condominium conversion] context have not fared well."[45]

---

[43] 39 Cal. 3d 256, 703 P.2d 339 (1985).

[44] *See also* Gilbert v. City of Cambridge, 932 F.2d 51 (1st Cir.) (ordinance to slow trend of condominium conversions by requiring that parties seek a permit to convert upheld), *cert denied*, 502 U.S. 866 (1991); Silverman v. Barry, 727 F.2d 1121 (D.C. Cir. 1984), *cert. denied*, 488 U.S. 956 (1988).

[45] *Silverman*, 727 F.2d 1121. *See generally* Note, *The Validity of Ordinances Limiting Condominium Conversion*, 78 MICHIGAN L. REV. 124, 132–35 (1979).

Housing Preservation Regulations

Some cities have cloaked restrictions on residential building changes behind housing preservation laws. When the housing market shifts, property owners often seek to convert old hotels or single room–occupancy arrangements into more profitable investments. However, under certain housing preservation laws landlords have been restrained to the point where they lose control of their buildings.[46] The leading case in this area is without question *Seawall Associates v. City of New York* because it clearly shows the outer limits of regulation.[47]

In *Seawall*, owners of single room–occupancy (SRO) buildings brought a taking challenge against a New York City ordinance that compelled owners to be residential landlords and required them to rehabilitate and offer their properties for rent. New York's highest court held that the ordinance was a per se physical taking and a facially invalid regulatory taking, reasoning that the SRO owners were forced to accept tenants with whom there was no existing landlord-tenant relationship. This lack of a previous relationship was paramount to the court's decision, and distinguishes *Seawall* from cases in which the landlord unsuccessfully tried to raise a physical or regulatory taking claim.[48]

An example of an unsuccessful attempt to use a takings claim against a preservation ordinance was seen in *Nash v. City of Santa Monica*.[49] The subject ordinance prevented removal or destruction of rental units unless the apartment owner acquired a permit. Nash wanted to demolish his building in hopes that the land would appreciate in value and insisted that he had a property right unjustifiably withheld by the city ordinance.[50] The Supreme Court of California found no taking on the basis of *Penn Central*, noting that the regulation "[does not] interfere with the [property] owner's primary investment-backed expectations and [does] not render the owner

---

[46]*See, e.g.,* Seawall Assocs. v. City of New York, 74 N.Y.2d 92, 542 N.E.2d 1059 (local law facially invalid), *cert. denied,* 493 U.S. 976 (1989).

[47]*Id.*

[48]*See, e.g.,* Yee v. City of Escondido, 503 U.S. 519 (1992).

[49]37 Cal. 3d 97 , 688 P.2d 894 (1984), *appeal dismissed,* 470 U.S. 1046 (1985).

[50]Nash's property was occupied by persons of very low, low, or moderate income. However, Nash's desire to demolish the building was because of his growing disenchantment with owning the property. 37 Cal. 3d at 101–02.

unable to receive a reasonable rate of return on his investment."[51] In response to *Nash*, the California Legislature passed the Ellis Act, California Government Code section 7060, "[permitting] landlords to go out of business."[52]

The Chosen Few: Miscellaneous Takings Cases that Broaden the Takings Analysis

Other types of regulatory takings claims have been made by landlords or tenants when the government speaks on issues affecting their relationships with third parties.

In one case, an ordinance to deter the use or sale of illegal drugs brought about a takings claim! The ordinance allowed an administrative board to declare any site a public nuisance when used for the sale or delivery of illegal drugs. The apartment building owner, in *City of St. Petersburg v. Bowen*,[53] argued that the city took his property when the board declared his building a public nuisance and ordered it closed for one year without compensation. Florida's District Court of Appeal held that a taking occurred because the ordinance deprived the apartment owner of all economic use of his property.

Tenants may also bring a takings claim. In *Naegele Outdoor Advertising, Inc. v. City of Durham*,[54] a tenant was aggrieved by an ordinance prohibiting commercial advertising on several properties he had leased. He claimed compensation, for among other things, the loss in market value of billboards. The court held that there was no taking of property because there was no physical invasion, and the tenant was not deprived of all economically viable use of the property. The state's desire to improve the appearance of the city, through regulation, by restricting advertising was deemed to be reasonable.

---

[51]*Id.* at 102.

[52]Javidzad v. City of Santa Monica, 204 Cal. App. 3d 524, 527, 251 Cal. Rptr. 350 (1988) (state statute preempts rent control section of city charter).

[53]675 So. 2d 626 (Fla. Dist. Ct. App. 1996), *review denied*, 680 So. 2d 421 (Fla. 1996), *cert. denied*, 117 S. Ct. 1120 (1997). *But see* Zeman v. City of Minneapolis, 552 N.W.2d 548 (Minn. 1996) (rental dwelling license revoked due to drug deals, violence; no regulatory taking; ordinance based on legitimate public interest).

[54]803 F. Supp. 1068 (M.D.N.C. 1992), *aff'd without op.*, 19 F.3d 11 (4th Cir.), *cert. denied*, 513 U.S. 928 (1994).

(For more on this subject, see chapter 26.) The *Naegele* court added that the state cannot be the guarantor of investment risks that people choose to make.

The state's police power appeared to be limited in *Bowen*, but the *Naegele* court seemed more willing to tolerate government action that burdened an individual for the good of the public. Perhaps the difference in approach is due to the difference between a Florida appeals court (*Bowen*) and a federal trial court in North Carolina (*Naegele*). Whatever the reason for their different approaches, the cases are unique. However, they share the benefit of illustrating that regulatory takings claims can be brought by either of the parties in a landlord-tenant relationship.

Conclusion

Takings law in the landlord-tenant area is turbulent. The standards that courts have developed for regulatory takings analysis generally lead to a decision that the regulation at issue is constitutional because of the government's interest in protecting the public's welfare, health, and safety. However, because of the ambiguities inherent in the economic considerations of regulatory takings cases, such cases will be a continuing source of controversy.

Chapter 20

Historic Preservation

When done by government, historic preservation in the United States happens in two key ways: designation of individual landmarks and historic districting. Indeed, the vast majority of preservation ordinances provide for both. It appears that no takings court has attached significance to which technique was used in a given case, at least since a 1978 dissent by Justice Rehnquist.[1] Nonetheless, the two approaches offer a convenient way to organize the discussion.

Landmark Designation

In 1963, New York City's historic Penn Station was demolished to make way for the new Madison Square Garden. The resulting outcry provoked a sharp turn in the course of historic preservation law—a new focus on the preservation of individual landmarks.[2] Within two years, New York City passed a landmarks law. By 1989, about 1,500

---

[1]Penn Central Transp. Co. v. New York City, 438 U.S. 104, 138 (1978) (Rehnquist, J., dissenting). *See, e.g.,* St. Bartholomew's Church v. City of New York, 914 F.2d 348, 355 (2d Cir. 1990) ("differences are of no consequence"), *cert. denied,* 499 U.S. 905 (1991).

[2]Paul Goldberger, *A Commission That Has Itself Become a Landmark,* N.Y. Times, April 15, 1990, at H36.

local governments had followed the city's lead by enacting some type of historic preservation ordinance.[3]

Yet in some cases, preserving individual, privately owned landmarks has been controversial. Not unexpectedly, owners whose property is designated over their objections often decry the resulting use restrictions and maintenance duties.[4] Then, too, an old building is not always adaptable to profitable use; the owner may prefer to replace it with a new one. And unlike owners in historic districts, where everyone labors under the same restrictions, landmark owners may feel they are being singled out—asked to bear a cost their neighbors are not.[5] Finally, deciding whether a building or site is worth preserving can in some measure be a subjective call; by definition, it involves aesthetics. Ingredients such as these send some historic landmark owners to takings lawyers.

Landmark preservation largely has withstood takings challenges. The guiding light in the field is the Supreme Court's decision in *Penn Central Transportation Co. v. New York City*,[6] rejecting a taking attack on a municipal landmark ordinance and widely viewed as a broad judicial endorsement of historic preservation. We will return to this decision later. Heavily influenced by *Penn Central*, state courts have been similarly inclined to spurn such takings claims.[7] Such

[3]AMERICAN PLANNING ASS'N, RESPONDING TO THE TAKINGS CHALLENGE 23 (Planning Advisory Serv. Report No. 415) (Richard J. Roddewig & Christopher J. Duerksen eds., 1989). The text figure includes both landmark and districting ordinances. *See also* NATIONAL ALLIANCE OF PRESERVATION COMM'NS, THE UNITED STATES PRESERVATION COMMISSION IDENTIFICATION PROJECT (Aug. 1994) (finding 1863 historic preservation commissions in United States, an increase of 117 percent since 1981) (hereinafter NATIONAL ALLIANCE).

[4]Designation with the *consent* of the landmark owner, followed by government action in conformance with the terms of that consent, does not raise takings issues. A recent survey indicates that about 40 percent of local historic preservation commissions require such consent. NATIONAL ALLIANCE, *supra* note 3, App. B.

[5]Something similar may happen when the boundaries of historic districts are drawn; owners of individual parcels may dispute being included in (or excluded from) the district.

[6]438 U.S. 104 (1978).

[7]*See, e.g.*, 900 G Street Assoc. v. Department of Hous. & Community Dev., 430 A.2d 1387 (D.C. App. 1981); Shubert Org., Inc. v. Landmarks Preservation Comm'n, 166 A.D.2d 115, 570 N.Y.S.2d 504 (1991), *cert. denied*, 504 U.S. 946 (1992); United Artists Theater Circuit, Inc. v. City of Philadelphia, 535 Pa. 370, 635 A.2d 612 (1993).

courts, while giving lip service to the three-factor *Penn Central* test, often require complete elimination of economic use for a taking[8]— which *Penn Central* does not.

In contrast with the states, the federal government has only a limited presence in the preservation of privately owned historic sites. Federally recognized sites are not subject to any direct regulation, though such recognition may trigger constraints on the use of nearby lands under other federal and state programs.[9] Courts have noted the possibility of takings based on such constraints, but no taking has yet been found.[10]

History of Landmarks Preservation

From the 19th century until the 1960s, private individuals and historical societies preserved landmark properties by purchasing them, while government did little. In a few instances, governments preserved particular landmarks by acquiring them through eminent domain.[11] Scant legislation addressed the subject, although a few cities, such as Charleston and New Orleans, enacted ordinances protecting historic districts as early as the 1930s.

Early attempts by state and local governments to preserve landmarks through unauthorized withholding of demolition permits or through special legislative action affecting only single properties were

---

[8]*See* discussion of *Penn Central* later in this chapter.

[9]*See* especially National Historic Preservation Act § 106, 16 U.S.C. § 470f (requiring federal agencies to "take into account" effect of their "undertakings" or "licenses" on any place included in or eligible for inclusion in National Register).

[10]*See, e.g.,* Ainsley v. United States, 8 Cl. Ct. 394 (1985) (federal ban on surface mining near national historic site may be a taking); Department of Natural Resources v. Indiana Coal Council, Inc., 542 N.E.2d 1000 (Ind. 1989) (state designation of archeological site, eligible for National Register, as unsuitable for mining is not taking). *See also* Historic Green Springs, Inc. v. Bergland, 497 F. Supp. 839 (E.D. Va. 1980) (federal landmark designation may "impede or discourage" commercial development in area near landmark site), *vacated on other grounds,* 12 ENVTL. L. 20, 100 (E.D. Va. 1981).

[11]*See, e.g.,* United States v. Gettysburg Elec. Ry. Co., 160 U.S. 660 (1896) (federal government's use of eminent domain to preserve Gettysburg battlefield upheld); Roe v. Kansas *ex rel.* Smith, 278 U.S. 191 (1929) (state's use of eminent domain to preserve historic Shawnee Mission upheld).

struck down—though not on takings grounds.[12] Courts viewed such ad hoc preservation efforts with suspicion.

Witness a comparatively recent such case, *Benenson v. United States*.[13] There, a decade-long parade of inconsistent government pronouncements, unsuccessful negotiations, and construction moratoria was held to inflict a taking. Initially, federal plans called for the acquisition of land along Pennsylvania Avenue, including the historic Willard Hotel, to create a "national square." But federal funds never came. Between 1965 and 1975, both the federal and District of Columbia governments conducted fruitless negotiations with the hotel owner to trade property, denied demolition permits, and enacted two year-long construction moratoria. In 1974, the federal plan changed and the hotel was designated to be preserved. The court held that the protracted government actions barring demolition, taken while the government recognized it was uneconomic to operate the hotel,[14] were confiscatory.

In the mid-1960s, local governments began to enact *comprehensive* legislation to preserve landmarks. These ordinances typically provide that buildings designated landmarks may not be demolished or significantly altered without government approval, often supplied by a historical commission. In contrast with the foregoing ad hoc approach, which lacks a unifying legal framework, comprehensive landmark ordinances have fared well in the courts. From their inception, they have generally been upheld.[15] Landmark ordinances were

---

[12]People *ex rel.* Marbro Corp. v. Ramsey, 28 Ill. App. 252, 171 N.E.2d 246 (1960) (city's attempt to preserve 17-story theater and office building by withholding a vested demolition permit found unconscionable when unwilling owner required to bear expense); Keystone Assocs. v. Moerdler, 19 N.Y.2d 78, 224 N.E.2d 700 (1966) (state legislative declaration establishing private corporation to condemn Old Metropolitan Opera Building and 180-day moratorium on demolition, as well as capping compensation for demolition delay, declared invalid; if upheld would be taking).

[13]548 F.2d 939 (Ct. Cl. 1977).

[14]Ironically, the hotel was ultimately restored and has been operating, apparently successfully, for more than a decade.

[15]*See, e.g.,* Manhattan Club v. City of New York, 51 Misc. 2d 556, 273 N.Y.S.2d 848 (1966) (first test of city landmark ordinance finding no taking). *See also* Maher v. City of New Orleans, 516 F.2d 1057 (5th Cir. 1975) (upholding New Orleans' historic district ordinance against facial taking claim), *cert. denied,* 420 U.S. 905 (1976). Although *Maher* concerns historic district legislation, it is influential.

Willard Hotel in Washington, D.C., just blocks from the White House. Government efforts to block demolition of this historic structure triggered the case of *Benenson v. United States.*

further buttressed against takings challenges by the Supreme Court's 1978 decision in *Penn Central*, explored below. Indeed, most experts view this decision as the real catalyst for the widespread adoption of historic preservation ordinances.[16]

New York City's landmark preservation law, enacted in 1965, has served as a national prototype.[17] At the outset, it creates a landmarks preservation commission empowered to designate landmark structures. To qualify as a landmark, a structure must be at least thirty years old.[18] Once designated, a property is subject to regulatory controls—in particular, the commission must approve any significant

[16]*See, e.g.,* RICHARD J. RODDEWIG, PREPARING A HISTORIC PRESERVATION ORDINANCE, PAS Rept. No. 374 (American Planning Ass'n 1993).

[17]N.Y. City Admin. Code § 25-301 et seq.

[18]This particular feature has not been widely replicated. Except for a few local ordinances in the West, most jurisdictions either do not impose an age requirement or follow the criteria for listing in the National Register, which uses a threshold of 50 years, unless the property has "exceptional importance." 36 C.F.R. § 60.4.

alteration or demolition by issuing a "certificate of appropriateness." To limit the impact on the landmark owner, the ordinance has a "hardship provision" whereby an owner of designated property who is incapable of earning a reasonable return under the designation may more easily obtain a certificate of appropriateness.[19]

Although landmark ordinances are the most prominent contemporary method, landmarks can be preserved by other means. The large majority of states also use a "conservation easement" approach, under which public and some private entities are empowered to hold nonpossessory interests protecting landmarks.[20] In other cases, state environmental laws protecting historical resources may preserve individual landmark properties.[21]

Penn Central Transportation Co. v. New York City

This Supreme Court decision,[22] famous chiefly for its important three-factor test for regulatory takings, involved an equally monumental landmark. Grand Central Terminal, the imposing Beaux Arts railway station built in 1913, was designated a landmark under New York City's landmark ordinance in 1967. Later, the terminal's owners sought approval to construct a 55-story office tower atop the terminal. The city's landmarks commission denied approval of this and a later 53-story proposal. The owners cried taking.

---

[19]About one-third of historic preservation commissions have explicit authority in their ordinances to make economic hardship determinations. Personal communication, Legal Department, National Trust for Historic Preservation (Mar. 6, 1996).

[20]A conservation easement is created through an agreement between the property owner and the easement holder that entitles the latter to enforce limitations or affirmative obligations on the property owner—in this case, to preserve historic aspects of the property. See generally NATIONAL TRUST FOR HISTORIC PRESERVATION, ESTABLISHING AN EASEMENT PROGRAM TO PROTECT HISTORIC, SCENIC, AND NATURAL RESOURCES (1995). The large majority of the states expressly authorize use of the conservation easement for historic preservation.

[21]See, e.g., Minnesota v. County of Hennepin, 495 N.W.2d 416 (Minn. 1993) (county violated Minnesota Environmental Rights Act in approving demolition of national guard armory); London v. Art Comm'n, 190 A.D.2d 557, 593 N.Y.S.2d 233 (1993) (city's decision on whether to remove Central Park bandshell requires prior inquiry into applicability of State Environmental Quality Review Act).

[22]438 U.S. 104 (1978).

In addressing the taking claim, the Supreme Court opened by endorsing the preservation of structures and areas with special historic, architectural, or cultural significance as a legitimate government goal—an unsurprising statement, but hailed nonetheless as a symbolic victory by preservationists. The only real issue before the Court was whether pursuit of that goal had imposed a taking in this case. It had not, said the Court, for reasons both general and particular.

As a general matter, it was immaterial that the Commission's action deprived the terminal's owners of all use of their "air rights" above the terminal;[23] the relevant parcel for takings analysis was the entire city block designated as the historic site. As to *that* property, economic use remained: The owners had conceded (in what surely was a tactical blunder) that they could continue to earn a reasonable return from the terminal without the office tower.

Further good news for historic preservationists came with the majority opinion's view that the distinctions between historic districting and individual landmark preservation were unimportant for takings purposes. The danger in the latter of discriminatory treatment—singling out a parcel for less favorable treatment than neighboring ones—was largely mitigated, said the Court, by the ordinance's comprehensive, citywide approach. Nor was the Court impressed by the argument that only in the case of historic districts (and zoning generally) is there a rough balance between the burdens on the property owner and the benefits to him or her from the use of similar restrictions on surrounding properties.[24] The Court was unwilling to conclude that the owners had in no way been benefitted by the landmarks law. All in all, a small step for New York City, and a giant leap for landmarks preservation.

Moving from the general to the particular, the Court found the ordinance's impact on the terminal's owners fell short of a taking. The law did not affect the present use of the terminal, and so did not

---

[23]Actually, the commission's actions may not have deprived plaintiff of all air rights. As the Court explained elsewhere in its opinion, rejection of the 55- and 53-story tower proposals did not foreclose the possibility that scaled-down proposals, which the station's owners never bothered to submit, might have been approved. Thus, some have argued that the taking issue in this canonical (dare we say, landmark) case was not ripe.

[24]This argument was pressed by Justice Rehnquist, author of the three-justice dissent. *Penn Central*, 438 U.S. at 138. As noted at the outset, however, later court decisions have not picked up on his position.

interfere with the owners' primary expectation for the parcel.[25] Nor, as mentioned, was there any showing that the owners could not continue to earn a reasonable return without an office tower above the terminal. Finally, to the extent the owners were denied use of airspace, those rights were transferable to several parcels in the vicinity—the seminal use by a court of "transferable development rights" to deflect a taking claim.[26]

One can see that beyond its fame as a jurisprudential manifesto, *Penn Central* offers valuable teaching on how to design a judicially acceptable landmarks law.

Use of the *Penn Central* Factors in Landmarks Cases

Courts evaluating landmarks laws since *Penn Central* have targeted two of the takings factors announced in that decision: economic impact and, less frequently, interference with investment-backed expectations.

Economic impact. Generally, a landmark designation is not a taking if the owner retains an economically viable use—any economically viable use—of the site.[27] If the owner can continue to use the property as he or she has been, courts often accept this as sufficient, seeming to assume that in the absence of proof otherwise, a continued use must be an economic one.[28] Cases turn on economic use,

[25]Not widely known is that Grand Central Terminal was designed and constructed to take a 35-story office tower. This fact, had it been noted in *Penn Central*, might have raised an argument of frustration of investment-backed expectations.

[26]At least one effort to secure city approval of a transfer of development rights from Grand Central Terminal was unsuccessful. 383 Madison Assocs. v. City of New York, 193 A.D.2d 518, 598 N.Y.S.2d 180 (1993) (rejecting "constitutional claims" of would-be recipient of such rights), *cert. denied,* 511 U.S. 1081 (1994).

[27]United Artists Theater Circuit v. City of Philadelphia, 535 Pa. 370, 635 A.2d 612 (1993); Lubelle v. Rochester Preservation Bd., 158 A.D.2d 975, 551 N.Y.S.2d 127 (1990); M.B. Assocs. v. District of Columbia, 456 A.2d 344 (D.C. 1982); 900 G Street Assocs. v. Department of Hous. and Community. Dev., 430 A.2d 1387 (D.C. 1981).

[28]International College of Surgeons v. City of Chicago, 1994 U.S. Dist. LEXIS 18989 (N.D. Ill. 1994) (no taking where plaintiff failed to show it would suffer economic hardship by continuing existing use), *reversed on jurisdictional grounds,* 91 F.3d 981 (7th Cir. 1996), *rev'd on jurisdictional grounds,* 118 S. Ct. 523 (1997); Shubert Org., Inc. v. Landmarks Preservation Comm'n, 166 A.D.2d

explicitly or implicitly, in part because this is the takings test, but also because many ordinances, like that of New York City, have hardship provisions easing restrictions when the owner would otherwise lose all economic use.[29]

As with other owners of regulated property, owners of landmark buildings are not entitled to highest and best use, but only to an economically viable use. The difference between the property's value under the landmark regulation and without it can be great and still not be a taking.[30]

Two other landmark preservation situations in which the economic impact factor is salient involve maintenance and repair as well as transferable development rights. Maintenance and repair requirements obviously impose an affirmative duty on the landmark owner to spend money. Recognizing this, courts have said that such requirements may work a taking when the cost is so high that continued use is uneconomic.[31] The burden of proof is on the property

---

115, 570 N.Y.S.2d 504 (1991) (no taking where owners could continue use as theaters). *See also* St. Bartholomew's Church v. City of New York, 914 F.2d 348 (2d Cir. 1990) (no taking where church could still use building for charitable and religious purposes), *cert. denied*, 499 U.S. 905 (1991).

[29]*See, e.g.,* 900 G Street Assocs., 430 A.2d at 1389–90. The landmarks ordinance at issue expressly defined "hardship" as being a taking of property without just compensation.

Use of such a takings-based standard for proof of hardship is the usual practice. New York City's economic hardship provision is very unusual in defining a specific "reasonable rate of return" (6 percent). N.Y. City Admin. Code § 25-302 v.

[30]No post-*Lucas* decision has had occasion to tell us whether landmark ordinances may constitute "background principles of property law" under that decision—though an archeological protection statute has been so held. Hunziker v. Iowa, 519 N.W.2d 367 (Iowa 1994). If landmark ordinances are viewed similarly, those who buy historic buildings *after* the adoption of a landmark ordinance will confront an added obstacle in their pursuit of compensation relief. *See* chapter 12.

[31]Citizens' Comm'n to Save Historic Rhodes Tavern v. District of Columbia, 432 A.2d 710, 718 (D.C. 1981) (requiring parties to spend substantial sum to preserve landmarks with little or no public assistance could be taking), *cert. denied*, 454 U.S. 1054 (1981); State v. Erickson, 301 N.W.2d 324 (Minn. 1981) (permanently denying owner beneficial use of his property by requiring substantial repairs would be taking).

owner, however, and in very few of the cases is a taking actually found.[32] On the other hand, note that some limitation on the use of maintenance and repair requirements is imposed by the aforementioned economic hardship provisions.

Broadview Apartments Company v. Commission for Historical and Architectural Preservation[33] neatly illustrates the problem. The owner of an historic apartment building was denied a demolition permit to construct a parking garage on the site. He sued, presenting three studies concluding that due to the extensive repairs needed, the structure could not be profitably restored and rented. The city relied upon a single cost study that did not take into account the cost of servicing debt on the property, any recovery of the purchase price, and the cost of replacing the structure's roof. The court of appeals found that the permit denial was a taking—"where restrictions deprive the landowner of all reasonable beneficial use of the property, compensation must be paid."[34]

In the extreme case, historic designation can shift the burden of restoring highly degraded buildings to property owners. Plainly, this is where the takings argument is strongest, especially when the renovation cost is greater than the probable market value of the property after the renovation.[35] Renovation in such cases would seem essentially a public burden.

Turn now to transferable development rights (TDR) programs, under which unused building densities at landmark sites may be transferred to other sites, and are thus given economic value.[36]

[32]A suspiciousness of a certain inability-to-maintain claims was voiced in *International College of Surgeons,* 1994 U.S. Dist. LEXIS 18989: "[A] property owner could deliberately neglect its property, or even damage it, and then claim that land-use regulations effect a taking because the property is so far gone—for reasons unrelated to the regulations—that the owner's proposed redevelopment is the only remaining viable use."

[33]433 A.2d 1214 (Md. Ct. Spec. App. 1981).

[34]*Id.* at 1217.

[35]*See, e.g.,* Weinberg v. City of Pittsburgh, 13 PRES. L. REP. 1068 (Pa. Ct. Comm. Pleas Nov. 29, 1993), *aff'd,* 651 A.2d 1182 (Pa. Commw. Ct. 1994). In reversing the historic commission's decision denying a demolition permit, the appellate court was undeterred by the fact that the building owner had purchased with full knowledge of historic preservation restrictions.

TDRs are particularly useful at landmark sites, where the building density permitted by the zoning ordinance often is not used up. The *Penn Central* decision, recall, asserts that as an offset to the costs imposed by a landmark law, TDRs decrease the chance that the economic impact factor will point to a taking.[37] Although apparently no subsequent case turns on the existence of a TDR program, its role in softening the economic impact of landmark restrictions doubtless will continue to undercut takings claims.[38]

Investment-backed expectations. In landmark preservation cases, this element of the *Penn Central* test has been variously translated as whether the owner bought the property knowing it was subject to landmark restrictions or bought with "reasonable expectations of profit."[39] In the former instance, courts presume that the buyer paid a price appropriately discounted for the regulation's impact.[40]

Landmark restrictions need not be in force when the building is purchased to undercut a buyer's reasonable expectations; lesser government actions can put buyers on notice. In *900 G Street Ass'n v. Department of Housing and Community Development*,[41] a District

---

[36]*See generally* Dwight H. Merriam, *Making TDRs Work,* 56 N. CAROLINA L. REV. 77, 90–100 (1978).

[37]The relevance of TDRs to the taking claim was more fully explored in the state high court ruling below. *Penn Central,* 42 N.Y.2d 324, 366 N.E.2d 1271 (1977). The fact that the value of the transferred rights might not equal the value of the lost development rights at the historic site, explained the court, did not necessarily mean that a taking had occurred. *See generally* DANIEL R. MANDELKER, LAND USE LAW § 11.34 (3d ed. 1993).

[38]*See, e.g.,* Shubert Org., Inc. v. City of New York, 166 A.D.2d 115, 570 N.Y.S.2d 504 (1991) (landmark designation of 22 Broadway theaters was not a taking where, among other factors, TDR program was in place; TDR program here assumed to have economic benefit), *cert. denied,* 504 U.S. 946 (1992).

The Supreme Court decision in Suitum v. Tahoe Regional Planning Agency, 117 S. Ct. 1659 (1997), did not disturb *Penn Central's* use of TDRs to offset economic impact and lessen the chance of a taking.

[39]900 G Street Assocs. v. Department of Hous. & Community Dev., 430 A.2d 1387, 1390 (D.C. 1981).

[40]*See, e.g.,* Atlas Enter. Ltd. Partnership v. United States, 32 Fed. Cl. 704, 708 (1995).

[41]430 A.2d 1387 (D.C. 1981).

of Columbia developer bought a building weeks before a new, stricter
landmark ordinance took effect. The builder later sought a demolition permit, which was denied. In finding that the ordinance did not
work a taking, the court noted that the building was listed on "designated historical rosters"; that, in the buyer's negotiations with the
prior owners, the latter's difficulties in getting a demolition permit
were likely discussed; and that the new owners had to be aware of the
well-publicized efforts of the local government to enact stricter landmark protection.[42] All these factors, said the court, "must have influenced the price which petitioner was willing to pay for the property
[and] its realistic expectations for the uses which could be made of the
property. . . ."[43] The *900 G Street* analysis has since been applied to
an even earlier stage, where the building was bought before it was
designated a landmark.[44]

At the opposite pole, ambiguous landmark regulation may fail to
give notice to a purchaser and thus leave investment-backed expectations intact. In one taking case,[45] the dispute arose from the disapproval of a development plan that would have left intact only the facade of an historic building. At issue was whether the building owner
knew at the time of purchase that this preservation method was not
permitted. The court found the preservation regulations ambiguous,
owing to inconsistent government interpretion. Hence the court
could not hold that the building owner had necessarily been unreasonable in expecting, as of the time of purchase, to demolish all but
the facade. Further evidence on the issue was needed.

Landmarks with a Charitable or Religious Purpose

Early on, courts recognized that the "economically viable use" takings test was inappropriate for landmark properties not in economic
use, such as those serving charitable or religious purposes. So the
courts evolved a more appropriate (and difficult to meet) standard:

---

[42]*Id.* at 1390.

[43]*Id.*

[44]Kalorama Heights Ltd. Partnership v. District of Columbia, 655 A.2d 865,
871–72 (D.C. 1995) (no taking where building bought seven months prior to
landmark designation; there were "strong preservationist trends in the area,
chance of obtaining variances was only fifty percent, and purchase amounted to
'gamble'").

[45]Atlas Enter. Ltd. Partnership v. United States, 32 Fed. Cl. 704 (1995).

Landmark regulation imposes a taking when it seriously interferes with the charitable or religious purpose.[46]

An early case adopting this specialized test, *Lutheran Church in America v. City of New York*,[47] involved the former residence of J.P. Morgan in Manhattan. Purchased by a church, it had been used for administrative purposes but soon was outgrown. In 1965, the church sought a demolition permit in order to build a larger office structure, which the city denied. It was uncontested that the existing building was inadequate for the church's expanding needs. For that reason, the court found that designation would prevent or at least seriously interfere with the carrying out of the church's charitable purpose, and so would be a taking.

This teaching—that interference with a charitable institution's *expansion* is a taking—was reexamined later under *Penn Central*, despite that decision's focus on economic, rather than nonprofit, activities. In *St. Bartholomew's Church v. City of New York*[48] a court denied a church's taking claim in circumstances similar to *Lutheran Church in America*. The church in *St. Bartholomew's* sought to replace its "community house," a designated landmark, with an office tower. The city denied permission under its landmarks law. Despite such denial "drastically restrict[ing] the Church's ability to raise revenues,"[49] the court saw no taking because the church could continue its charitable and religious activities in its current facility. "Although the regulation may 'freeze' the Church's property in its existing use and prevent the Church from expanding or altering its activities, *Penn Central* explicitly permits this."[50] More accurately, we might

[46]*See, e.g.*, Sailor's Snug Harbor v. Platt, 29 A.D.2d 376, 288 N.Y.S.2d 314 (1968); Lutheran Church in America v. City of New York, 35 N.Y.2d 121, 316 N.E.2d 305 (1974); Society for Ethical Culture v. Spatt, 51 N.Y.2d 449, 415 N.E.2d 922 (1980) (rejecting plaintiff's taking claim but reaffirming rule for charities).

Beyond our scope here is an additional issue raised by landmark designation of churches—whether a designation interferes with the free exercise of religion. For example, a recent Supreme Court decision involving historic preservation of a church hinged on the constitutionality of the federal Religious Freedom Restoration Act, though a taking claim was raised in the trial court. Boerne v. Flores, 117 S. Ct. 2157 (1997).

[47]35 N.Y.2d 121, 316 N.E.2d 305 (1974).

[48]914 F.2d 348 (2d Cir. 1990), *cert. denied*, 499 U.S. 905 (1991).

[49]914 F.2d at 355.

[50]*Id.* at 356. *Accord* Canisius College v. City of Buffalo, 217 A.D.2d 985, 629 N.Y.S.2d 886, *appeal denied*, 86 N.Y.2d 709, 658 N.E.2d 221 (1995).

The "community house" (low building) adjacent to St. Bartholomew's Church in Manhattan, New York City. As with the Grand Central Terminal only a half-mile away, city efforts to block upward expansion of this designated historic structure led to an important takings case: *St. Bartholomew's Church v. New York City*.

observe, *Penn Central* allows a defense that the existing use remains viable where that use offers a reasonable *economic* return.

How to deal with the nonprofit owner of a historic landmark—i.e., what constitutes "economic hardship" in such a case—has also been addressed legislatively.

Interiors

Preservation ordinances may allow for designation of building interiors as well as exteriors.[51] New York City's landmark ordinance, for example, specifically contemplates landmarking of interiors that are at least thirty years old and normally open or accessible to the public.[52] Without specific authorization in the ordinance, however, a city may not have the power to designate interiors.[53]

Because government regulation of interiors seems somehow more intrusive, and more likely to thwart economic use, early decisions suggested it warrants heightened scrutiny for takings.[54] Notwithstanding, courts have generally upheld interior designations against takings challenges.[55] As with the exterior cases, the building owner's ability to continue the existing use of the property poses a serious obstacle to obtaining compensation.

A facial challenge, for example, was brought by a District of Columbia theater owner claiming that *any* designation of a building's interior fails to serve a legitimate public interest, requires public invasion of the property, and denies economic use.[56] The court disagreed, holding that interior designation was not a facial taking because public viewing of the interior was not necessary.[57] Several of the ordinance's legitimate public purposes, such as preserving cultural history,

---

[51]A recent survey indicates that about 11 percent of historic commissions have authority to regulate interiors. NATIONAL ALLIANCE, *supra* note 3, App. B.

[52]N.Y. City Admin. Code § 25-302.

[53]United Artists Theater Circuit v. City of Philadelphia, 535 Pa. 370, 635 A.2d 612 (1993) (historic commission lacked authority to designate interior of building under landmark ordinance).

[54]*See, e.g.*, Manhattan Club v. City of New York, 273 N.Y.S.2d 848 (Sup. Ct. 1966).

[55]*See generally* Scott R. Rothstein, Comment, *Takings Jurisprudence Comes in from the Cold: Preservation of Interiors Through Landmark Legislation*, 26 CONNECTICUT L. REV. 1105 (1994).

[56]Weinberg v. Barry, 634 F. Supp. 86 (D.D.C. 1985).

[57]*Id.* at 92.

did not depend on the public's having interior access. And, even if public viewing was necessary, there were compatible uses.[58]

The designation of a restaurant interior also has been held no taking, the court finding that the owner was "not substantially deprived of the economic benefit of this space."[59]

Historic Districts

Most states have passed enabling legislation for historic districts that is independent of zoning enabling laws,[60] even though designation of historic districts may be authorized under the zoning enabling laws.[61] The typical enabling legislation makes historic preservation districts a part of zoning. As with other zoning, local government has broad legislative discretion in designing regulations and mapping the districts. Historic districts are usually overlay districts that do not alter the underlying use and dimensional standards of the existing land-use regulations. Overlay districts are discussed in more detail in chapter 15.

Some historic district enabling legislation is detailed, giving local governments the authority to delineate historic districts, to establish district commissions, and to provide specific regulatory authorization and procedures for implementing districts. In addition, this legislation often authorizes a commission to survey areas that might be designated historic areas.

The owners of buildings within a historic district must obtain specific permission for any exterior alterations, demolition, or new construction. Proposed changes are examined for appropriateness or consistency with the district. An owner attempting to change a building must apply for a "certificate of appropriateness."

[58]Theater owners challenging designation of interiors also fared poorly in New York City. Shubert Org., Inc. v. City of New York, 166 A.D.2d 115, 570 N.Y.S.2d 504 (1991) (landmark designation of 22 Broadway theaters, including interiors, was not a taking where the properties could still be used for theater productions), *cert. denied*, 504 U.S. 946 (1992).

[59]Teachers Ins. & Annuity Ass'n v. City of New York, 185 A.D.2d 207, 586 N.Y.S.2d 262, 264 (1992), *aff'd*, 603 N.Y.S.2d 399 (1993).

[60]*See* N.Y. Gen. Mun. Law § 96-a.

[61]City of Santa Fe v. Gamble-Skogmo, 73 N.M. 410, 389 P.2d 13 (1964) (statutes provide enabling authority for zoning).

The first historic districts were for areas of exceptionally significant historic relevance.[62] The courts do not generally have difficulty upholding historic district regulation when there is obvious significant historic value. However, over the years there has been a trend to include within districts some geographic areas and buildings that have neither unique nor significant historic value. Remember, we are not talking about designating individual buildings as we were earlier in the chapter, but we are considering the impact of large-area zoning or zoning-like districts that sweep up everything in their path, including the 1960s raised ranch between two Victorians.[63] It is with more common types of structures where the courts may differ with the findings of a historic district commission.

The takings issue arises most frequently in historic districts when demolition of relatively common older structures is proposed, a commission denies a permit to build a new structure, or a commission requires maintenance and repair of a building. For example, in Albany, New York, a petitioner wanted to demolish a common, 150-year-old structure in the Center Square/Hudson Park Historic District.[64] The Historic Resources Commission denied an application for a "certificate of appropriateness." The City Zoning Board of Appeals agreed. The petitioner sued for permission to demolish the structure, claiming the denial caused a taking. The court considered the building's age and serious deterioration, including decaying roof, missing floors, and damage from fire and rot.

The building owner presented evidence of the cost of restoration and the potential income if restored. The court noted that government does not have the right to impose on an owner the sole burden of an economically unfeasible restoration for the general benefit of society-at-large.[65] In addition, the court found that the petitioner's

[62]See In re Opinion of the Justices to Senate, 333 Mass. 773, 128 N.E.2d 557 (1955) (upheld historic district in Town of Nantucket). See also City of New Orleans v. Pergament, 198 La. 852, 5 So. 2d 129 (1941) (municipal council and commission have authority to preserve Vieux Carre); In re Opinion of the Justices to Senate, 333 Mass. 783, 128 N.E.2d 563 (1955) (preservation of Beacon Hill in Boston upheld).

[63]One of the authors successfully represented the owner of a nondescript 1946 Cape Cod–style home who petitioned to have the boundaries of a colonial-era historic district altered to include his home because of the cachet and protection the district would provide.

[64]Lemme v. Dolan, 146 Misc. 2d 817, 552 N.Y.S.2d 506 (Sup. Ct. 1990), rev'd, 163 A.D.2d 717, 558 N.Y.S.2d 991 (1990).

[65]Id. at 823.

property was structurally unsound and a threat to public health, safety, and welfare. The decisions of the Historic Resources Commission and the Zoning Board of Appeals were held to be arbitrary and capricious and a taking.[66]

However, a New York appellate court reversed the lower court because the commission's interpretation of the ordinance had been reasonable and consistent with statutory language; granting of a variance was possible; the owner did not seek waiver or variance; and some important factual questions had not been determined.[67]

In a similar case, a court held that if the historic value of a property and the costs of restoration are substantial, and society seeks to preserve the historic nature of the property, then government should condemn the property and pay to restore it.[68] Forcing the burden on the landowner would cause a taking.[69] It is unconstitutional to force the owner "to assume the cost of providing a benefit to the public without recoupment".[70] Moreover, when the action deprives the owner of all profitable use of the property, just compensation is required.[71]

While owners do not have to bear the costs of benefits to society in general, they do have an affirmative responsibility to maintain property.[72] But, where the maintenance expense is unreasonable, a

[66]See also Wolk v. Reisen, 67 A.D.2d 819, 413 N.Y.S. 2d 60 (1979) (denial of certificate of appropriateness overturned because building was seriously deteriorated, fire damaged, unsafe and dangerous).

[67]Lemme, 163 A.D.2d 717, 558 N.Y.S.2d 991 (1990).

[68]See FGL & L. Property Corp. v. City of Rye, 66 N.Y.2d 111, 485 N.E.2d 986 (1985).

[69]Lutheran Church in Am. v. New York, 35 N.Y.2d 121, 129, 316 N.E.2d 305 (1974) (commission cannot convert property to public use by simply invading "owner's right to own and manage").

[70]Fred F. French Investing Co. v. City of New York, 39 N.Y.2d 587, 596, 350 N.E.2d 381 (zoning amendment invalid as unreasonable, depriving owner of all property rights except bare title and "dubious future reversion of full use"), cert. denied, appeal dismissed, 429 U.S. 990 (1976).

[71]Benenson v. United States, 212 Ct. Cl. 375, 548 F.2d 939 (1977) (taking where hotel located in historic district forced to cease operations because repair, rehabilitation costs prohibitive). But see Park Home v. City of Williamsport, 680 A.2d 835, 837 (Pa. 1996) (request to demolish building within historic district denied; no taking because owner did not meet burden of proving denial of "any profitable use").

[72]Two influential decisions are Maher v. City of New Orleans, 516 F.2d 1051 (5th Cir. 1975) (requiring maintenance of historic buildings as a potential taking), cert. denied, 426 U.S. 905 (1976), and Lafayette Park Baptist Church v.

maintenance requirement may constitute a taking. An alternative argument has its basis in *Penn Central*.[73] It might be argued that an equitable distribution of benefits is similar to the "average reciprocity of advantage"[74] in that all district property owners share both the responsibility and benefits of maintenance.[75] Courts must often balance the general benefit to society from historic districts against the costs of restoration to individual property owners.

This balancing, and the linkage and overlap between the preservation of individual landmarks and the use of historic districts, are illustrated in the effort to preserve the few remaining elegant homes along Lake Shore Drive in Chicago. The city council designated the seven remaining houses as an historic district, "Seven Houses on Lake Shore Drive District," under the city's Landmarks Ordinance.[76] Shortly thereafter, the International College of Surgeons (ICS) sought to demolish all but the front facades of two houses to construct a 41-story, mixed-use condominium tower. The Landmarks Commission denied the demolition request and ICS challenged the action in court.[77]

The court found that the plaintiff's traditional use of the property remained and necessary repairs could be completed at a reasonable cost.[78] There were several reasonable alternative uses, including uses as homes or consulates. China had offered $6.5 million for the ICS building and although use as a consulate would require a zoning

---

Scott, 553 S.W.2d 856 (Mo. Ct. App. 1977) (city's decision not to permit demolition of church in historic district).

[73]438 U.S. 104, 133 (1978) (no taking; landmarks law restrictions substantially relate to promoting general welfare and permit reasonable beneficial use).

[74]Keystone Bituminous Coal Ass'n v. DeBenedictis, 480 U.S. 470, 491 (1987) (no taking for various reasons, including that public interest in preventing activities similar to public nuisances can outweigh owner's interests).

[75]*But see Layfayette Park Baptist Church*, 553 S.W.2d 856 (Mo. Ct. App. 1977) (restoration may not be economically feasible). *See also* Figarsky v. Historic Dist. Comm'n, 171 Conn. 198, 368 A.2d 163 (1976) (cost of repairs for compliance with building code prohibitive).

[76]International College of Surgeons v. City of Chicago, 1994 U.S. Dist. LEXIS 18989 at 3 (N.D. Ill. December 30, 1994), *rev'd, remanded,* 91 F.3d 981 (7th Cir. 1996), *reversed, remanded,* 118 S. Ct. 523 (1997).

[77]1994 U.S. Dist. Lexis 18989 at 5–8. Relevant factors for the court included whether the property contained landmark features or whether denying demolition would cause economic hardship to the owner.

[78]*Id.* at 59–64.

variance, it seemed reasonable to assume one might be granted given that the Polish consulate was next door. Concluding that ICS was not denied all reasonable and beneficial economic return on the property, the court upheld denial of both the demolition permits and use of the economic hardship exception. The court said that it need determine only whether ICS was deprived of "all reasonable return, as opposed to the highest and best return." A taking does not occur wherever a designation prevents a landowner from developing the property to its highest and best use.[79]

However, the Circuit Court of Appeals for the Seventh Circuit reversed and remanded the case to the Circuit Court of Cooke County, where the case had begun.[80] The defendants had removed the case to federal court, but the Seventh Circuit held that the property owner's claims did not properly belong there.

The U.S. Supreme Court reversed the Seventh Circuit.[81] The Court held that the federal trial court "properly exercised . . . jurisdiction over the federal claims in ICS's complaints, and properly recognized that [the trial court] could thus also exercise supplemental jurisdiction over ICS's state law claims."[82] After reversing the Seventh Circuit, the Court remanded the case to the appeals court for further proceedings.[83]

In some cases, the individual-building claim and the district-created takings claim are combined. For example, a property owner may seek to demolish or alter a structure, claiming that the project qualifies for a special merit exception to district requirements. In the District of Columbia,[84] an owner sought a special merit exception because the proposed luxury condominium project would increase tax revenues, among other things. The issues were whether the project outweighed the public interest in preserving the building and whether there were no feasible alternatives to demolition. The court denied

---

[79]*Id.* at 99–100. *See also Penn Central,* 438 U.S. 104, 131 (diminution in value alone does not support finding of taking); United Artists Theater Circuit, Inc. v. City of Philadelphia, 535 Pa. 370, 635 A.2d 612 (1993) (no taking in designation of private building as historic).

[80]*Surgeons,* 91 F.3d 981 (7th Cir. 1996), *reversed, remanded,* 118 S. Ct. 523 (1997).

[81]118 S. Ct. 523, 528–29 (1997).

[82]*Id.* at 530.

[83]*Id.* at 534.

[84]Kalorama Heights Ltd. Partnership v. District of Columbia Dep't of Consumer & Regulatory Affairs, 655 A.2d. 865 (D.C. 1995).

the special merit exception because the owner failed to show that alternatives to demolition were found unfeasible.[85] If there was a reasonable alternative use, there could be no taking, said the court, even if the property was reduced in value or if there were a number of "higher" or better land uses available.[86]

Another case before the courts now in Cumberland, Maryland, involves a 149-year-old Roman Catholic Church monastery and chapel.[87] The facility occupies an entire city block and in 1978 was designated as part of the Washington Street Historic District. The monastery and chapel have been vacant since 1986 because they are in disrepair; maintenance and reconstruction costs are prohibitive. The parish decided to raze the buildings to remove the financial liability and applied for a certificate of appropriateness. The application was denied.

The parish responded with a multicount complaint including charges that the city effected a taking of property by denying the demolition permit. The defendant moved to dismiss all the counts, but the takings claim survived. The court found that the high cost of renovations rendered the church property "economically useless."[88] Thus, the court found a taking, and offered the church the opportunity to prove money damages.[89] In such a situation, if the public considers the benefit to society to be important, then the public should pay for this benefit.[90]

In a Massachusetts case with a twist on the usual demolition permit problem, a property owner first sought and received permission to demolish three structures that the parties agreed had no historical

---

[85]Id. at 870.

[86]A proposed project on vacant land within an historic district is also subject to requirements designed to preserve the historic character of the neighborhood. See Dupont Circle Citizens Ass'n v. Barry, 455 A.2d 417 (D.C. 1983).

[87]Cardinal Keeler v. Mayor & City Council of Cumberland, 928 F. Supp. 591 (D. Md.), summ. judgment granted in part, denied in part, 940 F. Supp. 879 (D. Md. 1996).

[88]Cardinal Keeler, 940 F. Supp. 879.

[89]The court also denied an attempt to dismiss the case on statutory grounds. However, the court allowed the church summary judgment on its claims that the city had violated its right to free exercise under both the First Amendment and the Maryland Declaration of Rights.

[90]See Lutheran Church in Am. v. New York, 35 N.Y.2d 121, 129, 316 N.E.2d 305 (1974) (if public wants to prevent owner's free use of building, public should condemn the property).

significance.[91] During demolition, the owner had a change of heart with regard to one building—an old garage. His request to change the certificate of appropriateness was denied by the regional historic commission. That decision was challenged as arbitrary and capricious. The state appellate court found that the commission had no rational basis for denying the change as the building was not incompatible with the historic character of the district. The Supreme Judicial Court of Massachusetts then overruled the appellate court, noting that the local committee balanced the interests of the property owner and the public. Also, the commission possessed substantial discretion in determining congruity with the historic district.[92]

Creating an historic district is the last step to regulation. Fearing the restrictions from such a designation, some have challenged the very creation of an historic preservation district as a taking. For example, in Connecticut the City of Norwich established an historic district, including a colonial-era town green and about 100 nearby buildings and lots.[93] Property owners who wanted to demolish a building within the district challenged the historic district commission's denial of their proposal. They lost one court appeal; the Connecticut Supreme Court, however, granted their request for review of their as-applied taking claim.

The Connecticut high court first found that the ordinance creating the historic district was a valid exercise of the police power.[94] The owners had faulted the "aesthetic considerations" language of the ordinance as too vague, but the court found that a statute provided needed guidance. Also, aesthetic considerations were not the sole factor used to invoke the police power. In addition, the court found that the law was not settled about the relationship of aesthetic considerations to exercise the police power. Next, the court considered whether even the valid ordinance could have effected a taking of the plaintiffs' property. The property owners had the burden of proving that the ordinance caused their property to have no value; they did not meet that burden, the court found.

---

[91]Harris v. Old King's Highway Regional Dist. Comm'n, 38 Mass. App. Ct. 447, 648 N.E.2d 1296 (1995), *superseded,* 421 Mass. 612, 658 N.E.2d 972 (1996). Though this is not a taking case, it is important, with the later decision by the Supreme Judicial Court of Massachusetts, for the economic analysis that is applicable in the takings context.

[92]*Harris,* 421 Mass. 612, 617, 658 N.E.2d 972 (1996).

[93]Figarsky v. Historic Dist. Comm'n, 171 Conn. 198, 368 A.2d 163 (1976).

[94]171 Conn. at 209.

Two cases, though they did not involve takings claims, illustrate how ad hoc regulation can precipitate such claims. For example, some municipalities have tried to use historic district rules to deny a demolition permit to a property outside the district's boundaries. The Supreme Court of South Dakota ruled that Deadwood could not deny a demolition permit for the Treber Ice House because the building was not an historic property as defined by the state enabling legislation.[95] In addition, the property was outside the city's historic district and though "eligible" was not listed on the National Register.

In the City of South Pasadena, California, homeowners seeking to construct an addition were informed by the City Building and Planning Division that their home was a "qualified historic[al] structure"[96] under the State Historical Building Code. This required an evaluation of the project's impact on the "historical environment."[97]

The court found no basis for South Pasadena's interpretation because the city did not create an historic zone to contract with the owners for preservation nor did it enact a regulatory historic district in the neighborhood.[98] Consequently, as discussed previously, "eligibility" for listing in the National Register of Historic Places is not enough to prohibit alterations to the owners' home. The city could not use the California Environmental Quality Act (CEQA) as a substitute for a proper zoning ordinance, the court noted.

In summary, creation of an historic district is, by itself, not likely to be successfully challenged as a taking. However, attempts to regulate alterations or demolition of historic properties in the absence of an historic district or individual-building designation can be risky.

The designation of individual landmarks and the creation of historic districts can be mutually reinforcing in protecting historic resources. Individual buildings sometimes merit individual designation because of their importance or because they are outside a district. Districts preserve structures and space in ways that individual designation cannot. Furthermore, districts permit consideration of how structures and space contribute to the larger context—an essential analysis of preservation. Importantly, districts can protect individual landmarks. Both individual designations and districts can create takings problems. Are we considering an individual landmark or is its

[95]Donovan v. City of Deadwood, 538 N.W.2d 790, 793 (S.D. 1995).
[96]Cal. Health & Safety Code §§ 18950–61.
[97]Prentiss v. City of South Pasadena, 15 Cal. App. 4th 85, 18 Cal. Rptr. 2d 641 (1993), *review denied,* 1993 Cal. LEXIS 3766 (July 15, 1993).
[98]15 Cal. App. 4th at 95.

designation and evaluation in the context of the district the basis for the claim? Carefully drafted district regulations, adopted after broad-based public participation and consensus-building on the district's objectives, have the potential to substantially reduce takings claims. The ad hoc, crisis-driven approach, largely based on denial of a demolition permit, hurts all concerned and can be avoided in large measure through careful planning. The stakes are too high—private property rights can be damaged or historic resources lost—to depend on the reactive regulation that seems to result in so much litigation.

Chapter 21

Airplanes and Airports

Those who reside near airports will be forgiven if their feelings about the wonders of aviation are mixed. The noise, vibrations, and soot from low-flying aircraft can undercut substantially the quality of life on land nearby, impairing conversation, sleep, and radio and TV reception, while rattling windows, frightening animals, stopping work, etc. This is particularly so for jet aircraft, the advent of which in the 1950s and 1960s spawned an entire generation of aircraft takings litigation.[1] Defendants in almost all cases have been the local governments that own the airports—or the United States in connection with military aircraft operations, whether or not at federally owned bases.

Here we first survey the takings case law stemming from the operation of aircraft per se, then turn to the litigation prompted by preemptive government efforts to restrict development near airports.

---

[1]Many court decisions of this period are explicit that it was only when overflights of propeller aircraft from defendant's airport were supplanted by those of jets that the taking cause of action became viable. *See, e.g.,* Martin v. Port of Seattle, 64 Wash. 2d 309, 391 P.2d 540 (1964), *cert. denied,* 379 U.S. 989 (1965). *Cf.* Bacon v. United States, 295 F.2d 936 (Ct. Cl. 1961) (taking occurred only when jets using nearby Air Force base were replaced by bigger jets, with their "terrifying" noise).

Aircraft Operations

Causby and *Griggs*

A 1946 opinion of the Supreme Court, *Causby v. United States*,[2] remains unbowed today as the leading pronouncement in the field.[3] The landowner operated a small chicken farm 2,000 feet from the end of a civilian airport runway. After leasing rights at the airport in 1942, the United States began flying heavy bombers and fighters over the farm at altitudes as low as 83 feet. The result was devastating noise, causing chickens to hurl themselves into walls and destroying the property's usability for that business.

The Court rejected the common law doctrine that landownership extends outward to the universe, accepting federal statutory claims that airspace above the minimum safe altitude is publicly owned. Notwithstanding, the Court insisted, the landowner must have exclusive control over the "immediate reaches" above his property. Invasions of airspace at this low altitude, affecting as they do the use of the land, equate with invasions of the surface itself.

Apparently limiting itself to such low flights directly over the claimant's land, the Court set forth the fundamental rule: To be a taking, flights must be "so low and so frequent as to be a direct and immediate interference with the use and enjoyment of land."[4] Finding such interference on the facts presented, the Court held that the United States, through its overflights, had bought itself an "avigation easement."

Most intriguing about *Causby* is its infusion of the common law concepts of trespass and nuisance into the takings brew. Trespass is implicated by the Court's several mentions that the flights were directly over the plaintiff's land, rather than merely nearby. This emphasis may also reflect the view, well-settled in takings law even when this case was decided, that physical invasions are the most suspect of government interferences with private land. And since physical invasions are held takings largely independent of their economic impact, it was unsurprising that the *Causby* Court saw a taking even though non-chicken-farm uses of plaintiff's land remained. But nuisance thinking also entered the picture, leading the Court to limit takings to

[2] 328 U.S. 256 (1946).

[3] *See generally* Jay M. Zitter, Annotation, *Airport Operations or Flight of Aircraft as Constituting Taking or Damage of Property*, 22 A.L.R.4th (1983).

[4] *Causby*, 328 U.S. at 266.

those trespassory overflights that interfered substantially with the use and enjoyment of land.[5]

The Supreme Court's other foray into the overflight/takings area, *Griggs v. Allegheny County*,[6] turned from the question of *whether* to *who*. Where a local government made the decision to build the airport, chose its location, and was its promoter and owner, the Court declared, it was the taker. Although the airport was designed to federal requirements and under federal supervision, the United States was deemed to have taken nothing.[7] Presumably, the same result would apply where the locals prohibit certain land uses near a proposed airport in order to qualify for federal construction grants.

The Direct Overflights Prerequisite

The trespass/nuisance split personality of *Causby* underlies the most consistent difference between the federal and state flight cases. The federal cases, stressing the trespass basis of *Causby*, generally limit takings recovery for airplane overflights to those directly over one's land. By contrast, almost all state cases, highlighting the nuisance basis of *Causby*, allow recovery regardless of whether the land owner's airspace was invaded.

The federal rule was first announced in 1962 in *Batten v. United States*,[8] in which homeowners near an Air Force base alleged a taking based on noise, vibrations, and smoke from jet aircraft operating from the base, despite the absence of flights directly overhead. "No amount of sympathy" for the homeowners, said the court, can alter the fact that the Supreme Court sees no taking when government activities do not

---

[5]A private nuisance is an intentional act that interferes with another person's use and enjoyment of his land, which interference is both substantial and unreasonable under the circumstances. PROSSER AND KEETON ON THE LAW OF TORTS 622–23 (W.P. Keeton ed., 1984). *See* Long v. City of Charlotte, 306 N.C. 187, 293 S.E.2d 101 (1982) (criticizing, in airplane overflights context, the inadequacies of nuisance and trespass approaches individually).

[6]369 U.S. 84 (1962).

[7]Would the Supreme Court have felt as strongly about local liability had the case arisen after City of Burbank v. Lockheed Air Terminal, Inc., 411 U.S. 624 (1973)? There, the Court held that local controls over airport operations, when aimed at noise reduction, are preempted by federal enactments. Should local authorities be held liable for takings based on the noise from aircraft takeoffs and landings when they lack authority to regulate such noise?

[8]306 F.2d 580 (10th Cir. 1962), *cert. denied*, 371 U.S. 955 (1963).

directly encroach on private property, except in the extreme case. To hold otherwise, said the court, would obliterate the careful distinction between "damage" and "taking," noting that no cases hold the United States liable for noise, vibrations, and smoke without a physical invasion. A dissenter, however, questioned why takings should depend on whether the government physically invaded.

Picking up on the *Batten* dissent, an important early state case on aircraft disturbances, *Thornburgh v. Port of Portland*, jettisoned the direct overflights prerequisite later the same year.[9] Noting that *Causby* used the language of nuisance as well as that of trespass, this court phrased the issue as whether a nuisance that affects the landowner in the same manner as a trespass can amount to a taking. Answering yes, the court stated the takings criterion as whether government has substantially deprived the owner of useful possession, either by repeated trespasses or by repeated nontrespassory interferences called nuisances. "Logically," said the court, "the same kind and degree of interference with the use and enjoyment of one's land can also be a taking even though the noise vector may come from some direction other than the perpendicular."[10] *Thornburgh*, by the way, is not based on a state constitution that prohibits "taking or damaging."[11]

Despite major overhaul of takings jurisprudence since these decisions were handed down, the schism between federal and state courts on the question of direct overflights largely persists. Until 1997, direct overflights appeared to be indispensable for the federal courts.[12] Such courts refused to discern takings based on noise, soot, and vibrations from flights over nearby properties,[13] taxiing operations,[14] or the testing of jet engines at a nearby military air base (despite the exhausts facing plaintiff's property).[15] Important in rejecting some of

[9]376 P.2d 100 (1962) (en banc). *See also* Martin v. Port of Seattle, 64 Wash. 2d 309, 391 P.2d 540, 545–46 (1964) (*Batten* dissent is more likely the correct reading of *Causby*), *cert. denied*, 379 U.S. 989 (1965).

[10]*Thornburgh*, 376 P.2d at 106.

[11]*See* chapter 2 (discussing state constitutions).

[12]Recent affirmations of the federal rule are in Brown v. United States, 30 Fed. Cl. 23, 35 (1993), *rev'd on other grounds*, 73 F.3d 1100 (Fed. Cir. 1996), and Stephens v. United States, 11 Cl. Ct. 352, 359 (1986).

[13]Town of East Haven v. Eastern Airlines, Inc., 331 F. Supp. 16 (D. Conn. 1971).

[14]*Id.*

[15]Bellamy v. United States, 235 F. Supp. 139 (E.D.S.C. 1964); Leavell v. United States, 234 F. Supp. 534 (E.D.S.C. 1964).

these claims was the fact that plaintiffs continued to live in their homes, suggesting to the courts that while a substantial interference with use and enjoyment of land may exist, there was no near-complete destruction of interests as seen to be required of nontrespassory flights.[16] In 1997, however, the Federal Circuit opened the door to takings claims based at least in part on non-overhead flights, where there is a "peculiarly burdensome" pattern of activity.[17]

Patterning after *Thornburgh,* the large majority of state court cases emphasize the comparability of nuisance and trespass and, accordingly, dispense with concern that the flights be over the property.[18] Finding "irrelevant" the issue whether "the wing-tip of the aircraft passes through some fraction of an inch of the airspace directly over plaintiff's land," one state supreme court explained that plaintiffs are not seeking recovery for a trespass, but for interference with use and enjoyment of land.[19] A few state courts, however, base the rejection of a direct overflights prerequisite at least in part on the broader scope of those state constitutions that demand compensation for both the "taking" and "damaging" of property.[20]

[16]Batten v. United States, 306 F.2d 580 (10th Cir. 1962), *cert. denied,* 371 U.S. 955 (1963); *Leavell,* 234 F. Supp. 534 (E.D.S.C. 1964).

[17]Argent v. United States, 124 F.3d 1277 (Fed. Cir. 1997). *Argent* affirmed that under *Causby,* takings compensation would continue to be denied for "normal aircraft operations, not passing directly overhead." *Id.* at 1284.

[18]*See, e.g.,* Jackson v. Metro. Knoxville Airport Auth., 922 S.W.2d 860 (Tenn. 1996); City of Philadelphia v. Keyser, 45 Pa. Commw. 271, 407 A.2d 55 (1979); Alevizos v. Metro. Airports Comm'n, 298 Minn. 471, 216 N.W.2d 651 (1974); Henthorn v. Oklahoma City, 453 P.2d 1013 (Okla. 1969); Johnson v. City of Greenville, 222 Tenn. 260, 435 S.W.2d 476 (1968); Jacksonville v. Schumann, 167 So. 2d 95 (Fla. Dist. Ct. App. 1964); Martin v. Port of Seattle, 64 Wash. 2d 309, 391 P.2d 540 (1964), *cert. denied,* 379 U.S. 989 (1965). *See also* Nestle v. City of Santa Monica, 6 Cal. 3d 920, 496 P.2d 480 (1972) (en banc) (discussing landowners' taking claims based on airport operations without noting whether flights were directly overhead). The minority state view, that direct overflights *are* a prerequisite, is stated in Louisville and Jefferson County Air Bd. v. Porter, 397 S.W.2d 146 (Ky. 1965), and Fergusson v. City of Keene, 108 N.H. 409, 238 A.2d 1 (1968). *But see* Sundell v. Town of New London, 119 N.H. 839, 409 A.2d 1315 (1979) (softening, and arguably overruling, *Fergusson*).

[19]*Martin,* 391 P.2d at 545.

[20]*See, e.g.,* Aaron v. City of Los Angeles, 40 Cal. 3d 471 (1974), *cert. denied,* 419 U.S. 1122 (1975); *Martin,* 391 P.2d at 546.

Takings Factors

Merely having to endure the low rumble of nearby aircraft operations is not sufficient, of course, to make out a taking claim—even in the federal courts when there are many direct overflights. Courts implicitly recognize the indispensability of airports to contemporary society. Thus, the stringent *Causby* "direct and immediate interference" standard must always be satisfied. (If satisfied, the government acquires an "avigation easement" over the entire tract at the lowest altitude frequently flown, for all types of planes that do not further increase the burden on the land.)

Application of the *Causby* standard is flexible, looking at the totality of circumstances.[21] Generally, however, the interference must be substantial; indeed almost all successful overflight/takings cases involve land within a mile of airports, with planes flying over regularly at less than 1,000 (usually less than 500) feet. Those injured by aircraft flights less than "substantially" are better advised to seek relief from the political branches of government.

Substantiality of impact is particularly clear where the landowner is unable to continue the existing land use—recall the chicken farm in *Causby*. Such inability is present in almost all the successful overflight/takings claims. In a recent case, however, the United States was rebuffed when it argued that because the overflights did not impair a ranch's existing uses (for cattleraising and recreational hunting), a taking was precluded. The Federal Circuit explained that the "enjoyment" in the *Causby* standard refers to *future* feasible uses of the land as well as current ones.[22] To adopt the government's proposal of a categorical no-taking rule, it said, would mean the government could effectively preclude future lawful uses of the property—a particular loss to the landowner where the property, as here, is being put to only non-intensive uses.

---

[21]In a multiple-plaintiff case, the direct and immediate interference must be established for each parcel, and the finding of a taking as to one parcel does not, without more, support a finding of a taking as to the others. Persyn v. United States, 34 Fed. Cl. 187, 196 (1995), *aff'd without pub. op.*, 106 F.3d 424 (Fed. Cir. 1996), *cert. denied*, 117 S. Ct. 1697 (1997). *See, e.g.*, City of San Jose v. Superior Ct., 12 Cal. 3d 447, 525 P.2d 701 (1974) (en banc) (taking claims brought by owners of land in vicinity of airport could not be maintained as class action in light of particularized facts necessary to support each claim).

[22]Brown v. United States, 73 F.3d 1100 (Fed. Cir. 1996).

In addition, though the impact on the future use must still be substantial, substantiality can be measured, according to the Federal Circuit, with reference to only the overflown portion of the land.[23] This narrowing of focus to the affected portion can be particularly pivotal where the government overflies only a small portion of a large tract.[24]

The altitude and frequency of overflights are plainly key elements in the takings case. First, altitude. Since *Causby*, the altitude of 500 feet has emerged as a guideline in the Court of Federal Claims for segregating regular overflights that effect a *Causby* "direct and immediate interference" and hence a taking (below 500 feet) from those that do not (above 500 feet).[25] The origin of this constitutional Rubicon is the administratively fixed minimum safe altitude for flights over uncongested areas,[26] adopted by statute as the floor of "navigable airspace."[27] When the impacts are severe enough, however, the claims court has departed from the benchmark—in the leading case finding a taking on the basis of unusually frequent and noisy overflights at altitudes no lower than 600 feet.[28] Thus, the federal rule is

---

[23]*Id.* This abrogation of the "parcel as a whole" rule is a dubious development. To be sure, aircraft overflights constitute a physical invasion, and we remember that the relevant-parcel rule does not apply in such instances. But the *Causby* standard for overflight takings is not a pure physical invasion standard. Because it demands consideration of the degree of impact on the landowner, it is more akin to regulatory takings approaches, which generally do not allow segmentation of the parcel. *See* discussion of parcel as a whole doctrine in chapter 12.

[24]In *Brown*, planes overflew "at least 100 acres" of the 6,858-acre ranch.

[25]*Persyn*, 34 Fed. Cl. 187, Stephens v. United States, 11 Cl. Ct. 352 (1986); Powell v. United States, 1 Cl. Ct. 669, 673 (1983); Hero Lands Co. v. United States, 554 F. Supp. 1262 (Cl. Ct.), *aff'd without pub. op.*, 727 F.2d 1118 (Fed. Cir. 1983), *cert. denied*, 466 U.S. 972 (1984); A.J. Hodges Indus., Inc. v. United States, 355 F.2d 592, 594 (Ct. Cl. 1966); Aaron v. United States, 311 F.2d 798, 801 (Ct. Cl. 1963).

[26]14 C.F.R. § 91.119(c).

[27]49 U.S.C. § 1301(29). Use of congressionally declared navigable airspace does not guarantee freedom from liability for a taking. Griggs v. Allegheny County, 369 U.S. 84 (1962); Martin v. Port of Seattle, 64 Wash. 2d 309, 391 P.2d 540 (1964), *cert. denied*, 379 U.S. 989 (1965).

[28]Branning v. United States, 654 F.2d 88 (Ct. Cl. 1981). *Branning* has been said to confer a "very limited exception [to the navigable airspace rule] when the Air Force consciously selects and imposes an egregious burden on a plaintiff's land." *Persyn*, 34 Fed. Cl. at 195. A less restrictive view of this exception, however, is suggested in Argent v. United States, 124 F.3d 1277, 1282–83 (Fed. Cir. 1997).

best stated as a rebuttable presumption: "when overflights occur in navigable airspace, a presumption of non-taking exists which can be overcome by proof of destruction of, or substantial impairment to the property."[29] Conversely, overflights at less than 500 feet do not ensure compensability.[30]

In the state courts, use of a nuisance approach to overflight takings has lessened the importance of the federal "500-foot rule." However, the rule still seems to have some influence, as the phrase "under 500 feet" appears in claims and judicial summaries of the facts. In the leading case, holding that flights over 500 feet may nonetheless be a taking, the court explained: "Logically, it makes no difference to a plaintiff . . . whether the disturbing flights pass 501 feet or 499 feet above his land. . . . The barring of actions when the flights are above 500 feet is also difficult to reconcile with the theory that recovery should be based on nuisance concepts rather than upon trespass theory."[31] Thus, the only sure guideline in the state courts seems to be the unsurprising one that the lower the altitude of flights, the more likely a taking will be found.[32]

Moving from the altitude of the flights to their frequency, the absence of any judicial guidepost becomes total. The frequency of offending flights is often noted in the opinions, at least to say whether they are "regular," but no particular frequency has emerged from the haze to become determinative.[33]

Another overflight/takings factor, the diminution in plaintiff's property value caused by the offending overflights, is noted occasion-

---

[29]*Stephens*, 11 Cl. Ct. at 362.

[30]Brown v. United States, 73 F.3d 1100 (Fed. Cir. 1996).

[31]Thornburgh v. Port of Portland, 233 Or. 178, 376 P.2d 100, 109 (1962).

[32]For a representative sampling of cases, *see* Cochran v. City of Charlotte, 53 N.C. App. 390, 281 S.E.2d 179 (1981) (flights as low as 105 feet effect taking); Cunliffe v. County of Monroe, 63 Misc. 2d 62, 312 N.Y.S.2d 879 (1970) (flights between 250 and 1,000 feet are not a taking); and Hillsborough County Aviation Auth. v. Benitez, 200 So. 2d 194 (Fla. Dist. Ct. App. 1967) (flights between 250 and 500 feet constitute taking).

[33]*See, e.g., Persyn*, 34 Fed. Cl. 187, 199 (1995) ("no set formula" as to requisite frequency; type of aircraft must be considered). For illustrative purposes, *see* Aaron v. United States, 311 F.2d 798 (Ct. Cl. 1963) (takings line crossed when flights per day increased from 4 to 10 or 12); Petition of Ramsey, 31 Pa. Commw. 182, 375 A.2d 886 (1977) (no taking where three to five flights daily and no direct overflights); and Henthorn v. Oklahoma City, 453 P.2d 1013 (Okla. 1969) (taking where seven flights per day under 500 feet).

ally by courts. In a few states, courts have elevated this element to the status of a formal takings criterion, embellishing the *Causby* standard. (In practice, of course, this will weed out few potential claimants, since any property satisfying the tough *Causby* test surely must suffer major value loss.) No court, however, appears to have insisted that the landowner demonstrate any exact amount of value loss. Minnesota courts call for a "definite and measurable" diminution;[34] Florida, for a "substantial loss in market value;"[35] Washington, for a "measurable decline in market value."[36] Other courts have weighed in as well.[37]

An interesting issue arises in the "decreased increase" cases—that is, when the affected property has *increased* in value during the period in question, but not as much as similar properties further from the airport. Most cases hold that such a situation does not rule out a taking, on the ground that there is no basis for excluding from the property's value immediately before the date of the alleged taking that component of value attributable to appreciation.[38]

No particular noise level appears to be determinative.

Time Considerations

Airports evolve. An airfield may have been built in the '30s, expanded in the '40s, begun using jets in the '50s (bigger ones in the '60s), and later still changed its prescribed take-off and landing approaches or extended a runway. Precisely when in such a sequence of events one acquired a parcel, and when one filed the taking suit, define whether,

[34]Alevizos v. Metro. Airports Comm'n, 317 N.W.2d 352, 358 (Minn. 1982).

[35]Fields v. Sarasota-Manatee Airport Auth., 512 So. 2d 961, 965 (Fla. Dist. Ct. App. 1987), *rev. denied*, 520 So. 2d 584 (Fla. 1988).

[36]Martin v. Port of Seattle, 64 Wash. 2d 309, 391 P.2d 540, 547 (1964), *cert. denied*, 374 U.S. 989 (1965).

[37]Long v. City of Charlotte, 306 N.C. 187, 293 S.E.2d 101, 110 (1982); Kupster Realty Corp. v. State, 93 Misc. 2d 843 404 N.Y.S.2d 225 (1978).

[38]*See, e.g.,* City of Atlanta v. Starke, 192 Ga. App. 267, 384 S.E.2d 419 (1989) (increased value does not preclude taking where property would have been worth $25,000 more without overflights); State v. Doyle, 735 P.2d 733 (Alaska 1987) (taking claim lies where rate of appreciation reduced by overflights). For the minority voice, see Fields v. Sarasota-Manatee Airport Auth., 953 F.2d 1299 (11th Cir. 1992) (Florida taking standard for overflights, requiring "substantial adverse impact on market value," cannot be satisfied merely by decreased increase in value).

and for what, a landowner is compensated. The acquisition date matters because the plaintiff cannot obtain compensation on a taking theory for circumstances already present at acquisition. For one thing, those are presumably discounted in the purchase price.[39] For another, takings law limits recovery to those holding a property interest as of the date of the taking.

The filing date of the litigation matters because of federal and state statutes of limitations (*see* chapter 6), which may require the court to fix the exact date (or dates) in the airport's growth history when the complained-of taking (or takings) occurred. Any of the above changes in airport configuration or operations may define a date of taking if it is one that precipitated a substantial incremental harm to the landowner.[40] Thus, the fact that an airport already has acquired an overflight easement does not preclude a subsequent taking if later overflights are noisier, more numerous, or at lower altitudes.[41] (Of course, only those harm-aggravating events that occur within the limitations period are compensable.)

In addition to pointing to a recent change in operations, land owners may be able to get around the statute of limitations on takings claims by arguing a nuisance theory. A leading California case holds that the nuisance created by an airport is an ongoing one that daily restarts the limitations period.[42]

The Court of Federal Claims recently clarified that there is no requirement that the number of low overflights *peak* before the taking cause of action accrues.[43] And quite sensibly so, for where airport op-

[39]*See, e.g.,* Joseph v. Bond, 507 F. Supp. 453, 454 (D.D.C. 1981).

[40]The requirement of an objective change within the statute of limitations' time span apparently can be circumvented under the analysis of Provident Mut. Life Ins. Co. v. City of Atlanta, 864 F. Supp. 1274, 1283 (N.D. Ga. 1994). There, a taking challenge to airport operations was held not necessarily time barred, despite the vintage of the most recent increase in overflights, where the alleged taking was based on a characterization of the airport's operations as a continuing nuisance. Such use of nuisance law to define the date of taking blurs the objective-change rule and is an unwelcome development.

[41]*Id.* at 1283 n.3; Avery v. United States, 330 F.2d 640, 643 (Ct. Cl. 1964). In one case, the court asserted the possibility of a new taking when the number of flights returned to earlier high levels after a 15-year-long substantial decrease. Argent v. United States, 124 F.3d 1277 (Fed. Cir. 1977).

[42]Baker v. Burbank-Glendale-Pasadena Airport Auth., 39 Cal. 3d 862, 705 P.2d 866 (1985).

[43]Persyn v. United States, 34 Fed. Cl. 187 (1995), *aff'd without pub. op.,* 106 F.3d 424 (Fed. Cir. 1996), *cert. denied,* 117 S. Ct. 1697 (1997).

erations continue to grow, such a prerequisite could delay by years, even decades, the time when compensation relief could be sought. Rather, said the court, the cause of action accrues when the United States "*begins* to operate its aircraft at low elevations and with such frequency that they substantially interfere with the use and enjoyment of the land, with the intent to continue such flights indefinitely."[44] (Emphasis in original.)

Zoning Near Airports

Airport Zoning

One of the objectives of zoning is to regulate land use so as to avoid nuisance conflicts. An early illustration is the casebook classic, *Hadacheck v. Sebastian*, where an ordinance made it unlawful to operate a brickyard or kiln within certain areas of Los Angeles. The ordinance was upheld as a good-faith prohibition that promoted the health, safety, and general welfare of the public.[45] For similar purposes, in recent years many local governments have adopted airport zoning.[46] It is designed to separate the airspace at existing airports from incompatible land uses, encroaching development, and, even, tree growth. The attempts to adopt and regulate under such zoning

---

[44]*Id.* at 197.

[45]Hadacheck v. Sebastian, 239 U.S. 394 (1915).

[46]In Pennridge Dev. Enter., Inc. v. Volovnik, 154 Pa. Cmmw. 609, 624 A.2d 674 (1993), the Commonwealth Court of Pennsylvania upheld an airport zoning ordinance as applied to an existing airport use that the property owner claimed as a nonconforming use, but the court found to be a conforming use under the new conditional use regulations. For an especially interesting account, both factually and legally, of the interjurisdictional and intergovernmental disputes that can arise in a complex situation, you would do well to read the trilogy of the Westchester County, New York, airport cases, County of Westchester v. Town of Greenwich, 745 F. Supp. 951 (S.D.N.Y. 1990) (*Westchester I*); 756 F. Supp. 154 (S.D.N.Y. 1991) (*Westchester II*); and 793 F. Supp. 1195 (S.D.N.Y. 1992) (*Westchester III*), *question certified*, County of Westchester v. Commissioner of Transp., 986 F.2d 624 (2d Cir.), *certified question answered*, County of Westchester v. Town of Greenwich, 227 Conn. 495, 629 A.2d 1084, *and rev'd, remanded*, County of Westchester v. Commissioner of Transp., 9 F.3d 242 (2d Cir. 1993), *cert. denied*, 511 U.S. 1107 (1994). *See also* Powers v. Ulichny, 185 Conn. 145, 147 n.3, 440 A.2d 885 (1981) (citing six articles on airport zoning).

have led to many challenges. Such zoning can help prevent overflight takings claims, of the type discussed in the previous section, by separating the airport use from potentially impacted uses. However, the zoning itself may cause a taking.

Typical Zoning Efforts

Monroe County, Florida, created a new zoning classification throughout the county called "PA-Private Airport."[47] The purpose of the district was "to ensure the continued use of existing private airports."[48] To protect private airports from encroaching uses that could potentially object to the airport, the ordinance limited the uses of land within and adjacent to the district and established a proscription.

This case involved potentially developable property adjacent to the airport. The court analyzed the takings issue by considering whether the zoning deprived the landowner of all economically viable use of the property and interfered with investment-backed expectations. The court found no taking because economically viable alternative uses of the property existed under the PA zoning (alternatives that were potentially quite profitable).

The Court of Appeals for the Eleventh Circuit affirmed, holding that the rezoning did not deprive the property owner of the right to exclude others because the regulation "did nothing to require [the property owner] to open its property to the public for use just as the public wished."[49] As to whether the property owner had been deprived of all economically viable uses of the property, the Eleventh Circuit did not disagree with the trial judge that other potential uses included: "a private airport, . . . construction of boat slips, a beach club, or dry storage space for boats."[50] Finally, the Eleventh Circuit rejected an equitable estoppel argument, finding that the original zoning of the area alone was not sufficient to constitute a property interest.[51]

Airport zones, which are typically overlay zones limiting the types of uses and the height of structures in approach and departure areas,

[47]New Port Largo, Inc. v. Monroe County, 873 F. Supp. 633 (S.D. Fla. 1994), aff'd, 95 F.3d 1084 (11th Cir. 1996), cert. denied, 117 S. Ct. 2514 (1997).

[48]Id. at 636 n.5 (quoting Ord. No. 14-1979 (later codified as §§ 19-295 to 19-302 of the Monroe County Code)).

[49]New Port Largo, 95 F.3d at 1088.

[50]Id. at 1089.

[51]Id. at 1090.

are often used around military airfields. In 1987, the U.S. Air Force issued a study of zoning in the vicinity of McConnell Air Force Base in Sedgwick County, Kansas.[52] Based on the study findings, the metropolitan planning department recommended establishing Airport Overlay Districts (AODs) north and south of the Air Force base, aligned with the runways, 3,800 feet wide, and running several thousand feet north and south of the ends of the runways. In the AODs, land-use restrictions were applied like restrictions in other overlay zones in that they were were supplemental to the underlying restrictions.

The owners of an eighty-acre commercially zoned tract within the AOD sued, claiming a taking, because although their current uses were acceptable under the AOD regulations, they wanted to further develop their property with heavy industrial and commercial uses.

Their as-applied challenges were dismissed as not ripe (see chapter 10). However, the court did hear the facial challenge to the AODs, including evidence from the owners that the risk of an airplane crash was less than 1 in 19,547 years in one area of the AOD and less than 1 in 43,268 years in another area of the AOD.[53] The court found that the AOD land-use restrictions were facially valid, reasonable, not arbitrary and capricious, and did not effect a taking.[54]

So long as underlying reasonable and beneficial economic uses remain in airport overlay districts, it will be very difficult to demonstrate a taking, particularly in a facial attack, even though statistics may show a very low risk from the overflights. The inability to further develop a property that already has some economic use is not likely to support a successful taking claim.[55]

---

[52]Harris v. City of Wichita, 862 F. Supp. 287, 289 (D. Kan. 1994), *aff'd without op.*, 74 F.3d 1249 (10th Cir. 1996).

[53]*Id.* at 292.

[54]In another case involving an airport study, the U.S. Court of Federal Claims dismissed a taking claim, reiterating from earlier claims cases that a study of zoning near airports is merely advisory. Davis v. United States, 35 Fed. Cl. 392, 396 (Fed. Cl. 1996).

[55]This is not to say, however, that a prohibition on a particular use within an airport zoning area could not fail under substantive due process analysis, as we discuss in chapter 2. *See* Banks v. Fayette County Bd. of Airport Zoning Appeals, 313 S.W.2d 416 (Ky. 1958) (land-use restriction void for not bearing reasonable relationship to purpose of eliminating airport hazards). *See also* Brown v. United States, 73 F.3d 1100 (Fed. Cir. 1996) (property owners' affidavits sufficient to raise issue whether aircraft overflights constitute taking; cause remanded).

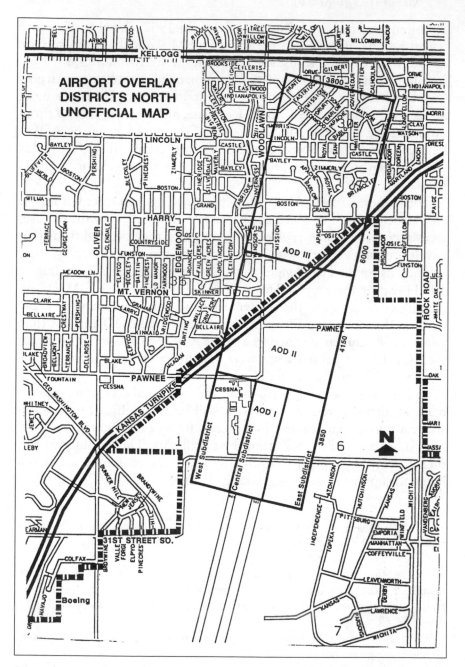

Map of airport overlay districts (AOD II and AOD III) at issue in *Harris v. City of Wichita*.

Height Restrictions

Most of the early airport zoning ordinances dealt only with the obvious—restricting the height of structures to keep airplanes from flying into them. The two questions in these cases are whether the height restrictions are just a backdoor (inverse condemnation) method of acquiring an avigation easement without paying for it and whether the height restrictions leave any reasonable, beneficial economic use. A valid claim for inverse condemnation can be based on a height restriction around an airport, especially if the restriction can be shown to reduce the fair market value of the property.[56]

Sometimes the taking claim arising out of the designation of an airport zone is inextricably tied to a taking claim based on overflights.[57] Additionally, the designation of a zone around an airport to create a so-called "clear zone" may later become the basis for an eminent domain action. This is a logical approach to addressing the just compensation issue—it cannot be inverse condemnation if it is direct condemnation. For example, in the mid-1960s, the City of West Memphis, Arkansas, enacted an ordinance to establish a clear zone over properties adjacent to the airport. Property owners sued claiming an inverse condemnation and the city then filed a counterclaim to condemn avigational easements and to request that compensation be determined by a jury.[58] The jury awarded relatively modest damages of $2,500 to each of the owners.

Nonetheless, there are real restrictions on the government in exercising its eminent domain power, including the requirement that it be shown that the property is being taken for a public use or purpose. Warren County, Kentucky, attempted to take about 25 acres of a 100-acre cattle ranch, for a "public airport safety zone and other public

---

[56]Sneed v. County of Riverside, 218 Cal. App. 2d 205, 32 Cal. Rptr. 318 (1963) (property owner's taking claim valid; ordinance in effect "takes" avigation easement). *But see* Fitzgarrald v. City of Iowa City, 492 N.W. 2d 659 (Iowa 1992) (city may adopt zoning ordinance establishing height and use restrictions around airport, diminishing market value of nearby properties, without causing a taking), *cert. denied*, 508 U.S. 911 (1993).

[57]Beachy v. Board of Aviation Comm'rs of the City of Kokomo, Ind., 699 F. Supp. 742 (S.D. Ind. 1988).

[58]Minkowitz v. City of West Memphis, 241 Ark. 207, 406 S.W.2d 887 (1966); Highland Realty, Inc. v. Indianapolis Airport Auth., 182 Ind. App. 439, 395 N.E.2d 1259 (1979) (property condemned for airport clear zone; statutes so authorize).

purposes. . . ."[59] Prior to the taking, the owner said he would be willing to accept land in exchange for the area the county needed, but those negotiations broke down. After the legislative body voted to condemn the property, the owner offered to restrict the land to agricultural use and to give the airport a noise easement and/or an easement prohibiting trees, residential development, and the erection of any structures up to the building restriction line at the airport. The county would not agree and went ahead with the condemnation.

The trial court dismissed the petition for condemnation and the appellate court affirmed on the ground that a fee-simple acquisition was not necessary for the intended public purpose.[60] The decision suggests that condemnation conducted together with or independent of airport zoning should be limited to the acquisition of the least interest necessary to protect the airport and its operations as well as the surrounding users of land.

There is indeed overlap between the overflight physical-invasion claim cases and the regulatory takings cases where properties near airports are affected by both the overflights and regulatory restrictions. Iowa City and Johnson County, Iowa, adopted an "Approach Overlay Zone" and "Clear Overlay Zone" in areas adjacent to the Iowa City Airport.[61] Like other typical approach zones, this one includes a wedge-shaped area beginning 200 feet from the end of the runway that defines the maximum height of structures. The Iowa City Approach Overlay Zone used a 34 to 1 slope. An extension of one of the runways would cause a portion of the approach slope to cut through the middle of a private residence, which would be allowed to remain as a nonconforming use.

The Clear Overlay Zone prohibited all but lowest-density uses in buildings and further prohibited twelve different categories of uses, from campgrounds to sanitary landfills to motels to theaters. The Supreme Court of Iowa affirmed the trial court's decision that there was no physical-invasion taking because there was no measurable decrease in market value from the overflights. The court also affirmed that though there may be a reduction in value from the airport zoning restrictions, the deprivation was not so severe as to be a taking under Iowa law.[62]

[59]City of Bowling Green, Ky. v. Cooksey, 858 S.W.2d 190 (Ky. Ct. App. 1992).
[60]Id. at 193.
[61]Fitzgarrald, 492 N.W.2d at 661–62.
[62]Id. at 666.

A typical airport zoning ordinance and taking by overregulation is described in *Peacock v. County of Sacramento*.[63] There, Sacramento County adopted an ordinance to maintain clear airspace for the existing runway. The ordinance prohibited any structure or vegetation with a height above zero feet at a distance of up to 200 feet from either end of the runway and then a clear airspace with a slope of 20 to 1 from that point out for the next 10,000 feet. For example, 400 feet into this wedge-shaped airspace, no structure or vegetation could grow higher than 20 feet (400 divided by the 20 to 1 slope equals 20).[64] The trial court found and the appellate court agreed that the airport zoning denied the property owners "any practical or beneficial use of their affected property."[65]

Height restrictions have been routinely upheld in the courts, so long as there is an underlying use. The height restrictions may even be upheld where they are more restrictive and preserve larger areas of airspace than the Federal Aviation Administration (FAA) requires.[66]

Use Restrictions

Airport zoning typically includes both height restrictions and use restrictions, so it is sometimes difficult to separate one from the other in a taking claim. For example, the City of Caldwell, Idaho, adopted an airport ordinance restricting both the elevation of structures within certain areas around the local airport runway-approach areas and limiting uses within those areas. In one area the only permitted use was agriculture. In a decision that for its time, over thirty years ago, provided a useful summary of the overflight and zoning cases, the Supreme Court of Idaho found that the ordinance caused a taking of property. In doing so, the court quoted from one of the early and often-cited airport zoning cases:

[63]271 Cal. App. 2d 845, 77 Cal. Rptr. 391 (1969).

[64]*Id.* at 848.

[65]*Id.* at 862.

[66]La Salle Nat'l Bank v. County of Cook, 34 Ill. App. 3d 264, 340 N.E.2d 79 (1975) (preemption not an issue because goals of federal, local governments differ). For a discussion of the issue of federal preemption of state law in the context of airport noise, *see* City of Atlanta v. Watson, 267 Ga. 185, 475 S.E.2d 896 (Ga. 1996) (federal Aviation Safety Noise Abatement Act of 1979 preempted state law in suit seeking redress for airport noise).

> The City may not under the guise of an ordinance acquire . . .
> rights in private property which it may only acquire by . . . pur-
> chase or by the exercise of its power of eminent . . . domain.[67]

Similarly, the City of Faribault, Minnesota, created two zones in the vicinity of the airport.[68] The most restrictive zone closest to the airport prohibited above-ground structural uses. The second zone limited population density to fifteen persons per acre with a minimum lot size of three acres. The court found the second zone designation invalid as it left owners with no reasonable use of their property. The city was given the choice of repealing the ordinance or paying compensation.[69] The court also explained that an injunction was the appropriate remedy, but if the injunction proved inadequate, damages might be available. By contrast other court decisions have upheld residential land-use restrictions in the vicinity of airports as a reasonable prohibition on the grounds that the level of aircraft noise would make residential use unbearable. Such limitations are more defensible if they are part of a general or comprehensive plan for the city or the airport area.[70]

In San Antonio, Texas, thirty-four neighbors of Kelly Air Force Base brought an action claiming an avigation easement by physical taking from overflights of aircraft using the base as noted earlier in this chapter.[71] The residents' properties were located within Accident Potential Zones (APZ1 and APZ2) that extended off the end of the airport runways. These accident zones did not themselves restrict development, but subsequent action by the City of San Antonio resulted

[67]Roark v. City of Coldwell, 87 Idaho 557, 565, 394 P.2d 641 (1964) (citing Yara Eng'g v. City of Newark, 132 N.J.L. 370, 40 A.2d 559 (1945). *See also* Provident Mut. Life Ins. Co. v. City of Atlanta, 864 F. Supp. 1274 (N.D. Ga 1994) (commercial property exposed to direct path of landing and departing aircraft denied participation in airport program to purchase properties from exposed residents; ordinance invalid as taking of property without just compensation; Fifth Amendment taking claim not ripe but taking-by-nuisance claim remanded), *summ. j. granted, mot. granted*, 938 F. Supp 829 (N.D. Ga. 1995) (nuisance claim barred by statute of limitations; taking-by-nuisance claim similarly barred).

[68]McShane v. the City of Faribault, 292 N.W.2d 253 (Minn. 1980).

[69]*Id.* at 259.

[70]Eck v. the City of Bismarck, 302 N.W.2d 739 (N.D. 1981) (zoning ordinance valid; master plan included plans for new runway).

[71]Persyn v. United States, 34 Fed. Cl. 187 (1995).

in a restrictive zoning ordinance. The property owners contended that the APZs constituted a deliberate campaign to induce fear among prospective purchasers. In addition, they argued that they were exposed to noise, increased potential for accidents and low-level overflights, resulting in a decreased market value for their properties. The owners lost because the court said there can be no taking based on flights in navigable airspace.[72] Airspace above 1,000 feet of the highest obstacle within a horizontal radius of 2,000 feet of an aircraft in the congested areas of cities, towns, or villages, and 500 feet above the surface in uncongested areas (except over open water or sparsely populated areas) is considered navigable, or public airspace.[73] The plaintiffs could not show that the flights occurred below 500 feet over each property.[74] The effective application of airport zoning can reduce these kinds of potential conflicts.

Noise is one of the most significant airport nuisances. An effective land-use plan for the area around an airport will significantly alleviate existing and potential problems. Today, state and federal agencies including the FAA have encouraged effective land-use planning near airports.[75] Coordinated land-use planning, consistency among land-use plans and use restrictions, and the linkage to valid goals and objectives enhance reasonableness and consequently increase the likelihood that such restrictions will be upheld by the courts. A consistent continuing planning effort will go a long way in reducing the potential for land-use conflicts arising from overflights near airports—and most important for all concerned—reduce the number of takings claims. Airport zoning is an integral part of this planning.

---

[72]See also Lacy v. United States, 219 Ct. Cl. 551, 553, 595 F.2d 614, 615 (1979).

[73]Navigable airspace is defined in 14 C.F.R. § 1.1 The definition refers to the Minimum Safe Altitudes section of the same title, § 91.119.

[74]See Hoyle v. City of Charlotte, 276 N.C. 292, 172 S.E.2d 1 (1970) (residence in industrial zone exposed to more overflights at lower attitudes, 90 feet to 300 feet, as a result of extended runways and larger aircraft; new trial ordered); Cochran v. City of Charlotte, 53 N.C. App. 390, 406, 281 S.E.2d 179 (1981) (taking found based on (1) frequency of flights, (2) altitude, (3) type of aircraft, and (4) duration of exposure), petition denied, 304 N.C. 725, 288 S.E.2d 380 (1982).

[75]Scott Dvorak, The Trouble with Airports, ZONING NEWS, May 1996, at 2.

Chapter 22

Contracts and Development Agreements

Land development depends on contracts of many types. Chief among them is the contract to buy or develop a property.[1] Development contracts have evolved to include not only agreements between private parties, but also those between private developers and government regulators.

Naturally, when something goes awry in the development process, allegations of takings arise. This is an enormous, complex, and exceedingly untidy area of the law made worse by the uncomfortable interplay of the Contracts Clause[2] with the Takings Clause. The Contract Clause says, in essence, that no state shall pass any law impairing the obligation of contracts.

Contract rights deserve protection because they promote the efficient allocation of resources and the growth of commerce.[3] Where a regulation impairs a contract right, it may in narrow circumstances also constitute a taking under the Fifth Amendment Takings Clause.[4]

In 1934, the U.S. Supreme Court rejected a Contracts Clause challenge to state regulation that allegedly interfered with a contract.[5] The

[1]*See, e.g.,* Kaiser Dev. Co. v. City & County of Honolulu, 649 F. Supp. 926 (D. Haw. 1986) (agreement between property owner and developer did not create protectable interest in property being developed), *aff'd*, 898 F.2d 112 (9th Cir.), *cert. denied*, 499 U.S. 947, 954 (1991).

[2]U.S. Const. art. I, § 10, cl. 1.

[3]For a comprehensive view of the contract clause, see Leo Clarke, *The Contract Clause: A Basis for Limited Judicial Review of State and Economic Regulation*, 39 U. MIAMI L. REV. 183 (1985).

[4]*Id.* at 186.

[5]Home Bldg. & Loan Ass'n v. Blaisdell, 290 U.S. 398 (1934).

Court found an implied reservation of the police power in all contracts. In other words, valid police power regulation, subject only to minimal review under the rational relationship test, became an exception that swallowed the rule.[6] But while the exception is onerous, it is not insurmountable.[7] There have been some successful Contracts Clause cases. Importantly, in a 1977 decision, the U.S. Supreme Court held that a stricter standard should be used when analyzing state laws affecting contracts between private parties and the state itself.[8]

Generally, the elements of a successful Contracts Clause claim include a valid contract, substantial impairment of it, public regulation that does not justify impairment of the contract,[9] and reason to assume that the contract might be impaired by government action.[10]

What is the inherent nature of the interest? Is it merely a contract right, such as the right to purchase, or is it the underlying interest in the property itself?

The federal government enacted the Redwood Park Expansion Act, then condemned timber-producing land, preventing the owners from performing a contract to provide timber to a sawmill.[11] The Court of Appeals for the Ninth Circuit held that the sawmill only had a "prospective business opportunity"—no property interest under the Fifth Amendment—thus no taking.

The same result—no property interest, no taking—can be found both where apartment management contracts were canceled upon

---

[6]Keystone Bituminous Coal Ass'n v. DeBenedictis, 480 U.S. 470 (1987), is a good example of the effect of this exception. *Keystone* is discussed more fully in chapter 25.

[7]*See, e.g.*, Allied Structural Steel v. Spannaus, 438 U.S. 234, 244 (1978) (state pension law as applied to company caused severe impacts and violated Contracts Clause).

[8]United States Trust Co. v. New Jersey, 431 U.S. 1 (1977).

[9]Generally, the application of a regulatory statute within the government's powers may not be defeated by private contract. Concrete Pipe & Prods. of Cal., Inc. v. Construction Laborers Pension Trust for S. Cal., 508 U.S. 602, 641–47 (1993).

[10]If the government action does not impair the contract at all, the claim fails from the beginning. Urbatec v. City of Whittier, 1995 U.S. App. LEXIS 22463 (9th Cir. 1995).

[11]PVM Redwood Co. v. United States, 686 F.2d 1327 (9th Cir. 1982), *cert. denied*, 459 U.S. 1106 (1983).

government condemnation of buildings[12] and when a pipeline company that had recovered only 73 percent of its irrevocable contract quota lost its contract and its investment in the pipe because the land was appropriated by the government.[13]

Contract zoning—a deal between the government and developers—has historically been disfavored in the law and among planners on several grounds.[14] Such zoning raises even more difficult questions of what property interest, if any, may be at issue.[15] An early case avoided considering the validity of such deals with a simple pronouncement: A regulation offering developers a density bonus in return for a "gift" of developable land to the local government is not contract zoning.[16] Then with the contract zoning issue conveniently eliminated, the court held that the developer who had conveyed land to the city had "vested contractual rights" in the increased density and that the city was equitably estopped from downzoning the property proposed for a higher-density use.

The generic term "contract zoning" covers many types of local approvals and processes, including "conditional zoning" that often

[12]Hooten v. United States, 405 F.2d 1167 (5th Cir. 1969); 767 Third Ave. Assocs. v. U.S., 48 F.3d 1575, 1581–83 (Fed. Cir. 1995) (no taking of lease interest when government ordered all Federal Republic of Yugoslavia property interests in U.S. "blocked"); Omnia Commercial Co. v. United States, 261 U.S. 502 (1923).

[13]United States v. 677.50 Acres of Land, 420 F.2d 1136 (10th Cir.), cert. denied, 398 U.S. 928 (1970).

[14]See Hartnett v. Austin, 93 So. 2d 86, 89 (Fla. 1956) ("municipality cannot contract away the exercise of its police powers"); Ford Leasing Dev. Co. v. Board of County Comm'rs, 528 P.2d 237, 240 (1974) (contract zoning can be invalid as "ultra vires"—beyond statutory powers). But see Stephens v. City of Vista, 994 F.2d 650, 656 (9th Cir.) (government may contract for specific development "without surrendering control of its land use power"), amended on other grounds, reh'g denied, reported in full, 1993 U.S. App. LEXIS 19877 (9th Cir. May 20, 1993).

For a comprehensive treatment of this subject, see Judith W. Wegner, Moving Toward the Bargaining Table: Contract Zoning, Development Agreements, and the Theoretical Foundations of Government Land Use Deals, 65 North Carolina L. Rev. 957 (1987). An intriguing argument for applying takings law to a public contract case is found in Michael L. Zigler, Takings Law and the Contract Clause: A Takings Law Approach to Legislative Modifications of Public Contracts, 36 Stanford L. Rev. 1447, 1484 (1984).

[15]Bruce M. Kramer, Contract Zoning—Old Myths and New Realities, 34 Land Use L. & Zoning Dig. No. 8, at 4 (1982).

[16]Baltimore v. Crane, 352 A.2d 786, 791-92 (Md. 1976).

requires exactions from the developer.[17] For example, what happens if a developer, hoping to build 650 residential units and almost 3 million square feet of other uses on 550 acres, enters into a complex rezoning agreement with the county? The developer agrees to provide many exactions: dedicating open space and buffers; preserving trees; screening its property from neighbors; and providing storm water drains, a trail system, and a community swimming pool. The developer also conveys 16.05 acres to the county for road construction. But, a citizens coalition opposes the development in its location adjacent to the Manassas Battlefield Park and lobbies Congress. It takes the development site by eminent domain (private property taken for public use by state, municipalities, or authorized entities) and incurs an obligation to pay the developer.[18]

Does the county have a compensable property interest in the contract with the developer for all the exactions proposed upon rezoning, and are the 16.05 acres previously given and now taken?

First, the agreement did not convey any property to the county, but only promoted regulation of land development through the police power. Thus, the agreement is not compensable. As for the 16.05 acres conveyed in fee simple for future roads, it was an unencumbered fee-simple grant; the county has a compensable interest. The limited-purpose intent of the conveyance doesn't matter.

Contract zoning will seem tame after comparing it to an all-encompassing development agreement between a government/landowner and a developer.[19] If such agreements are property under the Takings Clause, they may materially affect vesting. Vesting protects a developer from the imposition of more restrictive regulation. In one

---

[17]*But see* Delucchi v. County of Santa Cruz, 179 Cal. App. 3d 814, 225 Cal. Rptr. 43 (county permitted to reduce residential density despite contrary agreement), *cert. denied, appeal dismissed*, 479 U.S. 803 (1986). *Cf.* O'Dell v. Board of City Comm'rs, 910 S.W.2d 436, 437 (Tenn. Ct. App. 1995) (no contract zoning in consent order) *with* Warner Co. v. Sutton, 274 N.J. Super. 464, 644 A.2d 656, 666 (App. Div. 1994) (consent order substantially altering zoning must go through regular zoning amendment process); Prock v. Town of Danville, 655 N.E.2d 553 (Ind. Ct. App. 1995).

[18]This subject is covered in chapter 32.

[19]Board of Supervisors of Prince William County v. United States, 48 F.3d 520 (Fed. Cir. 1995), *cert. denied*, 516 U.S. 812 (1995). This case is of special interest. It is from an influential court, it is recent, it discusses exactions and their history, it has a wonderful analysis of what "property" is and it is only eight pages long.

case, a court rejected a developer's equal protection claim that it was unreasonable to protect developers who had development agreements, but not those without such agreements, especially if the "withouts" had invested heavily in infrastructure improvements.[20]

A property owner who cannot win under either the Takings Clause or Contracts Clause may still have a cause of action in common-law breach of contract.[21] And that remedy may be enough to cut off a property rights claim brought under section 1983 (a federal remedies statute described in chapter 7).[22] A development agreement with a city may further limit a developer to a court order that a public official, entity, or lower court perform a specified duty.[23] Sometimes there may be no remedy at all. Consider a developer who enters into a memorandum of understanding intended to produce a development agreement, but no agreement results. Such a claim is not ripe for decision.[24]

In what may be considered a typical case, the owners of land in Michigan entered into a conditional purchase and sale agreement

[20]A good overview of this vast subject is David L. Callies, *Developers' Agreements and Planning Gain,* 17 Urban Lawyer 599 (1985), which discusses the statutory basis for such agreements.

A LEXIS search of the term "development agreement" in the ALLCDE files of both the STATES and CODES libraries produced 499 "hits" (July 3, 1997). Selected statutes are listed by state from the citations list: Alaska Stat. § 38.05.027; Ariz. Rev. Stat. § 9-500.05; Cal. Gov't. Code §§ 65460.10, & 65864–69.5; Fla. Stat. chs. 161.0531, 163.3227–3229, & 163.3235–.3241; Haw. Rev. Stat. §§ 46-121 to -132; Idaho Code § 67-6511A.

Also, La. Rev. Stat. §§ 33:4780.21 to -.33; N.D. Cent. Code § 48-02.1-03 to -09; Or. Rev. Stat. §§ 94.504–.528; S.C. Code Ann. §§ 6-31-10 to -160; Tenn. Code. Ann. § 4-17-302; Wash. Rev. Code §§ 36.70B.170 to -210. *See also* Del Oro Hills v. City of Oceanside, 31 Cal. App. 4th 1060, 1081–82, 37 Cal. Rptr. 2d 677, *review denied,* 1995 CA Sup. Ct. Minutes 04 19, *cert. denied,* 516 U.S. 823 (1995). Other states also have statutes addressing development agreements: Colo. Rev. Stats. §§ 24-68-102, 24-68-104; Md. Ann. Code Art. 28 § 7-121, Md. Ann. Code Art. 66B § 13.01; Minn. Stats. 462.358 sub. 3c; Nev. Rev. Stat. Annot. § 278.0201; and N.J. Stats. 40.55D-45.2.

[21]*DeLucchi,* 179 Cal. App. 3d 814, 820–24.

[22]LaSociete Generale Immobiliere v. Minneapolis Community Dev. Agency, 44 F.3d 629, 640–41 (8th Cir. 1994), *cert. denied,* 516 U.S. 810 (1995).

[23]Thrust IV Inc. v. Styles, 1995 U.S. Dist. LEXIS 5634, at 5 (N.D. Calif. Apr. 27, 1995).

[24]Lodestar Co. v. County of Mono, 946 F.2d 898 (9th Cir. 1991). The Ninth Circuit's decision is not to be published and may not be cited by 9th Cir. courts except as provided by Ninth Cir. Rule 36-3. Ripeness is discussed in chapter 5.

under which the buyer's duties included obtaining approval for a lot division.[25] The township denied the lot division; the prospective purchaser appealed, but lost. The sellers elected to terminate the agreement. Predictably, the court held that the prospective purchaser had no property interest in the development contract after failure to win approval of the lot split.

Does the owner of property proposed for development as a shopping center and subject to a city-developer development agreement have a taking claim when the city fails to fulfill the agreement and condemn the property? No, because the property owner's right to sell or use the property was never hindered.[26]

Where do we find ourselves at the end of this discussion? The law in this area gives little protection to developers. Assuming that will not appreciably change, parties to these contracts must bargain for their own protection. In the government-developer development agreement, remedies and damages, including liquidated damages, should be specified, along with alternative dispute resolution. Developers of property owned by someone else should avoid the usual conditional purchase and sale agreement or option and instead structure the deals with interest sufficient to constitute a property interest. Developers might close in escrow or close on a fractional interest before proceeding with approvals. In some states this or even less might be enough, such as binding language in the agreement. The key: Ask the "Is it property" question at the very beginning.[27]

This is perhaps one of those Takings Clause issues that could be addressed through federal and state legislation. Such legislation need not redefine takings, but should ensure access to a forum where troubling cases of large losses and wipeouts could be tried.

The complex modern processes of land development and preservation can slice and dice fee-simple interests in real property into so many parts as to defy categorization. And related to these interests in land are many other rights, some of which are, and some of which are not, crowned with the title of being no less than property protected by the Takings Clause. Confusion within and between the cases exists. The important rule of precedent imposes its powerful inertia on this area of law. Movement seems difficult, if not impossible, yet problems arising from contemporary land development must be addressed.

[25]G.M. Eng'rs & Assocs., Inc. v. West Bloomfield Township, 922 F.2d 328 (6th Cir. 1990).

[26]Armour & Co., Inc. v. Inver Grove Heights, 2 F.3d 276 (8th Cir. 1993).

[27]This is exactly the point in Pro-Eco, Inc. v. Board of Comm'rs of Jay County, Ind., 57 F.3d 505 (7th Cir. 1995), *cert. denied*, 516 U.S. 1028 (1995).

Part V

Environmental Programs Raising Takings Issues

Chapter 23

Wetlands

At the dawn of this century, our nation's highest court branded wetlands "the cause of malarial and malignant features" and opined that "the police power is never more legitimately exercised than in removing such nuisances."[1] Today, the received wisdom is diametrically opposite. Wetlands are ecologically revered, and the fact that 50 percent of the wetlands in the contiguous 48 states have been lost since the nation was founded is cited as a cause for great alarm.[2] The lead federal wetlands agency, the U.S. Army Corps of Engineers, has had to virtually reinvent its institutional culture, installing environmental protection alongside its traditional focus on safeguarding navigation.[3] Both the Bush and Clinton Administrations have embraced a policy of "no net loss" of wetlands, though a coherent implementation of that policy has yet to be realized.

In our heightened sensitivity to wetlands, however, lies a problem. Wetlands are predominantly in private hands, and many have little

---

[1]Leovy v. United States, 177 U.S. 621, 636 (1900).

[2]*See, e.g.,* Peter Steinhart, *No Net Loss,* AUDUBON, July 1990, at 18 (90 percent of wetlands in California and Connecticut are gone; 95percent of those in Iowa).

[3]Reacting to growing national concern for the environment, the Corps in 1968 invented a "public interest review" process for passing upon wetlands permit applications. Besides navigation, the Corps would consider such factors as fish and wildlife, conservation, aesthetics, and ecology. Public interest review received its first judicial test in Zabel v. Tabb, 430 F.2d 199 (5th Cir. 1970), *cert. denied,* 401 U.S. 910 (1971), which upheld a Corps permit denial for fish and wildlife reasons, not reasons related to navigation.

economic utility unless filled, drained, or dredged.[4] As a result, federal, state, and local efforts to block destruction of private wetlands by regulatory fiat have been for decades a prime generator of takings litigation[5]—and more recently a target of property rights activists.

The functions of wetlands are well understood today; courts often recite them at the outset of wetlands/takings cases.[6] Wetlands, we are told, are among the most biologically productive of ecosystems. They provide habitat for wildlife, both resident and migratory, and in particular may act as spawning grounds for ocean-dwelling species. Wetlands serve as aquifer recharge areas (through increased water "residence time"), provide filtration that maintains water quality, and attenuate the severity of floods by acting as a buffer. No doubt as well, the new-found scenic and open-space benefits of wetlands have played a role in the drive to preserve them.

The legislative response to the destruction of privately owned wetlands has taken several forms.[7] Many states have adopted laws specifically directed at wetlands conservation; others embed wetlands preservation in broad environmental laws. The latter is the federal approach—through a permit program under section 404 of the Clean

---

[4]Recognizing the developmental restraints that federal wetlands regulation imposed on a particular private wetland, a state tax court reassessed it from $19,978,100 to $976,500. Bergen County Assocs. v. Borough of E. Rutherford, 12 N.J. Tax 399 (1992).

[5]There were about 400 reported wetlands regulatory cases from 1960 to 1990, of which about one half raised a taking issue. Jon Kusler & Erik J. Meyer, *Takings: Is the Claims Court All Wet?*, NATIONAL WETLANDS NEWSLETTER (Envtl. L. Inst.), Nov./Dec. 1990, at 6. There are more takings challenges to federal regulatory actions under the Clean Water Act § 404 (wetlands protection) program than to any other federal environmental program. *See generally* U.S. GENERAL ACCOUNTING OFFICE, CLEAN WATER ACT: PRIVATE PROPERTY TAKINGS CLAIMS AS A RESULT OF THE SECTION 404 PROGRAM (RCED-93-176FS 1993); Richard C. Ausness, *Regulatory Takings and Wetland Protection in the Post-Lucas Era*, 30 LAND & WATER L. REV. 349 (1995).

[6]*See especially* Vatalaro v. DER, 601 So. 2d 1223, 1125–27 (Fla. Dist. Ct. App. 1992); Moskow v. Commissioner, 384 Mass. 530, 427 N.E.2d 753 (1981). *See generally* COUNCIL ON ENVIRONMENTAL QUALITY, OUR NATION'S WETLANDS: AN INTERAGENCY TASK FORCE REPORT (1978).

[7]*See generally* MARK S. DENNISON & JAMES F. BERRY, WETLANDS: GUIDE TO SCIENCE, LAW AND TECHNOLOGY (1993). For an up-to-date survey of state wetlands laws, see WILLIAM L. WANT, LAW OF WETLANDS REGULATION (looseleaf service).

Water Act governing the discharge of "dredged and fill material" into covered wetlands.[8] In addition, most states with wetlands laws, and to a limited extent the federal government, authorize subordinate governments to implement the program when minimum standards are met. Finally, governments use various nonregulatory approaches, in the form of both sticks and carrots—such as the federal "swamp-buster" program for agricultural wetlands.[9]

As one would expect, only the regulatory approaches to wetlands preservation have sparked takings litigation.[10] For this reason, and perhaps to head off legislative efforts to cut back substantially on regulatory control of wetlands, the Army Corps of Engineers has sought to lessen the impact of wetlands regulations on the private property owner.[11] Other innovative approaches, both regulatory and nonregulatory, abound in the states.[12]

Due to the large volume of wetlands/takings cases, this chapter does not explore related case law arising from regulation of floodplains, coastal zones, and beach erosion and access.

[8]33 U.S.C. § 1344. *See generally* ENVIRONMENTAL LAW PRACTICE GUIDE ch. 19 (Michael B. Gerrard ed., 1992). Prior to the enactment of section 404 in the Federal Water Pollution Control Act of 1972 (renamed Clean Water Act in 1977), federal regulation of the disposal of dredged and fill material was done under section 10 of the Rivers and Harbors Act of 1899 (RHA), 33 U.S.C. § 403. RHA section 10 remains on the books, but has been largely superseded by the 404 program. The 1972 Act left responsibility for implementing RHA section 10 with the Corps of Engineers, but called for shared responsibility between the Corps and the Environmental Protection Agency over the 404 program.

[9]16 U.S.C. § 3821. The swampbuster program is further discussed in chapter 32.

[10]Nonregulatory government actions have provoked numerous takings claims in the context of federal water improvement projects, when physical invasions have been imposed on private landowners. *See, e.g.*, Applegate v. United States, 35 Fed. Cl. 406 (1996) (harbor project allegedly causing erosion of beachfront properties); Turner v. United States, 23 Cl. Ct. 447 (1991) (stream channelization project found to cause flooding, sediment deposit on downstream private land).

[11]*See, e.g.*, Issuance of Nationwide Permit for Single-Family Housing, 60 Fed. Reg. 38,650 (1995) (allowing greatly expedited approval where landowner seeks to fill in up to one-half acre of wetland related to construction or expansion of single-family home).

[12]Wetlands mitigation banking is a key initiative.

The Historic Pendulum

In the many decades since the first wetlands/takings cases, one can discern three more or less distinct eras—major swings in judicial perception of the public benefits and private burdens involved. The era a case falls in often goes a long way to explaining its outcome.

The first era, in the 1960s and early 1970s, saw several state courts respond sympathetically to the aggrieved private wetlands owner, probably because the public goals of the new wetlands statutes were contrary to prevailing attitudes about such ecosystems. Typical of the period is *Morris County Land Improvement Co. v. Township of Parsippany-Troy Hills*,[13] addressing a township zoning ordinance. The court found "[o]f the highest legal significance" that the prime object of the zoning was to retain plaintiff's land substantially in its natural state—that is, in the court's view, to secure a public benefit rather than prevent a harm. Hence, it was likely compensable.[14]

The second era, comprising the remainder of the 1970s and 1980s, saw a dramatic judicial pendulum swing from suspicion to acceptance of wetlands regulation. As if to justify the swing, many cases from early in this period contain extended discussion of the public interest promoted by wetlands. Few cases during this period find takings, even though an increasing number of states were putting wetland protection regimes into place. *Just v. Marinette County*, an environmentalist favorite from Wisconsin, probably represents the high water mark of judicial sensitivity to wetlands.[15] Other states particularly well represented in the case law of this period are Connecticut, Florida, Massachusetts, Michigan, New Hampshire, and New York.[16] These courts appeared to accept the special status of

[13]40 N.J. 539, 193 A.2d 232 (1963).

[14]Other takings holdings in favor of wetland owners during this period include Commissioner of Natural Resources v. S. Volpe & Co., 349 Mass. 104, 206 N.E.2d 666 (1965) (on remand, lower court found taking); State v. Johnson, 265 A.2d 711 (Me. 1970); and Bartlett v. Town of Old Lyme, 161 Conn. 24, 282 A.2d 907 (1971).

[15]56 Wis. 2d 7, 201 N.W.2d 761 (1972).

[16]The parade of cases from New Hampshire, beginning in 1975, is particularly long. All of them find no taking. Highlights include the earliest case, Sibson v. State, 115 N.H. 124, 336 A.2d 239 (1975), followed by Claridge v. New Hampshire Wetlands Bd., 125 N.H. 745, 485 A.2d 287 (1984); New Hampshire Wetlands Bd. v. Marshall, 127 N.H. 240, 500 A.2d 685 (1985), and Rowe v. Town of North Hampton, 131 N.H. 424, 553 A.2d 1331 (1989).

Limestone quarrying (top) and processing (bottom) in Dade County, Florida. Denial of a permit to quarry limestone at another Dade County site was at issue in *Florida Rock Industries, Inc. v. United States.*

Between a Rock and a Harbor

In 1956 a developer bought a 250-acre, mostly wetlands lot on a New Jersey barrier island, in the hope of subdividing it. In 1972 a mining company purchased 1,560 acres of wetlands west of Miami, Florida, intending to quarry limestone. Thus began two of the most often dissected, and certainly longest running, ordeals in takings law.

For the developer, the takings story began in the 1970s. By then, the developer had filled in and constructed hundreds of homes on 199 acres of its lot. Plans to develop the remaining 51 acres, however, ran into a snag. The state initially refused a wetlands permit, which compelled the U.S. Army Corps of Engineers to deny the federal permit. (The Clean Water Act and Coastal Zone Management Act prohibit issuance of federal wetlands permits until specified state permits have been issued.) Eventually the state agreed to allow development on 12.5 of the 51 acres, with the developer promising to convey to the state a conservation easement on the remaining 38.5 acres. This time, the Corps did not follow the state's lead, denying the federal permit again in 1982. After the developer's attack on the validity of the Corps' denial was spurned by a federal district court, it filed a taking claim.

In the ensuing years, the case of *Loveladies Harbor, Inc.* v. *United States* generated several court decisions and broke new ground in takings law. It is best known for its narrow definition of the "parcel as a whole," under which the court found a 99 percent reduction in property value.

---

wetlands and often stretched to find noncompensable even the strictest of regulations.

For the United States as well, the 1970s and at least the early 1980s were a time of government friendly rulings.[17] Court decisions cited the Supreme Court's tendency to uphold land-use restrictions if soundly based on public interest, even where landowners suffer precipitous value loss. Also, the challenged permit denials were held not to deny all reasonable uses of the landowner's property *as a whole—* either because the property included uplands not affected by the permit denial, or because a permit had been granted for the filling in of some, even if not all, of the wetlands on the parcel.

[17]The leading decisions are Deltona Corp. v. United States, 657 F.2d 1184 (Ct. Cl. 1981), *cert. denied*, 455 U.S. 1017 (1982), and Jentgen v. United States, 657 F.2d 1210 (Ct. Cl. 1981), *cert. denied*, 455 U.S. 1017 (1982).

But it also spoke to the meaning of *Lucas*, the burdens of proof and going forward in a regulatory taking case, claims court jurisdiction, and so on. In 1994 the Federal Circuit agreed with the trial court that a taking had occurred. The next year, the case was settled and the developer—or rather, a charitable trust that had been set up when the developer died—received almost $8 million for the 51 undeveloped acres. Much of the $8 million reflected accumulated interest.

Turn now to the mining company. In 1978 Florida Rock Industries, Inc. applied for a Corps wetlands permit to allow limestone quarrying on 98 of its 1,560 acres (the Corps would not consider a broader application). In 1980 the permit was denied—chiefly, in the trial court's view, because of the threatened loss of valuable wetlands. The mining company filed a taking action.

Florida Rock Industries, Inc. v. United States has been a judicial yo-yo. Since the first trial court decision in 1985, the case has gone up on appeal twice, and it is now before the trial court for the third time. Like *Loveladies*, it is a legal trailblazer—undoubtedly part of the reason for its long duration. The most recent decision in the case opens up the possibility of "partial regulatory takings" when the government eliminates only a moderate fraction of a property's value, and suggests that certain property rights can be looked at separately from others the owner has in the same tract. At this point, it is almost certain that a taking will be found. The question is, by what rationale?

By the mid-1980s, the winds of change were blowing again—possibly because the federal wetlands program had now taken hold and confronted a more conservative federal bench. In 1983, a federal wetlands permit denial was seen by a court to be a taking for the first time.[18] Then followed two important interim rulings favorable to wetland owners. In 1986, in *Florida Rock Industries v. United States*, the Federal Circuit again weighed the public interest in wetlands preservation against the landowner's loss, as it had in the early 1980s. But this time it tipped toward the landowner—same court, different result.[19] Two years later, a key ruling on the "parcel as a whole" issue went against the United States in another wetlands/taking case— *Loveladies Harbor, Inc. v. United States*.[20] When the U.S. Claims

[18]1902 Atlantic Ltd. v. Hudson, 574 F. Supp. 1381 (E.D. Va. 1983) (dictum).
[19]791 F.2d 893 (Fed. Cir. 1986), *cert. denied*, 479 U.S. 1053 (1987).
[20]15 Cl. Ct. 381 (1988). The "parcel as a whole," or relevant parcel, issue is treated later in this chapter and in chapter 12.

Court finally reached the takings questions in *Florida Rock* and *Loveladies Harbor*, it found takings in both—on the same day.[21]

People started to take notice. These decisions, and other claims court rulings of the time, took an unmistakably less deferential attitude toward the public interest in wetlands than did earlier federal decisions. *Florida Rock* and *Loveladies Harbor* in particular decided key unresolved issues of takings law against the government. (In the most recent round, the Federal Circuit affirmed *Loveladies*[22] and remanded *Florida Rock*[23] with guidance to the trial court likely to produce a decision for the property owner.) Plainly, this latest period is witnessing a fundamental change in the attitude of these two federal courts toward the wetland owner. To be sure, it is not a swing of the pendulum to the opposite extreme—government always loses. Indeed, the United States has won more wetlands/takings cases than it has lost in the new era. Once, however, the United States could count on a win; today, it must do its homework and fight it out case by case.

A comparable shift in the state courts is not yet apparent. It is not clear that in the late 1980s and 1990s, more state courts than previously are making states and localities pay when property value is impaired by wetlands development restrictions.[24]

Ripeness

Several issues as to ripeness (see chapter 5) recur in the wetlands area. A few have even achieved that rarity in takings law—resolution. The Supreme Court has said unequivocally, and state courts have agreed,

[21]*Loveladies Harbor*, 21 Cl. Ct. 153 (1990); *Florida Rock*, 21 Cl. Ct. 161 (1990).

[22]28 F.3d 1171 (Fed. Cir. 1994).

[23]18 F.3d 1560 (Fed. Cir. 1994), *cert. denied*, 513 U.S. 1109 (1995).

[24]Recent wetlands cases from this period finding no taking include Alegria v. Keeney, 687 A. 2d 1249 (R.I. 1997); Gazza v. New York State, 89 N.Y.2d 1035, *cert. denied*, 118 S. Ct. 58 (1997); FIC Homes of Blackstone, Inc. v. Conservation Comm'n, 673 N.E.2d 61 (Mass. App. 1996), *review denied*, 424 Mass. 1104, 676 N.E.2d 55 (1997); Zealy v. City of Waukesha, 201 Wis. 2d 365, 548 N.W.2d 528 (1996); and Mock v. DER, 154 Pa. Commw. 380, 623 A.2d 940 (1993), *aff'd*, 542 Pa. 357, 667 A.2d 212 (1995), *cert. denied*, 517 U.S. 1216 (1996). In Gardner v. New Jersey Pinelands Comm'n, 125 N.J. 193, 593 A.2d 251 (1990), the vitality of a 1960s state court decision finding a wetlands taking was said to have eroded due to the subsequent rise in societal environmental awareness.

that a claim of permanent taking generally is not ripe until the permit is actually applied for and denied.[25] Thus, an agency's mere designation of a parcel as coming under its permit program cannot by itself be a taking, since it leaves open the possibility that the permit, if applied for, will be granted.[26] The same holds true when the government orders construction on a wetland to cease until the owner secures a permit.[27] Little better is the incomplete permit application. Rejection of incomplete applications through a "denial without prejudice" confers no ripeness, unless judicial scrutiny reveals that in actual fact rejection was based on the proposal's wetlands impact.[28]

Not surprisingly, the U.S. Court of Federal Claims does not invoke ripeness to send takings plaintiffs back to the Corps of Engineers to exhaust variance possibilities and administrative appeals, since the section 404 process currently allows for neither.

Other ripeness issues, however, remain murky. For how long must a wetlands permit applicant wrangle with the government over what permit conditions (e.g., for compensatory mitigation) are mutually acceptable?[29] Can a taking claim based on the *entire* wetland owned be ripe if based on a permit denial covering only a fraction thereof?[30]

[25]A claim of *temporary* regulatory taking may dispense with the permit denial prerequisite—as when the complaint is of unreasonable delay in an agency's processing of the permit application.

[26]United States v. Riverside Bayview Homes, Inc., 474 U.S. 121 (1985). *Accord* Carabell v. DNR, 191 Mich. App. 610, 478 N.W.2d 675 (1991); Bond v. DNR, 183 Mich. App. 225, 454 N.W.2d 395 (1989); Wedinger v. Goldberger, 71 N.Y.2d 488, 522 N.E.2d 25 (1988).

[27]Tabb Lakes, Ltd. v. United States, 10 F.3d 796, 800–01 (Fed. Cir. 1993).

[28]*Cf.* City Nat'l Bank v. United States, 33 Fed. Cl. 759 (1995) (ripe notwithstanding Corps' describing permit denial as "without prejudice," since denial actually merits based) *with* Heck v. United States, 134 F. 3d 1468 (Fed. Cir. 1998) (no ripeness, since denial without prejudice was, as Corps asserted, based solely on application's incompleteness).

[29]In Plantation Landing Resort, Inc. v. United States, 30 Fed. Cl. 63 (1993), *aff'd without pub. op.*, 39 F.3d 1197 (Fed. Cir. 1994), *cert. denied*, 514 U.S. 1095 (1995), the court said it could not view a Corps permit denial as a taking when the denial was the result of a failure to reach agreement with the landowner on mitigation requirements. Though the decision was not couched in the language of ripeness, since the permit was denied, it nonetheless highlights the duty of the wetland owner to pursue reasonable negotiations as to permit conditions before claiming a taking.

[30]*Cf.* Florida Rock Indust., Inc. v. United States, 791 F.2d 893 (Fed. Cir. 1986) (claim that entire parcel was taken by denial of permit for portion is premature), *cert. denied*, 479 U.S. 1053 (1987) *with* Formanek v. United States, 18 Cl. Ct. 42 (1988) (claim that entire parcel was taken is ripe).

Particularly important in actions against nonfederal agencies: Can a court reach the taking issue when only the owner's *first submitted* development proposal was rejected? Or must the owner then submit scaled-down versions to achieve the ripeness prerequisite of a final decision?[31]

Statutes may affect the ripeness determination. In New Jersey, a "safety valve" provision in the state's wetlands statute was judicially interpreted to mean that the state and land developer must confer whenever the state takes an initial position that would be a taking.[32] Because the process leading to permit denial was thus seen to be incomplete until the state decides whether its opening-shot regulations might be relaxed, the taking claim was held not to be ripe until then.

The key exception to these ripeness requirements of permit application, negotiation, and (if initially denied) reapplication, is the doctrine of futility (see chapter 5)—the notion that a landowner should not be made to seek government approvals when doing so would be pointless or illusory. Courts have often invoked this "futility exemption" to ripeness prerequisites where the government's conduct, or its rationale for denying the permit, indicates that no development of economically viable extent would be acceptable on the wetland. Use of the exemption to excuse making the *initial* permit application, however, is problematic;[33] the exemption is generally applied to soften the requirement for later, scaled-down or reconfigured proposals.[34] Moreover, the wetlands owner cannot plead futility "whenever faced with long odds or demanding procedural requirements."[35]

[31]*See, e.g.*, Hoffman v. Town of Avon, 28 Conn. App. 262, 610 A.2d 185 (1982) (no taking where plaintiff submitted only one application); Carabell v. DNR, 191 Mich. App. 610, 478 N.W.2d 675 (1991) (likewise). If the scaled-down proposals are too similar to the original, reapplications will not achieve ripeness. *See* Gil v. Town of Greenwich, 219 Conn. 404, 593 A.2d 1368 (1991).

[32]East Cape May Assocs. v. New Jersey, 300 N.J. Super. 325, 693 A.2d 114 (App. Div. 1997).

[33]Heck v. United States, 134 F. 3d 1468 (Fed. Cir. 1998) (citing Southern Pac. Transp. Co. v. City of Los Angeles, 922 F.2d 498, 504 (9th Cir. 1990)).

[34]*See, e.g.*, Marks v. United States, 34 Fed. Cl. 387 (1995), *aff'd without op.*, 116 F.3d 1496 (Fed. Cir. 1997), *cert. denied*, 118 S. Ct. 852 (1998); Loveladies Harbor, Inc. v. United States, 21 Cl. Ct. 153, 157 (1990), *aff'd* 28 F.3d 1171 (1994); Formanek v. United States, 18 Cl. Ct. 785, 792–93 (1989); Orion Corp. v. State, 109 Wash. 2d 621, 747 P.2d 1062, 1068 (1987) (en banc), *cert. denied*, 486 U.S. 1022 (1988).

[35]Heck v. United States, 37 Fed. Cl. 245, 252 (1997), *aff'd*, 134 F.3d 1468 (Fed. Cir. 1998).

The Regulatory Taking Test: Permission to Fill Denied

State and federal courts have phrased their tests differently for when denial of permission to dredge or fill a wetland is a taking—though it is not always clear to what practical effect. By and large, at least so far, both types of courts have demanded a very high degree of interference before compensation is awarded. Moreover, as the Supreme Court has evolved its takings jurisprudence in the past two decades, state courts are moving toward the federal norm. *Lucas* (total takings) and the three-factor *Penn Central* test (partial takings) are becoming the majority standard.

State Courts

Despite convergence with the federal norm, the takings jurisprudence of the state courts seems more tilted toward the regulator than that of the Court of Federal Claims. Perhaps the reason is that state courts more often than federal ones speak of the public benefit (or public trust) in wetlands, often finding it to outweigh even substantial detriments to the wetland owner. Then, too, most state courts insist outright that for a regulatory taking to be discerned as a result of frustrated development, the plaintiff must have lost virtually *all* economic use of the parcel. Said one court: "[u]ntil . . . plaintiff has been finally deprived . . . of the reasonable and proper use of the property," there is no taking.[36] Moreover, in the eyes of many state courts, rather modest residual uses may deflect the landowner's total-deprivation argument. Uses deemed sufficient have included seasonal placement of a trailer,[37] camping,[38] a single-family home,[39] and agricultural/open-space use.[40] The recent trend in some states, however, seems to be to relax the use-deprivation showing required of the owner.[41]

[36]Brecciaroli v. Commissioner of Envtl. Protection, 168 Conn. 349, 362 A.2d 948 (1975). *Accord* Vatalaro v. DER, 601 So. 2d 1223 (Fla. Dist. Ct. App. 1992); Wedinger v. Goldberger, 71 N.Y.2d 488, 522 N.E.2d 25 (1988); Mock v. DER, 154 Pa. Commw. 380, 623 A.2d 940 (1993) *aff'd*, 542 Pa. 357, 667 A.2d 212 (1995), *cert. denied*, 517 U.S. 1216 (1996); State v. Capuano Bros., Inc., 120 R.I. 58, 384 A.2d 610 (1978).

[37]Hall v. Board of Envtl. Protection, 528 A.2d 453 (Me. 1987).

[38]Claridge v. New Hampshire Wetlands Bd., 125 N.H. 745, 485 A.2d 287 (1984).

[39]Moskow v. Commissioner, 384 Mass. 530, 427 N.E.2d 750 (1981).

[40]April v. City of Broken Arrow, 775 P.2d 1347 (Okla. 1989).

[41]*See, e.g.*, East Cape May Assocs. v. New Jersey, 300 N.J. Super. 325, 693 A.2d 114 (1997) ("minimal uses" insufficient to undermine taking claim, citing *Lucas*). In a related vein, the California Supreme Court in 1997 offered its first recognition that a less-than-total loss of use or value could be a taking. Kavanau v. Santa Monica Rent Control Bd., 16 Cal. 4th 761, 941 P.2d 851 (1997), *cert. denied*, 118 S. Ct. 856 (1998).

Interwoven with the current majority-view state test is the classic distinction in takings law between government actions that prevent harm (generally not takings) and those that secure public benefits (often takings). Most state courts have long embraced this dichotomy to find wetlands preservation efforts noncompensable as a prevention of public harm—either specific harms, such as pollution and resultant economic harm, or more diffuse ones, such as nonitemized "community welfare."[42] One court explained that the wetlands restriction before it was not to be thought of as securing a benefit by maintaining land in its natural state; rather, it prevented harm from the change in the natural character of the land that, given its location on a lake, would pollute water and degrade fishing and scenic beauty.[43] The vigor of the harm/benefit distinction was lessened in 1992, however, by the Supreme Court's rejection of it as manipulable and value-laden.[44] Indeed, the Court used wetlands protection as a prime example of government action that could be (and has been) characterized as both.

From the traditional judicial characterization of wetlands protection as a harm preventer rather than benefit provider, it was not difficult for courts to reach back to the even older public trust doctrine (see chapter 14). Under this amorphous, much-debated concept, there *is* no right to use property impressed with the trust in a manner that impairs trust interests, however one defines them. Plainly, viewing the waters of a state as natural resources infused with a public trust serves to bolster wetlands regulation against takings challenges.[45]

One variant of the public trust doctrine is in *Just v. Marinette County*: "[a]n owner of land has no absolute and unlimited right to change the essential natural character of his land so as to use it for a

[42]*See, e.g.*, Tahoe Sierra Preservation Council, Inc. v. Tahoe Regional Planning Agency, 638 F. Supp. 126, 135 (D. Nev. 1986), *aff'd in part, rev'd in part on other grounds*, 911 F.2d 1331 (9th Cir. 1990), *cert. denied*, 499 U.S. 943 (1991); Graham v. Estuary Properties, 399 So. 2d 1374 (Fla.) (conceding that harm/benefit dichotomy unclear), *cert. denied*, 454 U.S. 1083 (1981); Moskow v. Commissioner, 384 Mass. 530, 427 N.E.2d 753 (1981); Sibson v. State, 115 N.H. 124, 336 A.2d 239 (1975); Just v. Marinette County, 56 Wis. 2d 7, 201 N.W.2d 761 (1972).

[43]*Just*, 201 N.W.2d at 768.

[44]Lucas v. South Carolina Coastal Council, 505 U.S. 1003, 1024–26 (1992).

[45]*See, e.g.*, Orion Corp. v. State, 109 Wash. 2d 621, 747 P.2d 1062 (1987) (en banc), *cert. denied*, 486 U.S. 1022 (1988). However, few courts have directly addressed the issue whether application of the public trust doctrine provides a complete defense to a taking claim.

purpose for which it was unsuited in its natural state and which injures the rights of others."[46] Relying on this principle, the court
found no taking in a county ordinance's requirement that a permit be
secured to fill in wetlands along a pristine lake, where such fill might
harm water quality and recreational values. At the same time, the
court explained that it would not find the requisite injury to the rights
of others in *all* instances of wetlands destruction, as in the case of an
"isolated swamp unrelated to a navigable lake or stream."[47] The *Just*
rule, doubtless the pinnacle of judicial protection of wetlands, has
been adopted in a handful of states.[48]

A tantalizing question is whether the public trust doctrine in any of
its incarnations will be accepted by courts as the kind of "background
principle of property . . . law" referred to in *Lucas*. At least in those
states in which the doctrine is well-established, it would seem to
qualify.[49] If so accepted (there is little case law so far), the doctrine
could be a significant obstacle to takings claimants. The same question
of "background principle" eligibility has been raised about some other
common law doctrines affecting wetlands. *Lucas* itself makes crystal
clear only that common law *nuisance* is a background principle.[50]

[46]201 N.W.2d at 768.

[47]*Id.* at 769.

[48]Rowe v. Town of North Hampton, 131 N.H. 424, 553 A.2d 1331, 1335 (1989);
Graham v. Estuary Properties, Inc., 399 So. 2d 1374, 1382 (Fla.), *cert. denied*, 454
U.S. 1083 (1981); American Dredging Co. v. State Department of Envtl. Protection,
391 A.2d 1265, 1271 (N.J. Super. Ct., Ch. Div., 1978), *aff'd*, 169 N.J. Super. 18, 404
A.2d 42 (1979). *Just* has also been reaffirmed recently in its state of origin. Zealy v.
City of Waukesha, 201 Wis. 2d 365, 548 N.W.2d 528 (1996) (clarifying that *Just* rule
goes beyond geographic limits of traditional public trust doctrine).

[49]*See* Hope M. Babcock, *The Impact of* Lucas v. South Carolina Coastal Council
on *Wetlands and Coastal Barrier Beaches*, 19 HARVARD ENVTL. L. REV. 1 (1995); Paul
Sarahan, *Wetlands Protection Post-*Lucas: *Implications of the Public Trust Doctrine
on Takings Analysis*, 13 VIRGINIA ENVTL. L.J. 537 (1994) (arguing that interrelated
hydrology may make doctrine applicable to wetlands *adjacent* to public trust waters
and suggesting that when restricting wetlands development, states develop data on
probable impact on those waters). *See also* Mary K. McCurdy, *Public Trust Protection for Wetlands*, 19 ENVTL. L. 683 (1989) (pre-*Lucas* view of public trust).

[50]505 U.S. at 1029. *See, e.g.*, Palazzolo v. Coastal Resources Management
Council, No. 88–0297 (R.I. Super. Ct. Oct. 24, 1997) (wetlands fill proposal
amounting to public nuisance can be blocked without compensation, even if total
taking). *See generally* Fred P. Bosselman, *Limitations Inherent in the Title to Wetlands at Common Law*, 15 STANFORD ENVTL. L.J. 247, 327–37 (1996) (suggesting
that English common law of wetlands could be relevant to determining "background
principles" under *Lucas*).

Federal Courts

In the Court of Federal Claims and its appellate court, the takings canon is *Lucas* and the *Penn Central* test.[51] In practice, however, two elements of the latter, economic impact and (less so) interference with investment-backed expectations, have eclipsed the third—character of the government action.[52] The weighing of the public interest in wetlands protection against the private burden, part of the "character of the government action" factor, is today a minor player in these courts.[53]

The economic impact factor largely translates into a simple percentage calculation of the loss in the parcel's fair market value from before to after the permit denial.[54] Thus, the Court of Federal Claims has found takings in section 404 permit-denial cases chiefly on the basis of resulting land value losses of 99, 95, 92, and 88 percent.[55] Federal wetlands managers should not be complacent that the takings thresholds will always remain so high, however. In 1994, a ruling in *Florida Rock* asked, in introducing the concept of a "partial regulatory taking," whether a value diminution of only 62 percent might be

[51]*See generally* Merlyn W. Clark, *Wetlands: Compensation for "Taking" by Denial of the Section 404 Permit*, 29 Idaho L. Rev. 41 (1992–93).

[52]*See, e.g.*, Florida Rock Indus., Inc. v. United States, 18 F.3d 1560, 1567 (Fed. Cir. 1994) (citing *Penn Central* solely for its "economic impact" factor), *cert. denied*, 513 U.S. 1109 (1995); Good v. United States, 39 Fed. Cl. 81 (1997) (investment-backed expectations pivotal).

[53]However, the Federal Circuit recently admonished the Court of Federal Claims to address all three *Penn Central* factors, including character of the government action, when deciding a regulatory taking case. Broadwater Farms Joint Venture v. United States, 121 F.3d 727 (Fed. Cir. 1997) (unpublished wetlands case).

[54]*Florida Rock*, 18 F.3d at 1567.

[55]The text percentages are found in: Loveladies Harbor, Inc. v. United States, 28 F.3d 1171 (Fed. Cir. 1994) (99 percent); Florida Rock Indus., Inc. v. United States, 21 Cl. Ct. 161 (1990), *vacated and remanded*, 18 F.3d 1560 (Fed. Cir. 1994) (trial court used improperly low "after value"; that such value warranted finding a taking not disputed), *cert. denied*, 513 U.S. 1109 (1995) (95 percent); Bowles v. United States, 31 Fed. Cl. 37 (1994) (finding 100 percent value loss, but holding that even if only 92 percent value loss, there was taking); and Formanek v. United States, 26 Cl. Ct. 332 (1992) (88 percent). See also 1902 Atlantic Ltd. v. United States, 26 Cl. Ct. 575, 579 (1992) (88 percent value loss satisfies "economic impact" factor, though no taking found).

sufficient to "take."[56] (At the opposite end, losing the use of 15 percent of one's land while still able to turn a profit is not a taking.[57])

As in land valuation generally, where the government seeks to support its valuation of a permit-denied wetland by alleging remaining uses, they must meet a "showing of reasonable probability that the land is both physically adaptable for such use *and* that there is a demand for such use in the reasonably near future."[58] (Emphasis in original.)

The Court of Federal Claims and the Federal Circuit take a narrow view of the *Lucas* "background principles," a view which they have articulated mostly in their wetlands decisions. Depending on the decision consulted, these courts accept as background principles only the state's common law of (1) nuisance,[59] or (2) nuisance and property,[60] or (3) the latter plus state statutes rooted therein.[61] Federal law is excluded, although the United States may defend wetlands/takings actions through the federal navigational servitude (*see* chapter 14), when wetlands are within the servitude's shoreward reach.[62] And unlike some state courts, the Court of Federal Claims and the Federal Circuit have shown no disposition to embrace anything resembling a public trust doctrine.

The Regulatory Taking Test: Project Delays

Even where development of a privately owned wetland is ultimately allowed to proceed, takings claims based on the period of delay have been pressed. Little wonder, given that project delays can rack up significant costs. So far, two important situations have arisen.

First, courts have grappled with the sometimes lengthy processing time before a permit is issued, holding that the key factor in the

[56]18 F.3d at 1567.
[57]Forest Properties, Inc. v. United States, 39 Fed. Cl. 56 (1997).
[58]Loveladies Harbor, Inc. v. United States, 21 Cl. Ct. 153, 158 (1990), *aff'd*, 28 F.3d 1171 (Fed. Cir. 1994).
[59]Loveladies Harbor, Inc. v. United States, 28 F.3d 1171, 1179 (Fed. Cir. 1994).
[60]*Forest Properties*, 39 Fed. Cl. 56.
[61]Good v. United States, 39 Fed. Cl. 81 (1997).
[62]In Marks v. United States, 34 Fed. Cl. 387 (1995), *aff'd without op.*, 116 F.3d 1496 (Fed. Cir. 1997), *cert. denied*, 118 S. Ct. 852 (1998), for example, the court readily rejected on navigational servitude grounds the portion of a wetlands taking claim based on lands below the high-water mark. *See also Good*, 39 Fed. Cl. at 96–97, (affirming *Marks* but holding that United States failed to show that all limitations on plaintiff's property overlapped servitude).

takings analysis is whether the wait was unreasonable or extraordinary. Was it unduly protracted in light of the complexity of the regulatory scheme? Did the owner fail to take actions that might have shortened the processing time? To date, federal courts have held that waiting periods for section 404 permits of fifteen months, sixteen months, and two years, respectively, were not takings.[63]

A second delay scenario is when an agency's assertion of jurisdiction over a wetland, or its denial of a permit, is judicially set aside. Consider, for example, *Tabb Lakes, Inc. v. United States*,[64] in which the U.S. Army Corps of Engineers issued a cease and desist order requiring a developer to stop subdivision work until it obtained a section 404 permit, but was judicially informed three years later that its claim of jurisdiction was defective. No taking, said the Federal Circuit. The cease and desist order had specifically left the door to development open through obtaining a permit. Invoking a powerful principle for government planners, the court further noted that "mere fluctuations in value during . . . government decisionmaking, absent extraordinary delay, . . . cannot be considered a taking."[65]

Both delay scenarios, therefore, suggest that a wetland owner's temporary taking case stands or falls mainly on the existence of "unreasonable" or "extraordinary" delay—though, at least in wetlands cases, the courts rarely define these terms, nor find the requisite delay to exist. In any event, the determination surely will continue to be made on a case-by-case basis.

A potent source of confusion is the takings role of a project's economic return during the restricted period. The *Tabb Lakes* trial court homed in on the existence of lot sales and tax returns showing profitability during the development prohibition. This seems misguided. The better view is that at least where the restriction is plainly temporary, as in the *Tabb Lakes* cease and desist order, economic viability during the restricted period is irrelevant. The strong likelihood of *future* economic use supports *present* economic value.

[63]1902 Atlantic Ltd. v. United States, 26 Cl. Ct. 575, 579 (1992) (15 months); Dufau v. United States, 22 Cl. Ct. 156 (1990) (16 months); Lachney v. United States, 22 Envtl. Rptr. (Cases) 2031 (Fed. Cir. 1985) (two years).

[64]10 F.3d 796 (Fed. Cir. 1993).

[65]*Id.* at 801 (quoting Agins v. City of Tiburon, 447 U.S. 255, 263 n.9 (1980)). *See also* Littoral Dev. Co. v. San Francisco Bay Conservation & Dev. Comm'n, 33 Cal. App. 4th 211, 39 Cal. Rptr. 2d 266 (1995) (agency's assertion of wetlands jurisdiction invalidated; resultant delay not taking because government's legal arguments plausible though erroneous; use of property continued during dispute).

Parcel as a Whole

The "parcel as a whole" conundrum (*see* chapter 12) has played a pivotal role in wetlands takings cases, since the parcel in question usually consists of both regulated wetlands and unregulated uplands. Applying the general rule against segmenting a parcel in the taking analysis, courts historically have rejected takings claims whenever a wetland owner could not show that economic use of the unrestricted portion of the property was infeasible.

But what *is* the parcel as a whole in a particular case? The answer is easy only where a wetlands permit denial affects only a small or moderate fraction of a contiguous, unsubdivided parcel, in the same ownership whose bounds have not changed in the relevant time period. Unsurprisingly, it is that entire parcel.[66] At the very least, the Supreme Court's pronouncements mean that such a straightforward tract is not to be divided up for the purpose of isolating the wetlands affected by the use restriction.

But reality is often not straightforward. What is the relevant parcel when plaintiff owns noncontiguous parcels on the date of the alleged taking? Should *they* be added in when determining the regulation's impact on the property owner? What about portions of the original lot that were sold off before the regulatory scheme went into effect, or before permit denial? And what is to be done when a tract is subdivided or in different zoning classifications, or the restricted portion is almost the entire parcel? Where such complicating factors are present, the Supreme Court's absolutely worded insistence on nonsegmentation, aimed primarily against segmentation to isolate the regulated portion, may not be relevant guidance.[67]

An early federal wetlands case took a broad view of the parcel as a whole. After asserting that contiguous uplands had to be included in the relevant parcel, the court in *Deltona Corp. v. United States* suggested inclusion as well of sections of the original purchase that had been developed and sold off prior to the permit denial on the contested section.[68] In *Loveladies Harbor*, however, the federal Claims

---

[66]*See, e.g.*, Fox v. Treasure Coast Regional Planning Council, 442 So. 2d 221 (Fla. Dist. Ct. App. 1983); Moskow v. Commissioner, 384 Mass. 530, 427 N.E.2d 750 (1981); American Dredging Co. v. New Jersey, 169 N.J. Super. 18, 404 A.2d 42 (App. Div. 1979).

[67]One might still wish that lower courts would trouble to mention the Supreme Court law on parcel as a whole and make an effort to distinguish it.

[68]657 F.2d 1184, 1192 (Ct. Cl. 1981), *cert. denied*, 455 U.S. 1017 (1982).

Court went with a narrow definition, refusing to factor in two pieces of the developer's original 250-acre purchase: the lots it had developed and sold off by the date of the alleged taking (193 acres), and developed but unsold upland lots that were not contiguous with the land for which the permit was denied (6 acres).[69]

On appeal, the Federal Circuit in *Loveladies Harbor* said the parcel-as-a-whole determination was an ad hoc one, sensitive to factual nuances.[70] So, the divergent results in *Deltona* and *Loveladies Harbor*, it argued, were consistent; they were simply the products of the different facts in each case. The Federal Circuit affirmed the Claims Court's acreage exclusions, endorsing its newly minted rationale that land "developed or sold before the regulatory environment existed" should not be included.[71] The 193 acres had been sold, and the 6 upland acres at least developed, before the "regulatory environment" of Clean Water Act section 404 was enacted in 1972. Such remains the rule in this important circuit.[72]

Other applications of the ad hoc approach to relevant-parcel determinations have proved less hospitable to landowners. How the developer treated the acreage in question has proved key. In *Ciampitti v. United States*,[73] the Claims Court lumped a developer's wetland with a nearby—but noncontiguous—upland it owned that was "inextricably linked in terms of purchase and financing" with the wetland. Similarly, in *Forest Properties v. United States*,[74] the court

[69]15 Cl. Ct. 381, 391–93 (1988). The six acres of uplands were valued at $2.4 million near the time of the taking, compared with the $300,000 paid by the developer for the entire 250-acre tract. These figures make plain that the court's exclusion of this small fragment of the original tract was essential to its finding of a taking.

[70]*Accord* East Cape May Assocs. v. New Jersey, 300 N.J. Super. 325, 693 A.2d 114 (App. Div. 1997).

[71]*Loveladies Harbor*, 28 F.3d 1171, 1181 (Fed. Cir. 1994). In Volkema v. DNR, 214 Mich. App. 66, 542 N.W.2d 282 (1995), a state court expressly adopted this "developed or sold" rule, using it to remove from a wetlands taking analysis half of the original 45-acre tract. Still, no taking was found, since the restricted wetland constituted only one-fourth of the remaining acreage.

[72]*But see* Broadwater Farms Joint Venture v. United States, 35 Fed. Cl. 232 (1996) (sector developed and sold off before *date of alleged taking* not included in relevant parcel where no evidence of strategic behavior), *vacated and remanded*, 121 F.3d 727 (Fed. Cir. 1997) (unpublished) (affirming discussion of relevant parcel).

[73]22 Cl. Ct. 310 (1991).

[74]39 Fed. Cl. 56 (1997).

found that the developer had treated the combined lake-bottom/upland parcel as one income-producing unit for purposes of financing, planning, and development. It could not now segregate the wetland portion, said the court, for purposes of deciding the taking claim.

To the same effect in the state courts is *K & K Construction Co. v. Department of Natural Resources*,[75] holding that where a permit application contemplated a single comprehensive development encompassing several tracts in common ownership, the relevant parcel was at least those tracts. Indeed, the single development proposal negated the fact that the tracts were zoned differently.

Other wetlands decisions of the Court of Federal Claims and the Federal Circuit have differed over whether individual subdivision lots in common ownership should be considered together for takings purposes. The more extended analyses, dealing with lots that were both purchased and sought to be developed together, have strongly rejected individual consideration.[76] A state wetlands decision appears to be of the same view.[77]

As noted, what to include in the relevant parcel is of more than academic interest. The party that prevails on the relevant-parcel issue most likely will win on the taking issue as well. Deeming the restricted wetland portion alone to be the relevant parcel almost ensures that the court will find complete loss of economic use—a *Lucas* "total taking."[78]

Finally, removing acreage from the takings calculus arguably encourages strategic behavior by the developer in advance of applying for a wetlands permit—i.e., behavior that seeks to put the developer

[75]456 Mich. 570, 575 N.W.2d 531 (1998).

[76]Tabb Lakes, Inc. v. United States, 10 F.3d 796 (Fed. Cir. 1993); *Broadwater Farms*, 121 F.3d 727 (unpublished). *Cf.* Bowles v. United States, 31 Fed. Cl. 37, 41 n.4 (1994) (taking claim based on permit denial for one subdivision lot; plaintiff's 10 adjacent lots purchased at same time not considered).

[77]*See, e.g.*, FIC Homes of Blackstone, Inc. v. Conservation Comm'n of Blackstone, 41 Mass. App. 681, 673 N.E.2d 61 (1997).

[78]In *Tabb Lakes*, 10 F.3d at 802, the Federal Circuit refused to narrow the parcel as a whole to solely the wetlands portion of a tract, explaining that wetlands permit denials "would [then], ipso facto, constitute a taking in every case. . . ." In Loveladies Harbor, Inc. v. United States, 28 F.3d 1171 (Fed. Cir. 1994), the same court's narrowing of the relevant parcel to only the acreage involved in the permit denial allowed it to find a complete elimination of economic use, hence a taking. *See generally* Stephen M. Johnson, *Defining the Property Interest: A Vital Issue in Wetlands Taking Analysis After* Lucas, 14 J. ENERGY, NAT. RES. & ENVTL. L. 41 (1994).

in the best position for bringing a taking action if a permit is denied. For example, a developer might sell the nonwetland portion of a property before applying to the Corps of Engineers to fill in the wetland still owned and then, if a permit is denied, claim a severe percentage loss in value of the still-owned acreage.[79] Since *Lucas* teaches that takings law protects the understandings and expectations one has at the time land is acquired, it would seem that a substantial return from any significant portion of a tract, whether or not still owned at the time of permit denial, cuts against a taking claim based on what happens to be owned at the date of taking.

Prior Knowledge

Can a wetlands buyer have a reasonable expectation of being able to develop when it was "on notice" at time of purchase that a wetlands permit would have to be applied for and might be denied? Or does such foreknowledge, without more, defeat a taking claim? If it does not, would prepurchase knowledge of additional facts suggesting that a permit is likely to be denied foreclose a viable taking suit? Need such knowledge be actual, or can it be imputed by law?

A growing number of state cases seem to say that the existence of a wetlands regulatory regime at the time of purchase cuts strongly against a taking claim. The issue is discussed either in deciding whether the wetland owner has a property right to develop or in terms of *Penn Central's* "interference with distinct investment-backed expectations." Consider, for example, *Claridge v. New Hampshire Wetlands Bd.*: "A person who purchases land with notice of statutory impediments to the right to develop that land can justify few, if any, legitimate investment-backed expectations of development rights which rise to the level of constitutionally protected property rights."[80]

---

[79]The United States pressed this argument in *Loveladies Harbor*, 28 F.3d at 1181. The court may have found merit in it, since the court's adopted rule—land developed or sold before the regulatory environment existed is excluded—could act to minimize strategic behavior. Later Court of Federal Claims decisions on wetlands/taking claims have also shown awareness of the strategic behavior issue. *See, e.g.*, Forest Properties, Inc. v. United States, 39 Fed. Cl. 56, 73 (1997).

[80]125 N.H. 745, 485 A.2d 287, 291 (1984). *Accord,* City of Virginia Beach v. Bell, 1998 WL 120262 (Va. S. Ct. Feb. 27, 1998); Alegria v. Keeney, 687 A.2d 1249 (R.I. 1997); FIC Homes of Blackstone, Inc. v. Conservation Comm'n of Blackstone, 41 Mass. App. 681, 673 N.E.2d 61 (1996), *review denied*, 424 Mass. 1104, 676 N.E.2d 55 (1997); Namon v. State, 558 So. 2d 504 (Fla. Dist. Ct. App. 1990); Rowe v. Town of North Hampton, 131 N.H. 424, 553 A.2d 1331 (1989). The minority

The wetland owner faces a particularly uphill climb where the amount paid for the wetland clearly reflected diminished development expectations.[81]

Federal decisions as well seem favorably inclined toward some sort of foreknowledge exception, but have not yet embraced an absolute rule barring takings whenever regulation precedes purchase. In *Deltona Corp. v. United States*, the Court of Claims first articulated the defense in a wetlands taking case.[82] The developer, it said, *knew* when it bought the property that development could take place only with the necessary permit. More recently, the Claims Court spurned a taking action after noting that the developer had ample warning before purchase "that the property was encumbered by a likelihood it could not be developed."[83] In yet another instance, the court confined the defense to instances when the plaintiff lacked an "objectively reasonable" belief that it could build.[84]

The most important endorsement of the "on notice" defense is in the latest *Florida Rock* opinion. The investment-backed expectations factor of *Penn Central*, it says, limits takings to "owners who . . . bought their property in reliance on a state of affairs that did not include the challenged regulatory regime."[85] Many issues are raised by this statement, however, such as whether the court intended an absolute bar to takings actions filed after the critical date and whether that date is necessarily when the regulatory regime goes into effect for the population at large or is known to apply to the landowner-plaintiff in particular.

The Court of Federal Claims and the Federal Circuit now lean toward use of the preexisting regulatory scheme in the takings analysis through the *Penn Central* "investment-backed expectations" factor, rather than in the prior inquiry into plaintiff's property interest.[86]

Adoption of an absolute rule disabling takings claims in every instance where regulation predates purchase seems unwise. Though

view, that regulatory foreknowledge does not disable the taking claim, is embodied in Vatalaro v. DER, 601 So. 2d 1223 (Fla. Dist. Ct. App. 1992). *Vatalaro* and *Namon*, both Florida cases, are difficult to reconcile.

[81]*See, e.g.*, Gazza v. New York State, 89 N.Y.2d 603, 679 N.E.2d 1035 (purchaser who paid $100,000 for previously designated wetland worth $396,000 if unregulated cannot complain of taking when development permit is denied).

[82]657 F.2d 1184 (Ct. Cl. 1981), *cert. denied*, 455 U.S. 1017 (1982).

[83]Ciampitti v. United States, 22 Cl. Ct. 310 (1991).

[84]Bowles v. United States, 31 Fed. Cl. 37 (1994).

[85]28 F.3d at 1177.

[86]*See, e.g.*, Loveladies Harbor, Inc. v. United States, 28 F.3d 1171, 1177 (Fed. Cir. 1994); Forest Properties, Inc. v. United States, 39 Fed. Cl. 56 (1997).

takings law certainly is starved for bright-line rules, this one would be at the expense of fairness. For openers, the regulatory landscape and the definition of a wetland may evolve after the wetland is bought. This factor alone makes it inequitable to always reject takings claims where the wetland was bought after some sort of wetlands preservation program was on the books. Even when the definition of a wetland has not changed over the relevant time span, the judgmental leeway in applying the definition can leave buyers unclear as to what they bought. Finally, physical changes in the land may occur—what constitutes a wetland when the government acts to regulate may not have been one when bought.

Even when it is clear at the time of purchase that the property has wetland, and the regulatory landscape stays constant between purchase and restriction, there remains a large element of uncertainty in how the government agency will react to the permit application. The Corps of Engineers, for example, undertakes an amorphous "public interest review" of such applications, balancing many broad factors. In short, there are many contingencies that must fall into place before a general statutory scheme is transformed into restrictions on a specific property. The query in each case must be, is it reasonable to charge the land buyer with the expectation that the contingencies leading to restricted development of that land would in fact occur?[87]

One way for a prospective wetlands buyer to defeat the prior knowledge barrier may be to have the *seller* submit the development application in instances where the seller's title predates the regulatory regime. Case law has yet to address how such a strategic maneuver should be treated.

Speculators and "After Value"

Even if permit denial robs a wetland of all *immediate* economic use, the land may retain value for those willing to gamble that restrictions on the tract may lessen in the future. After all, the pendulum of societal priorities swings both ways. The Federal Circuit has been in the

---

[87]The decision in Good v. United States, 39 Fed. Cl. 81 (1997), pushes the envelope as to which future development restrictions a land buyer reasonably should be expected to anticipate. There, the court found that a prepurchase version of the statute, though nonregulatory, put the buyer on notice of future restrictions and precluded reasonable expectations of development.

forefront on this issue, taking the view that "after value" necessarily includes the value of land to speculators.[88]

At the same time, post–permit denial offers from speculators are adequate to establish residual value only if the speculator can reasonably be assumed knowledgeable of all regulatory restrictions. Offers from "suckers"—e.g., victims of fraud or persons unfamiliar with American law—must be discarded, but this standard does not require a detailed inquiry into the sophistication of each buyer of a comparable parcel. Though clearly discrepant sales may be disregarded, "an assessor may not disregard an *entire* market as aberrational."[89] (Emphasis in original.)

Who Is Liable?

Further deepening the wetlands/takings quagmire is the attribution issue—who is responsible for a taking when, as often happens, more than one level of government is regulating the same site. Who should pay, for example, when permission to fill or drain the wetland is denied by both the state or local government and the United States? Is the fact that the restriction is imposed under a delegated program sufficient to impute takings liability to the delegating government? The possibility of state or local takings liability reportedly has become a disincentive to states' assuming responsibility for the federal section 404 programs within their borders—partly as a result of the more landowner friendly takings jurisprudence developed in the Court of Federal Claims and the Federal Circuit in the past decade.

The few cases to wrestle with this point so far suggest that when a government's action is truly coerced, absolution will be granted. Thus, a state court granted a county's motion to be dismissed from a taking case, since the county had acted to restrict the wetland owner under the direction and control of the state—that is, had acted as the state's agent.[90] In contrast, the Court of Federal Claims has ruled that

[88]Florida Rock Indus., Inc. v. United States, 791 F.2d 893, 902–03 (Fed. Cir. 1986), *cert. denied*, 479 U.S. 1053 (1987).

[89]Florida Rock Indus., Inc. v. United States, 18 F.3d 1560, 1567 (Fed. Cir. 1994), *cert. denied*, 513 U.S. 1109 (1995).

[90]Orion Corp. v. State, 109 Wash. 2d 621, 747 P.2d 1062 (1987) (en banc), *cert. denied*, 486 U.S. 1022 (1988). Minnesota has legislatively mandated that whenever its counties impose wetlands restrictions pursuant to state requirements, the state bears any statutory compensation liability. 1996 Minn. Laws ch. 462, § 36.

when a county comprehensive plan imposes a wetland development ban only remotely linked to federal Clean Water Act requirements, the resulting value loss may be considered in evaluating a taking claim based on subsequent federal permit denial. Using the locally impaired value as its baseline, the court discerned no further value reduction from the later federal permit denial, hence no federal taking.[91]

Arguably the denial of a federal wetlands permit based on prior state denials is an instance that falls in between the foregoing cases. On the one hand, the Corps of Engineers has no choice under the governing statutes but to refuse the permit.[92] On the other hand, the United States voluntarily imposed the denial requirement on the Corps in enacting those statutes. In the only case to address this circumstance, the court rejected the Corps' argument that the compulsory nature of the permit denial creates a per se defense to takings liability.[93] At the state level, takings claims have been brought against state agencies whose opposition allegedly compelled the Corps' permit denials.[94]

Regrettably, the question of whether the mere fact of delegation points the taking finger at the delegator appears not to have been addressed.[95] To be sure, a state that takes over the federal wetlands program does so voluntarily, suggesting that takings law would not transfer liability to the United States. If, however, delegated states are regarded as instrumentalities of the United States for program pur-

[91]City Nat'l Bank of Miami v. United States, 33 Fed. Cl. 759, 764 (1995) ("The fact that the Federal Government shares a common goal with states and localities in protecting water quality does not open the Federal Government to liability for the effects of a similar local planning tool."). This is an important holding, since frequently a wetland burdened with a federal permit denial has already been zoned by the local government for agricultural use, open space, or wetlands.

[92]See Clean Water Act § 401; Coastal Zone Management Act § 307 (both prohibiting the Corps from granting wetlands permits until applicants have received specified state approvals).

[93]Ciampetti v. United States, 18 Cl. Ct. 548, 555–56 (1989) (ruling so despite fact that permit denials are "without prejudice"—i.e., subject to owner eventually obtaining state approvals). See 33 C.F.R. § 320.4(j)(1) (defining permit denials without prejudice).

[94]See, e.g., Ventures Northwest, Ltd. v. State, 914 P.2d 1180 (Wash. Ct. App. 1996).

[95]The Court of Federal Claims has indicated awareness of the issue, however, in City Nat'l Bank of Miami, 33 Fed. Cl. at 763 n.4.

poses, the picture becomes less clear.[96] One supposes that here, as elsewhere in takings jurisprudence, ad hocery will reign.

Conclusion

Wetlands regulation puts the takings issue in high relief. Unlike many other forms of environmentally inspired land-use restriction, when a development permit is denied on a wetland, economic use may evaporate. Because most parcels contain both wetlands and uplands, the parcel-as-a-whole issue is recurring, and pivotal. Thus, wetlands cases are numerous and one of the prime vehicles for judicial exploration of the many unresolved quagmires of takings law. In pursuing this exploration, conflicting philosophical strands as to the nature of property rights in an age of heightened environmental awareness lie just below the surface.[97] The special legal status historically accorded to water-related property adds a further layer of consideration.

[96]A wetland owner recently argued that because a state's water quality certification program was created solely to satisfy the statutory prerequisites for a federally issued section 404 permit, the state's denial of such certification should be imputed to the United States for takings liability purposes. Heck v. United States, 134 F.3d 1468 (Fed. Cir. 1998) (issue not reached).

[97]See Joseph L. Sax, *Property Rights and the Economy of Nature: Understanding* Lucas v. South Carolina Coastal Council, 45 STANFORD L. REV. 1433 (1993); Eric T. Freyfogle, *The Owning and Taking of Sensitive Lands*, 43 UCLA L. REV. 77 (1995).

Chapter 24

Wildlife

Heedless of the swirling property rights debate, spotted owls and grizzly bears continue to roam according to ancient evolutionary rhythms rather than the legal bounds of private land. If only they knew. Government efforts to protect wildlife, particularly endangered and threatened species, spark heated debate over the impact on the private landowner, embracing not only direct impacts such as legal constraints on land use but secondary ripples as well, such as difficulty in obtaining loans when endangered species may be present on land used as collateral. Accounts of landowner hardship from the property rights movement abound. And the debate is due to widen, as calls are increasingly heard for ecosystem (rather than species-by-species) management and biodiversity preservation.[1]

Right now, the volume of legal challenges to wildlife protection founded on property rights is small given the decibel level of the public debate, and those rulings that do exist are largely in favor of government.[2] But the pace of litigation is quickening, and shifts in the judicial mood toward greater protection of property owners should not be ruled out.

[1]*See* David Farrier, *Conserving Biodiversity on Private Land*, RESOURCE LAW NOTES no. 32 (Univ. of Colo. 1994).

[2]*See generally* Stephen P. Foley, *Does Preventing "Take" Constitute an Unconstitutional Taking?: An Analysis of Possible Defenses to Fifth Amendment Taking Claims Based on the Endangered Species Act*, 14 UCLA J. ENVTL. L. & POL'Y 327 (1996); Lynn E. Dwyer & Dennis D. Murphy, *Property Rights Case Law and the Challenge to the Endangered Species Act*, 9 CONSERVATION BIOLOGY 725 (1995); Robert Meltz, *Where the Wild Things Are: The Endangered Species Act and Private Property*, 24 ENVTL. L. 369 (1994).

Types of Private Land Impacts: Direct-Use Restraints

Certainly a key impact that wildlife laws have on landowners is the direct-use restraint—the government's determination that an activity on private land must be barred, or at least modified, to avert injury to wildlife or its habitat. And certainly the key enactment in this impact category is the federal Endangered Species Act (ESA).[3] Given this Act's starring role in both the public and congressional property-rights drama, the steps by which it imposes land-use constraints— and seeks to mitigate them—warrant a close look.

The ESA Process

The ESA process begins when the Fish and Wildlife Service (FWS) "lists" a species as endangered or threatened. Listing must be done without reference to any economic or private property impacts it might have by virtue of the ESA restrictions triggered.[4] Along with listing, the ESA says that the FWS must, when "prudent and deter-minable," designate the "critical habitat" of the species—areas essential to its conservation.[5] In sharp contrast with listings, critical habitat designations are to be based *both* on scientific data and "economic impact and any other relevant impact,"[6] allowing the consequences for private lands to be weighed. This ESA distinction between listing and habitat designation, allowing analysis of property impacts only with the latter, was made by Congress quite deliberately.[7]

The listing of a species under the ESA brings on an array of prohibitions, including, for endangered animal species, a bar against "taking" individuals of that species.[8] A FWS rule extends these ESA

[3]16 U.S.C. §§ 1531–44. *See generally* U.S. GENERAL ACCOUNTING OFFICE, ENDANGERED SPECIES ACT: INFORMATION ON SPECIES PROTECTION ON NONFED-ERAL LANDS (RCED-95-16 1994) (90 percent of domestic listed species for which U.S. Fish & Wildlife Service responsible have some or all habitat on non-federal lands).

[4]ESA § 4(b)(1)(A), 16 U.S.C. § 1533(b)(1)(A). For marine species, the National Marine Fisheries Service makes the listing determination.

[5]ESA § 4(a)(3), 16 U.S.C. § 1533(a)(3).

[6]ESA § 4(b)(2), 16 U.S.C. § 1533(b)(2). The FWS has *formally* excluded territory from designated critical habitat for economic reasons only once, in the case of the northern spotted owl. The agency often considers economic impacts informally, however, as it develops its initial critical habitat proposal.

[7]H.R. REP. NO. 567, 97th Cong., 2d Sess. 12 (1982); H.R. CONF. REP. NO. 835, 97th Cong., 2d Sess. 19 (1982).

prohibitions to threatened species as well.[9] The term "take" is defined broadly in the Act—including "to harass, harm, pursue, [and] hunt" a listed animal[10]—and applies to actions on private as well as public land. (Thus, "take" in the ESA context has nothing to do with its use in the constitutional sense.)

While the definition of "take" might, by itself, preclude a smattering of private land uses, its impact on property owners was made potentially far more sweeping when the FWS defined the component term "harm" to embrace *"significant habitat modification* or degradation where it actually kills or injures wildlife by significantly impairing essential behavioral patterns. . . ."[11] (Emphasis added.) Now a landowner might violate the ESA without directly encountering a species member, but merely by substantially altering the habitat of the species.

The significance of the FWS interpretation of "harm" for the property rights debate, and for the future of the ESA, was lost on no one. Thus, the anticipation was intense when the Supreme Court in 1995 agreed to decide the interpretation's validity. The case was an appeal from a District of Columbia Circuit decision holding, two judges to one, that FWS's reading was invalid. "Harm," said the majority, embraces only "the perpetrator's direct application of force against the animal taken."[12] The Supreme Court rejected this narrow view and upheld the government's habitat-modification reading as reasonable.[13]

The ESA also enlists federal agencies in a way that can limit private property use, calling on them to consult with the FWS to ensure that their actions are "not likely to jeopardize the continued existence of any [listed] species, or result in the destruction or adverse modification of" designated critical habitat.[14] ESA afficionados call this the

[8]ESA § 9(a)(1), 16 U.S.C. § 1538(a)(1).

[9]50 C.F.R. § 17.31 (wildlife), § 17.71 (plants).

[10]ESA § 3(19), 16 U.S.C. § 1532(19).

[11]50 C.F.R. § 17.3.

[12]Sweet Home Chapter of Communities for a Great Oregon v. Babbitt, 17 F.3d 1463, 1465 (D.C. Cir. 1994). On two previous occasions, the Ninth Circuit had sustained the FWS. Palila v. Hawaii, 639 F.2d 495 (9th Cir. 1981), 852 F.2d 1106 (9th Cir. 1988).

[13]Babbitt v. Sweet Home Chapter of Communities for a Great Oregon, 515 U.S. 687 (1995).

[14]ESA § 7(a)(2), 16 U.S.C. § 1536(a)(2).

"federal nexus" provision, as it impinges on the private landowner only when his or her development aspirations require federal approvals, grants, or other assistance. For example, this section might preclude the Corps of Engineers from issuing a wetlands fill permit.[15]

With more than a thousand domestic species listed as endangered or threatened and hundreds more awaiting consideration, these ESA prohibitions pose, in the minds of some, a ubiquitous threat to private property.[16] Yet the Act seeks to soften its prohibitions and accommodate development in several ways—ways which Secretary of the Interior Babbitt, mindful of intense political pressures to ease ESA restrictions, has been trying to expand.[17] These devices in the Act include principally the exemption for "incidental takes"—takings of listed animals, within acceptable limits, that are merely incidental to the purpose of a proposed activity. When an activity on private land involves no federal approvals or grants (no "federal nexus"), incidental "takes" are permitted following the landowner's preparation of a "habitat conservation plan" (HCP) and its approval by FWS.[18]

The HCP process has been controversial, however, its cost prohibitive for some small landowners and the resultant delays nettlesome to developers. To make it more workable, the Department of the Interior has adopted innovations such as the "no surprises" policy.[19] The no surprises policy is just what it says: People who participate in an HCP are assured that even if additional measures are later found necessary to preserve a species covered by the plan, they will not be called on to contribute more land, mitigation, or money, barring extraordinary circumstances.[20] In another move, the FWS is

---

[15]*See, e.g.,* Good v. United States, 39 Fed. Cl. 81 (1997).

[16]*See, e.g.,* Ike C. Sugg, *Caught in the Act: Evaluating the Endangered Species Act, Its Effects on Man and Prospects for Reform,* 24 CUMBERLAND L. REV. 1 (1993–94); Stuart L. Somach, *What Outrages Me About the Endangered Species Act,* 24 ENVTL. L. 801 (1994).

[17]Bruce Babbitt, *The Endangered Species Act and "Takings:" A Call for Innovation Within the Terms of the Act,* 24 ENVTL. L. 355 (1994); Ira M. Heyman, *Property Rights and the Endangered Species Act: A Renascent Assault on Land Use Regulation,* 25 PACIFIC L.J. 157 (1994).

[18]ESA § 10(a)(1)(B); 16 U.S.C. § 1539(a)(1)(B).

[19]62 Fed. Reg. 29,091 (1997) (proposed rule codifying FWS policy in effect since 1994).

[20]The number of approved HCPs has risen rapidly in recent years. As of June 30, 1997, the FWS reports approval of 213 incidental take permits with accom-

seeking to negotiate HCPs with regional governments more capable than small landowners of paying for HCP preparation. A different procedure, using federally prepared biological assessments rather than HCPs, is used to bless incidental takings when a federal nexus exists.[21]

Recall as well that critical habitat must be designated only where "prudent," and that, when designated, boundaries may reflect economic impacts. For whatever reason, the FWS has designated critical habitat for only a small portion of listed species, a fact that plainly reduces the potential for takings clashes.

Other bows to economic growth and property rights under active consideration by Secretary Babbitt are advance multispecies planning (to avoid "train wrecks," as he puts it),[22] greater use of the ESA's heightened flexibility for managing threatened (as opposed to endangered) animal species,[23] primary reliance on federally owned lands for conservation efforts, and greater use of federal-state cooperative agreements.[24] Beyond this, the Act also provides for a cabinet-level Endangered Species Committee (popularly, the "God Squad"), a cumbersome, seldom-used mechanism that may permit large projects to proceed despite the threat of species extinction.[25]

Case Law

Because each of these flexibility-enhancing features of the ESA program has its limitations, few would claim that they explain a peculiar

---

panying HCPs, a big increase over the 20 approved as of early 1994. Not everyone is satisfied with the no surprises policy, however; some have questioned whether the ESA authorizes it.

[21]ESA § 7(b)(4)(B); 16 U.S.C. § 1536(b)(4)(B).

[22]By acting before a species is on its ecological deathbed, it is envisioned that preservation measures can be less draconic and more flexible, hence less onerous to the landowner. Held up as a model is the ecosystem planning approach in California's Natural Community Conservation Planning Act, Cal. Fish & Game Code §§ 2800-40. See generally Craig Manson, *Natural Communities Conservation Planning: California's New Ecosystem Approach to Biodiversity*, 24 ENVTL. L. 603 (1994).

[23]ESA § 4(d), 16 U.S.C. § 1533(d). For example, in the Pacific Northwest the Department of the Interior has proposed a "4(d) rule" for the threatened northern spotted owl. This would relieve owners of forested tracts of 80 acres or less of the general prohibition against incidental "takes" of such owls. 60 Fed. Reg. 9,484 (1995).

[24]ESA § 6(c), 16 U.S.C. § 1535(c).

[25]ESA § 7(e), 16 U.S.C. § 1536(e).

fact: as yet, there appears to be not a single reported court decision finding a taking based on an ESA land-use restriction.[26] One cannot glibly attribute this dearth solely to the high hurdles facing takings plaintiffs generally, since another federal environmental program— regulating private wetlands—has sparked a hefty number of takings cases. It is more likely that the ESA produces comparatively more moderate impacts that fall short of the total or near-total elimination of economic use demanded by contemporary takings law. As important, the availability of an HCP/incidental "take" process under the ESA may be raising ripeness doubts in the minds of attorneys considering a taking suit prior to invoking this process. Once the incidental take permit is granted, the restrictions may be beyond takings challenge on the ground that, strictly speaking, they are consented to by the affected landowners.

There appear to be only a few court decisions dealing with land-use limits under federal wildlife law—one, an old case involving the Migratory Bird Treaty Act;[27] another, a 1997 ruling under the ESA. The latter decision, *Good v. United States*,[28] holds that even granting that development would cause an ESA "take" of endangered species on the property, no *Lucas* "total taking" is shown. The property need not necessarily be maintained in its natural state, since both the "take" prohibition and the "federal nexus" section of the Act exempt incidental takes. Stretching the *Penn Central* concept of investment-backed expectations, *Good* also found that land purchased immediately before ESA enactment did not support landowner expectations of government noninterference when pre-ESA federal and state law had signalled a general government interest in protecting rare species. *Good* is now on appeal.

It is hardly taking a risk to predict more ESA-based takings litigation in the future. For example, additional takings lawsuits based on timbering restrictions to protect the threatened northern spotted owl would seem likely, given the restrictions' geographic breadth. One need not look hard to find other acrimonious ESA-related property rights disputes that could breed litigation.

[26]Moreover, there are few cases, reported or pending, that even address such takings challenges.

[27]In *Bailey v. Holland*, 126 F.2d 317 (4th Cir. 1942), the court discerned no taking in application of a Migratory Bird Treaty Act hunting ban to private land near a wildlife refuge, allegedly rendering the land almost worthless.

[28]39 Fed. Cl. 81 (1997).

A majority of states also have endangered species laws, plus laws of the more traditional game-protection variety.[29] As with the ESA, such laws have not generated much case law in the land-use restriction category, possibly the result of conservation efforts that rely chiefly on state-owned lands, formal acquisition of habitat, and private incentives. While almost every state provides statutory protection for endangered or threatened species on the federal list in addition to those on their own list, few go quite as far as the federal enactment in protecting privately owned habitat.

What litigation there is has been filed largely by land developers. A Vermont ruling grappled with the state's denial of a permit for a vacation home development that would overlap a state-protected "deeryard area."[30] The court saw no physical taking (based on the invading deer), though the majority opinion is questionable given its use of a multifactor test in place of the customary per se rule for permanent physical occupations.[31] A Florida decision held that a developer suffered no taking when part of a subdivision development had to be left undisturbed for several years while occupied by a nesting pair of bald eagles.[32] The temporary regulatory claim was rejected on the grounds that the plaintiff was deprived of only its ideal use of the land, and the restricted portion constituted only a third of the entire tract.[33] And a Washington ruling saw no taking in a county's denial of a developer's preliminary plat as inadequate to protect eagle habitat.[34] The developer had failed to show denial of all economic use, said the court, in that the county's decision left open the possibility of a less dense development. Bucking the trend, however, the

[29]See generally RUTH S. MUSGRAVE & MARY A. STEIN, STATE WILDLIFE LAWS HANDBOOK (1993).

[30]Southview Assoc., Ltd. v. Bongartz, 980 F.2d 84 (2d Cir. 1992), cert. denied, 507 U.S. 987 (1993). A deeryard is a place with shrubs and low growth, providing shelter and a food source for deer, especially in winter.

[31]The regulatory taking claim was dismissed on ripeness grounds, but an extended obiter dictum by the chief judge repays close reading. Id. at 100, 105–09.

[32]Florida Game & Fresh Water Fish Comm'n v. Flotilla, Inc., 636 So. 2d 761 (Fla. Dist. Ct. App.), review denied, 645 So. 2d 452 (1994).

[33]In another case, the restriction's confinement to only a modest portion of the tract was instrumental in defeating a taking claim against a timbering limit imposed to protect deeryards. Seven Islands Land Co. v. Maine Land Use Regulation Comm'n, 450 A.2d 475 (Me. 1982).

[34]State v. Lake Lawrence Pub. Lands Protection Ass'n, 92 Wash. 2d 656, 601 P.2d 494 (1979), cert denied, 449 U.S. 830 (1980).

Ninth Circuit has affirmed a jury verdict awarding $1.45 million when a developer was required by the city to scale down a proposed seaside resort in order to, among other things, preserve habitat for an endangered butterfly.[35]

Frustrated developers such as these, of course, are mainstays of the takings debate. In a more exotic scenario, a landowner brought an unsuccessful taking challenge to a state's restriction on the number of hunting permits allowed for his land.[36]

Types of Private Land Impacts: Limits on Defensive Measures

A second impact of wildlife laws on land stems from the restrictions such laws place on the landowner's use of defensive measures against nuisance animals. Depredations by protected animals include consumption of privately owned forage and crops, typically by deer and waterfowl, and attacks on livestock, by predators such as grizzly bears and wolves. The prototype for this type of impact, long preceding the ESA, arose under state hunting restrictions. To be sure, many states appear to recognize a state constitutional right to defend one's property from wild animals, even when contrary to state conservation laws.[37] In addition, landowners are often allowed statutorily to take animals that are destroying their crops, livestock, or other property, usually under permit. Still further, certain states allow for the compensation of wildlife depredations, upon proof of destruction by the landowner.[38] Notwithstanding, conflicts have occurred.

[35]Del Monte Dunes v. City of Monterey, 95 F.3d 1422 (9th Cir. 1996), *cert. granted*, 118 S. Ct. 1359 (1998).

[36]Clajon Prod. Corp. v. Petera, 70 F.3d 1566 (10th Cir. 1995) (restriction did not eliminate all economically beneficial use, nor fail to substantially advance legitimate state interest).

[37]*See, e.g.,* Cross v. State, 370 P.2d 371, 376–77 (Wyo. 1962) (state's due process clause read to guarantee "the inherent and inalienable right to protect property"). *See generally* Mountain States Legal Found. v. Hodel, 759 F.2d 1423, 1428 n.8 (10th Cir. 1986), *cert. denied*, 480 U.S. 851 (1987); J.C. Vance, Annotation, *Right to Kill Game in Defense of Person or Property*, 93 A.L.R.2d 1366 (1964) (noting that property protection right has been found in states having constitutional provision guaranteeing the right of protecting property, and those that do not).

[38]*See generally* MUSGRAVE & STEIN, *supra* note 29, (recommending general

The takings decisions, dating back to a 1917 ruling involving a ban on hunting state-reintroduced beaver, are almost all government wins.[39] Typically, the decisions invoke the sovereign's long-recognized interest in regulating the taking of wildlife (once expressed as state "ownership" of the wildlife within its borders), and government nonresponsibility for the acts of wild animals. The economic impact on the landowner is not closely examined. In the few instances where the plaintiff has been vindicated, it appears that the state's departure from its usual practice of purchasing protective easements was the culprit, not the animal-caused injury per se.[40]

The doctrine of government nonresponsibility running through these takings cases rests on the animals' status as *ferae naturae*—of a wild nature.[41] The hoary rule holds that no one, including governments, can be called to account for the actions of such animals before they have been "reduced to possession."[42] Put otherwise, the sovereign has no duty to control the movement of such animals.[43] For the plaintiff seeking to impose liability for wildlife injuries on the sovereign, the rule is a daunting obstacle, even when the sovereign has aggravated the extent of injury by restricting available defensive measures.

---

adoption of landowner compensation for wildlife damages, along with requirements that landowners attempt to mitigate such damages). A private analog is the wolf compensation fund established by a national environmental group. The fund, which pays livestock owners for losses due to wolf predation, was a major factor in assuaging ranchers' concerns when wolves were reintroduced into the Yellowstone National Park area.

[39]*See, e.g.,* Barrett v. State, 220 N.Y. 423, 116 N.E. 99 (1917) (government-reintroduced beavers); Maitland v. People, 93 Colo. 59, 23 P.2d 116 (1933) (protected deer); Platt v. Philbrick, 8 Cal. App. 2d 27, 47 P.2d 302 (1935) (animals in refuge might proliferate due to year-round hunting ban, damaging private garden); Collopy v. Wildlife Comm'n, 625 P.2d 994 (Colo. 1981) (goose hunting ban).

[40]State v. Herwig, 17 Wis. 2d 442, 117 N.W.2d 335, 340 (1962) (waterfowl hunting ban); Shellnut v. Arkansas, 222 Ark. 25, 258 S.W.2d 570 (1953) (deer hunting ban).

[41]BLACK'S LAW DICTIONARY 619 (6th ed. 1990).

[42]*See, e.g.,* Sickman v. United States, 184 F.2d 616, 618 (7th Cir. 1950), *cert. denied,* 341 U.S. 949 (1951).

[43]*See, e.g.,* Leger v. Louisiana Dep't of Wildlife & Fisheries, 306 So. 2d 391, 394 (La. Ct. App. 1975) (claim based on wildlife-caused damage denied on non-constitutional grounds), *review denied,* 310 So. 2d 640 (La. 1975).

Indeed, this doctrine of government nonresponsibility is so well entrenched as to apply full force, limited case law suggests, even when the marauding animals are introduced into the landowner's vicinity by the government itself.[44] If there are any bounds on the doctrine, one would expect to see them here. In one case, the California courts were unmoved by the plight of a rancher who claimed that Tule elk relocated to nearby state-owned land had migrated onto his land, damaging fences, eating crops raised for livestock, and aggravating streambed erosion.[45] In this case at least, the court held, government intervention did not undermine the animals' *ferae naturae* status because the state only briefly reduced the wild animals to possession, exercised no control after relocation, and employed the animals' historic range.

In recent times, federal wildlife controls have brought on their own share of depredation/takings cases. In contrast with some state constitutions, the federal Constitution has not been construed as affording an inherent right to defense of property, nor does the ESA explicitly allow such a defense in enforcement actions for violating the act. To protect persons, sometimes; but not property.[46] Rather, animal damage control is left in the exclusive hands of federal field agents. Under the ESA, for example, the FWS has promulgated special rules allowing its agents, but not private individuals, to "take" members of certain threatened species and experimental populations that have actually harmed property. So far, special rules cover the *threatened* grizzly bear and experimental populations of red wolves.[47] However, the ESA cannot easily be read to allow the FWS a similar freedom to abate property injuries if a species is listed as *endangered*.

---

[44]*See, e.g.,* Barrett v. State, 220 N.Y. 423, 116 N.E. 99 (1917). In *Barrett,* the state reintroduced beavers to a region of the Adirondack Mountains, where they destroyed hundreds of trees on plaintiff's valuable woodland. Reintroduction was not seen to be different in takings-law contemplation from increasing the beaver population by banning their destruction, which the court believed was surely no taking.

[45]Moerman v. State, 17 Cal. App. 4th 452, 21 Cal. Rptr. 2d 329 (Cal. Ct. App.), *review denied,* No. S034811 (Cal. 1993), *cert. denied,* 511 U.S. 1031 (1994).

[46]*See, e.g.,* ESA § 11(a)(3), 16 U.S.C. § 1540(a)(3) (protection of persons as civil defense); ESA § 11(b)(3), 16 U.S.C. § 1540(b)(3) (protection of persons as criminal defense).

[47]50 C.F.R. §§ 17.40(b)((i)(c)(grizzlies), 17.84 (c) (5) (red wolves).

After an early Migratory Bird Treaty Act (MBTA) ruling, finding no taking when protected geese damaged private crops,[48] the federal case law has accelerated in recent years with several more no-taking decisions. Courts continue to be unmoved by the government's contributory role through limitation of the landowner's defenses, and the doctrine of *ferae naturae*, by name or equivalent statement, remains firmly entrenched.

Most dramatic, and illustrative of the conflict between private property and the ESA, is *Christy v. Hodel*.[49] There, after losing many sheep to bears, a frustrated rancher shot a grizzly bear menacing his sheep and was assessed a civil penalty of $2,500 for his "take" of a threatened species. The court found no regulatory taking of Christy's sheep because, it said, FWS regulations left him with a complete bundle of property rights in them. Additionally, the court found no physical taking of the sheep because the United States neither owns nor controls the wildlife it protects; the rancher's loss is merely the "incidental . . . result" of reasonable regulation.

In other federal takings cases, compensation was denied when wild horses protected under the Wild Free-Roaming Horses and Burros Act consumed private livestock forage;[50] when water sources on federal land, used by ranchers under federal permits for their livestock, had to be shared with such horses;[51] and when compelled removal of a fence on a private ranch led to pronghorn antelope competing for forage with the cattle there.[52]

---

[48]Bishop v. United States, 126 F. Supp. 449, 452 (Ct. Cl. 1954), *cert. denied*, 349 U.S. 955 (1955). Another claim from this period, also involving migratory waterfowl, was brought under the Federal Tort Claims Act (FTCA). Sickman v. United States, 184 F.2d 616 (7th Cir. 1950), *cert. denied*, 341 U.S. 939 (1951). The plaintiff's theory was that by protecting the birds under the MBTA, the United States became responsible for ensuing crop damage. The court disagreed, holding that because individuals cannot be held liable under *ferae naturae* for the trespasses of animals in a state of nature, neither, under the FTCA, can the United States. *See* 28 U.S.C. § 2675(a).

[49]857 F.2d 1324 (9th Cir. 1988), *cert. denied*, 490 U.S. 1114 (1989).

[50]Mountain States Legal Found. v. Hodel, 799 F.2d 1423, 1430–31 (10th Cir. 1986), *cert. denied*, 480 U.S. 851 (1987).

[51]Fallini v. United States, 31 Fed. Cl. 53 (1994) (no taking), *vacated*, 56 F.3d 1378 (Fed. Cir. 1995) (complaint not timely filed), *cert. denied*, 116 S. Ct. 2496 (1996).

[52]United States *ex rel.* Bergen v. Lawrence, 848 F.2d 1502, 1507 (10th Cir.), *cert. denied*, 488 U.S. 980 (1988).

Cross-Cutting Issues

A few matters extend to *both* restrictions on private land use and limits on the landowner's defensive measures. Probably the most important is the fish or fowl question: whether to analyze wildlife law impacts as physical or regulatory takings. Plaintiffs often assert that wildlife laws should be seen as causing permanent physical occupation of land by the protected animals or as causing an appropriation of consumed livestock and forage. For the property owner, this approach has the advantage that takings law is intolerant of government appropriations and occupations of property. The downside for the property owner is that without exception, the courts embrace *ferae naturae* and refuse to attribute the animals' presence or depredations to government. Intense government management of a species, or capture and relocation of a herd, may be the only way to circumvent this entrenched legal doctrine.

By contrast, if wildlife laws are seen as land-use regulation, the barrier to the takings plaintiff is a factual one—proving total or near-total reduction in the value of the property viewed as a whole.[53] One suspects that in the overwhelming majority of cases, such a showing cannot be made, since economic uses of the property not constituting "takes" still remain. Owing to *ferae naturae*, courts seem to prefer the regulatory taking line of analysis.

Another cross-cutting matter is government's historic involvement with wildlife and the impact of *Lucas v. South Carolina Coastal Council*. On one level, *Lucas* will have little effect. Signals from the few federal cases suggest that regulation in the name of wildlife protection—even to avert extinction—will continue to be evaluated for takings under the same case-by-case standards as other government action affecting property. *Lucas* endorses this view. There, the Court specifically noted conservation of endangered species habitat as an example of a governmental purpose easily characterized as *both* prevention of public harm (traditionally deemed noncompensable) and creation of a public benefit (often held compensable).[54] At the very least, then, wildlife protection programs may not be able to circum-

---

[53]*See, e.g., Mountain States*, 799 F.2d at 1428 (Wild Free-Roaming Horses and Burros Act "is nothing more than a land-use regulation"), *cert. denied*, 480 U.S. 851 (1987).

[54]*Lucas*, 505 U.S. at 1024 n.11.

vent case-by-case balancing. In addition, *Lucas* is explicit that its rule of per se compensability for regulatory "total takings" generally applies regardless of the public interest advanced to justify the restraint.

Another facet of *Lucas*, however, opens the door through which government's historic interest in wildlife may enter the takings analysis. The *Lucas* decision pronounced that total takings are not compensable when the landowner's proposed actions are inconsistent with "background principles of the State's law of property and nuisance" existing when the property was acquired. It was earlier noted that this "background principles" concept cannot logically be confined to total takings—or, for that matter, to regulatory takings. Under this view, the historic involvement of states in wildlife regulation, if accepted as background principles, may shrink the already small probability that property owners will be able to prove takings in this area.[55] If the ESA and other federal wildlife laws are similarly embraced as background principles, one who purchases land after their enactment, or after a species is listed, may face a similar obstacle.[56]

Some observers have even suggested that quite apart from whether or not wildlife statutes exist at the time land is acquired, destruction of wildlife and its essential habitat may be brought within the *Lucas* exception as common law public nuisance.[57] Others have opined that that amorphous creature, the public trust doctrine, might be a basis for government restraints on wildlife-harming activities and a shield

[55]A California state court appears to be the only judicial forum to address this point thus far. In Sierra Club v. Department of Forestry & Fire Protection, 21 Cal. App. 4th 603, 26 Cal. Rptr. 2d 338, 347 (1993), the court noted in dictum that "wildlife regulation of some sort has been historically a part of the pre-existing law of property," and hence seems to qualify as a *Lucas* background principle. However, this decision was ordered "depublished" under California court rules and, therefore, may not be cited as precedent in California. 1994 Cal. LEXIS 1388 (March 18, 1994). *See generally* Oliver A. Houck, *Why Do We Protect Endangered Species, and What Does That Say About Whether Restrictions on Private Property to Protect Them Constitute "Takings"?*, 80 IOWA L. REV. 297, 308–21 (1995).

[56]Whether *Lucas* background principles extend to federal as well as state law, and to statutory as well as common law, remains unsettled.

[57]*See, e.g.,* Paula C. Murray, *Private Takings of Endangered Species as Public Nuisance*, 12 J. ENVTL. L. 119 (1993).

against any resulting takings actions.[58] For the moment, however, the courts appear committed to a straightforward "remaining economic uses" test for wildlife-related regulatory takings.

Conclusion

It has been said that while property rights are well analyzed in our legal and moral tradition, our legal and ethical duties to wildlife are novel and not universally accepted.[59] Foregoing development of private land that might harm a public drinking water source is a sacrifice most landowners might accept as noncompensable; having one's livelihood disrupted to preserve an endangered bird has proven a tougher call.

Ultimately, courts may have to confront head-on the question of whether there is a protectable property interest in private land uses that harm wildlife and wildlife habitat, and whether the specter of extinction makes any difference. The "background principles" concept of *Lucas* and the public trust doctrine prefigure this debate. For the near term, however, the Supreme Court seems unlikely to condone any approaches that shrink the envelope of constitutional protection, and takings analysis of wildlife cases should proceed within the customary ad hoc, case-by-case framework.

---

[58]*See, e.g.,* Anna R.C. Casperson, *The Public Trust Doctrine and the Impossibility of "Takings" by Wildlife,* 23 BOSTON COLLEGE ENVTL. AFF. L. REV. 357 (1996); Gary D. Meyers, *Variation on a Theme: Expanding the Public Trust Doctrine to Include Protection of Wildlife,* 19 ENVTL. L. 723 (1989).

[59]Holmes Ralston, III, *Property Rights and Endangered Species,* 61 U. COLORADO L. REV. 283, 283 (1990).

Chapter 25

Mining

It is one of the world's oldest economic pursuits. So it is only fitting that mining gave rise to the Supreme Court's first decision recognizing the concept of regulatory takings, in 1922.[1] Since that year, mining-related takings cases have made regular appearances on the Court's docket, from the wartime seizure and shutdown cases of the 1950s,[2] to quarrying in the 1960s,[3] to the surface mining, elimination of stale claims, and prevention-of-subsidence decisions of the 1980s.[4] A surface mining case from the lower federal courts has given us what may be the largest regulatory taking settlement (or, for that matter, judgment) in American legal history—$200 million.[5]

A survey of the mining takings cases reveals the broad spectrum of environmental stresses that this admittedly necessary economic activity can inflict. The cases spring from government prohibition of

[1]Pennsylvania Coal Co. v. Mahon, 260 U.S. 393 (1922).

[2]United States v. Central Eureka Mining Co., 357 U.S. 155 (1958) (no taking by federal wartime shutdown of nonessential gold mines); United States v. Pewee Coal Co., 341 U.S. 114 (1951) (taking by federal wartime seizure of coal mine).

[3]Goldblatt v. Town of Hempstead, 369 U.S. 590 (1962) (no taking through ordinance barring excavation below water table).

[4]Discussed *passim*.

[5]Whitney Benefits, Inc. v. United States, 926 F.2d 1169 (Fed. Cir.), *cert. denied*, 502 U.S. 952 (1995). This settlement, reached in 1995, terminated litigation in which a taking of plaintiff's mineral estate was found as a direct result of Congress's action in enacting the Surface Mining Control and Reclamation Act of 1977. It is not an instance of taking by discretionary agency action, as in the usual case.

mining that disrupts alluvial valley floors,[6] prime farmlands,[7] wetlands,[8] steep slopes,[9] and ecosystems generally,[10] or pollutes streams[11] and, in the case of oil and gas, ocean waters of the continental shelf.[12] Other cases have arisen from government proscription of mining seen to threaten the public safety—as through the subsidence effects of underground mining or with open quarrying in populated areas.[13] Still other mining takings decisions are borne of regulatory efforts to protect special areas, such as burial sites,[14] mountains,[15] national parks, historic sites, homes, schools, and churches,[16] or to avoid waste.[17]

But mining prohibitions are not the only ways in which government actions have prompted takings cases in this area. Other takings issues have been spawned by the contested constitutional status of the partial and inchoate property interests often involved in mining activities, and by government efforts to weed out long-dormant claims, apply new requirements (environmental and economic) to existing mining operations, require disclosure of sensitive information, clean up contaminated mining sites, and so on. Given this diversity of

[6]*Id.*

[7]Hodel v. Indiana, 452 U.S. 314 (1981).

[8]Florida Rock Indus., Inc. v. United States, 18 F.3d 1580 (Fed. Cir. 1994), *cert. denied*, 513 U.S. 1109 (1995).

[9]Hodel v. Virginia Surface Mining & Reclamation Ass'n, 452 U.S. 264 (1981).

[10]Michigan Oil Co. v. Natural Resources Comm'n, 71 Mich. App. 667, 249 N.W.2d 135 (1977).

[11]Rybacheck v. United States, 23 Cl. Ct. 222 (1991); Commonwealth v. Barnes & Tucker Co., 472 Pa. 115, 371 A.2d 461 (1977).

[12]Sun Oil Co. v. United States, 572 F.2d 786 (Ct. Cl. 1978); Union Oil Co. v. Morton, 512 F.2d 743 (9th Cir. 1975).

[13]*See* Goldblatt v. Town of Hempstead, 369 U.S. 590 (1962); Bernardsville Quarry, Inc. v. Borough of Bernardsville, 129 N.J. 221, 608 A.2d 1377 (1992).

[14]Thompson v. City of Red Wing, 455 N.W.2d 512 (Minn. Ct. App. 1990); Department of Natural Resources v. Indiana Coal Council, 542 N.E.2d 1000 (Ind. 1989).

[15]Rissler & McMurry Co. v. State, 917 P.2d 1157 (Wyo. 1996) (taking claim unripe due to failure to exhaust administrative remedies), *cert. denied*, 117 S. Ct. 765 (1997).

[16]Hodel v. Virginia Surface Mining & Reclamation Ass'n, 452 U.S. 264, 294 n.36, 296 n.37 (1981).

[17]Big Piney Oil & Gas Co. v. Wyoming, 715 P.2d 557 (Wyo. 1986).

factual settings, we first provide a general takings overview, then divide the topic of mining and takings by factual setting.[18]

The takings cases generated by mining restrictions do not stray far from the takings law mainstream. The government action's impact on the mine operator must be severe before the taking line is crossed, the state mining cases holding to the general state court view that *all* economically viable use must be eliminated.[19]

This high hurdle may not be as daunting in the mining cases as it has been elsewhere, however. First, consider the owner of land in fee simple. While such owners usually have residual uses after a government restriction is imposed, undermining the taking claim, it may happen that the mining company fee-owner does not. The company may be able to demonstrate that it paid so much for the land that no use other than mining generates enough profit to be a reasonable return on investment.[20] Or, there may be special circumstances, such as wetlands mining, where mining is the only economic use.[21]

A greater advantage for winning a taking action inures to the mine operator who owns something less than an unqualified fee-simple interest, as such operators often do. By virtue of owning only a mineral estate or possessing only a leasehold, a mining enterprise is far more

[18]*See generally* Jan G. Laitos, *Regulation of Natural Resources Use and Development in Light of the "New" Takings Clause*, 34 ROCKY MTN. MIN. L. INST. 1-1 (1988); Mary A. Viviano, *The Takings Clause: A Protection to Private Property Rights in Federal Oil and Gas Leases*, 74 TULSA L.J. 43 (1988); Marla E. Mansfield, *Regulatory Takings, Expectations, and Valid Existing Rights*, 5 J. MIN. L. & POL'Y 431 (1989–90); Patrick C. McGinley, *Of Pigs and Parlors: Regulatory Takings in the Coal Fields*, 5 J. MIN. L. & POL'Y 473 (1989–90).

[19]*See, e.g.*, Miller Bros. v. DNR, 203 Mich. App. 674, 513 N.W.2d 217, 220, *appeal denied*, 447 Mich. 1038, 527 N.W.2d 513 (1994); Thompson v. City of Red Wing, 455 N.W.2d 512 (Minn. Ct. App. 1990); Massimo v. Town of Naugatuck, 41 Conn. Supp. 196, 564 A.2d 1075 (Super. Ct. 1989).

[20]This line of argument bumps up against the vagueness of the economically viable use concept in takings law. Many courts have not made clear that a property use generating positive cash flow cannot be an economically viable use for purposes of takings law when such cash flow fails to provide a reasonable return on investment.

[21]The mining-in-a-wetland case of Florida Rock Industries, Inc. v. United States complicates the text assertion, however. There, the Federal Circuit held that the economically viable use factor in takings law embraces not only immediately available use of the property, but sale to knowledgeable speculators as well. *Id.*, 791 F.2d 893, 901–03 (Fed. Cir. 1986), *cert. denied*, 479 U.S. 1053 (1987).

likely than the fee-simple owner of land to be in a position to claim that it lost *all* the rights it had at the hands of government—and hence suffered a taking.[22] A prohibition on mining leaves a mineral estate holder with nothing;[23] the fee-simple landowner likely has other possibilities.

There appears to be a small exception to the strategic disadvantage of broader property interests. It occurs when the mineral interest owner holds an ancillary property interest solely to facilitate mineral development. In *Keystone Bituminous Coal Ass'n v. DeBenedictis*, a "support estate" recognized by state law as a separate interest in land was found incapable of supporting a taking action.[24] As a practical matter, said the Court, the support estate's value derives entirely from the mineral or surface estate to which it is attached. Thus, it must be "bundled" with the primary estate for purposes of determining whether a regulatory taking occurred. That being so, a state antisubsidence law that did not interfere with exploitation of a mineral estate sufficiently to be a taking, did not take the associated support estate.[25]

Certainly one of the key questions a takings court faces in connection with mining restrictions, particularly after *Keystone* and *Lucas*, is whether mining constitutes a nuisance. If so, the taking claim is usually dealt a fatal blow. As nuisance law requires, whether a particular mine is a public nuisance depends on whether the court sees it as a threat to public health and safety.

The opposing Supreme Court decisions in *Pennsylvania Coal* and *Keystone* neatly make the point. In *Pennsylvania Coal*, the Supreme Court buttressed its holding of a taking by finding that the subsidence statute in question was "not justified as a protection of personal

[22]*See, e.g.,* Miller Bros v. DNR, 203 Mich. App. 674, 513 N.W.2d 217, *appeal denied*, 447 Mich. 1038, 527 N.W.2d 513 (1994); Western Energy Co. v. Genie Land Co., 227 Mont. 74, 737 P.2d 478 (1987).

[23]As stated in *Pennsylvania Coal:* "For practical purposes, the right to coal consists in the right to mine it." 260 U.S. 393, 414 (1922).

[24]480 U.S. 470, 501–02 (1987).

[25]Similar belittling of property interests ancillary to the primary mineral interest occurred in Whitney Benefits, Inc. v. United States, 926 F.2d 1169, 1174 (Fed. Cir.) (taking claim based on surface mining ban not deflected by plaintiff's ownership of surface acreage solely to allow exploitation of claim), *cert. denied*, 112 U.S. 406 (1991), and Murphy v. Amoco Prod. Co., 729 F.2d 552 (8th Cir. 1984) (legislative abolishment of right to damage surface without compensating surface owner is not taking since mineral estate must be viewed as a whole).

safety."[26] In *Keystone*, the Court's rejection of the taking attack on a similar subsidence law was based in part on its labeling of deep mining that causes subsidence as "tantamount to [a] public nuisance[]."[27] Rulings from lower courts have also come down on both sides. For example, the Federal Circuit found surface mining on alluvial valley floors not to be a nuisance, because the controlling statute permitted most mining in such areas and the government claimed no safety threat. A taking was found.[28] By contrast, the same court held that deep mining that threatened breakage of gas, water, and electric lines as well as collapse of surface structures, was a substantial risk to public health and safety and could be proscribed without compensation.[29] State court decisions likewise straddle the nuisance issue based on the facts presented.[30]

As with the nuisance determination, a mining takings case also may stand or fall on the "parcel as a whole" issue. The towering decision is *Keystone*, which affirmed the rule against carving up property into segments for purposes of takings analysis not once, but twice.[31] First, said the Court, the state's requirement that 50 percent of the coal under surface structures be left in the ground to prevent subsidence is not a taking of the left-behind coal. That coal does not constitute a separate segment of property under takings law.[32] Second, the fact that the state recognizes a support estate separate

[26]260 U.S. at 414.

[27]480 U.S. at 491. *See also* Hodel v. Indiana, 452 U.S. 314, 329 (1981).

[28]*Whitney Benefits*, 926 F.2d 1169. *See also* Eastern Minerals Int'l v. United States, 36 Fed. Cl. 541 (1996) (coal mining may constitute nuisance in certain circumstances, but not shown to be nuisance here; taking found).

[29]M & J Coal Co. v. United States, 47 F.3d 1148 (Fed. Cir. 1995), *cert. denied*, 516 U.S. 808 (1995).

[30]*Cf.* Aztec Minerals Corp. v. Colorado, 940 P.2d 1025, 1032 (Colo. App. 1996) (abandoned mine polluting site and downstream waters is public nuisance) and Bernardsville Quarry, Inc. v. Borough of Bernardsville, 129 N.J. 221, 608 A.2d 1377 (1992) (quarry that might be "attractive nuisance" held a public nuisance-like activity) *with* Miller Bros. v. DNR, 203 Mich. App. 674, 513 N.W.2d 217 (1994) (nuisance law aims to protect adjoining owner, not, as here, surface owner), *appeal denied*, 447 Mich. 1038, 527 N.W.2d 513 (1994) and Western Energy Co. v. Genie Land Co., 227 Mont. 74, 737 P.2d 478 (1987) (surface mining is not a nuisance in this state; no suggestion of safety threat).

[31]480 U.S. at 496–502 (1987).

It's All Relative . . .

Twenty-seven million tons of coal sounds like a large amount to have to leave in the ground. It *is* a large amount. But takings law deals in how the property that is restricted relates to the full quantum of property owned.

In *Keystone,* the Supreme Court confronted a Pennsylvania law that sought to prevent the evils of surface subsidence from underground bituminous coal mining.

It did this by requiring coal companies to leave 50 percent of their bituminous coal in the ground as supporting pillars, when that coal is below surface structures. The coal companies suing in *Keystone* argued that this requirement meant, as applied to their mines, that 27 million tons of coal had to be left behind. However, the total amount of coal in the companies' mines was 1.46 *billion* tons—making the left-behind portion less than two percent of what the plaintiffs owned *in toto.*

How did the Court deal with this? At the outset, it lamented that it could not be sure how much of the 27 million tons had to be abandoned

---

from the mineral or surface estate does not alter the outcome. Though the value of the mine operators' support estate was arguably completely destroyed, the Court rejected use of "legalistic distinctions within a bundle of property rights."[33] The value of the support estate, it found, was merely part of the bundle of sticks held by either the coal or surface owner.

With this overview in mind, let us turn now to some takings issues peculiar to mining.

---

[32]*Contra*, Miller Bros. v. DNR, 203 Mich. App. 674, 513 N.W.2d 217, 220 (1994) (where slant drilling under protected area would not allow removal of all oil and gas, there was taking of unextractable portion), *appeal denied*, 447 Mich. 1038, 527 N.W.2d 513 (1994).

In *Keystone*, it should be noted, the restricted and unrestricted coal was contiguous. Generally, a court is unlikely to fold into the relevant parcel a mine operator's *noncontiguous* mineral holdings in the area. Western Energy Co. v. Genie Land Co., 227 Mont. 74, 737 P.2d 478, 483 (1987). *See* Lucas v. South Carolina Coastal Council, 505 U.S. 1003, 1016 n.7 (1992).

[33]Keystone, 480 U.S. at 500.

solely because of the anti-subsidence law. (Other reasons may prevent the extraction of coal.) More important, the Court reasserted its "property as a whole" rule: Takings law does not allow the conceptual segmenting of property so that the landowner can assert that the restricted portion suffered the threshold use deprivation. Here, the rule meant that the 27 million tons of coal were not to be analyzed separately, but rather as a small portion of the plaintiffs' aggregate holdings. Viewed that way, the Court felt the mining companies had not even come close to showing the kind of severe economic impact, or severe interference with investment-backed expectations, that is needed to find a taking.

But make no mistake: *Keystone* was a squeaker. While five justices felt that making 2 percent of the coal nonextractable was insufficient, a four-justice dissent felt otherwise. The dissent argued that at least where the government eliminates all use of an identifiable segment of property, as it did here, that segment should stand alone in the takings analysis. As yet, this view has not become the majority position on the Supreme Court.

Conflicts Between Mineral and Surface Use: Subsidence

In the late 19th century, the concept of vertical severance of land-ownership was born. If the right to mine ("mineral estate") could be separated from rights in the overlying surface ("surface estate"), it was claimed, then both mining company and surface owner could benefit. In poorer regions in particular, the opportunity to acquire cheaper land (from a seller reserving mineral rights) or needed cash (from sale of one's underlying mineral estate) proved an irresistible arrangement. Typically, the mineral estate holder also purchased or reserved the right to cause subsidence of the overlying surface without liability to the surface owner.

A simple-enough scheme—until the mining advances from far-off possibility to imminent certainty. Then the existence of severed estates creates difficult issues as to concurrent use and development.[34] Subsidence of the severed surface is but one example.

In 1921, Pennsylvania undertook to rescue surface owners faced with imminent deep mining under their lots from certain consequences of such a severance deal, made forty-three years earlier. In

[34]*See generally* 6 AMERICAN LAW OF MINING ch. 200 (1994).

the Kohler Act enacted that year, the state forbade the mining of an-
thracite coal in such a manner as to cause subsidence of the land, but
restricted the Act's application largely to land where the surface was
owned by someone other than the mineral owner. This narrow scope
allowed the Supreme Court to characterize the case, *Pennsylvania
Coal Co. v. Mahon*, as infused with little public interest.[35] Rather, it
was seen to involve no more than the state's attempt to give surface
owners "greater rights than they bought," at the expense of complete
elimination of the mining company's interest. This the Court could
not condone—it found a taking of the mineral rights.

Now skip ahead to modern times, where several courts have held
subsidence statutes *not* to effect takings. What has changed? At least
as the courts describe it, it is the more public nature of the interest
that the state claims to be advancing. In the leading recent case, *Keystone Bituminous Coal Ass'n v. DeBenedictis*, the Supreme Court asserted (five justices to four) that the challenged subsidence law displayed "[n]one of the indicia of a statute enacted solely for the benefit
of private parties."[36] The statute recited a litany of public purposes:
protection of health and safety, enhancement of tax value, preservation of surface water drainage, and so on. Moreover, unlike in *Pennsylvania Coal*, the statutory mining prohibition here made no exception for land where the surface was owned by the owner of the
coal—showing that something more than a private-benefit statute
rescuing only severed surface owners was contemplated.[37]

A significant lower court voice on the subsidence matter is *M & J
Coal Co. v. United States*. *M & J* found no taking after a federal
agency, to prevent further subsidence, required that an ongoing mine
operation leave more coal behind than the company had envisioned
when it bought the mining rights.[38] Though the mining company had
acquired the right of subjacent support, that fact did not immunize it
against regulatory action to abate the threat of utility line breakage,
surface fissures hazardous to children, and dangerous sinkholes—
harms of a distinctly public sort.

[35] 260 U.S. 393 (1922).

[36] 480 U.S. 470, 486 (1987). *See also* Old Ben Coal Co. v. Department of
Mines & Minerals, 204 Ill. App. 3d 1062, 562 N.E.2d 1202 (1990) (using *Keystone* public-purpose rationale to hold that state law effected no taking of mining
company's surface support waivers).

[37] *Keystone* involved a facial challenge; the Court did not address whether the
impact of the Act on a specific property might be a taking.

[38] 47 F.3d 1148 (Fed. Cir. 1995), *cert. denied,* 516 U.S. 808 (1995).

Plainly, statute drafters should take care that both the legislative findings and the structure of subsidence laws reasonably support a broad public purpose, rather than merely protecting surface owners who made a shortsighted real estate deal.[39]

Conflicts Between Mineral and Surface Use: Issues Other than Subsidence

The extreme surface disruption caused by strip mining, as compared to that of underground mining, has long fueled efforts to thwart strip mining when not consented to by the surface owner. One setting for this drama has been the "broadform deed," a type of deed for severing the surface estate from the mineral estate on a parcel that was in common use by Appalachian coal companies around the turn of the century. The broadform deed, however, was silent as to the method of extraction contemplated. At the time, deep mining was the prevailing technique, but technological advances in ensuing decades made strip mining an economically attractive way to extract. Early efforts to convince courts that the broadform deed contemplated extraction only by the techniques known at the time of signing—that is, underground mining—were generally unsuccessful.

In 1988, Kentucky adopted a constitutional amendment saying that in severance transfers not specifying the method of coal extraction, it shall be held, absent clear evidence to the contrary, that the parties' intention was that extraction be by methods in use in the area at the time the instrument was executed. No taking of the mineral holders' rights, said the state supreme court—four justices to three.[40] The amendment, the court explained, simply codified a rule of contract construction designed to give effect to the original intention of the parties. It didn't hurt, either, that the amendment's reading of that original intent was seen by the court to be correct, reflecting the

[39]*See, e.g.*, Natural Resources Comm'n v. Amax Coal Co., 638 N.E.2d 418 (Ind. 1994), where a surface mine operator cried taking based on the state's restricting its groundwater use to avert subsidence *off-site*. These facts deprived the mining company of a *Pennsylvania Coal*-type argument that the state was merely seeking to relieve surface owners of an improvident deal. No taking was found.

[40]Ward v. Harding, 860 S.W.2d 280 (Ky. 1993), *cert. denied*, 510 U.S. 1177 (1994).

growing dissatisfaction in its recent decisions with its early acceptance of strip mining under broadform deeds. A spirited dissent, however, accused the majority of ignoring long-standing precedent and bowing to the popular clamor for reform.

A useful contrast may be drawn between the foregoing case and one in which no plausible argument existed that the mineral interest at issue was confined to deep mining. In the latter case, a state statute requiring surface-owner consent before a strip mining permit could be granted was found indistinguishable from the antisubsidence statute in *Pennsylvania Coal*, hence a taking.[41]

Mining on Government Land: Status, Scope of the Claim

Prospecting on federal- or state-owned land may lead to the government's granting any of an assortment of property interests: unpatented claims, leaseholds, or, after patent, fee title.[42] That leaseholds and fee titles should fall under the protection of the Fifth Amendment is hardly surprising[43]—they are traditional property rights known to every first-year law student. Less obvious is that unpatented claims to minerals on federal lands—a mere possessory in-

---

[41]Western Energy Co. v. Genie Land Co., 227 Mont. 74, 737 P.2d 478 (1987).

[42]Under the General Mining Law of 1872, 30 U.S.C. §§ 21–54, persons may enter federal lands to prospect for certain "hard" minerals (gold, silver, etc.) and file claims therefor. In order to be valid, claims must be "located" and recorded in accordance with prescribed procedures, and must be on legally available land. In order to *remain* valid, claims must be maintained by making yearly improvements. The claim holder can file for a "patent," and thus obtain fee-simple title to the land. Because of the extremely low charge extracted for these land patents, the absence of environmental controls on ensuing operations, and other reasons, the General Mining Law has been the subject of congressional reform efforts for more than a decade.

Mining of certain "soft" minerals (coal, oil, gas, phosphates, etc.) on federal lands plays out under the Mineral Lands Leasing Act of 1920, 30 U.S.C. §§ 181–287, through a leasing system rather than conveyance of outright title.

[43]*See, e.g.,* Foster v. United States, 607 F.2d 943 (Ct. Cl. 1979) (lease from private party); Sun Oil Co. v. United States, 572 F.2d 786 (Ct. Cl. 1978) (lease under federal Outer Continental Shelf Lands Act). On occasion, the fact that plaintiff holds a lease causes judicial confusion as to whether the challenge should be treated as sounding in taking or breach of contract.

terest based on location of valuable minerals—should also be firmly entrenched as property within the ambit of takings law.

Yet this has long been so. A valid, unpatented claim gives the claim holder only the right to possess land for the purpose of developing and extracting mineral resources; the United States retains legal title to the land and may regulate disturbance of surface resources under several statutory and constitutional authorities.[44] Courts have universally labeled unpatented mining claims as "property."[45] The claimant is said to enjoy "a valid, equitable title in the claim, possessing all of the incidents of real property;"[46] it is "property in the fullest sense of the term."[47] Thus, the Takings Clause limits the government's ability to regulate or limit access to, and clearly to divest, valid mining claims.[48] As elsewhere, however, no taking occurs as long as regulation of surface disturbance does not seriously interfere with exploitation of the claim.[49]

It is fundamental that to be valid, claims must be on federal lands that have not been withdrawn from location (that is, have not been set aside for other purposes). Thus, claims filed after withdrawal cannot support a taking claim, since no property right ever existed.[50] Noncompensability is the rule as well when the claim is filed during a period when the government believed the land locatable, only to be judicially informed later that it had committed legal error making the claim void from the outset.[51] Indeed, the same outcome may result even when a claim initially valid is later rendered invalid by govern-

[44]See, e.g., 30 U.S.C. § 612(b). Said the Supreme Court: "The United States, as owner of the underlying fee title to the public domain, maintains broad powers over the terms and conditions upon which the public lands can be used. . . ." United States v. Locke, 471 U.S. 84, 104 (1985).

[45]Locke, 471 U.S. at 104; Kunkes v. United States, 78 F.3d 1549, 1551 (Fed. Cir. 1996); United States v. Bagwell, 961 F.2d 1450 (9th Cir. 1992); Freese v. United States, 6 Cl. Ct. 1, 10 (1984), aff'd, 770 F.2d 177 (Fed. Cir. 1985); Oil Shale Corp. v. Morton, 370 F. Supp. 108, 124 (D. Colo. 1973).

[46]Kunkes v. United States, 32 Fed. Cl. 243, 252 (1994), aff'd, 78 F.3d 1549 (Fed. Cir. 1996).

[47]Wilbur v. Kruishnic, 280 U.S. 306, 316 (1930).

[48]However, the Takings Clause may not be used to overturn a Department of the Interior determination that a claim is invalid. That must be attempted through an Administrative Procedure Act suit in federal district court. Hafen v. United States, 30 Fed. Cl. 470, 473 (1994).

[49]Freese, 6 Cl. Ct. at 16.

[50]Clawson v. United States, 24 Cl. Ct. 366, 369 (1991).

[51]Id.

ment action, if the court is confronted with the wrong plaintiff. Thus, the hapless purchaser who buys a claim that was minable under then-existing agency interpretation of a statute, only to see that interpretation judicially reversed, gets no relief under takings law. As a general rule, takings law compensates only the owner of property as of the date of the government action—here, the statute's effective date.[52]

As the United States has shifted over the past century from a policy of conveying away title to the public lands towards one of retention in federal ownership with permitted private uses, a new issue has arisen. If a holder of an unpatented mining claim under the 1872 General Mining Law is blocked from proceeding to patent (fee ownership), does that offend the Takings Clause? Put differently, is the right to obtain full fee ownership a property right in itself, distinct from either the unpatented claim or the desired patent? The answer, says limited case law, is that the right to receive a patent is indeed a separate property right, but only once a claim holder fully complies with the extensive procedures in federal mining law for obtaining a patent. Thus, a claim holder not in full compliance with such law as of the effective date of a law creating a new national recreation area was not owed compensation as a result of the law's ban on issuance of further patents.[53]

Finally, questions may arise as to the scope of the mineral interest, often due to ambiguous wording in the governing legal instruments. Government efforts to thwart mining activity while adjudicating the bounds of the mineral right in good faith do not constitute a taking. A closer call, however, is when the government blocks a long-standing mining operation and then leaves initiation of judicial proceedings (ultimately holding the government action invalid) to the unfortunate miner.[54]

Additional Regulation of an Existing Operation

Having gotten the needed approvals and begun exploration or devel-

---

[52]Fixel v. United States, 26 Cl. Ct. 353 (1992).

[53]Freese v. United States, 639 F.2d 754 (Ct. Cl.), *cert. denied*, 454 U.S. 827 (1981). *See also* NRDC v. Berklund, 609 F.2d 553 (D.C. Cir. 1980).

[54]Yuba Goldfields, Inc. v. United States, 723 F.2d 884 (Fed. Cir. 1983).

opment, a mining operator should not become complacent. Government may, for a variety of reasons, draw further regulatory arrows from its quiver. New, sometimes costly, conditions on the exercise of mining rights require the operator first to ascertain whether the governing statute, regulations, or lease terms contemplate the imposition of new conditions. If so, no taking exists.[55]

One would expect that where new environmental awareness points to hitherto unknown dangers of mining, all but the severest restrictions could be added by government without effecting a taking. Moreover, as the Supreme Court has said in a taking case, "[t]hose who do business in the regulated field cannot object if the legislative scheme is buttressed by subsequent amendments to achieve the legislative end."[56] Because constitutional compensation is uncertain, legislatures may have to pick up the compensation ball in some instances if mining companies nervous about the possibility of future restrictions are to make large capital commitments. Illustrative is the Outer Continental Shelf Lands Act, which sets out a mechanism for agency compensation of oil and gas leaseholders under the Act when outright cancellation of a lease is required to avert serious environmental harm.[57]

Economic motives also may animate government to impose new burdens. Thus, dissatisfaction with the low royalty that lessees were paying for publicly owned coal led to the Federal Coal Leasing Amendments Act of 1976, raising the royalty for existing leases to 12.5 percent of coal value.[58] Lessees claimed a taking based on the fact that their leases provided for "reasonable" royalty readjustment which, they argued, demanded individualized consideration of each lease.[59] Noting that interpretations that immunize entities from sovereign power are disfavored, the court found no unmistakable sur-

---

[55]Recall M & J Coal Co. v. United States, 47 F.3d 1148 (Fed. Cir. 1995) (added restrictions within statutory remedial authority existing when mining rights acquired, hence no taking), *cert. denied*, 516 U.S. 808 (1995).

[56]Concrete Pipe & Prod. of Ca. v. Construction Laborers Pension Trust, 508 U.S. 602, 645 (1993) (quoting FHA v. The Darlington, Inc., 358 U.S. 84, 91 (1958)). Some caution is appropriate in extrapolating this principle from the economic regulation cases in which it usually appears to the land-use context involved in mining cases.

[57]43 U.S.C. § 1334(a)(2)(C).

[58]30 U.S.C. § 207.

[59]Western Fuels-Utah, Inc. v. Lujan, 895 F.2d 780 (D.C. Cir. 1990).

render of Congress's power to change the law of coal leasing. So, it concluded, the leases did not confer a vested right to reasonable, individualized readjustments into the indefinite future, and no taking occurred.

Finally, government may act to weed out stale or worthless claims and mineral interests, as by imposing new filing requirements on the claim- or interest-holder. The new filings demanded are typically minimal, but the penalty for noncompliance or less-than-rigorous punctuality may be severe: even vested interests can be extinguished entirely. The Supreme Court has twice sustained such extinguishments against takings challenge. First, in *Texaco, Inc. v. Short*, it upheld an Indiana statute saying that a mineral interest unused for twenty years reverts to the surface owner, unless the mineral owner timely files in the county recorder's office.[60] There is little doubt, said the Court, that government has the power to condition the retention of property rights on the performance of *reasonable* conditions indicating intention to retain the interest.

Relying on this holding, the High Court in *United States v. Locke* later rejected a taking attack on a federal recording system designed to rid federal lands of stale mining claims.[61] In this factually striking case, the Court upheld the federal Bureau of Land Management's refusal to accept an annual filing made just *one day* after the statutory deadline. Plaintiffs' mineral deposits thus escheated to the United States. After confirming Congress's affirmative power to condition the retention of property rights on reasonable conditions furthering legitimate government goals, the Court found no taking: "Regulation of property rights does not 'take' private property when . . . reasonable investment-backed expectations can continue to be realized as long as [the owner] complies with reasonable regulatory restrictions. . . ."[62]

---

[60]454 U.S. 516 (1982). Relying on *Texaco* is Georgia Marble Co. v. Whitlock, 260 Ga. 350, 392 S.E.2d 881 (1990) (statute giving surface owner right to reclaim ownership of severed mineral rights where mineral owner neither works nor pays taxes on rights held no taking), *cert. denied*, 498 U.S. 1026 (1991).

[61]471 U.S. 84 (1985).

[62]*Id.* at 107. *Accord* Nequoia Ass'n v. Department of the Interior, 626 F. Supp. 827 (D. Utah 1987). Going beyond *Locke* is Kunkes v. United States, 78 F.3d 1549 (Fed. Cir.), *cert. denied*, 117 S.Ct. 74 (1996). There, unlike in *Locke*, the claimants' failure to comply with new requirements for maintaining existing claims involved no neglect. Rather, plaintiffs alleged inability to pay. Notwithstanding, said the court, the new requirement was similar to preexisting ones and not unreasonable. So, no taking occurred.

"Valid Existing Rights"

Time and again, the status of preexisting property interests has arisen when federal and state governments set aside public lands for designated purposes, enclose private holdings within government-designated natural areas, or regulate surface mining. Our concern here, of course, is when those preexisting interests involve the right to mine. Federal statutes have on numerous occasions immunized "valid existing rights" (VERs) as of the date of enactment from operation of the particular restriction involved. In the Wild and Scenic Rivers Act, for instance, Congress asserted that "subject to valid existing rights," minerals in federal lands within the Wild and Scenic Rivers System are withdrawn from the mining and leasing laws.[63]

Not once, apparently, has Congress defined what a VER is. In carrying out the federal Surface Mining Control and Reclamation Act (SMCRA), however, the Department of the Interior (DOI) has tried mightily to do so, in order to decide which surface coal mining operations may proceed in areas that by statute or agency designation are deemed unsuitable for that purpose.[64] In 1979, the DOI defined VER to require the proffer of a binding document evidencing a coal right as of when the lands were designated unsuitable, and a showing that either (1) the coal is needed for and immediately adjacent to a valid surface coal mining operation existing by the required date, or (2) as of when the land was designated unsuitable, the person asserting VER possessed "all state and federal permits necessary to conduct" mining operations. A judicial quibble with this test led to the DOI's suspending the "all permits" element of the test and accepting a good faith effort to obtain all permits as sufficient.[65]

In 1983, the DOI made its first attempt to fuse the VER definition and takings law. At that time, Secretary Watt promulgated a revised rule defining VER as any interest interference with which would be a constitutional taking, adopting the view that Congress wanted to avoid such takings under its statutes.[66] This rule was judicially invalidated on procedural grounds. A second effort to combine VER and takings came in 1991, when the DOI proposed a new rule purportedly defining VER as rights the denial of which would constitute a

[63]16 U.S.C. § 1280.
[64]SMCRA § 522(e); 30 U.S.C. § 1272(e) (agency designation).
[65]45 Fed. Reg. 51,548 (1980).
[66]48 Fed. Reg. 41,312 (1983).

taking. This time, however, the proposal did not use the constitutional taking standard, but rather the concept of takings in President Reagan's executive order on federal agency takings.[67] That concept has been widely criticized as generally overstating the danger that federal agency actions might effect takings.[68] As a result of this and the proposal's generally expansive view of VERs, a Bush administration proposal to finalize the rule provoked a firestorm of public criticism and its eventual withdrawal.

Thus, the VER standard currently in effect for all but two states is the "good faith/all permits" standard, with an added "needed for and adjacent" test (modified 1979 standard). In Illinois and West Virginia, the 1983 Fifth Amendment takings test applies.[69]

An important state court decision held that VER covers only the area covered by the mining permits or permit applications (existing as of the requisite date), not the entire site under lease.[70] If the environment is to be protected, said the court, it could not allow an entire-site reading of VER. Neither did such a reading effect a taking, since no evidence had been presented of value loss and the parcel as a whole had been productively mined for thirteen years.

Required Disclosure of Information

In the course of exploration and production, mining companies generate mounds of data as to the likelihood of commercially producible

---

[67]Exec. Order No. 12,630, 3 C.F.R. 554 (1988), *reprinted in* 5 U.S.C. § 601 note.

[68]Congressional Research Service, *Comparison of Taking Principles in Executive Order No. 12630 with Supreme Court Taking Jurisprudence, and Related Questions* (memorandum for various members of the House of Representatives, Dec. 19, 1988) (on file with Robert Meltz); James McElfish, *The Takings Executive Order: Constitutional Jurisprudence or Political Philosophy?*, 18 ENVTL. L. REP. 10474 (1988).

[69]These states had adopted the takings test and declined to revise it in response to DOI's court losses. *See generally* JAMES M. MCELFISH, JR. & ANN E. BEIER, ENVIRONMENTAL REGULATION OF COAL MINING: SMCRA'S SECOND DECADE 271–74 (Envtl. L. Inst. 1990) (history of DOI's attempts to define VER); *Symposium on Valid Existing Rights*, 5 J. MIN. L. & POL'Y 381 (1989–90) (spectrum of views on VER, including relationship to takings).

[70]Cogar v. Faerber, 179 W. Va. 600, 371 S.E.2d 321 (1988).

resources in specific locations. Many states require disclosure of this confidential business information to either state agencies, who use it in managing the state's resources, or to the public, in order to broaden participation in resource development. Disclosure to the public often follows an initial confidentiality period when the data remains in the exclusive possession of the state government.

It is well settled that such confidential data, despite their intangible nature, are property protected by both the federal and state constitutions.[71] The more nuanced question is whether the required disclosure of that information constitutes a taking of that property. The 1984 Supreme Court decision in *Ruckelshaus v. Monsanto*, also dealing with government use or disclosure of submitted trade secrets, doubtless will set the analytical mold.[72] There, the takings analysis hinged almost entirely on the interference with reasonable investment-backed expectations factor of the *Penn Central* test. The Court saw a taking, a betrayal almost, where trade secrets submitted to EPA during a period when the governing statute created an expectation that they would not be compromised were then used or disclosed by the agency pursuant to later congressional enactment.

A straightforward application of *Ruckelshaus* to mining is found in a state case where oil companies challenged use of oil well data by a state agency for its own internal purposes.[73] The court found nothing in the law or practice at the time the data was submitted to support an argument that an expectation of nonuse of the data was reasonable. Nor was there any evidence that companies investing in the particular well had relied on an assumption of government nonuse (as opposed to public disclosure) in deciding to invest. Of course, where regulations expressly and clearly require permit applicants to disclose pro-

[71]The confidentiality of the data is key. *See, e.g.,* City of Northglenn v. Grynberg, 846 P.2d 175 (Colo. 1993) (no taking where town's publication of report showing mineral lease not to contain producible quantities was based on public data).

[72]467 U.S. 986 (1984).

[73]State Dep't of Natural Resources v. Arctic Slope Regional Corp., 834 P.2d 135 (Alaska 1991). One may question the precedential viability of pre-*Ruckelshaus* decisions in this area that fail to make the temporal distinctions in that decision. *See, e.g.,* Noranda Exploration, Inc. v. Ostrom, 113 Wis. 2d 612, 335 N.W.2d 596 (1983) (state disclosure law held a taking with no discussion of whether mining exploration data was generated before or after enactment).

duction data generated under the permit, complaints of a taking are particularly hollow.[74] It is not "a taking for the Government to impose financial obligations upon the recipient of a benefit if, as here, the benefit may be declined."[75]

In most cases, state laws compelling public disclosure of submitted data provide for an initial confidentiality period of a few years, the rationale being that release after this period does little economic harm to the submitter. Depending on particularities, such confidentiality periods may or may not tip the court against finding a taking.[76]

Conclusion

The mining takings cases are strikingly diverse. They involve a wide array of mining restrictions, from minor filing requirements to outright prohibitions. On the receiving end are a gamut of property interests (unpatented mining claims, rights to patents, leaseholds, etc.) and estates (surface, support, and mineral). The threats provoking the government action may be public (highway subsidence, broken gas mains) or private (residential subsidence). And the mining may occur on land that is either public or private. Valid existing rights, whatever they are eventually defined to be, may or may not be involved. Compare this diversity with the average wetlands takings case, which generally stems from the same core fact: denial of a permit.

Quite naturally, therefore, it is difficult to generalize from the mining takings cases. Decisions are likely to be based on general Supreme Court takings principles, rather than the mining takings cases that have gone before.

These are difficult cases, made no easier by the fact that the

---

[74]*See, e.g.*, United States v. Geophysical Corp. of Alaska, 732 F.2d 693 (9th Cir. 1984) (oil and gas permits under the Outer Continental Shelf Lands Act).
[75]*Id.* at 700.
[76]*Cf. Noranda Exploration*, 335 N.W.2d 596, 604–05 (1983) (3-year and 13-year confidentiality period too short to bring disclosure requirement within police power) *with* Hartman v. State Corp. Comm'n, 215 Kan. 758, 529 P.2d 134, 147 (1974) (two-year confidentiality period, extendable on showing that more time is needed, undercuts taking argument).

amounts of money involved may be quite large. As well, mining conflicts are often more intractable than other land-use conflicts because the density transfer techniques so useful in the usual land-use context may not be available here—the tradable resource may simply not be present.[77] Thus, we may assume that government regulation of mining will continue to make a deep impression on the takings landscape.

---

[77]See, e.g., Whitney Benefits, Inc. v. United States, 752 F.2d 1554, 1555–56 (Fed. Cir. 1985) ("no agreement in sight" after five years of negotiations between mineral estate holder and United States over possible land exchange).

Chapter 26

Billboard Controls

I think that I shall never see
A billboard lovely as a tree
Indeed, unless the billboards fall
I'll never see a tree at all.

       — OGDEN NASH (*Song of the Open Road*)

Ogden Nash's satirical jab reflects a view of billboards and the billboard industry held by many Americans. Once viewed as an inherent feature of the open road and Americana, billboards have in more recent years been targeted as aesthetic and safety nuisances, at least in nonurban portions of the country. Indeed, billboard regulation was one of the first recognized applications of land-use control based principally on aesthetic concerns.

Nevertheless, the billboard industry has proven a most formidable foe in the face of efforts by federal, state, and local governments to limit the placement and control the maintenance of billboards. The industry has repeatedly invoked the Takings Clause, together with other constitutional theories, in a largely unsuccessful effort to block billboard regulation through court action. The industry has been far more successful in the legislative arena, however, obtaining statutory relief that often limits or postpones the adverse economic impacts of billboard regulation. Indeed, the manner in which the conflict between private property rights and government regulation has played out in the billboard arena may well be a precursor to broader legislative efforts to balance private and public interests. (*See* chapter 34.)

Increased Regulation of Billboards

Until the latter part of this century, billboard control in the United States was largely voluntary or nonexistent, with the only serious efforts to limit them being pursued by a handful of states and municipalities. Federal regulation of outdoor advertising began in 1958, when Congress enacted the Federal Aid Highway Act.[1] This voluntary legislation simply allowed participating states to control billboards either by exercising their police power or the power of eminent domain. Its practical effect was virtually nil.

Public pressure to address the proliferation of billboards in suburban and rural America continued to mount. The movement gained a key spokesperson in the mid-1960s when then–First Lady "Lady Bird" Johnson made billboard regulation one of her top priorities. Congress responded in 1965 by passing the Federal Highway Beautification Act.[2] Focusing primarily on the Interstate Highway System, the Act declared that "the erection and maintenance of outdoor advertising signs, displays, and devices in areas adjacent to the Interstate System, and the primary system should be controlled in order to protect the public investment in such highways, to promote the safety and recreational value of public travel, and to preserve natural beauty."[3] The Act looked primarily to the states to accomplish those objectives: Each state was required to develop a program restricting construction of new billboards and requiring removal of existing, nonconforming signs within "federal corridors" (i.e., designated areas within 660 feet of interstate and federally funded primary highways).[4]

The outdoor advertising industry's economic interests were protected by other, key features of the Act, however. Congress required that each state elect between losing 10 percent of its federal highway funds or implementing a statutory system of "just compensation." Under the Act, compensation is required as a condition of compelled removal of those billboards "lawfully erected under State law" but prescribed under the subsequent, federal Act.[5] Congress coupled that regulatory stick with an important fiscal carrot: The Act provides for

[1]Pub. L. No. 85-381, 72 Stat. 89, § 122 (1958).
[2]Pub. L. No. 89-285, 79 Stat. 1028, *codified as amended* at 23 U.S.C. § 131.
[3]23 U.S.C. § 131(a).
[4]23 U.S.C. § 131(b).
[5]23 U.S.C. § 131(g).

a 75 percent federal share of such mandated compensation to bill-board owners.[6]

The federal legislation quickly spawned similar legislation at the state level encompassing land uses and areas extending well beyond the highway corridors addressed in the Act. Many of these state laws replicate key features of the Act, including provisions requiring statutory compensation.[7] Some states have in turn expressly required their political subdivisions to regulate billboard advertising.[8] While the billboard industry quickly attacked this broader form of state legislation as preempted by the federal Act, that theory has been rejected by federal and state courts alike.[9]

Litigation Challenging Billboard Regulation

Regulatory systems governing the prohibition, maintenance, and removal of outdoor advertising have not gone unchallenged. To the contrary, billboard regulation has been one of America's most litigated forms of land-use regulation in recent decades. As the U.S. Court of Appeals for the Ninth Circuit recently observed: "The continuing efforts of [governments] to eradicate what they perceive to be a visual blight and safety hazard has resulted in billboard litigation raising complicated constitutional and statutory claims."[10]

Over the years the billboard industry has invoked a variety of legal theories in response to ever-increasing efforts at billboard regulation.

[6]*Id. See also* Georgia Outdoor Advertising Inc. v. City of Waynesville, 900 F.2d 783, 788 (4th Cir. 1990).

[7]*See, e.g.*, Cal. Bus. & Prof. Code §§ 5412, 5412.6; N.C. Gen. Stat. § 136-131.1; 49 Zoning Digest 1045 (describing 1997 Idaho legislation barring government entities from removing legally placed outdoor advertising signs without payment of compensation).

[8]*See, e.g.*, Florida's Local Government Comprehensive Planning & Land Development Regulation Act, Fla. Stat. § 163.3202(2)(f), requiring each local government in that state to adopt ordinances controlling billboards, signs, etc.

[9]*See, e.g.*, Art Neon Co. v. City of Denver, 488 F.2d 118, 123 (10th Cir. 1973) *cert. denied,* 417 U.S. 932 (1974); E.B. Elliott Advertising Co. v. Metropolitan Dade County, 425 F.2d 1141, 1150 (5th Cir. 1970) *cert. dismissed,* 400 U.S. 805 (1970); Tahoe Regional Planning Agency v. King, 233 Cal. App. 3d 1365, 1388–92, 285 Cal. Rptr. 335, 345 (1991); Lamar-Orlando Outdoor Advertising v. City of Ormond Beach, 415 So. 2d 1312, 1320 (Fla. 1982).

[10]Outdoor Sys., Inc. v. City of Mesa, 997 F.2d 604, 607 (9th Cir. 1993).

Many such suits are brought on constitutional grounds such as the First Amendment, federal preemption, due process, and equal protection. There is no clear trend to the First Amendment cases, except that they have generated a set of constitutional principles even more obtuse and incomprehensible than those developed under the Takings Clause.[11] Indeed, when compared to the First Amendment billboard decisions, the inverse condemnation cases discussed below seem a model of clarity.

Freedom of speech issues aside, constitutional challenges to government regulation of billboards have generally proven unsuccessful. This has been especially true of claims that billboard regulations violate private property rights under the Takings Clause. And the pattern holds in both state and federal courts, where state and local billboard control measures are frequently challenged.

Illustrative of the federal courts' perspective on these issues are the Ninth Circuit's decision in *Outdoor Systems, Inc. v. City of Mesa*[12] and the Fourth Circuit's opinion in *Naegele Outdoor Advertising, Inc. v. City of Durham*.[13] In *City of Mesa*, two Arizona municipalities regulated the size, location, and height of commercial signs; additionally, they required nonconforming billboards to eventually be removed under a variety of circumstances. The Ninth Circuit rejected a multifaceted regulatory taking challenge to the sign ordinances. The court of appeals first concluded—as these decisions invariably do—that the cities' interest in billboard regulation is legitimate, and that this interest is advanced by ordinances such as those being challenged in *City of Mesa*.[14] The Ninth Circuit then assessed the economic im-

---

[11]The principal case on billboard controls and the First Amendment, Metromedia, Inc. v. San Diego, 453 U.S. 490 (1981), is distinctive both for its lack of a majority opinion and the abject confusion and disparate results it has spawned in lower federal and state court cases. *See, e.g.,* Naegele Outdoor Advertising, Inc. v. City of Durham, 844 F.2d 172, 173–74 (4th Cir. 1988), *cert. denied,* 513 U.S. 928 (1994) (rejecting First Amendment challenge); Union City Bd. of Zoning Appeals v. Justice Outdoor Displays, Inc., 266 Ga. 393, 467 S.E.2d 875, 882 (Ga. 1996) (ordinance favoring signs based on content violates First Amendment); Desert Outdoor Advertising v. City of Moreno Valley, 103 F.3d 814, 819–20 (9th Cir. 1996) *cert. denied,* 118 S. Ct. 294 (1997) (local sign ordinance violates First Amendment); Ackerley Communications v. Krochalis, 108 F.3d 1095, 1099–100 (9th Cir. 1997) (city's aesthetic-based restriction on billboards is constitutional regulation of commercial speech).

[12]997 F.2d 604 (9th Cir. 1993).

[13]844 F.2d 172 (4th Cir. 1988).

[14]997 F.2d at 616.

pact of the ordinances, applying the "ad hoc, factual inquiry" made famous by the U.S. Supreme Court in its regulatory takings decisions. Noting that government's compelled *immediate* removal of privately owned billboards would produce a more difficult constitutional question, the court observed that: (1) The required *eventual* removal of the signs is constitutional; and (2) under long-standing law of nonconforming uses, "it cannot be an unconstitutional taking to require a nonconforming billboard to be removed once the land on which it stands changes use."[15]

In *City of Durham*, a local government prohibited off-premise commercial billboards except alongside interstate or federally funded highways (i.e., those falling under the Federal Highway Beautification Act discussed earlier). A billboard firm challenged the ban as a compensable taking of its property. As in *City of Mesa*, the Fourth Circuit first opined in *City of Durham* that the ordinance "advances a legitimate state interest in aesthetics."[16] Like *City of Mesa*, the Fourth Circuit found the more complex question to be whether the measure deprived the company of economically viable use of its property. The court in *City of Durham*, like *City of Mesa*, found the answer to this question to depend upon application of the relevant facts to the multipart inquiry announced by the U.S. Supreme Court in *Penn Central* and its progeny:

> The [trial] court should make findings pertaining to every aspect of Naegele's business that will be affected by the ordinance, including the number of billboards that can be economically used for noncommercial advertising, the number that are economically useless, the terms of Naegele's leases for billboard locations, the land Naegele owns for locations and whether it has any other economic use, the cost of billboards and their actual life expectancy, the income expected during the grace period, the salvage value of the billboards that cannot be used, the loss of sharing revenue, the percentage of affected signs compared to the remaining signs in Naegele's business unit, the relative value of affected and remaining signs, whether the amortization period is reasonable, and any other evidence presented by the parties the court deems relevant.[17]

[15]*Id.* at 617.
[16]844 F.2d at 174–76 (citing the Fourth Circuit's earlier opinion in Georgia Outdoor Advertising, Inc. v. Waynesville, 833 F.2d 43, 46 (4th Cir. 1987)).
[17]844 F.2d at 178.

While such a legal inquiry sounds both complex and formidable, most billboard measures ultimately seem to pass constitutional muster under the Takings Clause. Indeed, that was the eventual result when the City of Durham case was remanded to the district court for application of the above-quoted constitutional criteria.[18]

State courts that have adjudicated regulatory takings challenges to local billboard control measures have reached similar results, although sometimes without the detailed level of constitutional analysis found in federal decisions such as those summarized above. An apt example is *National Advertising Co. v. Village of Downers Grove*.[19] The challenged ordinance in *Downers Grove* limited the size of off-premise signs. After the local zoning board denied the billboard company's application for a billboard of excessive size, the company sued under the Fifth Amendment. The Illinois Supreme Court was unimpressed:

> [National] has not suffered a taking as a result of the Downers Grove ordinance. Downers Grove has not physically invaded National's property rights. Rather, it has enacted a program that applies to everyone to promote the common good of traffic safety and esthetics, a program that . . . substantially advances legitimate interests of the Village.[20]

The reviewing court further concluded that the billboard company lacked "legitimate investment-backed expectations" because the company was on notice that its proposed signs violated the ordinance.[21]

Another state court decision that relied largely upon the perceived need of local government to reconcile competing land uses to reject a taking challenge to billboard regulation is *In re Condemnation by the Delaware River Port Authority*.[22] In that case the court found that a landowner whose billboards were obstructed by government's erection of highway sound barriers lacked a viable claim to compensation. The court found that the government had not removed the billboard,

---

[18]Naegele Outdoor Advertising, Inc. v. City of Durham, 803 F. Supp. 1068 (M.D.N.C. 1992). *See also* Outdoor Graphics, Inc. v. City of Burlington, 103 F.3d 690 (8th Cir. 1996) (similar analysis, identical result).

[19]204 Ill. App. 3d 499, 561 N.E.2d 1300 (1990), *cert. denied*, 501 U.S. 1261 (1991).

[20]*Id.* at 1309.

[21]*Id.*

[22]667 A.2d 766 (Pa. Commw. 1995).

and that the landowner "had no property right in the view either from or to its sign."[23]

Most takings challenges to billboard regulation focus upon *local* ordinances. This is understandable, because most such regulation takes place at the local government level. In recent years, however, state and regional governments have enacted their own billboard control measures. Predictably, takings litigation has followed to challenge these state and regional efforts. Just as predictably, these challenges have been no more successful than those summarized above.

Two recent state court decisions from California illustrate this trend. In *Tahoe Regional Planning Agency v. King*,[24] a bi-state land-use planning agency sued advertising companies and property owners to compel the removal of certain billboards in the Lake Tahoe Basin under the agency's land-use plan. That plan prohibits off-premise advertising signs and provides for amortization of nonconforming signs. The defendants responded to TRPA's enforcement efforts by claiming that the land-use plan effected a regulatory taking of their property interests. After first concluding that the regional agency's billboard restrictions were not preempted by federal or state law,[25] the California court proceeded to address the regulatory takings claim. The *King* court held in a wide-ranging opinion that: (1) Such aesthetic and scenic zoning is a legitimate subject of land-use regulation; (2) amortization is a constitutionally appropriate method for the elimination of nonconforming uses; and (3) whether a billboard regulation is so onerous as to trigger an unconstitutional taking requires an ad hoc factual determination.[26] Regarding the third standard, the California Court of Appeal specifically embraced the multi-factored constitutional standard first articulated by the Fourth Circuit in *City of Durham* and quoted above.[27]

Another California state appellate court came to a similar conclusion in *Patrick Media Group, Inc. v. California Coastal Commission*.[28] There, the California Coastal Commission had conditioned approval of a state coastal development permit upon the developer's

[23]*Id.* at 769. *See also* Naegele Outdoor Advertising Co. v. City of Lakeville, 532 N.W.2d 249 (Minn. Ct. App. 1995) (accord).

[24]233 Cal. App. 3d 1365, 285 Cal. Rptr. 335 (1991).

[25]233 Cal. App. 3d at 1390–92.

[26]*Id.* at 1393–1402.

[27]*Id.* at 1401–02 (quoting and applying Naegele Outdoor Advertising v. City of Durham, supra, 844 F.2d 172 (4th Cir. 1988)).

[28]9 Cal. App. 4th 592, 11 Cal. Rptr. 2d 824 (1992).

removal of billboards located on the property. The billboard company lessee filed a regulatory taking lawsuit against the commission. While the court held the company's challenge to be barred on procedural grounds, it also concluded that the state billboard act's amortization requirement was a relevant defense to any such takings claim.[29]

Several subissues of regulatory takings law tend to emerge regularly in billboard cases. Since many billboards exist under fixed-term leases, and often the lessors are government managers of publicly owned lands, the question arises as to a government lessor's obligation under the Takings Clause to *renew* such leases. Not surprisingly, the courts have answered in the negative, finding that a billboard lessee has no reasonable, investment-backed expectation that such a lease would be renewed.[30]

Another issue relates to the proper plaintiff in billboard takings cases: Several courts have observed that both the owner of the underlying real property and the owner of the billboard itself have cognizable interests under the Takings Clause, and that those interests are conceptually distinct.[31] And a related question is the "denominator" question addressed in comprehensive fashion in chapter 12. Particularly when the plaintiffs are multimillion dollar advertising corporations operating in many states or even nationwide, how broadly a re-

---

[29]9 Cal. App. 4th at 603–04 (citing Cal. Bus. & Prof. Code §§ 5412, 5412.6).

[30]*See, e.g.,* Ryan Outdoor Advertising v. United States, 559 F.2d 544, 557 (9th Cir. 1977). *Cf.* National Advertising Co. v. Village of Downers Grove, 204 Ill. App. 3d 499, 561 N.E.2d 1300, 1309 (Ill. App. Ct 1990), *cert. denied,* 501 U.S. 1261 (1991) (billboard company lacked reasonable, investment-backed expectation that nonconforming billboards would be allowed under municipal ordinance); Patrick Media Group v. DuPage Water Comm., 258 Ill. App. 3d 1068, 630 N.E.2d 958 (Ill. App. Ct. 1994) (accord); Whiteco Indus. v. City of Tucson, 168 Ariz. 257, 812 P.2d 1075 (Ariz. Ct. App. 1990) (since billboard leases expired prior to eminent domain action, billboard owner had no compensable interest).

[31]Outdoor Sys., Inc. v. City of Mesa, 997 F.2d 604, 617 (9th Cir. 1993) ("There are two distinct property interests involved . . . a landowner's . . . and the billboard owner's. . . . For purposes of analysis we will consider these interests separately."). *See also* Patrick Media Group, Inc. v. California Coastal Comm'n, 9 Cal. App. 4th 592, 11 Cal. Rptr. 2d 824 (1992) (billboard company lessee has property interest distinct from that of owner of underlying real property).

viewing court views the relevant property interest is likely to have a considerable influence on the ultimate question of takings liability.[32]

The one issue of seemingly overriding significance in the billboard takings decisions is the presence in virtually all cases of an amortization component. As noted above, most state and local programs that limit billboards have replicated the Federal Highway Beautification Act's amortization provisions. Such amortization schemes have the effect of rounding off the rough edges of an aggressive program of billboard regulation or proscription. They allow billboard companies and their lessors a period of time in which to recoup their investments and earn a reasonable (if temporary) economic return. Amortization programs dovetail nicely with the traditional notion of land-use planning that nonconforming uses should be phased out gradually rather than terminated immediately.

From a legal perspective, the existence of an amortization component allows government defenders of billboard programs to argue that such programs don't cause an economic "wipeout" that would trigger the *Lucas*, virtual per se rule of takings liability; instead, the program can be characterized as one that *limits* economic return and therefore falls under *Penn Central*'s ad hoc, balancing approach. That the existence of such amortization provisions is relevant to the liability phase of a regulatory taking case is by now well settled.[33] Their importance in sustaining the validity of billboard regulation schemes is reiterated in virtually all of the reported decisions.[34] Indeed, those few reported decisions intimating that certain government programs restricting billboards may trigger regulatory takings liability have focused on those programs' *lack* of such amortization

[32]*See, e.g.*, Naegele Outdoor Advertising, Inc. v. City of Durham, 844 F.2d 172, 178 (4th Cir. 1988) ("The appropriate unit [of Naegele's property] is that which will be substantially affected by the ordinance."); Georgia Outdoor Advertising Inc. v. City of Waynesville, 900 F.2d 783, 787–88 (4th Cir. 1990).

[33]*City of Durham*, 844 F.2d at 177 ("The allowance of an amortization period . . . is one of the facts that the district court should consider in defining the character of the governmental action, which is the third factor mentioned in *Penn Central*."); Tahoe Regional Planning Agency v. King, 233 Cal. App. 3d 1365, 1393, 285 Cal. Rptr. 335, 351 (1991) ("an ordinance prohibiting existing billboards may be enforced as a constitutionally valid exercise of the state's police power which does not require compensation if a reasonable amortization period for discontinuance of the use is provided").

[34]*See, e.g.*, Newman Signs, Inc. v. Hjelle, 268 N.W.2d 741, 758 (N.D. 1978).

provisions.[35] In recent years, most takings challenges to those bill-board programs containing amortization provisions necessarily focus on the *reasonableness* of those provisions. To date, most courts seem willing to give government the benefit of the doubt on that score.[36] And that in turn is a key reason why regulatory takings challenges to billboard controls are unlikely to succeed.[37]

Property rights advocates often bemoan the fact that courts rarely find compensation to be required in regulatory takings litigation brought under the Fifth Amendment. Government officials simultaneously complain that the specter of takings liability constrains their ability and willingness to enact necessary regulatory programs. Regulatory takings claims will doubtless continue to be advanced to challenge various programs limiting or banning commercial billboards. Nevertheless, the fact that such challenges are seldom if ever successful is due in large measure to the *statutory* or *regulatory* amortization (i.e., compensation) provisions which are a cornerstone of the billboard regulatory programs. There's a message in that, one would think.

[35]*See, e.g.*, State Highway Dep't v. Branch, 222 Ga. 770, 152 S.E.2d 372, 373 (1966). *Cf.* League to Save Lake Tahoe v. Crystal Enters., 685 F.2d 1142, 1145 (9th Cir. 1982) (recognizing the "doubtful constitutionality of compelling the immediate discontinuance of nonconforming uses").

[36]*E.g.*, E.B. Elliott Advertising Co. v. Metropolitan Dade County, 425 F.2d 1141, 1155 (5th Cir. 1970), *cert. dismissed*, 400 U.S. 805 (1970).

[37]One recent exception to the rule is Lamar Advertising of S. Ga., Inc. v. City of Albany, 260 Ga. 46, 389 S.E.2d 216, 217 (1990) (local ordinance requiring sign removal effects a taking requiring compensation). Significantly, Georgia is one of the few states whose billboard control statutes contain no amortization provision. *Id.* at 216.

Chapter 27

Rails to Trails

It was an idea whose time had come. For a century, the railroads had been a dominant transportation mode, encouraged and heavily subsidized by legislatures. Since 1916, however, the number of miles of operating line had been in decline, as the railroads lost out to new, alternative modes of transportation.[1] With the railroads' eclipse came a problem: What to do with the thousands of miles of unused rail corridors? By and large, these corridors had been assembled when land was cheap but had grown considerably more valuable as open space became scarce and urban and suburban growth pushed land values ever upward. To allow the selling off of these now-unused rights-of-way meant, in all probability, that they would be lost forever.

With the environmental 1960s and 1970s came an appealing solution: Convert the unused railroad rights-of-way to recreational trails for the use of hikers, bikers, cross-country skiers, and horseback riders. The advantages are plain enough.[2] Suburban sprawl often removes outdoor recreational venues to great distances from where most of us live; close-to-home oases from congestion, such as verdant,

---

[1]In 1916, railroads in the United States reached their peak of total operating line, at 254,037 miles. D. PHILIP LOCKLIN, ECONOMICS OF TRANSPORTATION 86 (6th ed. 1966). By 1987, the number had dropped to 145,000 miles. Charles H. Montange, *Rail to Trail Conversions in Railroad Abandonment Proceedings*, 12 COLUMBIA J. ENVTL. L. 91, 95 n.14 (1987).

[2]*See generally* Montange, *supra* note 1.

Portion of the Capital Crescent Trail in Bethesda, Maryland. A nearby segment of this rails-to-trails conversion was at issue in *Chevy Chase Land Co. v. United States.*

unused rail corridors, are a tempting resource. In rural areas, trail use of unused railroad rights-of-way may complement existing recreational resources. At the same time, preservation of rail corridors ensures that if public or commercial interest in railroads is someday rekindled, the reassembly of such corridors will not be prohibitively expensive.

Enter the property owner. This individual holds title to the land abutting or traversed by the discontinued rail line and may have long believed that when the railroad neighbor someday ceased operating, its right-of-way would revert to him or her. The landowner's belief is based on an understanding that the railroad in question holds something less than a full and unlimited interest in its right-of-way, as many railroads undeniably do. Many of these qualified property interests, whether created by voluntary conveyance or condemnation, are limited expressly or impliedly to rail use, giving rise to a credible argument that if rail use ends, the right-of-way reverts to the original landowner (or that owner's successor in interest). And so, one might conclude, government actions to turn the corridor over to hikers and bikers cheat the reversionary interest holder of a property right, working a taking.[3] Otherwise put, are the hikers and bikers "government-invited gatecrashers"?[4]

A brief, we hope painless, excursion into the lexicon of real property is unavoidable here.[5] A railroad may own its right-of-way[6] in "fee simple absolute," in which case its ownership is unqualified and the former owner retains no interest, present or future. In this circumstance, discontinuance of railroad use has no effect on either party's interests. The former owner cannot complain of a taking.

In other cases, of greater interest here, the terms of the conveyance or condemnation limit use of the railroad's right-of-way to rail purposes, or to a broader purpose (such as "public travel") that includes rail operation. These more limited right-of-way interests take several forms, the most common being the fee-simple determinable and the easement. With the fee-simple determinable, the railroad acquires actual title to the right-of-way, the grantor retaining only a "possibility of reverter." The possibility of reverter is called a future interest, because it is just that: Title returns to the holder if and when some specified future event (such as discontinuance of rail use) occurs. By contrast, with an easement the railroad obtains only a right of use. Title remains with the owner of the underlying land (the "servient tenement"), who may continue to use the right-of-way in any manner that does not interfere with rail use.[7]

---

[3]*See generally* Michael M. Berger, *Rails-to-Trails Conversions: Has Congress Effected a Definitional Taking?*, 1990 INST. ON PLANNING, ZONING, & EMINENT DOMAIN ch. 8 (Southwestern Legal Found.); Comment, *The Use of Discontinued Railroad Rights-of-Way as Recreational Hiking and Biking Trails: Does the National Trails System Act Sanction Takings?*, 33 ST. LOUIS UNIV. L.J. 205 (1988).

[4]LAURENCE TRIBE, AMERICAN CONSTITUTIONAL LAW 602 (2d ed. 1988).

[5]*See generally* National Wildlife Fed'n v. ICC, 850 F.2d 694, 703 (D.C. Cir. 1988).

[6]We use the term "right-of-way" in the sense of the physical strip of land on which the railroad builds its roadbed. In other contexts, the term is also used to refer to the *right* to use the strip of land, a meaning akin to the concept of an easement.

[7]Easements are the dominant form of railroad rights-of-way west of the Missouri River. Montange, *supra* note 1, at 111.

It is these limited property interests that implicate the takings issue when reversion is blocked in order to create a trail.[8]

The National Trails System Act

The most prominent rails-to-trails program is the federal one, chartered by section 8(d) of the National Trails System Act (NTSA).[9] Section 8(d) came about after earlier congressional efforts at promoting conversion of abandoned rail lines proved inadequate.[10] A key reason was that prior local efforts to convert were being blocked by state courts on the ground that after abandonment, the railroad had no interest to convey.[11] Under the provision, Congress authorized the Interstate Commerce Commission (ICC), now replaced by the Surface Transportation Board (STB),[12] to preserve for possible future railroad use rights-of-way no longer in service, and to allow interim use of the land as recreational trails. (Note: We use both acronyms, as appropriate.)

Section 8(d) operates by the magic wand of redefinition. A railroad seeking to shut down a route may negotiate with a state, municipality, or private group that is prepared to assume responsibility for managing the trail. If agreement is reached, the land may be turned over to the trail operator for interim trail use—"interim" because trail use is seen as only transitional until rail service is someday resumed (hence the term "rail banking"). The magic wand is the declaration in section 8(d) that such trail use shall not be deemed by the STB to be a rail line abandonment—though it may look like one to the reversionary interest owner. Without an STB certificate of abandonment, state-created reversionary interests cannot mature.

Either you buy it or you don't. Either you regard trail use under section 8(d) and similar state programs as a genuinely temporary

---

[8]Actually, it is more proper to speak of an easement "lapsing" or being "extinguished." "Reversion" is a term reserved for the fee-simple determinable and related interests where the railroad obtains *title* to the right-of-way. Notwithstanding, we follow the common practice of using "reversion" for both.

[9]16 U.S.C. § 1247(d). Implementing regulations are at 49 C.F.R. § 1152.29.

[10]See the legislative history of section 8(d), especially H.R. REP. No. 28, 98th Cong., 1st Sess. 8 (1983), and SEN. REP. No. 1, 98th Cong., 1st Sess. 9 (1983).

[11]Pollnow v. State DNR, 88 Wis. 2d 350, 276 N.W.2d 738 (1979); Schnabel v. City of DuPage, 101 Ill. App. 3d 553, 428 N.E.2d 671 (1981).

[12]Under the ICC Termination Act, the ICC was abolished as of Dec. 31, 1995, and all functions pertinent to rail abandonments transferred to the newly created Surface Transportation Board. Pub. L. No. 104-88, 109 Stat. 803.

phase until a possible resumption of rail service, warranting the STB in denying abandonment certification, or you see rail banking as a ruse to legitimize a brazen denial of reversionary property rights created under state law.[13] Whichever, the takings issue is present.

Preseault in the Supreme Court

The rails-to-trails concept has made one ascent to the U.S. Supreme Court, in the form of a petition for review of the ICC's section 8(d) rule. In *Preseault v. ICC*, the Court found it unnecessary to address the merits of the taking claim.[14] Right claim, wrong remedy, it said. The landowners, who claimed a reversionary interest underlying the abandoned rail line, had failed to pursue compensation for the alleged taking, the exclusive remedy for federal takings and one available to the landowners in the U.S. Claims Court under the Tucker Act. Nothing in the NTSA, said the Court, unambiguously suggested repeal of the Tucker Act compensation remedy. Hence, the landowners' effort to have section 8(d) invalidated was premature.[15]

Despite not reaching the taking issue, two things about the Supreme Court's *Preseault* decision are important. First, the majority opinion acknowledges in dicta that for certain less-than-fee interests held by railroads, interim use as a recreational trail might indeed bring about a taking of underlying reversionary interests.[16]

Second, the analytical framework for rails-to-trails takings claims set out in the three-justice concurrence by Justice O'Connor is persuasive. The concurring justices' point is that while Congress un-

---

[13]*See, e.g.,* National Wildlife Fed'n v. ICC, 850 F.2d 694 (D.C. Cir. 1988) (declining to find rail banking a fiction, though seeing as significant that ICC rules under section 8(d) do not require a determination that resumption of service is likely).

[14]494 U.S. 1 (1990). For a view of this decision by the attorney who argued the case for the Preseaults, *see* Michael M. Berger, *Is the Rails-to-Trails Statute a Taking? Only the Claims Court Knows,* 13 ZONING & PLANNING LAW REPORT 33 (May 1990), *reprinted in* ZONING AND PLANNING LAW HANDBOOK ch. 9 (Kenneth H. Young ed., 1991).

[15]*See also* Glosemeyer v. Missouri-Kansas-Texas R.R., 879 F.2d 316 (8th Cir. 1989) (equitable relief not available if landowner prevails on claim that rails-to-trails statute effects taking of reversionary interest, since compensation available under Tucker Act).

[16]*Preseault,* 494 U.S. at 13, 16.

Hot on the Trail

Paul and Patricia Preseault own some attractive lakefront acreage in Burlington, Vermont, on which they have a home. They enjoy their property, but so do up to two hundred people per hour who, on a warm weekend, walk and bike the trail that crosses the property. This trail was once a railroad line.

The Preseaults' rails-to-trails story began long ago, in 1899. Back then the Rutland-Canadian Railway Co. acquired a right-of-way over what became the Preseaults' property. Rutland-Canadian installed its track and began to operate its trains over the line. In the 1970s the successor to Rutland-Canadian, Vermont Railway, stopped using the line, removing all switches, bridges, and track from the portion on the Preseaults' land. And here the fun begins.

First, in 1981, the Preseaults went to state court and claimed that by ending operations and removing its equipment, Vermont Railway had abandoned its easement. As a result, the Preseaults argued, the easement was extinguished and the right of way was reverted to them as owners of the title to the land. The state court replied, however, that it had no power over the matter. The ICC, it said, had not authorized abandonment of the route and thus still had exclusive control.

So, logically enough, the Preseaults went to the ICC for a certificate of abandonment. But in the meantime, the federal Rails-to-Trails Act had been enacted in 1983, and the ICC invoked it in 1986 to approve an agreement between the State of Vermont (the railroad's lessor) and the City of Burlington, which transferred the right-of-way to the city for interim use as a public trail.

doubtedly had the *power* to postpone reversions, it is an entirely separate question whether the exercise of that power effects a *taking*. The STB may say there is no abandonment of a rail line, as NTSA section 8(d) instructs it to do when interim trail use has been negotiated, but it cannot redefine the reversionary interest created under state law. The NTSA may preempt the operation of state rail abandonment laws, but it does not displace state law as the source from which property rights generally are derived. To hold otherwise, said Justice O'Connor, would "threaten[] to read the Just Compensation Clause out of the Constitution."[17] We return soon to this concurring view, and to the holdings of the federal appellate courts.

[17]*Id.* at 23.

Begin judicial phase two. Now the Preseaults attacked the ICC order in federal court, arguing that the act was a taking on its face. The Second Circuit thought otherwise, however, and said further that the Act qualified the Preseaults' property rights. On appeal, the U.S. Supreme Court refused to even touch the taking question, because in its view the taking claim should have been brought first before the Court of Federal Claims.

Which triggered the third (and perhaps final) judicial phase. Accepting the Supreme Court's advice, the Preseaults turned to the U.S. Court of Federal Claims in Washington, D.C. There, they sued the United States as well as the State of Vermont. With the court's first ruling, in 1992, the Preseaults' fortune seemed to change—the court accepted their argument that the railroad held only an easement. Later the same year, however, the court held that despite that limited interest, there had been no taking. And the Federal Circuit, or rather, a three-judge panel of that court, agreed.

Apparently unsatisfied with the panel decision, the full Federal Circuit decided to rehear the case before all the judges of the court. In November 1996, six of the nine judges voted to reverse the lower court's judgment (though only four judges, less then a majority, clearly endorse all parts of the rationale supporting that ruling). The opinion touched all aspects of the case. Yes, it said, the railroad and the state had only an easement. Yes, it had been abandoned before that whole rails-to-trails matter came along, but even if it had not, the easement was not broad enough to include trail use. And yes, the federal government had effected a taking by approving the trails conversion. The Preseaults would have to endure the hikers and bikers passing by not far from their house, but they would be paid.

As we go to press, the trial court has yet to decide how much money the Preseaults are to be paid for the taking. That ruling, when it comes, might well go up on appeal again.

Defining the Property Interest

The first step in evaluating whether a proposed trail conversion might work a taking is the obvious one: Determine what interest the railroad has. As noted at the outset, if the railroad holds the right-of-way in fee simple absolute, the taking issue evaporates instantly, since retention of such an interest does not hinge on continued rail use.[18]

[18]*See, e.g.,* City of Manhattan Beach v. Superior Ct., 13 Cal. 4th 232, 914 P.2d 160 (1996), *cert. denied,* 117 S. Ct. 511 (1996). There, the state supreme court found that the right-of-way acquired by a railroad in 1888 was in fee simple, not an easement. As a result, the heirs of the grantor had no remedy when the railroad's successor in interest entered into an agreement with the city to create a park on the right-of-way.

If, on the other hand, the railroad holds only an easement or fee-simple determinable, the picture is murkier. Precisely which right-of-way uses were contemplated by grantor and grantee when the easement or fee-simple determinable was created? More to the point, can recreational trail use be fairly regarded as among them? The answer to these two questions—What is the property interest? If an easement or contingent fee, how broad?—taps into a rich, century-old, but ambiguous body of case law in which courts look at the language of conveyance, state rules governing its interpretation, and (especially in the case of the western railroads) several federal statutes.[19]

The recent en banc Federal Circuit decision in *Preseault* illustrates both questions.[20] The court closely examined the language of the conveyance documents from 1899, finding that under Vermont law they had conveyed to the railroad an easement, not a fee.[21] The fee was not broad enough to include recreational trail use. The Vermont courts, it observed, had not accepted the "doctrine of shifting uses," under which the original scope of an easement can flex to reflect changed modes of transportation. To be sure, the general common law, too, allows adjustment of an easement in the face of changing times. But, concluded the court, it is hard to stretch that principle to the point where it blesses a shift from railroad commercial transportation to recreational outings by hikers and bikers.

A state case on the scope-of-the-easement problem is *Lawson v. Washington*,[22] arising under a state rails-to-trails statute. The result was the same as in *Preseault*. Initially, the trial court found that the right-of-way granted to the railroad was a perpetual public easement, so that change to another form of transportation—that is, hiking and biking—did not constitute abandonment. The appellate court reversed, citing Washington cases holding that when an easement is created by private conveyance, it is not a perpetual public easement at all. Rather, where the deed conveys an easement for railroad pur-

---

[19]*See generally* Charles F. Kalmbach, Jr., *The Rededication of Lightly Used or Abandoned Rail Rights of Way to Other Uses*, 7 Transp. L.J. 99, 104–09 (1975); A. E. Korpela, Annotation, *Deed to Railroad Company as Conveying Fee or Easement*, 6 A.L.R.3d 973 (1966).

[20]100 F.3d 1525 (Fed. Cir. 1996).

[21]In Chevy Chase Land Co. v. United States, 37 Fed. Cl. 545 (1997), a similar exhaustive survey of Maryland's property law led to the conclusion that the railroad had acquired a fee-simple absolute, not an easement. As a result, the trail conversion caused no taking.

[22]107 Wash. 2d 444, 730 P.2d 1308 (1986).

poses only, uses inconsistent with rail use constitute abandonment. Nor would the court accept the state's argument that rails-to-trails conversion is akin to the typical historical evolution of an electric railroad into a motor-bus line, a subsequent use generally held to be within even narrowly drawn railroad easements.[23] *Lawson* is not alone in holding that where the easement is for railroad purposes only, a change to trail use amounts to abandonment.[24]

At the other end of the spectrum are cases in which the easement is deemed to be for public travel or general public use, with no limitation to railroad use. Here, reversion is held not to be triggered by trail use and other traversings.[25] These cases are quick to point out that under a well-settled rule of construction, the holder of an easement is not limited to the use in vogue when the easement was acquired— more particularly, that hikers and bikers are using the right-of-way for transportation just as the railroad once did. State and federal statutes encouraging rails-to-trails conversion are deemed by the courts to support this view.

There is yet another issue as to the nature of the property interest involved, an issue raised by one of the most important questions in current takings law. In *Lucas*,[26] the Supreme Court had stressed more than courts had previously the expectations and understandings of the property owner at the time the land was acquired, based on laws then existing. Only those expectations, it implied, were compensable.

In 1992, the Court of Federal Claims in *Preseault* took this notion of compensable expectancies and ran with it.[27] The court reviewed the long history of increasing federal regulation of railroads—in particular, the government's incremental legislative steps toward the modern rails-to-trails program. In light of how late in this history the Preseaults acquired the fee beneath the railroad right-of-way in question, the court held they had no compensable expectancy that con-

---

[23]A dissenting judge, however, did buy this argument. He argued that one must look beyond "railroad purposes only" language to the purpose of the deed, which, if viewed as creating a transportation corridor, might well encompass recreational trail use.

[24]*Accord* McKinley v. Waterloo R.R. Co., 368 N.W.2d 131 (Iowa 1985); Schnabel v. County of DuPage, 101 Ill. App. 3d 553, 428 N.E.2d 671 (1981).

[25]A rails-to-trails example is Minnesota v. DNR, 329 N.W.2d 543 (Minn.), *cert. denied*, 463 U.S. 1209 (1983). *See also* Rieger v. Penn Central Corp., 1985 WL 7919 (Ohio Ct. App. 1985).

[26]Lucas v. South Carolina Coastal Council, 505 U.S. 1003 (1992).

[27]27 Fed. Cl. 69 (1992).

version to recreational use would result in reversion. By the time of acquisition, it said, the Preseaults should not have been surprised at being denied possession in light of where congressional efforts to preserve rail corridors were then headed. Hence, their taking claim was rejected. A three-judge panel of the Federal Circuit affirmed on a similar rationale.

On rehearing, however, the full Federal Circuit vigorously rejected this line of reasoning, at least when used to deflect taking claims based on physical invasions of property rather than use restrictions.[28] And physical invasions, said the court, were precisely what the rails-to-trails program was all about. Indeed, the court indicated that even land bought after the 1983 enactment of the Rails-to-Trails Act (the Preseaults had their parcels by 1980) came with an undiminished bundle of rights.

Is There a Taking?

Suppose, then, that the railroad holds an interest in the right-of-way that, upon conversion of the right-of-way to trail use, would trigger a reversion—but for the postponing of reversion by a rails-to-trails program. Is this postponement, of potentially very long duration, to be viewed as a taking?[29]

The majority view finds such postponement a taking, often by explicit reference to the per se takings rule for permanent physical invasions of property. Consider first the case where reversion is prevented by the federal rails-to-trails program. The government argument is that because NTSA section 8(d) *defines* STB certification for interim trail use as not constituting abandonment, this must under the Supremacy Clause of the Constitution[30] take precedence over state law notions of abandonment. Since there is no abandonment until the

---

[28]*Preseault,*100 F.3d 1525, 1537–40 (Fed. Cir. 1996).

[29]Note that on proper facts, the landowner may be able to argue that the railroad's easement was abandoned *before* the rails-to-trails conversion was effected. In this posture, a taking claim is easily made, based on the government's outright appropriation of a new easement. No issue as to the scope of the original easement arises, since it no longer exists. In *Preseault*, the majority held as an alternative ground for finding a taking that the Vermont Railway had abandoned its easement in 1975, long before the trails conversion. *Id.* at 1549.

[30]U.S. Const. art. VI.

STB says there is, the argument concludes, conversion to trail use under STB approval can never be a taking.

Not so, said the court in *National Wildlife Federation v. ICC*.[31] The issue is not whether Congress has the power to encourage conversion of rights-of-way to trails and in the process postponement of reversionary interests. It unquestionably does. Rather, the issue is whether under the Takings Clause it must pay when it does so. The questions are entirely separate: While the state or local government's ability to bring about a reversion is preempted, the state-created property interest is not.[32] Two years after *National Wildlife Federation*, the O'Connor concurrence in *Preseault*, noted earlier, echoed this line of reasoning.[33] And a majority of the judges in the en banc Federal Circuit decision in *Preseault* hewed to this same rationale.

A contrary holding, affirming the ICC view that trail use under section 8(d) can *never* result in a taking, is found in the Second Circuit's ruling in *Preseault v. ICC*.[34] If the ICC says abandonment is inappropriate, no reversionary interest can vest. One may seriously question the continued vitality of the court's rationale, which the Supreme Court on appeal seemed to repudiate.

One final matter: *If* there is a taking, who is liable for it? The United States might argue that it is the local government that actually effects the trails conversion. The local government might contend that it did so only because of the federal rails-to-trails program that allowed the conversion to occur without bringing on an STB determination of abandonment.[35] In the Federal Circuit's *Preseault* decision, the plurality opinion came down in favor of federal liability, noting that the state acted under federal authority pursuant to an STB order.[36]

---

[31]850 F.2d 694 (D.C. Cir. 1988).

[32]*Accord* McKinley v. Waterloo R.R. Co., 368 N.W.2d 131 (Iowa 1985) (serious taking question would arise if court accepted contention that federal act preempted state property law).

[33]In an analogous sentiment, the Supreme Court has declared that government may not, simply by declaration, "transform private property into public property without compensation, even for . . . limited duration. . . . " Webb's Fabulous Pharmacies, Inc. v. Beckwith, 449 U.S. 155, 164 (1980).

[34]853 F.2d 145 (2d Cir. 1988), *aff'd on other grounds*, 494 U.S. 1 (1990).

[35]The wetlands chapter (chapter 23) discusses similar issues as to where responsibility for takings should lie when both federal and state agencies are involved.

[36]100 F.3d 1525, 1551.

Conclusion

By analyzing rails-to-trails taking claims as potential physical takings, rather than regulatory ones, the courts have ensured rulings for the property owner. Of course, there are still many instances where the railroad has a fee simple absolute, or an easement broad enough to embrace recreational trail use. These instances remain above the takings fray. In other circumstances, however, the *Preseault* case fires a warning shot (despite its fractionated opinions) that trail conversion may depend on either property owner consent or compensation.

Chapter 28

Hazardous Wastes and Contaminated Site Cleanup

The fastest-growing areas of natural resource law and policy over the past decade, along with regulatory takings, have been hazardous substance control and contaminated site cleanup. Until recently, however, there has been little examination of the Takings Clause in these areas.[1]

That state of affairs is beginning to change. There has been an explosion of litigation in recent years brought under various state and federal statutes governing control of toxic substances and cleanup of hazardous waste sites. Most prominent is the federal Comprehensive Environmental Response, Compensation and Liability Act (CERCLA, or Superfund)[2] and its state law equivalents, which focus on remediation of historic environmental contamination. Governmental efforts to clean up sites, along with private landowners' attempts to resist those efforts and (especially) fiscal accountability for costly remediation projects, are bringing inverse condemnation claims to center stage.

---

[1]Several recent law review articles have attempted partially to fill this void. *See, e.g.*, Daniel R. Hansen, *Environmental Regulation and Just Compensation: The National Priorities List as a Taking*, 2 N.Y.U. ENVTL. L.J. 1 (1993); James P. Downey, *Environmental Cleanup Actions, the Valuation of Contaminated Properties, and Just Compensation for Affected Property Owners*, 8 J. LAND USE & ENVTL. L. 325 (1993); Stephen D. Blevit, *A Tale of Two Amendments: Property Rights and Takings in the Context of Environmental Surveillance*, 68 SO. CAL. L. REV. 885 (1995).

[2]42 U.S.C. §§ 9601–75.

Private property claims will likely increase in the future as a result of so-called "brownfield" initiatives. "Brownfield" is a term commonly used to describe an abandoned or underused industrial or commercial site containing contamination from a prior industrial or commercial use. State and federal regulators have announced ambitious plans to remediate and redevelop brownfields into revitalized and economically productive properties. In the long term, such brownfield initiatives can yield substantial social, economic, and environmental benefits. In the short term, however, they will likely further exacerbate the tension between private property rights and government-sponsored toxic cleanup activities.

The relative handful of reported decisions dealing with Takings Clause principles in the hazardous waste context reveal some disparate judicial responses to an often intractable land-use problem.

Contaminated Site Cleanup

Private Landowner/Operator Responsibility for Remediation

A few private landowners or hazardous waste site operators have relied upon the Takings Clause to challenge direct responsibilities imposed on them to remediate hazardous waste problems. Such efforts have generally proven unsuccessful.

Illustrative is *Atlas Corporation v. United States*.[3] *Atlas* involved a uranium producer who for years had been operating under contract with the federal government. In the 1970s, Congress was made aware of potential health hazards associated with radioactive mill tailings, a by-product of the uranium mining process. Congress responded in 1978 by enacting legislation requiring uranium producers to undertake often-costly measures to stabilize and decontaminate the mill tailings. The processors in *Atlas* did so, but then sued the federal government under the Takings Clause to recover their expenses.

The Federal Circuit rejected the taking claim. After noting that the federal statute effected no *physical* invasion of plaintiffs' property, the court of appeals proceeded to analyze the claim under a regulatory takings analysis. Applying the multifactor *Penn Central* test, the court focused in particular on the "character of the governmental action" criterion. It found that the producer's statutory obligation to

[3]895 F.2d 745 (Fed. Cir. 1990), *cert. denied*, 498 U.S. 811 (1990).

deal with the radioactive waste by-products of its uranium mining operation was a reasonable governmental response to a serious public health and safety problem and did not constitute a taking.[4]

As if further rationalization were necessary, the *Atlas* court went on to conclude that the statutory cleanup requirement did not impose an undue, deleterious economic impact upon the uranium processors, nor did it interfere with their legitimate investment-backed expectations.[5]

Sometimes, the private responsibilities created by government's hazardous waste abatement activities are indirect rather than direct. One example is section 107 of CERCLA, which imposes financial liability on landowners for government's incurred hazardous site cleanup costs. In *United States v. Shell Oil Co.*,[6] for example, federal and state officials brought an action under section 107 against landowners and oil companies to recover their response costs, incurred in cleaning up a hazardous waste site. The private defendants challenged that claim as a taking of Shell's property (i.e., money). The court disagreed, noting in particular that under CERCLA the landowners had an express right to obtain "contribution" (i.e., reimbursement) from responsible third parties under another section of the same statute.[7] *Shell Oil* is consistent in analysis and result with other decisions that have addressed takings challenges to CERCLA's cost recovery provisions.[8]

Compelled Government Access to Private Property to Conduct Cleanup

More difficult constitutional questions are presented when government enters private property to abate hazardous waste problems. Courts have reached differing conclusions as to whether such action can be taken without offending the Takings Clause.

The prevailing view is that government may occupy private property without compensating the landowner when such action is

---

[4]*Id.* at 757–58, Keystone Bituminous Coal Ass'n v. DeBenedictis, 480 U.S. 470 (1987); *Mugler v. Kansas*, 123 U.S. 623 (1887).

[5]*Id.* at 758.

[6]841 F. Supp. 962 (C.D. Cal. 1993).

[7]*Id.* at 974.

[8]United States v. Northeastern Pharmaceutical Chemical Co., 810 F.2d 726, 734 (8th Cir. 1986); United States v. Iron Mountain Mines, Inc., 812 F. Supp. 1528, 1545–46 (E.D. Cal. 1992).

necessary to abate hazardous waste problems on the site. Perhaps the most well-known articulation of this position is the Supreme Judicial Court of Massachusetts' 1986 decision in *Nassr v. Commonwealth of Massachusetts*.[9] In *Nassr*, state officials occupied a private site for 18 months in order to clean up toxic pollutants deposited on the site by the landowners' lessee. The landowners originally acceded to the entry, but later claimed that the commonwealth's cleanup operation constituted a temporary taking of their property. The Massachusetts court rejected the contention:

> In this case, the Commonwealth acted under the authority of [a state statute] to remove the hazardous material and thereby to prevent the risks of groundwater contamination, fires and explosions, and life threatening disease. The Commonwealth's actions were classic exercises of the State's police power to maintain the public health.[10]

This result, and the judicial reliance on the "nuisance exception" to inverse condemnation liability, was mirrored in *Brown v. California*,[11] a case involving the McColl Superfund site in Southern California. When private landowners abandoned the site rather than accept responsibility for the cleanup of toxic wastes there, the State of California assumed those responsibilities as authorized under both CERCLA and state law. Years later, private lienholders sued the state in inverse condemnation, claiming that the ten-year government cleanup project resulted in the state's "exclusive possession" of the site to the detriment of the lenders. The California Court of Appeal rejected that claim, finding that: (1) In order for a compensable taking to occur the public must be furnished with the use and enjoyment of the property (it wasn't here); and (2) any damage to the lienholders resulted from a legitimate and necessary exercise of the police power and is therefore not compensable.[12]

A quite different result is found in the Federal Circuit's controver-

---

[9]394 Mass. 767, 477 N.E.2d 987 (1985).

[10]*Id.*, 477 N.E.2d at 990–91.

[11]21 Cal. App. 4th 1500, 26 Cal. Rptr. 2d 687 (1994).

[12]21 Cal. App. 4th at 1505–06, 26 Cal. Rptr. 2d at 689–90 ("[The State's] interest in protecting the surrounding residents from injury arising from the hazardous waste and resulting pollutants, and in protecting the underground aquifers from contamination is surely 'a legitimate government objective in furtherance of which the police power may be exercised'").

sial decision, *Hendler v. United States.*[13] *Hendler* involved another Superfund site in Southern California—the notorious Stringfellow Acid Pits. Hendler owned property immediately adjacent to the Stringfellow site. The federal government, in conjunction with the State of California, wanted to locate groundwater wells and related monitoring equipment on Hendler's parcel as part of the government's cleanup activities for the Stringfellow site under CERCLA. When Hendler refused to consent to this activity, the government invoked its policy power authority, entered onto Hendler's property, and installed twenty-two wells and associated equipment. Hendler then sued in the Court of Federal Claims, alleging an unconstitutional physical and regulatory taking of his property.

In a decision that came as a considerable shock to government regulators, the Federal Circuit upheld the taking claim in most respects. As to the claim that the government's administrative order authorizing federal and state access to the Hendler property effected a *regulatory* taking, the court found that mere *issuance* of the order did not do so. But the court left little doubt that *implementation* of the order could have precisely that effect:

> The Government does not have the right to declare itself a co-tenant-in-possession with a property owner. Among a citizen's—including a property owner's—most cherished rights is the right to be left alone.[14]

The Federal Circuit in *Hendler* then addressed the landowner's alternate theory, that the government's cleanup and monitoring activities triggered a *physical* taking. The court found that it did and was unmoved by the government's claim that its abatement activities on the parcel were temporary rather than permanent.[15] *Hendler* repeatedly stressed that the government was acting for a proper, even compelling, public purpose when it entered the subject property as part of

---

[13]952 F.2d 1364 (Fed. Cir. 1991).

[14]*Id.* at 1374–75. The principle that hazardous waste cleanup orders do not themselves effect a taking, but that implementation of such orders can do so, has been embraced in several other federal decisions. *See, e.g.,* Scogin v. United States, 33 Fed. Cl. 568, 576 (1995); United States v. Charles George Trucking Co., Inc., 682 F. Supp. 1260, 1270–71 (D. Mass. 1988) (CERCLA provision authorizing government entry not a per se taking, though implementation may be compensable in particular circumstances). *See also* United States v. Fisher, 864 F.2d 434, 438–39 (7th Cir. 1988) (accord).

[15]*Hendler,* 952 at F.2d 1377.

its congressionally mandated toxic pollution control efforts. Yet the federal court saw this fact as wholly irrelevant to the taking inquiry,[16] a conclusion seemingly at variance with U.S. Supreme Court jurisprudence.

One might argue that *Hendler* can be reconciled with the *Nassr* and *Brown* cases. After all, in *Hendler* the hazardous site was *adjacent* to the plaintiff's property while in the latter two decisions the claimants' parcels were themselves the source of the hazardous wastes. Yet there is nothing in the *Hendler* opinion that limits its reasoning to the former situation. And *Nassr* and *Brown*'s reliance on the nuisance exception to the Takings Clause finds precious little support in *Hendler*.

Will state and federal cases find the *Nassr/Brown* precedents more compelling than *Hendler* in future takings cases involving hazardous waste sites?[17] Should the fact that substantial public funds are often required to clean up contaminated private properties somehow be factored into the takings inquiry in a more prominent fashion?[18] Intriguing questions.

Miscellaneous Issues

Speaking of an Extreme Case . . .

Takings principles sometimes do not coexist easily with hazardous waste problems. One prominent illustration is provided by the infa-

[16]*Id.* at 1378. In subsequent decisions in the same case, the Court of Federal Claims has largely eviscerated the victory achieved by the Hendlers in the Federal Circuit. *See* Hendler v. United States, 36 Fed. Cl. 574 (1996) (on remand from Federal Circuit, nominal damages awarded for physical taking of private property resulting from government's placement of monitoring wells to assess groundwater pollution; landowners' regulatory taking claim rejected based on *Lucas's* nuisance exception); Hendler v. United States, 38 Fed. Cl. 611 (1997) (nuisance exception reaffirmed; landowners not entitled to compensation for temporary physical taking; special benefits conferred on landowners by government monitoring efforts outweigh any financial injury from temporary taking).

[17]In *Scogin*, 33 Fed. Cl. 568, the Court of Federal Claims was able to avoid this dilemma, on very similar facts; it found that the landowner had executed valid agreements and leases granting the government and its contractors access to carry out remediation activities on Scogin's Superfund-designated site. *Id.* at 578.

[18]*See, e.g., Hendler*, 38 Fed. Cl. 611.

mous Summitville Mine in southwestern Colorado. The owners of the mine simultaneously sued the State of Colorado for allegedly allowing that toxic waste site to happen, and the federal government for spending taxpayer funds to clean it up. The first suit, filed in state court, claimed that Colorado officials were negligent in issuing a mining permit to its predecessors-in-interest.[19] A second federal court lawsuit charged that the U.S. Environmental Protection Agency violated the mine owners' Fifth Amendment rights by implementing a long-term cleanup strategy at the site, when a less expensive and faster remediation plan allegedly would have sufficed. As a result, said the owners, they could not mine or sell the property. Hence, they concluded, their property was taken.

The reaction of one local observer to the two-front Summitville Mine takings strategy is both apt and succinct: "What's a body to do? If you permit a mine, it's a taking. If you don't, it's a taking, and if you clean it up, it's a taking."[20]

Municipal Landfills

Related to the question of how hazardous waste sites are treated under the Takings Clause is the problem of solid waste disposal sites generally. Landfills are an increasingly controversial land use, often made more so by the existence within such sites of toxic substances having a particularly negative effect on surrounding areas. Controversies over the siting and operation of these landfills can often precipitate legal claims under the Takings Clause.

One recent and somewhat unusual example arose in New York. The Town of Esopus operated its municipal landfill under a license issued by state environmental authorities. In the late 1980s, state officials discovered various hazardous materials at the landfill site, eventually ordering its closure. The town did not challenge the closure order, but instead commenced an inverse condemnation lawsuit against the State of New York. However, the reviewing court spurned the town's takings claim, concluding that the state was pursuing valid health and safety concerns. The court further noted that not all

---

[19] Aztec Minerals Corp., et al. v. Colorado, Rio Grande County Dist. Ct., No. 94 CV 50. The Colorado trial court subsequently dismissed the action in an unreported 1995 opinion.

[20] R.E. Baird, *Was Cleanup a "Taking"?*, High Country News (Feb. 20, 1995).

possible uses of the site were precluded under the state's closure order, and that the landfill site retained residual economic value.[21]

A somewhat more conventional confrontation between a private landfill operator and a municipality was resolved by the Connecticut Supreme Court in *Bauer v. Waste Management of Connecticut, Inc.*[22] At issue there was whether a municipally imposed, ninety-foot height limitation could be enforced consistent with the Takings Clause. Relying on a variety of regulatory takings principles analyzed elsewhere in this volume, the state supreme court ruled that the height limitation was constitutional.[23]

Effect of Toxic Contamination on Fair Market Value

One issue that arises with ever-increasing frequency is how property contaminated with hazardous wastes should be valued under the Takings Clause. This question most often has been confronted in the context of direct condemnation actions but, of course, it is equally relevant in the case of inverse condemnation claims.

The former situation is illustrated by a recent state court decision, *Tennessee v. Brandon*.[24] In that eminent domain action, the Tennessee Court of Appeals held that evidence of environmental contamination on the private property to be condemned, as well as the cost of reasonable remediation efforts, was relevant to the issue of fair market value payable by the government.[25]

A more unique situation was presented in *Penn Central Corp. v. United States*.[26] There various railroads to whom railyard properties had been conveyed filed suit against the federal government. The railroads' goal was to insulate themselves from liability under CERCLA for site contamination occurring before they obtained the railyard properties. One claim of the railroads was based on the Fifth Amendment; the theory was that since they had already paid for the acquired

[21]Town of Esopus v. New York, 166 Misc. 2d 36, 631 N.Y.S.2d 213 (N.Y. Ct. Cl. 1995).

[22]234 Conn. 221, 662 A.2d 1179 (1995).

[23]*Id.*, 662 A.2d at 1195–98 ("The financial effect on a particular owner must be balanced against the health, safety and welfare of the community").

[24]898 S.W.2d 224 (Tenn. Ct. App. 1995).

[25]*Id.* at 227. *See also* City of Olathe v. Stott, 253 Kan. 687, 861 P.2d 1287, 1288 (1993); Florida v. Finkelstein, 629 So. 2d 932, 933–34 (Fla. Dist. Ct. App. 1993) (accord).

[26]862 F. Supp. 437 (Regional Rail Reorg. Ct. 1994).

railyards, the companies shouldn't subsequently be required to reimburse the government for cleanup costs under CERCLA.

A specially convened federal court disagreed:

> Penn Central has misconstrued the nature of a CERCLA claim; we thus side with the government. Penn Central's. . . potential responsibility for the cleanup costs comes from its responsibility for creating the contamination. . . . [W]hile a CERCLA claim relates in a sense to the physical condition of the properties, it concerns a fundamentally different subject—the protection of human health and the environment. . . .[27]

Conclusion

Application of Takings Clause principles to hazardous waste control activities places in particularly sharp focus the ongoing tension between private property rights and government's exercise of the police power. Safeguarding the public from the poisoning of its land, air, and water supplies is one of the most fundamental exercises of government's police power. Yet the containment of hazardous wastes and contaminated site cleanup activities can have dramatic, often draconian effects on private property rights. It is perhaps no wonder that the cases that have struggled with this problem to date have reached sometimes inconsistent results.

[27]*Id.* at 450.

Chapter 29

Water Rights

The intersection of the Takings Clause and water rights is a subject of increasing controversy, especially in the water-short, generally arid states west of the 100th meridian. This tension is the product of two key and interrelated phenomena: first, the steady and often dramatic increases in population in a region with more finite resource limits than other parts of the country; and second, heightened interest in such "instream uses" as recreation, species preservation and propagation, and aesthetics. Together, these trends have increased greatly the multifaceted demands on a finite supply of water.

It is therefore little wonder that increased judicial and academic interest in regulatory takings principles has manifested itself in the often-arcane world of water rights law. For over a century, the Takings Clause has occasionally been invoked to challenge governmental decisions allocating water rights. But it has only been in the last decade or so that intensive scrutiny has been given to this topic. It is virtually certain that the number of Takings Clause–based attacks on water rights determinations will increase in the coming years.

Water Rights as Property

Traditionally, water rights allocation decisions have been made at the state level and are governed by state law.[1] No two states, seemingly,

---

[1] A general overview of water rights law is obviously beyond the scope of this work. Three excellent treatises on the subject are Water and Water Rights (Robert Beck ed., Mitchie Co. 1991); Wells A. Hutchins, Water Rights in the Nineteen Western States (1981); Dan Tarlock, Law of Water Rights and Water Resources (1994). This chapter also draws substantially on the scholarship of Stanford University law professor Barton H. Thompson, Jr.

possess identical water rights systems. A common thread, however, seems to be that virtually every jurisdiction recognizes that water rights qualify as property which is subject to at least *some* measure of constitutional protection.[2] But the nature of that property right is perceived differently from state to state and, indeed, often depends on the nature of the water right being invoked.

Under established water law principles, for example, riparian water rights are private interests appurtenant to real property bordering the water source; the holder of a riparian water right is entitled to the reasonable use of that water, correlatively with other riparian owners. Appropriative water rights, by contrast, are not an attribute of the ownership of real property and may be used for specific purposes on the property, irrespective of its location relative to the watercourse, according to a system of prioritized uses and rights.[3]

It is generally recognized for Fifth Amendment purposes, however, that the property interest in water rights is distinct from, and less powerful than, private interests in *real* property. The Supreme Court has stressed, for example, that real property interests are subject to heightened constitutional protection under the Takings Clause, as contrasted with other types of property. The Court has predicated this dichotomy both on the more limited expectations of owners of non-real property interests, and on government's traditionally high degree of control over property interests other than land.[4] Accordingly, most courts have been careful to distinguish, at least for inverse condemnation purposes, privately held water rights from private interests in real property.[5]

The Supreme Court has similarly stressed that inasmuch as property interests are created under state law, courts adjudicating regulatory takings claims must carefully review the property law of the ap-

---

[2]*See, e.g.*, Madera Irrigation Dist. v. United States, 985 F.2d 1397, 1401 (9th Cir. 1993), *cert. denied*, 510 U.S. 813 (1993); Public Service Comm'n. v. Federal Energy Regulatory Comm'n., 754 F.2d 1555, 1564 (10th Cir. 1985), *cert. denied*, 474 U.S. 1081 (1986); Hale v. Colorado River Mun. Water Dist., 818 S.W.2d 537, 541–42 (Tex. Ct. App. 1991); Department of Ecology v. Adsit, 103 Wash. 2d 698, 705–07, 694 P.2d 1065, 1069–70 (1985); Lux v. Hagin, 69 Cal. 255, 374–75, 10 P. 674 (1886).

[3]*See generally* sources identified in note 1, *supra*.

[4]*See, e.g.*, Lucas v. South Carolina Coastal Council, 505 U.S. 1003, 1027–28 (1992).

[5]*See, e.g.*, United States v. Willow River Power Co., 324 U.S. 499, 510 (1945) ("Rights, property or otherwise, which are absolute against all the world are certainly rare, and water rights are not among them.").

plicable state. The purpose of this inquiry is to determine whether challenged governmental restrictions to the exercise of private property rights "inhere in the title itself, in the restrictions that background principles of the State's law of property and nuisance already place upon" those private property rights.[6]

The net effect of these principles, it would seem, is to promote a balkanization of regulatory takings rules that is especially pronounced when it comes to water rights. Because the viability of Takings Clause challenges are largely dependent upon state law–based rules of property, and since those state law rules are perhaps nowhere more diverse than in the area of water rights, inverse condemnation challenges to government's regulation of private water rights are likely to lead to disparate results. As noted below, that trend is already under way.

Legal Limits on the Scope of Water Rights as Property Interests

Traditionally, a number of reasons have been advanced to support the principle that privately held water rights are not subject to a significant degree of protection under the Takings Clause—and certainly to less deference than is real property. The three perhaps most prominent such justifications are summarized briefly below. These rationales are closely related to one another and often overlap. To date, state and federal courts have relied on one or more of these principles to reject the vast majority of regulatory takings challenges to government restrictions on the private exercise of water rights.

Water Rights as Being Incapable of Private Ownership

Some states—and courts—have taken the view that whatever private "rights" may exist to the resource, water rights are simply incapable of private ownership.[7] It is axiomatic, so the argument goes, that

---

[6]*Lucas*, 505 U.S. at 1029. *Cf.* Stevens v. City of Cannon Beach, 317 Or. 131, 854 P.2d 449 (1993), *cert. denied*, 510 U.S. 1207 (1994) (rejecting inverse condemnation claim to government's refusal to permit seawall construction, on ground that landowner's claimed property interest was subject to long-standing public rights that precluded takings claim).

[7]*See, e.g.*, Pratt v. State Dep't of Natural Resources, 309 N.W.2d 767, 772 (Minn. 1981); F. Arthur Stone & Sons v. Gibson, 230 Kan. 224, 630 P.2d 1164, 1174 (1981).

there can be no taking if there is no private property interest to "take." And it is equally settled that "not all economic interests are 'property rights'; only those economic advantages are 'rights' which have the law back of them."[8] If the holder of a water right lacks a protectable property interest in that right, the Fifth Amendment is by definition inapplicable, and there can be no compensable taking.

Supporters of this view cite the fact that several state constitutions or statutes contain express provisions that water is the property of the state or public at large, rather than that of private persons or interests.[9] And the Supreme Court has opined that the protections of the Takings Clause are not available where a property right is expressly conditioned on the right of the government to nullify or severely compromise that right.[10]

The Usafructuary Nature of Water Rights

Under long-standing principles of property law, private rights to water have always been considered less absolute and fundamentally different in kind than fee interests in real or even personal property. Water rights have traditionally been characterized as "usufructuary" in nature.[11]

The right of use, as contrasted with a right of ownership, has been cited in numerous court decisions as a justification for according holders of water rights weaker constitutional protection under the Fifth Amendment than owners of other types of property.[12]

---

[8]United States v. Willow River Power Co., 324 U.S. 499, 502 (1945). *See also* Peterson v. Department of the Interior, 899 F.2d 799, 807 (9th Cir. 1990), *cert. denied*, 498 U.S. 1003 (1990).

[9]Wyo. Const. art. 8, § 1; Mont. Const. art. III, § 15; Idaho Code § 42-101; Cal. Water Code § 102 ("All water within the State is the property of the people of the State. . . .").

[10]*Cf*. Dames & Moore v. Regan, 453 U.S. 654, 674 n.6 (1981).

[11]The California Supreme Court described the concept as follows nearly 150 years ago: "The right of property in water is *usufructuary*, and consists not so much of the fluid itself as the advantage of its use. . . . The right is not in the *corpus* of the water, and only continues with its possession." Eddy v. Simpson, 3 Cal. 249, 252 (1853) (emphasis in original). *See also* current Cal. Water Code § 1001 (accord).

[12]*See, e.g.*, Town of Chino Valley v. City of Prescott, 131 Ariz. 78, 638 P.2d 1324, 1328 (Ariz. 1981), *appeal dismissed*, 457 U.S. 1101 (1982); Pratt v. State Dep't of Natural Resources, 309 N.W.2d 767, 772 (Minn. 1981).

Paramount Public Interest in Water

Perhaps the most oft-cited reason why water rights obtain substantially less protection under the Takings Clause than do interests in real property is the abiding and continuing public interest in the allocation of limited water resources.[13] The most famous articulation of this view is Supreme Court Justice Oliver Wendell Holmes' 1908 opinion for the Court in *Hudson County Water Co. v. McCarter:*

> [F]ew public interests are more obvious, indisputable, and independent of particular theory than the interest of the public of a state to maintain the rivers that are wholly within it substantially undiminished, except by such drafts upon them as the guardian of the public welfare may permit for the purpose of turning them to a more perfect use. . . . [W]e are of the opinion that the private property of riparian proprietors cannot be supposed to have deeper roots. *Whether it be said that such an interest justifies the cutting down by statute, without compensation, in the exercise of the police power, or that, apart from statute, those rights do not go to the height of what the defendant seeks to do, the result is the same.* . . . The private right to appropriate is subject . . . to the initial limitation that it may not substantially diminish one of the great foundations of public welfare and health.[14] (Emphasis added.)

This "paramount public interest" has manifested itself in many aspects of western water rights law. It has been codified, for example, as part of the constitutions and statutory schemes of several states.[15]

The public trust doctrine, similarly, holds that certain public resources are incapable by their nature of full private ownership. The doctrine imposes on resource managers an affirmative and continuing duty to manage those resources for the continuing benefit of the

---

[13]*See, e.g.,* In re Hood River, 114 Or. 112, 227 P. 1065, 1092–93 (1924), *appeal dismissed,* 273 U.S. 647 (1926); Baumann v. Smrha, 145 F. Supp. 617, 625 (D. Kan. 1956), *aff'd,* 352 U.S. 863 (1956); Baeth v. Hoisveen, 157 N.W.2d 728, 732 (N.D. 1968).

[14]209 U.S. 349, 356 (1908).

[15]*See, e.g.,* Cal. Const. art. X, § 2; Cal. Water Code §§ 102, 1243.5, 1394.

general public.[16] Efforts to apply the public trust doctrine to water rights determinations have met with mixed results in various states.[17] For those jurisdictions that have embraced the doctrine in the water rights context, public trust principles would seem a formidable barrier to a successful takings claim. The courts of at least two states, Texas and California, have so suggested.[18]

The doctrine of paramount public rights in water similarly manifests itself in the so-called "reasonable and beneficial use" doctrine, embraced in several states. That principle bars the waste of water, and prescribes a rule of reasonable and beneficial use, method of use, and method of diversion in the exercise of water rights. More to the point, it provides that a water holder's property rights in water exist only so long as those rights are exercised consistently with contemporary social needs and values.[19]

[16]Academic treatment of the public trust doctrine has been voluminous. Two of the best expositions are Joseph Sax, *The Public Trust Doctrine in Natural Resources Law: Effective Judicial Intervention*, 68 MICHIGAN L. REV. 471 (1970), and Jan S. Stevens, *The Public Trust: A Sovereign's Ancient Prerogative Becomes the People's Environmental Right*, 14 U.C. DAVIS L. REV. 195 (1980).

[17]*Cf.* United Plainsmen Ass'n v. North Dakota State Water Conservation Comm'n., 247 N.W.2d 457 (N.D. 1976) (public trust doctrine requires state officials to gauge effect of permit on existing and future state requirements, and to devise water conservation plan) and National Audubon Soc'y v. Superior Ct., 33 Cal. 3d 419, 658 P.2d 709 (1983), *cert. denied*, 460 U.S. 997 (1983) (accord); Kootenai Envtl. Alliance, Inc. v. Panhandle Yacht Club, 105 Idaho 622, 671 P.2d 1085, 1094 (accord); *with* Seven Springs Ranch, Inc. v. Arizona, 156 Ariz. 471, 753 P.2d 161, 165 (Ariz. Ct. App. 1987) (public trust doctrine inapplicable to determinations made under Arizona's comprehensive Groundwater Management Act). For a detailed discussion of the intersection of water rights, the public trust doctrine, and the Takings Clause, *see* Douglas L. Grant, *Western Water Rights and the Public Trust Doctrine: Some Realism About the Takings Issue*, 27 ARIZ. ST. L.J. 423 (1995).

[18]In re Guadalupe River Basin, 642 S.W.2d 438, 445–446 (Tex. 1982); National Audubon Society v. Superior Court, *supra*, 33 Ca.3d 419, 440, 658 P. 2d 709 (no unconstitutional divestment of private property right in light of fact that public trust interest inherently reserved by sovereign and never passed into private ownership; *cf. People v. California Fish Co.*, 166 Ca. 576, 599–601, 138 P. 79 (1913) (rejecting on public trust grounds claim that government's fixing of harbor lines effects taking of private property).

[19]*See, e.g.*, Brian E. Gray, *In Search of Bigfoot: The Common Law Origins of Article X, Section 2 of the California Constitution*, 17 HASTINGS CONST. L.Q. 225, 227, 271–72 (1989).

In *Gin S. Chow v. City of Santa Barbara*, the California Supreme Court explicitly upheld the reasonable and beneficial use doctrine, as codified in that state's constitution, against a regulatory takings challenge: "It has been long established that all property is held subject to the reasonable exercise of the police power and . . . constitutional provisions declaring that property shall not be taken without due process of law have no application in such cases." [20]

The Takings Clause as Applied to Particular Water Law Disputes

The above principles individually and collectively have been relied upon by the courts to reject nearly all claims in which government decisions to allocate finite water supplies have been challenged under the Takings Clause. In recent years, regulatory takings claims continue to fare relatively less successfully than analogous legal claims attacking restrictions on the use and development of *real* property, i.e., land.

Nevertheless, the general increase in inverse condemnation litigation prompted by the judiciary's recently stated, more expansive view of Takings Clause principles in general has been mirrored by similar growth in regulatory takings challenges to water rights decisions. And, at least on occasion, those challenges have proven successful.

Takings Challenges Following Modifications of State Water Law Systems

Various states have over time modified their water rights systems in a manner that reduces or abolishes previously existing rights. Sometimes these alterations take the form of a shift from a common law–based system of water allocation to a statutory system of one kind or another. Another example is when previously unregulated water rights are made subject to allocation controls for the first time. Such changes can provoke legal challenges under the Takings Clause.

One often-litigated example of such a shift is the effort by a number of western states to abolish unexercised riparian rights

[20]217 Cal. 673, 703, 22 P.2d 5 (1933). *See also* Bamford v. Upper Republican Natural Resource Dist., 245 Neb. 299, 512 N.W.2d 642, 651–52 (1994), *cert. denied*, 513 U.S. 874 (1994).

legislatively in favor of a comprehensive permit system based on prior appropriation. Riparians who suffer under such legislatively mandated changes have filed regulatory takings challenges in almost every state in which this reform was implemented. Predictably, the courts have rejected those challenges in virtually all jurisdictions.[21] The response of the Washington Supreme Court is illustrative: "[I]t is well established that riparian rights may be extinguished or limited by statute."[22]

A notable variation from this trend, and one that shows the increased uncertainty in this area of inverse condemnation law, is the 1993 case of *Franco-American Charolaise, Ltd. v. Oklahoma Water Resources Board*.[23] In that decision a closely divided Oklahoma Supreme Court struck down state legislation limiting the exercise of both future and previously validated riparian water uses. The court held that riparian rights constitute private property rights protected under the Oklahoma Constitution, and determined that the legislative changes effected a taking of that property for public use—by permitting competing appropriators to divert the water—rather than merely restricting or restructuring riparians' rights.[24]

In recent years, federal courts have been relatively more willing than their state counterparts to question changes to state or local water rights systems on takings grounds. Perhaps the most notable example is a controversy over Hawaiian water rights.

In *McBryde Sugar Co. v. Robinson*, the Hawaii Supreme Court held in 1973 that long-standing Hawaiian principles of water rights were no longer workable, and that they should be abolished in favor of a modern system based on riparian rights.[25] That decision produced a *federal* Takings Clause challenge, and the federal district court went so far as to find that the state court decision effected a

---

[21]McBryde Sugar Co. v. Robinson, 55 Haw. 260, 517 P.2d 26 (1973); In re Water Rights of Guadalupe River Basin, 642 S.W.2d 438 (Tex. 1982); Belle Fourche Irrigation Dist. v. Smiley, 176 N.W.2d 239 (S.D. 1970); In re Hood River, 114 Or. 112, 227 P. 1065 (1924), *appeal dismissed*, 273 U.S. 647 (1926); Baumann v. Smrha, 145 F. Supp 617 (D. Kan. 1956), *aff'd*, 352 U.S. 863 (1956); Department of Ecology v. Abbott, 103 Wash. 2d 686, 694 P.2d 1071 (1985). *Cf.* In re Waters of Long Valley Creek Stream System, 25 Cal. 3d 339, 599 P.2d 656 (1979).

[22]*Abbott*, 694 P.2d at 1077.

[23]855 P.2d 568 (1993).

[24]*Id.* at 577.

[25]54 Haw. 174, 504 P.2d 1330 (1973).

compensable taking of those previously secure Hawaiian water rights.[26] The Court of Appeals for the Ninth Circuit subsequently scaled back that holding, concluding that the state court had the ability to change the common law insofar as it affects future rights; but rights previously vested due to compliance with and reliance upon preexisting law remain vested and can only be divested through condemnation accompanied by payment of just compensation.[27]

A more recent illustration of this phenomenon is the Ninth Circuit's 1991 decision in *McDougal v. County of Imperial*.[28] At issue in that case was a county groundwater control ordinance that, if implemented, would limit the landowner's extractive rights. After the district court had upheld the measure as designed to address the legitimate state interest in preventing overdrafting of groundwater basin, the court of appeals reversed and remanded. It instructed the district court to determine both whether the severity of the private deprivation outweighed the public interest involved and whether the groundwater measure was, on the facts, the product of an improper governmental motive.[29]

Regulatory Takings Challenges to Federal Programs Affecting Privately Held Water Rights

An equally controversial, recent application of Takings Clause principles is to *federal* programs that affect the private use of water. The federal government, prompted by a variety of both congressional enactments and presidential initiatives, has steadily shifted its natural

---

[26]Robinson v. Ariyoshi, 441 F. Supp. 559 (D. Haw. 1977).

[27]Robinson v. Ariyoshi, 753 F.2d 1468 (9th Cir. 1985), *vacated and remanded*, 477 U.S. 902 (1986), *opinion vacated*, 887 F.2d 215 (9th Cir. 1989). The litigation was ultimately dismissed on ripeness grounds. While the continued viability of *Robinson* is thus less than clear, the litigation raises the key issue of whether *courts*, as opposed to legislatures and executive branch officials, can "take" property. That topic is discussed further in chapter 12 of this book.

[28]942 F.2d 668 (9th Cir. 1991).

[29]*Id.* at 676–80. Notably, groundwater ordinances of this kind have been routinely upheld by state courts against inverse condemnation challenges. *See, e.g.*, Bamford v. Upper Republican Natural Resource Dist., 245 Neb. 299, 512 N.W.2d 642, 651–52 (1994), *cert. denied*, 513 U.S. 874 (1994); Town of Chino v. City of Prescott, 131 Ariz. 78, 638 P.2d 1324 (Ariz. 1981), *appeal dismissed*, 457 U.S. 1101 (1982); Peterson v. Department of Ecology, 92 Wash. 2d 306, 596 P.2d 285 (1979); Knight v. Grimes, 127 N.W.2d 708 (S.D. 1964).

resource policy in recent decades from one promoting private use of public resources for utilitarian goals to the pursuit of preservationist and ecological objectives.[30] This major shift in federal policy has precipitated regulatory takings challenges in a variety of contexts.

First, federal reclamation law reform. Beginning around the turn of the century, the federal government encouraged the settlement and cultivation of western lands through the construction of numerous expensive dam, reservoir, and aqueduct projects, the water from which was delivered to ranchers and farmers at below-market leasing rates. More recent congressional enactments have cut back on those reclamation programs, citing both economic and environmental concerns. Water subsidies have been reduced, as have deliveries, to a variety of western water users. Predictably, these developments have been resisted by those same users, who have at times relied upon litigation and the Takings Clause.

To date, such inverse condemnation challenges to federal reclamation reform efforts have been unsuccessful. In *Peterson v. U.S. Department of the Interior*, for example, the Ninth Circuit held that although water recipients have a property interest in their water delivery contracts with the federal government, the government has rather wide latitude to modify the terms of those contracts notwithstanding Takings Clause principles.[31] And in *Madera Irrigation Dist. v. Hancock*, the same court ruled that the U.S.' conditioning of renewal of federal water contracts upon the payment of funds for operation and maintenance costs attributable to the original contract terms did not violate the constitutional rights of water users.[32]

Congress has recently undertaken still more ambitious efforts to reform federal reclamation policy, including passage of the Central Valley Project Improvement Act of 1993.[33] Federal efforts to implement that legislation have been challenged under the Takings Clause,

---

[30]*See, e.g.,* Federal Land Policy and Management Act of 1976, 43 U.S.C. § 1701 *ff.*; Central Valley Project Improvement Act of 1993, Pub. L. No. 102-575, 106 Stat. 4706; Joseph Sax, *Property Rights and the Economy of Nature: Understanding* Lucas v. South Carolina Coastal Council, 45 STANFORD L. REV. 1433 (1993).

[31]899 F.2d 799, 812–13 (9th Cir. 1990), *cert. denied*, 498 U.S. 1003 (1990) ("hammer clause" contained in Reclamaton Reform Act of 1982 withstands inverse condemnation challenge).

[32]985 F.2d 1397, 1403–05 (9th Cir. 1993), *cert. denied*, 510 U.S. 813 (1993).

[33]Pub. L. No. 102-575, 106 Stat. 4706.

though judicial rulings to date have not yet reached the merits of those claims.[34]

Second, the federal Endangered Species Act (ESA), which is closely related to reclamation law reform. That statute directs federal officials to protect plant and animal species listed as threatened or endangered under the statute, along with the habitats upon which they depend. This mandate has been interpreted by the federal government to encompass changes in the operation of federal water projects necessary to promote ESA objectives.[35]

As noted elsewhere in this work, no court has yet declared governmental action undertaken pursuant to the Endangered Species Act to effect an unconstitutional taking of private property.[36] But such efforts, particularly when they affect long-standing private interests in water supplies, are likely to produce future challenges under the Takings Clause.

Third, federal reserved water rights claims. The federal reserved water rights doctrine is largely a judicially created doctrine which holds that when the United States withdraws land from the public domain and reserves the land for a federal purpose, the right to use then-unappropriated water that is necessary for reservation-related purposes is implicitly reserved. For example, federal regulators might assert a reserved water rights claim to provide for healthy wildlife habitat in a national forest. A federal reserved water right is implicitly limited to the amount of water necessary to accomplish the specific purpose of the federal reservation. A federal reserved right, moreover, vests on the date of the reservation and is superior to the rights of future appropriators. It is a right that, once established, takes its place in the priority of state water rights. While this reserved water right is created pursuant to federal law, it is generally asserted in a state adjudicatory forum.[37]

[34]*See, e.g.*, Westlands Water District v. United States, 850 F. Supp. 1388, 1409–11 (E.D. Cal. 1994) (dismissing, on jurisdictional grounds, taking challenge to Central Valley Project Improvement Act).

[35]*See, e.g.*, Carson-Truckee Water Conservancy Dist. v. Clark, 741 F.2d 257 (9th Cir. 1984), *cert. denied*, 470 U.S. 1083 (1985).

[36]*See* Chapter 24.

[37]*See, e.g.*, Cappert v. United States, 426 U.S. 128, 138 (1976); United States v. New Mexico, 438 U.S. 696, 700 (1978). Congress has waived the federal government's sovereign immunity in order to allow itself to be joined in general water adjudications, which usually are resolved in the state courts. *See* 43 U.S.C. § 666 (the so-called McCarran Amendment).

The federal government's periodic efforts to assert such reserved water rights draw strong support from environmentalists, Native Americans, recreationists, and other interest groups who stand to benefit from the use (or nonuse) of such water. Private property owners and western states are just as adamantly opposed to these federal reserved claims, in part because such claims, if successful, necessarily reduce the amount of water available to be appropriated by the states to other users and uses. Regulatory takings principles are likely to be one set of legal arguments advanced to resist the assertion of these federal reserved water rights claims in the future.

Fourth, federal activities indirectly affecting water rights. Private property owners have occasionally challenged on inverse condemnation grounds federal regulatory and proprietary activities that have an indirect, but significant, effect on the exercise of their water rights. Three recent examples of this relatively recent trend are *Broughton Lumber Co. v. United States*,[38] *Fallini v. United States*,[39] and *Hage v. United States*.[40]

In *Broughton Lumber*, a lumber company sued the United States to recover compensation for the claimed taking, through passage of federal legislation, of the alleged right to apply a state-granted water right to the generation of hydroelectric power for commercial purposes. (The company's continued use of the water for logging purposes was no longer economical, and it sought a license from the Federal Energy Regulatory Commission (FERC) to pursue a hydroelectric project to which it planned to devote its state water rights.) Intervening federal environmental legislation made those latter plans infeasible. The company argued that the passage of the federal statute deprived it of a compensable, reasonable investment-backed expectation in the use of its water right.

The Court of Federal Claims disagreed, finding that the FERC application process is fraught with uncertainty and that the vast majority of such applications are never granted.[41]

In *Fallini*, Nevada ranchers grazed cattle on public lands within a Bureau of Land Management allotment. The ranchers sued the United

---

[38]30 Fed.Cl. 239 (1994).

[39]31 Fed. Cl. 53 (1994), *judgment vacated as untimely filed*, 56 F. 3d 1378 (Fed. Cir. 1995), *cert. denied*, 517 U.S. 1243 (1996).

[40]35 Fed. Cl. 147 (1996).

[41]"[P]laintiff's desire to develop its water right into a profitable enterprise through a change in use is not based on a reasonable expectancy. Thus it does not rise to the level of a compensable property interest." 30 Fed. Cl. at 243.

States in inverse condemnation, claiming that the government's management of wild horses on the public domain had effectively appropriated water "owned" by the ranchers. The Court of Federal Claims rejected the regulatory taking claim on two distinct grounds.[42] First, the ranchers had failed to perfect their water rights under state law and therefore lacked a necessary prerequisite to any taking claim: ownership or title to the property at issue. Second, under the federal grazing/leasing regime, the plaintiffs lacked a compensable expectancy in the exclusion of wild horses from the allotment or exclusive use of the water claimed.

In *Hage*, ranchers claimed that the federal government's cancellation of a permit to graze livestock on federal lands effectively "took," among other things, the ranchers' state-issued water rights in violation of the Fifth Amendment. While the Court of Federal Claims did not resolve that question in its 1996 decision, it came to the rather startling conclusion that it had the authority to adjudicate the rancher's water rights claims for purposes of the taking challenge, separate and apart from the existing and elaborate state water rights adjudication system.[43] Significantly, the *Hage* court also opined that water rights are subject to the same degree of protection under the Fifth Amendment as are rights to real property.[44] *Hage* thus stands in stark contrast with other judicial rulings on this last point.

Water-Use Restrictions as a Limit on Land-Use Development

Perhaps the closest intersection of water rights and land-use development (the latter being the traditional crucible for regulatory takings claims) is in the case in which water shortages, or the absence of adequate water delivery systems, are cited as a basis for government refusing to permit development of land. In some instances, lack of adequate water supply has been used as an explicit or implicit rationale to restrict land-use development.

Such policies have been challenged under the Takings Clause. Until recently, most courts have rejected these claims, in large part based on

[42]The court's decision is worth discussing even though it was later vacated on statute-of-limitations grounds.

[43]35 Fed. Cl. at 159–60.

[44]"This is particularly true in the West where water means the difference between farm and desert, ranch and wilderness, and even life and death. This court holds that water rights are not 'lesser' or 'diminished' property rights unprotected by the Fifth Amendment." *Id.* at 172.

the view that landowners lack any absolute right under the Constitution to obtain water deliveries.[45]

One case suggesting that trend may be shifting is the Ninth Circuit's 1990 decision in *Lockary v. Kayfetz*.[46] In that case, the court held that a property owner can establish a compensable taking if it demonstrates that a moratorium on new water deliveries prevents all practical or economically viable use of its property. (The chances of a successful regulatory taking claim in this context would be understandably enhanced if it were demonstrated that the refusal to provide water service was based on a subjective "no growth" policy, rather than objectively verifiable lack of adequate water resources or delivery infrastructure.)

Conclusion

The interplay between water rights and regulatory takings law, largely ignored for the first two centuries of this nation's history, has become a subject of far greater judicial scrutiny in the past two decades. And competing pressures for finite water resources are bound to increase in the years to come—spurred both by an ever-burgeoning population and by expanded demands that those resources satisfy "non-consumptive uses" such as wildlife preservation, recreation, and aesthetics. The Takings Clause promises to figure prominently as those competing demands for water are sorted out by claimants and the courts.

---

[45]*See, e.g.*, Gilbert v. California, 218 Cal. App. 3d 234, 249–58, 266 Cal. Rptr. 891 (1990); Hollister Park Inv. Co. v. Goleta County Water Dist., 82 Cal. App. 3d 290, 147 Cal. Rptr. 91, 93 (1978).

[46]917 F.2d 1150 (9th Cir. 1990).

Part VI

Remedies

Chapter 30

Invalidation and Other Equitable Relief

In this chapter we discuss money damages and other types of monetary recovery available in takings cases. But first, we cover invalidation and other types of equitable relief that are less used today. You will likely find that, although invalidation after the *First English* decision of 1987 is less important, there are compelling reasons why a taking claimant should continue to pursue a variety of remedies.

Invalidation, rendering something illegal or depriving it of legal effect,[1] was the remedy of choice among landowners with takings headaches at the beginning of this country's takings jurisprudence.[2] But the popularity of invalidation has diminished in recent years as more courts have begun to award money damages. The *First English* decision had an enormous impact on takings, virtually displacing the invalidation remedy with money damages in all jurisdictions, both federal and state.

You may be asking yourself at this point: If invalidation is the Tyrannosaurus rex of takings remedies today, should we study it? Yes, because invalidation is often bundled with remedies for other claims in a takings case, and prospective invalidation by the government after a court finds a taking is the characteristic way to cut off future money damages by converting a potential permanent taking into

---

[1]BALLENTINE'S LAW DICTIONARY 661 (3d ed. 1969).

[2]*See* Pennsylvania Coal Co. v. Mahon, 260 U.S. 393 (1922) (state's exercise of its police power declared void in response to taking claim).

a temporary one.[3] Moreover, invalidation and other forms of equitable relief are still appropriate takings remedies when no forum is available to hear a compensation claim. Thus, invalidation and other equitable remedies have played an important part in takings litigation and will continue to do so, despite the increased emphasis on money damages today.

Invalidation and Other Equitable Relief: Some Definitions

There are three types of equitable relief commonly requested in takings cases. As distinguished from remedies at law, which are principally those of money damages (*see* Chapter 31), a remedy in equity is considered an "extraordinary" remedy that invokes the special powers of courts to do justice by weighing the equitable rights and obligations of the parties.[4] Three types of equitable relief often requested by takings plaintiffs are a writ of mandamus, declaratory judgment, and an injunction.

A writ of mandamus is an order from the court to a public official to do his or her duty, such as to issue a building permit or zoning approval.[5] Such a writ is available only where the function is "ministerial" (i.e., legally required) as compared to "discretionary."[6] The prerequisites for a writ of mandamus generally include:

1. that the plaintiff have a clear right to the relief sought;
2. that the defendant have a clear duty to perform the act requested; and
3. that there be no other available remedy.[7]

[3]*See* First English Evangelical Lutheran Church v. County of Los Angeles, 482 U.S. 304, 321 (1987) (once court determines that taking has occurred, government has option of amending or withdrawing offending regulation or exercising power of eminent domain).

[4]*See* Sherman v. City of Colorado Springs Planning Comm'n, 763 P.2d 292, 295 (Colo. 1988).

[5]*See id.*

[6]This distinction is not as clear is it appears to be, as a court may also grant a writ of mandamus that orders a zoning agency to exercise a discretionary responsibility, although the court cannot order the agency to act in a particular manner. Teed v. King County, 36 Wash. App. 635, 677 P.2d 179, 184 (1984) (court cannot compel rezoning).

[7]*Sherman*, 763 P.2d at 295. *See also* Schrader v. Guilford Planning & Zoning Comm'n, 36 Conn. Supp. 281, 418 A.2d 93, 94 (Super. Ct. 1980).

Another commonly requested remedy in takings cases is declaratory judgment, which, as its name says, declares the respective rights of the parties.[8] The Uniform Declaratory Judgment Act, which has been widely adopted, authorizes declaratory judgment proceedings challenging municipal ordinances such as zoning regulations.

Declaratory judgment is often requested to challenge the constitutionality of a zoning restriction, seeking a declaration that the plaintiff's land has been rendered "valueless" and, therefore, that the regulation is invalid.[9] This type of request is very similar to (and is often brought in conjunction with) the third form of equitable remedy, injunction.

Courts issue injunctions to compel someone to do, or not to do, something.[10] Like a writ of mandamus, an injunction may not compel a discretionary decision, nor is it available if there is an alternative legal remedy. Unlike mandamus, however, in most states a citizen may bring an injunction action to enforce a zoning ordinance against another citizen. Finally, similar to declaratory judgments, a request for injunctive relief often results in invalidation of a zoning restriction that effects a taking of private property.

You are not alone if you find these requests for relief and the courts' treatment of them to be a curious admixture. Because landowners sometimes file "shotgun" pleadings claiming every violation of every law since the Magna Carta, as well as requesting every type of relief available and not available, the courts are often left sorting out conflicting and inconsistent claims and requests for relief. As a result, courts have differed greatly as to the appropriateness of certain remedies in takings cases, and, despite the landmark *First English* decision, the issue remains somewhat unresolved to this day.

---

[8]A declaratory judgment is defined as "[a] binding adjudication of the rights and status of litigants even though no consequential relief is awarded." BLACK'S LAW DICTIONARY 409 (6th ed. 1990).

[9]*See, e.g.*, Davis v. Pima County, 121 Ariz. 343, 590 P.2d 459 (Ct. App. 1978) (plaintiffs alleged county wrongfully refused to rezone their property; sought declaratory relief, other remedies; sole remedy was undoing legislation), *cert. denied*, 442 U.S. 942 (1979); Agins v. City of Tiburon, 24 Cal. 3d 266, 598 P.2d 25 (1979) (plaintiffs sought, among other relief, declaratory judgment, claiming ordinance had completely destroyed property value; relief denied; development not precluded), *aff'd on other grounds*, 447 U.S. 255 (1980).

[10]An injunction is defined as "[a] court order prohibiting someone from doing some specified act or commanding someone to undo some wrong or injury." BLACK'S LAW DICTIONARY 784 (6th ed. 1990).

Invalidation and Other Equitable Remedies
Available Prior to *First English*

Before 1987, when the Supreme Court definitively resolved the issue of the availability of damages for takings claims in *First English*, many state and federal courts held that only equitable relief was available to remedy unconstitutional takings. It all started with the 1922 *Pennsylvania Coal* opinion, where landowners sought to enjoin a coal company from causing subsidence due to the company's underground mining.[11] Making the often-quoted statement, "[t]he general rule at least is, that while property may be regulated to a certain extent, if regulation goes too far it will be recognized as a taking," the Court declared void the exercise of police power that had limited the company's use of its mineral rights.[12] Since the Court did not discuss the possibility of damages, many courts concluded that damages were inappropriate in takings cases.[13]

One such court to make this assumption was the California Supreme Court, in *Agins v. City of Tiburon*.[14] In this case, the court reviewed the availability of inverse condemnation as a landowner's remedy when a public agency had adopted a zoning ordinance that substantially limited the use of his property.[15] As support, the court cited previous California decisions similarly limiting remedies available to takings plaintiffs as well as the *Pennsylvania Coal* decision.[16]

Unfortunately, the U.S. Supreme Court failed to resolve this issue when *Agins* was appealed in 1980. Instead, the Court found no

[11]*Pennsylvania Coal*, 260 U.S. at 412.

[12]*Id.* at 415–16.

[13]*Cf. Davis*, 590 P.2d at 459; Bama Investors, Inc. v. Metropolitan Dade County, 349 So. 2d 207 (Fla. Dist. Ct. App. 1977), *cert. denied*, 359 So. 2d 1217 (Fla. 1978); Mailman Dev. Corp. v. City of Hollywood, 286 So. 2d 614 (Fla. Dist. Ct. App. 1973), *cert. denied*, 293 So. 2d 717 (Fla.), *cert. denied*, 419 U.S. 844 (1974); Fred F. French Investing Co. v. City of New York, 39 N.Y.2d 587, 350 N.E.2d 381, *appeal dismissed and cert. denied*, 429 U.S. 990 (1976), all limiting remedy for a regulatory taking to equitable relief, *with* Nemmers v. City of Dubuque, 764 F.2d 502 (8th Cir. 1985); Corrigan v. City of Scottsdale, 149 Ariz. 538, 720 P.2d 513 (1986); Lomarch Corp. v. Mayor & Common Council, 51 N.J. 108, 237 A.2d 881 (1968); City of Austin v. Teague, 570 S.W.2d 389 (Tex. 1978), all holding that money damages are a required remedy under the Fifth Amendment.

[14]598 P.2d 25.

[15]*Id.* at 26.

[16]*Id.* at 28–29.

taking had actually occurred, so it was not required to consider whether a state may limit the remedies available to a person whose land has been temporarily taken.[17]

One year later, the Supreme Court again left open the question as to the proper remedy for a landowner whose property had been taken by a regulatory ordinance in *San Diego Gas & Electric Co. v. City of San Diego*.[18] This time around, the Court dismissed the appeal from a California Court of Appeal decision that, in light of *Agins*, the plaintiff could not recover monetary damages through inverse condemnation. The court of appeal found instead that, because the record presented factual disputes not covered by the trial court, mandamus and declaratory relief would be available if the appellant desired to retry the case.[19]

Since the California court had not decided whether any taking had, in fact, occurred, but instead contemplated remanding to the trial court for further proceedings, the Supreme Court declined to hear the appeal because the judgment of the state court was not yet final.[20] Thus, the issue of the appropriate remedy in takings cases remained unresolved.[21] Six years later the Supreme Court's *First English* decision finally resolved this issue, totally changing the landscape of available remedies in takings cases.

Invalidation and Other Equitable Remedies in a Post-*First English* World

Finally presented with a case ripe for Supreme Court adjudication,[22] the Court held in *First English* that damages are constitutionally

---

[17]*Agins*, 447 U.S. at 263.

[18]450 U.S. 621 (1981).

[19]The final court of appeal decision was unpublished, *but see* the Supreme Court decision, 450 U.S. at 623–30, for an informative review of the proceedings.

[20]450 U.S. at 631–33. *See also* chapter 5.

[21]The Supreme Court attempted to address the invalidation/damages question two more times after *San Diego Gas & Elec. Co.*, only to again find itself unable to do so given the perceived procedural inadequacies of each of the cases the Court had selected to review. *See* MacDonald, Sommer & Frates v. County of Yolo, 477 U.S. 340 (1986); Williamson County Regional Planning Comm'n v. Hamilton Bank, 473 U.S. 172 (1985).

[22]*First English*, 482 U.S. at 311–13.

required in regulatory takings cases.[23] In coming to this precedential conclusion, the Court considered the purpose of the Fifth Amendment:

> [I]t is designed not to limit the governmental interference with property rights per se, but rather to secure compensation in the event of otherwise proper interference amounting to a taking. Thus, government action that works a taking of property rights necessarily implicates the "constitutional obligation to pay just compensation."[24]

Thus, where the government's activities have already worked a taking of all use of property, no subsequent action by the government can relieve it of the duty to provide monetary compensation for the period of the taking.[25]

Since the availability of monetary compensation was assured after *First English*, the availability of equitable relief in pure takings cases fell into jeopardy. Indeed, the Supreme Court has declared that "[e]quitable relief is not available to enjoin an alleged taking of private property for a public use, duly authorized by law, when a suit for compensation can be brought against the sovereign subsequent to the taking."[26] Thus, in a pure taking case (with no other constitutional claims mixed in), equitable relief should be unavailable.[27]

---

[23]*Id.* at 322. Justice Brennan, who voted with the majority in *First English*, presaged this view in his earlier dissent in *San Diego Gas & Elec. Co.*, 450 U.S. at 661 n.26 (Brennan, J., dissenting).

[24]*First English*, 482 U.S. at 315 (quoting Armstrong v. United States, 364 U.S. 40, 49 (1960)).

[25]*First English*, 482 U.S. at 321. Ironically, the Court concluded with a reference to the *Pennsylvania Coal* decision, reiterating Justice Holmes' statement that "a strong public desire to improve the public condition is not enough to warrant achieving the desire by a shorter cut than the constitutional way of paying for the change." *Id.* at 321–22.

[26]Ruckelshaus v. Monsanto Co., 467 U.S. 986, 1016 (1984) (takings challenge not ripe because remedy available under Tucker Act). Indeed, this sentiment of the Court long predates *First English*. See, e.g., Hurley v. Kincaid, 285 U.S. 95, 104 (1932) (even if a taking had occurred, no injunction if compensation for taking could be had in an action at law).

[27]*See* Preseault v. ICC, 494 U.S. 1, 11–17 (1990) (denying equitable relief claim because compensation available under Tucker Act); various opinions in *Preseault* were issued from 1992–1996, with the most recent holding that the property owners are entitled to just compensation. 100 F.3d 1525 (Fed. Cir. 1996). *See also* Clouser v. Espy, 42 F.3d 1522, 1539–40 (9th Cir. 1994), (equi-

As is the case with all rules, there are exceptions to the general non-availability of equitable relief in pure takings cases. The most important exception occurs when no forum is available to hear the compensation claim, such as when Congress has explicitly withdrawn the Tucker Act remedy for challenges to certain statutes. In this situation, equitable relief is still appropriate.[28]

Moreover, there have also been instances since *First English* where equitable relief, rather than monetary compensation, has been granted for takings, apparently ignoring the *First English* mandate. For example, the U.S. Supreme Court recently upheld an appellate court's declaration that despite amendments intended to soften its impact, section 207 of the Indian Land Consolidation Act effected a taking of certain small interests in Indian lands.[29] The first amendment involved a calculation based on the income-generating capacity of the interest, but by focusing on income generated rather than value of the parcel, the amendment "misses the point."[30] A second amendment allowed transfer of fractional interests to a limited class of individuals, yet "severely restricts the right of an individual to direct the descent of his property."[31] A third amendment allowed tribes to create their own codes to govern descent of fractional interests, but this provision was not used to defend the statute (and tribes have apparently not developed such codes).[32] Besides affirming the taking declaration, the Court upheld the trial court's injunction preventing Congress from acting under amended section 207.[33] Without reference to *First English*, the Court of Appeals for the Ninth Circuit had determined that the "amended [statute] continues to completely

---

table not monetary relief sought in taking claim; dismissed because exclusive remedy is suit for money damages under Tucker Act), *cert. denied*, 515 U.S. 1141 (1995); Town Bd. v. Greenfield Mills, Inc., 663 N.E.2d 523, 528 (Ind. 1996) (no judicial review of taking claim because only injunctive relief, not damages, requested).

[28]*See Ruckelshaus*, 467 U.S. at 1016 ("Generally, an individual claiming that the United States has taken his property can seek just compensation under the Tucker Act."). *See also* Williamson County Regional Planning Comm'n v. Hamilton Bank, 473 U.S. 172, 194–95 (1985).

[29]Youpee v. Babbitt, 519 U.S. 234 (1997).

[30]*Id.* at 733.

[31]*Id.*

[32]*Id.* at 733–34.

[33]*Id.* at 732.

abolish one of the sticks in the bundle of rights for a class of Indian landowners," and had declared the statute an impermissible regulation of Indian lands.[34]

Though equitable relief is generally unavailable in pure takings cases, it is rare to see a pure takings claim because most plaintiffs allege a mixture of violations when the value of their land has been affected by governmental action. A single fact pattern can encompass several disparate claims, such as procedural due process, substantive due process, equal protection, and First Amendment as well as takings violations.[35] To stir the pot even more, takings plaintiffs often add a request for relief under 42 U.S.C. section 1983, the Civil Rights Act, which creates no new rights but does provide additional means of redress for those whose federal constitutional and statutory rights are violated.[36] The courts are then left to analyze various claims in each takings case, and they do not always take care to separate the claims from the remedies.[37] As a result, it is still common to see invalidation and other equitable remedies awarded in takings cases, though these remedies are often more appropriately justified under the Due Process rather than the Takings Clause.[38]

---

[34]Youpee v. Babbitt, 67 F.3d 194, 200 (9th Cir. 1995).

[35]See Eide v. Sarasota County, 908 F.2d 716, 720–23 (11th Cir. 1990) (outlining four types of constitutional claims and remedies for challenging commercial zoning's effect on property), cert. denied, 498 U.S. 1120 (1991).

[36]See chapter 7 for a discussion of this claim in takings cases.

[37]Some courts are not very receptive to this mixture of claims in takings cases. See, e.g., First Bet Joint Venture v. Central City, 818 F. Supp. 1409, 1412 (D. Colo. 1993). But cf. Guimont v. Clarke, 121 Wash. 2d 586, 593–94, 854 P.2d 1, 5 (1993) (land-use regulation may be challenged as either or both an unconstitutional taking and violation of substantive due process), cert. denied, 510 U.S. 1176 (1994).

[38]Note that remedies may also be limited due to factors not related to the constitutional underpinnings of a taking plaintiff's claim. See, e.g., Pro-Eco, Inc. v. Board of Comm'rs, 57 F.3d 505, 512 (7th Cir.) (landfill moratorium ordinance invalidated; no compensation because owner knew about ordinance before buying property), cert. denied, 516 U.S. 1028 (1995); Thrust IV, Inc. v. Styles, 1995 U.S. Dist. LEXIS 5634, at 15-16 (N.D. Cal. Apr. 27, 1995) (remedies limited by contract).

Conclusion

Though the award of damages has virtually supplanted that of equitable relief in pure takings cases, invalidation and other forms of equitable relief still have a role to play in takings litigation today. Despite *First English*'s authorization of damage awards in takings, equitable relief is available if no forum is open to hear a claim for compensation, and it is appropriately awarded when there is a violation of other constitutional or statutory rights in addition to the Fifth Amendment Takings Clause. As a result, the takings plaintiff would be wise to press related legal theories as well and should continue to include requests for equitable relief in addition to those for just compensation. That way, all bases of the takings game are covered.

Chapter 31

Money Damages, Interest, and Fees

The most controversial question of regulatory takings law for the decade preceding 1987 was whether money damages are a constitutionally compelled remedy in inverse condemnation cases. (*See* chapter 30.) Before then, state and federal courts alike had split on the issue,[1] and the conflict had precipitated a vigorous academic debate.[2] After several false starts,[3] the U.S. Supreme Court effectively

---

[1]Before 1987, a number of jurisdictions had limited the remedy for a regulatory taking to invalidation of the offending regulation. *See, e.g.,* Agins v. City of Tiburon, 24 Cal. 3d 266, 598 P.2d 25 (1979), *aff'd on other grounds,* 447 U.S. 255 (1980); Fred F. French Inv. Co. v. City of New York, 39 N.Y.2d 587, 350 N.E.2d 381, *cert. denied,* 429 U.S. 990 (1976); Mailman Dev. Corp. v. City of Hollywood, 286 So. 2d 614 (Fla. 1974), *cert. denied,* 419 U.S. 844 (1974); Citadel Corp. v. Puerto Rico Hwy. Auth., 695 F.2d 31 (1st Cir. 1982), *cert. denied,* 464 U.S. 815 (1983).

[2]*Cf.* Norman Williams, Jr., et al., *The White River Junction Manifesto,* 9 VERMONT L. REV. 193 (1984) (damages remedy in regulatory takings cases warranted by neither constitutional precedent nor policy considerations) with Michael Berger & Gideon Kanner, *Thoughts on the White River Junction Manifesto: A Reply to the 'Gang of Five's' Views on Just Compensation for Regulatory Taking of Property,* 19 LOYOLA L.A. L. REV. 685 (1986) (taking the contrary view).

[3]The Supreme Court had attempted to answer the invalidation/damages question in *four* separate decisions in the 1980s, only to find itself unable to do so given the perceived procedural inadequacies of each of the individual cases the Court had selected for review. *See* Agins v. City of Tiburon, 447 U.S. 255 (1980); San Diego Gas & Elec. Co. v. City of San Diego, 450 U.S. 621 (1981); Williamson County Regional Planning Comm'n v. Hamilton Bank, 473 U.S. 172 (1985); MacDonald, Sommer & Frates v. County of Yolo, 477 U.S. 340 (1986). Instead (and somewhat ironically) these four decisions wound up developing another subissue of regulatory takings law—the ripeness doctrine. *See* chapter 5.

ended the dispute in 1987 when it held in *First English Evangelical Lutheran Church v. County of Los Angeles* that damages are constitutionally required and, indeed, the preferable remedy in regulatory takings cases.[4] But neither *First English* nor the Supreme Court, which authoritatively addressed the question of how such damages should be measured.

Even in the decade since *First English*, courts, litigants, and scholars have devoted relatively little attention to the damages issue. The vast majority of the legal community's focus has instead continued to be on the antecedent question of whether and under what circumstances a government defendant will be deemed *liable* for a taking. This state of affairs may be chiefly attributable to the fact that government has won and still wins a large majority of inverse condemnation lawsuits, and that those cases in which liability *is* found often settle on a damages figure before the compensation question is litigated. On the academic front, most scholars seem far more interested in the liability aspects of inverse condemnation law than upon the vaguely green-eyeshade-tinged debate over money damages.

Nevertheless, the question of how damages should be calculated in regulatory takings cases has taken on an increasingly important role in recent years, as courts become more favorably disposed to property owners on the threshold liability issue. In the wake of a judicial determination that government regulators are culpable under the Fifth Amendment, it is incumbent upon litigants and courts alike to be able to answer the question, "What do we do now?"

The subject of damages for regulatory takings is, in fact, firmly grounded in eminent domain law. Subsequent experience and precedent, however, reveal that the analogy works only in part. As discussed below, well-settled valuation principles from eminent domain and physical takings law apply better to *permanent* regulatory takings than to temporary ones.

---

[4]482 U.S. 304 (1987). The *First English* decision discusses the legal and policy underpinnings of the compelled damages remedy. *Id.* at 314–22. Justice Brennan, who voted with the *First English* majority, presaged those views in his earlier dissent in *San Diego Gas & Elec. Co.*, 450 U.S. at 661 n.26 (Brennan, J., dissenting).

Current view of Lutherglen, formerly the church-owned and -operated campground in the Angeles National Forest, Los Angeles County, California, and the site involved in *First English Evangelical Lutheran Church v. County of Los Angeles*.

Basic Principles in Awarding Damages for a Regulatory Taking

Basic principles, primarily imported from eminent domain law and physical invasion cases, do apply equally to the assessment of money damages in regulatory takings litigation. They include:

- the amount of compensation awarded under the Fifth Amendment must be "just" to both the property owner *and* the public;[5]
- in the event of a temporary regulatory taking, compensation is owed for the "fair value for the use of the property during the period of the taking";[6]
- the burden of proof in establishing the value of private property subject to just compensation is on the owner;[7]

[5]United States v. Miller, 317 U.S. 369, 374–75 (1943).

[6]*First English*, 482 U.S. at 319, 322.

[7]United States *ex rel.* Tenn. Valley Auth. v. Powelson, 319 U.S. 266, 273–76 (1943); United States v. Land, 62.50 Acres, 953 F.2d 886, 890 (5th Cir. 1992). *Cf.* Loveladies Harbor, Inc. v. United States, 21 Cl. Ct. 153, 157 (1990).

- the focus is necessarily on the owner's monetary loss, *not* on the government's gain;[8]
- consequential damages (such as lost profits, relocation costs, loss of goodwill, etc.) are generally not compensable under the Fifth Amendment; [9] and
- in determining the amount of damages to be awarded, the trial court must engage in an essentially ad hoc analysis, applying the most appropriate valuation standard in the particular factual setting involved.[10]

"Fair Market Value"—the Constitutional Touchstone

When property is "taken" as a result of government action, it is by now axiomatic that the proper measure of just compensation is normally based on the property's "fair market value."[11]

Fair market value, in turn, has been defined by a host of state and federal courts, most often in direct condemnation actions. In general, it means the highest amount of money that would be paid for the

[8]*First English*, 482 U.S. at 319; Kimball Laundry Co. v. United States, 338 U.S. 1, 6 (1949). *Cf.* San Diego Gas & Elec., 450 U.S. at 656–57 (Brennan, J., dissenting) ("If the regulation denies the private property owner the use and enjoyment of his land and is found to effect a 'taking,' it is only fair that the public bear *the cost of benefits received.* . . ." (emphasis added)).

[9]*See, e.g.,* Yuba Natural Resources, Inc. v. United States, 904 F.2d 1577, 1581–82 (Fed. Cir. 1990) (citing *Kimball Laundry Co.,* 338 U.S. at 7); United States v. General Motors Corp., 323 U.S. 373, 379–80 (1945); Herrington v. County of Sonoma, 790 F. Supp. 909, 915 (N.D. Cal. 1991), *aff'd,* 12 F.3d 901 (9th Cir. 1993); Burligh Assembly of God v. Zoning Bd., 247 N.J. Super. 285, 588 A.2d 1297, 1299–1300 (N.J. Super. Ct. App. Div. 1990). *But see* State v. Hammer, 550 P.2d 820, 823 (Alaska 1976); Louisiana Dep't of Highways v. Constant, 369 So. 2d 699 (La. 1979) (both finding such consequential damages to be compensable). For one commentator's view that the law governing consequential damages should be liberalized, *see* Michael Debow, *Unjust Compensation: The Continuing Need for Reform,* 46 So. CAL. L. REV. 579, 582–88 (1995).

[10]*See, e.g.,* Yuba Natural Resources v. United States, 821 F.2d 638, 640–41 (Fed. Cir. 1987) (citing United States v. Miller, 317 U.S. 369, 373–74 (1943)); Corrigan v. City of Scottsdale, 149 Ariz. 538, 720 P.2d 513, 518–19 (Ariz. 1986), *cert. denied,* 479 U.S. 986 (1986).

[11]*See, e.g.,* Yuba Natural Resources, 904 F.2d at 1580; *Loveladies Harbor,* 21 Cl. Ct. at 161.

property in question by a willing but unpressured, informed buyer to a willing but unpressured, informed seller.[12] A number of state legislatures have gone so far as to codify the concept.[13]

Courts do not view market value as the *exclusive* measure of just compensation, however. Occasionally, decisions find it an inappropriate or unavailable measure of damages, and in those cases adopt other than market value damages.[14]

A related principle imported from eminent domain jurisprudence to regulatory takings law is that property must be valued at its "highest and best use." This means that in determining fair market value, one must consider not only the property's existing use. In addition, the present and prospective possibility of devoting the property to other reasonable, legal, realistic, physically adaptable, and more profitable uses must be assessed.[15]

However, only objectively measurable values are compensable.[16] Indeed, "it is not at all unusual that property uniquely adapted to the owner's use has a market value on condemnation which falls far short of enabling the owner to preserve that use"; rather, compensation is properly assessed only for the market value of the property taken by the government from the owner.[17] Similarly, government is only required to pay compensation for the interest it has taken, not for the economic value that the property owner may have lost.[18] Purely

[12]United States v. Miller, 317 U.S. 369, 374–75 (1943); Masketer v. Ohio Holding Co., 38 Ohio App. 2d 49, 313 N.E.2d 413, 416–17 (Ohio Ct. App. 1973), *cert. denied*, 419 U.S. 835 (1974); Sacramento & S.R.R. v. Heilbron, 156 Cal. 408, 104 P. 979 (1909).

[13]*See, e.g.*, Cal. Code Civ. Proc. § 1263.320(a).

[14]*See, e.g.*, United States v. Cors, 337 U.S. 325, 332 (1949) (holding that special purpose for property might be considered in place of "market value"); Port Auth. Trans-Hudson Corp. v. Hudson Rapid Tubes Corp., 20 N.Y.2d 457, 468, 231 N.E.2d 734, 738 (1967), *cert. denied*, 390 U.S. 1002 (1968) (accord). *Cf.* Cal. Code Civ. Proc. § 1263.320(b).

[15]McCandless v. United States, 298 U.S. 342 (1936); DICTIONARY OF REAL ESTATE APPRAISAL AIREA 152 (1984).

[16]Kimball Laundry Co. v. United States, 338 U.S. 1, 5 (1949). *See also* United States *ex rel.* Tenn. Valley Authority v. Powelson, 319 U.S. 266, 282 (same).

[17]United States v. 564.54 Acres of Land (Lutheran Synod), 441 U.S. 506, 514 (1979).

[18]United States v. General Motors Corp., 323 U.S. 373, 380 (1945).

speculative value or uses are excluded from the fair market value and "highest and best use" analyses.[19]

Courts have often grappled with particular factors that should be considered in assessing property's fair market value for Fifth Amendment purposes. For example, it is relatively well settled that existing regulatory restrictions and contingencies, especially those associated with *potential* uses, must be taken into account in determining just compensation due for taken property.[20] (If, on the other hand, the law purporting to make a use illegal is itself unconstitutional, then the use can properly be considered in determining the property's value and the particular law is disregarded.)[21] A related, and relatively recent, concern is real property that suffers from contamination by hazardous substances. Evidence of such contamination is similarly admissible as a (negative) element of a property's fair market value for purposes of the Just Compensation Clause.[22]

The question often arises in regulatory takings cases, *when* is the date on which fair market value is to be determined and just compensation calculated? The simple answer is: the time of the government taking.[23] That date is usually (but not always) readily ascertainable in the case of eminent domain proceedings or physical invasion cases. It is sometimes more difficult to fix in regulatory takings litigation.[24] And this problem is exacerbated when *temporary*

[19]Olson v. United States, 292 U.S. 246, 257 (1934); United States v. Land, 62.50 Acres, 953 F.2d 886, 890 (5th Cir. 1992).

[20]*Powelson*, 319 U.S. at 284; *Land, 62.50 Acres,* 953 F.2d at 890; United States v. 174.12 Acres of Land, 671 F.2d 313, 316 (9th Cir. 1982).

[21]Florida Rock Indus. v. United States, 791 F.2d 893, 905 (Fed. Cir. 1986), *cert. denied,* 479 U.S. 1053 (1987).

[22]Finkelstein v. Department of Transp., 656 So. 2d 921 (Fla. 1995) (holding that "evidence of contamination is relevant and admissible on the issue of market value in a valuation trial if there is sufficient factual predicate upon which to conclude that the contamination does affect the market value of the property taken"). *See also* 8 NICHOLS, LAW OF EMINENT DOMAIN § 14C.06[1] (3d ed. Rev. 1997) ("the knowledgeable buyer would be concerned about the direct costs of remediation").

[23]First English Evangelical Lutheran Church v. County of Los Angeles, 482 U.S. 304, 320 (1987); San Diego Gas & Elec. Co. v. City of San Diego, 450 U.S. 621, 658–59 (1981) (Brennan, J., dissenting); Yuba Natural Resources, Inc. v. United States, 904 F.2d 1577, 1580 (Fed. Cir. 1992); Loveladies Harbor, Inc. v. United States, 21 Cl. Ct. 153, 161 (1990).

[24]*See* Whitney Benefits, Inc. v. United States, 752 F.2d 1554, 1559–60 (Fed. Cir. 1985), *aff'd,* 926 F.2d 1169 (Fed. Cir.), *cert. denied,* 502 U.S. 952

regulatory takings are involved, inasmuch as the date on which the taking begins *and ends* must be determined by the court.[25] This business of when the taking occurs is an interesting and complex one. (*See* chapter 13.)

Permanent Regulatory Takings of Fee Interests

American courts have adopted fundamentally different principles in calculating damages in *permanent* and *temporary* regulatory takings cases. Before getting to that, it is essential to note that the government is in the driver's seat when it comes to deciding whether a taking is temporary or permanent. The U.S. Supreme Court emphasized in *First English* that when a court finds a regulation compensable, government officials have the choice of either: (1) leaving the offending measure in place, thereby making the taking permanent; or (2) repealing the regulation as applied to the plaintiff's property, and thus limiting the government's liability to the payment of interim, or temporary, damages.[26] Of course, other legal or policy mandates may constrain the official's options.

Analogies to established principles of eminent domain law work far better for permanent regulatory takings than for temporary ones. In general, the rule in permanent takings cases is that compensation is to be measured by the value of the property on the date of taking, plus interest (or other delay damages) from the date of the taking to the date of payment, minus any rents or profits that the owner was able to obtain from the property after the time of its taking.[27]

Direct condemnation principles have evolved three basic standards of assessing fair market value which are often used for permanent regulatory takings as well.

(1991) (regulatory taking occurs when government action effectively prevents economic development of a landowner's property, e.g., upon enactment of a statute).

[25]*See, e.g.,* Hensler v. City of Glendale, 8 Cal. 4th 1, 24–25, 876 P.2d 1043 (1994), *cert. denied,* 513 U.S. 1184 (1995), and cases cited therein. *See also* discussion of statute of limitations issue in regulatory takings cases, in chapter 6.

[26]482 U.S. 304, 319 (1987).

[27]INSTITUTE ON PLANNING, ZONING, AND EMINENT DOMAIN § 12.02[1] (Matthew Bender 1989) (citing Kimball Laundry Co. United States, 338 U.S. 1, 6 (1949); United States v. 564.4 Acres, 441 U.S. 506 (1979)).

- *Comparable sales approach.* In this, the most widely used appraisal method, the property value is determined by analyzing sales data of similar properties. A real estate appraiser compares the sales to the property being valued in terms of size, shape, applicable zoning, topography, location, use, and time of sale. Adjustments are then made for differences among the "comparables" in order to arrive at a value for the appraised property.

  The comparable sales approach is generally considered the preferred method of determining a property's fair market value, since it involves the least degree of speculation.[28]

- *Cost approach.* The "cost approach" seeks an estimate of the investment that would be required to develop a property to its present condition. Stated differently, an appraiser seeks to determine the depreciated replacement cost of the subject property. This is done in four steps that involve:

  1. estimating the land's value as vacant;
  2. estimating the current cost of reproducing the existing improvements;
  3. estimating the depreciation of those improvements and deducting that depreciation from the reproduction costs of the improvements; and
  4. then adding the value of the land to the depreciated reproduction cost of the improvements to arrive at the fair market value under the "cost approach."[29]

- *Capitalization of income approach.* Under the "capitalization of income" method of appraising fair market value, the property is valued on the basis of the future income that it may produce. The appraiser, in effect, is required to determine the present value of future revenues lost as a result of the taking.[30]

---

[28]United States v. 564.54 Acres of Land (Lutheran Synod), 441 U.S. 506, 513–14 (1979); United States v. 100 Acres of Land, 468 F.2d 1261, 1265 (9th Cir. 1972), *cert. denied*, 414 U.S. 822 (1973); Front Royal & Warren County Indus. Park Corp. v. Town of Front Royal, 749 F. Supp. 1439, 1448 (W.D. Va. 1990), *vacated on other grounds*, 945 F.2d 760 (1991), *cert. denied*, 503 U.S. 937 (1992).

[29]United States v. 99.66 Acres of Land, 970 F.2d 651, 655 (9th Cir. 1992).

[30]Julius Sackman, 5 NICHOLS LAW OF EMINENT DOMAIN § 19.05 (rev. 3d ed. 1997).

Critical to the capitalization of income approach is the *type* of income that is deemed relevant and admissible by the courts. Most jurisdictions preclude evidence of income that could conceivably be produced from a business conducted on the property, while allowing actual rents received or expected to be received from the parcel.[31] The distinction derives from the perception that business income is inherently speculative and a poor indication of a property's market value because it depends heavily on various factors other than the land's producing capacity.[32]

Each of the above-described methods has inherent limitations. Most authorities, for example, find the "cost approach" wholly inapplicable to undeveloped land and the income capitalization method to be of only limited utility in that context.[33] Yet it is raw land that is most often at issue in regulatory takings cases. And several courts have identified the limited utility of any of the "fair market value" approaches with respect to *temporary* regulatory takings.[34]

Less-than-Fee and Other Interests

On occasion, less-than-fee property interests (such as easements) form the basis of a regulatory takings claim. Similarly, government restrictions on the right to use and develop fee interests in real property are themselves often analogized to less-than-fee interests in land, i.e., a conservation easement or a government-held option on the parcel during the period of the alleged unconstitutional taking.[35] The basic Fifth Amendment remedy remains the same, however: The landowner must be fairly compensated for the property interest that has been lost. "The value of that interest, in turn, is determined by

---

[31]*See, e.g.,* People v. Dunn, 46 Cal. 2d 639, 641, 297 P.2d 964, 966 (1956); Julius Sackman, 5 NICHOLS LAW OF EMINENT DOMAIN §§ 19.07–19.10 (3d ed. rev. 1997).

[32]*Id.*

[33]*See, e.g.,* THE APPRAISAL OF REAL ESTATE at 129 (American Institute of Real Estate Appraisers, 4th ed., 1964).

[34]*See, e.g.,* Yuba Natural Resources, Inc. v. United States, 904 F.2d 1577, 1580–81 (Fed. Cir. 1990) (citing *First English*).

[35]*See, e.g.,* City of Austin v. Teague, 570 S.W.2d 389 (Tex. 1978); Lomarch Corp. v. Mayor of Englewood, 51 N.J. 108, 237 A.2d 881 (1968); RICHARD F. BABCOCK, THE ZONING GAME: MUNICIPAL PRACTICES AND POLICIES 168–72 (1966).

isolating it as a component of the overall fair market value of the affected property."[36]

Less-than-fee and other property interests that have been the subject of regulatory takings claims include: mineral rights;[37] possessory interests in rent-controlled mobile-home park pads;[38] water rights and flowage easements; [39] federal licenses and permits;[40] and billboard leases. [41] Quantification of money damages in such cases raises often-nettlesome valuation questions.[42]

Temporary Takings

Assessing damages in regulatory takings cases is especially controversial when it comes to "temporary takings." This issue first took on nationwide focus a decade ago, in the wake of the Supreme Court's *First English* decision. That decision recognized that government defendants found liable for a regulatory taking are given the option by the Court of rescinding the offending measure. Whereas such a rescission had previously spelled the end of the matter in at least some jurisdictions, *First English* made it clear that regulators choosing the rescission alternative remain liable for "compensation for the period during which the taking was effective."[43]

---

[36]Wheeler v. City of Pleasant Grove, 833 F.2d 267, 270 (11th Cir. 1987) [hereinafter *Wheeler III*]. *See also* Cal. Code Civil Proc. § 1260.220(a).

[37]*Yuba Natural Resources*, 904 F.2d 1577 (Fed. Cir. 1990); NRG Co. v. United States, 24 Cl. Ct. 51 (1991).

[38]*See, e.g.*, Azul Pacifico, Inc. v. City of Los Angeles, 948 F.2d 575 (9th Cir. 1991), *overruled on other grounds*, Yee v. City of Escondido, 503 U.S. 519 (1992). The *Azul Pacifico* decision contains a provocative discussion of how monetary damages for the "loss" of a possessory interest in a mobile-home pad are to be calculated. 948 F.2d at 584–86.

[39]Hemmerling v. Tomlev, 67 Cal. 2d 572, 63 Cal. Rptr. 1 (1967).

[40]United States v. 42.13 Acres of Land, 73 F.3d 953 (9th Cir. 1996), *cert. denied*, 518 U.S. 1017 (1996) (hydropower license); Fallini v. United States, 31 Fed. Cl. 53, 58 (1994), *vacated and remanded on other grounds*, 56 F.3d 1378 (Fed. Cir. 1995). *See also* United States v. Fuller, 409 U.S. 488, 492 (1973).

[41]Ryan Outdoor Advertising, Inc. v. United States, 559 F.2d 554 (9th Cir. 1977).

[42]*Id. See also* Cordeco Dev. Corp. v. Vasquez, 539 F.2d 256 (1st Cir. 1976), *cert. denied*, 429 U.S. 978 (1976).

[43]482 U.S. at 321.

Although *First English* referred to post–World War II cases dealing with temporary *physical* takings,[44] it did not otherwise discuss the unique problems associated with calculating compensation for property temporarily taken by government's regulatory activities. Only a handful of post–*First English* decisions have had occasion to contribute to the jurisprudence on this subject, as noted above. Commentators have addressed the question, however, often reaching disparate conclusions on the appropriate method by which temporary takings damages should be measured.[45]

A threshold problem is that the far more established methodologies by which damages for *permanent* takings are calculated are not readily applicable to temporary takings cases. Specifically, the temporary physical takings cases cited in *First English* explicitly reject the "fair market value" standard that forms the touchstone of damages assessment in permanent takings actions.[46] The Supreme Court has instead opined that the proper measure of monetary compensation in

[44]*See, e.g.,* Kimball Laundry Co. v. United States, 338 U.S. 1 (1949); United States v. Petty Motor Co., 327 U.S. 372 (1946); United States v. General Motors Corp., 323 U.S. 373 (1946).

[45]Some of the more thoughtful articles on this question include Jay Harris Rabin, *It's Not Just Compensation, It's a Theory of Valuation as Well: Valuing "Just Compensation" for Temporary Regulatory Takings,* 14 COLUMBIA J. ENVTL. L. 247 (1989); Joseph P. Mikitish, *Measuring Damages for Temporary Regulatory Takings: Against Undue Formalism,* 32 ARIZONA L. REV. 985 (1990); J. Margaret Treatbar, *Calculating Compensation for Temporary Regulatory Takings,* 42 KANSAS L. REV. 201 (1993) [hereinafter *Calculating Compensation*]; Clynn S. Lunney, *Compensation for Takings: How Much Is Just?,* 42 CATHOLIC U. L. REV. 721 (1993); Richard J. Roddewig & Christopher Duerksen, *Measuring Damages in Takings Cases: the Next Frontier,* in 1993 ZONING AND PLANNING LAW HANDBOOK 273; DANIEL MANDELKER ET AL., FEDERAL LAND USE LAW § 4A.06.

Some pre-*First English* commentaries have proven prescient on the subject of measuring damages in regulatory takings cases as well. *See, e.g.,* DONALD G. HAGMAN & DEAN MISCZYNSKI, WINDFALLS FOR WIPEOUTS (APA 1978); Douglas Kmiec, *Regulatory Takings: the Supreme Court Runs Out of Gas in San Diego,* 57 INDIANA L.J. 45 (1982); Alan F. Ciamporcero, *"Fair" is Fair: Valuing the Regulatory Taking,* 15 U.C. DAVIS L. REV. 741 (1982).

[46]*See, e.g., Kimball Laundry Co.,* 338 U.S. 1, 18 (temporary interruptions require increased measure of compensation because they greatly narrow the "range of alternatives" open to the condemnee).

interim regulatory taking cases is the value of the use of the property during the period of the temporary taking.[47]

Care must be taken in devising any interim damages remedy to avoid a result which winds up compensating the property owner *in excess of* the fair market value of the subject property. Such a result would be particularly inequitable in light of the fact that the plaintiff in a temporary taking case retains title to and long-term use of the property, while a permanent taking presumably results in the government obtaining title to the parcel.[48]

Experience has shown that, as with many aspects of inverse condemnation law, the devil is in the details. The handful of courts that have to date addressed the issue of how interim damages for regulatory takings are to be measured have come up with a broad array of approaches.[49]

Rental Value

The rental value of property over the period of the temporary regulatory taking is frequently cited as an appropriate basis for calculating interim damages.[50] This method is the one most analogous to that used in temporary *physical* takings.[51] Under the rental value formula, the appropriate fair rental value is multiplied by the period of the temporary taking to obtain the proper damages figure.[52]

One serious limitation on the rental value method is that it is generally only considered suitable when the property at issue has a pre-existing use at the time the regulation takes effect. The typical regu-

[47]*First English*, 482 U.S. at 319, 321. *See also* Yuba Natural Resources v. United States, 821 F.2d 638, 641 (Fed. Cir. 1987) (discussing "the distinction between temporary and permanent takings and the concurrent distinction between measures of compensation applicable to those two situations").

[48]*First English*, 428 U.S. at 319, 321.

[49]For a more thorough explication of these varying methodologies, *see, e.g., Calculating Compensation, supra* note 45.

[50]*See* Yuba Natural Resources, Inc. v. United States, 904 F.2d 1577, 1581 (Fed. Cir. 1990); France Stone Co., Inc. v. Charter Township of Monroe, 802 F. Supp. 90, 106–07 (E.D. Mich. 1992); State Dep't of Health v. The Mill, 809 P.2d 434, 436–38 (Colo. Ct. App. 1991); Snyder v. City of Minneapolis, 441 N.W.2d 781, 789 (Minn. 1989).

[51]Kimball Laundry Co. v. United States, 338 U.S. 1 (1949); United States v. Petty Motor Co., 327 U.S. 372 (1946).

[52]*Kimball Laundry Co.,* 338 U.S. 1; *Petty Motor Co.,* 327 U.S. 372.

latory taking case, on the other hand, involves government restrictions on the *planned* use of property rather than existing use. And frequently, no rental market exists for the unused property. Thus, courts and commentators generally discourage use of the rental value method for undeveloped property.[53] A related criticism is that the rental value method is relatively speculative—especially when future, anticipated uses are urged as the basis of fair rental value—and has the potential for windfall awards.[54]

Before-and-After ("Developer's") Approach

Some courts have measured damages by comparing the value of the property before the regulation with the subsequent value of the parcel.[55] This standard is fairly easy to calculate, and is measured in one of two ways. Under the first, a court determines the difference between the market value of the fee on the date of the regulatory taking and its market value on the date the taking ceases. The second valuation method calculates the difference between the property's value immediately before the regulation became effective and the property's value immediately following its imposition.[56]

While at least one court has utilized the before-and-after approach in a regulatory takings case,[57] it has generally been rejected by appellate courts in favor of other methodologies in recent years.[58]

[53]*See, e.g.,* City of Austin v. Teague, 570 S.W.2d 389, 395 (Tex. 1978) ("Anticipated rentals from land that is presently undeveloped is just as speculative and uncertain as measuring anticipated profits from a presently unestablished business."); Jay Harris Rabin, *supra* note 45, at 256.

[54]*Calculating Compensation, supra* note 45, at 222 n.162 ("[T]he fair rental method, while ostensibly logical and undoubtedly appropriate for temporary physical takings, presents a great opportunity for large, windfall awards.").

[55]Cordeco Dev. Corp. v. Santiago Vasquez, 539 F.2d 256, 261 (1st Cir. 1976); Washington Market Enters. v. City of Trenton, 68 N.J. 107, 343 A. 2d 408, 416–17 (1975); Knight v. City of Billings, 642 P.2d 141 (Mont. 1982).

[56]*Calculating Compensation, supra* note 45 at 225.

[57]*Washington Market,* 343 A.2d at 408.

[58]*See, e.g.,* Wheeler v. City of Pleasant Grove, 896 F.2d 1347, 1350–51 (11th Cir. 1990) [hereinafter *Wheeler IV*] (overturning district court's application of before-and-after standard); City & County of Honolulu v. Market Place Ltd., 55 Haw. 226, 517 P.2d 7 (1973); Contra Costa Water Dist. v. Bar-C Properties, 5 Cal. App. 4th 652, 7 Cal. Rptr. 2d 91 (1992). *Cf.* Kimball Laundry Co. v. United States, 338 U.S. 1, 7 (1949) (rejecting before-and-after approach in temporary physical taking case).

Option Value

At least one state, New Jersey, has measured temporary takings damages by determining the value of a fictional option to purchase the affected property for the period in which the invalidated regulation was in effect.[59] The value of the option is generally calculated by using the market value of the property without any zoning restrictions; this is intended to avoid requiring the court to speculate as to the level of a constitutionally valid restriction government regulators would impose on the affected property.[60]

The option value method can be an accurate measure of the property interest actually taken. Because there is often a market for options to purchase undeveloped land, this approach is more appropriate than the rental value method when such vacant property is at issue. On the other hand, the value of an option does not necessarily bear any relation to the property owner's actual losses. It is thus best suited to cases in which there is no present use of the land and the regulation prevents an anticipated sale or is enacted in contemplation of public acquisition of the property.[61]

Market Rate of Return

Probably no damages method has attracted as much attention in temporary takings cases as the market rate of return approach. Under this method, the property owner is compensated by an amount designed to approximate the temporary loss of the ability to produce income or profits. Applications of this formula typically apply a market rate of return to the difference between the value of the subject property with and without the challenged regulation. Several variations of the market rate of return method exist, and different versions can produce dramatically different results.[62]

[59]Lomarch Corp. v. City of Englewood, 51 N.J. 108, 237 A.2d 881, 884 (1968) (city imposed year-long development freeze); Sheerr v. Evesham Township, 184 N. J. Super. 11, 445 A.2d 46, 74–75 (N.J. Super. Ct. App. 1982) (change in zoning deprived owner of ability to sell property). *See also* N.J. Rev. Stat. § 40:55D-44 (option value the proper method of calculating just compensation when "the reservation of public areas" constitutes a taking).

[60]*Sheerr,* 445 A.2d at 74.

[61]*Id.; Lomarch,* 237 A.2d at 884; *Calculating Compensation, supra* note 45, at 226–27.

[62]*Calculating Compensation, supra* note 45, at 227.

The simplest formulation of this method of valuation is to apply an appropriate rate of return to the difference between the market value of the property *with* and *without* the challenged restriction, calculated over the period in which the measure was in effect. The difference should, in theory, reflect a market estimation of future profits and development costs concerning the property.[63] The Court of Appeals for the Eighth Circuit embraced this approach in 1985, calculating damages by first subtracting the value of the land zoned for residential purposes—the designation improperly applied by the city—from the value of the land under an industrial designation. The court of appeals then applied a designated market rate of return to the difference.[64] The Eleventh Circuit temporarily embraced the same approach, suggesting that it compensates the owner for actual losses, i.e., "the property's potential for producing income or an expected profit."[65] Commentators believe this variant of the market rate of return approach works best when there is no existing use of the land at the time the regulation is imposed, and the regulation effects a change in value that is readily measured in the marketplace.[66]

Equity Interest Approach

In *Wheeler IV*, the Eleventh Circuit departed from its previously approved market rate of return method by holding that the proper yardstick of the value of the subject property without the invalid restriction is the value the parcel would have upon completion of the planned project. The court of appeals then subtracted from this figure the value of the property owner's equity interest in the property with the invalid restriction. Finally, it determined that the proper measure of damages was the market rate of return on the difference between the owner's equity interest in the contemplated development and the

---

[63]Nemmers v. City of Dubuque, 764 F.2d 502, 505 (8th Cir. 1985); *Wheeler III*, 833 F.2d 267, 271 (11th Cir. 1987); Usdin v. State Dep't of Envtl. Protection, 173 N.J. Super. 311, 414 A.2d 280, 283 (N.J. Super. Ct. App. 1980).

[64]*Nemmers*, 764 F.2d at 505. This approach varies from the fair rental value method discussed earlier, since the latter generally uses the value of the property without *any* restrictions, rather than its value prior to the invalidated ordinance (as was the case in *Nemmers*).

[65]*Wheeler III*, 833 F.2d at 271.

[66]Mikitish, *supra* note 45, at 999.

owner's equity interest in the undeveloped land.[67] This methodology departs from the more conventional market rate of return method in several pertinent respects.[68]

The equity interest approach has been followed by at least two other federal courts,[69] but has generated substantial criticism from judges and commentators alike for its perceived inadequacies. Foremost among these flaws are concerns that: The equity interest method improperly relies on speculation that a project will meet its developer's full expectations; fails to consider the developer's construction costs; neglects to consider alternative, available uses of the property under the challenged regulation; and omits consideration of alternate investment opportunities for capital that would otherwise have gone into the development.[70]

Herrington (Probability) Method

In *Herrington v. County of Sonoma*, a federal district court in California articulated still another approach to calculating compensation for a temporary regulatory taking.[71] The court initially rejected as unsuitable the previously announced standards for calculating interim damages, noting the "speculativeness" inherent in any determination regarding the level of use a landowner would be allowed but for the unconstitutional regulation.[72] Like the Eleventh Circuit in *Wheeler III*, the district court expressed concern that the property owner not suffer injury from the delay in earning income from a pro-

---

[67]Wheeler v. City of Pleasant Grove (*Wheeler IV*), 896 F.2d 1347, 1350-51 (11th Cir. 1990).

[68]*See Calculating Compensation, supra* note 45, at 231.

[69]Corn v. City of Lauderdale Lakes, 771 F. Supp. 1557, 1570–71 (S.D. Fla. 1991), *aff'd in part, rev'd in part,* 997 F.2d 1369 (11th Cir. 1993); Front Royal & Warren County Indus. Park v. Town of Front Royal, 749 F. Supp. 1439, 1445 (W.D. Va. 1990), *vacated on other grounds,* 945 F.2d 760 (4th Cir. 1991), *cert. denied,* 503 U.S. 937 (1992).

[70]*Corn,* 771 F.Supp. at 1570–71; Roddewig & Duerksen, *supra* note 45, at 285; *Calculating Compensation, supra* note 45, at 232.

[71]790 F. Supp. 909 (N.D. Cal. 1991), *aff'd,* 12 F.3d 901 (9th Cir. 1993). *Herrington* involved damages awarded in the wake of a successful substantive due process claim rather than a regulatory taking, but the analysis seems fully applicable to the latter situation as well. *Id.; Calculating Compensation supra* note 45, at 232, n.234.

[72]*Herrington,* 790 F. Supp. at 915.

posed real estate development. On the other hand, the *Herrington* court sought to take into account the reasonable uncertainty about whether the development would have received final approval even in the absence of the invalid restriction. Similarly, the court attempted to provide compensation for the increased costs of construction due to the regulatory delay, discounted by the possibility that the project would not have been approved. Accordingly, *Herrington* adopts a "probability" formula that focuses on "the relevant issues involved in the Herringtons' subdivision application and assesses the probability of approval based on criteria normally considered by the County in processing subdivision approvals."[73]

Specifically, the probability formula takes into account the highest valuation of the property proposed by the parties and the lowest valuation as so-called boundary values. The full difference between these boundary values may only be awarded to the landowners, however, if they can prove "that there was a 100% probability that their subdivision proposal would have been approved but for the County's illegal acts." The *Herrington* method then applies a reasonable market rate of return (representing the length of time the owners were improperly denied the right to develop) to the difference derived from this probability analysis.[74]

The *Herrington* probability method is noteworthy in that it attempts to address and minimize the speculation inherent in damages calculations of this type, and to incorporate considerations of risk inherent in the land development business. The U.S. Court of Appeals for the Ninth Circuit affirmed the district court's innovative approach, characterizing it as the product of "a careful and searching analysis."[75] The *Herrington* approach has similarly received support from several commentators.[76]

---

[73]*Id.* at 915.

[74]*Id.* at 915. *See also Calculating Compensation, supra* note 45, at 233. *Herrington* is also notable for its discussion of the appropriate rate of return that should be applied in the formula. The district court ultimately concluded that the 52-week U.S. Treasury bill rate should be used to determine the proper rate of return. 790 F. Supp. at 922–23.

[75]*Herrington v. County of Sonoma*, 12 F.3d 901, 903 (9th Cir. 1993).

[76]Roddewig & Duerksen, *supra* note 45, at 285; *Calculating Compensation, supra* note 45 at 241 ("The *Herrington* approach . . . comes closest to estimating what the real future value of a piece of property was at the time of the taking.").

Section 1983–Based Damages Approach

As noted in chapter 7, regulatory takings cases are increasingly being brought under the federal Civil Rights Act of 1871, 42 U.S.C. section 1983. Several cases have explicitly held that section 1983 is the proper procedural mechanism for securing just compensation under the Fifth Amendment.[77] A great deal of case law independent of regulatory takings litigation has developed on the question of how money damages should be measured and assessed in section 1983 cases. That jurisprudence has developed separately from the real estate–based methodologies summarized immediately above.

If these broader, section 1983–based principles are applied in the temporary regulatory takings context, different and often lower damages awards will likely result. This conclusion is based in major part on the grounding of section 1983 claims in traditional tort law principles.[78] For example, a cardinal precept of section 1983 is that damages awarded under that statute are compensatory in nature, and that a plaintiff may therefore only recover them if he or she is able to prove actual loss or injury resulting from the illegal government act.[79]

A landowner subject to an invalid regulation may have a formidable task proving damages under this standard. For example, if real property is not being used at the time an invalid regulation is enacted, it is difficult to contemplate a compelling showing of "injury" for purposes of establishing liability under section 1983.[80] Several courts have embraced this tort-like measure of damages in temporary regulatory takings cases, which generally result in much smaller monetary

[77]*See, e.g.,* Azul Pacifico, Inc. v. City of Los Angeles, 973 F.2d 704, 705 (9th Cir. 1992). *See generally* Lynch v. Household Fin. Co., 405 U.S. 538, 552 (1972) (rights in property are basic civil rights protected by § 1983); San Diego Gas & Elec. Co. v. City of San Diego, 450 U.S. 621, 656 n.23 (1981) (Brennan, J., dissenting).

[78]*See, e.g.,* Carey v. Piphus, 435 U.S. 247, 253 (1978) (§ 1983 "was intended to '[create] a species of tort liability'" for persons deprived of rights secured to them by Constitution.).

[79]Memphis Community School Dist. v. Stachura, 477 U.S. 299, 315 (1987); Corrigan v. City of Scottsdale, 149 Ariz. 538, 720 P.2d 513, 519, (Ariz. 1986) *cert. denied,* 479 U.S. 986 (1986).

[80]*Calculating Compensation, supra* note 45, at 238.

awards than the potential "windfalls" available under one or more of the eminent domain–based standards summarized earlier.[81]

Some observers have suggested that the tort-based principles underlying section 1983 seem somewhat inconsistent with those underlying the Takings Clause. They argue that to the extent the former would reduce monetary awards available to compensate for temporary regulatory takings, they should be disregarded in favor of the more generous judgments awardable under other methods of calculating money damages.[82]

Each of the above-described methods for calculating interim damages for regulatory takings has its advantages and deficiencies. Accordingly, state and federal courts have been reluctant to prescribe a "one size fits all" temporary damages rule. To the contrary, several courts and scholars have explicitly embraced an ad hoc approach, noting that the potential array of factual settings in regulatory takings cases is broad, and that different methodologies work better in different cases.[83]

Government-Created Value

In recent years, some commentators have argued that the damages calculation in regulatory takings litigation is unfairly skewed because it fails to account for the *increase* in private property values created by a wide array of government programs and projects. Government acts to increase private property values through capital improvements including streets, parks, utility lines, transit systems, and public buildings. Its provision of police and fire protection, public medical facilities, and the like have a similar, positive effect on property value. So too, the argument goes, do a broad array of land-use regulations that prevent destruction of community resources and enhance value by preventing incompatible uses and densities.

---

[81]*See, e.g.,* City of Austin v. Teague, 570 S.W.2d 389, 395 (Tex. 1978) (limiting damages in temporary regulatory takings case to "actual losses"); *Corrigan,* 720 P.2d at 518–19 (requiring proof of "actual loss"). *See also Calculating Compensation, supra* note 45 at 238.

[82]Rabin, *supra* note 45, at 262–63; *Calculating Compensation, supra* note 45, at 236–40.

[83]*Corrigan,* 720 P.2d at 518; Mikitish, *supra* note 45, at 1001–02; *Calculating Compensation, supra* note 45, at 241.

Proponents of this view ask: If these governmental actions increase the value of private property, do such acts constitute a "giving" of public resources for private use? And, at least in the case where landowners claim government regulations have devalued their property, shouldn't such "givings" be offset against the fiscal damage attributable to the regulatory taking?[84]

Like the origins of regulatory takings jurisprudence, advocates of the government "giving" theory find precedent for their theory in the law of eminent domain. Condemnation law addresses the issue of government-created value in at least two ways. First, it provides that the government "may not be required to compensate a condemnee for elements of value that the Government has created, and that it might have destroyed under the exercise of governmental authority other than the power of eminent domain."[85] Thus, for example, in the regulatory takings context, value created by government through a nearby subway station or a permit to use adjacent public lands would not be considered private property subject to compensation under the Takings Clause. Second, eminent domain law provides that a property owner need not be compensated for value added to the remainder parcel by the very project for which the "take" parcel was condemned: "if governmental activities inflict slight damages upon land on one respect and actually confer great benefits when measured in the whole, to compensate the landowner further would be to grant him a special bounty."[86] Thus, for example, increases in the value of private property caused by community height and design standards could be offset against the decrease in value caused by those same regulations when applied to the subject property.

To date, no court has explicitly embraced this reciprocal theory of takings and "givings" in the inverse condemnation context. Problems of valuation, causation, and general feasibility have been cited as making such a system impracticable to administer.[87] Nevertheless,

---

[84]*See, e.g.,* Donald Elliott, *Givings and Takings,* LAND USE LAW & ZONING DIGEST 3 (Jan. 1996); HAGMAN & MISCZYNSKI, *supra* note 45, at 15–18, § 311 et seq.

[85]United States v. Fuller, 409 U.S. 488, 492 (1973); Elliott, *supra* note 84, at 6.

[86]United States v. Sponenbarger, 308 U.S. 256, 266–67 (1939); Los Angeles County Metro. Transp. Auth. v. Continental Dev. Corp., 16 Cal. 4th 694, 714, 941 P.2d 809 (1997); Elliott, *supra* note 84, at 7.

[87]Elliott, *supra* note 84, at 8-9; HAGMAN & MISCZYNSKI, *supra* note 45, at 18–19.

the concept of government-created property value is intriguing and serves as an instructive counterpoint to the more traditional (and one-sided) debate over proper measurement of damages in regulatory takings controversies.

Interest, Attorney Fees, and Costs

Interest in the Federal Courts

The Supreme Court has long held that the Takings Clause does not require just compensation to be paid contemporaneously with the taking; it may be paid later.[88] It could hardly be otherwise, of course, since in most cases the occurrence of a taking is not clear until a court rules. In any event, when the government tenders compensation after the date of the taking, it must pay interest calculated from that date.[89]

Strictly speaking, the interest required in a taking case is different from that imposed by the court as prejudgment interest in, say, a breach of contract case. Takings interest is conceived to be mandated by the Constitution; it is a component of the "just compensation" promised by the Takings Clause. Indeed, some prefer not to call it interest at all, but rather "delay compensation." Under whatever term, it is designed to place the property owner "in as good a position pecuniarily as he would have occupied if the payment had coincided with the appropriation."[90] Because takings interest is constitutionally based, it is held to be outside the rule that interest on court judgments does not lie against the United States in the absence of a statute or contract to the contrary.[91]

Interest against the United States is computed from the date of the taking to the date on which payment is actually tendered to the property owner. As noted, the considerable lengths of time that have elapsed in the past between these two dates—five years, ten years— can make interest a formidable component of the ultimate award.

In the influential Court of Federal Claims where most takings ac-

---

[88]Preseault v. Interstate Commerce Commission, 494 U.S. 1, 11 (1990); Kirby Forest Indus., Inc. v. United States, 467 U.S. 1, 10 (1984).

[89]*Kirby*, 467 U.S. at 10; Yaist v. United States, 17 Cl. Ct. 246, 261 (1989).

[90]*Kirby*, 467 U.S. at 10.

[91]*See, e.g.*, Library of Congress v. Shaw, 478 U.S. 1 (1984). The general rule for nontakings actions is applied to the Court of Federal Claims by 28 U.S.C. § 2516(a).

tions against the United States start out, the judges since 1980 have usually adopted as inverse condemnation interest rates those set by the Secretary of the Treasury under another statute often litigated in that court—the Contract Disputes Act (CDA).[92] To be sure, statutes do not absolutely control the judicial award of takings interest, since it is constitutionally based.[93] But the CDA rates, taking into consideration "current private commercial rates of interest for new loans maturing in approximately five years,"[94] are thought by the court to be a fair and just "adjustment" to the value of the property taken, reflecting the passage of time since the taking. CDA interest rates peaked out during the high inflation years of the early 1980s at 15 ½ percent, but in recent times have stayed between 6 and 8 percent.[95]

Every bit as important as the interest rate, given the often long time periods involved, is whether interest should be computed on a simple or compound basis. The general rule in the Court of Federal Claims until recently has been simple interest. Absent "special circumstances," the Court has said repeatedly that simple interest puts the plaintiff in "as good a position pecuniarily" as if payment had coincided with taking.[96] Until recently, "special circumstances" were found almost exclusively in patent infringement cases; rarely elsewhere.

Since 1990, however, the Chief Judge of the Court of Federal Claims has widened the special circumstances exception to virtually swallow the simple-interest rule, imposing compound interest against the United States in a series of high-profile regulatory takings decisions.[97] To be sure, compound interest is probably more faithful to the constitutional make-the-plaintiff-whole standard, since it better reflects how the typical landowner would have invested the compen-

[92]41 U.S.C. § 611.

[93]Miller v. United States, 620 F.2d 812, 837 (Ct. Cl. 1980); United States v. Blankenship, 543 F.2d 1272, 1275–76 (9th Cir. 1976).

[94]The quote derives from 50 U.S.C. App. § 1215(b)(2), a section of another statute, the Renegotiation Act, to which CDA rates are tied.

[95]Two recent departures by the Court of Federal Claims from the CDA-rates standard are NRG, Inc. v. United States, 31 Fed. Cl. 659 (1994) (using 52-week Treasury bill rate adopted by Congress in 1986 for "quick take" condemnations) and Eastern Minerals Int'l, Inc. v. United States, 39 Fed. Cl. 621 (1997) (using Internal Revenue Code rate for tax overpayments).

[96]See, e.g., Paul v. United States, 21 Cl. Ct. 415, 428 (1990).

[97]See, e.g., Whitney Benefits, Inc. v. United States, 30 Fed. Cl. 411 (1994); Florida Rock Indus., Inc. v. United States, 23 Cl. Ct. 653 (1991).

sation payment had he or she received it at the time of the taking. Still, it would be more direct if simple interest were to be relegated to history, if that is what the court wishes to do, through an upfront recognition of economic reality, rather than by stretching the concept of special circumstances.

Perhaps in recognition of how money actually is invested, Congress in 1986 specified the use of compound interest when computing the liability of the United States for formal condemnation "quick takes."[98] Since then, plaintiffs have pressed the argument in many takings cases that while not formally applicable, the quick-take model should be adopted by courts in takings cases as well.

For the foregoing reasons, it is very probable that the Chief Judge's embrace of compound interest will be endorsed in the future by other judges of the Court of Federal Claims.[99]

Interest in the State Courts

The rule in the state courts on the subject of interest payments largely parallels that of their federal counterparts. State tribunals generally find interest on inverse condemnation damages to be constitutionally mandated. The rationale is precisely that noted above— an award of interest is required in order to make the property owner whole.[100]

As in the case of federal litigation, this leaves unresolved the issue of what the appropriate measure of interest is to be. Occasionally, state legislatures have attempted to address that question by statute. Most courts have construed such legislation to be advisory at best, inasmuch as the ultimate determination of the rate of interest required for "just compensation" is a judicial function.[101] Precisely what interest rate is appropriate varies from state to state and, quite

---

[98]40 U.S.C. § 258e-1(2).

[99]Results so far are mixed, however, perhaps reflecting that old habits die hard. *Cf.* Goodwyn v. United States, 32 Fed. Cl. 409 (1994) (simple interest) *with* Eastern Minerals Int'l, Inc. v. United States, 39 Fed. Cl. 621 (1997) (compound interest).

[100]City of Gary v. Belovich, 623 N.E.2d 1084, 1086 (Ind. 1993); Customer Co. v. City of Sacramento, 10 Cal. 4th 368, 390, 895 P.2d 900 (1995), *cert. denied,* 516 U.S. 1116 (1996).

[101]*Customer Co.,* 10 Cal. 4th at 390; State by Humphrey v. Baillon Co., 480 N.W.2d 673, 676 (Minn. Ct. App. 1992).

often, from case to case. At times, courts refer to particular state statutes, "usual market rates," or other criteria.[102]

Far less amorphous is the question of when interest begins to accrue on an inverse condemnation damage award. State courts have rather consistently rejected the notion advanced by government defendants that interest should run only from the time the inverse condemnation lawsuit is commenced. Instead, the settled rule is that interest is to be calculated from the government taking itself—presumably an earlier date and one that increases the aggregate amount of money awarded to a successful takings plaintiff.[103]

While there is little state jurisprudence on the simple-versus-compound-interest issue, it seems likely that most state courts will eventually emulate the compound-interest preference of the U.S. Court of Federal Claims' Chief Judge, for precisely the policy reasons set out above.[104]

Attorney Fees and Other Costs in the Federal Courts

In contrast with interest, these other additions to the property-value award are held not to be an element of constitutional "just compensation."[105] The rationale for such noninclusion is founded on the

---

[102]Cf. *Customer Co.*, 10 Cal. 4th at 390–91 (characterizing state statute, which in turn cited to floating rate of earnings of state's Surplus Money Investment Fund); Buffalo v. J.W. Clement Co., 28 N.Y.2d 241, 269 N.E.2d 895 (1971) (state statutory rate advisory); Redevelopment Agency v. Gilmore, 38 Cal. 3d 790, 797–98, 700 P.2d 794 (1985) (citing Kirby Forest Indus., Inc. v. United States, 467 U.S 1, 11 n.16 (1984) for proposition that constitutionally proper interest must reflect market conditions); Lehigh Valley Trust Co. v. Pennsylvania Turnpike Comm'n, 401 Pa. 135, 163 A.2d 86 (1960) (court would disregard prevailing prime commercial interest rate in favor of higher, legal rate of interest prescribed by state law).

[103]Coeur D'Alene Garbage Serv. v. City of Coeur D'Alene, 114 Idaho 588, 759 P.2d 879 (1988); Simmons v. Board of Comm'rs, 624 So. 2d 935 (La. Ct. App. 1993); *Customer Co.*, 10 Cal. 4th at 390. Of course, precisely when a takings claim begins to accrue can be a topic of considerable debate. That question is treated separately in chapter 13.

[104]Cf. Sintra, Inc. v. City of Seattle, 131 Wash. 2d 640, 935 P. 2d 555, 565–66 (1997) (simple, rather than compound, interest appropriate unless former fails to afford "just compensation").

[105]United States v. Bodcaw, 440 U.S. 202, 203 (1979); Dohany v. Rogers, 281 U.S. 362, 368 (1930).

ancient takings law canard that Fifth Amendment takings compensation "is for the property, and not to the owner."[106] Otherwise put, the government need pay only for what it takes, not for all the attendant harms.

But while there is no constitutional basis for the recovery of attorney fees and other costs in federal takings cases, there is a statutory one. Under the lengthily named Uniform Relocation and Real Property Acquisition Policies Act (URA), the United States has agreed to pay "reasonable costs, disbursements, and expenses, including reasonable attorney, appraisal, and engineering fees" whenever a court renders judgment for a takings plaintiff or the Attorney General settles a case.[107]

Of course, the URA is inapplicable to takings claims brought in federal court against state or local governments. In such cases, federal courts are generally unwilling to award attorney fees in takings cases absent some other congressional statute specifically authorizing such an award.[108]

As discussed in more detail in chapter 7, one such statute is the federal Civil Rights Act. Attorney fees are in fact commonly awarded to prevailing property owners in takings cases brought under that legislation, codified at 42 U.S.C. section 1983. A separate provision of the Civil Rights Act expressly provides for an award of fees in such cases, which can be brought in either federal or state courts.[109]

Attorney Fees and Other Costs in the State Courts

The relative unanimity with which state courts have addressed the

---

[106]Monongahela Navigation Co. v. United States, 148 U.S. 312, 326 (1893).

[107]42 U.S.C. § 4654(c). Another federal statute, the Equal Access to Justice Act, also allows successful takings claimants against the United States to recover fees and costs. 28 U.S.C. § 2412(b). However, constraints on the use of this statute have led plaintiffs to strongly prefer the URA.

[108]See, e.g., Richmond Elks Hall Ass'n v. Richmond Redevelopment Agency, 561 F.2d 1327, 1333 (9th Cir. 1977) (citing Dohany v. Rogers, 281 U.S. 362, 368 (1930) (rejecting landowners' claim that federal courts must look to state law regarding award of costs and attorney fees in inverse condemnation actions)).

[109]42 U.S.C. § 1988. See Williams v. Horvath, 16 Cal. 3d 834, 837, 548 P.2d 1125 (1976) (state and federal courts have concurrent jurisdiction to adjudicate claims brought under section 1983).

question of interest in inverse condemnation cases has not been replicated when it comes to attorney fees in such litigation.[110] Nor do most states provide an easy "fix" to the problem via a statutory provision analogous to the federal laws noted earlier. The result is a diversity of state approaches and results when it comes to the award of attorney fees in regulatory takings cases.

The starting point in state takings litigation is the venerable and oft-debated "American Rule" governing award of attorney fees. Under that principle—which departs from the practice in virtually all other legal systems around the world—each party to a civil lawsuit in this country is expected to bear his or her own attorney fees, regardless of the outcome of the case.[111] Traditionally, the only exceptions to the American Rule recognized by the courts were those instances in which Congress or state legislatures had enacted explicit statutory exceptions; more recently, state courts have begun carving out some common law fee-shifting exceptions as well.[112]

Nonetheless, there is a perception among many states that it would be particularly inequitable for a prevailing property owner in an inverse condemnation lawsuit to be forced to bear the often-formidable expenses associated with retaining legal counsel. Accordingly, some state legislatures have enacted specific statutory exceptions to the American Rule in such litigation; in other jurisdictions, state judges have reached the same conclusion on their own.

California provides an apt illustration. California Code of Civil Procedure section 1036, originally enacted as part of that state's Eminent Domain Law, expressly provides for a prevailing plaintiff in an inverse condemnation action to recover his or her attorney fees and costs. While early California precedents applied this provision only in cases involving physical damage to private property, recent state court decisions have expressly declared an award of attorney fees

---

[110]State jurisprudence is, however, consistent with the federal courts' holding that the award of attorney fees and costs is not constitutionally required. *See, e.g.*, Holtz v. Bay Area Rapid Transit Dist., 17 Cal. 3d 648, 658, 552 P.2d 430 (1976).

[111]Alyeska Pipeline Co. v. Wilderness Soc'y, 421 U.S. 240, 269 (1975); Serrano v. Priest, 20 Cal. 3d 25, 569 P.2d 1303 (1977).

[112]*Serrano*, 20 Cal. 3d 25. By contrast, the U.S. Supreme Court has held that federal courts may not create common law exceptions to the American Rule, but instead must look to Congress for explicit authority in order to shift attorney fees to the losing party. *Alyeska*, 421 U.S. at 269.

mandatory in successful regulatory takings litigation as well.[113] Several other states have taken a similarly expansive view.[114]

The policy underpinnings of this result were forcefully stated by the New Hampshire Supreme Court in one of the earliest state cases finding government liability in a regulatory takings case. In *Burrows v. City of Keene,* the court found that an award of attorney fees to a prevailing landowner was fully warranted: "Because a citizen should not be compelled to bear the financial burden of protecting himself from unconstitutional abuses of power, we hold that the plaintiffs are entitled to reasonable counsel fees. . . ."[115] Most states have taken the same view,[116] although a few jurisdictions continue to refuse to award attorney fees to a prevailing property owner.[117]

While the majority rule among state courts thus appears to be that attorney fees are awardable to prevailing property owners in inverse condemnation cases, most states have rejected the related argument that contingency fees of the type common in garden-variety tort cases are appropriate in takings litigation.[118]

Unlike the case with attorney fees, civil court costs are awarded to the prevailing party in virtually all state court systems. Takings litigation is no exception. In inverse condemnation cases, a prevailing landowner can expect to recover a host of costs including filing fees, expert witness, and appraisal expenses.[119] Some states allow such costs to be recovered even for reasonable expenses incurred before the takings lawsuit is filed.[120] Of course, the bilateral nature of cost

[113]Hensler v. City of Glendale, 8 Cal. 4th 1, 15, 896 P.2d 1043, 1046 (1994).

[114]*See, e.g.,* City of Garrett v. Terry, 512 N.E.2d 405, 407 (Ind. 1987) (construing state statute awarding court costs and expenses to successful landowners in inverse condemnation cases to include attorney fees). *Accord,* Cody v. Department of Transp., 60 N.C. App. 724, 300 S.E.2d 25, 28–29 (1983).

[115]121 N.H. 590, 432 A.2d 15, 22 (1981).

[116]Peoples Natural Gas Co. v. Every, 497 N.W.2d 872 (Iowa 1993); Fortin v. Manchester Hous. Auth., 133 N.H. 154, 574 A.2d 945 (1990).

[117]*See, e.g.,* Raymond v. Chittenden Circumferential Highway, 604 A.2d 1281, 1285 (Vt. 1992) (construing Vermont statute).

[118]City of Minnetonka v. Carlson, 298 N.W.2d 763, 766–67 (Minn. 1980); Prucka v. Papio Natural Resources Dist., 206 Neb. 234, 292 N.W.2d 293, 296 (1980); Salton Sea Marina, Inc. v. Imperial Irrigation Dist., 172 Cal. App. 3d 914, 954, 218 Cal. Rptr. 839 (1985). *Sintra Inc.* v. City of Seattle, 131 Wash. 2d 640, 935 P.2d 555, 568–569 (1997).

[119]Los Angeles v. Beck, 40 Cal. App. 3d 763, 115 Cal. Rptr. 569 (1974).

[120]*See, e.g.,* Customer Co. v. City of Sacramento, 10 Cal. 4th 368, 390, 895 P.2d 900 (1995), *cert. denied,* 516 U.S. 1116 (1996).

awards also means that a property owner whose takings claim is rejected by the court can expect to be required to reimburse the prevailing government defendant for its litigation costs.[121]

Conclusion

Questions as to the award of interest, costs, and attorney fees in inverse condemnation cases seem particularly well-suited to legislative action—as existing enactments in this area suggest. Many of the above-described issues that have caused uncertainty in the courts—simple-versus-compound interest, for example—could profitably be addressed through legislation. The substance of regulatory takings law is sufficiently (and perhaps inevitably) convoluted; legislatures should redouble their efforts to clarify the related procedural questions.

Legislative attention is especially appropriate because these procedural questions have strong policy underpinnings and consequences. For instance, the matter of attorney-fee shifting has major implications for litigants and justice system alike. Should a prevailing property owner in a taking case be allowed to secure attorney fees from a government defendant? Should a prevailing government similarly recoup its attorney costs from the unsuccessful landowner? Or should American courts in takings cases adopt the English solution to the attorney fees debate and leave it to the sound discretion of the trial court to allocate fees as appropriate in a given case?

The key point is that seemingly technical questions of calculation of damages, interest rates, court costs, and attorney fees can have enormous practical effect on the willingness of litigants to file, settle, abandon, and litigate takings cases. In this way, these procedural rules can—and quite often do—have a major impact on the substance of inverse condemnation law.

[121]*See, e.g.,* Locklin v. City of Lafayette, 7 Cal. 4th 327, 377, 867 P.2d 724 (1994).

Part VII

Lessening the Public/Private Conflict

Chapter 32

Voluntary Initiatives, Incentives, and Direct Acquisition

Besides moving toward more flexible regulation and more property rights–sensitive programs, there are other ways to avoid conflicts between landowner and government. A short and unabashedly incomplete survey of this miscellany is offered here—just enough to whet the reader's interest. The main "sticks" in this bundle of topics are voluntary initiatives, incentives, and direct acquisition.

There is little doubt we will be seeing more of these nonregulatory approaches in the near future. America's commitment to private property—socially, economically, and politically—is unlikely to abate. To be sure, as environmental values themselves become a national commitment, property rights may undergo adjustment, possibly some contraction. But the broad scope of our environmental programs is unlikely to be matched by a commensurately shrinking concept of property. Conflicts will remain, particularly since so many of the resources to be protected are on private land: 75 percent of wetlands are located on private property, 90 percent of endangered species depend for at least some of their habitat on private property, etc. Plainly, we cannot protect these environmental components adequately through initiatives on the public lands alone.[1]

The experience with nonregulatory approaches is still in its infancy. One thing that can be said with certainty, however, is that they are less likely than regulatory controls to provoke landowners and

---

[1]*See generally* David Farrier, *Conserving Biodiversity on Private Land: Incentives for Management or Compensation for Lost Expectations?*, 19 HARVARD ENVTL. L. REV. 303 (1995).

property rights activists. Correctly or not, such activists see traditional regulation as eviscerating the institution of property—removing the core of the concept (the owner's rights of use) and leaving
only a hollow shell (title and the duty to pay real property taxes). The
approaches grouped here largely remain above this criticism. Voluntary initiatives, incentives, and disincentives leave the property owner
free to choose, and usually involve more landowner participation
than does regulation. Though disincentives (or the loss of incentives)
may feel like coercion in some instances, property owners can still appreciate that with the former, they incur no formal penalty for not
going along.

Voluntary Efforts

It is not unusual today for developers to tout the environmental
amenities that a particular subdivision offers—open space, wildlife,
beautiful views. New communities with overt environmental themes
are a growing, though still limited, market.[2] The preservation of these
land-related values through covenants and easements in conveyance
documents has grown commensurately. These private agreements are
enforceable in court by the beneficiaries of such agreements. A similar
use of covenants has been proposed for government transfers of land
into private hands—incorporating density or use restrictions, open
space and viewplane dedication requirements, etc.[3]—though the
modest quantity of such transfers does not support this as a principal
conflict-reducing strategem.

Another important category involves efforts to increase voluntary
landowner participation in government programs. Included here is
participation motivated by the owner's desire to stave off regulatory
prescriptions, admittedly not voluntary in the purest sense. Endangered species conservation has probably prompted more innovative
thought than most other programs in this regard. We noted earlier
(*see* chapter 24) some ideas recently implemented by the U.S. Department of the Interior under the Endangered Species Act. Particularly
noteworthy is the "safe harbor" program, under which a landowner

[2]*See, e.g.*, Stefan Fatsis, *New Communities Make It Easy Being Green*, WALL
ST. J., Nov. 10, 1995, at B14.
    [3]DAVID L. CALLIES, PRESERVING PARADISE: WHY REGULATION WON'T WORK
103 (1994).

voluntarily agrees to take a species-beneficial action (or avoid a harmful one) in return for federal assurances that his or her duties under the Act will not be increased thereby.

A generally admired species conservation effort, often praised by Secretary of the Interior Babbitt, is California's Natural Communities Conservation Planning Act (NCCPA).[4] Under it, the state may enter into voluntary agreements with all affected parties (public and private) for developing and implementing an areawide conservation plan—a preventive, multispecies approach to avoid the "emergency room" approach of the federal Endangered Species Act.

A nonpartisan stab at how to enhance voluntary participation in endangered species conservation is that of the nonpartisan Keystone Center. Its 1995 report[5] proposes: NCCPA-like conservation agreements under which stakeholders (again, public and private) work together to stabilize species *before* endangered status requires draconian recovery measures; technical, material, and financial assistance to landowners; an award or other mechanism to recognize voluntary actions by private landowners to preserve species; and other ideas along the lines of the federal innovations.

Economic Incentives and Disincentives

Instances of primarily economic approaches to preserving or bringing about government-desired land uses are found readily at federal, state, and local levels. As for incentives, a successful example is the federal Partners for Wildlife program, created in 1987 and administered by the Fish and Wildlife Service (FWS). Working with conservation districts, the program assists farmers, ranchers, and other landowners to protect wetlands and other wet habitat on their property—often, fields that are too wet to farm. FWS acquires no property interests. Rather, the means is project cost-sharing and technical assistance, under voluntary agreements with the landowner for a minimum of 10 years. At the agreement's expiration, project elements become the landowner's property.

---

[4]Cal. Fish & Game Code §§ 2800–40.
[5]The Keystone Center, The Keystone Dialogue on Incentives for Private Landowners to Protect Endangered Species: Final Report (Colo. 1995).

Of course, a time-honored technique for molding private conduct is tax incentives, and the use of private property is no exception. The donation of scenic easements and life-estate remainder interests[6] to environmental groups (those primarily involved in land preservation and those with wider agendas), land trusts, and government itself, has long been encouraged by tax codes—in particular, by the charitable deduction, and by reductions in property and estate taxes. Where private donee groups are recognized as tax-exempt entities, donations to which are deductible,[7] they can often get the property interest at lower than market price—allowing subsequent conveyance to government at discounted prices. Land owned by such groups may qualify for exemption from local real property taxes, depending on the use actually made of the property and the status of the owning entity. The Wildlands Project, an embryonic but ambitious effort to enhance protection of America's remaining wild areas, is one of the newest environmental initiatives to look to the tax code.[8] Landowners who are so inclined could contribute "ecological reserve easements" that permanently incorporate such lands into a state or national wildlands reserve system.

Lately, further interest in the use of tax incentives has been sparked by proposals from anti-regulatory members of Congress to amend the Endangered Species Act. Ideas that have surfaced in recent congressional bills include allowing an enhanced value for the deduction of the value of an endangered species easement to the United States, creating a tax credit for costs incurred by landowners under "Endangered Species Conservation Agreements" with the federal government, the deferral of estate taxes on land that directly contributes to the conservation of an endangered species,[9] and a habitat-acquisition fund checkoff for tax overpayments.[10]

---

[6]A life-estate remainder interest comes about when a landowner arranges to hold onto property until such time as the owner (and, typically, his or her spouse) dies, at which time the land goes to the designated organization or government.

[7]26 U.S.C. §§ 170, 501(c)(3).

[8]See, e.g., Jamie Sayen, The Role of Private Lands in an Ecological Reserve System, 6 WILD EARTH 50 (Summer 1996).

[9]The use of tax credits and estate tax reform has also been endorsed by some environmentalists. Michael J. Bean & David S. Wilcove, Ending the Impasse, ENVTL. FORUM (Envtl. Law Inst.) 22 (July/Aug. 1996).

[10]Use of the tax code is also the focus of the species-preservation incentives discussion in KEYSTONE CENTER, supra note 5.

The shift toward market-based incentives for pollution control has also spawned new approaches. A 1992 report from the Progressive Policy Institute in Washington, D.C., concludes that use of pollution charges in place of command-and-control regulation can solve many of the weaknesses of the traditional regulatory approach.[11]

Other land-use programs couple economic incentives with more traditional approaches. This is a common pattern with the federal government, which for federalism reasons seeks to minimize the use of direct land controls. The approach is to use federal incentives to get states or localities to adopt such controls. Thus, the Coastal Zone Management Act dangles federal program-implementation funds before states to encourage their adoption of coastal zone management plans meeting federal standards,[12] while the National Flood Insurance Program makes the availability of such insurance contingent on local adoption of floodplain development controls.[13]

Economic *dis*incentives—typically, the loss of government benefits if private land is put to undesired use—are also receiving new attention. Federal examples include the "sodbuster" and "swampbuster" programs for agricultural lands. The sodbuster initiative was born of concern that cultivating certain lands, such as hillsides and dry soils, could greatly enhance their erosion rate by exposing topsoil. Under sodbuster,[14] those who cultivate such highly erodible land not cultivated between 1981 and 1985 are ineligible for most major farm program benefits, including price supports. Indeed, those benefits are lost for all the land the farmer operates. However, a producer is not subject to these provisions if he or she cultivates the highly erodible land using an approved conservation plan.

Swampbuster is a key agricultural wetland's protection program.[15] Under swampbuster, a farmer who alters a wetland to enable agricultural production loses the same federal farm program benefits as would be lost under sodbuster. Adverse reaction from the agricultural

[11]THE GREENING OF AMERICA'S TAXES: POLLUTION CHARGES AND ENVIRONMENTAL PROTECTION.

[12]16 U.S.C. §§ 1451–64.

[13]42 U.S.C. § 4022.

[14]16 U.S.C. §§ 3811–13.

[15]16 U.S.C. §§ 3821–23. *See generally* Daryn McBeth, *Wetlands Conservation and Federal Regulation: Analysis of the Food Security Act's "Swampbuster" Provisions as Amended by the Federal Agricultural Improvement and Reform Act of 1996*, 21 HARVARD ENVTL. L. REV. 201 (1997).

community, however, led to the addition of flexibility-enhancing mechanisms in the 1996 farm bill, such as giving the Secretary of Agriculture discretion to determine which benefits violators are ineligible for. We never said that avoiding regulation absolutely guarantees an easy time.

Another federal stalwart is the Coastal Barrier Resources Act of 1982,[16] one of the few items of new environmental legislation supported by the deregulation-minded Reagan administration. This initiative seeks to stem the rush of development on certain coastal barrier islands along the Atlantic and Gulf Coasts. It aims to do so without regulating, but simply by eliminating the federal benefits that had formerly been available. In particular, those wishing to purchase land or build (for most purposes) on these islands must do without federally insured mortgages, federal flood insurance (a big item on barrier islands), and federal disaster relief. The United States saves money, and property uses deemed undesirable for reasons of public safety and fragile environment are discouraged. The barrier islands program also shows the importance of removing counterproductive subsidies first—before contemplating regulation, government should at least make sure it is not promoting the very behavior it proposes to control.[17]

Government and Private Land Acquisition

At the risk of stating the obvious, one of the most straightforward ways to avoid takings litigation is for government simply to acquire privately owned land for public use and enjoyment. Government's authority to do so is largely unquestioned.[18] Indeed, property rights advocates often promote public land acquisition as a preferable al-

---

[16]16 U.S.C. §§ 3501–10.

[17]The same point has been made in connection with agricultural subsidies, which are said to promote environmental degradation by encouraging crop production on marginal lands. POLITICAL ECONOMY RESEARCH CENTER, REINVENTING ENVIRONMENTALISM IN THE NEW ERA 10 (Terry L. Anderson ed., 1995).

[18]In most such cases, the only issue is the dollar amount necessary to fairly compensate the private owner for the property interest acquired. Occasionally, government acquisition is challenged as not being for a "public use," but the courts have given government extremely broad latitude on that score. One prominent example of this free hand is the U.S. Supreme Court's decision in Hawaii Housing Authority v. Midkiff, 467 U.S. 229 (1984).

ternative to government regulation—at least when the ultimate objective of regulation in a particular case is beyond reasonable debate.

President Abraham Lincoln was one of the first American leaders to perceive the value of public acquisition of land for conservation purposes. It was during Lincoln's administration that the United States created its first national park—the Yosemite Valley and the nearby Mariposa Grove in California. An entire system of national parks, preserves, and monuments has been created in the subsequent 134 years. In some cases, they have been reserved from the public domain, in others obtained through voluntary acquisitions from private parties, and in still others acquired through formal exercise of government's power of eminent domain. But overall, creation of the national parks system has served an important lesson: Where unique and irreplaceable natural resources are involved, the best way to ensure their long-term protection is often through a focused program of public acquisition and management. Takings Clause problems simply don't emerge in the absence of private property interests.[19]

State and local governments have followed the example of the federal government, often heading off private property disputes before they arise through aggressive land acquisition programs. Many years ago, for example, the State of Oregon embarked on an effort to acquire numerous parks and beaches along its spectacular coast. The result: a most impressive chain of publicly owned preserves and recreational areas that have largely insulated Oregon from the coastal land-use wars waged in recent years in neighboring California and many other coastal states.

Similarly, the City of Boulder, Colorado, has guaranteed the long-term preservation of its scenic vistas by buying up open space surrounding the town. This has forestalled suburban encroachment without the need for regulatory fixes such as land-use moratoria, which often transmute into regulatory takings claims.

One of the biggest acquisition successes to date can be found in the Lake Tahoe Basin, which straddles the California–Nevada border. That success is the product of cooperative efforts by California,

---

[19]This is not to say that public-private land-use conflicts cannot arise in the national parks system. They can, and do. The creation of national parks and preserves is often steeped in controversy, and usually the product of political compromise. *See, e.g.,* Althaus v. United States, 7 Cl. Ct. 698 (1985) (Voyageurs National Park); Drake's Bay Land Co. v. United States, 424 F.2d 574 (Ct. Cl. 1970) (Point Reyes National Seashore).

Nevada, and the federal government, and warrants closer attention here.

Lake Tahoe is among the world's most pristine mountain lakes, along with Oregon's Crater Lake and Lake Baikal in Siberia. The crown jewel of the Sierra Nevada mountain range, Lake Tahoe is surrounded by steep slopes composed of thin and highly erodible soils. The watershed feeding the lake is largely composed of wetlands, and a single stream provides Tahoe's only outlet. The net effect of these topographic and hydrological conditions is that the pure waters of Lake Tahoe are particularly vulnerable to pollution and sedimentation from the surrounding upland areas.

The Lake Tahoe Basin's spectacular beauty and proximity to major population centers have made it a popular resort and second-home area. This popularity has spawned many ill-considered development proposals over the years (including numerous "paper subdivisions" in environmentally fragile areas), which, when constructed, began to degrade Lake Tahoe's world-renowned clear waters. Alarmed regulators responded by adopting an increasingly strict system of building restraints, beginning in the late 1960s. The result? A multitude of legal challenges brought by disappointed property owners anxious to develop and enjoy their particular piece of alpine paradise. Most of those challenges included a claim for just compensation under the Takings Clause. Government regulators won the vast majority of these cases, but the political controversy remained. Indeed, it worsened as Lake Tahoe's water quality declined and government responded with more and more severe land-use limits.[20]

In the 1980s, state and federal officials began to realize that while they were winning the incremental legal battles, they were in real danger of losing the war for Lake Tahoe's long-term future. They responded with a series of legislative initiatives designed to remove sensitive properties in the Lake Tahoe Basin from the threat of development, simultaneously provide a fair economic return to private property owners, and thereby help preserve Lake Tahoe's water quality and the basin's related environmental values. Congress acted first, enacting the Santini-Burton Act in 1980.[21] Santini-Burton authorized the public sale of about 7,000 acres of federally owned lands near urban Las Vegas. The proceeds from these sales were used to

[20]These developments are chronicled in greater detail in the excellent book, TAHOE: AN ENVIRONMENTAL HISTORY, by DOUGLAS H. STRONG (U. Neb. Press 1984).

[21]Pub. L. No. 96-586, 94 Stat. 3381 (1980).

Two views of the tract in El Dorado County, California, acquired by the State of California as part of the Lake Country Estates litigation settlement: Washoe Meadows State Park and Lake Valley State Recreation Area (top) and Angora Creek and Washoe Meadows (bottom).

fund a program administered by the U.S. Forest Service to purchase environmentally sensitive lands in the Lake Tahoe Basin from willing sellers, for fair market value. Using nearly $80 million in Santini-Burton Funds,[22] the U.S. Forest Service has acquired approximately 3,500 environmentally sensitive parcels at Lake Tahoe, totaling about 11,500 acres.[23]

Similar, complementary programs were enacted in California and Nevada. California voters enacted the Lake Tahoe Acquisitions Bond Act in 1982, authorizing the sale of $85 million in state bonds to finance the purchase of additional environmentally sensitive lands from willing sellers on the California side of the Tahoe Basin.[24] To date the California program has expended over $50 million in bond act funds for the purchase of approximately 4,040 fragile lots aggregating over 5,000 acres.

The Nevada electorate responded in kind in 1986, approving a separate $31 million bond act designed to acquire fragile lots on the Nevada side of the Lake Tahoe Basin.[25] Under the Nevada program, approximately 500 Nevada parcels totaling 230 acres have been acquired by that state.

The effect of these aggressive federal and state programs to acquire environmentally sensitive lots in the Lake Tahoe Basin has been both dramatic and multifaceted. The number of regulatory takings cases at Lake Tahoe brought against federal, state, and local regulators has declined dramatically. Moreover, a number of takings lawsuits

----

[22]For a variety of reasons, the contemplated sales of federal lands near Las Vegas failed to generate the revenues necessary to fully undertake the ambitious federal buyout program at Lake Tahoe. Subsequent congressional appropriations have been required to pursue the task.

[23]Recently, certain property rights advocates have complained to Congress that the Forest Service was administering the Santini-Burton program in a way that deprived private sellers of fair market value for their Tahoe lots and effected a taking of their properties. In an investigation and audit requested by Nevada Senator Harry Reid, the General Accounting Office (GAO) ultimately found such allegations to be without merit. The GAO concluded that the Forest Service's acquisition program had been conducted within the legal parameters established by the Santini-Burton Act, that the private lot owners had in fact received just compensation for their properties, and that no taking had thus transpired. U.S. GEN. ACCOUNTING OFFICE, FOREST SERVICE: LAND ACQUISITIONS WITHIN THE LAKE TAHOE BASIN (GAO No. RCED-95-22 1995).

[24]Cal. Gov't Code § 66952 et seq.

[25]Nev. Rev. Stat. ch. 585 (1985).

pending at the time these acquisition programs were created have subsequently been settled through public purchase of the litigation parcels. Perhaps even more important, much of the contentiousness which historically plagued land-use decisions at Lake Tahoe has dissipated. The availability of these federal and state "willing seller" acquisition programs has provided property owners with an economic alternative to pursuing development of fragile lands. From the public's perspective, government acquisition of these lots permanently saves them from the threat of ill-considered development, expands available open space in the Tahoe Basin, and has already had a beneficial (albeit incremental) impact on Lake Tahoe's water quality. In short, acquisition has created a "win-win" situation for Lake Tahoe—one that would have been impossible through regulatory solutions alone.

The Lake Tahoe experience is being replicated in other parts of the nation. The Clinton administration has recently announced ambitious plans to protect and restore the Everglades by spending hundreds of millions of dollars to purchase approximately 100,000 acres of land. That acquisition would be designed to take out of production farmland, the runoff from which is despoiling the Everglades, and to restore a more natural flow of fresh water across Florida's swampy southern region.[26]

In Massachusetts, Nantucket officials have created a land bank designed to protect their island's remaining open space by purchasing beaches and moors threatened with development. The Nantucket land bank is supported by revenue bonds which are in turn funded through a local real estate transfer tax.[27]

In Northern California, a legal and policy battle has raged for years over the future of the ancient redwoods within the privately owned, 4,700-acre Headwaters Forest. The corporate owners of these forest lands want to log them, an unsurprising goal in light of the fact that the redwood trees are worth up to $200,000 apiece as lumber. Environmentalists, on the other hand, cite the fact that these unique forests contain trees that are over 1,000 years old and contend that their removal would cause incalculable damage to the habitat of

[26]John H. Gusman, Jr., *Clinton Backing Vast Effort to Restore Florida Swamps,* N.Y. TIMES, Feb. 18, 1996, at A1.

[27]Robert Guenther, *Nantucket Races Developers to Preserve Its Open Spaces,* WALL ST. J., Mar. 27, 1985, at 39.

The Lake Country Estates Saga: Evolution from Litigation to Acquisition Solutions

One particularly striking example of the often salutary shift from litigation to acquisition-based approaches to resolving property disputes is the saga of the Upper Truckee Marsh in the Lake Tahoe Basin. In the 1960s and 1970s, private owners of a large amount of wetlands-dominated property near Lake Tahoe sought governmental permits for an ambitious commercial and residential development project. Approval of that project would have meant the elimination of the largest remaining, privately-owned wetlands area in the Tahoe Basin, and an acceleration in the decline of Lake Tahoe's water quality. When state and regional land-use officials rejected the project, the developers sued in 1973, claiming a regulatory taking. The litigation raged for years, even reaching the U.S. Supreme Court at one point. (In *Lake Country Estates, Inc. v. Tahoe Regional Planning Agency*, 440 U.S. 391 (1979), the Supreme Court's decision dealt, perhaps predictably, with threshold procedural matters, ensuring several additional years of litigation.)

Eventually becoming weary of open-ended litigation (and its attendant expense and delay), the parties searched for an alternate solution. One became available on the eve of trial in 1984, when the State of California obtained a lucrative infusion of cash from the federal government in settlement of an unrelated offshsore oil revenue dispute. A portion of those funds was appropriated for settlement of the *Lake Country* case, and the

numerous endangered species. So far, state and federal regulators have refused to allow logging in the Headwaters Forest, triggering regulatory takings lawsuits by the corporate landowners against California and the federal government. Recently, however, negotiations have taken place between the parties. The most likely alternatives to continued litigation are a government-funded purchase of the Headwaters Forest or its exchange for other, less environmentally valuable public lands. In either case, the pending litigation would become moot and the Headwaters would receive permanent protection from development.[28]

[28]*See, e.g.,* Charles McCoy, *Maxxam's Hurwitz Nears Pact to Swap Redwood Grove for Thousands of Acres,* WALL ST. J., July 19, 1996, at A4; Editorial, *New Hope to Preserve Old-Growth Headwaters,* S.F. CHRON., July 30,

negotiators went to work. Eventually California agreed to pay the owner/developer $5 million and, in exchange, the state received 777 acres of environmentally sensitive Tahoe watershed and a dismissal of the *Lake Country* lawsuit.

Today, the former development site provides an array of public recreational opportunities. A portion of the property, the Lake Tahoe Valley State Recreation Area, is a championship golf course, available for public play; in the winter, snowmobile rentals are available. Another segment of the property is a state park. This area remains undeveloped, offering hiking trails and cross-country skiing opportunities. Because of its retention in its natural, wetlands state, the park helps to ensure the permanent protection of the Tahoe watershed and Lake Tahoe's still-unique water quality.

And what of the developers? They took the funds obtained from the state in the litigation settlement (having made a tidy profit when compared to their own acquisition costs) and devoted them to less controversial development opportunities in Southern California.

An epilogue to the Lake Country Estates saga: This litigation settlement and accompanying public acquisition set the stage for several more at Lake Tahoe in subsequent years. This informal resolution of regulatory takings disputes became a common trend at Lake Tahoe, with negotiated compensation being paid to numerous developers by the government, and the public receiving title to several environmentally sensitive parcels in the Lake Tahoe Basin.

In contrast to federal, state, and local efforts that target specific resources for public acquisition, some regulatory programs contain generic acquisition components. One example is section 5 of the federal Endangered Species Act, which directs the U.S. Secretaries of the Interior and Agriculture to embark upon a land acquisition program "to conserve fish, wildlife, and plants, including those which are listed as endangered species or threatened species. . . ."[29] The

---

1996, at A16. As this book goes to press, a tentative settlement and proposed government acquisition of a portion of the Headwaters Forest had been negotiated between the corporate landowners, the federal government and the State of California.

[29]16 U.S.C. § 1534.

Migratory Bird Conservation Act similarly directs federal officials to acquire lands for migratory bird conservation and habitat purposes.[30]

Acquisition is sometimes used in government regulatory programs for pollution control as well. Illustrative is section 104(j) of the federal Comprehensive Environmental Response, Compensation and Liability Act (CERCLA, also known as Superfund Act).[31] That section authorizes the United States to acquire any contaminated property that is needed to conduct a remedial action under the Act's hazardous substance cleanup provisions.

Unfortunately, these acquisition provisions have been little used by government officials, despite the fact that they often represent more "user-friendly" alternatives to the regulatory constraints for which the above-described statutes are far better known. Why? Explanations range from a lack of adequate funding for acquisition strategies to the belief that federal officials are more comfortable advancing traditional regulatory strategies than they are pursuing more novel acquisition-based approaches. With increased attention being paid to "regulatory reform" initiatives, however, it is likely that the acquisition option will come under increased scrutiny as a potential way around the all too common regulation-begets-takings-claims scenario.

Less-than-Fee Interests

It may seem to the casual observer that public acquisition represents an all-or-nothing alternative to regulatory approaches. Not so. First year law students are indoctrinated early with the fact that property interests can be carved up in any number of ways. The "bundle of sticks" representing landownership can be surrendered incrementally just as well as totally. From the government's perspective, public acquisition of less-than-fee interests in land may serve the same policy objectives as does outright purchase, but at far less public expense and with far fewer land management responsibilities. From the landowner's standpoint, surrendering merely some fractional interest in the land allows the owner to retain title while simultaneously realizing tax benefits and satisfying the government resource management objectives.

---

[30]16 U.S.C. §§ 715a, 715c, 715d. *See also* 16 U.S.C. § 668dd(b)(3) (public acquisition by exchange in national wildlife refuge system).

[31]42 U.S.C. § 9604(j).

Illustrative is the conservation easement. In exchange for money or some form of government benefit, a landowner can agree to devote his or her property to a particular type of use. For example, a farmer may be willing to agree that he will use his property for agricultural purposes only for a specified period of time, thereby promoting the community objective of preserving scarce agricultural lands in the region. In exchange for the farmer's execution and recording of an agricultural easement memorializing that agreement, the government affords the farmer benefits in the form of tax breaks, cash payments, off-site development credits, etc.[32]

Closely related is the open-space easement, under which a private landowner agrees to restrict development. Again, the incentives to agree to such an open-space easement are intensified and can include compensating development opportunities off-site; tax benefits; monetary payments; or a combination thereof.[33]

The majority of such less-than-fee interests are negotiated between private property owners and local governments. While state and federal governments often specifically authorize and support such locally bargained-for transactions, they occasionally take a more direct role. One example is the Conservation Reserve Program (CRP) created by Congress and administered by the U.S. Department of Agriculture.[34] The objective of the CRP is to discourage agricultural cultivation of highly erodible and other environmentally sensitive cropland. The CRP is implemented through payments by the federal government to farmers who let their land lie fallow, guaranteed through a CRP agreement. To date over 36.5 million acres have been enrolled in the CRP, representing a total financial commitment by the federal government of over $19.5 billion.[35] Similarly, the federal

[32]In California, local governments are authorized to offer such agricultural easements to farmers under the Williamson Act. Cal. Gov't Code §§ 51200–95. In exchange for a farmer's agreement to devote land exclusively to agriculture for at least 10 years, the statute allows the local government to provide the farmer with substantial property tax relief. *See also* that state's Agricultural Land Stewardship Act, Cal. Pub. Res. Code § 10200 et seq. (state grants program to facilitate acquisition of agricultural conservation easements by local governments and private nonprofit groups).

[33]*See, e.g.*, Cal. Gov't Code § 51070 et seq. (California Open Space Easement Act); Cal. Civ. Code § 815 et seq. (Conservation Easement Act).

[34]16 U.S.C. § 3831–3136.

[35]*See* Farrier, supra note 1, at 329–34.

Wetlands Reserve Program (WRP) seeks to discourage agricultural cultivation of wetlands and encourage wetlands restoration.[36]

Sometimes the objective is to create a "holding action" during which the land cannot be developed irreversibly to some unwanted use. The objective may also be to acquire it in the future. To meet these goals, there are several other alternatives. The government or private party could lease the land for a term of years. They could acquire, by purchase or gift, a "right of first refusal" that would allow them to purchase the property if it ever became available for sale. Acquisition of covenants and easements on property do not have to be forever; they can be for a term of years, just enough to preserve the land while plans and funding are put together for future acquisition.

The Critical Role of Public and Private Land Trusts

Regulatory agencies, for all their expertise and authority, often lack the wherewithal to acquire and manage interests in land. This deficiency may be attributable to a lack of jurisdictional authority, funding, expertise, interest, or a combination of these factors. In any event, conventional regulatory agencies are at times ill-equipped to explore fully nonregulatory initiatives that avoid or render moot inverse condemnation disputes. This important task has, accordingly, fallen to a new breed of government agency, and to a wide array of private organizations.

Some jurisdictions have been more active in this area than others. The State of California has been particularly aggressive in creating numerous land conservancies, each empowered to acquire, manage, and rehabilitate lands in discrete regions of that state possessing special resource sensitivity. Specifically, California has established separate conservancies with jurisdiction over California's 1,100-mile coastline, San Francisco Bay, the Santa Monica Mountains (the largest recreational open space remaining in greater Los Angeles), the California side of Lake Tahoe Basin, the Coachella Valley in the Southern California desert, and the Central Valley's San Joaquin River. While the details vary, each of California's regional land conservancies is responsible for land acquisition and management programs designed to promote public recreational and access

---

[36]16 U.S.C. §§ 3837–3837f, *discussed in* Farrier, *supra* note 1, at 334–37.

opportunities, preservation of open space, protection of wildlife habitat, and resource restoration.[37]

Some resource agencies at the local and federal levels similarly undertake land trust–type activities, usually as part of their larger mission. Local park districts are an example.

Government has not been able to tackle the challenges of land acquisition and management by itself. Fortunately, a wide array of private organizations has sprung up in recent years to fill the gap. They range from prominent, national nonprofit organizations, such as the Trust for Public Lands, the Nature Conservancy, and the American Farmland Trust, to ad hoc neighborhood groups committed to preserving particular local resources. Private land trusts, conservancies, and the like possess a number of practical advantages over their government counterparts. The private nonprofits can act quickly to acquire and preserve lands threatened with imminent development, complete land transactions free of the bureaucratic constraints that at times shackle government agencies, and have greater latitude in their fundraising activities.

Land trusts are not a strictly private versus public proposition, however. Often, public and private land trust organizations are able to work together to accomplish joint objectives. Success stories involving joint public/private entities can be found in New York, Vermont, Rhode Island, and many other jurisdictions.[38]

Conclusion

Those concerned with the preservation of finite natural resources—be they private environmentalists or government managers—must be prepared to look beyond purely regulatory strategies. At best, litigation offers a temporary fix to legal, technical, and ecological problems that require big-picture solutions. Such solutions often can be realized only through nonregulatory approaches.

As this chapter suggests, such approaches are both numerous and promising. One of the benefits of the current takings law conundrum is the incentive it creates for parties to pursue nonregulatory strategies. That is something from which all concerned can take some comfort.

[37]See, e.g., California Tahoe Conservancy, Progress Report: 1985–1991 (1991).

[38]For an excellent overview, see Land Conservation Through Public/Private Partnerships (Eve Endicott ed., Island Press 1996).

Chapter 33

Alternative Dispute Resolution

In areas of human conflict where time-consuming and expensive litigation have become the norm, hopeful eyes inevitably turn to the techniques of alternative dispute resolution (ADR). Facilitation, mediation, arbitration, mini-trials, etc.—all these methods have been employed to increase the speed and decrease the cost (and adversial nature) of conflict resolution relative to the traditional courtroom battle.

In this chapter, we look solely at ADR in the takings litigation context as it is evolving in suits against the United States. The federal focus is compelled by the absence of survey material on comparable efforts in the states.[1] In addition, the federal government has recently been innovating in this area.

Probably the chief authority for use of federal ADR is General Order No. 13 of the U.S. Court of Federal Claims, issued in 1987. Order 13 seeks to facilitate settlement of takings cases before the court, and thus is not ADR in the fuller sense of techniques that avoid litigation altogether. Nonetheless, the promise it offers for more streamlined resolution of such cases makes a closer look worthwhile.

The ADR methods of Order 13 are voluntary on each side; both parties must agree to the technique that is used. The rule particularly encourages use of its approaches where the parties anticipate a lengthy discovery and a protracted trial (more than one week). Because Order 13 techniques employ additional judges, a case must be

---

[1]Leading examples of state ADR efforts in the land-use conflict area are those of Florida and Maine. These programs go well beyond resolution of takings litigation, however.

referred to Order 13 ADR by the presiding judge. Should the ADR effort fail, the case is returned to the presiding judge's docket.

The first, and simpler, Order 13 technique is use of a settlement judge—a judge of the same court, other than the presiding judge, who will sit down with the parties and point out the strengths and weaknesses of each side's case. ADR specialists call this "early neutral evaluation." The hope is that by fostering a more realistic assessment of such strengths and weaknesses, areas of difference are narrowed and chances of settlement raised.

The other Order 13 technique is the mini-trial—an expedited procedure in which each party presents an abbreviated version of its case to, once again, a judge other than the presiding judge in the case. The mini-trial judge then assists the parties in negotiating a settlement. Availability of this technique is limited to cases that involve factual disputes and are governed by "well-established principles of law." Participation of principals (agency officials, senior management) is expressly encouraged.

Use of Order 13 techniques in the U.S. Court of Federal Claims appears to have been limited so far—in part, no doubt, because both parties must agree to their use. It has been suggested as well that the techniques work best when the takings dispute has been narrowed and the dispositive questions have been agreed upon. Further, the fact that a landowner's action turns on an undeveloped area of takings law, all too often the case, does not augur well for settlement through Order 13. Notwithstanding, it would seem that given the unrealistic expectations that some property owners bring into takings litigation—based on lack of familiarity with the boundaries and nuances of takings law—making greater use of Order 13 is something to be considered.

Broader use of ADR in the takings context may be fostered by the confluence of a few factors. First is the pressure on government nowadays to ease the private property impacts of regulatory programs. As noted in connection with property rights legislation (*see* chapter 34), ADR is one of a number of possible "process" reforms that might vent the pressure created by the property rights movement without the troublesome implications of some proposed "takings" laws. Like many of those process reforms, ADR in the takings litigation context may not (although it can) lighten the regulatory burden itself, but may expedite the Fifth Amendment cure.

A second factor fostering takings ADR is its broad endorsement by the U.S. Department of Justice's Environment and Natural Resources

Division,[2] which contains the unit assigned the land-use-related takings cases. An Office of Alternative Dispute Resolution was established in the Department in 1995, and a pilot ADR program for takings cases is now in an early stage. The pilot program, drawn from current authority in court rules and employed only when all parties agree, involves seeking a ninety-day stay of Court of Federal Claims proceedings during which the program agency and property owner exchange confidential information documents. Such exchange, it is hoped, will promote more settlements, or at least focus discovery and the issues that need to be developed in the takings litigation. Between 150 and 200 claimants in takings actions against the United States are now enrolled in this program.

In September, 1995, the Department of Justice also abandoned its long-held position that the Constitution forbids the use of binding arbitration by federal agencies.[3] An executive order to the same effect soon followed.[4] The Department's now repudiated argument held that any entity exercising binding authority over an entity within the Article II branch of the federal government has to be appointed pursuant to the Appointments Clause of the Constitution,[5] which arbitrators typically are not. Still, it is a big step from conceding there is no constitutional objection to federal agencies submitting to binding arbitration, to embracing its use in a given context, such as takings litigation.

Moving a step earlier in the process, before the action is filed, the federal government seems to be embracing ADR in a range of administrative circumstances to avert more acrimonious property rights

---

[2]Catherine M. Flanagan, *Getting to Justice*, LEGAL TIMES SPECIAL REPORT 28 (May 13, 1996).

[3]"Constitutional Limitations on Federal Government Participation in Binding Arbitration," memorandum from Walter Dellinger, Ass't Att'y Gen., to John Schmidt, Assoc. Att'y Gen. (Sept. 7, 1995).

[4]Exec. Order No. 12,988, 61 Fed. Reg. 4,729 (Feb. 5, 1996). Section 12 revoked an earlier executive order barring federal lawyers from entering into binding arbitration.

[5]U.S. Const. art. II, § 2, cl. 2. The Appointments Clause sets forth the exclusive mechanisms by which an officer of the United States may be appointed. There does not appear to be any dispute that arbitrators are not officers of the United States. Rather the issue has been whether the Appointments Clause contains a negative inference—that only officers of the United States appointed pursuant to the Appointments Clause may exercise significant federal authority.

disputes down the road. The Negotiated Rulemaking Act, enacted in 1990, allows for mediated negotiations during a federal agency's development of its informal rules.[6] The Administrative Dispute Resolution Act, enacted the same year but much broader than its aged peer, sets out rules for the use of ADR in any controversy that relates to an administrative program.[7] More recently, the Clinton administration's Reinventing Government initiative has recommended greater use of ADR.

In the case of the Endangered Species Act program, a veritable vortex of landowner-government disputes, greater attention is being given to using the "habitat conservation planning" process in that statute as an avenue for bringing in ADR.[8]

[6] 5 U.S.C. §§ 561–70.
[7] 5 U.S.C. §§ 571–82.
[8] 16 U.S.C. § 1539(a)(2)(A).

Chapter 34

Property Rights Legislation

How times change. In early 1988, the phenomenon of property rights legislation and executive orders was entirely unknown. Today, the federal government and some two dozen states have laws or executive orders on the books that speak to the topic.[1] Since 1990, virtually every state legislature has at least considered property rights bills.

The reasons for this legislative cascade seem clear enough. Greatly increased regulation of land use, a swing of the national political pendulum toward skepticism of government, and Supreme Court opinions calling attention to takings—all these things set the stage. A perception by some that the takings jurisprudence developed by the courts is too heavily weighted in favor of government regulators provided impetus. To be sure, it might be noted that this legislative burst of activity occurs at precisely the time when at least the U.S. Supreme Court is moving toward greater protection of property rights under the Takings Clause. There is no paradox, however, since to the property rights activist, the doctrinal shift of the Court is too slow and too modest. Legislatures to the rescue.

Of course, there is nothing wrong with our elected governing bodies being players on this field. Indeed, given the importance of the societal choices implicit in how we regard private property, legislative involvement may be seen as preferable to leaving the matter entirely

---

[1]Useful surveys of the legislation include ROBERT MELTZ, "PROPERTY RIGHTS" LAWS IN THE STATES (Cong. Research Service report for Congress, No. 97-21, 1996); American Resources Information Network, *Summary of State Takings Legislation* (available at http://www.arin.org/arin/states.html); and David Coursen, *Property Rights Legislation: A Survey of Federal and State Assessment and Compensation Measures*, 26 ENVTL. L. RPTR. 10239 (1996).

with the courts and disjointed case-by-case litigation of takings cases. As the Chief Judge of the U.S. Court of Federal Claims put it:

> The government here had little guidance from the law as to whether its action was a taking. . . . The citizen likewise had little more precedential guidance. . . . There must be a better way. . . . Courts, however, cannot produce comprehensive solutions. They can only interpret the . . . Constitution in very specific factual circumstances. . . . Judicial decisions are far less sensitive to societal problems than the law and policy made by the political branches. . . .[2]

Arguably, then, the debate is not *whether* the private property impacts of government programs should be tossed into the political cauldron, but only *how* they should be dealt with. No small question. And reflecting the debate's complexity, the range of seriously proposed answers runs the gamut from modest reforms in the government programs that most commonly give rise to landowner complaints, to making the government pay for almost every loss in property value it directly causes.

The Players

Partisans in the debate fall into clearly defined groups. Favoring legislation are, first, certain landowners—those who have encountered government frustration of their land-use plans and those who fear they might. Many such landowners are rural; some join a grassroots group in the loosely organized network known as the "property rights movement." It is these small landowners whose encounters with government regulators provide the stuff of the many hardship stories that drive the property rights issue. Some of these stories have been discredited,[3] but many others have not.

Second, and overlapping the first category, are business sectors with an economic interest both in the reduced regulation of private property and in greater access to public resources (or to private inter-

---

[2]Bowles v. United States, 31 Fed. Cl. 37, 40 (1994).

[3]*See, e.g.*, Michael A. Wolf, *Overtaking the Fifth Amendment: The Legislative Backlash Against Environmentalism*, 6 FORDHAM ENVTL. L.J. 637 (1995) (disputing veracity of some horror stories and questioning whether compensation legislation addresses landowners' plights).

ests on public lands). Prominent in this group are developers, farmers, ranchers, and the extractive industries (mining, timber, oil, and gas). National and state farm bureaus have been particularly active. The third category embraces conservatives, libertarians, and others espousing political or economic philosophies of limited government, minimal regulation, and free-market solutions.

Opponents of property rights legislation include a broad spectrum of groups whose agendas stress the collective benefits deriving from government's ability to control private land use. Though environmentalists are plainly out front, others have been only slightly less vehement. They include groups representing historic preservationists, hunting and fishing interests, labor, the disabled, senior citizens, and consumers. Some civil rights, public health, and religious groups have weighed in as well. And while many states have enacted property rights legislation, a variety of organizations representing state and local government have passed resolutions against such laws, especially those of the compensation variety (described below).

A Quick History

The modern property rights movement, born in the late 1980s, did not invent the notion that government should be sensitive to property rights. Long before, Congress and the states were enacting legislation with explicit private property safeguards. For example, by the late 1980s the phrase "valid existing rights" appeared in the U.S. Code over 100 times, most of them instances where Congress, in creating new land-use controls, mandated that settled property expectations be left alone.[4] Statutory preconditions imposed on the exercise of federal agency eminent-domain powers also evidence a legislative awareness of the disruptive potential of taking private land.[5]

---

[4]*See, e.g.,* Surface Mining Control and Reclamation Act, 16 U.S.C. § 1272(e); Wilderness Act, 16 U.S.C. §§ 1133(c) (using similar phrase "existing private rights"), § 1133(d)(3); Wild and Scenic Rivers Act, 16 U.S.C. §§ 1279(b), 1280; Alaska Native Claims Settlement Act, 43 U.S.C. § 1613(g).

[5]Two preconditions used in the U.S. Code with some regularity are (1) a specified maximum acreage that may be condemned; and (2) in natural preserves, a requirement that the condemning agency leave to the owner of noncommercial residential land a right to use and occupancy for some period of time, as long as the property is not used inconsistently with the preserve's purposes.

Yet what we today call "property rights legislation" has distinct qualities not seen before. The approaches favored by property rights activists often take the form of statutory provisions that speak explicitly of property rights, generally apply governmentwide, and may find themselves in freestanding bills devoted exclusively to property rights.

The curtain-raising event of this modern era was Executive Order No. 12,630, signed by President Reagan on March 15, 1988.[6] The order, styled "Government Actions and Interference with Constitutionally Protected Property Rights" created a risk management mechanism. As implemented by Attorney General guidelines, it required each federal agency to prepare a written "takings impact assessment" (TIA) whenever the agency proposed an action that "could" effect a constitutional taking. Through such before-the-fact analysis, the order asserted, the government could minimize inadvertent drains on the federal fisc through takings claims, and at the same time sensitize federal agencies to their actions' impacts on private property.

Had the order stopped with a TIA requirement, it might have been uncontroversial. But it went further, setting out what it represented as a distillation of Supreme Court takings jurisprudence, plus a set of restrictive preconditions on those agency actions aimed at protecting public health and safety. Commentators seized on these latter components of the order to argue that it was more ideological manifesto than internal executive-branch housekeeping;[7] and when the Reagan administration left town in early 1989, the perception was that agency implementation of the order slacked off.

The belief that Executive Order No. 12,630 was not being enforced led to the first piece of "property rights legislation" in the contemporary sense of the phrase. In 1990, Senator Steve Symms (R-Idaho) introduced a floor amendment declaring that regulations promulgated by certain environmental agencies could not take effect until the agency was certified by the Attorney General as in compliance with the order.[8] While the amendment was rejected, the vote was close[9] de-

[6]3 C.F.R. 554 (1988), *reprinted in* 5 U.S.C. § 601 note.

[7]*See, e.g.,* Jerry Jackson & Lyle D. Albaugh, *A Critique of the Takings Executive Order in the Context of Environmental Regulation,* 18 Envtl. L. Rptr. 10463 (Nov. 1988); James M. McElfish, Jr., *The Takings Executive Order: Constitutional Jurisprudence or Political Philosophy?,* 18 Envtl. L. Rptr. 10474 (Nov. 1988).

[8]136 Cong. Rec. S10,909 (daily ed. July 27, 1990).

[9]*Id.* at 10,917.

spite a minimum of persuasive effort by its sponsor. Partisans in the debate took notice.

Following 1990, momentum picked up—slowly at first, far more quickly after the Republican election sweep of 1994. By 1995, not only the political base, but the diversity of approaches in property rights legislation, had widened considerably. To the Symms assessment approach (expanded in later bills to cover *all* federal agencies) were added new ideas: a statutorily declared threshold for compensation of property owners, prohibitions on federal agency personnel entering upon private property to collect information without the owner's consent, use of alternative dispute resolution, administrative appeals of agency actions restricting property use, expansions of court jurisdiction to allow compensation and invalidation claims to be filed in the same court, a requirement that agencies pay for takings liability (under Constitution or statute) out of their own appropriations, and so forth.

In the states, the buildup of political pressure was concurrent, though with far more proposals actually being enacted. Within two years of the Reagan executive order, the governors of California and Colorado signed assessment orders along similar lines.[10] In 1991, Washington became the first state to enact legislation supported by the property rights movement,[11] with Delaware and Arizona close on its heels in 1992 (Arizona's was later rescinded by referendum). By 1995, every state had at one time or another considered property rights legislation, and some two dozen had enacted some version or another. Possibly reflecting the perceived political message of the November 1994 elections, almost half these enactments occurred in 1995.

In intriguing contrast with its success in legislatures, property rights legislation has been rejected on both occasions when it was put to popular vote. First, Arizona voters in 1994 rejected, by 60 percent to 40 percent, that state's takings assessment law.[12] Then a Washington referendum in 1995 repealed, by the same wide margin, a very aggressive compensation (plus assessment) statute enacted just a half year earlier by initiative and legislative passage.[13] To add one more,

---

[10]Cal. Exec. Order No. D-78-89 (Dec. 20, 1989); Colo. Exec. Order No. D-0152-89 (Nov. 28, 1989).

[11]Wash. Rev. Code § 36.70A.370.

[12]Proposition 300.

[13]Referendum 48.

Rhode Islanders adopted by popular vote in 1986 a constitutional amendment that appears to declare that land-use regulation for environmental purposes cannot be a taking under that state's constitution.[14] How to interpret this 3-for-3 defeat of the pro-property rights position in popular votes is uncertain, though not surprisingly the combatants have been quick to put their own spins on it.

Let us now turn to a dissection of the different genres of *enacted* legislation; comment on their strengths and weaknesses in lessening the public/private conflict; and, finally, recommend a middle, possibly less acrimonious, path. We focus more on principles than particularities, since the pace of change in this area is so fast.

The Assessment Approach

Assessment bills are the property rights activists' answer to the National Environmental Policy Act (NEPA).[15] Each takes the view that some important impact of government action is being slighted by agency decision-makers, and that legislative intervention is needed. Intervention in each instance takes the form of a requirement that the agency create a formal process, including a written "impact statement" in some cases, to address the erstwhile overlooked impacts on a par with the agency's historical mission and values.[16]

Assessment bills thus take a front-end approach (dubbed "look before you leap" by property rights advocates), requiring agencies to gauge the takings, or property rights, implications of their proposed actions. In their pure form, they are strictly procedural; there is no supplementation of the constitutional standard for takings.

Arguments made in favor of assessment bills are, first and foremost, that they would minimize unnecessary government encroachments on private property. Given the centrality of private property in our society, activists argue, this is a worthy goal in and of itself, inde-

[14]R.I. Const. art. 1, § 16.

[15]42 U.S.C. §§ 4321–61.

[16]The structural parallel between NEPA—or, more precisely, a state "little NEPA"—and assessment legislation is made explicit in Montana, which simply engrafted its property rights assessment approach onto the Montana Environmental Policy Act. Mont. Code Ann. §§ 75-1-102, 75-1-103, 75-1-201. In addition, drafters of the U.S. Attorney General's guidelines under Exec. Order No. 12,630 (unpublished) borrowed several concepts from the Council on Environmental Quality regulations implementing NEPA. 40 C.F.R. parts 1500–08.

pendent of whether an adequate constitutional or statutory remedy for the encroachment exists. At the federal level, the contention is that President Reagan's executive order is being half-heartedly implemented, in part because it is unenforceable by those outside the federal government. And, of course, it can be revoked by a stroke of the presidential pen. Thus, property rights activists conclude, the order needs to be codified and given teeth.

Opponents of assessment bills see them as adding yet another layer of red tape to delay agencies contemplating regulatory action. Moreover, TIAs cannot achieve their intended purpose, they say, since whether a taking will occur as a result of agency action can be evaluated only as to a specified site, in an "as applied" analysis.[17] Indeed, one leading property rights champion appears to agree, at least as to agency actions of broad application and effect.[18] Hence, TIAs on many agency actions may be little more than guesswork, phrased in boilerplate. And since courts find takings under the Fifth Amendment only infrequently, it is claimed that the costs of doing TIAs will be excessive compared to the dollar amount of the compensation awards avoided.[19]

The assessment-bill opposition also objects to the requirement in some bills that TIAs be made available to the public, and that a private cause of action exist for enforcing TIA provisions. Public disclosure, it is argued, will provide the aggrieved property owner with a roadmap for conducting takings litigation against the government—and thus may foment lawsuits rather than reduce them. In point of fact, the firm policy of the federal executive branch under Executive Order No. 12,630 has always been to keep TIAs confidential—officials citing, in addition to the litigation concern, attorney-client privilege and the Freedom of Information Act exemption for internal,

[17]Recall the Supreme Court's stated preference for adjudication of takings claims in an as-applied context. *See* chapter 10.

[18]Nancie G. Marzulla, *State Private Property Rights Initiatives as a Response to "Environmental Takings," in* NAT'L LEGAL CENTER FOR THE PUBLIC INTEREST, REGULATORY TAKINGS: RESTORING PRIVATE PROPERTY RIGHTS 107 (Roger Clegg ed., 1995). Another writer predicts that agencies' takings determinations will be "nearly meaningless." *Recent Legislation, Property—Constitutional Law—Takings—Utah Requires Agencies and Localities to Conduct Takings Impact Analyses,* 108 HARVARD L. REV. 519, 521 (1994).

[19]A study concludes that the costs of preparing TIAs in the states have been "minimal." NATIONAL CONFERENCE OF STATE LEGISLATURES, STATE LEGISLATIVE REPORT: EVALUATING THE EFFECTS OF STATE TAKINGS LEGISLATION 3 (Jan. 1998).

pre-decisional memoranda.[20] Allowing a private cause of action, it is felt, can only paralyze agencies further—which, indeed, is argued to be the true purpose of such a device.

All the property rights bills enacted in the early years—1991 through 1993—were of the assessment type, and this approach remains far more common than others. State assessment laws show a strong preference for assessment by the program agency rather than the state's attorney general. Often, however, the demand for program-agency assessments is fused with a requirement that the attorney general set up a "process" for the assessing, perhaps supply the agency with a "checklist" of takings indicators, or offer other guidance as to what constitutes a taking under the state and federal constitutions.[21] Whether this preference for agency evaluation is simple mimicry of the federal order, or instead results from more substantive reasons, is not clear.[22] Most, though not all, states require that their TIAs be held confidential, and that judicial review, if any, be limited. Some extend their assessment mandate to local as well as state agencies.

Most tantalizing is what these bills envision as the legal consequence when the proposed action is determined by the agency or AG to have significant takings implications—"tantalizing" because it is so important, yet not always made plain. Some state enactments say nothing, allowing the inference that takings implications need only be considered, but do not dictate agency choices. This approach tracks NEPA, under which federal agencies must consider the environmental impacts of alternative proposed actions, but need not elect

[20]5 U.S.C. § 552(b)(5).

[21]States in which the attorney general (AG) is required to do the assessing are Delaware and Indiana. States in which the program agency does the assessing, with or without AG guidance or checklists, are Colorado (health and safety actions only), Idaho, Kansas, Louisiana (agricultural and forest land only), Michigan, Missouri, Montana, Nebraska, North Dakota, Oregon (forestry restrictions only), Tennessee, Texas, Utah, Virginia, Washington, West Virginia, and Wyoming.

[22]Given the fact-intensiveness of takings analysis, perhaps a hybrid approach is preferable. The program agency, having an intimate familiarity with program details, clearly has a role to play; it is not practical for the AG's office to amass comparable knowledge on a broad front. On the other hand, the attorney general's office needs to have a coordinating approach, to prevent agencies from adopting inconsistent interpretation of takings case law.

the one that minimizes environmental harm if countervailing agency priorities outweigh. The Reagan executive order appears to be in this camp.[23]

Other property rights enactments go a step further, saying that the property impacts must be minimized, but not necessarily eliminated, before the agency can proceed. And still others appear to take the absolute position that the action may not be taken until modified to remove all takings implications. The last group raises significant questions as to whether an override of program mandates was intended and, given the vagueness of takings law, query whether there is a potential for political mischief in an agency's having such wide discretion to void otherwise lawful courses of action.

A variation on the usual assessment mold has been adopted in Maine, where the law requires advance review of agency rules for whether they contain variance provisions adequate to ensure that Fifth Amendment takings will not occur.[24]

The Compensation/Regulatory Relief Approach

In contrast with the assessment approach, compensation/regulatory relief proposals take a back-end approach, often prescribing a statutory standard for when owners should be compensated for government restrictions on property use. Almost always, the impact of concern is a drop in the private property's market value, and the compensation threshold is stated as a percentage of value lost due to the government action. Recognizing that some uses of private property are inherently noxious, however, all compensation enactments to date immunize government action restricting certain uses—often referred to generically as "nuisance exemptions."

---

[23]Section 1(b) of the order calls upon agencies to review their actions so as to avoid "unnecessary" takings. The attorney general guidelines under the order state: "In those instances in which a range of alternatives are [sic] available, each of which would meet the statutorily required objective, prudent management requires selection of the least risk alternative." Attorney General's Guidelines for the Evaluation of Risk and Avoidance of Unanticipated Takings § I.A. ("Policy, Purpose, and Mandate").

[24]1996 Me. Laws ch. 537.

Arguments in Favor

Arguments in favor of compensation/regulatory relief legislation start with the premise that the constitutional remedy now in place is inadequate. It is said to be too time-consuming and unpredictable, and in most cases requires too severe an impact on the landowner (almost complete elimination of land value) to prevail. Assertions along the lines of "most landowners don't have 10 years and $500,000 in attorneys' fees to litigate a takings case," though not reflective of the typical case, were made repeatedly during the 1995 House floor debate on the "Contract with America" property rights bill.[25] Having a single, unvarying value-loss threshold as a compensation trigger affords greater certainty to both landowner and government agency (leaving aside vaguely worded exceptions to liability). And, property rights activists say, setting the threshold lower than the constitutional trigger corrects the lax reading courts give the Takings Clause. This will instill a proper respect for private property among government bureaucrats, who now have no incentive to factor private property impacts into their decisions.

Nor would such bills be budget busters, property rights advocates continue, since the prospect of massive liability would make agencies "mend their ways"—that is, search for less property-intrusive means of accomplishing goals.[26] At a minimum, agencies would be more willing to talk with affected landowners before acting. These salutary effects would be especially likely if the legislation stipulates that compensation payments come out of the offending agency's appropriated funds.[27] Direct accountability, who can dispute, gets the agency's attention. As an additional safeguard against unlimited outlays, the leading federal compensation bills today make explicit that the property owner's right to compensation is conditional upon avail-

[25] *See* CONGRESSIONAL RECORD for March 1 through March 3, 1995.

[26] A Congressional Budget Office cost estimate on the compensation provisions of S. 605, a leading property rights bill in the 104th Congress, echoes this view: "CBO expects that enacting the bill would cause federal agencies to attempt to avoid paying compensation by modifying their decisions, processing permits more quickly, or otherwise changing their behavior." Cost estimate sent to Senator Orrin Hatch, Chairman, Committee on the Judiciary, Oct. 17, 1995 (hereinafter *CBO Report*).

[27] Currently, judgments and settlements in takings actions against the United States usually are paid from an off-budget separate appropriation known as the Judgment Fund, not from an agency's appropriation. 31 U.S.C. § 3104.

ability of agency appropriations. All of these counter-arguments to the charge of budget-busting gain added strength, of course, if the legislature rewrites the governing statute to authorize or require less intrusive regulation.

Arguments Against

Quite expectedly, it is not assessment legislation that opponents of property rights bills get most exercised about—it is compensation legislation. An assessment requirement, depending on its scope and reviewability, may indeed call for a major investment of agency resources. Yet to many in the opposition, such requirements are generally regarded as but a nuisance—a vague symbol of deregulatory sentiment. By contrast, compensation bills are seen as taking a painful, program-debilitating bite. To the compensation opponent, such legislation is naught but a surrogate for deregulation, particularly at the low compensation thresholds (ranging from anything-greater-than-zero to 50 percent value loss) used in such bills. In tight budgetary times, they argue, even a moderate outflow of government funds to affected property owners will cripple program implementation.[28]

At a conceptual level, opponents point out that compensation bills do not take account of the offsetting benefits that the landowner reaps from the restriction-imposing program. *The owner* can't tear down that historic building, but neither can others in the community tear down theirs—conferring neighborhood amenities on one and all. More broadly, opponents observe, life in civilized society inevitably involves a mix of benefits and burdens, a balancing of private rights and public rights as they evolve over time. Thus, it makes no sense—not to mention being a gargantuan task—to compensate for every modest impact.[29] When the burden on the landowner is particularly severe, the constitutional remedy is available. If significant impacts on landowners

---

[28]According to a study, states report that through March 1997, no litigation had been filed against a state agency or local government under state takings laws that provide for compensation or regulatory relief causes of action. National Conference of State Legislatures, *supra* note 19, at 3.

[29]*See, e.g.,* Carol M. Rose, *A Dozen Propositions on Private Property, Public Rights, and the New Takings Legislation,* 53 Washington & Lee L. Rev. 265 (1996); Frank I. Michelman, *A Skeptical View of "Property Rights" Legislation,* 6 Fordham Envtl. L.J. 409, 415 (1995) (reading *Lucas* to say that most regulatory restrictions on land use are regarded by Americans as part of the normal give-and-take of society).

are too common, then a search should be launched for ways to reform the program so that its goals are achieved with less impact.

Opponents of compensation legislation are fond of claiming that such bills require the government to pay polluters for not polluting.[30] Supporters parry the charge by pointing to the exemptions in such bills insulating the government from having to compensate when the activity it is restricting constitutes a nuisance. The riposte, however, is that nuisance doctrine (private or public) has various limitations that make it unlikely to cover many instances of pollution, including the typical case where a factory emits a small amount of pollutant that combines with that of many others to cause an injury many miles (and perhaps years) distant.[31]

Another tack of opponents is to lay claim themselves to being the true defenders of property rights. Discouraging government from acting against a proposed harmful use of land, they contend, may result in the harm (pollution, socially undesirable uses) being visited upon the downwind, downslope, or nearby lands of others. Thus, compensation bills endorsed by the property rights groups arguably protect one landowner's property at the expense of many others' rights.

Further, the government does not require reimbursement when its actions *increase* the value of private property (as by proximity to a highway exit); why then should government pay every time it *decreases* values?[32]

Finally, opponents target the workability of property-owner compensation schemes. If, as supporters argue, costs will be contained by conditioning payments on the availability of appropriations, then the grand rhetoric in compensation bills as to every property owner's compensation entitlement may prove but an empty promise. In addi-

[30]The charge assumes that pollution laws may restrict the use of property, or affected portions of property, sufficiently to meet the compensation bill's threshold.

[31]The gap between the reach of compensation bills and that of their nuisance exemptions is narrowed somewhat by the use in some bills of a supplementary exemption for land uses that threaten public health and safety.

[32]Property rights activists assert that contrary to the text, the government *does* require reimbursement when its actions increase property value—through higher property taxes. A lively debate has ensued as to whether such higher taxes fully offset the received benefit. *See generally* WINDFALLS FOR WIPEOUTS: LAND VALUE CAPTURE AND COMPENSATION (Donald Hagman & Dean Misczynski eds., 1978).

tion, such bills will generate a large bureaucracy of claims processors, not to mention an army of lawyers and real estate appraisers. Landowners will shop for appraisers willing to find the requisite value diminution as a result of government use restriction.

Enactments

The history of compensation/regulatory-relief legislation is a brief one. As noted, the early bills and enactments were all of the assessment variety; compensation legislation did not achieve prominence until roughly 1994. Today, a handful of states have enacted some form of compensation legislation, each with its own important wrinkles.

In contrast with the approaches recently ascendant on Capitol Hill, the principal state enactments do not establish an *automatic* compensation entitlement. Rather, the state agency is given options. Florida and Texas are the leading examples.[33] In Florida, when a state or local action "inordinately burdens" an existing (or reasonably foreseeable) use of real property, the owner first must submit a claim to the pertinent agency. If the agency agrees with the claim, it may give the owner a number of options—including an adjustment in the land-use restriction, transferable development rights, purchase of the land, etc. Adjustment of land-use restrictions, where part of the offer, must still protect the public interest—and a court must so certify. Only if the agency offer is rejected may the owner file a court action to determine whether, even considering the offer, the property is "inordinately burdened." The compensation amount must be the value loss, considering the agency's final settlement offer.

Texas's approach is somewhat different—call it "invalidation with a compensation option." Under this law, real property owners who believe that their property has lost 25 percent or more of its value by virtue of a state or local use restriction may file claims. If a claim is approved, the agency/court must order a rescission of the offending action, as it applies to the complainant. The government agency then may elect to pay damages, whereupon the agency or court must withdraw the rescission order, reinstating the use restriction.

[33]Fla. Stat. Ann. § 70.001; Tex. Gov't Code Ann. § 2007 et seq. (both statutes enacted 1995). *See generally* David L. Powell et al., *Florida's New Law to Protect Private Property Rights*, 23 ENVTL. & URBAN ISSUES 10 (Fall 1995), and responsive comments at 20–35; Note, *Land Use Regulation—Compensation Statutes—Florida Creates Cause of Action for Property Owners*, 109 HARVARD L. REV. 542 (1995).

A useful framework for thinking about the compensation component of these laws is how they address, or fail to address, some of the most ubiquitous issues of Fifth Amendment jurisprudence. First, when is the taking claim ripe (*see* chapter 5)? None of the state enactments trudges into this thorny thicket, with the exception of the Florida statute which defines a claim under the statute as ripe once the state agency issues a "ripeness decision" identifying the allowable uses on the property (or failing to do so within the requisite time).

Second, where should the line between taking and nontaking be drawn; how far is "too far" (*see* chapter 12)? Most of the enacted compensation laws opt for a simple percentage of lost value—20 to 40 percent is the range at present. Florida's law appears to be unique in taking a nonnumerical course, making "inordinately burdens" the standard and defining it to mean that the property owner is unable to attain reasonable investment-backed expectations or is left with only unreasonable uses.

Third, how broad is the "nuisance exemption" (*see* chapter 14)— a question of special cogency after *Lucas*. State laws and pending federal bills offer several shadings here. Thus, Florida exempts government responses to common law public nuisances or noxious uses, while Texas immunizes actions to restrict nuisances, to protect public health and safety, to prevent construction in floodplains, and so on.

Fourth, what is the relevant parcel (*see* chapter 12)? Supreme Court takings orthodoxy continues to insist that one must look at the entire parcel, not merely the affected segment, in gauging the impact of government action. Legislatures, for the most part, have taken the more property owner friendly course and done precisely the opposite. Thus, a Mississippi law declares that state or local action causing more than a 40 percent loss in the value of a forest or agricultural land parcel—or portion thereof—gives rise to the compensation right.[34] Though such laws (and recent federal bills taking the same approach) state no minimum portion size, there may be practical limitations on pressing claims based on regulations affecting only very small portions.[35]

---

[34]Miss. Code Ann. §§ 49-33-1 to 49-33-17. Taking a similar approach is Louisiana Act No. 302 (1995), and the leading property rights bills in the 104th Congress (H.R. 9, S. 605, and S. 1954).

[35]The Congressional Budget Office asserts that small affected portions of larger parcels would be unlikely to give rise to compensation claims since they have little market value independent of the property as a whole. *CBO Report, supra* note 26.

Fifth, what role should be played by the property owner's expectations or understandings as of the date the property was acquired (*see* chapters 3 and 12)? This element of takings law, introduced by *Penn Central* and expanded by *Lucas*, is of growing importance in the lower-court case law, but is only marginally reflected in the compensation legislation. An exception is the Florida statute, which defines its compensation threshold—"inordinately burdens"—partially in terms of whether the property owner is unable to attain reasonable investment-backed expectations. The reason for the scarcity of expectations-inclusive approaches, possibly, is that the concept of expectations does not lend itself to a simply worded trigger. Even the Florida law does little more than restate Supreme Court canon.

In grappling with some of these key issues, the compensation laws live up to their drafters' conviction that judicial interpretation of the Takings Clause is too weighted toward the government and must be rectified. In most instances, the legislation provides not only a clearer compensation standard, but, of critical importance, one that is far more attractive to the property owner than any plausible interpretation of the constitutional case law. For instance, while federal and state courts usually require almost complete elimination of economic use or market value before discerning a constitutional taking, state compensation laws, as noted, use triggers of 20 to 40 percent for affording relief.[36] (The leading federal compensation bill in the 105th Congress, S. 781, uses 33 percent.) In addition, while the U.S. Supreme Court steadfastly declines to segment property in regulatory takings analysis, two state compensation laws (and the federal bills) require that percentage value loss be computed on only the parcel's affected portion. It has been argued that by choosing a tight enough delineation of the "affected portion," *any* percentage threshold may be met.[37]

[36]Louisiana Act No. 302 (1995) (20 percent); Miss. Code Ann. §§ 49-33-1 to 49-33-17 (40 percent). Another property rights law with a percentage threshold is Oregon Sen. Bill No. 1156 (1995), using 10 percent; but meeting this threshold triggers administrative, not monetary, relief.

[37]*See, e.g.,* Rose, *supra* note 29, at 290–91. A unique approach to the "affected portion" debate would shift the analysis from portion of the parcel to portion of the property' owner's *total worth*. The owner would be compensated whenever the government-caused loss in property value exceeded a set portion of the owner's assets, including those other than the affected parcel. William M. Treanor, *The* Armstrong *Principle, the Narratives of Takings, and Compensation Statutes*, 38 WILLIAM & MARY L. REV. 1151 (1997).

Other Approaches

A measure of the growing maturity of the property rights movement is that supporters of legislative intervention are moving beyond the "classical" assessment and compensation approaches. Innovative approaches, often having superior traits such as fewer transaction costs, call for attention in state legislatures.

A popular entry among these new tacks is the "codification" of the "essential nexus" test of *Nollan* and the "rough proportionality" test of *Dolan*. It is not codification in the strict sense—*that* would involve enactments stating a test for when compensation is due. Rather, these laws often call an absolute prohibition: State agencies may not attach conditions to permits that fail the essential nexus or rough proportionality tests, whether or not they are willing to compensate.[38] This metamorphosis from compensation precondition to absolute prohibition has something to be said for it. *Nollan* and *Dolan* are based on the "substantially advance" prong of the *Agins* test, a due process–like standard drawn from an early due process case. The remedy for due process violations is, as we know, to prohibit the government activity, not to offer the plaintiff compensation. Thus, the condition-to-prohibition conversion in these state laws makes fundamental sense and seems fair as well. Less altruistically, states may want to minimize the chance of incurring compensation liability under *Nollan* and *Dolan*.

A second recurring approach is to mandate that if a state court or agency finds that a state action is a taking under some constitutional or statutory standard, property value assessments used in calculating the landowner's tax liability be commensurately reduced.[39] This seems only reasonable. A closer question, however, arises where the payment moves in the opposite direction—from the government to the landowner. In particular, should the government, when purchasing a property, be allowed to benefit from value losses that the government itself imposed? Apparently the only statutory answer to this question so far arises from the Congress, which, as part of the California Desert Protection Act of 1994, required that lands acquired by the Secretary of the Interior under the statute be appraised

---

[38]Examples are Ariz. Rev. Stat. Ann. § 9-500.12 et seq., §11-810 et seq., Cal. Gov't Code §§ 66,000–007, and Utah Code Ann. § 63-90-4(2). Arizona's bill, enacted in 1995, was drafted by the same legislator who authored an assessment bill that went down to defeat in a closely watched 1994 referendum.

[39]*See, e.g.,* Kan. H.B. 2015 (enacted 1995); N.D. Sen. Bill 1156 (enacted 1995), and Tenn. Code Ann. § 12-1-204.

without regard to the presence of endangered or threatened species, and any consequent federal restrictions on land use.[40] However, where the prohibited property use poses a threat more alarming to the popular perception than loss of a species, such as harmful pollution, the idea of a government purchaser having to refund the value lost as a result of the prohibition seems less palatable.

Other state laws provide more fodder for the legislative imagination. Arizona has created an ombudsman's office to represent the interests of private property owners in state proceedings;[41] in Utah, a similar office serves more of an advisory and mediating role.[42] Florida has established a dispute resolution scheme whereby a property owner who believes that state or local action is "unreasonable or unfairly burdens" property use may appear before a special master.[43] The master must recommend alternatives, which may include adjustment of land development standards, that protect the public interest while easing the restraints on property use. In a two-year demonstration program, Oregon provides that a timber owner who can prove that a state harvest restriction will cause more than a 10 percent loss may apply for approval of an alternate plan that provides the greatest protection possible while reducing the loss below 10 percent.[44]

Another idea put forward for legislative consideration is greater use of burden shifting—moving from the landowner's to the government's shoulders the task of making some critical showing in the land-use dispute (already adopted in the *Nollan/Dolan* statutes discussed earlier).

Process and Program Changes: The Middle Way

Our survey of enacted state property rights legislation shows an overwhelming preference for assessment laws over compensation

---

[40]16 U.S.C. § 410aaa-80.

[41]Ariz. Rev. Stat. Ann. §§ 41-1311 to 41-1313.

[42]Utah Code Ann. § 63-34-13.

[43]Fla. Stat. Ann. § 70.51. This procedure may be used by the property owner before turning to the courts under other provisions in the statute. Maine has established a mediation program, available whenever a landowner has suffered "significant harm" as a result of government action regulating land use. Me. Rev. Stat. Ann. tit. 5, § 3341.

[44]Oregon Sen. Bill 1156 (1995).

laws.[45] Indeed, many of these assessment laws were enacted as compromises after compensation bills failed to garner the requisite political support. One does not have to search far to find the reasons legislatures favor assessment over compensation—lower costs, less complexity, and less chilling effect on state programs.

But, the property rights champion might say, less justice for the landowner as well. The response to this charge, assuming one agrees that there is a looming government threat to private property, is that assessment approaches need not be used in isolation. Other process approaches deserve debate. In fact, one could well argue from the perspective of 1998 that process approaches have better political prospects than others, legislatures having tired of the compensation debates.

Indeed, 1997 and 1998 in the U.S. Congress are the years of the process bill. Two aproaches are being taken. First, a bill originally drafted by the National Association of Home Builders (H.R. 1534, S. 1204, S. 1256) takes aim at the abstention and ripeness barriers erected by federal courts to avoid reaching the merits of takings-based section 1983 claims brought against local governments. Studies showed that a very high percentage of these takings claims are resolved on those threshold issues.[46] The bill and its later versions propose to bar federal courts from invoking abstention in this litigation unless state law claims were made as well. As to ripeness, the bills address both prongs of the seminal ripeness decision in *Williamson County Regional Planning Comm'n v. Hamilton Bank*. The first prong, the requirement of a final, authoritative decision as to what uses of the subject property are permitted, is reduced to a statutory definition. The thrust of the definition is to limit the number of applications and variance requests required of the landowner, ending the current ambiguity and its potential for judicial abuse. The second prong of *Williamson County*, the demand that the landowner exhaust state forums for obtaining compensation before coming to federal court, would be eliminated entirely.

The battle over the abstention/ripeness bill has been fought so far

---

[45]*See generally* Ellen Perlman, *Property Rights: A Revolt Under Construction*, 9 GOVERNING 28 (Oct. 1995).

[46]*See, e.g.,* Brian W. Blaesser, *Closing the Federal Courthouse Door to Property Owners: The Ripeness and Abstention Doctrines in Section 1983 Land Use Cases*, 2 HOFSTRA PROP. L. J. 73 (1988).

on the field of federalism. Would such a bill, for example, invite the federal courts to become involved prematurely in local land-use matters? Or should the federal courthouse door be as open to Fifth Amendment takings claims as other federal constitutional claims, even when purely local land-use regulation is involved? The House of Representatives passed H.R. 1534 by a comfortable margin in 1997, though not comfortable enough to override the threatened presidential veto.

The second process approach ascendant in 1997–1998 involves takings claims only against the United States. This approach (H.R. 992, S. 1256) seeks to rectify a jurisdictional split in the federal courts, under which takings claims against the United States (for more than $10,000) must be filed in the U.S. Court of Federal Claims, while most other claims against the national government must be filed in the federal district courts. The bills would give each of these courts the jurisdiction it now lacks, allowing the landowner to claim a taking and challenge the validity of the government action in either one.

Elsewhere, we have already noted Arizona's and Utah's ombudsman laws. Additional ideas might be greater availability of administrative appeals of agency actions that restrict property use, greater access to alternative dispute resolution, and an expedited small claims procedure for takings claims up to a certain amount. An alternative dispute resolution approach already in place is that of General Rule No. 13, U.S. Court of Federal Claims (*see* chapter 33). Rule 13 allows use of "settlement judges" (a neutral advisor who informs each party of the strengths and weaknesses of its case) and mini-trials (an expedited procedure in which each party presents an abbreviated version of its case to a neutral advisor, who then assists with settlement negotiations), though it applies only when litigation has been filed and only when both parties consent.

However the compensation versus process-changes debate plays out, there can be little disagreement that legislatures and agencies should weigh the private property impacts of alternative courses of action. For whatever its more extreme proposals, the property rights movement has had the salutary effect of putting private property on the decisionmaker's radar screen. As a result of this government sensitization, and partly, no doubt, for the purpose of undercutting more extreme proposals, congressional moderates and federal agencies with vulnerable programs have done the obvious. They have embarked on a search for how existing programs could be modified so as to lessen their impact on property rights without unduly sacrificing program effectiveness. A case in point is the series of administrative reforms launched by Secretary of the Interior Bruce Babbitt in the Endangered Species Act program—entirely within the four corners of the existing statute (*see* chapter 24).[47]

One can also be sure that in the future when government confers benefits or grants approvals (as for use of public land), it will seek greater use of clauses explicitly disclaiming the creation of any compensable property rights.

At this late date, it seems that the impressive political strength of the property rights groups ensures that they will not be ignored. As said, the question is not if legislatures will find ways to make a bow in their direction, but how. We suggest that accommodation of property rights activists' concerns may be possible without the considerable difficulties, noted earlier, in most of the recently popular compensation approaches. The current waning of legislative interest in mechanistic compensation formulae may be a reflection of this.

---

[47]None of these reforms has been tested in court yet, however.

Conclusion

Consider these recent actions of the Supreme Court in takings cases arising from land-use controls. First, a quadruplet of February 1997 decisions from the New York Court of Appeals, each involving the foundational question of how a land buyer's development expectations are to figure into the takings (or condemnation) analysis, is presented to the Supreme Court for review. It declines to hear all of them.[1] Second, the Court deliberates over a land-based taking case involving ripeness, raising hopes that it would provide guidance in this knotty and inconsistent body of law that has figured in hundreds of lower court rulings. When the decision comes down, it is narrowly drawn and does not even lay down an absolute rule.[2]

Now consider what the Court has done with takings claims *not* involving land. In June 1997, the High Court agreed to hear a takings challenge to a Texas program under which the interest on certain lawyers' client-funds accounts is used by the state to pay for legal services to the poor.[3] In October 1997, the Court accepted a taking case attacking a federal program under which companies that were once

[1]Gazza v. Department of Envtl. Conservation, 89 N.Y.2d 603, 679 N.E.2d 1035, *cert. denied*, 118 S. Ct. 58 (1997); Basile v. Town of Southampton, 89 N.Y.2d 974, 678 N.E.2d 489, *cert. denied*, 118 S. Ct. 264 (1997); Kim v. City of New York, 90 N.Y.2d 1, 681 N.E.2d 312, *cert. denied*, 118 S. Ct. 50 (1997); Anello v. Zoning Bd. of Appeals, 89 N.Y.2d 535, 678 N.E.2d 870, *cert. denied*, 118 S. Ct. 2 (1997).

[2]Suitum v. Tahoe Regional Planning Agency, 117 S. Ct. 1659 (1997).

[3]Phillips v. Washington Legal Found., *cert. granted*, 117 S. Ct. 2535 (June 27, 1997) (U.S. No. 96-1578). On June 15, 1998, the Supreme Court held that the interest in question was the property of the attorneys or their clients, not of the state of Texas. 118 S. Ct. 1925. The case was then remanded for a determination on the taking issue.

parties to coal miner collective bargaining agreements are made liable for miner-retiree health benefits.[4]

Taking a longer view, it turns out that many of the regulatory takings cases decided or agreed to be decided by the Supreme Court since the vaunted 1987 trilogy has little to do with land. Even more surprising are the issues raised in the land-related cases the Court has taken. Not a single Supreme Court case decided or agreed to be decided in this decade-long period deals with the garden-variety land-use situation that developers and zoners routinely confront—a use restriction (absent exaction conditions) that causes a moderate or serious, but not total, loss in land use or value. How, one might well ask, has the Court found the time and will to adjudicate the arcane takings implications of car forfeiture,[5] what to include in a utility's rate base,[6] interest on lawyers' accounts,[7] and amendments to the federal welfare statute,[8] but not these basic, everyday land-use questions?

Recall some of the basic conundrums of regulatory takings law today. First, when is the taking claim ripe? Following its seminal decisions in the mid-1980s, the Court has bestowed but one narrow ruling on the role of transferable development rights in the ripeness determination. Second, how much economic impact is a taking? Today, we have only a rule for the rare situation where a total loss of use or value occurs. Third, what role is to be given the development expectations of the land buyer in light of the law at date of purchase? And the related question: What types of law are included in the *Lucas* concept of "background principles? Supreme Court decisions offer contradictory cues as to which types of law delimit the bundle of sticks, and to what degree. Fourth, what is the "relevant parcel"? The Court tells us that a parcel is not to be segmented just to isolate the regulated portion. But in all but the simplest situations, there are

---

[4]Eastern Enterprises v. Apfel, *cert. granted*, 118 S. Ct. 334 (Oct. 20, 1997) (U.S. No. 97-42). On June 25, 1998, the Supreme Court held this benefits-funding program unconstitutional on a 5 to 4 vote. 118 S. Ct. 2131. The five justices voting for unconstitutionality divided, however, on whether takings or substantive due process was the applicable constitutional provision. The four justices in dissent all favored use of substantive due process.

[5]Bennis v. Michigan, 516 U.S. 442 (1996).

[6]Duquesne Light Co. v. Barasch, 488 U.S. 299 (1989).

[7]*Phillips*, 117 S. Ct. 2535.

[8]Bowen v. Gilliard, 483 U.S. 587 (1987).

other ambiguities about what belongs in the relevant parcel, with little judicial guidance on how to make the cut. Unsatisfying, indeed.

What is the reason for this jurisprudential vacuum in the land-use area? Perhaps it is because until now, the Court has been amply occupied by relatively easy or easily circumscribed takings issues—e.g., permanent physical occupations. The low-hanging fruit, it is said, get eaten first. More likely, however, it is not only the attractiveness of these cases, but active avoidance of the tough ones. The everyday regulatory situation to which we refer—say, a 70 percent loss in value, no complicating factors—implicates maddeningly difficult line-drawing questions. We may never, the Court seems to be hinting by its selection of cases to hear, stray into this trackless territory far from the tightly circumscribed comfort of the total taking, the permanent physical occupation, and the exaction condition on development permits.

But the Court has let the regulatory taking genie out of the bottle, and it cannot now refuse to discipline it.[9] As to ripeness, the Court might give better markers for determining when agency responses to development proposals on a tract have established a "final decision." Presumably, for example, there is no need for the developer to waste time seeking approval of proposals scaled down to the point of non-profitability. Also, after which proposal denials does the landowner need to pursue a variance rather than a reconfigured development scheme? And when does the "futility exception" (noted briefly in a Supreme Court footnote, and now routinely discussed in the lower courts) excuse further dealings with the land-use authority?

As to the required degree of economic impact, is there some threshold above which, absent egregious factors, the probability of a taking is greatly increased? Or below which the probability drops precipitously? Is economic impact to be measured by a multifactor approach, or simply by valuation? Do we focus on remaining value or remaining use?

The landowner expectations factor raises two clusters of issues the Court might usefully clarify. First, where in the analytic framework should the expectations of the land purchaser be inserted? Only in the three-factor *Penn Central* balancing test, or in some "antecedent inquiry" into what property rights the plaintiff acquired at purchase? Does it matter that the landowner claims a physical taking, rather than a regulatory one?

---

[9]We are indebted to Mr. David Coursen, U.S. EPA Office of General Counsel, for suggesting this theme.

Second, which expectations are reasonable to consider? Must development expectations be fully formed and documentable as of the date of acquisition in order to be counted? Is it enough to discount a development expectation that the regulatory program under which the restriction was imposed predates land acquisition? And does the "background principles" notion in *Lucas* include only the common law of nuisance, as its author seemed to suggest, or other sources of law—federal as well as state? Whatever the included sources, need the law be of great vintage, or may it be freshly minted?

Finally, the "parcel as a whole" or "relevant parcel" factor. Is lack of contiguity fatal to a claim that acreage be fused into the relevant parcel? When should a portion of an original parcel that has been sold off prior to the date of taking be included in the relevant parcel? How can the parcel as a whole be defined so as to discourage strategic behavior by landowners (for example, selling off nonwetland acreage before applying for a permit on the wetland portion of a tract)?

In the Court of Federal Claims and the Federal Circuit, where most takings challenges to federal action are adjudicated, other problem areas beg for High Court guidance. There are ubiquitous federal-state issues, such as when state action may be imputed to the United States for purposes of takings liability. (Do states become "agents" of the United States when implementing a federal program, even though acting voluntarily?) And when should prior state-imposed restrictions be factored into a property's "before value" when calculating the impact of federal action? Only when the state action has no federal nexus whatsoever?

Persistent issues arise, too, as to the boundary between breach of contract and takings actions. Are the two theories coextensive owing to the oft-repeated bromide that contract rights are property?

We do not minimize the difficulty the Court faces in making the calls and drawing the lines here. The diversity of circumstances under which government/property owner disputes come up is virtually infinite. The government may assert compelling interests to support its land-use restrictions, or relatively marginal ones. The property owner may bear the burden alone or with the great majority of property owners in the area. The burden may be a total surprise or in line with expectations.

Adding to the daunting task, recent takings decisions in the courts are beginning to highlight the complex nature of property itself. It has long been commonplace to observe that property is an historically fluid construct. Now courts are plumbing the depths of *Lucas'* "background principles" notion, and expectations generally, to establish that property interests are molded as well by the legal and factual circumstances of the particular landowner. To some extent the Court is likely to be a societal sounding board in this definitional enterprise. Competing normative notions of the nature and purpose of property in our market society vie for the justices' sympathies. An economic model? A biocentric, ecological one? Something else again?

Then, too, the Court knows full well that any significant shift it might make (or decline to make) in the line between taking and nontaking is more than interpretation of the Fifth Amendment. It is a statement about the very role of government. Current takings law makes it fairly difficult for the nonphysically invaded property owner to win. That approach embodies one view of government and its ability to achieve public ends without compensation liability. If takings cases are made much easier to win, that will embody a more restrictive conception of the proper bounds on government action. It is blind to say that takings law is concerned only with whether government must pay, not whether it may take the action giving rise to the duty to pay. Government coffers are finite. If an agency must pay, actions of the kind in question will rarely be taken.

This last paragraph points out an added difficulty, as if one were needed. Many key takings decisions of the Supreme Court in 1987 and afterward were decided by close votes, some by five to four. The political philosophies of the justices are plainly a factor in their votes in these cases. Indeed, to some observers the outcome of a Supreme Court taking case devolves to a simple logic. The conservative block (Rehnquist, Scalia, Thomas, and, on the takings issue, O'Connor) will see a taking. The liberal/moderate wing (Breyer, Ginsburg, Stevens, and Souter) will find no taking. Thus, all that matters is how will Justice Kennedy vote?

An ideologically polarized Supreme Court is, of course, not the most promising forum for shining light into the dark recesses of regulatory takings law. Yet that light cannot come from anywhere else. Legislatures have their responsibility, as we have noted. They can and should design more property-sensitive programs, with more escape valves for the occasional hardship case. And other promising legislative approaches are on the horizon: giving an agency a chance to rethink its regulation when a taking occurs, or streamlining the process for asserting takings claims in court. But as we suggested in the chapter on property rights legislation, the search for a mechanically applied, absolute, and universal rule for which government actions should be compensable is likely a futile one. The recent shift in the focus of congressional property rights bills—away from compensation and toward process—attests to this difficulty.

The Supreme Court should shoulder its duty and wade cautiously into the mire. The framework laid out in *Penn Central* two decades ago is a *potentially* workable one for landowner and government regulator alike.

Appendix A

Key Supreme Court Takings Decisions Involving Land Use: The Short Course

Penn Central Transportation Co. v. New York City
438 U.S. 104 (1978)
in which the Supreme Court sets out the now-ubiquitous three-factor balancing test for regulatory takings and signals its renewed interest in the field.

In 1967, the Landmarks Preservation Commission of New York City designated the Grand Central Terminal an historic landmark under that city's landmarks preservation law. The following year, the terminal owners sought permission from the commission to build a 55-story office tower atop the terminal, in keeping with similar properties in the area. Permission was denied.

Held, no taking. Before announcing this holding, however, the Court sought to lend some order to the ad hoc and amorphous takings law existing at the time. Three factors, it said, have particular significance: (1) the economic impact of the regulation on the landowner, (2) the extent to which the regulation interferes with distinct (in later cases, usually "reasonable") investment-backed expectations, and (3) the "character" of the government action. This expansive theorizing was an important signal that the Court's half-century of neglecting land-use-based takings claims had come to an end.

There was no taking here, however. The owner could still earn a reasonable return from Grand Central Terminal without the office tower, and more modest additions to the existing structure might still be approved. The availability of transferable development rights also softened the impact of the proposal rejection. Finally, the Court rejected the owner's effort to focus the taking analysis solely on the infringed air rights over the terminal. Takings law, said the Court, does not divide a parcel into discrete segments.

Agins v. City of Tiburon
447 U.S. 255 (1980)
announcing a new two-part regulatory takings test of uncertain relation to that of *Penn Central*.

The Aginses purchased an unimproved five-acre lot overlooking San Francisco Bay, in the City of Tiburon. Afterward the city, as required by state law, adopted a zoning ordinance under which the Agins' property could be used for between one and five single-family residences. Without seeking approval for development of their tract under the ordinances, the Aginses sued the city alleging a taking.

Held, no facial taking. Before reaching this holding, however, the Court did two things. First, because the owners had not submitted a development plan under the ordinance, the Court found that any as-applied taking claim was unripe. Thus, the only question properly before the Court was the facial claim—whether the mere enactment of the zoning ordinance was a taking.

Second, to resolve the facial claim, the Court laid out a new regulatory takings test, without clarifying its scope of application, or whether it supplemented or replaced the three-factor *Penn Central* test announced only two years earlier. "The application of a general zoning law . . . effects a taking," it said, "if the ordinance does not substantially advance legitimate state interests . . . or denies an owner economically viable use of his land."

In this case, said the Court, the zoning ordinance substantially advances the legitimate governmental goal of preserving open space. Moreover, the Aginses will benefit by the application of the ordinance to others. Nor has denial of economically viable use been shown, since up to five houses may be permitted on the property. Hence, the ordinance effects no taking on its face.

Loretto v. Teleprompter Manhattan CATV Corp.
458 U.S. 419 (1982)
in which the per se rule for permanent physical occupations of land is announced.

Jean Loretto purchased a five-story apartment building on the Upper West Side, New York City, in 1971. Previously, the local cable TV company had installed cable on the building to service other properties. Two years after Loretto's purchase, the company connected a line for Loretto's own tenants. Under a 1973 state statute, however, Loretto was entitled to only one dollar for this installation on her property.

Held, a taking occurred. In the past, said the Court, we have invariably found a taking when government effects a permanent physical occupation of private property—importantly, without regard to whether the occupation achieves an important public benefit or has only minimal economic impact on the owner. The rationale is that such an appropriation is perhaps the most serious form of invasion of an owner's interests. In particular, it interferes with the owner's right to exclude unwanted occupiers, one of the most treasured strands in an owner's bundle of property rights.

Williamson County Regional Planning Commission v. Hamilton Bank
473 U.S. 172 (1985)
wherein the Court lays out the basic two-prong test for when a taking claim in federal court is ripe.

In 1973, a developer submitted a preliminary plat for the cluster development of its tract, Temple Hills Country Club Estates (Tennessee), to the county planning commission. Upon approval, the developer conveyed to the county an open-space easement for a golf course and began building roads and installing utility lines. It spent $3 million building the golf course. In 1980, with a more restrictive zoning ordinance in effect, the commission asked the developer to submit a revised preliminary plat before it sought final approval for the remaining sections of the subdivision. This the developer did, but the commission disapproved it. The developer then appealed to the Zoning Board of Appeals, which determined that the commission should apply the earlier ordinance.

At this point, Hamilton Bank acquired through foreclosure the portion of the subdivision that had not yet been developed. In 1981, the bank submitted two preliminary plats to the commission, which denied them for eight stated reasons, while also asserting that the board lacked jurisdiction to hear appeals from the commission.

Held, the taking claim is not ripe. There are two prongs to the takings ripeness test, announced the Court, neither of which is met here. First, a land-use taking claim under the U.S. Constitution is not ripe until the government entity has reached a final decision regarding the application of the regulations to the property at issue. In particular, the owners of the property here did not seek variances that would have allowed them to develop the property according to the proposed plat. Second, a federal taking claim presented to a federal court must be preceded by landowner efforts to obtain compensation from the state, as through a taking action in the state courts. If a state provides an adequate procedure for obtaining compensation, the property owner cannot claim a violation of the Takings Clause in federal court until it has used the procedure and been denied compensation. No state remedies were pursued in this case.

First English Evangelical Lutheran Church v. County of Los Angeles
482 U.S. 304 (1987)
in which the Court ends the long-standing confusion as to what remedy the Takings Clause requires for a regulatory taking.

In 1957, the church bought a 21-acre parcel along the banks of the Middle Fork of Mill Creek in the Angeles National Forest, California. There, it built Lutherglen, a campground for handicapped children. In 1977, a forest fire denuded the hills upstream from Lutherglen, creating a flood hazard. Such flooding indeed occurred in 1978, destroying the buildings of Lutherglen. In response to the flooding, the County of Los Angeles adopted an "interim ordinance" barring the construction or reconstruction of buildings within an interim flood protection area that included Lutherglen.

Held, the Takings Clause requires the government to pay *monetary compensation* when it effects a temporary regulatory taking; *invalidation* of the regulation is not a sufficient remedy. (The existence of a taking on the facts presented was assumed by the Court solely for purposes of discussion.) Thus, said the Court, when a regulation is found to work a taking, the government's withdrawal of the regulation does not eliminate the compensation requirement, since at that point in time the taking has already occurred (when the regulation took effect). However, withdrawing the regulation does keep a temporary taking from becoming a permanent one, holding down the amount of compensation owed.

The Court clarified that its decision did not deal with the "quite different questions" that arise with normal delays in obtaining building permits, changes in zoning ordinances, variances, and the like.

Nollan v. California Coastal Commission
483 U.S. 825 (1987)
requiring a sufficient nexus between a dedication or exaction condition on a land development permit and the purpose of the permit scheme itself.

The Nollans leased a beachfront lot in Ventura County, California, with an option to buy. On the lot was a small bungalow, which they rented to summer vacationers. After years of rental use, the building fell into disrepair. The Nollans sought to purchase the property and replace the bungalow with a three-bedroom house, in keeping with the neighborhood. To do so, however, they needed a coastal development permit from the California Coastal Commission. The commission granted the permit subject to the condition that the Nollans record a deed restriction granting the public an easement to pass along the beach portion of their property, separated from the buildable portion by an eight-foot seawall. Such easement would allow easy passage by the public between publicly owned beaches a quarter mile above, and a quarter mile below, the Nollans' property.

Held, a taking occurred. Given that requiring the Nollans to convey an easement outright would clearly be a taking, the issue is whether demanding the same thing in the form of a *condition* for issuing a land-use permit alters the outcome. The answer is yes, said the Court—demanding the easement as a permit condition is *not* a taking, but only so long as the condition serves the same legitimate police power purpose as a refusal to issue the permit. Unless this "essential nexus" is present, the building restriction is not a valid regulation of land use but an "out-and-out plan of extortion."

The condition imposed here, concluded the Court, does not meet this test. The stated purpose of the permit scheme is to ensure "visual access" to the beach by people driving past the Nollans' (and other) property on its landward side. The Nollans' new house would interfere with that visual access, arguably lessening the public's desire to use the beach. The condition on the Nollans' permit, however, has nothing to do with this purpose. Rather, it seeks to allow increased beach use by people already on the beach. Thus, no essential nexus between permit purpose and permit condition exists.

Lucas v. South Carolina Coastal Council
505 U.S. 1003 (1992)
wherein the Court lays down a per se rule for regulation that completely eliminates the beneficial use of land—outside of "background principles."

In 1986, David Lucas paid $975,000 for two beachfront lots on the Isle of Palms, a barrier island in South Carolina that he and others had been extensively developing.

Lucas intended to build a single-family home on each lot—one for his own use, one for sale. Two years later, the state enacted a Beachfront Management Act, under which the state coastal council was to establish a baseline connecting the landward-most points of shoreline erosion during the past forty years. Because Lucas' lots were seaward of this baseline, the Act as implemented barred him from building any permanent habitable structures on them. During the pendency of Lucas's state court taking action, however, the state amended the Act (in 1990) to allow the coastal council to issue special permits in certain circumstances for the construction of habitable structures seaward of the baseline.

Held, regulation that *completely* eliminates the economically beneficial use of property is a *per se* taking, unless the regulated-away use is one that could have been barred under "background principles of the State's law of property and nuisance" existing at the time the property was acquired. The *per se* portion of the rule is necessitated by the functional similarity between complete elimination of use and an outright physical appropriation of the property, the latter indisputably a taking. The background-principles exception to the *per se* rule is dictated by the obvious fact that the government cannot be held accountable when it removes a right the property owner never acquired.

The Supreme Court remanded *Lucas* to the South Carolina high court to determine whether background principles of the state's nuisance and property law prohibit the use Lucas desired to make of his lots in the circumstances in which the lots were found. For this purpose, admonished the Court, reliance by the state court on conclusory statutory assertions that such use is not in the public interest is insufficient.

Dolan v. City of Tigard
512 U.S. 374 (1994)
supplementing the 1987 *Nollan* test with a requirement that the dedication/exaction condition impose no more than a proportionate degree of burden on the landowner.

Florence Dolan owned a plumbing and electric supply store on a 1.67-acre parcel in downtown Tigard, Oregon. Desiring to replace the store with one nearly twice as large, and to pave a 39-space parking lot on the site, Mrs. Dolan applied to the city planning commission for a permit. The permit was granted on the condition that she dedicate the portion of her property within the 100-year floodplain for improvement of a storm drainage system along Fanno Creek, and that she keep it open for public recreation. Further, she must dedicate an additional 15-foot strip of land adjacent to the floodplain as a pedestrian/bicycle pathway. The total area subsumed by these dedications was about 10 percent of the property and could be counted toward the 15 percent open-space requirement in the city's zoning scheme.

Held, a taking occurred. The takings test for analyzing dedication/exaction conditions on development permits has two parts, declared the Court. The first was announced in *Nollan v. California Coastal Commission* (above, this appendix): The nature of the permit condition must relate to, must have the same purpose as, the underlying permit. In *Dolan*, the Court added a second part: The degree of burden imposed on the property owner by the permit condition must be "roughly proportional" to the estimated impact of the proposed development on the community. Moreover, the burden of demonstrating rough proportionality is on the government; it is not on the property owner to show absence of same. "No precise mathematical calculation is involved, but the city must make some sort of individualized determination that the required dedication [condition] is related both in nature and extent to the impact of the proposed development."

The city's conditions easily meet the *Nollan* test, the Court held. For example, the pedestrian/bicycle pathway plainly addresses the likely increase in traffic congestion from enlarging Mrs. Dolan's store. But the newly minted *Dolan* test is not satisfied. As to the flood-plain easement, enlarging Mrs. Dolan's store and paving her parking lot, thereby increasing the amount of impervious surface, concededly will increase storm-water flow from her property. And barring development in the floodplain will offset that flooding pressure on Fanno Creek. However, the city has not shown why allowing the public to walk through this greenway is necessary for its flood control purpose. A private greenway seemingly would serve the purpose as well.

As to the pedestrian/bicycle pathway, the Court held that the city had not met its burden of showing that the additional number of vehicle and bicycle trips generated by Dolan's expanded operation are "roughly proportional" to the city's requirement for a dedication of the pathway. Its finding that the pathway "could" offset some of the increased traffic is not enough.

Appendix B

How a Court Might Analyze a Land-Use-Related Takings Claim

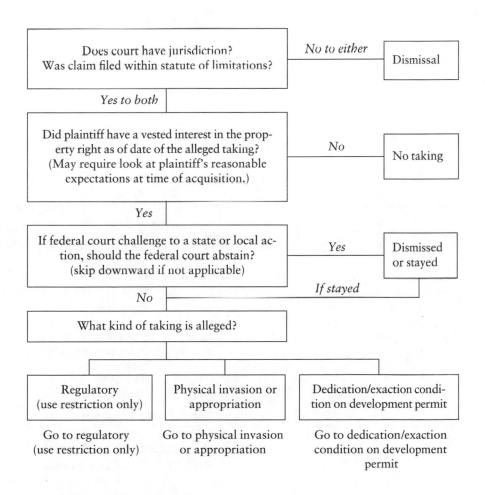

| Does court have jurisdiction? Was claim filed within statute of limitations? | *No to either* | Dismissal |

Yes to both

| Did plaintiff have a vested interest in the property right as of date of the alleged taking? (May require look at plaintiff's reasonable expectations at time of acquisition.) | *No* | No taking |

Yes

| If federal court challenge to a state or local action, should the federal court abstain? (skip downward if not applicable) | *Yes* | Dismissed or stayed |

If stayed

No

What kind of taking is alleged?

| Regulatory (use restriction only) | Physical invasion or appropriation | Dedication/exaction condition on development permit |

| Go to regulatory (use restriction only) | Go to physical invasion or appropriation | Go to dedication/exaction condition on development permit |

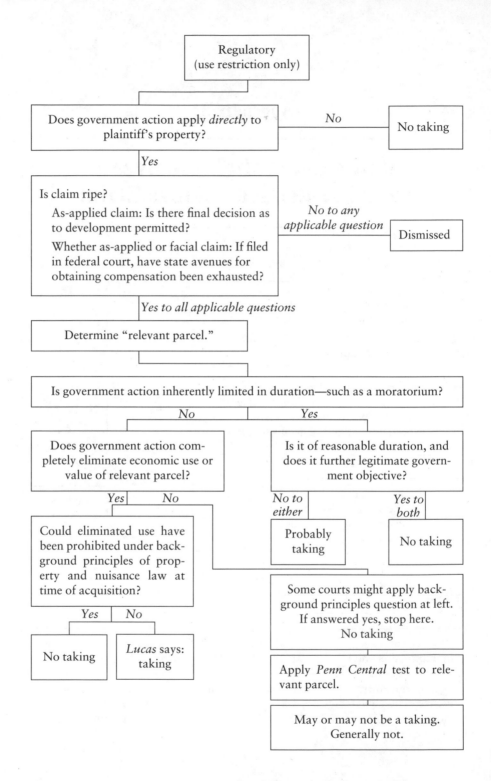

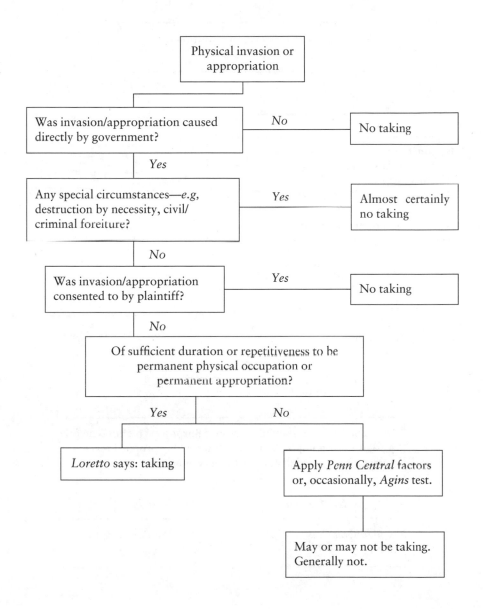

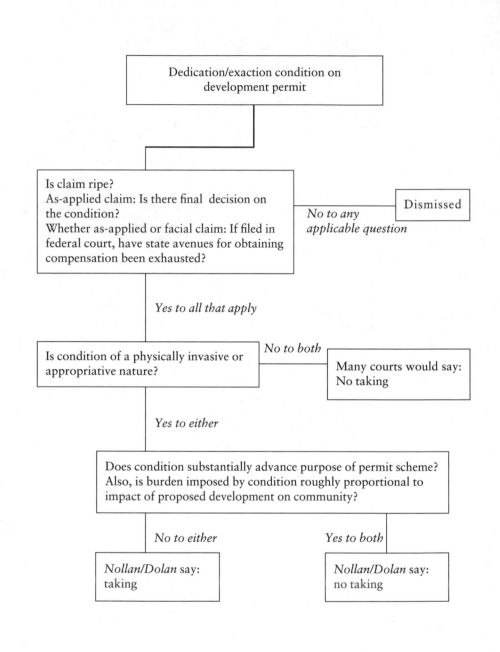

Index

Absolute immunity, 9192
Abstention doctrine, 74–77, 552
Acquisition of private property by
  government:
  by condemnation, *see*
    Condemnation
  direct, *see* Direct acquisition
  regulatory takings, *see* Regulatory
    takings
Acquisitory intent cases, *see*
  Precondemnation activities
Ad hoc approach:
  to determining takings, 8, 9, 104,
    105
  relevant parcel issue, 151–54
Administrative Dispute Resolution
  Act, 534
Aesthetics:
  billboards and, 425
  open space zoning, 226–27
Agins v. City of Tiburon, 111, 217,
  271, 275, 476–77
  open-space protective zoning, 227
  two-part test, 139, 227, 246
  denial of all economically viable
    use, 137, 138, 227, 246
  substantially advances a legitimate

governmental interest, 137–38,
  227, 246, 550
Aircraft operations, 337–47
  altitude of overflights, 343
  Causby v. Griggs, 338–39, 342
  diminution in plaintiff's property
    value, 344–45
  direct overflights prerequisite,
    339–41
  schism between state and federal
    courts, 340–41
  factors for takings, 342–45
  frequency of flights, 344
  fundamental rule for takings, 338
  Griggs v. Allegheny County, 339
  nuisance and, 341, 346
  time considerations, 345–47
  trespass and, 338, 339, 341
  see also Airports, zoning near
Airports, zoning near, 337, 347–55
  height restrictions, 351–53
  noise and, 355
  typical efforts at, 348–50
  use restrictions, 353–55
  see also Aircraft operations
Air rights, *Penn Central* case and,
  319, 320

Alaska court decisions, 237, 238
Albany, New York, historic district
    in, 329–30
Alternative dispute resolution (ADR),
    531–34
American Farmland Trust, 529
American Rule for awarding
    attorneys' fees, 89, 508
Americans with Disabilities Act
    (ADA), 296
Andrus v. Allard, 145–46
Animals, *see* Wildlife
Anti-takings resolutions, 206–207
Apartment building conversions, reg-
    ulations preventing, 308
Appropriative water rights, 458
Arbitration, binding, 533
Archeological sites, state statutes
    governing, 176–77
Arizona, 551, 553
    property rights movement and, 539
Armstrong v. United States, 195
Army Corps of Engineers, *see* U.S.
    Army Corps of Engineers
As-applied claims:
    facial claims versus, 107–16
    confusion in distinguishing,
        113–16
    ripeness of, 62–63, 109
    statute of limitations and, 109
    time of accrual of, 73
Assessment approach to property
    rights, 538, 539, 540–54
Atlas Corporation v. United States,
    448–49
Attorneys' fees, 506–10
    American Rule, 89, 508
    in federal courts, 506–507
    Section 1983 cases, 35, 61, 89, 507
    in state courts, 507–10
Authority issues, 77–80
    authority of agency to act, 77–79
    authority of agency to condemn,
        79–80
Average reciprocity of advantage

principle, 216–17, 219–20
Avigation easements, 342, 351
*Aztec Minerals Corp., et al. v.
    Colorado,* 453

Babbitt, Bruce, 394, 395, 515, 554
*Babbitt v. Sweet Home Chapter of
    Communities for a Greater
    Oregon,* 393
Background principles of *Lucas* deci-
    sion, *see* Exceptions to takings,
    state law-based limits on use
    of private property
Banta, John, xv
Batten v. United States, 339–40
*Bauer v. Waste Management of
    Connecticut, Inc.,* 454
Before-and-after ("developer's") ap-
    proach for valuing temporary
    takings, 495
Beneficial use test, futility exception
    and, 66
Benenson v. United States, 316
Berman v. Parker, 226
*Bernardsville Quarry v. Borough of
    Bernardsville,* 191
Billboard controls, 425–34
    amortization component of,
        433–34
    challenges to, 427–34
    First Amendment, 428
    to local ordinances, 431
    proper plaintiff in, 432
    relevant property issue, 432–33
    history of, 426–27
    renewal of billboard leases, 432
    state statutes, 427, 431
Bill of Rights, 6, 10
    Fifth Amendment:
    Due Process Clause, 13, 15–18
    Takings Clause, *see* Takings Clause
    First Amendment, 428
    Fourteenth Amendment, 88
    due process clause, 13–14, 15
    Fourth Amendment, 13, 18–19

Seventh Amendment, 93–94, 97
Blackstone, William, 25, 50, 250
Block v. Hirsch, 299
Bosselman, Fred, xv
Boulder, Colorado, land acquisition by, 519
Brandeis, Justice Louis, 19, 186
Breach of contract actions, 361, 558
Brennan, Justice William, 23, 86, 130, 247
Breyer, Justice Stephen G., 559
Bright-line rules, *see* Per se rules
Broadform deed, 413–14
Broadview Apartments Company v. Commission for Historical and Architectural Preservation, 322
Broughton Lumber Co. v. United States, 468
Brown v. California, 450, 452
Buegel v. City of Grand Forks, 230
"Bundle of sticks," property interests as, 26–27, 145–46
Burden of proof, 83–86, 551
  Dolan and, 85, 247, 253
  of facial claims, 107
Bureau of Land Management, 418
Burrows v. City of Keene, 509
Bush administration, 365

California:
  attorneys' fees, recovery of, 508–509
  consistency doctrine followed by, 204, 206–207
  Constitution of, 21
  court decisions, 21, 79, 126, 148–49
  aircraft operations, 346
  airport zoning, 353
  billboard controls, 431–32
  emergency exception, 194
  growth management programs, 266
  hazardous waste cleanup, 450

  historic districts, 335
  nuisance exception, 192
  precondemnation activities, 293–94
  public trust doctrine, 170–72
  rent regulations, 299–300, 301
  water rights, 463
  wildlife, 400
  Headwaters Forest, 523–24
  jurisdiction issues, 37, 38
  land acquisition by, 519–20, 522, 524–25
  land conservancies, 528–29
  Natural Communities Conservation Planning Act (NCCPA), 515
  property rights movement and, 539
  remedies for regulatory takings in, 35
California Desert Protection Act, 550–51
California Housing Securities, Inc. v. United States, 30–31
Callies, David, xv
Cannone v. Noey, 237
Capitalization of income approach to fair market value, 490–91
Cardinal Keeler v. Mayor & City Council of Cumberland, 333
Carpenter v. Tahoe Regional Planning Agency, 276–77
Casman v. United States, 41
Causby v. Griggs, 338–39, 342
Central Valley Project Improvement Act, 466–67
CERCLA, *see* Comprehensive Environmental Response, Compensation and Liability Act (CERCLA)
Charitable or religious purposes, landmarks with, 324–27
Christy v. Hodel, 401
Ciampitti v. United States, 151, 382
Cienega Gardens v. United States, 300–301

City National Bank of Miami v. United States, 207–208

City of Bowling Green, Ky. v. Cooksey, 351–52

City of Buffalo v. George Irish Paper Co., 288

City of St. Petersburg v. Bowen, 310, 311

Civil Rights Act of 1871, *see* Section 1983 claims

Clajon Production Corp. v. Petera, 153

Claridge v. New Hampshire Wetlands Bd., 384–85

Clean Water Act, 370
  section 404 for wetland protection, 366–67, 378, 382

Clinton administration, 365, 523
  Reinventing Government initiative, 534

Coastal Barrier Resources Act, 518

Coastal Zone Management Act, 370, 517

Collateral estoppel, 60–61

Colorado:
  hazardous waste site cleanup case in, 453
  property rights movement and, 539

Common law, 215
  custom and public access to shoreline and uplands, 174–75
  nuisance, *see* Nuisances
  Seventh Amendment and right to jury trial, 97

Community Concerned Citizens v. Union Township Board of Zoning Appeals, 229–30

Comparable sales approach to fair market value, 490

Compensable expectancies doctrine, 29–31, 443–44

Compensation remedy:
  basic principles in awarding damages, 485–86
  date of the taking and, 165

fair market value, *see* Fair market value

First English and, 39, 473, 477–78, 483–84, 489, 492–93

state compensation, 63–64, 76
  government-created value, 501–503

interest or "delay compensation," *see* Interest or "delay compensation"

permanent takings:
  of fee interests, 489–91
  of less-than-fee and other interests, 491–92

temporary takings, 489, 492–501
  approaches to measuring damages, 493–501
  before-and-after ("developer's") approach, 495
  equity interest approach, 497–98
  Herrington (probability) method, 498–99
  market rate of return, 496–97
  option value, 496
  rental value of, 494–95
  Section 1983-based damages approach, 500–501
  value of property during period of, 494

Comprehensive Environmental Response, Compensation and Liability Act (CERCLA), 447, 449, 450, 451, 454, 455
  acquisition of contaminated property under, 526

Comprehensive municipal zoning, 5, 16

Comprehensive plan, 199–208
  consistency states, 204–207
  relationship to zoning, 200–204, 221
  Standard State Zoning Enabling Act and, 200–201, 204
  states requiring a, 204

Conceptual severance principle, 148

Conclusions, 555–60
Concrete Pipe & Products of California, Inc. v. Construction Laborers Pension Trust, 146
Condemnation, 3
  authority of agency to condemn, 79–80
  defined, 281
  precondemnation activities, *see* Precondemnation activities
  right to jury trial, 94–95
Conditional use permits, 229–30
Conditional zoning, 359–60
Confederated Tribes of the Colville Reservation v. United States, 179–80
Connecticut court decisions, 334, 368, 454
Conservation easements, 318, 527
Conservation Reserve Program (CRP), 527
Constitution, U.S., 400
  Bill of Rights, *see* Bill of Rights
  Contracts Clause, 357–58
  Full Faith and Credit Clause, 60
  navigational servitude conferred by Commerce Clause of, 179
  Property Clause of, 183
  property protection in, 13–19
Contracts and development agreements, 357–63
Contract zoning, 359–60
Corn v. City of Lauderdale Lakes, 273–75
Corporation of the Presiding Bishop of the Church of Latter-Day Saints v. Hodel, 157–58
Cost approach to fair market value, 490, 491
Costs of litigation, compensation for, 506–10
Council on Environmental Quality, xv
Court of Federal Claims:

aircraft overflight takings cases, 346–47
authority to act rule, 77–78
General Order No. 13, 531–32, 553
interest awarded in, 504–505
jurisdiction, 39, 40–43, 553
relevant parcel issue and, 147
Covenants, 514
Crawford County, Georgia moratorium, 272–73
Criminal acts, fines and forfeitures for, 195
Cumberland, Maryland, 333
Cumulative impacts, problem of, 239
Customer Company v. City of Sacramento, 194

Damages, money, *see* Compensation remedy
Danforth v. United States, 284, 286, 293
Date of the taking, 161–65
  consequences of, 164–65
  determining, 161–64
  interest and, 165, 503
Declaratory judgment, 474, 475, 477
Dedications, 234
  fee-in-lieu of land, 233, 234, 241, 258
  see also Exactions
De facto takings, *see* Precondemnation activities
Delaware, property rights movement and, 539
Delay compensation, *see* Interest or "delay compensation"
Del Monte Dunes v. City of Monterey, 98, 100
Deltona Corp. v. United States, 381, 382, 385
Denominator issue, *see* Relevant parcel issue
Department of Agriculture v. Abbott, 464

Destruction by necessity exception to
    takings, 193–94
Developers:
    dedications, see Dedications
    development agreements, 357–63
    exactions, see Exactions
    property rights statutes and, 537
Development contracts, 357–63
Direct acquisition, 513
Direct land acquisition, 518–28
    history of, 518–19
    of less-than-fee interests, 526–28
Disclosure requirements for mining
    companies, 421–22
Disincentives to prevent
    government/landowner
    conflicts, 513, 515–18
Disposal of property, right to, 27
Dispute resolution, alternative
    (ADR), 531–34
District of Columbia, 332–33
Dodd v. Hood River County, 52–55
Dolan v. City of Tigard, 9, 21, 68,
    160, 247–58, 261, 550
    burden of proof and, 85, 247, 253
    facts and decision in, 247–54
    standard of review under, 9, 21
    unconstitutional conditions
        doctrine, 83, 143–44, 234,
        253, 256–58
Donovan v. City of Deadwood, 335
Downzoning, 222–26
Dreher v. Fuller, 239
Due process:
    clauses in Bill of Rights
        guaranteeing, 13–18
    state constitutions guaranteeing, 23

Easements, 514
    avigation, 342, 351
    compensation for takings of, 491,
        492
    conservation, 318, 527
    open-space, 527
    railroad, 437, 442–43

scenic, 516
Economic impact, 556, 557
    landmarks cases and, 320–23
    Penn Central decision, 132–33
    wetlands cases and, 378–79
Economic incentives to prevent gov-
        ernment/landowner conflicts,
        513, 515–18
Economic uses of property, 132–33
    barring of most profitable use, 133
    elimination of all beneficial use,
        132
    future profits, loss of, 133
Ehrlich v. City of Culver City, 257,
        259–60
Emergency exception to takings,
        193–94
Eminent domain, see Condemnation
Endangered Species Act:
    "federal nexus" provision, 393–94,
        514–15
    federal water projects and, 467
    habitat conservation plans,
        394–95, 396, 534
    "harm" interpreted by the Supreme
        Court, 393
    incidental takes, 394, 396
    land acquisition provision, 525
    proposed amendments to, 516
    protection process, 391–95
    rules allowing FWS agents to take
        members of threatened species,
        400
    "safe harbor" program, 514–15
Endangered species acts:
    federal, see Endangered Species Act
    state, 397
Endangered Species Committee
    ("God Squad"), 395
Endangered species conservation,
        voluntary landowner
        participation in, 514–15
Environmental law:
    federal, see specific statutes, e.g.
        Endangered Species Act

state statutes, 318
Epstein, Richard, 30, 256
Equitable relief, *see* Remedies, equitable relief
Equity interest approach to valuing temporary takings, 497–98
"Essential nexus" of dedication/exaction, 83, 143, 234, 235, 250, 254–55, 259–60, 550
Everglades, 523
Evictions, regulations restricting, 305–307
Exactions, 233, 241–61, 360
    Dolan and, *see Dolan v. City of Tigard*
    Ehrlich decision, 257, 259–60
    "essential nexus" test, 83, 143, 234, 235, 250, 254–55, 259–60, 550
    fee-in-lieu of, *see* Dedications, fee-in-lieu of land
    legal history of, 243–46
    takings analysis, 246
    Nollan and, *see Nollan v. California Coastal Commission*
    "roughly proportionate" test, 83, 143, 234, 250, 251–52, 254–55, 258, 259, 550
    substantive due process cases, 241–46
    unconstitutional conditions doctrine and, 256–58
    see also Dedications
Exceptions to takings, 141, 167–95
    emergency exception, 193–94
    federal law-based limits on use of private property, 168, 179–85
    "federalizing" the *Lucas* property law exception, 183–85
    Indian tribes, 182–83
    navigational servitude, 179–82
    public lands, protection of, 183
    fines and forfeitures, 195
    Lucas and, 141, 167–69, 170,

176–77, 180, 186, 187–89, 379, 403, 556, 558
    federalizing the *Lucas* exemption, 183–85
    "nuisance exception," 141, 168–69, 185–92, 379, 403
    historical background, 185–87
    in lower state and federal courts, 190–92
    Lucas and evolving role of, 187–89
    in post-*Lucas* era, 189–90, 409
    state law-based limits on use of private property, 168, 169–78, 403, 556, 558
    archaeological and historic sites, 176–77
    public access to shorelines and uplands, 173–76
    public access to waterways, 173
    public trust doctrine, 170–72
    Supreme Court warning on, 177–78
Exclusion of others from property, right to, 27, 117–18, 119–21, 150
    landlord takings claims, 296
Executive Order No. 12,630, 538, 541–42, 543
Exhaustion doctrine, moratoria and, 278–79

Facial claims:
    as-applied claims versus:
    confusion in distinguishing, 113–16
    burden of proof of, 107
    "no implementation" definition of, 114–15
    "no specifics" view of, 115, 116
    ripeness of, 62, 108, 112–13
    statute of limitations and, 109
    Supreme Court decisions, 111–13
    time of accrual of, 72
Fair Housing Amendments Act, 296

Fair market value, 486–89
  capitalization and income
    approach to, 490–91
  comparable sales approach to, 490
  cost approach to, 490, 491
  diminution of, 133
Fallini v. United States, 468–69
Farm bureaus, property rights
    statutes and, 537
*Fasano v. Board of County
    Commissioners of Washington
    County,* 220–21
FCC v. Florida Power Corp., 121–22
Federal Aid Highway Act, 426
Federal Aviation Administration,
    353, 355
Federal Circuit courts:
  jurisdiction of, 43, 553
  relevant parcel issue and, 147–48,
    151, 152–53
  see also specific takings issues
Federal Coal Leasing Amendments
    Act, 417
Federal courts:
  abstention doctrine and, 74–77,
    552
  circuit courts, *see* Federal Circuit
    courts
  Court of Federal Claims, *see* Court
    of Federal Claims
  district courts, *see* Federal district
    courts
  jurisdiction, *see* Jurisdiction,
    federal courts
  relevant parcel issue and, 147–48,
    151, 152–53
  see also specific takings issues
Federal district courts:
  jurisdiction of, 38–40, 41, 553
  see also specific takings issues
Federal Highway Beautification Act,
    426–47, 433
Federal reclamation law reform,
    466–67
Federal reserved water rights

  doctrine, 467–68
Federal Rules of Civil Procedure,
    right to jury trial and, 94–95
Fee simple absolute, 437, 441
Fee-simple determinable, 437, 442
Ferae naturae doctrine, 399–401,
    402
*Figarsky v. Historic District
    Commission,* 334
Fines, criminal, 195
*First English Evangelical Lutheran
    Church v. County of Los
    Angeles,* 9, 39, 228, 271
  compensation remedy and, 39,
    473, 477–78, 483–84, 489,
    492–93
  state compensation, 63–64, 76
  nuisance exception and, 190–91
  temporary takings, 141–42,
    266–67
Floodplain zoning, 227–29, 261
  nuisance exception applied to,
    190–91
Florida:
  consistency doctrine followed by,
    204
  court decisions, 126, 267–68, 310,
    311, 345, 397
  dispute resolution in, 551
  ripeness statute, 68
*Florida Game & Fresh Water Fish
    Comm'n v. Flotilla, Inc.,* 397
*Florida Rock Industries, Inc. v.
    United States,* 152, 153, 369,
    371–72, 378–79, 385
Footnotes, how to read legal, xix–x
Forest Properties v. United States,
    382–83
Forfeiture of property used in
    commission of crimes, 195
*Franco-American Charolaise, Ltd. v.
    Oklahoma Water Resources
    Board,* 464
Frankfurter, Justice Felix, 7
Fulcher v. United States, 97

Futility doctrine, 46, 57, 66–67, 374, 557

Future condemnation, *see* Precondemnation activities

Future real property interests, 437

General Mining Law of 1972, 416

General Order No. 13 of U.S. Court of Federal Claims, 531–32, 553

Gin S. Chow v. City of Santa Barbara, 463

Ginsburg, Justice Ruth Bader, 250, 559

G.M. Engineers & Assocs., Inc. v. West Bloomfield Township, 362

Goldblatt v. Town of Hempstead, 82, 245

Golden Valley Lutheran College v. City of Golden Valley, 269

Gold vs. Grain (Kelley), 192

Good v. United States, 396

Griggs v. Allegheny County, 339

Growth management programs, 263–80
  conclusions, 279–80
  definition of growth management, 264–66
  diminishing of property values under, 266
  moratoria, *see* Moratoria
  police power and, 265
  purposes of, 264, 265

Gunter v. Geary, 192

Habitat conservation plans, 394–95, 396, 534

Hadacheck v. Sebastian, 347

Hage v. United States, 468, 469

Hagman, Donald, 160

Hall v. City of Santa Barbara, 302

Harlan, Justice, 185

Harlow v. Fitzgerald, 92

Harris v. City of Wichita, 349–50

Hawaii court decisions, 155, 174–76, 464–65

Hazardous wastes and contaminated site cleanup, 447–55
  "brownfield" initiatives, 448
  CERCLA and its state equivalents, 447
  compelled government access to private property for cleanup, 449–52
  conclusion, 455
  extreme cases, 452–53
  fair market value, effect on, 454–55
  municipal landfills, 453–54
  private landowner/operator responsibility for remediation, 448–52

Headley v. Rochester, 211

Headwaters Forest, 523–24

Height restrictions in zoning near airports, 351–53

Hendler v. United States, 125, 451–52

Herrington probability method of valuing temporary takings, 498–99

Herrington v. City of Pearl, 278

Herrington v. County of Sonoma, 498–99

Historic districts, *see* Historic preservation, historic districts

Historic preservation, 313–36
  historic districts, 328–36
    certificate of appropriateness for exterior building changes, 328
    common scenario for taking actions, 329–30
    the first, 329
    maintenance costs, 330–31
    as overlay districts, 328
    state enabling laws, 328
  landmark designation, 313–28
    charitable or religious purposes, landmarks with, 324–27

Historic preservation—*cont.*
  federal involvement in, 315
  history of, 315–18
  interiors of buildings, 327–28
  local statutes, 313–14, 316–18
  Penn Central case and, 314, 317
  state courts and takings claims for,
    314–15
History of takings law, 4–11, 15, 35
  regulatory takings, 15, 104–105,
    129–30, 405
Hodel v. Virginia Surface Mining &
  Reclamation Ass'n, 112
Holmes, Justice Oliver Wendell, 104,
  159, 186, 461
Housing, low- and moderate-income
  rental, 300–301
Housing preservation regulations,
  309–10
Houston, Texas, 216
Hudson County Water Co. v.
  McCarter, 461
Hughes v. Washington, 155
Hunting restrictions, state, 398, 399
Hunziker v. Iowa, 176–77

Idaho court decisions, 353–54
Illinois, 420
Illinois Central Railroad v. Illinois,
  170
Immunity issues:
  Section 1983 claims, 91–92
Incentives to prevent
  government/landowner
  conflicts, 513, 515–18
Inconsistencies in takings law, 8, 105,
  138–39
  relevant parcel issue, 148, 152–53
Indian land claims, 28
  limitations on, 182–83
Indian Land Consolidation Act,
  479–80
Injunction, 474, 475, 479
In re Condemnation by the Delaware
  River Port Authority, 430–31

Interest (delay compensation), 489,
  503–505
  Court of Federal Claims and,
    504–505
  in state courts, 505–506
Interest or "delay compensation":
  date of the taking and, 165, 503
Interiors of buildings, landmark
  preservation of, 327–28
International College of Surgeons
  (ICS), 331–32
Interstate Commerce Commission
  (ICC), 438–41, 445
Invalidation remedy, 35, 39–40, 41,
  473–81
  definitions, 474–75
  after *First English,* 477–80
  prior to *First English,* 476–77
Inverse condemnation actions, *see*
  Taking actions
Investment-backed expectations, dis-
  tinct, 133–35, 384, 385, 430,
  556, 557–58

Johnson, "Lady Bird," 426
Joint Ventures, Inc. v. Department of
  Transportation, 267–68
Judicial takings, 154–59
  Hughes v. Washington, 155
  problems with theory of, 18–59
Jurisdiction, 35–43
  effect of section 1983, 35–36, 90
  federal courts, 35–36, 38–43
  Court of Federal Claims, 39,
    40–43, 553
  district courts, 38–40, 41, 553
  Federal Circuit, 43, 503
  First English and, 39
  property rights bills aimed at, 553
  state courts, 35, 36–38
Jury trial, right to, 93–100
  in direct condemnation actions,
    94–95
  limited case law, 93
  in regulatory takings cases, 95–100

in state courts, 99–100

suits against federal government in federal courts, 96–97

suits against state and local governments in federal courts, 97–99

Seventh Amendment to the Constitution, 93, 97

Just v. Marinette County, 191–92, 228, 368, 376–77

Kaiser Aetna v. United States, 180–81

K & K Construction Co. v. Department of Natural Resources, 383

Kanner, Gideon, 51, 293

Kawaoka v. City of Arroyo Grande, 270

Kelley, Robert, 192

Kelly v. Tahoe Regional Planning Agency, 275–76

Kennedy, Justice Anthony M., 184–85, 189, 250

Kentucky court decisions, 413–14

Keystone Bituminous Coal Ass'n v. DeBenedictis, 112, 132, 207, 408–11, 412

nuisance exception and, 186–87, 189, 409

"parcel as a whole" issue and, 409–10, 411

Keystone Center, 515

Kinzli v. City of Santa Cruz, 66

KLK, Inc. v. U.S. Department of Interior, 96

Klopping v. City of Whittier, 293–94

Kohler Act, 411–12

Lake Country Estates, Inc. v. Tahoe Regional Planning Agency, 524

Lake Shore Drive, Chicago, historic district of, 331–32

Lake Tahoe Acquisitions Bond Act, 522

Lake Tahoe Basin land acquisition program, 519–23, 524–25

Land acquisition, *see* Direct land acquisition

Landfills, municipal, 453–54

Landgate, Inc. v. California Coastal Commission, 79

Landlords and tenants, 295–311

apartment building conversions, regulations preventing, 308

conclusion, 311

evictions, regulations restricting, 305–307

housing preservation regulations, 309–10

illegal drug sales by third parties, 310

relationship between, 295–96

relocation assistance regulations, 307–308

rent regulations:

defined, 297–98

illustrative court decisions, 298–301

mobile-home parks and, 301–305

Penn Central multifactor analysis applied to, 298

reduction of regulated rent, 299–300

tenant-protection statutes, 296

tenant takings claims, 310–11

Landmark designation, *see* Historic preservation, landmark designation

"Landowners' Bill of Rights," 206–207

Land trusts, 516, 528–29

Land-use planning, *see* Planning

Land-use programs, 199–311

exactions, *see* Exactions

growth management, *see* Growth management programs

landlords and tenants, effect on, *see* Landlords and tenants

moratoria, *see* Moratoria

Land-use programs—*cont.*
planning, *see* Planning
precondemnation activities, *see* Precondemnation activities
subdivision, *see* Subdivision controls
zoning, *see* Zoning
Lawson v. Washington, 442–43
Leasehold interests, 414
Legal footnotes, how to read, xix–x
Legislative deference doctrine, 235
Life-estate remainder interests, 516
Lincoln, Abraham, 519
Lockary v. Kayfetz, 470
Locke, John, 10, 25
Long Beach Equities, Inc. v. Superior Court of Ventura County, 266
Long Cove Club Association v. Town of Hilton Head, South Carolina, 224
Loretto v. Teleprompter Manhattan CATV Corp., 119–21, 125, 296
Loveladies Harbor, Inc. v. United States, 151, 370–72, 381–82
Low- and moderate-income rental housing, 300–301
Lucas v. South Carolina Coastal Council, 9, 29, 30, 146, 226, 269, 377, 384
"background principles," *see* Exceptions to takings, state law-based limits on use of private property
burden of proof and, 85–86, 371
exceptions to takings, 141, 167–69, 170, 176–77, 180, 186, 187–89, 379, 403, 556, 558
federalizing of, 183–85
total takings, 140–41, 168–69, 187–88, 375, 433
wildlife protection and, 402–403
Lutheran Church in America v. City of New York, 325

McBryde Sugar Co. v. Robinson, 155, 156, 464–65
McDougal v. County of Imperial, 465
McShane v. the City of Faribault, 354
Madera Irrigation Dist. v. Hancock, 466
Madison, James, 25–26
Maine, 543
Maintenance and repair costs:
historic districts, 330–31
landmark designation and, 321–22
Mandelker, Daniel R., 257
M & J Coal Co. v. United States, 30, 183–85, 412
Manocherian v. Lenox Hill Hospital, 305–306
Maps of reservation, *see* Official map
Marketability test, futility exception and, 66
Market rate of return approach for valuing temporary takings, 496–97
Marshall v. Board of County Commissioners for Johnson County, Wyoming, 236
Maryland:
court decisions, 269
Massachusetts court decisions, 333–34, 368, 450
Michigan court decisions, 368
Mid Gulf, Inc. v. Bishop, 98, 273
Migratory Bird Treaty Act, 396, 401, 526
Miller v. City of Beaver Falls, 292
Miller v. Schoene, 193
Mineral estate, 407–408, 411
broadform deed, 413–14
Mineral rights:
compensation for takings of, 492
Mining, 405–23
broadform deed, 413–14
broad spectrum of mining takings cases, 405–407
conclusion, 422–23

disclosure requirements, 421–22
elimination of all economically
viable uses, 407
existing operation, additional regulation of, 416–19
on government land, 414–16
nuisance determination, 408–409
ownership of less than fee-simple
interest, 407–408
strip mining, 413–14
subsidence, 411–13
"valid existing rights" (VERs),
419–20
Minnesota court decisions, 127, 237,
268–69, 345, 354
Misczynski, Dean, 160
Mississippi court decisions, 278
Mobile-home parks, rent regulation
and, 301–305
physical invasion argument,
302–303
Yee v. City of Escondido, 303–304
Moerman v. State, 400
Money damages, see Compensation
remedy
Monroe County, Florida, 348
Montana court decisions, 239
Moratoria, 266–80
conclusions, 279–80
defensible, 272–78
uses available during and after,
275–78
defined, 266
duration of, 268–71
exhaustion doctrine and, 278–79
monetary damages, 279
"planning pause" cases, 272–73
precondemnation, 267–67
as temporary takings, 142–43,
266–67, 275–78
vested rights and, 267
Morris County Land Improvement
Co. v. Township of
Parsippany-Troy Hills, 368
Mugler v. Kansas, 185

Municipal Mapped Streets Act,
209–10

Naegele Outdoor Advertising, Inc. v.
City of Durham, 310–11, 428,
430
Nantucket, Massachusetts, 523
Nassr v. Commonwealth of
Massachusetts, 450, 452
National Advertising Co. v. Village of
Downers Grove, 430
National Association of Home
Builders, 552
National Audubon Society v.
Superior Court, 171–72
National Flood Insurance Program,
517
National Trails System Act (NTSA),
438–40
National Wildlife Federation v. ICC,
445
Natural Communities Conservation
Planning Act (NCCPA),
California, 515
Natural resources, state protection
under public trust doctrine of,
170–72
Nature Conservancy, 529
Navigational servitude, federal,
179–82, 379
Negotiated Rulemaking Act, 533–34
Nevada:
court decisions, 275–76, 368
land acquisition by, 520, 522
New Hampshire court decisions,
368, 509
New Jersey:
court decisions, 127, 191, 291
measurement of temporary takings
damages in, 496
wetland statute, 374
New Mexico court decisions, 270–
71
New Port Largo, Inc. v. Monroe
County, 97–98

New York City, New York:
  landmarks ordinance, 313–14,
    327
  Rent Stabilization Association,
    299
New York State:
  court decisions, 31, 148, 272,
    278–79
  evictions restrictions, 305–306
  historic districts, 330
  precondemnation activities, 288
  jurisdiction issues, 37
  land trusts, 529
  moratoria cases, 269–70, 272,
    278–79
  remedies for regulatory takings in,
    35
900 G. Street Ass'n v. Department
  of Housing and Community
  Development, 323–24
Noise and zoning near airports, 355
Nollan/Dolan and unconstitutional
  conditions doctrine, see
  Unconstitutional conditions
  doctrine
Nollan v. California Coastal
  Commission, 9, 122–24, 247,
  550
  standard of review under, 83
  "substantially advances" criterion,
    137–38, 250, 254, 550
  unconstitutional conditions
    doctrine, 143–44, 234,
    256–58
North Dakota court decisions, 230
Norwich, Connecticut, 334
Nuisances, 7, 377
  aircraft operations, 338–39, 341,
    346
  exceptions to takings for, see
    Exceptions to takings,
    "nuisance exception"
  "judicial zoning" and, 213–14
  mining as, 408–409

O'Connor, Justice Sandra Day, 178,
  250, 439, 440, 445, 559
Offen v. County Council for Prince
  George's County, Maryland,
  269–70
Official map, 208–13
Ohio court decisions, 230
Oklahoma court decisions, 464
Open space:
  easements, 27
  zoning for, 226–27
Option value approach for valuing
  temporary takings, 496
Oregon, 551
  court decisions, 174, 178, 220–21
  land acquisition program, 519
  Land Use Board of Appeals
    (LUBA), 37, 53, 59
Outdoor Systems, Inc. v. City of
  Mesa, 428–29
Outer Continental Shelf Lands Act,
  417
Overflight, see Aircraft operations

Palm Beach v. Wright, 212
Partial takings, 138, 375
  Penn Central test for, see Penn
    Central Transportation Co. v.
    New York City, three-factored
    test
Partners for Wildlife, 515
Patrick Media Group, Inc. v.
  California Coastal
  Commission, 431–32
Peacock v. County of Sacramento,
  353
Peduto v. City of North Wildwood,
  61
Penn Central Corp. v. United States,
  454–55
Penn Central Transportation Co. v.
  New York City, 7–8, 130–36,
  186, 245, 318–24, 325, 327
  landmarks designation and, 314,
    317, 320–24

relevant parcel issue, 145, 256
three-factored test, 138–39, 298,
    304, 315, 375, 433, 560
character of governmental action,
    135–36
distinct investment-backed expecta-
    tions, 133–35, 323–24, 384,
    385
economic impact of the regulation,
    132–33, 320–23
transferable development rights
    and, 320, 323
Pennell v. City of San Jose, 114
Pennridge Development Enterprises v.
    Volovnik, 230
Pennsylvania Coal Co. v. Mahon, 15,
    35, 159, 186, 405, 409, 412,
    476
Pennsylvania court decisions, 126–27,
    230, 292
People v. Gold Run Ditch & Mining
    Co., 192
Permanent takings, 489
    compensation remedy for, see
        Compensation remedy, perma-
        nent takings
    physical takings, 124–26, 444
Permits, conditional use, 229–30
Per se rules, 9
    for determining takings, 105
    physical takings, 117
    total takings, 140–41
Persyn v. United States, 354–55
Peterson v. U.S. Department of the
    Interior, 466
Physical improvements, requirements
    for, see Exactions
Physical takings, 117–28, 557
    conclusions, 128
    date of, determining, 163–64
    duration and extent of, 124–26
    examples of, 118
    by exercise of police power, 126–28
    government cleanup of hazardous
        waste sites as, 451–52

gray-area cases, 121–24
landmark case, 119–21
permanent, 124–26, 444
per se, 117, 118, 125, 444
rent regulation of mobile-home
    parks, 302–303
right to exclude and, 119–21
Pinewood Estates of Michigan v.
    Barnegat Township, 302
Plager, Judge Jay, 43
Planning, 199–213
    comprehensive plan, see
        Comprehensive plan
    official map, see Official map
    as precondemnation activity,
        291–92
    purpose of, 200
    zoning distinguished from, 200
Plat maps, 231–32
    as precondemnation activity,
        291–92
Police power, 16, 186, 193
    conditional permits and, rights
        under, 230
    contracts and, 358
    growth management programs as
        exercise of, 265
    historic district creation under, 334
    land-use regulations based on,
        214–15
    physical takings and, 126–28
    subdivision controls under the,
        233
    zoning under the, 214–15, 216, 217
Pollution control:
    CERCLA, see Comprehensive
        Environmental Response,
        Compensation and Liability Act
        (CERCLA)
    government land acquisition for,
        526
    market-based incentives for, 517
Possession of property, right of,
    27
Possibility of reverter, 437

Precondemnation activities:
abandonment of eminent domain
proceedings, 291
conclusions, 294
continuous versus mere threat of
condemnation, 286–88
delay in government action,
288–91, 294
economic effects of threat of
condemnation, 281–82
fact patterns of, 282–85
Klopping case, 293–94
mapping, planning, or platting,
291–92
moratoria as, 267–68
unreasonable government conduct,
285–86
value change and, 291
zoning and, 225
Prentiss v. City of South Pasadena,
335
Preseault v. ICC, 439–41, 442, 445,
446
Preseault v. United States, 31
Progressive Policy Institute, 517
Property and property interests,
558–59
as "bundle of sticks," 26–27,
145–46
compensable expectancies as,
29–31
defined, 25–26
relevant parcel issue, *see* Relevant
parcel issue
sources of, 27–29
Property rights movement, xv,
535–54
Property rights statutes, 535–54, 560
assessment approach, 538, 539,
540–43, 551–52
compensation/regulatory relief approach, 543–49, 551–52
arguments against, 545–47
arguments favoring, 544–45
enactments, 547–49
history of, 537–40

opponents of, 537
origins of, 535–36
other approaches to, 550–51
process approaches, 552–53
proponents of, 536–37
Public lands, federal restrictions on
private property to protect,
183
*Public Access Shoreline Hawaii v.
Hawaii County Planning
Commission ("PASH"),*
174–76
Public trust doctrine, 170–72,
376–77, 379
preventing harm to wildlife and,
403–404
water as resource and, 461–62

Qualified immunity, 92

Rails to trails, 435–46
abandonment issue, 438–40, 443,
444–45
conclusion, 446
determining a taking, 444–45
liability for a taking, 445
National Trails System Act
(NTSA), 438–39, 444
Preseault v. ICC, 439–41, 442,
445, 446
railroad's property interest:
determining, 441–44
understanding, 437
takings scenario, 435–37
Randolph, Patrick A., Jr., 258
Raskiewicz v. Town of New Boston,
89
Rate of return, reasonable, 132
Reagan, Ronald, 420
Executive Order No. 12,630, 538,
541–42, 543
Reagan administration, 518
property rights movement and, 538
Reciprocity of advantage principle,
159
Reclamation law reform, federal,

466–67
Redwood Park Expansion Act, 358
Regulatory "givings," 159–60
 calculation of damages and,
  501–503
Regulatory takings, 129–60
 avoiding, methods for, see Direct
  acquisition; Incentives to prevent government/landowner
  conflict; Voluntary initiatives
 criteria for:
 Agins, see Agins v. City of Tiburon
 Penn Central, see Penn Central
  Transportation Co. v. New
  York City, three-factored test
 uncertainty in, 138–39
 date of, see Date of the taking
 exceptions to takings, see
  Exceptions to takings
 history of takings law, 15,
  104–105, 129–30, 215, 405
 origin of concept of, 5, 15, 215,
  405
 partial takings, see Partial takings
 relevant parcel issue, see Relevant
  parcel issue
 takings actions, see Takings actions
 temporary, see Temporary takings
 total takings, see Total takings
 unconstitutional conditions
  doctrine, 143–44, 234, 253
Rehnquist, Justice William H., 187,
  250, 251, 313, 559
Reinventing Government initiative,
  534
Relevant parcel issue, 144–54, 556,
  558
 ad hoc approach versus objective
  criteria, 151–54
 billboards and, 432–33
 complexity of, 144–45
 downzoning and, 225–26
 key issues in relevant parcel
  inquiry, 149–51
 lower federal and state court treat-

ment of, 147–49, 151, 152–53
 in mining takings cases, 409–10,
  411
 Supreme Court decisions, 145–47,
  256
 wetlands and, 381–84
Religious or charitable purpose, landmarks with, 324–27
Relocation assistance regulations,
  307–308
Remedies, 473–510
 comparison of substantive due
  process and takings actions,
  18
 compensation, see Compensation
  remedy
 equitable relief, 473–81
 absent a forum to hear a compensation claim, 479, 481
 conclusion, 481
 declaratory judgment, 474, 475,
  477
 after *First English,* 477–80
 injunction, 474, 475, 479
 invalidation, see Invalidation
  remedy
 prior to *First English,* 35, 476–77
 writ of mandamus, 474, 477
 invalidation, see Invalidation
  remedy
 prior to *First English,* 35, 476–
  77
 "shotgun" pleadings, 475, 480
Rental value method for valuing temporary takings, 494–95
Rent regulations, see Landlords and
  tenants, rent regulations
Rent stabilization, 297
Rent Stabilization Ass'n v. Dinkins,
  299
Rent Stabilization Association of
  New York City (RSA), 299
Repairs, see Maintenance and repair
  costs
Res judicata, 60

Resolution Trust Corporation v. Diamond, 306–307

Reversionary property interests, rails to trails and, 437, 438, 439, 444, 445

Reynolds v. Georgia, 157

Rezoning, *see* Zoning, rezoning

Rhode Island:
land trusts, 529
property rights movement and, 539–40

Right of first refusal, 528

Right-of-way interests, railroad's, 437, 441–44

Riparian water rights, 458, 463–64

Ripeness, 22, 45–68, 556, 557
abstention and, 76–77
administrative remedies, exhaustion of, 64–65
as-applied claims, 62–63, 109
claim preclusion, 59–60
claim-splitting, 54–55
comparison of substantive due process and takings, 18
compensation requirement, 46, 51, 54
state compensation, 63–64
conclusions, 67–68
development of rule for land-use cases, 49–52
Dodd case, *see Dodd v. Hood River County*
facial claims, 62, 108, 112–13
final-decision requirement, 46, 51
exhaustion of administrative remedies, 64–65
hypothetical case, 46–48
futility doctrine, 46, 57, 66–67, 374, 557
issue preclusion, 59–61
policy implications of, 48–49
property rights bills aimed at, 552–53
"state compensation" prong, 63–64
Suitum case, 55–59

timing, importance of, 65–66
of wetlands claims, 372–74
Williamson case, *see Williamson County Regional Planning Commission v. Hamilton Bank*

River Oaks Marine, Inc. v. Town of Grand Island, 279

Roberts, Thomas E., 61

Robinson v. Ariyoshi, 155–56

"Roughly proportionate" test for dedication/exaction, 83, 143, 234, 250, 251–52, 254–55, 258, 259, 550
impact fees and, 258, 260

Ruckelshaus v. Monsanto Co., 134–35, 421

St. Bartholomew's Church v. City of New York, 325, 326

San Diego Gas & Electric Co. v. City of San Diego, 477

Santa Fe Village Venture v. City of Albuquerque, 270–71

Santini-Burton Act, 520–22

Scalia, Justice Antonin, 30, 114, 141, 146, 178, 185, 187–88, 226, 250, 559

Scenic easements, 516

Schulz v. Lake George Park Commission, 272

Seawall Associates v. City of New York, 148

Section 1500, Title 28 of United States Code, 41–43

Section 1983 claims, 53, 61, 87–92, 361, 480
attorneys' fees, recovery of, 35, 61, 89, 507
elements of, 87–88
elimination of exhaustion of administrative remedies requirement, 35
expansion of government liability under, 88–89
government defenses under, 91
immunity issues, 91–92

jurisdictional issues, 35–36, 39, 90
language of the statute, 87
limited to claims against state and
    local governments, 89
measurement of damages for,
    500–501
obstacles for property owners, 91
*Smith v. Zoning Board of Appeals of
    Town of Greenwich,* 239
"Sodbuster" programs for
    agricultural lands, 517
Souter, Justice David H., 57, 85, 189,
    250, 252, 559
South Dakota court decisions, 22,
    335
*Southview Associates, Ltd. v.
    Bongartz,* 51–52
Standard City Planning Enabling Act,
    201, 204, 209
Standard of review, 81–83
Standard State Zoning Enabling Act
    (SSZEA), 200–201, 215, 263
State constitutions, 539–40
    property protection in, 19–23
    takings clauses in, 3, 20–22
    water rights under, 460, 461, 463
State courts:
    interest awarded in, 505–506
    judicial takings and, 158
    jurisdiction, 35, 36–38
    relevant parcel issue and, 148–49
    *see also individual states and tak-
        ings issues*
State law:
    limits to takings based on, *see*
        Exceptions to takings, state
        law-based limits on use of pri-
        vate property
    as source of property interests,
        27–28
    *see also individual states and tak-
        ings issues*
*State v. Lake Lawrence Pub. Lands
    Protection Ass'n,* 397
Statutes of limitations, 69–74
    accrual of claim, 72–73

aircraft overflight takings cases,
    346
applicable limitations period,
    70–72
for as-applied claims, 109
date of the taking and, 165
for facial claims, 109
purpose of, 70
tolling of, 73–74
*Sterling v. Santa Monica Rent
    Control Board,* 299–300
Stevens, Justice John Paul, 8, 85,
    160, 187, 189, 250, 252, 253,
    559
Stevens v. Cannon Beach, 174, 178
Stewart, Justice Potter, 155
Subdivision controls, 230–40
    court standards for review of,
        234–35
    cumulative impacts, 239
    dedications and, *see* Dedications
    denial of all economically
        beneficial use of property,
        236–37
    due process limitations, 233, 235
    exactions and, *see* Exactions
    history of, 231–32
    imposing of local conditions absent
        state or local regulations, 238
    police power and, 233
    purposes of, 231
    reasonableness of, 233, 235
    review of plat by public
        authorities, 232–33, 234
    state and local statutes governing,
        231
    state enabling statutes and, 233
    temporary takings, 238
Subsidence, mining and, 411–13
*Suitum v. Tahoe Regional Planning
    Agency,* 55058
Summitville Mine, Colorado, 453
Superfund, *see* Comprehensive
    Environmental Response,
    Compensation and Liability
    Act (CERCLA)

Supreme Court, U.S., xv
  choice of takings cases, 555–57
  political philosophies of justices of,
    559
  state law-based limits on private
    property rights and, 177–78
  takings decisions, *see names of in-
    dividual cases*
  unresolved takings issues and,
    555–60
Surface estate, 411–12
  broadform deed, 413–14
Surface Mining Control and
  Reclamation Act (SMCRA),
  183–84, 419
Surface Transportation Board (STB),
  438–40, 444–45
"Swampbuster" programs for
  agricultural lands, 367,
  517–18
Symms, Steve, 538, 539

Tabb Lakes, Inc. v. United States,
  380
Tabb Lakes, Ltd. v. United States,
  151
Tahoe Regional Planning Agency
  (TRPA), 271, 275–77, 431
*Tahoe Regional Planning Agency v.
  King,* 431
Taking actions:
  abstention doctrine and, 74–77
  authority issues and, *see* Authority
    issues
  burden of proof, *see* Burden of
    proof
  comparison to substantive due
    process actions, 17–18
  date of the taking, 161–65
  consequences of, 164–65
  determining, 161–64
  determining a taking, *see* Takings,
    determining
  determining compensation in, *see*
    Compensation remedy

difficulty of winning, 559
history of takings law, *see* History
  of takings law
jurisdiction issues, *see* Jurisdiction
jury trial, right to, *see* Jury trial,
  right to
overview of, 3–4
remedies, *see* Remedies
ripeness of, *see* Ripeness
under Section 1983, *see* Section
  1983 claims
standard of review, 81–83
statutes of limitations, *see* Statutes
  of limitations
Taking impact assessment (TIA), 521,
  528
Taking Issue, The (Bosselman,
  Callies, and Banta), xv
Takings, determining, 4, 103–65
  ad hoc approach to, 104, 105
  overview, 103–105
  per se rules for, *see* Per se rules
  physical takings, *see* Physical tak-
    ings
  regulatory takings, *see* Regulatory
    takings
Takings Clause, xv, 3, 13, 14–15
  analysis of purpose of, 9, 10, 103
  comparison of substantive due
    process and takings theories,
    17–18
  remedies, *see* Remedies
*Tampa-Hillsborough County
  Expressway Authority v.
  A.G.W.S. Corp.,* 268
Tax incentives, 516
Tehema County, California, 206–207
Temporary takings, 266–67, 489
  compensation for, *see*
    Compensation remedy, tempo-
    rary takings
  erroneous assertion of regulatory
    jurisdiction as, 142
  moratoria as, 142–43, 266–67,
    275–78

normal delays, 142
subdivisions and, 238
types of, 141–43
Tenants, *see* Landlords and tenants
Tennessee v. Brandon, 454
Texaco, Inc. v. Short, 418
Thomas, Justice Clarence, 250, 559
Thornburgh v. Port of Portland, 340
Threatened species, *see* Endangered
     Species Act
Total takings, 139–41
     Lucas and, 140–41, 168–69,
          187–88, 375, 433
     nuisance exception to, 140–41,
          168–69, 187–88
Town of Esopus v. New York,
     453–54
Trails, *see* Rails to trails
Transferable development rights
     (TDRs), 320, 321, 322–23,
     556
Trespass, aircraft operations and,
     338, 339, 341
Troy Hill, Ltd. v. Renna, 306
Trust for Public Lands, 529
Trusts, land, 516, 528–29
Tucker Act, 39, 40, 42
     "little," 38
     statute of limitations under, 72
Tull v. United States, 100

Unconstitutional conditions doctrine,
     83, 143–44, 234, 253, 256–58
Uniform Declaratory Judgment Act,
     475
Uniform Relocation and Real
     Property Acquisition Policies
     Act (URA), 507
U.S. Army Corps of Engineers, 365,
     367, 370, 380, 386, 394
U.S. Department of Commerce, 209,
     263
     Zoning Advisory Committee, 215
U.S. Department of Housing and
     Urban Development (HUD),

300
U.S. Department of Justice:
     Environment and Natural
          Resources Division, 532–33
     Office of Alternative Dispute
          Resolution, 533
U.S. Department of the Interior, 419,
     514
U.S. Fish and Wildlife Service (FWS),
     392–95, 515
U.S. Forest Service, 522
U.S. Supreme Court, *see* Supreme
     Court, U.S.
*U.S. West Communications, Inc. v.
     Public Utilities Comm'n,* 22
United States v. Dickinson, 163, 164
United States v. Locke, 418–19
United States v. Reynolds, 94–95
United States v. Shell Oil Co., 449
Unpatented claims to minerals on
     federal lands, 414–16
Use of property, right of, 27
Utah, 551, 553
     court decisions, 267

"Valid existing rights" (VERs),
     419–20, 537
Vermont:
     court decisions, 397
     land trusts, 529
*Village of Euclid v. Ambler Realty
     Co.,* 215, 247
*Villas of Lake Jackson, Ltd. v. Leon
     County,* 273
Voluntary initiatives, 513, 514–15

Ward v. Harding, 413–14
Warren, Justice Earl, 6
Washington, 23
     court decisions, 307–308, 345,
          397, 464
     property rights movement and,
          539
Washington, D.C., *see* District of
     Columbia

Washington Market Enters, Inc. v. City of Trenton, 291

Waterways and water rights, 457–70
  appropriative water rights, 458
  challenges to regulatory takings, 463–70
  to federal programs affecting privately held water rights, 465–69
  following modification of state water law systems, 463–65
  as a limit on land-use development, 469–70
  conclusion, 470
  governed by state statutes, 457–58, 459
  legal limits on scope of water rights as property interests, 459–63
  incapable of private ownership, 459–61
  paramount public interest in water, 461–63
  navigational servitude, federal, 179–82, 379
  prior appropriation principle, 464
  public access to shorelands and uplands, 173–76
  public access to waterways, 173
  public trust doctrine and, 171–72
  riparian water rights, 458, 463–64
  water rights as property, 457–59

Watt, James, 419

Western Energy Co. v. Genie Land Co., 414

Western Land Equities, Inc. v. City of Logan, 267

West Virginia, 420

Wetlands, 365–89
  conclusion, 389
  denial of permission to dredge or fill, 375–79
  federal courts, 378–79
  state courts, 375–77
  federal protection of, 366–67
  historic pendulum in case law, 368–72

  importance of preserving, 365–66
  liable parties, 387–89
  prior knowledge of regulatory scheme, 384–86
  project delays, 379–80
  relevant parcel, 381–84
  ripeness of claims, 372–74
  speculators and "after value," 386–87
  state conservation and environmental statutes, 366
  "swampbuster" program for, 367, 517–18

Wetlands Reserve Program (WRP), 528

Wheeler v. City of Pleasant Grove (Wheeler IV), 497

Whitney Benefits, Inc. v. United States, 405

Wild and Scenic Rivers Act, 419

Wild Free-Roaming Horses and Burros Act, 401

Wildlands Project, 516

Wildlife, 391–404
  conclusions, 404
  cross-cutting issues, 402–404
  defensive measures against nuisance animals, limits on, 398–401
  direct-use restraints on private landowners, 391–98
  case law, 395–98
  Endangered Species Act process, 391–95
  public trust doctrine and, 171

Williamson County Regional Planning Commission v. Hamilton Bank, 22, 36, 50, 51, 63, 76, 552

Will v. Michigan Dept. of State Police, 91

Windfalls for Wipeouts (Misczynski and Hagman), 160

Wisconsin court decisions, 191–92, 228, 368, 376–77

Woodbury Place Partners v. Woodbury, 268–69, 271
Writ of mandamus, 474, 477
Wyoming court decisions, 236, 238

Yee v. City of Escondido, 122, 303–304
YMCA v. United States, 125

Zoning, 213–30
    in accordance with comprehensive plan, 200–201, 204, 208
    average reciprocity of advantage principle, 216–17, 219–20
    categorical takings, 218–19
    conditional, 359–60
    contract, 359–60
    historic districts, *see* Historic preservation, historic districts
    near airports, *see* Airports, zoning near
    planning distinguished from, 200
    police power and, 214–15, 216, 217
    as primary instrument of local land-use regulation, 216
    purpose of, 200
    reduction in land value due to, 218–20
    relationship to land-use planning, 200–204, 221
    rezoning, 220–30
        burden to obtain government permission to rezone, 221–22
        comprehensive, 222
        conditional uses, 229–30
        downzoning, 222–26
        economically viable use of the land, 223, 224–25
        floodplain regulations, 227–29
        limits to government rights, 223
        open space, designation of private property as, 226
        procedural differences, 220
        to reduce land values for cheap purchase by government, 225
        relevant parcel, 225–26
        substantially advancing legitimate state interests, 223–24
        upzoning, 222